THE NEW ECONOMIC SOCIOLOGY

THE NEW ECONOMIC SOCIOLOGY

A READER

EDITED BY FRANK DOBBIN

PRINCETON UNIVERSITY PRESS

PRINCETON AND OXFORD

Published by Princeton University Press, 41 William Street,
Princeton, New Jersey 08540
In the United Kingdom: Princeton University Press,
3 Market Place, Woodstock, Oxfordshire OX20 1SY

Library of Congress Cataloging-in-Publication Data

The new economic sociology : a reader / edited by Frank Dobbin.
p. cm.
Includes bibliographical references and index.
ISBN 0-691-04905-X (cloth : alk. paper)—ISBN 0-691-04906-8 (pbk. : alk. paper)
1. Economics—Sociological aspects. I. Dobbin, Frank.
HM548.N49 2004
306.3–dc22 2003060037

British Library Cataloging-in-Publication Data is available.

This book has been composed in Sabon

Printed on acid-free paper. ∞

www.pupress.princeton.edu

Printed in the United States of America

10 9 8 7 6 5 4 3 2 1

CONTENTS

ACKNOWLEDGMENTS ix

CHAPTER 1
The Sociological View of the Economy
Frank Dobbin 1

INSTITUTIONS

CHAPTER 2
From *The Protestant Ethic and the Spirit of Capitalism*
Max Weber 49

CHAPTER 3
Institutionalized Organizations: Formal Structure as Myth and Ceremony
John W. Meyer and Brian Rowan 86

CHAPTER 4
The Iron Cage Revisited: Institutional Isomorphism and Collective Rationality in Organizational Fields
Paul J. DiMaggio and Walter W. Powell 111

CHAPTER 5
From *Pricing the Priceless Child: The Changing Social Value of Children*
Viviana A. Zelizer 135

CHAPTER 6
The Social Construction of Organizations and Markets: The Comparative Analysis of Business Recipes
Richard Whitley 162

CHAPTER 7
The Decline and Fall of the Conglomerate Firm in the 1980s: The Deinstitutionalization of an Organizational Form
Gerald F. Davis, Kristina A. Diekmann, and Catherine H. Tinsley 188

NETWORKS

CHAPTER 8
From *The Division of Labor in Society*
Émile Durkheim 227

CHAPTER 9
Economic Action and Social Structure: The Problem of Embeddedness
Mark Granovetter 245

CHAPTER 10
Embeddedness and Immigration: Notes on the Social Determinants of Economic Action
Alejandro Portes and Julia Sensenbrenner 274

CHAPTER 11
A Structural Approach to Markets
Eric M. Leifer and Harrison C. White 302

CHAPTER 12
From *Structural Holes: The Social Structure of Competition*
Ronald S. Burt 325

CHAPTER 13
Embeddedness in the Making of Financial Capital: How Social Relations and Networks Benefit Firms Seeking Financing
Brian Uzzi 349

POWER

CHAPTER 14
From *The German Ideology*
Karl Marx 387

CHAPTER 15
From *The Transformation of Corporate Control*
Neil Fligstein 407

CHAPTER 16
From *Socializing Capital: The Rise of the Large Industrial Corporation in America*
William G. Roy 433

CHAPTER 17
From *City of Capital: Politics and Markets in the English Financial Revolution*
Bruce G. Carruthers 457

COGNITION

CHAPTER 18
From *The Elementary Forms of the Religious Life*
Émile Durkheim 485

CHAPTER 19
From *The Social Construction of Reality: A Treatise in the Sociology of Knowledge*
Peter L. Berger and Thomas Luckmann 496

CHAPTER 20
From *Organizations: Cognitive Limits on Rationality*
James G. March and Herbert A. Simon 518

CHAPTER 21
From *Sensemaking in Organizations*
Karl E. Weick 533

INDEX 553

ACKNOWLEDGMENTS

THANKS TO Lauren Dye, Michele Lamont, and John Meyer for suggestions on the introduction, to Peter Dougherty of Princeton University Press for championing the idea of such an anthology and for many useful conversations and suggestions, to Timothy Sullivan of the Press for excellent editorial suggestions, and to Richard Isomaki for superb copyediting.

Chapter 1

THE SOCIOLOGICAL VIEW OF THE ECONOMY

FRANK DOBBIN

AFTER SPENDING eighteen months among the Yanomamo of northern Brazil, Napoleon Chagnon (1968) described them as a fierce people respectful of quick tempers and casual violence. After spending a bit longer among the bond traders of Salomon Brothers, Michael Lewis (1987) described them as a guileful people respectful of quick wits and casual deception.

These peoples have different sorts of economies—systems for producing that with which they sustain life. They have different mechanisms for socializing the young. They have different cosmologies, or frameworks for making sense of the world. Both cosmologies tie social customs and physical objects to something bigger than society itself, in one case to a spirit world, in the other to a corpus of natural laws. The Yanomamo envision a world of departed ancestors that exists immediately above the visible sky and trace economic conventions (chest-beating contests) and physical objects (yams) to specific mythical ancestors. The bond traders envision a roster of social and physical laws that transcend time and space, and trace conventions (arbitrage) and objects (blowfish sushi) to specific laws. In each tribe, the average man on the street may not know everything about the ancestor spirits or scientific laws that govern the world, but he trusts that the experts know.

As a social scientist, what would you want to know to predict an episode of chest beating or bond trading? Chest beating and bond trading are economic behaviors, to be sure, for they determine how much of the group's resources one can claim. To predict an episode of either, it would help if you understood the basics of the local cosmology, embodied in customs and rituals. Is it broadly mystified, religious, philosophical, or rational? What are the established social roles—hunter, warrior, trader, investor? What is the meaning of the particular custom within the local cosmology? Is the chest beater or bond trader engaged in a show of plumage, of force, of business savvy? What is the wider role of the custom—to display a penchant for violence, to raise capital? The more you know, the better you will be at predicting episodes.

For the purpose of prediction, the concept of self-interest, which is at the center of most theories of economic behavior, does not get you very far. The Yanomamo and the bond trader may be self-interested, but their behavior is largely shaped by social institutions. Chest beating can only be understood in the context of the tribe's very particular cosmology. It is not that the Yanomamo warrior is a puppet of his culture. He reinterprets, challenges, and builds on his culture. He jokes about the ancestors who rule the earth and sky, rails at those ancestors when life treats him poorly, and devises new theories of fertility and weather. But the cosmology provides the lens through which he sees the world and the starting point for cultural change. The same goes for the bond trader. What the trader does makes sense only in the context of her special cosmology. She knows of no other way to interpret experience than through the lens of natural laws. She may chuck it all to join a Buddhist monastery, but she is not likely to question the laws of gravity or of supply and demand.

It is not just that the bond trader is rational and the Yanomamo belongs to a deluded cult that, incidentally, consumes a local hallucinogenic substance in large quantities. Economic practices also vary widely among modern, rationalized societies. Bond traders in Tokyo, Paris, and New York see the world through rationalized lenses, but through very different rationalized lenses. The same spirits do not rule the worlds of the Ndembu and the Yanomamo, and likewise the same laws of supply and demand do not obtain in Tokyo and New York. People in all of these places may be self-interested, but the concept of self-interest is of little use in explaining why people behave differently in different places.

Sociology's Distinct Approach to Economic Behavior

Economic modernization can be seen as a series of societal projects. There was the project of developing intercontinental trade routes, spearheaded by Europe's East India trading companies and colonizing monarchs. There was the project of building large-scale factories with wage labor forces nearby, spearheaded by early industrialists in Massachusetts and Manchester. There was also the project of divorcing the economy from society and polity, spearheaded by capitalists and politicians but also by philosophers and social observers. As Karl Polanyi argued in *The Great Transformation* (1944), British industrialization depended on the *idea* that the economy could be wrenched free of society—that a free labor market could be constructed by breaking traditional links between lords and serfs—as well as on the concrete public policies and capitalist practices.

One manifestation of the intellectual side of the project of splitting economy from society was the division of economics and sociology into distinct disciplines. In the nineteenth century, the dividing line between economics and sociology was difficult to draw. Most of the people who are now part of sociology's heritage studied economic behavior, and called themselves economists. Karl Marx was interested in how capitalism emerged from feudalism; Max Weber in how religious institutions hastened the development of capitalism; Émile Durkheim in the consequences of the division of labor. Empirical studies typically showed that the economy was not a distinct realm—that it was enmeshed in social life. In their struggle against this idea, economists increasingly turned to abstract theorizing in which they modeled behavior "as if" the economy could be treated as a world apart.

Sociologists continued to see economy and society as intertwined, but even sociologists came to accept the emerging division between the disciplines. Sociologists were inductive, deriving theories of social behavior by observing behavior. Economists were deductive, deriving theories of economic behavior from the axiom that self-interest drives individual behavior.

Economics thus came increasingly to resemble physics. As Paul Krugman (1994, xi) jokes, "An Indian-born economist once explained his personal theory of reincarnation to his graduate economics class. 'If you are a good economist, a virtuous economist,' he said, 'you are reborn as a physicist. But if you are an evil, wicked economist, you are reborn as a sociologist.'" For the economist, the pinnacle of the academic pyramid had become the most pristine science with the most immutable laws. Economists spelled out how people would behave if they followed pure principles of self-interest. Like physicists, they thought they were identifying universal laws. Like philosophers, they imagined an ideal world and worked out the details of how people would behave in it. They came to play the role that prophets played in another age, conjuring up a perfect world and its rules of behavior.

Sociology became increasingly empirical, based on in-depth studies of communities and corporations and sectors of the economy. Robert and Helen Lynd's *Middletown* (1929) depicted the changed economic institutions, changing network structure, and slowly changing culture of an average American city circa 1925. Philip Selznick's in-depth study of the agency established to fight Appalachian poverty during the depression, *TVA and the Grass Roots* (1949), showed how officials and corporations could subvert public policy's economic goals. C. Wright Mills's *The Power Elite* (1956) showed that power was becoming increasingly concentrated in business, government, and the military and that links between the elites in those sectors were increasing. Meanwhile Digby Baltzell's *The Protestant Establishment* (1964) showed the declining exclusivity of the Protestant elite and the rise of other groups in business and society. William H. Whyte's *The Organization Man* (1956) showed that corporate customs made middle managers conformist and complacent, undermining the work ethic and entrepreneurialism that Max Weber had described among capitalists. In these and other studies, sociologists found economy and society inextricably enmeshed, but left it to economists to theorize economic behavior.

Since about 1980, both sociologists and economists have been challenging this division of intellectual labor, in which economists explain economic behavior using deductive models and sociologists explain all other kinds of social behavior using inductive methods. Economists see economic behavior as shaped by society. Sociologists see family relations, religious systems, and political institutions as shaped by economics. And in particular, sociologists see social processes shaping economic behavior, not only at the margins, but at the center.

Sociologists began to explain economic behavior in terms of the same four social mechanisms they had observed shaping all sorts of social behavior. These mechanisms entered the common lexicon under the terms *institution*, *network*, *power*, and *cognition*.

Sociology's core insight is that individuals behave according to scripts that are tied to social roles. Those scripts are called conventions at the collective level and cognitive schemas at the individual level. Conventions and schemas make sense within a wider institutional framework, be it rational or religious or mystical. These conventions and schemas shape individual behavior, and so predicting economic behavior is a matter of comprehending conventions, schemas, and institutions. But prediction requires more than that, because conventions change. Understanding why they change is job one, and change can usually be traced to institutions, power, networks, and cognition. Economic *institutions* offer broad prescriptions for behavior. Institutions are sustained by occupational, industrial, and community *networks* that define social roles. *Power* shapes the evolution of new customs, when the powerful sanction the behavior of others and when they shape legal institutions. At the individual level, *cognition* is the carrier of conventions—it provides the schemas through which we make ongoing sense of conventions and through which we challenge them.

This anthology outlines the sociological view of economic behavior. It is divided into four parts, each focused on one of the social mechanisms that sociologists have discovered at the root of economic behavior. Each of the four groups of readings traces one social mechanism from its intellectual origins through studies that demonstrate its importance to studies that show how it meshes with the other mechanisms.

In this introductory chapter I endeavor to show that sociologists see these mechanisms as operating together to produce economic behavior patterns. I do so because it is easy to miss the forest for the trees. The economist Michael Piore describes economic sociology as "an enormous hodge-podge of ideas and insights, existing at all sorts of different levels of abstraction, possibly in contradiction with one another, possibly just incommensurate, without a basic theory or structure to sort them out, or order them" (1996, 742). This is a fair critique, to the extent that individual studies tend to focus on one of the four mechanisms, holding the others constant, and tend not to describe the big picture. Sociologists evaluate the effect of networks by artificially holding power constant just as physicists estimate the effect of gravity by holding atmospheric pressure constant. But sociologists have in fact been working toward an integrated theory of how economic customs arise and change. All four of these mechanisms play roles in that theory. My goal is to shine some light on that integrated theory.

Institutions

In common parlance people use *institution* to refer to sectors of society—the *institution* of organized religion. Sociologists use the term when talking about particular conventions, some defined by law and some by tradition. Institutions range in complexity from simple customs of exchange to elaborate modern states. The American state is, in the end, a huge agglomeration of smaller conventions, some informal and others codified. Institutions, large and small, shape human behavior not only by providing behavioral scripts, but by representing the relationships among things in the world—between the local totem and the harvest, or between antitrust and progress. For sociologists as for anthropologists (Geertz 1983; Douglas 1986), conventions and routines influence behavior in rationalized societies much as they do in mystified and religious societies. While social life in modern settings may be organized around ideas of progress rather than around ancestor worship, the individual makes particular decisions based on convention, just as she did when it was frog totems and not mathematical formulas that ruled the world. Today we reenact most conventions with an understanding of their rational purposes, but this is not to say that we actually make rational calculations every time we act. Our conventions may revolve around rationality and self-interest, but they are conventions just the same.

Networks

We learn how to be warriors, bond traders, teachers, witch doctors through social networks. What do you do when a buyer fails to pay, or when a drought fails to succumb to incantations? The prescriptions come from networks of others. *Network* theory builds on early French sociologist Émile Durkheim's idea that social location shapes identity and behavior. Your network influences how you behave and your understanding of how people in other roles should behave. Role behavior is defined by conventions, which take the form of conditional prescriptions for behavior; to wit, *if* you are a chief information officer in a large automobile company, *then* you should advocate the transfer of the firm's purchasing function to a Web-based bidding system. Other actors in your network define how you should dress (Brooks Brothers or loincloth), talk, comport yourself, and respond to bids for bonds. Social networks are the carriers of new economic practices and new ideas of what it means to be rational and efficient. Social networks also reward role-appropriate behavior, such as making good on a promise to sell bonds at a certain price, and sanction behavior that breaks norms, such as larceny.

Power

Karl Marx first defined *power* not merely as coercion, but as the ability to shape how others view the world and their own interests. From the dawn of capitalism, successful entrepreneurs and managers have defined economic conventions by proselytizing, telling the world that the best way to run a business is their way. Success itself gives these people the authority to define what rational behavior is. Economic power also goes hand in hand with the political power to determine public policies that shape how people see their interests and how they can behave. For instance, in chapter 16, William Roy finds that at the beginning of the twentieth century, a group of financiers who wanted to consolidate American manufacturing shaped the American view that oligopoly is natural and large firms are more efficient than small ones. In this way, power shaped the public policies that govern competition between firms and the pricing conventions of firms. This sort of power over economic institutions and economic norms operates through political networks, industry networks, and professional networks that serve as the conduits for new policy ideas and business strategies.

Cognition

Sociologists use the term *cognition* to refer to the psychological process of making sense of the world and its social conventions. Max Weber and Émile Durkheim articulated theories of social psychology as part of their theories of economic behavior. For them, the human mind is programmed to develop categories, causal frameworks, and maps of the world. Rather than looking for a single human cognitive archetype, Durkheim and Weber were interested in how "human nature" varies across social settings. Weber saw that many social systems produce individual psyches oriented to tradition rather than progress. He traced both the traditional and the modern psyche to the structure of religious institutions. In sociology, but also in cognitive psychology, behavioral economics, and cognitive science, the idea that core aspects of the psyche are situational rather than hard-wired has become commonplace. Economic sociologists are particularly interested in how ideas of rational self-interest vary with exposure to what Erving Goffman (1974) called different "frames" for understanding the world. For Goffman as for cognitive psychologists, cognitive frameworks are situated in individual consciousness, but they are shared among groups of people exposed to common institutions. Bond traders share a culture that shapes individual cognitive structures, and the same can be said for Yanomamo warriors. In modern social systems, people are exposed to different frameworks—market efficiency, economic justice, and so on (Boltanski and Thevenot 1991)—in different realms.

Why does economic sociology need a fourfold theory? A change in only one of these factors may result in a change in economic conventions, but the other factors matter along the way. Take the question of why America's largest companies reversed course in the 1970s and 1980s, abandoning a guiding business strategy of diversification for one of core competence. In 1970, big firms were buying companies in other industries to diversify their assets. General Electric bought NBC, and R. J. Reynolds bought Nabisco. By 1990, big firms were buying others in the same industry to take advantage of their core managerial competence—Daimler bought Chrysler. How did this shift happen? Neil Fligstein and Linda Markowitz (1993) and Gerald Davis, Kristina Diekmann, and Catherine Tinsley (1994) trace the changes. A change in legal *institutions* opened the way for the change in business conventions, when the Reagan administration relaxed antitrust enforcement to permit firms to buy related businesses. The spread of the core-competence strategy also depended on the rise of a *network* of institutional investors and securities analysts who came to define de-diversification as in their own interest, because it was easier to evaluate companies that were not diversified. They used their market *power* to reduce the value of diversified conglomerates, inviting hostile takeover artists and CEOs to restructure big corporations. Core competence hinged as well on the force of an existing *cognitive schema*, of managerialism, which gave managers and investors a shorthand for understanding the core-competence model and for challenging the corporation-as-portfolio schema behind the conglomerate. Managerialism defined executive expertise in an industry as key to a firm's success in that industry, providing a rationale for the core-competence firm. Take away any one of these factors and the American firm might still be structured much as it was in 1970. Can the change be explained by the superior efficiency of the new model? Perhaps it was more efficient in some cases, but it spread even to companies that had been very successful with the strategy of diversification, and thus efficiency alone did not drive the process. The social redefinition of corporate efficiency was at work.

What do we know about how these four mechanisms shape economic behavior? Next I trace the evolution of each idea since its inception by previewing the selections from this anthology and outlining their particular contributions. The anthology is organized around the four sociological camps that have focused on these mechanisms, but each section highlights work that brings in insights from the other schools.

Institutions and Economic Action

Human nature surely plays a role in determining behavior, as economic theory suggests, but it cannot easily explain variation across societies and over time in how people behave. Differences across societies, it goes without saying, can only be explained by something about society itself—by customs, institutions, resources. Society shapes the behavior of the individual. A newborn placed in the fold of Ndembu warriors will become a Ndembu warrior, and the very same newborn will become a bond trader among bond traders, a Catalan merchant among Catalan merchants, and a Calvinist preacher among Calvinist preachers. We know this from common sense more than from research, because university regulations prevent us from randomly assigning newborns to different tribes.

What we do know from previous research is that human behavior is highly predictable on average. You cannot always predict whether a particular Yanomamo will dig for yams this afternoon, but you can say with some certainty that in general the Yanomamo will dig for yams, and bond traders will trade bonds. To understand when and where these things will happen, you must grasp the logic underlying economic conventions. Is yam digging linked, in practice and in the minds of the natives, to the weather, to the days of the week, to the mood of totemic spirits? And bond trading? James Duesenberry's famous quip—"Economics is all about how people make choices; sociology is all about how they don't have any choices to make" (1960, 233)—captures this quality of social context. In these cases, it is not that the Yanomamo and the bond trader do not choose, but that they choose within cosmologies rather than across them.

Peoples' understandings of social customs are shaped by how the institutions around them express social order generally. When European institutions were broadly religious, they expressed social customs as an imperfect reflection of God's will. Kings, for instance, were thought to be chosen by God's own hand. Rationalization led to institutions that express social customs as an imperfect reflection of natural physical and social laws. Presidents, for instance, are thought to be chosen by the will of the people, because political philosophy defines democracy as humankind's natural state.

In religious and rationalized societies alike, people trace customs to something bigger than society itself. Rationalized societies trace customs not to the will of God but to physical and social laws inscribed in mathematical formulas. In each kind of society, people seek to divine the character of these exogenous forces by observation and epiphany. Thus, people read reason into the social practices they experience and understand worldly phenomena in terms of broader frames offered up by culture. Those of us born into a rationalized world spontaneously understand a thunderstorm with natural laws (low-pressure fronts) and not with spirit forces (displeased frog sprits) or the will of God. Comparative studies of capitalist societies show that they vary almost as richly in terms of causal imagery as do religious societies. Among societies oriented to salvation, institutions can direct human behavior toward prayer, warfare, or fulfilling a God-given calling. Among societies oriented to progress, institutions can direct human behavior toward market competition, coordination by large business groups, or state industrial planning.

In 1776, Adam Smith suggested that economic laws dictate that there is one best way to organize economic life. Trial and error would, he argued, reveal the details to nations. This suggested that modern societies would converge on one optimal set of economic institutions and behavior patterns. That assumption is now part of modern common sense, but comparative studies of capitalism do not bear it out. Some (Guillén 2001; Whitley and Kristensen 1996) find that different industrial systems have different comparative advantages, and suggest that countries are probably best served by recognizing and building on those advantages. Others (Fligstein and Byrkjeflot 1996) suggest that alternative market forms rely on different logics—labor markets, for instance, may rely on the logic of vocationalism or on that of managerialism—and that differences across countries may represent functional alternatives rather than, as Adam Smith might have argued, different stages in the evolution of rationalization.

Many similarities in economic conventions among rationalized societies, students of comparative capitalism argue, can be traced to mimicry or to the need to exchange goods and services across borders on common terms rather than to economic laws that make only one sort of fiscal policy (Campbell 2000) or incorporation law (Roy 1997) effective.

If America's economic conventions represent but one among many possible ways of efficiently organizing things, then understanding what shapes those conventions becomes an important sociological problem. Game theorists in economics explain differences in economic conventions across nations and over time with the idea of multiple Nash equilibria. How can economic systems generate different economic conventions, either over time or across space, even when all participants are behaving rationally? In a set of transactions that is repeated, the behavior of individuals may change from one round to the next (see Gibbons 1992). In consequence, given the parameters of the game and the stage of the game, different economic conventions may emerge.

Economic sociologists take a different view of why economic institutions differ across nations, why particular institutions persist, and what causes institutions to change. On the issue of why different kinds of economic systems arose in the first place, institutional analysts from political science and sociology argue that history has given different societies different material to begin with (Campbell 1998; Hall and Taylor 1996). For instance, in the late nineteenth century the French state planned and sponsored a network of railroads that linked Paris with all of the outlying regions, while the American state subsidized a handful of transcontinental railroads but left it to states and towns to subsidize various local and regional lines. Today the French state has a nationalized network of state-of-the-art high-speed trains that mirrors the network it planned in the nineteenth century, and the American state reluctantly subsidizes a semiprivate rail system with but one, slow, "high-speed" route. Why these persistent differences in the ways railways are planned and run in the two countries? They stem in part from the fact that with the threat of invasion from all sides, France had by the 1700s established an absolutist military regime and a corps of engineers to build roads, canals, and then railroads to its perimeter. The descendants of that corps still plan railroads. The United States had little in the way of a central state, and no pressing military need for a similar transport system in the 1700s (Dobbin 1994). Thus early institutional differences in nations shaped economic patterns.

On the issue of why different kinds of economic institutions persist, economic sociologists argue that institutions such as laws governing property typically survive until someone directly challenges them. "Path dependence" has been the most recent shorthand among sociologists and political scientists for describing how systems retain essential characteristics over time (Campbell 1998; Hall and Taylor 1996; Stark 1992). Once a group or nation goes down one path, toward antitrust or state industrial planning, for instance, future paths will necessarily lead off from that first choice. Different ways of organizing economies tend to be sticky, or resistant to change, and many different approaches may prove sufficiently efficient to persist. The institutional economist Douglass North, who won the Nobel Prize in economics in 1993, adopted the idea in his book on institutions and institutional change (North 1990). Social institutions that arise for reasons of chance survive to shape future economic behavior. The idea is not incompatible with game-theorists' idea of multiple equilibria, but the focus is on how institutions shape basic forms of rational behavior.

Max Weber suggested that institutions persist not only because they develop structural inertia but because they come to make sense to people, and that understanding what kind of sense they make is the key to understanding why they persist. Weber insisted that sociologists take what anthropologist Clifford Geertz later called the "native's point of view"—that they explore the meaning of social conventions to the people practicing them. Understandings of particular behaviors, it turns out, vary widely even across rationalized societies. Take cartels. In late-nineteenth-century Britain they were understood to be an efficient mechanism for coordinating industries. The government backed cartels as the wave of the future. Yet in the United States they were labeled an evil private invention that threatened both economic growth and democracy (Dobbin 1994). Joining a cartel meant something very different in Britain than it did in America.

Most customs have an implicit meaning, and enacting them in context reinforces that meaning. The Ndembu circumcision custom signifies the tribe's belief that the local totem increases fertility when invoked at the onset of adolescence. The custom of antitrust enforcement signifies the tribe's belief that price competition begets progress. These customs are usually enacted without much explanation, because everyone understands their meaning. Even anthropologists catch on pretty quickly. Both customs build on wider cosmologies, representing specific causal relationships between the tribal totem and fertility or between "market mechanisms" and progress. Weber insisted that we try to understand the meaning of customs to the groups who practice them, for people only practice customs that make sense to them. This is not to say that customs necessarily have the intended effects, and they may in fact serve functions that are invisible to those who enact them (Weber 1978, 4).

On the issue of why economic institutions change, Weber argued that change could originate in politics, in the law, in religious ideals. The model of change that most sociologists embrace is built on the idea of punctuated equilibrium that Stephen Jay Gould (1989) sketches for the biological world and Stephen Krasner (1984) adapts for the social world (and see Fligstein 2001). Customs tend to persist until something shakes up the social system, opening up the possibility of change. New customs are often worked out in power struggles, and they may or may not be more efficient than those they replace. The jury is still out, for instance, on whether the core-competence firm is ultimately more efficient than the diversified firm it replaced. Institutionalists from the field of economics (e.g., Williamson 1975) initially argued that institutions evolve toward increasingly efficient forms—that history is efficient when it comes to institutions. But even economic institutionalists (North 1990) have increasingly argued that change may be shaped by power and happenstance as well as by efficiency. Change in economic customs may more closely resemble random mutation than teleological progress.

Sociological thinking about institutions has evolved significantly since the time of Weber, particularly with the realization that different sorts of rationalized institutions have prospered alongside one another. Chapters 2 through 7 explore that evolution. In *The Protestant Ethic*, Weber traces the new spirit of capitalism among Calvinists, and the conventions of hard work and saving, to a new religious ethic—showing how a religious movement could produce rational economic conventions. In chapter 3, John Meyer and Brian Rowan discuss how new management conventions diffuse across fields of organizations, along with supporting rationales of efficiency. In chapter 4, Paul DiMaggio and Walter Powell build on this idea to show how three important mechanisms of diffusion operate, among networks of professionals, of business executives, or of organizations and the government agencies that regulate them. In chapter 5, Viviana Zelizer explores how the convention of child factory labor was put to an end by a social movement, which offered a new definition of the role of childhood in industrial society. In chapter 6, Richard Whitley explores the origins of different national "business systems" in East Asia, and the public policy institutions and private economic conventions that go along with them. Finally, in chapter 7, Gerald Davis, Kristina Diekmann, and Catherine Tinsley trace how a change in business conventions came about in large American firms, as the portfolio/conglomerate model was replaced by the core-competence model.

Where New Institutions and Customs Come From

Chapter 2 is an excerpt from Max Weber's *The Protestant Ethic and the Spirit of Capitalism.* Weber was a professor of economics in Germany, but with the publication of *The Protestant Ethic* he became one of the founders of modern sociology. Weber wondered how capitalism could arise in Europe out of the conservative economic traditions of feudalism and Catholicism, which did little to encourage people to work hard or to save. He found that those customs originated in early Calvinism, which taught predestination, or the idea that one's destiny in the afterlife was fixed prior to birth. What you did in life could not win you salvation, but it could signal your fate. God gave everyone an earthly calling—work to be done in His name—and demanded self-denial and asceticism. Commitment to these ideals might signal that one was destined for heaven. The idea of God's calling led Protestants to devote themselves to their work, whatever it was. Asceticism led them to save, for they were not to squander money on trinkets or religious icons. Devotion to work and saving became enduring customs—they became institutionalized. The customs spread even beyond the boundaries of Protestantism, and endured even when Protestantism took a new course that placed less emphasis on the calling and on asceticism.

In *The Protestant Ethic*, in his various studies of the world religions (1951, 1952, 1958, 1963), and in his opus on capitalism, *Economy and Society* (1978), Weber tried to understand the customs found in different social systems, the thinking behind those customs, and the forces that lead to changes in customs. Some (e.g. Novak 1993) argue that Catholicism was not so different from Protestantism and promoted the same kinds of behavior, but what was novel about Weber's ideas was not so much his particular argument as his vision of society. For Weber, the beliefs that underlie customs sustain them. In Calvinism, the belief in predestination—the belief that one is destined for heaven or hell at birth—sustains the custom of asceticism, because asceticism is thought to be a sign that one is bound for heaven. Weber argued, extending the concept, that in modern firms the belief in professional expertise sustains the custom of hierarchical authority. In *The Protestant Ethic* Weber explained how well-entrenched economic customs could change, as related parts of the social system change. In this case, a shift in religious beliefs was key, but Weber argued that changes in other parts of the social system—beliefs, political power, scientific knowledge—could lead to changes in economic conventions.

The Institutionalization of Rational Myths

Chapter 3 is John Meyer and Brian Rowan's seminal 1977 article sketching an approach to organizational sociology rooted in Weberian ideas. Weber argued that concrete economic customs made sense to people within the framework of a wider cosmology. Meyer and Rowan's "Institutionalized Organizations: Formal Structure as Myth and Ceremony" depicts how modern organizations adopt structures and practices that symbolize rationality and fairness. Their question: How do new ideas and practices spread among organizations to shape our understandings of progress?

When Meyer and Rowan's piece was first published, the prevailing view of the firm followed Adam Smith's thinking about national economies—that economic laws determined "best practices" for business and that those best practices would evolve everywhere eventually. If organizations looked alike, it was because they were subject to the same economic laws. If they had accounting departments and strategic planning teams and performance evaluations, it was because each organization had found each practice to be efficient. Meyer and Rowan described the rationalized practices found in organizations in terms of "myth and ceremony." Organizations adopt practices that embody myths of rationality with the goal of symbolizing their commitment to efficiency to the world. Organizational entrepreneurs who invent new practices often promote them directly to those in their networks and more widely in management magazines, through cover stories on quality teams or empowerment. New practices became "institutionalized"—taken for granted—as this process proceeds. New practices must conform to the wider understanding of what is rational, and so it is easier to sell certain kinds of practices in Osaka than in Omaha. In Meyer and Rowan's world, firms come to look alike because they jump on the same bandwagons, not because each discerns the (same) optimal way to organize itself.

How Fields Spread Rational Myths

In 1983, Paul DiMaggio and Walter Powell built on this idea, sketching the networks through which new rational customs diffuse among organizations—political networks, professional networks, and networks of firms. Schools were coming to look more like one another, and so were hospitals, auto factories, and charities. A growing body of standard practices could be found in each field. Like Meyer and Rowan, DiMaggio and Powell described the driving force behind institutionalization as social—managers of auto factories did not independently invent the same business practices; they copied those practices from leading firms.

Copying of organizational practices usually follows one of three patterns. Sometimes public policy encourages organizations to adopt new conventions ("coercive isomorphism"). For instance, federal regulations dictate that schools must meet certain standards, or give certain tests (Meyer and Scott 1983). Sometimes professional networks that span organizations promote new conventions ("normative isomorphism"). For instance, finance managers promoted the portfolio approach to corporate diversification in which the firm held a portfolio of different businesses (Fligstein 1990). Sometimes managers cannot figure out how to best proceed to achieve their goals, so they copy practices of successful organizations ("mimetic isomorphism"). For instance, American automakers copied Japanese production techniques after Japan made inroads into America's auto market. Mimetic isomorphism can have the character of a cargo cult, in which the tribe builds a wooden replica of a cargo plane in the hope that the replica will bear forth the same goods the real plane bore. Through these three processes, organizations within a sector come to look more and more alike.

Key business strategies often spread through mimetic isomorphism, and as Heather Haveman (1993) shows in a paper titled "Follow the Leader," firms that are defined as industry leaders due to high growth or sheer size are more likely than others to be copied by their peers. Among savings and loans, when industry leaders diversify into real estate or into commercial loans, other firms follow their lead. The very definition of what a savings and loan is is changed in the process.

The sectoral differences in management that DiMaggio and Powell describe have declined over the last few decades, with the rise of a more generic model of organizing (Meyer 1994). Social service agencies increasingly have CEOs, and hospitals increasingly have mission statements. But DiMaggio and Powell would surely see this as the natural extension of the process they document, as isomorphism increases across sectors as well as within them.

Meyer and Rowan and DiMaggio and Powell have charted how rational conventions spread through the forest of organizations to alter notions of rationality. The quality management movement, for example, turned the tide against the earlier movements of Taylorism and Fordism to encourage production workers to help design the production process (Cole 1989). The movement helped spread the idea that worker participation in job design could be more efficient than a strict division of labor between those who design assembly lines and those who work on them. To call the underlying idea of empowerment a rational myth is not to say that there is nothing to it, but rather, to suggest that such ideas diffuse much as customs diffuse in religious or mystical social systems.

For DiMaggio and Powell, as for Meyer and Rowan, new customs diffuse only when they accord with existing cognitive schemas. If the idea of school vouchers succeeds in the United States, it will be because Americans are inclined to think that public bureaucracies breed inefficiency and that the corrective is private competition.

Revolutions in Rational Customs

Chapter 5 excerpts one of Viviana Zelizer's rich Weberian analyses of how modern economic conventions came to be—in this case the convention of banishing child labor from factories. Zelizer's study shows how rationalized roles can be altered. Under early capitalism, children sold their labor by the hour, just as adults did. They had no special role in the factory, and they had no special role in the family, in that every able member contributed his or her labor. Social institutions of all sorts supported this view of the role of children. Life insurance for children was designed to replace children's income. Foster parents favored older boys because of their earning potential. The courts compensated parents of children killed in accidents for the child's lost wages. Early capitalism had rationalized the role of children in parallel to that of adults.

Between 1870 and 1930, children's advocates sought to remove children from industry, changing the meaning of childhood. They described childhood as a sacred category, defining children's value to parents as primarily emotional rather than economic. This crusade succeeded, altering the treatment of children across realms. Most forms of child labor were outlawed. Life insurance for children was redefined to provide parents with compensation for their grief over the loss of a child. Adoptive parents came to favor baby girls, who were inferior earners but superior objects of emotional attachment. The courts awarded grieving parents compensation for their emotional loss rather than for the loss of their child's income. Weber had argued that change in economic institutions can come from many different corners. Zelizer shows that a new rational myth of childhood emerged out of a social movement. The agents of this change were social reformers with a new interpretation of childhood, just as the agents of change in Meyer and Rowan's depiction of organizational life are management consultants with new rational myths of management. In the new myth, children are an asset we invest in for the future rather than a source of labor for the present. In Zelizer's study, rationalized economic conventions can change form entirely, and if those changes persist, we attach rationalized significance to the new form just as we had attached rationalized significance to the old form. The abolition of child factory labor has the feel, in retrospect, of something that was natural and historically inevitable. But child factory labor represented a natural and efficient economic convention at the time, and the redefinition of childhood simply represented another rational interpretation of the role of the child, as worker-in-training through schooling rather than apprenticeship.

National Institutions and Business Recipes

In chapter 6 Richard Whitley's "national business system" approach does for the world's different forms of capitalism what Max Weber did for the world religions, sketching the principles underlying each form. Weber had shown that under Protestantism, Catholicism, Hinduism, Buddhism, and Judaism, different religious logics of salvation corresponded to different prescriptions for how to behave. Whitley finds that there are many different sorts of capitalist economic systems, each with its own conventions and its own logic of rationality.

Whitley begins with national economic and political institutions that affect the firm. National institutions offer a particular social construction of the economy—a particular understanding of the relationships between state and industry, buyer and supplier, finance and industry. They also offer concrete conventions for raising capital, buying components, offering goods for sale, and so on. Within each nation, every industry faces a unique kind of business environment, and successful "business recipes" are those that are best suited to the environment. A winning business recipe for telecommunications may fail miserably in a year or two as the environment changes.

Each industry faces unique circumstances, but general patterns can be seen within each nation. Japan, Hong Kong, Korea, and Taiwan illustrate. Because they operate on very different principles, these economies favor different sorts of business recipes (see also Hamilton and Biggart 1988; Johnson 1982; Cumings 1987; Westney 1987). For instance, the principal economic actors are quite different in these countries, for historical reasons, and the different sorts of actors correspond to different recipes for the pricing of parts. The primary economic actors have been the *kaisha*, or large corporation, in Japan; the *chaebol*, or family-controlled conglomerate, in Korea; and the Chinese Family Business (CFB) in Taiwan and Hong Kong. Cross-shareholding in Japan means that there is typically little competition among parts suppliers, each of whom is formally connected to a buyer. Suppliers are more likely to compete in Taiwan and in Hong Kong, where firms are smaller and where connections between them are weaker. In the end, these business systems depend on different logics, and they create efficiency in different ways. Whitley focuses on the logics underlying these different business systems, but others focus on how new business conventions come about and alter those logics (Gao 1977; Stark 1992).

Each national business system embodies a different conception of how capitalism operates—of the different collective actors involved (family-owned businesses versus monolithic firms) and the relationships among them. For Whitley, each system has a logic that comes to shape how individuals think about their own behavior; in consequence individuals have different cognitive maps of the economic world, and groups have different customs that accord with those maps.

How Rational Myths Emerge

In chapter 7, Davis, Diekmann, and Tinsley (1994) build on the insights of Meyer and Rowan and of DiMaggio and Powell about the role of fads in popularizing new business practices. They explain the shift from the conglomerate to the focused firm that came about in the 1980s as corresponding to a new myth of corporate rationality. The old prescription for how a firm should be run, based in portfolio theory, suggested that huge firms should spread risk through diversification. The challenger model, based in classical managerialism, suggested that huge firms should instead focus on the activities that their management teams are best equipped to manage—on the core industry and kindred industries. This chapter exemplifies the theoretical integration of the new economic sociology, because it uses ideas from institutional, network, power, and cognitive theories.

When the Reagan administration relaxed antitrust law, a change in *institutions* made it possible for firms to switch from diversifying acquisitions to same-industry acquisitions. The new core-competence model of the firm depended on the growing *power* of institutional investors, who control large blocks of stock and who dislike conglomerates because their prospects are difficult to assess. A *network* of hostile takeover specialists developed the model of buying and breaking up the large conglomerates that institutional investors had undervalued. The new strategy was compelling to business because it came along with a familiar *cognitive* framing—that firms should specialize in industries that made the best use of management expertise. Davis and colleagues thus build an explanation of this shift in corporate strategy that depends on all four of the core insights of economic sociology.

The chapters in the institutional section focus on how economic conventions come to be and on what makes them change, emphasizing how our understandings of conventions support them. Economic institutions and conventions provide broad frameworks for understanding the world, and this can be seen in the differences between Catholicism and Protestantism as Weber depicts them in chapter 2. They also provide concrete scripts for how to behave, and this can be seen in the work of John Meyer and Brian Rowan, who describe how new conventions spread across organizations that hope to appear rational and to be rational. For DiMaggio and Powell, dominant firms, professional groups, and nation-states promote new management conventions, contributing to the evolution of conventions. Zelizer shows how one rational convention—child factory labor—was altered forever, when a social movement succeeded in redefining the role of childhood in capitalism.

Whitley carries Weber's ideas in another direction, exploring the logics underlying different forms of capitalism just as Weber had explored the logics underlying the different world religions. For Whitley, each national business system depends on a peculiar set of economic customs, which reinforce one another and which thereby produce a sort of self-sustaining system. Finally, Davis and colleagues show how a change in business conventions can depend on the confluence of *powerful* actors introducing a new strategy, a *network* promoting the strategy, regulatory *institutions* that permit the change, and a *cognitive* framework that legitimates the new strategy.

Networks and Economic Conventions

Max Weber documented the daily customs, and wider institutions, found in different societies. He asked how economic conventions differed between feudal Catholicism and urban Protestantism, and how people's understandings of the world sustained those different conventions. For Weber, conventions survive only because people attach meaning to them—because they make some sort of sense to people. So to understand a society, he sought to grasp the logic running through its conventions and institutions. For Weber, conventions, institutions, and their meanings drive social behavior.

Émile Durkheim tackled society from another angle, trying to understand different sorts of societies through their networks and roles. For Durkheim, social and economic conventions were held in place by social networks. Social networks varied dramatically among the societies Durkheim studied, from the tribes of the South Pacific to the industrial societies of early-twentieth-century Europe. These differences were rooted in the division of labor. In tribal societies, gathering food, making clothing, and building shelters were common tasks. Men and women typically performed different tasks, but that is as far as the dividing up of tasks went. Shared experience was the glue of social life. Tribesmen identified with fellow tribesmen.

In industrial societies the tasks of everyday life were divided up, among ranchers, farmers, factory workers, railwaymen. People who shared an occupation shared common experiences. They learned the everyday routines of the job from the occupational network, and came to identify with that network and its routines. Occupation became a primary role. Interdependence was the glue of social life—ranchers and railwaymen may have had little in common, but they depended upon one another.

Network theorists build on Durkheim's core ideas about the importance of social milieu and of role. Interpersonal networks provide behavioral scripts, or conventions, suggesting, for instance, that managers should "empower" workers by giving them more autonomy. Those networks convey cultural frameworks—chunks of tribal cosmology—so that the new convention of "empowerment" arrives complete with a new theory of human motivation.

The five chapters that follow Durkheim's develop two themes. The first three explore how networks generate and reinforce the very economic conventions that the institutional studies in the first section document. In chapter 9, Mark Granovetter builds on Durkheim's insight that networks establish economic conventions and sanctions. The norm against price gouging is enforced informally by members of an industry network; a seller who is known for price gouging in times of scarcity will lose customers in times of plenty. Alejandro Portes and Julia Sensenbrenner, in chapter 10, build on Granovetter's idea that social networks enforce economic norms via informal sanctions, and show how those norms can have positive effects for the community. In chapter 11, Eric Leifer and Harrison White argue that producers choose from a set of socially defined market roles—price leader, luxury brand, volume discounter—each with a set of off-the-shelf conventions.

The final two chapters explore the structural effects of networks. They explore how networks produce concrete economic advantages that most economic theories ignore. In chapter 12, Ronald Burt's *Structural Holes* shows how missing links in networks create patterns of information asymmetry. People with ties that span these gaps have economic advantages. In chapter 13, Brian Uzzi shows that both intimate and arms-length ties to banks shape the interest rates that small businesses receive on loans. Taken together, these studies provide a striking picture of the role of networks in establishing business customs, in sanctioning firms that do not abide by accepted business practices, and in creating economic advantages for firms.

How Social Milieu Shapes Economic Roles and Behavior

Émile Durkheim pioneered the study of modern occupational networks. Durkheim's *The Division of Labor in Society*, excerpted in chapter 8, charts the origins of the division of labor and explores how social attachment was restructured with industrialization, as individuals developed primary attachments to their occupational groups rather than simply to their local communities. For Durkheim, the glue that held society together was now people's interdependence rather than their common situation. Identification with a group of peers remained important, but those peers now consisted of an occupational group at large.

Durkheim understood social attachment to differ between primitive societies without differentiated roles and modern societies where roles were highly differentiated. Under feudalism virtually everyone was a peasant and the basis of social attachment, and of identity, was the fact that serfs' lives and livelihoods were shared. In complex societies with elaborate divisions of labor an individual's identity was connected to an occupational community of others, many of whom the individual never met. Benedict Anderson (1983) would later call the modern nation an "imagined community," comprising people who identify with others they have never met.

Durkheim saw that in modern societies, identity was formed by religious affiliation and by nationality but also increasingly by occupation. Managers and workers, professionals and bureaucrats thus behave according to occupational scripts. Durkheim documented the increasingly fine-grained economic conventions that emerged in modern societies. He showed that occupational networks were becoming the source of the economic conventions and meanings that Weber saw at the heart of modern economic behavior. The division of labor generated a complex web of overlapping occupational networks, each with elaborate socialization processes that conveyed particular customs of work.

How Networks Constrain Economic Behavior

Sociologists have long been interested in why people behave according to economic conventions. Institutionalists, from Weber forward, have argued that customs that are socially defined as self-interested are not hard to explain. In rationalized societies, people believe they should act in their self-interest and are always on the lookout for new ways to behave self-interestedly. Economic customs that are socially defined as altruistic are harder to explain, but network theorists argue that we follow altruistic customs because we are embedded in social networks. Our reputation, prestige, and future capacity to buy and sell depend on our behavior in a network of peers.

Chapter 9 is Mark Granovetter's erudite "Economic Action and Social Structure: The Problem of Embeddedness," which in 1985 gave the new economic sociology a theoretical shot in the arm, challenging two extreme views of economic behavior and proposing a middle ground in the tradition of Durkheim. Sociology's oversocialized conception of economic behavior (Wrong 1961) suggested that we follow norms like lemmings following the crowd. Neoclassical economics' under-socialized conception of economic behavior seemed to suggest that individuals are atomized decision-making machines unaffected by culture and socialization.

Granovetter proposed instead that individual economic choices were embedded in social context. Workplace and professional networks shape behavior, determining the kinds of economic behavior people can imagine and constraining the kinds of economic behavior they can pursue. Granovetter thus explains how rational actors can decide to abide by economic conventions even when doing so costs them money.

To illustrate, Granovetter tackles Oliver Williamson's "transaction cost" theory from institutional economics, which addresses the conditions that encourage a firm to merge with its supplier rather than to use the open market to obtain supplies. Williamson argues that a firm will merge with its supplier (will "vertically integrate") where it is efficient to do so; in particular, where the supplier has the opportunity to price-gouge. Granovetter counters that suppliers often abide by the norm against price-gouging, because their reputations and identities depend on this convention. Networks, moreover, often punish price-gougers by denying them business. Thus firms do not have to buy suppliers who might have the chance to price-gouge, because social networks discourage gouging.

Granovetter's theory melds elements of the neoclassical economic view, that people are self-interested maximizers of income, with elements of the sociological view, that social milieu shapes behavior. In Granovetter's model, for instance, it may be rational in the long run for a seller to follow social norms about pricing even when, in the short run, those norms impinge on her profits. Francis Fukuyama's bestseller *Trust: The Social Virtues and the*

Creation of Prosperity (1995) builds on Granovetter's idea that trusting social networks confers economic advantage on a society by obviating the need for extensive regulation, generating spontaneous cooperation and assistance, and making economic relations collaborative rather than legalistic.

How Networks Produce Social Capital and Reinforce Conventions

Granovetter argues that people's social networks can constrain them to abide by economic conventions, such as that against gouging. Chapter 10 is Alejandro Portes and Julia Sensenbrenner's "Embeddedness and Immigration: Notes on the Social Determinants of Economic Action," which builds on Granovetter's idea of embeddedness coupled with the idea of "social capital." French sociologist Pierre Bourdieu introduced the idea that social networks offer a type of "capital" for achieving economic ends. James Coleman (1990) in sociology and Robert Putnam (1993) in political science later built on the idea. Like Granovetter, Portes and Sensenbrenner show that social networks can promote economic conventions that serve the community even if they do not serve individual interests, narrowly construed. Like Granovetter, they challenge the view that people make economic decisions in isolation and show that conventions persist because networks come to expect members to abide by them.

Portes and Sensenbrenner distinguish mechanisms through which social capital can confer advantages on group members. *Reciprocity exchanges* involve the trading of virtual chits across economic exchanges. By doing good for someone else, you place them in your debt and you can expect them to do good for you in the future. *Bounded solidarity* (Durkheim 1933) refers to solidaristic bonds that tie communities together and cause them to support members in need. *Enforceable trust* refers to group sanctioning of behavior, following Granovetter's idea that malfeasance and bad faith will become known to the group and will be punished in subsequent exchanges.

Portes and Sensenbrenner illustrate the cases of bounded solidarity and enforceable trust in immigrant communities. In the case of bounded solidarity, ties among members of an immigrant community cause them to stand together behind a community member who is threatened. This creates, for instance, a kind of premium-less insurance pool for legal expenses. In the case of enforceable trust, immigrant groups often establish informal financial networks and rotating credit associations. Having no legal hold on members, these groups depend on informal sanctions such as the threat of ostracism from the business community. Enforceable trust succeeds to the extent that members depend on others in the community for business and for future loans. This kind of social capital safeguards lenders while providing credit to group members who might not qualify for loans from traditional lenders. In other words, strong in-group networks can serve to enforce such conventions as loan repayment. For Portes and Sensenbrenner, then, social networks create, convey, and enforce economic conventions.

How Market Networks Produce Roles

Institutionalists argue that corporations copy very specific practices—deconglomeration—from their competitors. Sociologists who look at producer markets as networks argue that market networks also generate an array of conventional roles. Market roles are themselves institutionalized. Firms deliberately choose from among these roles, often in an effort to find a market niche that will shield them from competition. For network theorists of markets, the configuration of market roles (large-volume, low-cost manufacturer; elite, low-volume producer) is itself routinized and recognizable across industries. CEOs do not really create market strategies de novo, they adopt one socially defined market role or another.

In chapter 11, Eric Leifer and Harrison White (1987) expand on White's (1981, 2002) network theory of markets, in which sellers follow the customs for pricing that are established by other sellers rather than discovering what "the market will bear" by trial and error. Sellers look to their peers for signals about how to set prices, how to determine quantities produced, and how to assess the trade-off between quantity and quality. For White, it does not make sense to think of markets, pace neoclassical economists, as composed of atomized producers paying attention only to the price signals coming from buyers.

In "A Structural Approach to Markets" Leifer and White show that producers define their identities relative to those of other producers. They choose from roles such as price leader, luxury brand, and volume discounter. These roles, like the occupational roles Durkheim describes, come with a set of prescriptions for how to behave—that is, economic conventions. The roles are based, in large part, on a socially established menu of decisions about quality, quantity, and price of the product. Whereas the economist Michael Spence (1973) argued that in labor markets, people signaled their productivity with educational attainment, White argues that in production markets sellers send signals to other sellers to mark their market territory. A new frozen pizza maker signals her niche by her prices, quantities, and quality, and she chooses that niche based on her perception of the niches that existing producers have left open. The identity, or strategy, she selects—inexpensive but chic, or the best that money can buy—soon locks her into a market position.

Like the institutionalists, network theorists show that individuals draw their strategies from customs rather than making rational calculations, from scratch, in each situation they face. White goes one step further, arguing that even the dimensions on which economic actors distinguish themselves from the crowd are determined by convention (see Bothner 2000). They are institutionalized. While for Granovetter a producer is constrained to follow the convention against gouging by concern over his reputation among buyers, for Leifer and White a producer is constrained by the behaviors—the business strategies—of other producers.

How Network Position can Confer Social Capital

In the tradition of Durkheim, Ronald Burt and Brian Uzzi are concerned with how one's network provides information about roles, reputations, and economic opportunities. This information can confer economic advantage, and it can shape pricing decisions. For Burt, "structural holes" in social networks create information asymmetries—imbalances of information among individuals or firms—and opportunities. Economists George Akerlof (1970) and Joseph Stiglitz (2002), who shared the 2001 Nobel Prize in economics with Michael Spence, have explored the consequences of information asymmetry but have not seen it as a feature of networks. Akerlof's famous paper "The Market for Lemons: Quality Uncertainty and the Market Mechanism" (1970) illustrates the problem of information asymmetry with the market for used cars. Information asymmetry depresses the prices that buyers are willing to pay for used cars, because while each seller knows whether he has a good machine or a lemon, buyers must operate on the assumption that all cars on offer are lemons.

Burt focuses on network structures, arguing that there are "structural holes" in all social networks—missing links that create information asymmetries. Where (B) knows both (A) and (C), who are strangers, (B) may be able to take advantage of his position. The headhunting industry works on this principle, with headhunters connecting dissatisfied executives with firms in search of personnel. The headhunter is rewarded for his network position in the form of a commission. *Structural Holes* shows that one can profit from spanning a hole in a network. Burt's theory has obvious practical implications, for it suggests that people should tap into diverse networks to maximize their economic opportunities. Mark Granovetter's 1974 book, *Getting a Job*, illustrates one way in which structural holes create opportunities. In his study of how people actually make the connections that get them jobs, Granovetter finds that people typically find jobs through weak social ties rather than through strong ones. Strong ties tend to produce overlapping information. If you are looking for a job and you ask all of your current coworkers, you will discover that they know about the same job openings. If you search through weak as well as strong ties, asking your college friends, your dentist, and your dry cleaner, you tap into wider networks of information and are more likely to land a job.

Burt's theory of structural holes helps to explain many economic phenomena that others have not been able to explain. Firms that cooperate with industry peers do better than those that do not, and this has long been put down to collusion. Network theory suggests that there may be more to it. Ingram and Roberts (2000) find that hotels make more money when their managers have many friends among their competitors, because those friends pass on overflow clients and exchange information about the market. Wayne Baker's *Networking Smart* (1994) and *Achieving Success through Social Capital* (2000) have brought such insights to an audience of managers seeking to understand how to make the best strategic use of networks.

How Network Ties Influence Prices Paid

Burt's theory of structural holes suggests that networks can create information asymmetries that advantage the well connected. Brian Uzzi's structural studies of networks and pricing demonstrate that network connections shape reputations and thereby influence pricing. Economic sociologists have sometimes been criticized for not studying the most important economic phenomenon, price. In chapter 13, Uzzi does just this in an award-winning study that combines ethnographic analysis with quantitative analysis of data on bank loans to small firms.

Do firms with similar profiles pay the same interest rates, regardless of their ties to the banks they borrow from? Common sense and conspiracy theory suggest that close personal ties might get you lower rates. Uzzi shows that it is not so simple. It is true that firms with close personal ties to banks receive favorable rates, but it is firms that have both close ties and arm's-length ties that receive the best rates. Close social ties encourage banks to share resources, but arm's-length ties give them objective information about a firm's creditworthiness. Both kinds of network ties help firms. Uzzi and Lancaster (forthcoming) find an equally interesting pattern of relations between networks and prices in the legal industry. Close ties lower prices (legal fees), as in banking, but corporate board ties increase the prestige and expertise of a law firm in its prospective client's eyes, and thus raise legal fees.

Network theorists have developed a number of different insights about economic behavior. Durkheim argued that networks create behavioral norms—conventions—for occupational groups and for firms. Like institutionalists, Harrison White is concerned with how customs make sense to people, and hence he focuses on how concrete interpersonal networks provide individuals with examples of how to behave rationally—scripts for how a luxury producer, or a volume discounter, should play the game. Granovetter shows how networks influence reputation and identity and thereby cause members to adhere to economic conventions. Portes and Sensenbrenner stand on Granovetter's shoulders to show that dense networks can enforce such norms as loan repayment and thereby substitute for legal sanctions. Ronald Burt and Brian Uzzi develop structural theories of networks, asking how networks shape reputations and transmit economic information.

Following the chapters on network theory is a group of chapters that emphasizes how power influences economic conventions. For institutionalists, people use power to promote the business strategies and regulatory institutions that they want to see adopted. Thus, according to Davis and colleagues, in the 1980s and 1990s institutional investors and securities analysts had the power to lowball stock in diversified firms, pressuring such firms to join the core-competence bandwagon. Network theorists see corporate power being used to (*a*) sanction firms that practice malfeasance, according to Granovetter, (*b*) prevent potential competitors from entering markets, according to Leifer and White, and (*c*) gain advantage over isolated firms, according to Burt. In the coming section, the focus is on how the powerful are able to influence (*a*) public regulation of markets and (*b*) business conventions.

Power and Economic Conventions

Like institutionalists, power theorists try to explain how economic conventions arise. They ask how power shapes conventions. Karl Marx's analyses of feudalism and capitalism inform most contemporary power theories. His economic sociology was rich and variegated, but the idea that has most influenced contemporary economic sociologists stems from his observation that under capitalism as under feudalism, people seldom perceive the exercise of power. Serfs accepted their positions as part of the natural God-given order. Workers accepted *their* positions as part of the natural pecking order under capitalism, in the belief that aptitude and fate separated assembly-line workers from Henry Ford.

Marx's idea was that power relations are obscured by ideology. It is not the threat of force that is the key to power, but the capacity to cause people to see certain economic conventions as natural and inevitable. Powerful individuals, firms, and countries promote their favored economic conventions not merely as such, but as good for society at large. Once a country, a firm, or a tycoon has convinced the world of the efficacy of a new public policy or business strategy, that policy or strategy is held in place not by the sustained exercise of power, but by its own self-evident efficacy (Lamont 1989).

Power theory has increasingly come to parallel institutional theory, in that both build on the idea that we read utility into the social conventions and institutions that surround us. When we see antitrust law in action, we develop explanations of it as a necessary component of an efficient market. We do not naturally think of it as the legacy of a nineteenth-century power struggle among different groups. Charles Perrow's (2002) *Organizing America: Wealth, Power, and the Origins of Corporate Capitalism* takes this approach to its highest form by arguing that large-scale capitalism emerged not because it was more efficient than small-scale production, but because a wealthy few wanted to dominate the economy. What drove the evolution of huge firms was not the democratic striving for plenty, in Perrow's view, but the striving of a small group for control over the economy.

The four selections in the third section of the anthology treat two broad issues. The chapters by Karl Marx, Neil Fligstein, and William Roy explore how the powerful devise policy institutions and business conventions to serve their own interests, framing those institutions and conventions as neutral and efficient. In *The German Ideology*, Marx argues that modern states were built to reinforce the power of capitalists but that they survive under the guise of democracy and freedom of opportunity. Marx saw the rhetoric of democracy and freedom as a smokescreen for a system of economic regulation designed to enrich owners of firms and impoverish their employees. The chapters by Fligstein and Roy exemplify how power theorists now use Marx's insight in combination with institutional and network insights. In each, power played a role in the initial formulation of a new business convention, networks helped to diffuse that convention, and institutionalization (meaning-making) helped to ensure that it would become taken for granted. Fligstein shows that management subgroups have struggled over control of the modern corporation, with sales managers wresting control from production managers and finance managers, in turn, wresting control from sales managers. Roy shows how early financiers used power to win control over large portions of American manufacturing and how they consolidated huge firms in many industries. In chapter 17, Bruce Carruthers takes up a second theme prominent in economic sociology, showing not that power helps to shape core ideas about rational behavior, but that economic decisions are shaped by power and politics. In the early British stock market, sellers of stock preferred to sell to others in their political party to keep important corporations in the hands of their political cronies.

How Coercion Shapes Economic Scripts

Karl Marx was interested in how the world that people encounter shapes not merely their economic behavior but also their ideas. In *The German Ideology*, excerpted in chapter 14, Marx critiqued contemporary philosophy for being based entirely in abstract thought rather than in human experience, and sketched a theory of human history based in the evolution of production and of class relations. In Europe, lords had exploited serfs under feudalism, masters had exploited workmen under guild production, and capitalists now exploited wage laborers under capitalism. Each system portrayed these relations as natural and just, for God chose lords and kings under feudalism, the master craftsman earned his position by the sweat of his brow under guild production, and the factory owner won his position with cunning under capitalism.

For Marx, the modern state imposed laws favoring capitalists on a society in which the vast majority were not capitalists, and it did so under the rhetoric of democracy rather than under that of capitalist domination. In so doing, Marx argued, states made capitalism seem natural and just when it was in reality neither. Today power theorists rarely portray the nation-state as a tool of capitalists, but they have built on Marx's idea that states impose a particular set of rules, regulations, and institutions shaping economic life—a set of "property rights," in the language of institutional economists. These property rights are not dictated by economic laws, but are worked out by powerful groups. In support of the idea that economic laws do not dictate public policy, comparative studies of capitalism, such as Richard Whitley's "business systems" studies (chap. 6), demonstrate that there are many ways of organizing a capitalist economy efficiently.

Thus while today's power theorists accept the idea that capitalism is more efficient than other economic systems, they argue that power relations produce different forms of capitalism. From institutional theory (Meyer, Boli, and Thomas 1987; Berger and Luckmann 1966; Wuthnow 1987) they draw insights about why we believe that there must be "one best way" to organize economic activity under capitalism. The modern worldview depends on a scientific cosmology in which the world we experience is produced by universal laws governing nature and the economy. Those laws determine the best way to design a bicycle, just as they determine the best way to design a semiconductor market. When we encounter a bicycle, we presume that trial and error have produced the best possible outcome. We think about semiconductor markets in the same way.

For power theorists, people come to take for granted, and to interpret as rational, the economic conventions that surround them. Power shaped those conventions in the first place.

How Management Factions Shape Corporate Strategy

Neil Fligstein's *The Transformation of Corporate Control* brings to bear Marx's insights about power struggles among competing elite factions, found for instance in *The Eighteenth Brumaire of Louis Bonaparte* (1963), in explaining changes in leadership and strategy among America's largest corporations. Fligstein explores power struggles within management groups seeking to gain control of large corporations. His foil is Alfred DuPont Chandler, America's preeminent business historian who in *The Visible Hand* (1977), told the story of the evolution of corporate control from the perspective of business efficiency. Early firms were run by managers with backgrounds in production. Later, sales and marketing managers took over, as the axis of competition among firms shifted from production to marketing. Later still, finance managers took over, as firms shifted focus from sales and marketing to diversification. Chandler treats these changes as part of the natural progression of the modern firm.

Fligstein finds that these changes were the result of a series of power struggles among management factions. Each group succeeded in taking control of the large corporation by convincing investors that their management specialty held the key to corporate efficacy. The shift from sales to finance management was kicked off in 1950 when Congress passed the Celler-Kefauver Act, making it difficult for firms to acquire others in related businesses. Finance managers responded with a new business model, later reinforced by portfolio theory in financial economics, in which the large firm should not act like a marketing machine in a single sector, but like an investor with a diversified portfolio. Finance managers now argued before corporate boards and investors that the diversified conglomerate was the way of the future and that they, finance managers, were best qualified to manage conglomerates. They thereby came to displace experts in sales at the helms of the biggest corporations.

What now makes this story more compelling than Chandler's argument that the conglomerate prevailed because it was more efficient than the one-trick pony is that the one-trick-pony (the "core-competence" firm) has risen again. Today the smart money is on firms that focus on one or two businesses; investors argue that *they*—not corporations—should diversify their portfolios as they see fit; and it is difficult to find advocates of the portfolio theory of the firm. As Davis and colleagues show in chapter 7 (and see Fligstein and Markowitz 1993), "core competence" arose because institutional investors and securities analysts found it hard to place a value on the conglomerate and used their power (to rate firms and to invest funds) to raise the stock prices of firms that operated in a single industry. Power played a role in the rise of the diversification strategy, and in its demise as well.

How Capitalist Factions Shaped Corporate Strategy

Fligstein's work brings together insights from power theory (a power play for control of large corporations was central), from network theory (a network of finance managers was key), and from institutional theory (new business customs became taken for granted) to explain shifts in corporate conventions—firm structure and strategy—over the course of the twentieth century. William Roy, in *Socializing Capital: The Rise of the Large Industrial Corporation in America* (1997), excerpted in chapter 16, brings together these same three elements to explain a wave of mergers at the beginning of the twentieth century that produced huge industrial enterprises and a business model based on economies of scale.

In explaining the rise of finance managers with their conglomeration strategy, Fligstein finds that antitrust amendments circa 1950 changed the balance of power between different sorts of managers within the firm. In Roy's case, the initial enforcement of antitrust in 1897 had an unanticipated effect on the balance of power between large and small firms. Roy shows that it was not only economies of scale that gave big firms an edge, as Alfred Chandler (1977) contended, because small firms merged into big firms even in industries that could not benefit from economies of scale. Instead, Roy argues, when antitrust prevented firms from joining together to set prices, large firms demanded that smaller competitors sell out or face certain death in price wars. It was not that large firms were more efficient than small firms, it was that they had the power to threaten them after antitrust prevented firms from banding together to set prices.

The irony of early antitrust law was that while it was designed to prevent the concentration of economic power by outlawing collusion, it encouraged mergers. Small firms could no longer set prices together, but they could merge into a bigger firm that could set a single price. The huge concentrated firm, then, was born out of an unanticipated coincidence of public policy and private power. Public policy fostered price competition, and large firms forced their smaller competitors to sell out. Americans soon came to take the huge industrial enterprise for granted, and to presume that large firms are large because they enjoy economies of scale. Drawing on institutional theory, Roy argues that people came to believe that the huge oligopoly emerged for reasons of efficiency rather than for reasons of power.

Fligstein shows how power (among finance experts) shaped the rise of the diversified conglomerate and contributed to our taking it for granted as efficient. Roy does the same for the huge oligopoly at the dawn of the twentieth century, showing that power has an ongoing effect—once a power struggle establishes a new business convention (the oligopoly), we come to believe it must be efficient, and this belief sustains it. In this case, the theory of scale economies was articulated to reinforce the oligopoly. Thereafter, people believed that firms were big because big was efficient, not because medium-sized firms had gobbled up small rivals by threatening price wars—by exercising power.

How Political Alliances Shape Exchange Patterns

Bruce Carruthers's *City of Capital: Politics and Markets in the English Financial Revolution* (1996), excerpted in chapter 17, examines the role of power from a different angle. Rather than looking at how power shapes business conventions, Carruthers looks at how politics shapes trading. A tenet of price theory in economics is that each seller chooses the buyer offering the highest price. Carruthers looks at English stock trading in the early 1700s to show that politics influenced sellers' choices of buyers. Stockholders in politically important companies often chose to sell to other partisans even when it meant that they would not get the best price. There were strong political battle lines in place in the early 1700s, and large companies exercised significant influence over political decision-making. Who controlled the East India Company was of some political consequence. Carruthers finds that stockholders with strong political leanings tended to sell to partisans. Sellers might lose money by refusing to sell to their political rivals, but that is exactly what they did.

Carruthers's study carries forward an important tradition in economic sociology of showing that political motives influence economic behavior (see Zelizer 1988). In Granovetter's terms, Carruthers finds that stock traders are embedded in a wider political context that shapes their behavior—that traders are not isolated machines driven by price alone. If this is true in the pristine realm of stock trading, Carruthers implies, it is surely true throughout economic life.

From the muckraking stories of collusion among early railway barons and oil magnates to journalists' tales of accounting scandals among corporate giants at the dawn of the twenty-first century, most journalistic accounts caution that power must not infiltrate business dealings. For most economic sociologists, power is a regular part of economic life. Modern regulatory institutions and business conventions are shaped in the first place by power relations. This is particularly evident in the United States, where industries are typically regulated by former captains of industry (Useem 1984). The studies included in this part suggest that business conventions and forms we take entirely for granted as originating in the search for efficiency—the oligopolistic manufacturing firm and the diversified conglomerate—were shaped by power struggles.

Cognition and Economic Conventions

Whether they focus on the effects of institutions, networks, or power, economic sociologists share a common set of social psychological assumptions. Durkheim spelled out the core ideas, and they are now shared not only by economic sociologists but by many sociological constructionists, cognitive psychologists, organization behavior theorists, cultural anthropologists, cognitive scientists, and behavioral economists.

These ideas are different from those underlying mid-twentieth-century American economics, which began with the premises of methodological individualism and self-interest. Under methodological individualism, behavior can be traced directly to human nature—to instinct. The instinct of greed trumps other instincts. People are naturally calculating—conniving, even—and systematically so. In premodern societies, the story goes, superstition and myth interfered with the rational pursuit of self-interest, but at heart people were always self-interested. The idea was that you could explain economic conventions with a small set of mathematical formulas that capture how self-interest is played out. Those formulas were written by nature. Social structures evolve to allow people to pursue their self-interest—they do not alter human instincts, they facilitate them. Society, then, is merely the individual mind writ large.

Sociologists have taken the opposite view, that the human mind is society writ small (Douglas 1986). Individual consciousness comes to reflect social institutions. Social institutions take many different forms, and the differences come about by chance. Tribes worship frogs because the local environment is inundated with frogs. Or they worship at the altar of public transport planning (in France) because in the eighteenth century, their state built royal roads to bring troops to the front. Consciousness comes to reflect institutions that arose by historical happenstance. Because history has produced many different kinds of societies, it has produced many different cognitive structures. For sociologists, while the survival instinct may be innate, much of what people view as innate, self-interested, economic behavior is scripted by convention rather than by biology. Much of it is learned rather than hardwired by our genes.

The degree to which behavior is learned, rather than innate, varies by species. Horses leave the womb ready to walk. Tortoises leave their eggs with all the tools they need to get along. But much human behavior is learned, and the interesting differences across groups are, ipso facto, learned. Socialization theory and cognitive psychology offer starting points for thinking about what underlies these differences, better starting points than mid-twentieth-century microeconomics, which is based in the idea that humans have universal goals (Teutonic luxury cars) and universal scripts for how to achieve them (Stanford MBA followed by McKinsey). After all, in some settings people are socialized to pursue the goal of appeasing the ancestors by the means of sacrificing small animals. Most economic theories now stipulate that goals vary—that your goal may be Zen tranquility rather than the BMW 745—but retain the idea that the means to achieving goals are more or less part of human nature. This may be where economic sociology differs most starkly from neoclassical economics—in the idea that the scripts for achieving goals are social phenomena that become embedded in cognitive schemas. The idea is that scripts are no more given by nature than goals are.

Social institutions create mental maps of the world in individuals. Some call them schemas, others frames (Goffman 1974), others cultural tool-kits (Swidler 1986). Institutions produce broadly similar cognitive frameworks across members of a society. These frameworks encompass categorization schemes, maps of relationships among things, and maps of causal processes.

This view of the human psyche is widely shared among sociologists. Not only Durkheim, but Weber and Marx saw human actions, motives, and understandings as reflecting social structure. Weber (1978, 4) turned this observation into a methodological dictum, arguing that to understand social action, one must understand its meaning to the actor. The social scientist may think that a price reduction has an objective meaning, but she will not understand it unless she understands what it means to the actor (Schutz 1970). While economists' belief in methodological individualism dictates that they must trace behavior to human nature, Weber insists that we must trace behavior to its socially constructed meaning.

The four chapters in the part on cognition trace the evolution of this sociological idea, that cognition is driven by social conventions and their meanings to the group. In chapter 18, Durkheim examines pre-modern religious systems to find that the social classification of things and beings and the social construction of causal processes are fundamental to human nature. In Chapter 19, excerpted from Peter Berger and Thomas Luckmann's *The Social Construction of Reality*, the sociological view of objectivation is spelled out—the cognitive process by which we transform subjective interpretations of the world around us (as driven by the spirit world, or by laws of nature) into hard objective realities. Chapter 20, James March and Herbert Simon's "Cognitive Limits on Rationality," sketches how members of organizations develop rationalized routines for solving problems, and how they come to apply these routines as rationalized rituals to solve problems. Finally, in chapter 21, the psychologist Karl Weick explores cognitive sensemaking within organizations, showing how people explain their own behavior post hoc, to themselves and to others, in socially meaningful terms. We invent meaningful rationales for action after we have acted, simultaneously reinforcing existing rationales and justifying our own behavior.

Origins of the Meaning Underlying Economic Action

Whereas for early economists, the core human trait was self-interest, for Durkheim the core trait was sociality. Economists traced behavior to self-interest, and Durkheim traced it to the group processes of classification and meaning-making. He found these processes in primitive and modern societies alike. Pacific Islanders categorized the world in ways alien to Durkheim, lumping the tribe with the totem, animals with vegetables, and so on. Their categories were based on affinities between things defined by the spirit world. They constructed understandings of causality built on these categories, and based in mystical rather than in rational principles. Yet as in modern societies, the shared constructions of the world they developed structured the psyche.

Durkheim's revelation in *The Elementary Forms of the Religious Life*, excerpted in chapter 18, is that the totem is at once the group's deity and its flag. The totem—be it a frog or a bat—represents the tribe as distinct from other tribes and is also the object of worship. The totem symbolizes the idea that the group is more than the sum of its parts—that there is something transcendental in social life. This insight is the kernel of the social constructionist theory of cognition. For Durkheim, societies trace social conventions to something bigger than society. Tribes that worship their ancestors trace conventions to the spirit world and see what goes on in society as a reflection of the world of the ancestors. Religious societies likewise trace social order and customs to something outside of society—to God.

Durkheim's followers argue that rationalized societies are not so different from religious and mystified societies. Rationalized societies trace social conventions to something outside of society—to laws of nature, economy, and society that are unvarying across time and space. Social constructionists, such as Peter Berger and Thomas Luckmann, who are excerpted in chapter 19, argue that cognitive structures come to reflect social conventions and the universal laws that modern societies define as underlying them. For them, human cognition is a reflection of the surrounding social order. We are rational actors, but only because we live in a universe governed by scientific laws. In a universe directed by frog spirits, our cognitive structures would reflect the frog kingdom. Moreover, rational cognitive orientation comes in as many flavors as mystified cognitive orientation.

The best evidence for this view may come from the historian Albert Hirschman (1977), who has shown that the goals-and-interests framework itself arose relatively recently even in the West, to replace a view of human behavior as driven by a series of innate passions—greed and lust and hunger. Self-interest, it seems, is just one among many lenses through which we can view the modern soul. It is now popular to believe, following historical studies such as Avner Greif's (1993) analysis of early trading patterns, that a modern version of self-interest can be found in antiquity and thus that self-interest is innate and that the inclination to truck and barter is hardwired. It is certainly the case, as Weber (1978) and Richard Swedberg (2002) argue, that elements of modern self-interest can be found in early modern Europe. But Neil Smelser's (1993) review of anthropological evidence suggests that in aboriginal societies, members did not view self-interest as underlying their own behavior and did not create incipient modern markets. That the modern version of self-interest is a product of rationalized societies seems clear. How, then, do specific notions of self-interest arise and evolve?

How Cognition Carries Prescriptions for Economic Behavior

Durkheim did not find much in the way of rational, calculating self-interest among totemic societies, but he did find the same general form of meaning-making that he had seen in modern societies. In both settings, people categorized things to make sense of the world. In both, they traced physical and social patterns to forces outside of society—to a spirit world or to a system of natural laws. For Durkheim, it is human nature to make sense of the world.

In chapter 19, Peter Berger and Thomas Luckmann sketch a social constructionist view of human cognition, a view that has come to shape the other three strands of economic sociology, including the work of Meyer and Rowan in chapter 3, the work of Leifer and White in chapter 11, and the work of William Roy in chapter 16. Their ideas are based in social phenomenology. Berger and Luckmann (1966, 20) say that their task is to grasp "the objectivations of subjective processes (and meanings) by which the *inter*subjective commonsense world is constructed." How is it, in other words, that our subjective "knowledge" of the world comes to have the feel of an objective reality? The fact that our fellows share that subjective knowledge helps to give it the feel of objective fact. Understanding how we come to take for granted the world as it presents itself is key to understanding how economic conventions are stabilized, and how they can change. If everyone around us believes that economic success is a consequence of the local totem's sentiment, of God's will, or of market conditions, we will find that belief compelling and will come to see it as objective knowledge rather than subjective belief. This is how we make sense of the world, as Durkheim contends. We do not see the socially constructed reality around us—the belief in the connection between market conditions and economic success—as a social product. We see it as real. Gravity is what it is, a force of nature (not of the spirit world) as predictable as death and taxes.

Berger and Luckmann find that the inclination to assign objective status to intersubjective reality characterizes human societies. In mystified, religious, and rational settings alike, people know *why* the sun rises and sets just as surely as they know *that* it rises and sets. At the level of cognition, the individual makes causal connections on the basis of the wider system of meaning institutionalized in concrete customs. Americans, for instance, believe that a kind of Darwinian competition among firms creates progress, killing the less efficient and rewarding the more efficient. This is a simple cognitive model that guides behavior. Under Leifer and White's version of network theory, the understanding that you will face stiff competition if you enter a market in a segment with a dominant actor follows from this cognitive model. Leifer and White find that the model leads market entrants to seek niches where there is no competition. Other countries and industries operate with entirely different market customs and cognitive models, many of which are not organized around a Darwinian market. Where the state coordinates business groups, as in Japan, or enforces cartel agreements, as was long the case in Britain and Germany, market customs and cognition take different forms. You might not see it as suicidal to enter a market that already has one very big fish.

Cross-national studies of the human psyche confirm that societies impose very different models of social order on the mind. In psychology, experimental studies have shown that individuals describe the same picture in very different ways, Americans focusing on the subject and Japanese focusing on the context (Nisbett et al. 2001). Hence Americans are more likely to attribute the behavior of others to character, while Japanese are more likely to attribute it to context. Comparative studies of management practices and ideas (e.g. Hofstede 1980) show that across a wide range of countries, orientations to authority, innovation, and cooperation vary systematically. "National character"—sometimes a code word for ethnicity—used to be thought to explain these differences, but scholars increasingly trace them to differences in national institutions (e.g., Whitley and Kristensen 1996). The institution of lifetime employment for managers still prevails in Japan (Dore 2000), and it contrasts starkly with the custom of getting ahead by moving around that prevails in the United States. Such customs shape cognitive orientations and the means people use to pursue goals. How to succeed in business is understood differently in these two settings.

Understanding what the actor has in mind when she acts is important to Berger and Luckmann not only as an intellectual exercise, but because it facilitates prediction. For some forms of behavior, as March and Simon argue in chapter 20, local scripts are highly routinized. But for many, individuals have to draw on the general mental models of action available to them. If you know that the American psyche makes a Darwinian market the driving force of progress, you can reasonably predict that when Americans face a problem of efficiency, they will try to apply the model. And indeed even where economists think market mechanisms will not work—telecommunications, air transport, health care, education—Americans have favored market solutions. Mid-twentieth-century American economics saw such preferences as innate, whereas economic sociologists tend to see them as learned—as nurture, not nature.

How Cognition Shapes Economic Choices

In discussing subjectivity, Berger and Luckmann are implicitly comparing the cognitive frames found in diverse societies or groups. Eving Goffman (1974) popularized the concept of a *frame* as a shared map of reality. Pierre Bourdieu (1977) defines *habitus* as a class-based way of seeing the world. Luc Boltanski and Laurent Thevenot (1991) use the term *justification* to refer to the menu of standard ways of understanding social action. Ann Swidler (1986) uses *cultural tool-kit* to describe the shared cultural components that people use to act on the world and interpret it. The common point is that societies produce broadly different sorts of cognitive orientations—maps of reality. The Ndembu and Kansas tribes have different understandings of how to achieve a good harvest. In economic sociology, studies of cognition have generally taken place at the organizational level rather than at the national level, though in cultural anthropology and, increasingly, cultural psychology the same processes are studied cross-nationally.

James March and Herbert Simon's "Cognitive Limits on Rationality" (1958) stipulates a modern, rational society and explores the role of cognition in organizational decision-making. March, a sociologist, and Simon, a cognitive psychologist and recipient of the 1978 Nobel Prize in economics, sketch two ideas that have been widely used in economic sociology. The first idea concerns the limits of human cognitive capacity in rational decision-making. Managers are seldom able to identify the optimal means to a particular end because of the difficulty of assessing the costs and benefits of each imaginable strategy. They typically settle on solutions that meet minimal criteria for achieving a goal rather than searching for the ideal solution, "satisficing" rather than optimizing. George Stigler, in a famous essay titled "Economics and Information" from 1961, argued that people search for ways to achieve a goal with perfect efficiency—that they continue to search until precisely the point at which the marginal cost of searching exceeds the marginal benefit to be gained. March and Simon anticipate this argument, showing that decision makers lack the information to judge when further searching is worth the effort. Instead, they argue, people begin the search process with familiar solutions in mind. When faced with a problem, people typically think of an analogous problem from the past and apply the solution used in that case—"What did we do the last time there was a budget shortfall?" They go beyond off-the-shelf remedies only when no such remedy is available.

This brings us to the second idea, which concerns the menu of solutions that organizations offer. Organizations develop all sorts of problem-solving routines, ranging from very precise routines for dealing with common and predictable functions (filling an order) to very general routines for dealing with rare and unpredictable functions (writing a computer program). The routines exist as organizational culture at the level of the firm and as cognitive problem-solving scenarios in the minds of individuals. In chapter 20 March and Simon argue that customs and cognitive frameworks are really two sides of the same coin, for cognitive frameworks reflect the customs individuals encounter in their work organizations. Whereas institutionalists focus on the character of broad institutional systems—religious or scientific, Hindu or Protestant—and on the factors that lead those systems to change, cognitive theorists focus on the individual-level cosmologies or cognitive frameworks that those institutions generate. Institutions and conventions vary across nations, but March and Simon point to important variations even across work organizations in the same nation and industry, shaping workers' cognitive frameworks and hence their knee-jerk reactions to problems that arise.

For March and Simon, people in modern work organizations act rationally, in that they pursue rationalized solutions to problems. You will not encounter many rain dances at IBM. But the nature of human cognition is such that people do not devise optimal solutions for the problems they face. They mostly choose from among the organization's ritual, albeit rationalized, solutions. These rituals have shaped their cognitive structures, offering ready means to particular ends.

How Action Reinforces Cognitive Frames

In exploring the relationship between social structure and individual cognition, Durkheim's followers argue that most human customs are framed as driven by forces outside of society. The human inclination to categorize and generalize leads people to see the wider universe as the source of social and economic customs. Berger and Luckmann argue that different groups have different meaning systems, and that to understand and predict a social behavior, we must grasp its subjective meaning to the actor. Often this meaning is mundane, for most of what people do is mundane. But how people understand their own actions matters. It matters whether one knocks on a table to bring a meeting to order or to ward off the bad luck brought on by uttering a desire aloud. It matters for predicting behavior.

March and Simon describe how organizational customs persevere as problem-solving routines. Organizations attach them to legitimate cultural frameworks, so that a routine for decision making may be understood in terms of "democracy" or of "expertise," but not in terms of prowess with a six-shooter or of epiphany.

Karl Weick's *Sensemaking in Organizations* (1995) examines how frames for understanding the world are activated and manipulated by individuals. Weick does not see the meaning of an action as tightly wedded to the action itself, but instead sees individuals as operating with a range of interpretive frames. People make sense of much of their behavior retrospectively, using these interpretive frames. To illustrate, Weick cites Garfinkel's study of jury decisions, which shows that jury members tend to select a punishment first, and then make sense of the evidence so that the crime fits the punishment. For Weick, organizational behavior tends to follow the same pattern. People act, and then construct rationales for their behavior using common cognitive/rhetorical elements.

What may be most innovative about the sensemaking perspective is the idea that action shapes cognition—that we make cognitive sense of even our own actions after they have occurred. Decision making is often spontaneous, but we interpret it with customary points of view. This challenges Duesenberry's quip that sociology is the study of why people don't have any choices to make. Weick suggests that people not only choose how to behave, they choose from a range of interpretations of their own actions. It is not that their actions must make sense, but that their accounts of their actions must make sense given the wider system they operate in. When you raise prices for the disk drives you sell to a computer manufacturer, you can say, and think, that your labor costs have risen or that your components are in short supply. You cannot say, or think, that the Lord came to you in a dream and told you to buy your husband a new car.

This brings us full circle, to the issue of how customs and their meanings are articulated. Durkheim suggested that what is constant in the human condition is the inclination to try to make sense of the world by categorizing and generalizing from experience. For Weick and the other students of cognition, basic cognitive frameworks are shaped by experience with social customs. Each individual does not have to interpret customs on her own; rather, each custom comes equipped with cultural meaning, whether it is the custom of sacrificing a goat at harvest time or the custom of enforcing antitrust law.

The Four Mechanisms in Action: The Creation of the Amicable Merger

Before concluding, I offer a final illustration of how the four sociological mechanisms operate together to shape economic conventions (Dobbin and Dowd 1997, 2000). For economic sociologists, people typically enact economic conventions with little forethought. When conventions are challenged by public policy shifts or by private action, groups often vie to determine which alternative conventions will come to be defined as rational. Who wins depends on both power and networks, but the winning strategy must be accompanied by a cultural and cognitive framing that lines up with existing conceptions of efficiency.

The decline of the cartel and the rise of the amicable merger in railroading is a case in point. Between 1880 and 1910, business conventions in the American railroad industry were revolutionized, as firms went from participating in cartels to merging into regional monopolies. In Britain and elsewhere, cartels survived. What caused the change in the United States?

First, the cartel represented one *institutionalized* economic convention with a clear-cut cultural and cognitive rationale of efficiency. In response to early rate wars, railroaders created cartels and argued that in modern nations with large firms, only cartels could prevent price wars that could destabilize entire sectors.

Second, a *network* of ranchers, farmers, and small shippers formed to fight the cartel, arguing that cartels checked the freedom of small shippers. The breadth of this network gave it the *power* to pass anticartel legislation. It also succeeded because it built on an American way of thinking, found in the Constitution and reflected in popular cognitive orientations, in which concentrated power (whether in the federal government or in private industry) was undemocratic.

Third, when antitrust outlawed cartels, railroads divided into two camps. Financiers argued that firms should respond with amicable mergers, to preserve the value of the many railroads whose stock financiers held. Dedicated railroaders, who owned individual railroads, argued that firms should fight it out in price wars, with the strongest railroad taking the spoils in each region. Financers convinced dedicated railroaders to embrace amicable mergers by dint of their *power.* J. P. Morgan announced that financiers would withhold capital from predatory railroads.

The result was the institutionalization of a new business convention, the amicable merger. The convention was supported by the new theory, and *cognitive framework*, of the natural monopoly, in which price wars were destructive and pointless (consolidation was inevitable) and friendly mergers were the efficient remedy.

Thus in short order, a new equilibrium of business conventions was established. Firms did not coordinate prices in cartels, but when competition threatened to break out, they put their heads together to arrange mergers. Everything about how rational managers should behave vis-à-vis their competitors had changed. A new economic convention had been institutionalized. Was it more efficient than the cartel? Unlikely, as both had the goal of precluding competition. But it came to be seen as more efficient, and the cartel was shortly defined as an irrational relic of history.

This pattern can be seen in the empirical studies by Davis and colleagues (chap. 7), by Fligstein (chap. 15), and by Roy (chap. 16). In each case, a set of business *institutions* is challenged by an emergent *network*, different groups use *power* to try to define the new institutions that will replace the old, and the group that wins links new institutions to a compelling *cognitive* model of efficiency. What results looks to the world like the work of natural economic laws that replace inefficient business conventions with more efficient ones.

Conclusion

If you think about how a Dallas semiconductor manufacturer sets today's price, as economists do, you put yourself in her place and imagine how she perceives supply and demand. What kind of increase in demand would cause her to raise the price, given fixed supply? But if you think about how semiconductor manufacturers set prices in both Dallas and Osaka, as economic sociologists do implicitly or explicitly, you consider how context shapes their decisions. Conventions and institutions explain much of the difference in pricing decisions. You cannot help but ask, for instance, whether without the Department of Defense's early nurturing of chip manufacturers, the Dallas semiconductor seller would even exist. You cannot help but wonder whether, without antitrust law in place, she would think of competition among producers as the main factor influencing pricing. In Japan, you cannot help but ask whether without MITI's tutelage of high-tech industries, the Osaka seller would exist. You cannot help but wonder whether without state support for long-term contracting, the seller would think of a decades-old collaboration with one buyer as the main factor influencing pricing. How the Dallas and Osaka sellers decide on price is shaped by context.

Economic sociology's terrain is the effect of the social on economic behavior. People may make choices that they view as rational, but they do so with the battery of customs and prescriptions that society offers. In Karl Marx's (1963, 15) famous words, "Men make their own history, but they do not make it just as they please: they do not make it under circumstances chosen by themselves, but under circumstances directly encountered, given and transmitted from the past." The past has presented the Dallas and Osaka chip manufacturers with *different* rational conventions for setting prices. In Dallas it is rational to adjust price to demand; in Osaka it is rational to sustain a beneficial relationship with the buyer. Context also changes over time, and so a given American seller may use entirely different decision rules in 1980 and in 2000.

At the dawn of the twentieth century, the fields of economics and sociology were not far apart. Economists John R. Commons and Thorstein Veblen were preoccupied with explaining how social context determines economic behavior. So were sociologists Émile Durkheim and Max Weber. But by halfway through the century, the two camps had moved apart. Economists interested in how institutions shape real-world behavior had become a rarity, as had sociologists interested in economic behavior per se. Economists developed a theory of perfectly rational, socially isolated individuals. They experienced a sort of collective amnesia about the origins of this endeavor, forgetting that neoclassical theory had been a kind of thought experiment that assumed a single human instinct (self-interest) and imagined a world built up from that one instinct. The field consequently elaborated what Mark Granovetter (chap. 7) calls an "undersocialized" view of human behavior, in which social customs and collective understandings are all but irrelevant in explaining everyday economic decisions. Only stylized economic facts mattered.

Sociologists had been trying to understand how context shapes behavior all along, and from about 1980 they returned to the study of the economy with an array of implements refined in their studies of migration decisions, political choices, career strategies—all manner of social behavior. Forged by the founders of the field, who studied the rise of new economic patterns in the nineteenth century, these tools were refined on the premise that social and economic behavior alike originate not in the individual, but in society.

Sociologists see people as creatures of habit, driven by customs and routines that arise by chance, or by force. Modernity thus does not signal a fundamental shift in the character of the individual. It is not that people followed shamanism, voodoo, and animal magnetism for a hundred thousand years and then suddenly with the Enlightenment became calculating, rational actors. It is that at some point society began to organize customs around rationality rather than around spirituality, and people dropped customs backed by spiritual and mystical significance for customs backed by rationalized significance.

Sociologists thus consider the range of social forces that shape economic customs. This has led to a proliferation of insights under four theoretical tents. Some have built on the insights of Max Weber with an institutional approach that emphasizes the importance of meaningful social conventions. Others have built on the insights of Émile Durkheim and Georg Simmel with an approach linking economic behavior to social networks. Others have stood on Karl Marx's shoulders to explore how power shapes the emergence of new economic conventions. Still others have built on Durkheim's ideas about our inclination to categorize and make sense of the world and Weber's insights about customs and their meanings to examine how economic conventions become reflected, and made meaningful, in the human mind.

Economic sociologists have found that these four forces operate together to produce and sustain behavioral customs and market structures. Thus economic sociology, like the field of sociology more broadly, is undergoing an unusual sort of paradigm shift. When Thomas Kuhn (1970) observed paradigm shifts in the physical sciences, he saw the gradual replacement of one broad explanatory framework by another. Sociology has historically entertained several competing paradigms at once, and in recent years those paradigms have cross-fertilized to produce a rich theory of social action. In sociological studies of economic life, we increasingly see network ideas conjoined with Marxist ideas about power. We increasingly see ideas about cognition merged with Weberian ideas about institutional structure. Sociology's inductive, empirical method has produced studies that find these four core mechanisms shaping social behavior in all sorts of settings. The field is increasingly coming to see them as part of a single sociological explanation of behavior.

If sociologists have often settled for proving the effects of one element of the fourfold paradigm at once, holding the other elements constant, they have done so for good reason. It is difficult to create a reliable natural experiment in which all four elements are in motion at once, just as it is difficult to observe the effects of gravity, temperature, and wind resistance at once. The evolution of economic conventions is a multifold process, and as in physics, it remains difficult to disentangle the elements except by observing one at a time.

Recent studies sketch how these factors work together. Neil Fligstein's *The Architecture of Markets* (2001), Harrison White's (2002) *Markets from Networks*, and William Roy's *Socializing Capital* (1997) develop synthetic theories of economic life and many of the chapters in this anthology draw on two, three, or even four of these mechanisms. This sociological model of the evolution of economic conventions follows the logic of the model of evolution that biologists now embrace (Gould 1989) in describing evolutionary changes as fairly haphazard rather than as, of necessity, improving on the status quo. As long as random evolutionary changes do not doom a species, they may be sustained in the species. The same goes for the evolution of economic customs. New customs can be sustained so long as they do not lead to economic collapse. For the most part, it is impossible to discern whether a new convention hurts or helps in the aggregate. There are enough successful innovations in technology and management to mask the effects of the innovations that do more harm than good.

That economic conventions are socially produced does not mean that they are entirely random. Economic conventions are subject to natural selection as Darwin described it, to be sure (Aldrich 1999). Grossly inefficient customs die out, and some take their practitioners with them. Sociologists' comparative studies of capitalism, however, suggest that for any given economic goal, a number of different means may be about equally efficient. If one accepts the premise that there is more than one way to skin most cats, then the whole world of economic conventions is opened to sociological analysis. If inefficiency did not doom the cartel or the conglomerate, it stands to reason that we need to explain what did. This is where sociology's convention-based approach to economic behavior comes in.

References

Akerlof, George A. 1970. "The Market for Lemons: Quality Uncertainty and the Market Mechanism." *Quarterly Journal of Economics* 84:488–500.

Aldrich, Howard. 1999. *Organizations Evolving*. Thousand Oaks, Calif.: Sage.

Anderson, Benedict. 1983. *Imagined Communities: Reflections on the Origin and Spread of Nationalism*. London: Verso.

Baker, Wayne E. 1994. *Networking Smart: How to Build Relationships for Personal and Organizational Success*. New York: McGraw-Hill.

———. 2000. *Achieving Success through Social Capital: Tapping the Hidden Resources in Your Personal and Business Networks*. San Francisco: Jossey-Bass.

Baltzell, E. Digby. 1964. *The Protestant Establishment: Aristocracy and Caste in America*. New Haven: Yale University Press.

Berger, Peter, and Thomas Luckmann. 1966. *The Social Construction of Reality: A Treatise on the Sociology of Knowledge*. Garden City, N.Y.: Doubleday.

Boltanski, Luc, and Laurent Thévenot. 1991. *De la justification: Les économies de la grandeur*. Paris: Gallimard.

Bothner, Matthew S. 2000. "Structural Position, Economic Performance, and Technology Adoption in the Global Computer Industry." Ph.D. diss., Columbia University.

Bourdieu, Pierre. 1977. *Outline of a Theory of Practice*. Trans. Richard Niel. Cambridge: Cambridge University Press.

Burt, Ronald S. 1992. *Structural Holes*. Cambridge: Harvard University Press.

Campbell, John L. 1998. "Institutional Analysis and the Role of Ideas in Political Economy." *Theory and Society* 27:377–409.

———. 2000. "Convergence or Divergence? Neoliberalism and Fiscal Policy in Postcommunist Europe." Working paper, Department of Sociology, Dartmouth College.

Carruthers, Bruce. 1996. *City of Capital: Politics and Markets in the English Financial Revolution*. Princeton: Princeton University Press.

Chagnon, Napoleon. 1968. *Yanomamo: The Fierce People*. New York: Holt, Rinehart, and Winston.

Chandler, Alfred D., Jr. 1977. *The Visible Hand: The Managerial Revolution in American Business*. Cambridge: Harvard University Press.

Cole, Robert E. 1989. *Strategies for Learning: Small-Group Activities in American, Japanese, and Swedish Industry.* Berkeley and Los Angeles: University of California Press.

Coleman, James. 1990. *Foundations of Social Theory.* Cambridge: Harvard University Press.

Cumings, Bruce. 1987. "The Origins and Development of the Northeast Asian Political Economy: Industrial Sectors, Product Cycles, and Political Consequences." In *The Political Economy of the New Asian Industrialism*, ed. Frederick C. Deyo. Ithaca, N.Y.: Cornell University Press.

Davis, Gerald F., Kristina A. Diekmann, and Catherine H. Tinsley. 1994. "The Decline and Fall of the Conglomerate Firm in the 1980s: The Deinstitutionalization of an Organizational Form." *American Sociological Review* 59:547–70.

DiMaggio, Paul J., and Walter W. Powell. 1983. "The Iron Cage Revisited: Institutional Isomorphism and Collective Rationality in Organizational Fields." *American Sociological Review* 48:147–60.

Dobbin, Frank. 1994. *Forging Industrial Policy: The United States, Britain, and France in the Railway Age.* Cambridge: Cambridge University Press.

Dobbin, Frank, and Timothy Dowd. 1997. "How Policy Shapes Competition: Early Railroad Foundings in Massachusetts." *Administrative Science Quarterly* 42: 501–29.

———. 2000. ""The Market That Antitrust Built: Public Policy, Private Coercion, and Railroad Acquisitions, 1825–1922." *American Sociological Review* 65:635–57.

Dore, Ronald 2000. *Stock Market Capitalism: Welfare Capitalism—Japan and Germany versus the Anglo-Saxons.* Oxford: Oxford University Press.

Douglas, Mary. 1986. *How Institutions Think.* Syracuse, N.Y.: Syracuse University Press.

Duesenberry, John. 1960. "Comment on Gary Becker's 'An Economic Analysis of Fertility.' " In *Demographic and Economic Change in Developed Countries*, ed. National Bureau of Economic Research. Princeton: Princeton University Press.

Durkheim, Émile. 1933. *The Division of Labor in Society.* Trans. George Simpson. New York: Free Press.

———. 1961. *The Elementary Forms of Religious Life.* Trans. Joseph Ward Swain. New York: Collier.

Fligstein, Neil. 1990. *The Transformation of Corporate Control.* Cambridge: Harvard University Press.

———. 2001. *The Architecture of Markets: The Economic Sociology of Twenty-First-Century Capitalist Societies.* Princeton: Princeton University Press.

Fligstein, Neil, and Haldor Byrkjeflot. 1996. "The Logic of Employment Systems." In *Social Differentiation and Social Inequality*, ed. James N. Baron, David Grusky, and Donald Treiman. Boulder, Colo.: Westview.

Fligstein, Neil, and Linda Markowitz. 1993. "Financial Reorganization of American Corporations in the 1980s." In *Sociology and the Public Agenda*, ed. William Julius Wilson. Beverly Hills: Sage.

Fukuyama, Francis. 1995. *Trust: The Social Virtues and the Creation of Prosperity.* New York: Free Press.

Gao, Bai. 1997. *Economic Ideology and Japanese Industrial Policy: Developmentalism between 1931 and 1965.* Cambridge: Cambridge University Press.

Geertz, Clifford. 1983. *Local Knowledge: Further Essays in Interpretive Anthropology.* New York: Basic.

Gibbons, Robert S. 1992. *Game Theory for Applied Economists.* Princeton: Princeton University Press.

Goffman, Erving. 1974. *Frame Analysis: An Essay on the Organization of Experience*. Cambridge: Harvard University Press.

Gould, Stephen Jay 1989: *Wonderful Life: The Burgess Shale and the Nature of History.* New York: Norton.

Granovetter, Mark. 1974. *Getting a Job: A Study of Contacts and Careers*. Cambridge: Harvard University Press.

———. 1985. "Economic Action and Social Structure: The Problem of Embeddedness." *American Journal of Sociology* 91:481–510.

Greif, Avner. 1993. "Contract Enforceability and Economic Institutions in Early Trade: The Maghribi Traders' Coalition." *American Economic Review* 83: 525–48.

Guillén, Mauro F. 2001. *The Limits of Convergence: Globalization and Organizational Change in Argentina, South Korea, and Spain*. Princeton: Princeton University Press.

Hall, Peter A., and Rosemary C. R. Taylor. 1996. "Political Science and the Three New Institutionalisms." *Political Studies* 44:936–58.

Hamilton, Gary G., and Nicole Woolsey Biggart. 1988. "Market, Culture, and Authority: A Comparative Analysis of Management and Organization in the Far East." *American Journal of Sociology* 94:S52-S94.

Haveman, Heather A. 1993. "Follow the Leader: Mimetic Isomorphism and Entry into New Markets." *Administrative Science Quarterly* 38:593–627.

Hirschman, Albert O. 1977. *The Passions and the Interests: Political Arguments for Capitalism before Its Triumph*. Princeton: Princeton University Press.

Hofstede, Geert. 1980. *Culture's Consequences: International Differences in Work Values*. Beverly Hills: Sage.

Ingram, Paul, and Peter W. Roberts. 2000. "Friendships among Competitors in the Sydney Hotel Industry." *American Journal of Sociology* 106:387–423.

Johnson, Chalmers. 1982. *MITI and the Japanese Miracle: The Growth of Industrial Policy, 1925–1975*. Stanford: Stanford University Press.

Krasner, Stephen D. 1984. "Approaches to the State: Alternative Conceptions and Historical Dynamics." *Comparative Politics* 17:223–46.

Krugman, Paul. 1994. *Peddling Prosperity: Economic Sense and Nonsense in the Age of Diminished Expectations*. New York: Norton.

Kuhn, Thomas. 1970. *The Structure of Scientific Revolutions*. Chicago: University of Chicago Press.

Lamont, Michele. 1989. "The Power-Culture Link in a Comparative Perspective." *Comparative Social Research* 11:131–50.

Leifer, Eric, and Harrison White. 1987. "A Structural Approach to Markets." In *Intercorporate Relations: The Structural Analysis of Business*, ed. Mark Mizruchi and Michael Schwartz. Chicago: University of Chicago Press.

Lewis, Michael. 1987. *Liar's Poker: Rising through the Wreckage of Wall Street*. New York: Norton.

Lynd, Robert, and Helen Lynd. 1929. *Middletown: A Study in Contemporary American Culture*. New York: Harcourt, Brace.

March, James, and Herbert Simon. 1958. *Organizations*. New York: Wiley.

Marx, Karl, 1963. *The Eighteenth Brumaire of Louis Bonaparte*. New York: International Publishers.

———. 1972. *The Germany Ideology.* In *The Marx-Engels Reader*, ed. Robert Tucker. New York: Norton.

Meyer, John W. 1994. "Rationalized Environments." In *Institutional Environments and Organizations: Structural Complexity and Individualism*; ed. W. Richard Scott and John W. Meyer. Thousand Oaks, Calif.: Sage.

Meyer, John, John Boli, and George Thomas. 1987. "Ontology and Rationality in the Western Cultural Account." In *Institutional Structure: Constituting State, Society, and the Individual*, eds. George Thomas, John Meyer, Ramirez Franisco, and John Boli. Newbury Park, Calif.: Sage.

Meyer, John W., and Brian Rowan. 1977. "Institutionalized Organizations: Formal Structure as Myth and Ceremony." *American Journal of Sociology* 83:340–63.

Meyer, John W., and W. Richard Scott, eds. 1983. *Organizational Environments: Ritual and Rationality.* Beverly Hills: Sage.

Mills, C. Wright. 1956. *The Power Elite.* Oxford: Oxford University Press.

Nisbett, Richard E., Kaiping Peng, Incheol Choi, and Ara Norenzayan. 2001. "Culture and Systems of Thought: Holistic versus Analytic Cognition." *Psychological Review* 108:291–310.

North, Douglass. 1990. *Institutions, Institutional Change, and Economic Performance.* Cambridge: Cambridge University Press.

Novak, Michael, ed. 1993. *The Catholic Ethic and the Spirit of Capitalism.* New York: Free Press.

Perrow, Charles. 2002. *Organizing America: Wealth, Power, and the Origins of Corporate Capitalism.* Princeton: Princeton University Press.

Piore, Michael. 1996. "Review of *The Handbook of Economic Sociology.*" *Journal of Economic Literature* 34:741–54.

Polanyi, Karl. 1944. *The Great Transformation: The Political and Economic Origins of Our Time.* New York: Rinehart.

Portes, Alejandro, and Julia Sensenbrenner. 1993. "Embeddedness and Immigration: Notes on the Social Determinants of Economic Action." *American Journal of Sociology* 98:1320–50.

Putnam, Robert D. 1993. *Making Democracy Work: Civic Traditions in Modern Italy.* Princeton: Princeton University Press.

Roy, William G. 1997. *Socializing Capital: The Rise of the Large Industrial Corporation in America.* Princeton: Princeton University Press.

Schutz, Alfred. 1970. "Interpretive Sociology." In *On Phenomenology and Social Relations*, ed. Helmut R. Wagner. Chicago: University of Chicago Press.

Selznick, Philip. 1949. *TVA and the Grass Roots: A Study in the Sociology of Formal Organization.* Berkeley and Los Angeles: University of California Press.

Smelser, Neil. 1993. "Economic Rationality as a Religious System." Department of Sociology, University of California at Berkeley.

Spence, Michael. 1973. "Job Market Signaling." *Quarterly Journal of Economics* 87:355–74.

Stark, David. 1992. "Path Dependence and Privatization Strategies in East Central Europe." *East European Politics and Societies* 6:17–51.

Stigler, George. 1961. "The Economics of Information." *Journal of Political Economy* 69: 213–25.

Stiglitz, Joseph E. 2002. "Information and the Change in the Paradigm in Economics." *American Economic Review* 92:460–501.

Swedberg, Richard. 2002. "The Case for an Economic Sociology of Law." Department of Sociology, Cornell University.

Swidler, Ann. 1986. "Culture in Action: Symbols and Strategies." *American Sociological Review* 51:273–86.

Useem, Michael. 1984. *The Inner Circle: Large Corporations and the Rise of Business Political Activity in the U.S. and U.K.*. Oxford: Oxford University Press.

Uzzi, Brian. 1999. "Embeddedness in the Making of Financial Capital: How Social Relations and Networks Benefit Firms Seeking Financing." *American Sociological Review* 64:481–505.

Uzzi, Brian, and Ryon Lancaster. Forthcoming. "Social Embeddedness and Price Formation in the Large Law Firm Market." *American Sociological Review.*

Weber, Max. 1951. *The Religion of China: Confucianism and Taoism*. Ed. and trans. Hans H. Gerth. Glencoe, Ill: Free Press.

———. 1952. *Ancient Judiasm*. Ed. and trans. Hans H. Gerth and Don Martindale. Ill: Free Press.

———. 1958. *The Religion of India: The Sociology of Hinduism and Buddhism*. Ed. and trans. Hans H. Gerth and Don Martindale. Glencoe, Ill: Free Press.

———. 1963. *The Sociology of Religion*. Trans. Ephriam Fischoff. Boston: Beacon.

———. 1978. "Basic Sociological Terms." In *Economy and Society: An Outline of Interpretive Sociology.* Ed. Guenther Roth and Claus Wittich. Trans. Ephraim Fischoff et al. 2 vols. Berkeley and Los Angeles: University of California Press.

———. 2002. *The Protestant Ethic and the Spirit of Capitalism*. Trans. Stephen Kalberg. Los Angeles: Roxbury.

Weick, Karl E. 1995. *Sensemaking in Organizations*. Thousand Oaks, Calif.: Sage.

Westney, Eleanor. 1987. *Imitation and Innovation; The Transfer of Western Organizational Forms to Meiji Japan*. Cambridge: Harvard University Press.

White, Harrison C. 1981. "Where Do Markets Come From?" *American Journal of Sociology* 87:517–47.

———. 2002. *Markets from Networks: Socioeconomic Models of Production*. Princeton: Princeton University Press.

Whitley, Richard. 1992. "The Social Construction of Organizations and Markets: The Comparative Analysis of Business Recipes." In *Rethinking Organization: New Directions in Organization Theory and Analysis*, ed. Michael Reed and Michael Hughes. London: Sage.

Whitley, Richard, and Peer Hull Kristensen, eds. 1996. *The Changing European Firm: Limits to Convergence*. New York : Routledge.

Whyte, William H., Jr. 1956. *The Organization Man*. New York: Simon and Schuster.

Williamson, Oliver E. 1975. *Markets and Hierarchies: Analysis and Antitrust Implications*. New York: Free Press.

Wrong, Dennis. 1961. "The Oversocialized Conception of Man in Modern Sociology." *American Sociological Review* 26:185–93.

Wuthnow, Robert. 1987. *Meaning and Moral Order: Explorations in Cultural Analysis*. Berkeley and Los Angeles: University of California Press.

Zelizer, Viviana A. 1987. *Pricing the Priceless Child: The Changing Social Value of Children*. New York: Basic.

———. 1988. "Beyond the Polemics on the Market: Establishing a Theoretical and Empirical Agenda." *Sociological Forum* 4:614–34.

INSTITUTIONS

Chapter 2

FROM *THE PROTESTANT ETHIC AND THE SPIRIT OF CAPITALISM*

Max Weber

Translated by Talcott Parsons

Religious Affiliation and Social Stratification[1]

A glance at the occupational statistics of any country of mixed religious composition brings to light with remarkable frequency[2] a situation which has several times provoked discussion in the Catholic press and literature,[3] and in Catholic congresses in Germany, namely, the fact that business leaders and owners of capital, as well as the higher grades of skilled labor, and even more the higher technically and commercially trained personnel of modern enterprises, are overwhelmingly Protestant.[4] This is true not only in cases where the difference in religion coincides with one of nationality, and thus of cultural development, as in eastern Germany between Germans and Poles. The same thing is shown in the figures of religious affiliation almost wherever capitalism, at the time of its great expansion, has had a free hand to alter the social distribution of the population in accordance with its needs, and to determine its occupational structure. The more freedom it has had, the more clearly is the effect shown. It is true that the greater relative participation of Protestants in the ownership of capital,[5] in management, and the upper ranks of labor in great modern industrial and commercial enterprises,[6] may in part be explained in terms of historical circumstances[7] which extend far back into the past, and in which religious affiliation is not a cause of the economic conditions, but to a certain extent appears to be a result of them. Participation in the above economic functions usually involves some previous ownership of capital, and generally an expensive education; often both. These are today largely dependent on the possession of inherited wealth, or at least on a certain degree of material well-being. A number of those sections of the old empire which were most highly developed economically and most favored by natural resources and situation, in particular a majority of the wealthy towns, went over to

Max Weber. 2001 (1930). *The Protestant Ethic and the Spirit of Capitalism*. Translated by Talcott Parsons. New York: Routledge, pp. 3–11, 39–41, 102–9, 115–16, 124–25, used by kind permission of the publisher.

Protestantism in the sixteenth century. The results of that circumstance favor the Protestants even today in their struggle for economic existence. There arises thus the historical question: why were the districts of highest economic development at the same time particularly favorable to a revolution in the Church? The answer is by no means so simple as one might think.

The emancipation from economic traditionalism appears, no doubt, to be a factor which would greatly strengthen the tendency to doubt the sanctity of the religious tradition, as of all traditional authorities. But it is necessary to note, what has often been forgotten, that the Reformation meant not the elimination of the church's control over everyday life, but rather the substitution of a new form of control for the previous one. It meant the repudiation of a control which was very lax, at that time scarcely perceptible in practice, and hardly more than formal, in favor of a regulation of the whole of conduct which, penetrating to all departments of private and public life, was infinitely burdensome and earnestly enforced. The rule of the Catholic Church, "punishing the heretic, but indulgent to the sinner," as it was in the past even more than today, is now tolerated by peoples of thoroughly modern economic character, and was borne by the richest and economically most advanced peoples on earth at about the turn of the fifteenth century. The rule of Calvinism, on the other hand, as it was enforced in the sixteenth century in Geneva and in Scotland, at the turn of the sixteenth and seventeenth centuries in large parts of the Netherlands, in the seventeenth in New England, and for a time in England itself, would be for us the most absolutely unbearable form of ecclesiastical control of the individual which could possibly exist. That was exactly what large numbers of the old commercial aristocracy of those times, in Geneva as well as in Holland and England, felt about it. And what the reformers complained of in those areas of high economic development was not too much supervision of life on the part of the church, but too little. Now how does it happen that at that time those countries which were most advanced economically, and within them the rising bourgeois middle classes, not only failed to resist this unexampled tyranny of Puritanism, but even developed a heroism in its defense? For bourgeois classes as such have seldom before and never since displayed heroism. It was "the last of our heroisms," as Carlyle, not without reason, has said.

But further, and especially important: it may be, as has been claimed, that the greater participation of Protestants in the positions of ownership and management in modern economic life may today be understood, in part at least, simply as a result of the greater material wealth they have inherited. But there are certain other phenomena which *cannot* be explained in the same way. Thus, to mention only a few facts: there is a great difference discoverable in Baden, in Bavaria, in Hungary, in the type of higher education which Catholic parents, as opposed to Protestant, give their children. That the percentage of Catholics among the students and graduates of higher educational institutions in general lags behind their proportion of the total population,[8] may, to be sure, be largely explicable in terms of inherited differences of wealth. But among the Catholic graduates themselves the percentage of those graduating from the institutions preparing, in particular, for technical studies and industrial and commercial occupations, but in general from those preparing for middle-class business life, lags still farther behind the percentage of Protestants.[9] On the other hand, Catholics prefer the sort of training which the humanistic gymnasium affords. That is a circumstance to which the above explanation does not apply, but which, on the contrary, is one reason why so few Catholics are engaged in capitalistic enterprise.

Even more striking is a fact which partly explains the smaller proportion of Catholics among the skilled laborers of modern industry. It is well known that the factory has taken its skilled labor to a large extent from young men in the handicrafts; but this is much more true of Protestant than of Catholic journeymen. Among journeymen, in other words, the Catholics show a stronger propensity to remain in their crafts, that is, they more often become master craftsmen, whereas the Protestants are attracted to a larger extent into the factories in order to fill the upper ranks of skilled labor and administrative positions.[10] The explanation of these cases is undoubtedly that the mental and spiritual peculiarities acquired from the environment, here the type of education favored by the religious atmosphere of the home community and the parental home, have determined the choice of occupation, and through it the professional career.

The smaller participation of Catholics in the modern business life of Germany is all the more striking because it runs counter to a tendency which has been observed at all times[11] including the present. National or religious minorities which are in a position of subordination to a group of rulers are likely, through their voluntary or involuntary exclusion from positions of political influence, to be driven with peculiar force into economic activity. Their ablest members seek to satisfy the desire for recognition of their abilities in this field, since there is no opportunity in the service of the state. This has undoubtedly been true of the Poles in Russia and eastern Prussia, who have without question been undergoing a more rapid economic advance than in Galicia, where they have been in the ascendant. It has in earlier times been true of the Huguenots in France under Louis XIV, the Nonconformists and Quakers in England, and, last but not least, the Jew for two thousand years. But the Catholics in Germany have shown no striking evidence of such a result of their position. In the past they have, unlike the Protestants, undergone no particularly prominent economic development in the times when they were persecuted or only tolerated, either in Holland or in England. On the other hand, it is a fact that the Protestants (especially certain branches of the movement to be fully discussed later) both as ruling classes and as ruled, both as majority and as minority, have shown a special tendency to develop economic rationalism which cannot be observed to the same extent among Catholics either in the one situation or in the other.[12]

Thus the principal explanation of this difference must be sought in the permanent intrinsic character of their religious beliefs, and not only in their temporary external historico-political situations.[13]

It will be our task to investigate these religions with a view to finding out what peculiarities they have or have had which might have resulted in the behavior we have described. On superficial analysis, and on the basis of certain current impressions, one might be tempted to express the difference by saying that the greater otherworldliness of Catholicism, the ascetic character of its highest ideals, must have brought up its adherents to a greater indifference toward the good things of this world. Such an explanation fits the popular tendency in the judgment of both religions. On the Protestant side it is used as a basis of criticism of those (real or imagined) ascetic ideals of the Catholic way of life, while the Catholics answer with the accusation that materialism results from the secularization of all ideals through Protestantism. One recent writer has attempted to formulate the difference of their attitudes toward economic life in the following manner: "The Catholic is quieter, having less of the acquisitive impulse; he prefers a life of the greatest possible security, even with a smaller income, to a life of risk and excitement, even though it may bring the chance of gaining honor and riches. The proverb says jokingly, 'either eat well or sleep well.' In the present case the Protestant prefers to eat well, the Catholic to sleep undisturbed."[14]

In fact, this desire to eat well may be a correct though incomplete characterization of the motives of many nominal Protestants in Germany at the present time. But things were very different in the past: the English, Dutch, and American Puritans were characterized by the exact opposite of the joy of living, a fact which is indeed, as we shall see, most important for our present study. Moreover, the French Protestants, among others, long retained, and retain to a certain extent up to the present, the characteristics which were impressed upon the Calvinistic churches everywhere, especially under the cross in the time of the religious struggles. Nevertheless (or was it, perhaps, as we shall ask later, precisely on that account?) it is well known that these characteristics were one of the most important factors in the industrial and capitalistic development of France, and on the small scale permitted them by their persecution remained so. If we may call this seriousness and the strong predominance of religious interests in the whole conduct of life otherworldliness, then the French Calvinists were and still are at least as otherworldly as, for instance, the north German Catholics, to whom their Catholicism is undoubtedly as vital a matter as religion is to any other people in the world. Both differ from the predominant religious trends in their respective countries in much the same way. The Catholics of France are, in their lower ranks, greatly interested in the enjoyment of life, in the upper directly hostile to religion. Similarly, the Protestants of Germany are today absorbed in worldly economic life, and their upper ranks are most indifferent to religion.[15] Hardly anything shows so clearly as this parallel that, with such vague ideas as that of the alleged otherworldliness of Catholicism, and the alleged materialistic joy of living of Protestantism, and others like them, nothing can be accomplished for our purpose. In such general terms the distinction does not even adequately fit the facts of today, and certainly not of the past. If, however, one wishes to make use of it at all, several other observations present themselves at once which, combined with the above remarks, suggest that the supposed conflict between otherworldliness, asceticism, and ecclesiastical piety on the one side, and participation in capitalistic acquisition on the other, might actually turn out to be an intimate relationship.

As a matter of fact it is surely remarkable, to begin with quite a superficial observation, how large is the number of representatives of the most spiritual forms of Christian piety who have sprung from commercial circles. In particular, very many of the most zealous adherents of Pietism are of this origin. It might be explained as a sort of reaction against mammonism on the part of sensitive natures not adapted to commercial life, and, as in the case of Francis of Assisi, many Pietists have themselves interpreted the process of their conversion in these terms. Similarly, the remarkable circumstance that so many of the greatest capitalistic entrepreneurs—down to Cecil Rhodes—have come from clergymen's families might be explained as a reaction against their ascetic upbringing. But this form of explanation fails where an extraordinary capitalistic business sense is combined in the same persons and groups with the most intensive forms of a piety which penetrates and dominates their whole lives. Such cases are not isolated, but these traits are characteristic of many of the most important churches and sects in the history of Protestantism. Especially Calvinism, wherever it has appeared,[16] has shown this combination. However little, in the time of the expansion of the Reformation, it (or any other Protestant belief) was bound up with any particular social class, it is characteristic and in a certain sense typical that in French Huguenot churches monks and businessmen (merchants, craftsmen) were particularly numerous among the proselytes, especially at the time of the persecution.[17] Even the Spaniards knew that heresy (i.e., the Calvinism of the Dutch) promoted trade, and this coincides with the opinions which Sir William Petty expressed in his discussion of the reasons for the capitalistic development of the Netherlands. Gothein[18] rightly calls the Calvinistic diaspora the seedbed of capitalistic economy.[19] Even in this case one might consider the decisive factor to be the superiority of the French and Dutch economic cultures from which these communities sprang, or perhaps the immense influence of exile in the breakdown of traditional relationships.[20] But in France the situation was, as we know from Colbert's struggles, the same even in the seventeenth century. Even Austria, not to speak of other countries, directly imported Protestant craftsmen.

But not all the Protestant denominations seem to have had an equally strong influence in this direction. That of Calvinism, even in Germany, was among the strongest, it seems, and the reformed faith[21] more than the others seems to have promoted the development of the spirit of capitalism, in the Wupperthal as well as elsewhere. Much more so than Lutheranism, as comparison both in general and in particular instances, especially in the Wupperthal, seems to prove.[22] For Scotland, Buckle, and among English poets, Keats, have emphasized these same relationships.[23] Even more striking, as it is only necessary to mention, is the connection of a religious way of life with the most intensive development of business acumen among those sects whose otherworldliness is as proverbial as their wealth, especially the Quakers and the Mennonites. The part which the former have played in England and North America fell to the latter in Germany and the Netherlands. That in East Prussia Frederick William I tolerated the Mennonites as indispensable to industry, in spite of their absolute refusal to perform military service, is only one of the numerous well-known cases which illustrates the fact, though, considering the character of that monarch, it is one of the most striking. Finally, that this combination of intense piety with just as strong a development of business acumen, was also characteristic of the Pietists, is common knowledge.[24]

It is only necessary to think of the Rhine country and of Calw. In this purely introductory discussion it is unnecessary to pile up more examples. For these few already all show one thing: that the spirit of hard work, of progress, or whatever else it may be called, the awakening of which one is inclined to ascribe to Protestantism, must not be understood, as there is a tendency to do, as joy of living nor in any other sense as connected with the Enlightenment. The old Protestantism of Luther, Calvin, Knox, Voet, had precious little to do with what today is called progress. To whole aspects of modern life which the most extreme religionist would not wish to suppress today, it was directly hostile. If any inner relationship between certain expressions of the old Protestant spirit and modern capitalistic culture is to be found, we must attempt to find it, for better or worse, not in its alleged more or less materialistic or at least antiascetic joy of living, but in its purely religious characteristics. Montesquieu says (*Esprit des Lois*, book 20, chap. 7) of the English that they "had progressed the farthest of all peoples of the world in three important things: in piety, in commerce, and in freedom." Is it not possible that their commercial superiority and their adaptation to free political institutions are connected in some way with that record of piety which Montesquieu ascribes to them?

Luther's Conception of the Calling

Now it is unmistakable that even in the German word *Beruf*, and perhaps still more clearly in the English *calling*, a religious conception, that of a task set by God, is at least suggested. The more emphasis is put upon the word in a concrete case, the more evident is the connotation. And if we trace the history of the word through the civilized languages, it appears that neither the predominantly Catholic peoples nor those of classical antiquity[25] have possessed any expression of similar connotation for what we know as a calling (in the sense of a life-task, a definite field in which to work), while one has existed for all predominantly Protestant peoples. It may be further shown that this is not due to any ethnical peculiarity of the languages concerned. It is not, for instance, the product of a Germanic spirit, but in its modern meaning the word comes from the Bible translations, through the spirit of the translator, not that of the original.[26] In Luther's translation of the Bible it appears to have first been used at a point in Jesus Sirach (11:20 and 21) precisely in our modern sense.[27] After that it speedily took on its present meaning in the everyday speech of all Protestant peoples, while earlier not even a suggestion of such a meaning could be found in the secular literature of any of them, and even, in religious writings, so far as I can ascertain, it is only found in one of the German mystics whose influence on Luther is well known.

Like the meaning of the word, the idea is new, a product of the Reformation. This may be assumed as generally known. It is true that certain suggestions of the positive valuation of routine activity in the world, which is contained in this conception of the calling, had already existed in the Middle Ages, and even in late Hellenistic antiquity. We shall speak of that later. But at least one thing was unquestionably new: the valuation of the fulfillment of duty in worldly affairs as the highest form which the moral activity of the individual could assume. This it was which inevitably gave everyday worldly activity a religious significance, and which first created the conception of a calling in this sense. The conception of the calling thus brings out that central dogma of all Protestant denominations which the Catholic division of ethical precepts into *proecepta* and *consilia* discards. The only way of living acceptably to God was not to surpass worldly morality in monastic asceticism, but solely through the fulfillment of the obligations imposed upon the individual by his position in the world. That was his calling.

Luther[28] developed the conception in the course of the first decade of his activity as a reformer. At first, quite in harmony with the prevailing tradition of the Middle Ages, as represented, for example, by Thomas Aquinas,[29] he thought of activity in the world as a thing of the flesh, even though willed by God. It is the indispensable natural condition of a life of faith, but in itself, like eating and drinking, morally neutral.[30] But with the development of the conception of *sola fide* in all its consequences, and its logical result, the increasingly sharp emphasis against the Catholic *consilia evangelica* of the monks as dictates of the devil, the calling grew in importance. The monastic life is not only quite devoid of value as a means of justification before God, but he also looks upon its renunciation of the duties of this world as the product of selfishness, withdrawing from temporal obligations. In contrast, labor in a calling appears to him as the outward expression of brotherly love. This he proves by the observation that the division of labor forces every individual to work for others, but his viewpoint is highly naive, forming an almost grotesque contrast to Adam Smith's well-known statements on the same subject.[31] However, this justification, which is evidently essentially Scholastic, soon disappears again, and there remains, more and more strongly emphasized, the statement that the fulfillment of worldly duties is under all circumstances the only way to live acceptably to God. It and it alone is the will of God, and hence every legitimate calling has exactly the same worth in the sight of God.[32]

That this moral justification of worldly activity was one of the most important results of the Reformation, especially of Luther's part in it, is beyond doubt, and may even be considered a platitude.[33] This attitude is worlds removed from the deep hatred of Pascal, in his contemplative moods, for all worldly activity, which he was deeply convinced could only be understood in terms of vanity or low cunning.[34] And it differs even more from the liberal utilitarian compromise with the world at which the Jesuits arrived. But just what the practical significance of this achievement of Protestantism was in detail is dimly felt rather than clearly perceived.

Asceticism and the Spirit of Capitalism

In order to understand the connection between the fundamental religious ideas of ascetic Protestantism and its maxims for everyday economic conduct, it is necessary to examine with especial care such writings as have evidently been derived from ministerial practice. For in a time in which the beyond meant everything, when the social position of the Christian depended upon his admission to the Communion, the clergyman, through his ministry, church discipline, and preaching, exercised an influence (as a glance at collections of *consilia*, *casus conscientia*, etc., shows) which we modern men are entirely unable to picture. In such a time the religious forces which express themselves through such channels are the decisive influences in the formation of national character.

For the purposes of this chapter, though by no means for all purposes, we can treat ascetic Protestantism as a single whole. But since that side of English Puritanism which was derived from Calvinism gives the most consistent religious basis for the idea of the calling, we shall, following our previous method, place one of its representatives at the center of the discussion. Richard Baxter stands out above many other writers on Puritan ethics, both because of his eminently practical and realistic attitude, and, at the same time, because of the universal recognition accorded to his works, which have gone through many new editions and translations. He was a Presbyterian and an apologist of the Westminster Synod, but at the same time, like so many of the best spirits of his time, gradually grew away from the dogmas of pure Calvinism. At heart he opposed Cromwell's usurpation as he would any revolution. He was unfavorable to the sects and the fanatical enthusiasm of the saints, but was very broad-minded about external peculiarities and objective towards his opponents. He sought his field of labor most especially in the practical promotion of the moral life through the church. In the pursuit of this end, as one of the most successful ministers known to history, he placed his services at the disposal of the parliamentary government, of Cromwell, and of the Restoration,[35] until he retired from office under the last, before St. Bartholomew's Day. His *Christian Directory* is the most complete compendium of Puritan ethics, and is continually adjusted to the practical experiences of his own ministerial activity. In comparison we shall make use of Spener's *Theologische Bedenken*, as representative of German Pietism, Barclay's *Apology* for the Quakers, and some other representatives of ascetic ethics,[36] which, however, in the interest of space, will be limited as far as possible.[37]

Now, in glancing at Baxter's *Saints' Everlasting Rest*, or his *Christian Directory*, or similar works of others,[38] one is struck at first glance by the emphasis placed, in the discussion of wealth[39] and its acquisition, on the Ebionitic elements of the New Testament.[40] Wealth as such is a great danger; its temptations never end, and its pursuit[41] is not only senseless as compared with the dominating importance of the kingdom of God, but it is morally suspect. Here asceticism seems to have turned much more sharply against the acquisition of earthly goods than it did in Calvin, who saw no hindrance to the effectiveness of the clergy in their wealth, but rather a thoroughly desirable enhancement of their prestige. Hence he permitted them to employ their means profitably. Examples of the condemnation of the pursuit of money and goods may be gathered without end from Puritan writings, and may be contrasted with the late medieval ethical literature, which was much more open-minded on this point.

Moreover, these doubts were meant with perfect seriousness; only it is necessary to examine them somewhat more closely in order to understand their true ethical significance and implications. The real moral objection is to relaxation in the security of possession,[42] the enjoyment of wealth with the consequence of idleness and the temptations of the flesh, above all of distraction from the pursuit of a righteous life. In fact, it is only because possession involves this danger of relaxation that it is objectionable at all. For the saints' everlasting rest is in the next world; on earth man must, to be certain of his state of grace, "do the works of him who sent him, as long as it is yet day." Not leisure and enjoyment, but only activity serves to increase the glory of God, according to the definite manifestations of his will.[43]

Waste of time is thus the first and in principle the deadliest of sins. The span of human life is infinitely short and precious to make sure of one's own election. Loss of time through sociability, idle talk,[44] luxury,[45] even more sleep than is necessary for health,[46] six to at most eight hours, is worthy of absolute moral condemnation.[47] It does not yet hold, with Franklin, that time is money, but the proposition is true in a certain spiritual sense. It is infinitely valuable because every hour lost is lost to labor for the glory of God.[48] Thus inactive contemplation is also valueless, or even directly reprehensible if it is at the expense of one's daily work.[49] For it is less pleasing to God than the active performance of his will in a calling.[50] Besides, Sunday is provided for that, and, according to Baxter, it is always those who are not diligent in their callings who have no time for God when the occasion demands it.[51]

Accordingly, Baxter's principal work is dominated by the continually repeated, often almost passionate preaching of hard, continuous bodily or mental labor.[52] It is due to a combination of two different motives.[53] Labor is, on the one hand, an approved ascetic technique, as it always has been[54] in the Western church, in sharp contrast not only to the Orient but to almost all monastic rules the world over.[55] It is in particular the specific defense against all those temptations which Puritanism united under the name of the unclean life, whose role for it was by no means small. The sexual asceticism of Puritanism differs only in degree, not in fundamental principle, from that of monasticism; and on account of the Puritan conception of marriage, its practical influence is more far-reaching than that of the latter. For sexual intercourse is permitted, even within marriage, only as the means willed by God for the increase of his glory according to the commandment, "Be fruitful and multiply."[56] Along with a moderate vegetable diet and cold baths, the same prescription is given for all sexual temptations as is used against religious doubts and a sense of moral unworthiness: "Work hard in your calling."[57] But the most important thing was that even beyond that labor came to be considered in itself[58] the end of life, ordained as such by God. St. Paul's "He who will not work shall not eat" holds unconditionally for everyone.[59] Unwillingness to work is symptomatic of the lack of grace.[60]

Here the difference from the medieval viewpoint becomes quite evident. Thomas Aquinas also gave an interpretation of that statement of St. Paul. But for him[61] labor is only necessary *naturali ratione* for the maintenance of individual and community. Where this end is achieved, the precept ceases to have any meaning. Moreover, it holds only for the race, not for every individual. It does not apply to anyone who can live without labor on his possessions, and of course contemplation, as a spiritual form of action in the kingdom of God, takes precedence over the commandment in its literal sense. Moreover, for the popular theology of the time, the highest form of monastic productivity lay in the increase of the *Thesaurus ecclesia* through prayer and chant.

Now only do these exceptions to the duty to labor naturally no longer hold for Baxter, but he holds most emphatically that wealth does not exempt anyone from the unconditional command.[62] Even the wealthy shall not eat without working, for even though they do not need to labor to support their own needs, there is God's commandment which they, like the poor, must obey.[63] For everyone without exception God's providence has prepared a calling, which he should profess and in which he should labor. And this calling is not, as it was for the Lutheran,[64] a fate to which he must submit and which he must make the best of, but God's commandment to the individual to work for the divine glory. This seemingly subtle difference had far-reaching psychological consequences, and became connected with a further development of the providential interpretation of the economic order which had begun in Scholasticism.

The phenomenon of the division of labor and occupations in society had, among others, been interpreted by Thomas Aquinas, to whom we may most conveniently refer, as a direct consequence of the divine scheme of things. But the places assigned to each man in this cosmos follow *ex causis naturalibus* and are fortuitous (contingent in the Scholastic terminology). The differentiation of men into the classes and occupations established through historical development became for Luther, as we have seen, a direct result of the divine will. The perseverance of the individual in the place and within the limits which God had assigned to him was a religious duty.[65] This was the more certainly the consequence since the relations of Lutheranism to the world were in general uncertain from the beginning and remained so. Ethical principles for the reform of the world could not be found in Luther's realm of ideas; in fact it never quite freed itself from Pauline indifference. Hence the world had to be accepted as it was, and this alone could be made a religious duty.

But in the Puritan view, the providential character of the play of private economic interests takes on a somewhat different emphasis. True to the Puritan tendency to pragmatic interpretations, the providential purpose of the division of labour is to be known by its fruits. On this point Baxter expresses himself in terms which more than once directly recall Adam Smith's well-known apotheosis of the division of labor.[66] The specialization of occupations leads, since it makes the development of skill possible, to a quantitative and qualitative improvement in production, and thus serves the common good, which is identical with the good of the greatest possible number. So far, the motivation is purely utilitarian, and is closely related to the customary viewpoint of much of the secular literature of the time.[67]

But the characteristic Puritan element appears when Baxter sets at the head of his discussion the statement that "outside of a well-marked calling the accomplishments of a man are only casual and irregular, and he spends more time in idleness than at work," and when he concludes it as follows: "and he [the specialized worker] will carry out his work in order while another remains in constant confusion, and his business knows neither time nor place[68] . . . therefore is a certain calling the best for everyone." Irregular work, which the ordinary laborer is often forced to accept, is often unavoidable, but always an unwelcome state of transition. A man without a calling thus lacks the systematic, methodical character which is, as we have seen, demanded by worldly asceticism.

The Quaker ethic also holds that a man's life in his calling is an exercise in ascetic virtue, a proof of his state of grace through his conscientiousness, which is expressed in the care[69] and method with which he pursues his calling. What God demands is not labor in itself, but rational labor in a calling. In the Puritan concept of the calling the emphasis is always placed on this methodical character of worldly asceticism, not, as with Luther, on the acceptance of the lot which God has irretrievably assigned to man.[70]

Hence the question whether anyone may combine several callings is answered in the affirmative, if it is useful for the common good or one's own,[71] and not injurious to anyone, and if it does not lead to unfaithfulness in one of the callings. Even a change of calling is by no means regarded as objectionable, if it is not thoughtless and is made for the purpose of pursuing a calling more pleasing to God,[72] which means, on general principles, one more useful.

It is true that the usefulness of a calling, and thus its favor in the sight of God, is measured primarily in moral terms, and thus in terms of the importance of the goods produced in it for the community. But a further, and, above all, in practice the most important, criterion is found in private profitableness.[73] For if that God, whose hand the Puritan sees in all the occurrences of life, shows one of his elect a chance of profit, he must do it with a purpose. Hence the faithful Christian must follow the call by taking advantage of the opportunity.[74] "If God show you a way in which you may lawfully get more than in another way (without wrong to your soul or to any other), if you refuse this, and choose the less gainful way, you cross one of the ends of your calling, and you refuse to be God's steward, and to accept His gifts and use them for Him when He requireth it: you may labour to be rich for God, though not for the flesh and sin."[75]

Wealth is thus bad ethically only insofar as it is a temptation to idleness and sinful enjoyment of life, and its acquisition is bad only when it is with the purpose of later living merrily and without care. But as a performance of duty in a calling it is not only morally permissible, but actually enjoined.[76] The parable of the servant who was rejected because he did not increase the talent which was entrusted to him seemed to say so directly.[77] To wish to be poor was, it was often argued, the same as wishing to be unhealthy;[78] it is objectionable as a glorification of works and derogatory to the glory of God. Especially begging, on the part of one able to work, is not only the sin of slothfulness, but a violation of the duty of brotherly love according to the apostle's own word.[79]

The emphasis on the ascetic importance of a fixed calling provided an ethical justification of the modern specialized division of labor. In a similar way the providential interpretation of profit making justified the activities of the businessman.[80] The superior indulgence of the seigneur and the parvenu ostentation of the nouveau riche are equally detestable to asceticism. But, on the other hand, it has the highest ethical appreciation of the sober, middle-class, self-made man.[81] "God blesseth His trade" is a stock remark about those good men[82] who had successfully followed the divine hints. The whole power of the God of the Old Testament, who rewards his people for their obedience in this life,[83] necessarily exercised a similar influence on the Puritan who, following Baxter's advice, compared his own state of grace with that of the heroes of the Bible,[84] and in the process interpreted the statements of the Scriptures as the articles of a book of statutes.

. . . . .

This worldly Protestant asceticism, as we may recapitulate up to this point, acted powerfully against the spontaneous enjoyment of possessions; it restricted consumption, especially of luxuries. On the other hand, it had the psychological effect of freeing the acquisition of goods from the inhibitions of traditionalistic ethics. It broke the bonds of the impulse of acquisition in that it not only legalized it, but (in the sense discussed) looked upon it as directly willed by God. The campaign against the temptations of the flesh, and the dependence on external things, was, as besides the Puritans the great Quaker apologist Barclay expressly says, not a struggle against the rational acquisition, but against the irrational use of wealth.

But this irrational use was exemplified in the outward forms of luxury which their code condemned as idolatry of the flesh,[85] however natural they had appeared to the feudal mind. On the other hand, they approved the rational and utilitarian uses of wealth which were willed by God for the needs of the individual and the community. They did not wish to impose mortification[86] on the man of wealth, but the use of his means for necessary and practical things. The idea of comfort characteristically limits the extent of ethically permissible expenditures. It is naturally no accident that the development of a manner of living consistent with that idea may be observed earliest and most clearly among the most consistent representatives of this whole attitude toward life. Over against the glitter and ostentation of feudal magnificence which, resting on an unsound economic basis, prefers a sordid elegance to a sober simplicity, they set the clean and solid comfort of the middle-class home as an ideal.[87]

On the side of the production of private wealth, asceticism condemned both dishonesty and impulsive avarice. What was condemned as covetousness, mammonism, etc., was the pursuit of riches for their own sake. For wealth in itself was a temptation. But here asceticism was the power "which ever seeks the good but ever creates evil";[88] what was evil in its sense was possession and its temptations. For, in conformity with the Old Testament and in analogy to the ethical valuation of good works, asceticism looked upon the pursuit of wealth as an end in itself as highly reprehensible; but the attainment of it as a fruit of labor in a calling was a sign of God's blessing. And even more important: the religious valuation of restless, continuous, systematic work in a worldly calling, as the highest means to asceticism, and at the same time the surest and most evident proof of rebirth and genuine faith, must have been the most powerful conceivable lever for the expansion of that attitude toward life which we have here called the spirit of capitalism.[89]

. . . . .

Now naturally the whole ascetic literature of almost all denominations is saturated with the idea that faithful labor, even at low wages, on the part of those whom life offers no other opportunities, is highly pleasing to God. In this respect Protestant asceticism added in itself nothing new. But it not only deepened this idea most powerfully, it also created the force which was alone decisive for its effectiveness: the psychological sanction of it through the conception of this labor as a calling, as the best, often in the last analysis the only means of attaining certainty of grace.[90] And on the other hand it legalized the exploitation of this specific willingness to work, in that it also interpreted the employer's business activity as a calling.[91] It is obvious how powerfully the exclusive search for the kingdom of God only through the fulfillment of duty in the calling, and the strict asceticism which church discipline naturally imposed, especially on the propertyless classes, was bound to affect the productivity of labor in the capitalistic sense of the word. The treatment of labor as a calling became as characteristic of the modern worker as the corresponding attitude toward acquisition of the businessman.

. . . . .

One has only to reread the passage from Franklin, quoted at the beginning of this essay, in order to see that the essential elements of the attitude which was there called the spirit of capitalism are the same as what we have just shown to be the content of the Puritan worldly asceticism,[92] only without the religious basis, which by Franklin's time had died away. The idea that modern labor has an ascetic character is of course not new. Limitation to specialized work, with a renunciation of the Faustian universality of man which it involves, is a condition of any valuable work in the modern world; hence deeds and renunciation inevitably condition each other today. This fundamentally ascetic trait of middle-class life, if it attempts to be a way of life at all, and not simply the absence of any, was what Goethe wanted to teach, at the height of his wisdom, in the *Wanderjahren*, and in the end which he gave to the life of his *Faust*.[93] For him the realization meant a renunciation, a departure from an age of full and beautiful humanity, which can no more be repeated in the course of our cultural development than can the flower of the Athenian culture of antiquity.

The Puritan wanted to work in a calling; we are forced to do so. For when asceticism was carried out of monastic cells into everyday life, and began to dominate worldly morality, it did its part in building the tremendous cosmos of the modern economic order. This order is now bound to the technical and economic conditions of machine production which today determine the lives of all the individuals who are born into this mechanism, not only those directly concerned with economic acquisition, with irresistible force. Perhaps it will so determine them until the last ton of fossilized coal is burned. In Baxter's view the care for external goods should only lie on the shoulders of the "saint like a light cloak, which can be thrown aside at any moment."[94] But fate decreed that the cloak should become an iron cage.

Since asceticism undertook to remodel the world and to work out its ideals in the world, material goods have gained an increasing and finally an inexorable power over the lives of men as at no previous period in history. Today the spirit of religious asceticism—whether finally, who knows?—has escaped from the cage. But victorious capitalism, since it rests on mechanical foundations, needs its support no longer. The rosy blush of its laughing heir, the Enlightenment, seems also to be irretrievably fading, and the idea of duty in one's calling prowls about in our lives like the ghost of dead religious beliefs. Where the fulfillment of the calling cannot directly be related to the highest spiritual and cultural values, or when, on the other hand, it need not be felt simply as economic compulsion, the individual generally abandons the attempt to justify it at all. In the field of its highest development, in the United States, the pursuit of wealth, stripped of its religious and ethical meaning, tends to become associated with purely mundane passions, which often actually give it the character of sport.[95]

Notes

1. From the voluminous literature which has grown up around this essay I cite only the most comprehensive criticisms. (1) F. Rachfahl, "Kalvinismus und Kapitalismus," *Internationale Wochenschrift für Wissenschaft, Kunst und Technik* (1909), nos. 39–43. In reply, my article: "Antikritisches zum Geist des Kapitalismus," *Archiv für Sozialwissenschaft und Sozialpolitik* (Tübingen), 20, (1910). Then Rachfahl's reply to that: "Nochmals Kalvinismus und Kapitalismus," 1910, nos. 22–25, of the *Internationale Wochenschrift*. Finally my "Antikritisches Schlusswort," *Archiv* 31. (Brentano, in the criticism presently to be referred to, evidently did not know of this last phase of the discussion, as he does not refer to it.) I have not incorporated anything in this edition from the somewhat unfruitful polemics against Rachfahl. He is an author whom I otherwise admire, but who has in this instance ventured into a field which he has not thoroughly mastered. I have only added a few supplementary references from my anticritique, and have attempted, in new passages and footnotes, to make impossible any future misunderstanding. (2) W. Sombart, in his book *Der Bourgeois* (Munich and Leipzig, 1913, also translated into English under the title

The Quintessence of Capitalism, London, 1915), to which I shall return in footnotes below. Finally (3) Lujo Brentano in part 2 of the appendix to his Munich address (in the Academy of Sciences, 1913) on *Die Anfänge des modernen Kapitalismus*, which was published in 1916. (Since Weber's death Brentano has somewhat expanded these essays and incorporated them into his recent book *Der wirtschaftende Mensch in der Geschichte*.—TRANSLATOR'S NOTE.) I shall also refer to this criticism in special notes in the proper places. I invite anyone who may be interested to convince himself by comparison that I have not in revision left out, changed the meaning of, weakened, or added materially different statements to, a single sentence of my essay which contained any essential point. There was no occasion to do so, and the development of my exposition will convince anyone who still doubts. The two latter writers engaged in a more bitter quarrel with each other than with me. Brentano's criticism of Sombart's book *Die Juden und das Wirtschaftsleben* I consider in many points well founded, but often very unjust, even apart from the fact that Brentano does not himself seem to understand the real essence of the problem of the Jews (which is entirely omitted from this essay, but will be dealt with later [in a later section of the *Religionssoziologie*—TRANSLATOR'S NOTE]).

From theologians I have received numerous valuable suggestions in connection with this study. Its reception on their part has been in general friendly and impersonal, in spite of wide differences of opinion on particular points. This is the more welcome to me since I should not have wondered at a certain antipathy to the manner in which these matters must necessarily be treated here. What to a theologian is valuable in his religion cannot play a very large part in this study. We are concerned with what, from a religious point of view, are often quite superficial and unrefined aspects of religious life, but which, and precisely because they were superficial and unrefined, have often influenced outward behavior most profoundly.

Another book which, besides containing many other things is a very welcome confirmation of and supplement to this essay insofar as it deals with our problem, is the important work of E. Troeltsch, *Die Soziallehren der christlichen Kirchen und Gruppen* (Tübingen, 1912). It deals with the history of the ethics of Western Christianity from a very comprehensive point of view of its own. I here refer the reader to it for general comparison instead of making repeated references to special points. The author is principally concerned with the doctrines of religion, while I am interested rather in their practical results.

2. The exceptions are explained, not always, but frequently, by the fact that the religious leanings of the laboring force of an industry are naturally, in the first instance, determined by those of the locality in which the industry is situated, or from which its labor is drawn. This circumstance often alters the impression given at first glance by some statistics of religious adherence, for instance in the Rhine provinces. Furthermore, figures can naturally only be conclusive if individual specialized occupations are carefully distinguished in them. Otherwise very large employers may sometimes be grouped together, with master craftsmen who work alone, under the category of "proprietors of enterprises." Above all, the fully developed capitalism of the present day, especially so far as the great unskilled lower strata of labor are concerned, has become independent of any influence which religion may have had in the past. I shall return to this point.

3. Compare, for instance, Schell, *Der Katholizismus als Prinzip des Fortschrittes* (Würzburg, 1897), 31, and von Hertling, *Das Prinzip des Katholizismus und die Wissenschaft* (Freiburg, 1899), 58.

4. One of my pupils has gone through what is at this time the most complete statistical material we possess on this subject: the religious statistics of Baden. See Martin Offenbacher, "Konfession und soziale Schichtung," *Eine Studie über die wirtschaftliche Lage der Katholiken und Protestanten in Baden* (Tübingen und Leipzig, 1901), vol. 4, part 5, of the *Volkswirt-schaftliche Abhandlungen der badischen Hochschulen.* The facts and figures which are used for illustration below are all drawn from this study.

5. For instance, in 1895 in Baden there was taxable capital available for the tax on returns from capital:

Per 1,000 Protestants	954,000 marks
Per 1,000 Catholics	589,000 marks

It is true that the Jews, with over four millions per 1,000, were far ahead of the rest. (For details see Offenbacher, *Studie*, 21.)

6. On this point compare the whole discussion in Offenbacher's study.

7. On this point also Offenbacher brings forward more detailed evidence for Baden in his first two chapters.

8. The population of Baden was composed in 1895 as follows:
Protestants, 37.0 percent; Catholics, 61.3 percent; Jewish, 1.5 percent. The students of schools beyond the compulsory public school stage were, however, divided as follows (Offenbacher, *Studie*, 16):

	Protestant (percent)	*Catholic (percent)*	*Jews (percent)*
Gymnasien	43	46	9.5
Realgymnasien	69	31	9
Oberrealschulen	52	41	7
Realschulen	49	40	11
Höhere Bürgerschulen	51	37	12
Average	48	42	10

(In the *Gymnasium* the main emphasis is on the classics. In the *Realgymnasium* Greek is dropped and Latin reduced in favor of modern languages, mathematics, and science. The *Realschule* and *Oberrealschule* are similar to the letter except that Latin is dropped entirely in favor of modern languages. See G. E. Bolton, *The Secondary School System in Germany* [New York, 1900].—TRANSLATOR'S NOTE.)

The same thing may be observed in Prussia, Bavaria. Würtemberg, Alsace-Lorraine, and Hungary (see figures in Offenbacher, *Studie*, 16 ff.).

9. See the figures in the preceding note, which show that the Catholic attendance at secondary schools, which is regularly less than the Catholic share of the total population by a third, only exceeds this by a few percent in the case of the grammar schools (mainly in preparation for theological studies). With reference to the subsequent discussion it may further be noted as characteristic that in Hungary those affil-

iated with the Reformed Church exceed even the average Protestant record of attendance at secondary schools. (See *Studie*, Offenbacher, 19).

10. For the proofs see Offenbacher, *Studie* 54, and the tables at the end of his study.

11. Especially well illustrated by passages in the works of Sir William Petty, to be referred to later.

12. Petty's reference to the case of Ireland is very simply explained by the fact that the Protestants were only involved in the capacity of absentee landlords. If he had meant to maintain more, he would have been wrong, as the situation of the Scotch-Irish shows. The typical relationship between Protestantism and capitalism existed in Ireland as well as elsewhere. (On the Scotch-Irish see C. A. Hanna, *The Scotch-Irish*, 2 vols. [New York: Putnam, 1902].)

13. This is not, of course, to deny that the latter facts have had exceedingly important consequences. As I shall show later, the fact that many Protestant sects were small and hence homogeneous minorities, as were all the strict Calvinists outside of Geneva and New England, even where they were in possession of political power, was of fundamental significance for the development of their whole character, including their manner of participation in economic life. The migration of exiles of all the religions of the earth, Indian, Arabian, Chinese, Syrian, Phoenician, Greek, Lombard, to other countries as bearers of the commercial lore of highly developed areas, has been of universal occurrence and has nothing to do with our problem. Brentano, in the essay to which I shall often refer, *Die Anfänge des modern Kapitalismus*, calls to witness his own family. But bankers of foreign extraction have existed at all times and in all countries as the representatives of commercial experience and connections. They are not peculiar to modern capitalism, and were looked upon with ethical mistrust by the Protestants (see below). The case of the Protestant families, such as the Muralts, Pestalozzi, etc., who migrated to Zurich from Locarno, was different. They very soon became identified with a specifically modern (industrial) type of capitalistic development.

14. Offenbacher, *Studie*, 58.

15. Unusually good observations on the characteristic peculiarities of the different religions in Germany and France, and the relation of these differences to other cultural elements in the conflict of nationalities in Alsace are to be found in the fine study of W. Wittich, "Deutsche und französische Kultur im Elsass," *Illustrierte Elsässische Rundschau* (1900, also published separately).

16. This, of course, was true only when some possibility of capitalistic development in the area in question was present.

17. On this point see, for instance, Dupin de St. André, "L'ancienne église réformée de Tours. Les membres de l'église," *Bull. de la soc. de l'hist. du Protest.* 4:10. Here again one might, especially from the Catholic point of view, look upon the desire for emancipation from monastic or ecclesiastical control as the dominant motive. But against that view stands not only the judgment of contemporaries (including Rabelais), but also, for instance, the qualms of conscience of the first national synods of the Huguenots (for instance 1st Synod, C. partic. qu. 10 in Aymon, *Synod. Nat.*, 10), as to whether a banker might become an elder of the church; and in spite of Calvin's own definite stand, the repeated discussions in the same bodies of the permissibility of taking interest occasioned by the questions of ultrascrupulous members. It is partly explained by the number of persons having a direct interest in the question,

but at the same time the wish to practice *usuraria pravitas* without the necessity of confession could not have been alone decisive. The same, see below, is true of Holland. Let it be said explicitly that the prohibition of interest in the canon law will play no part in this investigation.

18. Gothein, *Wirtschaftsgeschichte des Schwarzwalds* (Strasbourg: Treubner, 1892), 1:67.

19. In connection with this see Sombart's brief comments (*Der moderne Kapitalismus*, 1st ed., 380). Later, under the influence of a study of F. Keller (*Unternehmung und Mehrwen*, Publications of the Goerres-Gesellschaft, 12), which, in spite of many good observations (which in this connection, however, are not new), falls below the standard of other recent works of Catholic apologetics, Sombart, in what is in these parts in my opinion by far the weakest of his larger works (*Der Bourgeois*) has unfortunately maintained a completely untenable thesis, to which I shall refer in the proper place.

20. That the simple fact of a change of residence is among the most effective means of intensifying labor is thoroughly established (compare note 13 above). The same Polish girl who at home was not to be shaken loose from her traditional laziness by any chance of earning money, however tempting, seems to change her entire nature and become capable of unlimited accomplishment when she is a migratory worker in a foreign country. The same is true of migratory Italian laborers. That this is by no means entirely explicable in terms of the educative influence of the entrance into a higher cultural environment, although this naturally plays a part, is shown by the fact that the same thing happens where the type of occupation, as in agricultural labor, is exactly the same as at home. Furthermore, accommodation in labor barracks, etc., may involve a degradation to a standard of living which would never be tolerated at home. The simple fact of working in quite different surroundings from those to which one is accustomed breaks through the tradition and is the educative force. It is hardly necessary to remark how much of American economic development is the result of such factors. In ancient times the similar significance of the Babylonian exile for the Jews is very striking, and the same is true of the Parsees. But for the Protestants, as is indicated by the undeniable difference in the economic characteristics of the Puritan New England colonies from Catholic Maryland, the Episcopal South, and mixed Rhode Island, the influence of their religious belief quite evidently plays a part as an independent factor. Similarly in India, for instance, with the Jains.

21. It is well known in most of its forms to be a more or less moderated Calvinism or Zwinglianism.

22. In Hamburg, which is almost entirely Lutheran, the only fortune going back to the seventeenth century is that of a well-known Reformed family (kindly called to my attention by Professor A. Wahl).

23. It is thus not new that the existence of this relationship is maintained here. Lavelye, Matthew Arnold, and others already perceived it. What is new, on the contrary, is the quite unfounded denial of it. Our task here is to explain the relation.

24. Naturally this does not mean that official Pietism, like other religious tendencies, did not at a later date, from a patriarchal point of view, oppose certain progressive features of capitalistic development, for instance, the transition from domestic industry to the factory system. What a religion has sought after as an ideal, and what the actual result of its influence on the lives of its adherents has been, must be sharply distinguished, as we shall often see in the course of our discussion. On the specific

adaptation of Pietists to industrial labor, I have given examples from a Westphalian factory in my article "Zur Psychophysik der gewerblichen Arbeit," *Archiv für Sozialwissenschaft und Sozielpolitik* 28, and at various other times.

25. Of the ancient languages only Hebrew has any similar concept. Most of all in the word מְלָאכָה. It is used for sacerdotal functions (Exod. 35:21; Neh. 11:22; 1 Chron. 9:13, 23:4, 26:30), for business in the service of the king (especially 1 Sam. 8:16, 1 Chron. 4:23, 29:26), for the service of a royal official (Esther 3:9, 9:3), of a superintendent of labor (2 Kings 12:12), of a slave (Gen. 39:11), of labor in the fields (1 Chron. 27:26), of craftsmen (Exod. 31:5, 35:21, 1 Kings 7:14), for traders (Ps. 107:23), and for worldly activity of any kind in the passage, Sir. 11:20, to be discussed later. The word is derived from the root לאךְ, to send, thus meaning originally a task. That it originated in the ideas current in Solomon's bureaucratic kingdom of serfs (*Fronstaat*), built up as it was according to the Egyptian model, seems evident from the above references. In meaning, however, as I learn from A. Merx, this root concept had become lost even in antiquity. The word came to be used for any sort of labor, and in fact became fully as colorless as the German *Beruf*, with which it shared the fate of being used primarily for mental and not manual functions. The expression (חק), assignment, task, lesson, which also occurs in Sir. 11:20, and is translated in the Septuagint with διαθήκη, is also derived from the terminology of the servile bureaucratic regime of the time, as is דְּבַר־יוֹם (Exod. 5:13; cf. Exod. 5:14), where the Septuagint also uses διαθήκη for task. In Sir. 13:10 it is rendered in the Septuagint with κρίμα. In Sir. 11:20 it is evidently used to signify the fulfillment of God's commandments, being thus related to our calling. On this passage in Jesus Sirach reference may here be made to Smend's well-known book on Jesus Sirach, and for the words διαθήκη, ἔργον, πόνος, to his *Index zur Weisheit des Jesus Sirach* (Berlin, 1907). As is well known, the Hebrew text of the Book of Sirach was lost, but has been rediscovered by Schechter, and in part supplemented by quotations from the Talmud. Luther did not possess it, and these two Hebrew concepts could not have had any influence on his use of language. (See below on Prov. 22:29.)

In Greek there is no term corresponding in ethical connotation to the German or English words at all. Where Luther, quite in the spirit of the modern usage (see below), translates Jesus Sirach 11:20 and 21, *bleibe in deinem Beruf*, the Septuagint has at one point ἔργον, at the other, which however seems to be an entirely corrupt passage, πόνος (the Hebrew original speaks of the shining of divine help!). Otherwise in antiquity τὰ προσήκοντο is used in the general sense of duties. In the works of the Stoics κάματος occasionally carries similar connotations, though its linguistic source is indifferent (called to my attention by A. Dieterich). All other expressions (such as τάζις etc.) have no ethical implications.

In Latin what we translate as calling, a man's sustained activity under the division of labor, which is thus (normally) his source of income and in the long run the economic basis of his existence, is, aside from the colourless *opus*, expressed with an ethical content, at least similar to that of the German word, either by *officium* (from *opificium*, which was originally ethically colorless, but later, as especially in Seneca *de benef*; IV, p. 18, came to mean *Beruf*); or by *munus*, derived from the compulsory obligations of the old civic community; or finally by *professio*. This last word was also characteristically used in this sense for public obligations, probably being derived from the old tax declarations of the citizens. But later it came to be applied in the special modern sense of the liberal professions (as in *professio bene dicendi*), and in this narrower meaning had a significance in every way similar to the German *Beruf*, even in the more spiritual sense of the word, as when Cicero says of someone "non intelligit quid profiteatur," in the sense of "he does not know his real profession." The only difference is that it is, of course, definitely secular without any religious connotation. That is even more true of *ars*, which in imperial times was used for handicraft. The Vulgate translates the above passages from Jesus Sirach, at one point with *opus*, the other (verse 21) with *locus*, which in this case means something like social station. The addition of *mandaturam tuorum* comes from the ascetic Jerome, as Brentano quite rightly remarks, without, however, here or elsewhere, calling attention to the fact that this was characteristic of precisely the ascetic use of the term, before the Reformation in an otherworldly, afterwards in a worldly, sense. It is furthermore uncertain from what text Jerome's translation was made. An influence of the old liturgical meaning of מְלָאכָה does not seem to be impossible.

In the Romance languages only the Spanish *vocacion* in the sense of an inner call to something, from the analogy of a clerical office, has a connotation partly corresponding to that of the German word, but is it never used to mean calling in the external sense. In the Romance Bible translations the Spanish *vocacion*, the Italian *vocazione* and *chiamamento*, which otherwise have a meaning partly corresponding to the Lutheran and Calvinistic usage to be discussed presently, are used only to translate the κλῆσις of the New Testament, the call of the Gospel to eternal salvation, which in the Vulgate is *vocatio*. Strange to say, Brentano, *Die Anfänge des modernen Kapitalismus*, maintains that this fact, which I have myself adduced to defend my view, is evidence for the existence of the concept of the calling in the sense which it had later, before the Reformation. But it is nothing of the kind. κλῆσις had to be translated by *vocatio*. But where and when in the Middle Ages was it used in our sense? The fact of this translation, and in spite of it, the lack of any application of the word to worldly callings is what is decisive. *Chiamamento* is used in this manner along with *vocazione* in the Italian Bible translation of the fifteenth century, which is printed in the *Collezione di opere inedite e rare* (Bologna, 1887), while the modern Italian translations use the latter alone. On the other hand, the words used in the Romance languages for calling in the external worldly sense of regular acquisitive activity carry, as appears from all the dictionaries and from a report of my friend Professor Baist (of Freiburg), no religious connotation whatever. This is so no matter whether they are derived from *ministerium* or *officium*, which originally had a certain religious coloring, or from *ars*, *professio*, and *implicare* (*impeigo*), from which it has been entirely absent from the beginning. The passages in Jesus Sirach mentioned above, where Luther used *Beruf*, are translated: in French, v. 20, *office*; v. 21, *labeur* (Calvinistic translation); Spanish, v. 20, *obra;* v. 21, *lugar* (following the Vulgate); recent translation, *posto* (Protestant). The Protestants of the Latin countries, since they were minorities, did not exercise, possibly without even making the attempt, such a creative influence over their respective languages as Luther did over the still less highly rationalized (in an academic sense) German official language.

26. On the other hand, the Augsburg Confession only contains the idea implicitly and but partially developed. Article 16 (ed. by Kolde, p. 43) teaches: "Meanwhile it (the Gospel) does not dissolve the ties of civil or domestic economy, but strongly enjoins us to maintain them as ordinances of God and in such ordinances (*ein jeder nach seinem Beruf*) to exercise charity." (Translated by Rev. W. H. Teale [Leeds, 1842].)

(In Latin it is only "et in talibus ordinationibus exercere caritatem." The English is evidently translated directly from the Latin, and does not contain the idea which came into the German version.—TRANSLATOR'S NOTE.)

The conclusion drawn, that one must obey authority, shows that here *Beruf* is thought of, at least primarily, as an objective order in the sense of the passage in 1 Cor. 7:20.

And Article 27 (Kolde, p. 83) speaks of *Beruf* (Latin *in vocatione sua*) only in connection with estates ordained by God: clergy, magistrates, princes, lords, etc. But even this is true only of the German version of the *Konkordienbuch*, while in the German editio princeps the sentence is left out.

Only in Article 26 (Kolde, p. 81) is the word used in a sense which at least includes our present meaning: "that he did chastise his body, not to deserve by that discipline remission of sin, but to have his body in bondage and apt to spiritual things, and to do his calling." Translated by Richard Taverner, Philadelphia Publications Society, 1888. (Latin *juxta vocationem suam.*)

27. According to the lexicons, kindly confirmed by my colleagues Professors Braune and Hoops, the word *Beruf* (Dutch *beroep*, English *calling*, Danish *kald*, Swedish *kallelse*) does not occur in any of the languages which now contain it in its present worldly (secular) sense before Luther's translation of the Bible. The Middle High German, Middle Low German, and Middle Dutch words, which sound like it, all means the same as *Ruf* in modern German, especially inclusive, in late medieval times, of the calling (vocation) of a candidate to a clerical benefice by those with the power of appointment. It is a special case which is also often mentioned in the dictionaries of the Scandinavian languages. The word is also occasionally used by Luther in the same sense. However, even though this special use of the word may have promoted its change of meaning, the modern conception of *Beruf* undoubtedly goes linguistically back to the Bible translations by Protestants, and any anticipation of it is only to be found, as we shall see later, in Tauler (died 1361). All the languages which were fundamentally influenced by the Protestant Bible translations have the word; all of which this was not true (like the Romance languages) do not, or at least not in its modern meaning.

Luther renders two quite different concepts with *Beruf*. First the Pauline κλῆσις in the sense of the call to eternal salvation through God. Thus: 1 Cor. 1:26; Eph. 1:18, 4:1, 4; 2 Thess. 1:11; Heb. 3:1; 2 Pet. 1:10. All these cases concern the purely religious idea of the call through the Gospel taught by the apostle; the word κλῆσις has nothing to do with worldly callings in the modern sense. The German Bibles before Luther use in this case *ruffunge* (so in all those in the Heidelberg Library), and sometimes instead of "von Gott geruffet" say "von Gott gefordert." Second, however, he, as we have already seen, translates the words in Jesus Sirach discussed in the previous note (in the Septuagint ἔν τῷ ἔργῳ σου παλαιώθητι and καὶ ἔμμενε τῷ πόνῳ σου), with "beharre in deinem Beruf," and "bliebe in deinem Beruf", instead of "bliebe bei deiner Arbeit." The later (authorized) Catholic translations (for instance that of Fleischütz, Fulda, 1781) have (as in the New Testament passages) simply followed him. Luther's translation of the passage in the Book of Sirach is, so far as I know, the first case in which the German word *Beruf* appears in its present purely secular sense. The preceding exhortation, verse 20, στῆθι εν διαθήκη σου he translates "bliebe in Gottes Wort," although Sir. 14:1 and 43:10 show that, corresponding to the Hebrew חק, which (according to quotations in the Talmud) Sirach used, διαθήκη really did mean something similar to our calling, namely one's fate or assigned task. In its later and present sense the word *Beruf* did not exist in the German language, nor, so far as I can learn, in the works of the older Bible translators or preachers. The German Bibles before Luther rendered the passage from Sirach with *Werk*. Berthold of Regensburg, at the points in his sermons where the modern would say *Beruf*, uses the word *Arbeit*. The usage was thus the same as in antiquity. The first passage I know, in which not *Beruf* but *Ruf* (as a translation of κλῆσις) is applied to purely worldly labor, is in the fine sermon of Tauler on Ephesians 4 (*Works*, Basle edition, f. 117. v), of peasants who *misten* go: they often fare better "so sie folgen einfeltiglich irem Ruff denn die geistlichen Menschen, die auf ihren Ruf nicht Acht haben." The word in this sense did not find its way into everyday speech. Although Luther's usage at first vacillates between *Ruf* and *Beruf* (see *Werke*, Erlangen edition, p. 51), that he was directly influenced by Tauler is by no means certain, although the *Freiheit eines Christenmenschen* is in many respects similar to his sermon of Tauler. But in the purely worldly sense of Tauler, Luther did not use the word *Ruf*. (This against Denifle, *Luther*, 163.)

Now evidently Sirach's advice in the version of the Septuagint contains, apart from the general exhortation to trust in God, no suggestion of a specifically religious valuation of secular labor in a calling. The term πόνος, toil, in the corrupt second passage would be rather the opposite, if it were not corrupted. What Jesus Sirach says simply corresponds to the exhortation of the psalmist (Ps. 37:3), "Dwell in the land, and feed on his faithfulness," as also comes out clearly in the connection with the warning not to let oneself be blinded with the works of the godless, since it is easy for God to make a poor man rich. Only the opening exhortation to remain in the חק (verse 20) has a certain resemblance to the κλῆσις of the Gospel, but here Luther did not use the word *Beruf* for the Greek διαθήκη. The connection between Luther's two seemingly quite unrelated uses of the word *Beruf* is found in the first letter to the Corinthians and its translation.

In the usual modern editions, the whole context in which the passage stands is as follows, 1 Cor. 7:17 (English, King James Version [American revision, 1901]): "(17) Only as the Lord hath distributed to each man, as God hath called each, so let him walk. And so ordain I in all churches. (18) Was any man called being circumcised? let him not become uncircumcised. Hath any man been called in uncircumcision? let him not be circumcised. (19) Circumcision is nothing and uncircumcision is nothing; but the keeping of the commandments of God. (20) Let each man abide in that calling wherein he was called (ἐν τῇ κλήσει ῇ ἐκλήθη; an undoubted Hebraism, as Professor Merx tells me). (21) Wast thou called being a bondservant? care not for it; nay even if thou canst become free use it rather. (22) For he that was called in the Lord being a bondservant is the Lord's freedman; likewise he that was called being free is Christ's bondservant. (23) Ye were bought with a price; become not bondservants of men. (24) Brethren, let each man, wherein he was called, therein abide with God."

In verse 29 follows the remark that time is shortened, followed by the well-known commandments motivated by eschatological expectations: (31) to possess women as though one did not have them, to buy as though one did not have what one had bought, etc. In verse 20 Luther, following the older German translations, even in 1523 in his exegesis of this chapter, renders κλῆσις with *Beruf*, and interprets it with *Stand* (Erlangen ed., 51:51.)

In fact it is evident that the word κλῆσις at this point, and only at this, corresponds approximately to the Latin *status* and the German *Stand* (status of marriage, status of a servant, etc.). But of course not as Brentano, *Dic Anfänge des Mo der nen Kapitalismus*, 137, assumes, in the modern sense of *Beruf*. Brentano can hardly have read this passage, or what I have said about it, very carefully. In a sense at least suggesting it, this word, which is etymologically related to ἐκκλησία an assembly which has been called, occurs in Greek literature, so far as the lexicons tell, only once in a passage from Dionysius of Halicarnassus, where it corresponds to the Latin *classis*, a word borrowed from the Greek, meaning that part of the citizenry which has been called to the colors. Theophylaktos (eleventh–twelfth century) interprets 1 Cor. 7:20: ἐνοϊῳ βιῳ καὶ ἐν οἴῳ τάγματι καὶ πολιτεύματι ὤν ἐπίστενσεν. (My colleague Professor Deissmann called my attention to this passage.) Now, even in our passage, κλῆσις does not correspond to the modern *Beruf*. But having translated κλῆσις with *Beruf* in the eschatologically motivated exhortation, that everyone should remain in his present status, Luther, when he later came to translate the Apocrypha, would naturally, on account of the similar content of the exhortations alone, also use *Beruf* for πόνος in the traditionalistic and anti-chrematistic commandment of Jesus Sirach, that everyone should remain in the same business. This is what is important and characteristic. The passage in 1 Cor. 7:17 does not, as has been pointed out, use κλῆσις at all in the sense of *Beruf*, a definite field of activity.

In the meantime (or about the same time), in the Augsburg Confession; the Protestant dogma of the uselessness of the Catholic attempt to excel worldly morality was established, and in it the expression "einem jeglichen nach seinem Beruf" was used (see previous note). In Luther's translation, both this and the positive valuation of the order in which the individual was placed, as holy, which was gaining ground just about the beginning of the 1530s, stand out. It was a result of his more and more sharply defined belief in special Divine Providence, even in the details of life, and at the same time of his increasing inclination to accept the existing order of things in the world as immutably willed by God. *Vocatio*, in the traditional Latin, meant the divine call to a life of holiness, especially in a monastery or as a priest. But now, under the influence of this dogma, life in a worldly calling came for Luther to have the same connotation. For he now translated πόνος and ἔργον in Jesus Sirach with *Beruf*, for which, up to that time, there had been only the (Latin) analogy, coming from the monastic translation. But a few years earlier, in Prov. 22:29, he had still translated the Hebrew מְלָאכָה, which was the original of ἔργον in the Greek text of Jesus Sirach, and which, like the German *Beruf* and the Scandinavian *kald*, kallelse, originally related to a *spiritual* call (*Beruf*), as in other passages (Gen. 39:11), with *Geschaft* (Septuagint ἔργον, Vulgate *opus*, English Bibles *business*, and correspondingly in the Scandinavian and all the other translations before me).

The word *Beruf*, in the modern sense which he had finally created, remained for the time being entirely Lutheran. To the Calvinists the Apocrypha are entirely uncanonical. It was only as a result of the development which brought the interest in proof of salvation to the fore that Luther's concept was taken over, and then strongly emphasized by them. But in their first (Romance) translations they had no such word available, and no power to create one in the usage of a language already so stereotyped.

As early as the sixteenth century the concept of *Beruf* in its present sense became established in secular literature. The Bible translators before Luther had used the word *Berufung* for κλῆσις (as for instance in the Heidelberg versions of 1462–66 and 1485), and the Eck translation of 1537 says "in dem Ruf, worin er beruft ist." Most of the later Catholic translators directly follow Luther. In England, the first of all, Wyclif's translation (1382), used *cleping* (the Old English word which was later replaced by the borrowed *calling*). It is quite characteristic of the Lollard ethics to use a word which already corresponded to the later usage of the Reformation. Tyndale's translation of 1534, on the other hand, interprets the idea in terms of *status*: "in the same state wherein he was called," as also does the Geneva Bible of 1557. Cranmer's official translation of 1539 substituted *calling* for *state*, while the (Catholic) Bible of Rheims (1582), as well as the Anglican Court Bibles of the Elizabethan era, characteristically return to *vocation*, following the Vulgate.

That for England, Cranmer's Bible translation is the source of the Puritan conception of calling in the sense of *Beruf*, trade, has already, quite correctly, been pointed out by Murray. As early as the middle of the sixteenth century calling is used in that sense. In 1588 unlawful callings are referred to, and in 1603 greater callings in the sense of higher occupations, etc. (see Murray). Quite remarkable is Brentano's idea (*Die Anfänge des modernen Kapitalismus*, 139), that in the Middle Ages *vocatio* was not translated with *Beruf*, and that this concept was not known, because only a free man could engage in a *Beruf*, and freemen, in the middle-class professions, did not exist at that time. Since the whole social structure of the medieval crafts, as opposed to those of antiquity, rested upon free labor, and, above all, almost all the merchants were freemen, I do not clearly understand this thesis.

28. Compare with the following the instructive discussion in K. Eger, *Die Anschauung Luthers vom Beruf* (Giessen, 1900). Perhaps its only serious fault, which is shared by almost all other theological writers, is his insufficiently clear analysis of the concept of *lex naturae*. On this see E. Troeltsch in his review of Seeberg's *Dogmengeschichte*, and now above all in the relevant parts of his *Soziallehren der christlichen Kirchen*.

29. For when Thomas Aquinas represents the division of men into estates and occupational groups as the work of divine providence, by that he means the objective cosmos of society. But that the individual should take up a particular calling (as we should say; Thomas, however, says *ministerium* or *officium*) is due to *causae naturales*. *Quaest. quodlibetal*, VII, Art. 17c. "Hae autem diversificatio hominum in diversis officiis contingit primo ex divina providentia, quaeita hominum status distribuit . . . secundo etiam ex causis naturalibus, ex quibus contingit, quod in diversis hominibus sunt diversae inclinationes ad diversa officia . . ."

Quite similar is Pascal's view when he says that it is chance which determines the choice of a calling. See, on Pascal, A. Koester, *Die Ethik Pascals* (Tübingen, 1907). Of the organic systems of religious ethics, only the most complete of them, the Indian, is different in this respect. The difference between the Thomistic and the Protestant ideas of the calling is so evident that we may dismiss it for the present with the above quotation. This is true even as between the Thomistic and the later Lutheran ethics, which are very similar in many other respects, especially in their emphasis on providence. We shall return later to a discussion of the Catholic viewpoint. On Thomas Aquinas, see Maurenbrecher, *Thomas von Aquino's Stellung zum Wirtschaftsleben seiner Zeit* (1888). Otherwise, where Luther agrees with Thomas in details, he has probably been influenced rather by the general doctrines of Scholasticism than by Thomas in particular. For according to Denifle's investigations, he seems really not to have known Thomas very well. See Denifle, *Luther und Luthertum* (1903), 501, and on it, Köhler, *Ein Wort zu Denifles Luther* (1904), 25.

30. In *Von der Freiheit eines Cristenmenschen*, (1) the double nature of man is used for the justification of worldly duties in the sense of the *lex naturae* (here the natural order of the world). From that it follows (Erlangen ed., 27:188) that man is inevitably bound to his body and to the social community. (2) In this situation he will (p. 196: this is a second justification), if he is a believing Christian, decide to repay God's act of grace, which was done for pure love, by love of his neighbor. With this very loose connection between faith and love is combined (3) (p. 190) the old ascetic justification of labor as a means of securing to the inner man mastery over the body. (4) Labor is hence, as the reasoning is continued with another appearance of the idea of *lex naturae* in another sense (here, natural morality), an original instinct given by God to Adam (before the Fall, which he has obeyed "solely to please God." Finally (5) (pp. 161 and 199), there appears, in connection with Matt. 7:18 f., the idea that good work in one's ordinary calling is and must be the result of the renewal of life, caused by faith, without, however, developing the most important Calvinistic idea of proof. The powerful emotion which dominates the work explains the presence of such contradictory ideas.

31. "It is not from the benevolence of the butcher, the brewer, or the baker, that we expect our dinner, but from their regard to their own interest. We address ourselves, not to their humanity, but to their self-love; and never talk to them of our own necessities, but of their advantages" (*Wealth of Nations*, book 1, chap. 2).

32. "Omnia enim per to operabitur (Deus), mulgebit per te vaccam et servilissima quaeque opera faciet, ac maxima pariter et minima ipsi grata erunt" (*Exegesis of Genesis, Opera lat. exeget.*, ed. Elsperger, 7:213). The idea is found before Luther in Tauler, who holds the spiritual and the worldly *Ruf* to be in principle of equal value. The difference from the Thomistic view is common to the German mystics and Luther. It may be said that Thomas, principally to retain the moral value of contemplation, but also from the viewpoint of the mendicant friar, is forced to interpret Paul's doctrine that "if a man will not work he shall not eat" in the sense that labor, which is of course necessary *lege naturae*, is imposed upon the human race as a whole, but not on all individuals. The gradation in the value of forms of labor, from the *opera servilia* of the peasants upwards, is connected with the specific character of the mendicant friars, who were for material reasons bound to the town as a place of domicile. It was equally foreign to the German mystics and to Luther, the peasant's son; both of them, while valuing all occupations equally, looked upon their order of rank as willed by God. For the relevant passages in Thomas see Maurenbrecher, *Thomas von Aquino's Stellung*, 65ff.

33. It is astonishing that some investigators can maintain that such a change could have been without effect upon the actions of men. I confess my inability to understand such a view.

34. "Vanity is so firmly imbedded in the human heart that a camp-follower, a kitchen-helper, or a porter, boast and seek admirers." (Faugeres edition, 1:208. Compare Koester, *Die Ethik Pascals*, 17, 136ff.) On the attitude of Port Royal and the Jansenists to the calling, to which we shall return, see now the excellent study of Dr. Paul Honigsheim, *Die Staats und Soziallehren der französischen Jansenisten im 17ten Jahrhundert*, Heidelberg historical dissertation, 1914. It is a separately printed part

of a more comprehensive work on the *Vorgeschichte de französischen Aufklärung.* Compare especially 138ff.

35. See the excellent sketch of his character in Edward Dowden, *Puritan and Anglican: Studies in Literature* (London: K. Paul, Trench, Trübner, 1900). A passable introduction to Baxter's theology, after he had abandoned a strict belief in the double decree, is given in the introduction to the various extracts from his works printed in the *Works of the Puritan Divines* (by Jenkyn). His attempt to combine universal redemption and personal election satisfied no one. For us it is important only that he even then held to personal election, i.e. to the most important point for ethics in the doctrine of predestination. On the other hand, his weakening of the forensic view of redemption is important as being suggestive of baptism.

36. Tracts and sermons by Thomas Adams, John Howe, Matthew Henry, J. Janeway, Stuart Charnock, Baxter, Bunyan, have been collected in the ten volumes of the *Works of the Puritan Divines* (London, 1845–48), though the choice is often somewhat arbitrary. Editions of the works of Bailey, Sedgwick, and Hoornbeek have already been referred to.

37. We could just as well have included Voet and other continental representatives of worldly asceticism. Brentano's view that the whole development was purely Anglo-Saxon is quite wrong. My choice is motivated mainly (though not exclusively) by the wish to present the ascetic movement as much as possible in the second half of the seventeenth century, immediately before the change to utilitarianism. It has unfortunately been impossible, within the limits of this sketch, to enter upon the fascinating task of presenting the characteristics of ascetic Protestantism through the medium of the biographical literature; the Quakers would in this connection be particularly important, since they are relatively little known in Germany.

38. For one might just as well take the writings of Gisbert Voet, the proceedings of the Huguenot Synods, or the Dutch Baptist literature. Sombart and Brentano have unfortunately taken just the Ebionitic parts of Baxter, which I myself have strongly emphasized, to confront me with the undoubted capitalistic backwardness of his doctrines. But (1) one must know this whole literature thoroughly in order to use it correctly, and (2) not overlook the fact that I have attempted to show how, in spite of its antimammonistic doctrines, the spirit of this ascetic religion nevertheless, just as in the monastic communities, gave birth to economic rationalism because it placed a premium on what was most important for it: the fundamentally ascetic rational motives. That fact alone is under discussion and is the point of this whole essay.

39. Similarly in Calvin, who was certainly no champion of bourgeois wealth (see the sharp attacks on Venice and Antwerp in *Jes. Opp.*, III, 140a, 308a).

40. *Saints' Everlasting Rest*, chaps. 10, 12. Compare Bailey (*Praxis Pietatis*, 182) or Matthew Henry (*The Worth of the Soul*, *Works of the Puritan Divines*, 319). "Those that are eager in pursuit of worldly wealth despise their Soul, not only because the Soul is neglected and the body preferred before it, but because it is employed in these pursuits" (Ps. 127:2). On the same page, however, is the remark to be cited below about the sinfulness of all waste of time, especially in recreations. Similarly in almost the whole religious literature of English-Dutch Puritanism. See for instance, Hoornbeek's (*Theologia Practica*, X, chap. 18, 18) philippics against *avaritia*. This writer is also affected by sentimental pietistic influences. See the praise of *tranquillitas animi* which is much more pleasing to God than the *sollicitudo* of this world. Also Bailey, referring to the well-known passage in Scripture, is of the opinion that "A

rich man is not easily saved" (*Praxix Pietatis*, p. 182). The Methodist catechisms also warn against "gathering treasure on this earth." For Pietism this is quite obvious, as also for the Quakers. Compare Barclay, *An Apology for the True Christian Divinity*, 4th ed. (London, 1701), "and therefore beware of such temptations as to use their callings as an engine to be richer."

41. For not wealth alone, but also the impulsive pursuit of it (or what passed as such) was condemned with similar severity. In the Netherlands the South Holland Synod of 1574 declared, in reply to a question, that moneylenders should not be admitted to Communion even though the business was permitted by law; and the Deventer Provincial Synod of 1598 (Art. 24) extended this to the employees of moneylenders. The Synod of Gorichem in 1606 prescribed severe and humiliating conditions under which the wives of usurers might be admitted, and the question was discussed as late as 1644 and 1657 whether Lombards should be admitted to Communion (this against Brentano, who cites his own Catholic ancestors, although foreign traders and bankers have existed in the whole European and Asiatic world for thousands of years). Gisbert Voet (*Disp. Theol.*, IV, 1667, *de usuris*, 665) still wanted to exclude the Trapezites (Lombards, Piedmontese). The same was true of the Huguenot synods. This type of capitalistic classes were not the typical representatives of the philosophy or the type of conduct with which we are concerned. They were also not new as compared with antiquity or the Middle Ages.

42. Developed in detail in the tenth chapter of the *Saints' Everlasting Rest*. He who should seek to rest in the shelter of possessions which God gives, God strikes even in this life. A self-satisfied enjoyment of wealth already gained is almost always a symptom of moral degradation, If we had everything which we could have in this world, would that be all we hoped for? Complete satisfaction of desires is not attainable on earth because God's will has decreed it should not be so.

43. Richard Baxter, *A Christian Directory*, 2d ed. (London, 1678), pt. 1, pp. 375–76. "It is for action that God maintaineth us and our activities; work is the moral as well as the natural end of power. . . . It is action that God is most served and honoured by. . . . The public welfare or the good of the many is to be valued above our own." Here is the connecting-point for the transition from the will of God to the purely utilitarian viewpoint of the later liberal theory. On the religious sources of utilitarianism, see below in the text.

44. The commandment of silence has been, starting from the biblical threat of punishment for every useless word, especially since the Cluny monks, a favorite ascetic means of education in self-control. Baxter also speaks in detail of the sinfulness of unnecessary words. Its place in his character has been pointed out by John Sanford, *Studies and Illustrations of the Great Rebellion* (London: J. W. Parker and Son, 1858), 90ff.

What contemporaries felt as the deep melancholy and moroseness of the Puritans was the result of breaking down the spontaneity of the *status naturalis*, and the condemnation of thoughtless speech was in the service of this end. When Washington Irving (*Bracebridge Hall*, chap. 30) seeks the reason for it partly in the calculating spirit of capitalism and partly in the effect of political freedom, which promotes a sense of responsibility, it may be remarked that it does not apply to the Latin peoples. For England the situation was probably that (1) Puritanism enabled its adherents to create free institutions and still become a world power; and (2) it transformed that calculating spirit (what Sombart calls *Rechenhaftigkeit*), which is in truth essential to capitalism, from a mere means to economy into a principle of general conduct.

45. Baxter, *A Christian Directory*, pt. 1, p. 111.

46. Baxter, *A Christian Directory*, pt. 1, pp. 383f.

47. Similarly on the preciousness of time, see Barclay, *True Christian Divinity*, 14.

48. Baxter, *A Christian Directory*, pt. 1, p. 79. "Keep up a high esteem of time and be every day more careful that you lose none of your time, than you are that you lose none of your gold and silver. And if vain recreation, dressings, feastings, idle talk, unprofitable company, or sleep be any of them temptations to rob you of any of your time, accordingly heighten your watchfulness." "Those that are prodigal of their time despise their own souls," says Matthew Henry (*Worth of the Soul, Works of the Puritan Divines*, 315). Here also Protestant asceticism follows a well-beaten track. We are accustomed to think it characteristic of the modern man that he has no time, and for instance, like Goethe in the *Wanderjahren*, to measure the degree of capitalistic development by the fact that the clocks strike every quarter-hour. So also Sombart in his *Kapitalismus*. We ought not, however, to forget that the first people to live (in the Middle Ages) with careful measurement of time were the monks, and that the church bells were meant above all to meet their needs.

49. Compare Baxter's discussion of the calling, *A Christian Directory*, pt. 1, pp. 108ff. Especially the following passage: "Question: But may I not cast off the world that I may only think of my salvation? Answer: You may cast off all such excess of worldly cares or business as unnecessarily hinder you in spiritual things. But you may not cast off all bodily employment and mental labour in which you may serve the common good. Everyone as a member of Church or Commonwealth must employ their parts to the utmost for the good of the Church and the Commonwealth. To neglect this and say: I will pray and meditate, is as if your servant should refuse his greatest work and tie himself to some lesser, easier part. And God hath commanded you some way or other to labour for your daily bread and not to live as drones of the sweat of others only." God's commandment to Adam, "In the sweat of thy brow," and Paul's declaration, "He who will not work shall not eat," are also quoted. It has always been known of the Quakers that even the most well-to-do of them have had their sons learn a calling, for ethical and not, as Alberti recommends, for utilitarian reasons.

50. Here are points where Pietism, on account of its emotional character, takes a different view. Spener, although he emphasizes in characteristic Lutheran fashion that labor in a calling is worship of God (*Theologische Bedenken*, 3:445), nevertheless holds that the restlessness of business affairs distracts one from God, a most characteristic difference from Puritanism.

51. Baxter, *A Christian Directory*, pt. 1, p. 242, "It's they that are lazy in their callings that can find no time for holy duties." Hence the idea that the cities, the seat of the middle class with its rational business activities, are the seats of ascetic virtue. Thus Baxter says of his hand-loom weavers in Kidderminster: "And their constant converse and traffic with London doth much to promote civility and piety among tradesmen" in his autobiography (*Works of the Puritan Divines*, 38). That the proximity of the capital should promote virtue would astonish modern clergymen, at least in Germany. But Pietism also inclined to similar views. Thus Spener, speaking of a young colleague, writes: "At least it appears that among the great multitudes in the cities, though the majority is quite depraved, there are nevertheless a number of good

people who can accomplish much, while in villages often hardly anything good can be found in a whole community" (*Theologische Bedenken*, vol. 1, 66, p. 303). In other words, the peasant is little suited to rational ascetic conduct. Its ethical glorification is very modern. We cannot here enter into the significance of this and similar statements for the question of the relation of asceticism to social classes.

52. Take, for instance, the following passages (Baxter, *A Christian Directory*, 336f.): "Be wholly taken up in diligent business of your lawful callings when you are not exercised in the more immediate service of God." "Labour hard in your callings." "See that you have a calling which will find you employment for all the time which God's immediate service spareth."

53. That the peculiar ethical valuation of labor and its dignity was not originally a Christian idea nor even peculiar to Christianity has recently again been strongly emphasized by Harnack (*Mitt. des Ev.-Soz. Kongr.*, 14. Folge, 1905, nos. 3, 4, p. 48).

54. Similarly in Pietism (Spener, *Theologische Bendenken*, 3:429–30). The characteristic Pietist version is that loyalty to a calling which is imposed upon us by the Fall serves to annihilate one's own selfish will. Labor in the calling is, as a service of love to one's neighbor, a duty of gratitude for God's grace (a Lutheran idea), and hence it is not pleasing to God that it should be performed reluctantly (3:272). The Christian should thus "prove himself as industrious in his labour as a worldly man" (3:278). That is obviously less drastic than the Puritan version.

55. The significance of this important difference, which has been evident ever since the Benedictine rules, can only be shown by a much wider investigation.

56. "A sober procreation of children" is its purpose according to Baxter. Similarly Spener, at the same time with concessions to the coarse Lutheran attitude, which makes the avoidance of immorality, which is otherwise unavoidable, an accessory aim. Concupiscence as an accompaniment of sexual intercourse is sinful even in marriage. For instance, in Spener's view it is a result of the fall which transformed such a natural, divinely ordained process into something inevitably accompanied by sinful sensations, which is hence shameful. Also in the opinion of various Pietistic groups the highest form of Christian marriage is that with the preservation of virginity, the next highest that in which sexual intercourse is only indulged in for the procreation of children, and so on down to those which are contracted for purely erotic or external reasons and which are, from an ethical standpoint, concubinage. On these lower levels a marriage entered into for purely economic reasons is preferred (because after all it is inspired by rational motives) to one with erotic foundations. We may here neglect the Herrnhut theory and practice of marriage. Rationalistic philosophy (Christian Wolff) adopted the ascetic theory in the form that what was designed as a means to an end, concupiscence and its satisfaction, should not be made an end in itself.

The transition to a pure, hygienically oriented utilitarianism had already taken place in Franklin, who took approximately the ethical standpoint of modern physicians, who understand by chastity the restriction of sexual intercourse to the amount desirable for health, and who have, as is well known, even given theoretical advice as to how that should be accomplished. As soon as these matters have become the object of purely rational consideration the same development has everywhere taken place. The Puritan and the hygienic sex-rationalist generally tread very different paths, but here they understand each other perfectly. In a lecture, a zealous adherent of hygienic prostitution—it was a question of the regulation of brothels and prostitutes—defended the moral legitimacy of extramarital intercourse (which was looked upon as hygienically useful) by referring to its poetic justification in the case of Faust and Margaret. To treat Margaret as a prostitute and to fail to distinguish the powerful sway of human passions from sexual intercourse for hygienic reasons, both are thoroughly congenial to the Puritan standpoint. Similar, for instance, is the typical specialist's view, occasionally put forward by very distinguished physicians, that a question which extends so far into the subtlest problems of personality and of culture as that of sexual abstinence should be dealt with exclusively in the forum of the physician (as an expert). For the Puritan the expert was the moral theorist, now he is the medical man; but the claim of competence to dispose of the questions which seem to us somewhat narrow-minded is, with opposite signs of course, the same in both cases.

But with all its prudery, the powerful idealism of the Puritan attitude can show positive accomplishments, even from the point of view of race conservation in a purely hygienic sense, while modern sex hygiene, on account of the appeal to unprejudicedness which it is forced to make, is in danger of destroying the basis of all its success. How, with the rationalistic interpretation of sexual relations among peoples influenced by Puritanism, a certain refinement and spiritual and ethical penetration of marital relationships, with a blossoming of matrimonial chivalry, has grown up, in contrast to the patriarchal sentimentality (*Brodem*), which is typical of Germany even in the circles of the intellectual aristocracy, must necessarily remain outside this discussion. Baptist influences have played a part in the emancipation of woman; the protection of her freedom of conscience, and the extension of the idea of the universal priesthood to her were here also the first breaches in patriarchal ideas.

57. This recurs again and again in Baxter. The biblical basis is regularly either the passages in Proverbs, which we already know from Franklin (22:29), or those in praise of labor (31:16). Cf. *A Christian Directory*, pt. 1, pp. 377, 382, etc.

58. Even Zinzendorf says at one point: "One does not only work in order to live, but one lives for the sake of one's work, and if there is no more work to do one suffers or goes to sleep" (Plitt, *Zinzendorfs Theologie* [Gotha, 1869], 1:428).

59. Also, a symbol of the Mormons closes (after quotations) with the words: "But a lazy or indolent man cannot be a Christian and be saved. He is destined to be struck down and cast from the hive." But in this case it was primarily the grandiose discipline, halfway between monastery and factory, which placed the individual before the dilemma of labor or annihilation and, of course in connection with religious enthusiasm and only possible through it, brought forth the astonishing economic achievements of this sect.

60. Hence (*A Christian Directory*, pt. 1, p. 380) its symptoms are carefully analyzed. Sloth and idleness are such deadly sins because they have a cumulative character. They are even regarded by Baxter as "destroyers of grace" (pt. 1, pp. 279–80). That is, they are the antitheses of the methodical life.

61. See above, note 29.

62. Baxter, *A Christian Directory*, pt. 1, pp. 108ff. Especially striking are the following passages: "Question: But will not wealth excuse us? Answer: It may excuse you from some sordid sort of work by making you more serviceable to another, but you are no more excused from service of work . . . than the poorest man." Also, p. 376: "Though they [the rich] have no outward want to urge them, they have as great a necessity to obey God . . . God hath strictly commanded it [labor] to all."

63. Similarly Spener (*Theologische Bedenken*, 3:338, 425), who for this reason opposes the tendency to early retirement as morally objectionable, and, in refuting an objection to the taking of interest, that the enjoyment of interest leads to laziness, emphasizes that anyone who was in a position to live upon interest would still be obligated to work by God's commandment.

64. Including Pietism. Whenever a question of change of calling arises, Spener takes the attitude that after a certain calling has once been entered upon, it is a duty of obedience to Providence to remain and acquiesce in it.

65. The tremendous force, dominating the whole of conduct, with which the Indian religious teaching sanctions economic traditionalism in terms of chances of favorable rebirth, I have shown in the essays on the *Wirtschaftsethik der Weltreligionen*. It is an excellent example by which to show the difference between mere ethical theories and the creation of psychological sanctions with a religious background for certain types of conduct. The pious Hindu could advance in the scale of transmigration only by the strictly traditional fulfillment of the duties of the caste of his birth. It was the strongest conceivable religious basis for traditionalism. In fact, the Indian ethic is in this respect the most completely consistent antithesis of the Puritan, as in another respect (traditionalism of the caste structure) it is opposed to the Hebrew.

66. Baxter, *A Christian Directory*, pt. 1, p. 377.

67. But this does not mean that the Puritan viewpoint was historically derived from the latter. On the contrary, it is an expression of the genuinely Calvinistic idea that the cosmos of the world serves the glory of God. The utilitarian turn, that the economic cosmos should serve the good of the many, the common good, etc., was a consequence of the idea that any other interpretation of it would lead to aristocratic idolatry of the flesh, or at least did not serve the glory of God, but only fleshly cultural ends. But God's will, as it is expressed in the purposeful arrangements of the economic cosmos, can, so far as secular ends are in question at all, only be embodied in the good of the community, in impersonal usefulness. Utilitarianism is thus, as has already been pointed out, the result of the impersonal character of brotherly love and the repudiation of all glorification of this world by the exclusiveness of the Puritan *in majorem Dei gloriam*.

How completely this idea, that all idolatry of the flesh is inconsistent with the glory of God and hence unconditionally bad, dominated ascetic Protestantism is clearly shown by the doubts and hesitation which it cost even Spener, who certainly was not infected with democracy, to maintain the use of titles as ἀδιάφορον against numerous objections. He finally comforted himself with the reflection that even in the Bible the praetor Festus was given the title of κράτιστος by the apostles. The political side of the question does not arise in this connection.

68. "The inconstant man is a stranger in his own house," says Thomas Adams (*Works of the Puritan Divines*, 77).

69. On this, see especially George Fox's remarks in the *Friends' Library*, ed. W. and T. Evans, vol. 1 (Philadelphia, 1837), 130.

70. Above all, this sort of religious ethic cannot be regarded as a reflex of economic conditions. The specialization of occupations had, if anything, gone further in medieval Italy than in the England of that period.

71. For, as is often pointed out in the Puritan literature, God never commanded "love thy neighbor more than thyself," but only as thyself. Hence self-regard is also a duty. For instance, a man who can make better use of his possessions, to the greater

glory of God, than his neighbor, is not obliged by the duty of brotherly love to part with them.

72. Spener is also close to this viewpoint. But even in the case of transfer from commercial occupations (regarded as especially dangerous to virtue) to theology, he remains hesitant and on the whole opposed to it (*Theologische Bedenken*, 3:435, 443, 1:524). The frequent occurrence of the reply to just this question (of the permissibility of changing a calling) in Spener's naturally biased opinion shows, incidentally, how eminently practical the different ways of interpreting 1 Corinthians 7 were.

73. Such ideas are not to be found, at least in the writings, of the leading continental Pietists. Spener's attitude vacillates between the Lutheran (that of satisfaction of needs) and mercantilist arguments for the usefulness of the prosperity of commerce, etc. (*Theologische Bedenken*, 3:330, 332, 1:418: "the cultivation of tobacco brings money into the country and is thus useful, hence not sinful." Compare also 3:426–27, 429, 434). But he does not neglect to point out that, as the example of the Quakers and the Mennonites shows, one can make profit and yet remain pious; in fact, that even especially high profits, as we shall point out later, may be the direct result of pious uprightness (3:435).

74. These views of Baxter are not a reflection of the economic environment in which he lived. On the contrary, his autobiography shows that the success of his home missionary work was partly due to the fact that the Kidderminster tradesmen were not rich, but only earned food and raiment, and that the master craftsmen had to live from hand to mouth just as their employees did. "It is the pool who receive the glad tidings of the Gospel." Thomas Adams remarks on the pursuit on gain: "He [the knowing man] knows . . . that money may make a man richer, not better, and thereupon chooseth rather to sleep with a good conscience than a full purse . . . therefore desires no more wealth than an honest man may bear away" (*Works of the Puritan Divines*, li). But he does want that much, and that means that every formally honest gain is legitimate.

75. Thus Baxter, *A Christian Directory*, pt. 1, chap. x, 1, 9 (par. 24); pt. 1, p. 378, col. 2. In Prov. 23:24: "Weary thyself not to be rich" means only "riches for our fleshly ends must not ultimately be intended." Possession in the feudal-seigneurial form of its use is what is odious (cf. the remark, *A Christian Directory*, pt. 1, p. 380, on the "debauched part of the gentry"), not possession in itself. Milton, in the first *Defensio pro populo Anglicano*, held the well-known theory that only the middle class can maintain virtue. That middle class here means bourgeoisie as against the aristocracy is shown by the statement that both luxury and necessity are unfavorable to virtue.

76. This is most important. We may again add the general remark: we are here naturally not so much concerned with what concepts the theological moralists developed in their ethical theories, but, rather, what was the effective morality in the life of believers—that is, how the religious background of economic ethics affected practice. In the casuistic literature of Catholicism, especially the Jesuit, one can occasionally read discussions which—for instance on the question of the justification of interest, into which we do not enter here—sound like those of many Protestant casuists, or even seem to go farther in permitting or tolerating things. The Puritans have since often enough been reproached that their ethic is at bottom the same as that of the Jesuits. Just as the Calvinists often cite Catholic moralists, not only Thomas Aquinas,

Bernhard of Clairvaux, Bonaventura, etc., but also contemporaries, the Catholic casuists also took notice of heretical ethics. We cannot discuss all that here.

But quite apart from the decisive fact of the religious sanction of the ascetic life for the layman, there is the fundamental difference, even in theory, that these latitudinarian ideas within Catholicism were the products of peculiarly lax ethical theories, not sanctioned by the authority of the church, but opposed by the most serious and strictest disciples of it. On the other hand, the Protestant idea of the calling in effect placed the most serious enthusiasts for asceticism in the service of capitalistic acquisition. What in the one case might under certain conditions be allowed, appeared in the other as a positive moral good. The fundamental differences of the two ethics, very important in practice, have been finally crystallized, even for modern times, by the Jansenist controversy and the bull *Unigenitus*.

77. "You may labour in that manner as tendeth most to your success and lawful gain. You are bound to improve all your talents." There follows the passage cited above in the text. A direct parallel between the pursuit of wealth in the kingdom of Heaven and the pursuit of success in an earthly calling is found in Janeway, *Heaven upon Earth* (*Works of the Puritan Divines*, 275).

78. Even in the Lutheran Confession of Duke Christopher of Württemberg, which was submitted to the Council of Trent, objection is made to the oath of poverty. He who is poor in his station should bear it, but if he swore to remain so it would be the same as if he swore to remain sick or to maintain a bad reputation.

79. Thus in Baxter and also in Duke Christopher's confession. Compare further passages like: "the vagrant rogues whose lives are nothing but an exorbitant course; the main begging," etc. (Thomas Adams, *Works of the Puritan Divines*, 259). Even Calvin had strictly forbidden begging, and the Dutch synods campaigned against licenses to beg. During the epoch of the Stuarts, especially Laud's regime under Charles I, which had systematically developed the principle of public poor relief and provision of work for the unemployed, the Puritan battle-cry was: "Giving alms is no charity" (title of Defoe's later well-known work). Towards the end of the seventeenth century they began the deterrent system of workhouses for the unemployed (compare Leonard, *Early History of English Poor Relief* [Cambridge, 1900], and H. Levy, *Die Grundlagen des ökonomischen Liberalismus in der Geschichte der englischen Volkswirtschaft* [Jena, 1912], 69ff.).

80. The president of the Baptist Union of Great Britain and Ireland, G. White, said emphatically in his inaugural address before the assembly in London in 1903 (*Baptist Handbook*, 1904, 104): "The best men on the roll of our Puritan Churches were men of affairs, who believed that religion should permeate the whole of life."

81. Here also lies the characteristic difference from all feudal viewpoints. For the latter only the descendants of the parvenu (political or social) can reap the benefit of his success in a recognized station (characteristically expressed in the Spanish *Hidalgo = hijo d'algo = filius de aliquo* where the *aliquid* means an inherited property). However rapidly these differences are today fading out in the rapid change and Europeanization of the American national character, nevertheless the precisely opposite bourgeois attitude which glorifies business success and earnings as a symptom of mental achievement, but has no respect for mere inherited wealth, is still sometimes represented there. On the other hand, in Europe (as James Bryce once remarked) in effect almost every social honor is now purchasable for money, so long as the buyer has not himself stood behind the counter, and carries out the necessary metamorpho-

sis of his property (formation of trusts, etc.). Against the aristocracy of blood, see for instance Thomas Adams, *Works of the Puritan Divines*, 216.

82. That was, for instance, already true of the founder of the Familist sect, Hendrik Nicklaes, who was a merchant (Barclay, *Inner Life of the Religious Societies of the Commonwealth*, 34).

83. This is, for instance, definitely true for Hoornbeek, since Matt. 5:5 and 1 Tim. 4:8 also made purely worldly promises to the saints (*Theologia Practica*, 1:193). Everything is the work of God's providence, but in particular he takes care of his own. *Theologia Practica*, 1:192: "Super alios autem summa cura et modis singularissimis versatur Dei providentia circa fideles." There follows a discussion of how one can know that a stroke of luck comes not from the *communis providentia*, but from that special care. Bailey also (*Praxis Pietatis*, 191) explains success in worldly labors by reference to Providence. That prosperity is often the reward of a godly life is a common expression in Quaker writings (for example see such an expression as late as 1848 in *Selection from the Christian Advices*, issued by the General Meeting of the Society of Friends, London, 6th edition, 1851, p. 209). We shall return to the connection with the Quaker ethics.

84. Thomas Adam's analysis of the quarrel of Jacob and Esau may serve as an example of this attention to the patriarchs, which is equally characteristic of the Puritan view of life (*Works of the Puritan Divines*, 235): "His [Esau's] folly may be argued from the base estimation of the birthright" (the passage is also important for the development of the idea of the birthright, of which more later) "that he would so lightly pass from it and on so easy condition as a pottage." But then it was perfidious that he would not recognize the sale, charging he had been cheated. He is, in other words, "a cunning hunter, a man of the fields"; a man of irrational, barbarous life; while Jacob, "a plain man, dwelling in tents," represents the "man of grace."

The sense of an inner relationship to Judaism, which is expressed even in the well-known work of Roosevelt, Köhler (*Ein Wort zu Denifles Luther*) found widespread among the peasants in Holland. But, on the other hand, Puritanism was fully conscious of its differences from Hebrew ethics in practical affairs, as Prynne's attack on the Jews (apropos of Cromwell's proposals for toleration) plainly shows.

85. This is, as must continually be emphasized, the final decisive religious motive (along with the purely ascetic desire to mortify the flesh). It is especially clear in the Quakers.

86. Baxter (*Saints' Everlasting Rest*, 12) repudiates this with precisely the same reasoning as the Jesuits: the body must have what it needs, otherwise one becomes a slave to it.

87. This ideal is clearly present, especially for Quakerism, in the first period of its development, as has already been shown in important points by Weingarten in his *Englische Revolutionskirchen*. Also Barclay's thorough discussion (*Apology for the True Christian Divinity*, 519ff., 533) shows it very clearly. To be avoided are (1) worldly vanity; thus all ostentation, frivolity, and use of things having no practical purpose, or which are valuable only for their scarcity (i.e. for vanity's sake); (2) any unconscientious use of wealth, such as excessive expenditure for not very urgent needs above necessary provision for the real needs of life and for the future. The Quaker was, so to speak, a living law of marginal utility. "Moderate use of the creature" is definitely permissible, but in particular one might pay attention to the quality and durability of materials so long as it did not lead to vanity. On all this compare

Morgenblatt für gebildete Leser, 1846, pp. 216ff. Especially on comfort and solidity among the Quakers, compare M. Schneckenburger, *Vorlesungen über dic Lehrbegriffe der kleineren prutestantischen Kirchenparteien*, ed. Karl B. Hundeshagen (Frankfurt am Main: H. L. Brönner, 1863) 96f.

88. Adapted by Weber from *Faust*, act 1. Goethe there depicts Mephistopheles as "Die Kraft, die stets das Böse will, und stets das Gute schafft."—TRANSLATOR'S NOTE.

89. It has already been remarked that we cannot here enter into the question of the class relations of these religious movements (see the essays on the *Wirtschaftsethik der Weltreligionen*). In order to see, however, that for example Baxter, of whom we make so much use in this study, did not see things solely as a bourgeois of his time, it will suffice to recall that even for him in the order of the religious value of the callings, after the learned professions comes the husband-man, and only then mariners, clothiers, booksellers, tailors, etc. Also, under mariners (characteristically enough) he probably thinks at least as often of fishermen as of shipowners. In this regard several things in the Talmud are in a different class. Compare, for instance, in A. Wünsche, Der *Babylonian Talmud in seinen haggadischen Bestandteilen ubersetzt* (Leipsig, 1886–89), II, pp. 20, 21, the sayings of Rabbi Eleasar, which though not unchallenged, all contend in effect that business is better than agriculture. In between see II, 2, p. 68, on the wise investment of capital: one-third in land, one-third in merchandise, and one-third in cash.

For those to whom no causal explanation is adequate without an economic (or materialistic as it is unfortunately still called) interpretation, it may be remarked that I consider the influence of economic development on the fate of religious ideas to be very important and shall later attempt to show how in our case the process of mutual adaptation of the two took place. On the other hand, those religious ideas themselves simply cannot be deduced from economic circumstances. They are in themselves, that is beyond doubt, the most powerful plastic elements of national character, and contain a law of development and a compelling force entirely their own. Moreover, the most important differences, so far as nonreligious factors play a part, are, as with Lutheranism and Calvinism, the result of political circumstances, not economic.

90. Baxter's activity in Kidderminster, a community absolutely debauched when he arrived, which was almost unique in the history of the ministry for its success, is at the same time a typical example of how asceticism educated the masses to labor, or, in Marxian terms, to the production of surplus value, and thereby for the first time made their employment in the capitalistic labor relation (putting-out industry, weaving, etc.) possible at all. That is very generally the causal relationship. From Baxter's own viewpoint he accepted the employment of his charges in capitalistic production for the sake of his religious and ethical interests. From the standpoint of the development of capitalism these latter were brought into the service of the development of the spirit of capitalism.

91. Furthermore, one may well doubt to what extent the joy of the medieval craftsman in his creation, which is so commonly appealed to, was effective as a psychological motive force. Nevertheless, there is undoubtedly something in that thesis. But in any case asceticism certainly deprived all labor of this worldly attractiveness, today for ever destroyed by capitalism, and oriented it to the beyond. Labor in a calling as such is willed by God. The impersonality of present-day labor, what, from the standpoint of the individual, is its joyless lack of meaning, still has a religious justification

here. Capitalism at the time of its development needed laborers who were available for economic exploitation for conscience's sake. Today it is in the saddle, and hence able to force people to labor without transcendental sanctions.

92. That those other elements, which have here not yet been traced to their religious roots, especially the idea that honesty is the best policy (Franklin's discussion of credit), are also of Puritan origin, must be proved in a somewhat different connection (see the following essay [not translated here]). Here I shall limit myself to repeating the following remark of J. S. Rowntree (*Quakerism, Past and Present* [London: Smith, Elder, 1859], 95–96), to which E. Bernstein has called my attention: "Is it merely a coincidence, or is it a consequence, that the lofty profession of spirituality made by the Friends has gone hand in hand with shrewdness and tact in the transaction of mundane affairs? Real piety favours the success of a trader by insuring his integrity and fostering habits of prudence and forethought, important items in obtaining that standing and credit in the commercial world, which are requisites for the steady accumulation of wealth" (see the following essay). "Honest as a Huguenot" was as proverbial in the seventeenth century as the respect for law of the Dutch which Sir W. Temple admired, and, a century later, that of the English as compared with those continental peoples that had not been through this ethical schooling.

93. Well analyzed in Bielschowsky's *Goethe*, vol. 2, chap. 18. For the development of the scientific cosmos Windelband, at the end of his *Blütezeit der deutschen Philosophie* (vol. 2 of the *Geschicte der Neueren Philosophie*), has expressed a similar idea.

94. *Saints' Everlasting Rest*, chap. 12.

95. "Couldn't the old man be satisfied with his $75,000 a year and rest? No! The frontage of the store must be widened to 400 feet. Why? That beats everything, he says. In the evening when his wife and daughter read together, he wants to go to bed. Sundays he looks at the clock every five minutes to see when the day will be over—what a futile life!" In these terms the son-in-law (who had emigrated from Germany) of the leading dry-goods man of an Ohio city expressed his judgment of the latter, a judgment which would undoubtedly have seemed simply incomprehensible to the old man. A symptom of German lack of energy.

Chapter 3

INSTITUTIONALIZED ORGANIZATIONS: FORMAL STRUCTURE AS MYTH AND CEREMONY

JOHN W. MEYER AND BRIAN ROWAN

FORMAL ORGANIZATIONS are generally understood to be systems of coordinated and controlled activities that arise when work is embedded in complex networks of technical relations and boundary-spanning exchanges. But in modern societies formal organizational structures arise in highly institutionalized contexts. Professions, policies, and programs are created along with the products and services that they are understood to produce rationally. This permits many new organizations to spring up and forces existing ones to incorporate new practices and procedures. That is, organizations are driven to incorporate the practices and procedures defined by prevailing rationalized concepts of organizational work and institutionalized in society. Organizations that do so increase their legitimacy and their survival prospects, independent of the immediate efficacy of the acquired practices and procedures.

Institutionalized products, services, techniques, policies, and programs function as powerful myths, and many organizations adopt them ceremonially. But conformity to institutionalized rules often conflicts sharply with efficiency criteria, and, conversely, to coordinate and control activity in order to promote efficiency undermines an organization's ceremonial conformity and sacrifices its support and legitimacy. To maintain ceremonial conformity, organizations that reflect institutional rules tend to buffer their formal structures from the uncertainties of technical activities by becoming loosely coupled, building gaps between their formal structures and actual work activities.

This paper argues that the formal structures of many organizations in postindustrial society (Bell 1973) dramatically reflect the myths of their institutional environments instead of the demands of their work activities. The first part describes prevailing theories of the origins of formal structures and the main problem the theories confront. The second part discusses an alter-

John W. Meyer and Brian Rowan. 1977. "Institutionalized Organizations: Formal Structure as Myth and Ceremony." *American Journal of Sociology* 83:340–63.

native source of formal structures: myths embedded in the institutional environment. The third part develops the argument that organizations reflecting institutionalized environments maintain gaps between their formal structures and their ongoing work activities. The final part summarizes by discussing some research implications.

Throughout the paper, institutionalized rules are distinguished sharply from prevailing social behaviors. Institutionalized rules are classifications built into society as reciprocated typifications or interpretations (Berger and Luckmann 1967, 54). Such rules may be simply taken for granted or may be supported by public opinion or the force of law (Starbuck 1976). Institutions inevitably involve normative obligations but often enter into social life primarily as facts which must be taken into account by actors. Institutionalization involves the processes by which social processes, obligations, or actualities come to take on a rulelike status in social thought and action. So, for example, the social status of doctor is a highly institutionalized rule (both normative and cognitive) for managing illness as well as a social role made up of particular behaviors, relations, and expectations. Research and development is an institutionalized category of organizational activity which has meaning and value in many sectors of society, as well as a collection of actual research and development activities. In a smaller way, a No Smoking sign is an institution with legal status and implications, as well as an attempt to regulate smoking behavior. It is fundamental to the argument of this paper that institutional rules may have effects on organizational structures and their implementation in actual technical work which are very different from the effects generated by the networks of social behavior and relationships which compose and surround a given organization.

Prevailing Theories of Formal Structure

A sharp distinction should be made between the formal structure of an organization and its actual day-to-day work activities. Formal structure is a blueprint for activities which includes, first of all, the table of organization: a listing of offices, departments, positions, and programs. These elements are linked by explicit goals and policies that make up a rational theory of how, and to what end, activities are to be fitted together. The essence of a modern bureaucratic organization lies in the rationalized and impersonal character of these structural elements and of the goals that link them.

One of the central problems in organization theory is to describe the conditions that give rise to rationalized formal structure. In conventional theories, rational formal structure is assumed to be the most effective way to coordinate and control the complex relational networks involved in modern technical or work activities (see Scott 1975 for a review). This assumption derives from Weber's (1930, 1946, 1947) discussions of the historical emergence of bureaucracies as consequences of economic markets and centralized states. Economic markets place a premium on rationality and coordination. As markets expand, the relational networks in a given domain become more complex and differentiated, and organizations in that domain must manage more internal and boundary-spanning interdependencies. Such factors as size (Blau 1970) and technology (Woodward 1965) increase the complexity of internal relations, and the division of labor among organizations increases boundary-spanning problems (Aiken and Hage 1968; Freeman 1973; Thompson 1967). Because the need for coordination increases under these conditions, and because formally coordinated work has competitive advantages, organizations with rationalized formal structures tend to develop.

The formation of centralized states and the penetration of societies by political centers also contribute to the rise and spread of formal organization. When the relational networks involved in economic exchange and political management become extremely complex, bureaucratic structures are thought to be the most effective and rational means to standardize and control subunits. Bureaucratic control is especially useful for expanding political centers, and standardization is often demanded by both centers and peripheral units (Bendix 1964, 1968). Political centers organize layers of offices that manage to extend conformity and to displace traditional activities throughout societies.

The problem. *Prevailing theories assume that the coordination and control of activity are the critical dimensions on which formal organizations have succeeded in the modern world.* This assumption is based on the view that organizations function according to their formal blueprints: coordination is routine, rules and procedures are followed, and actual activities conform to the prescriptions of formal structure. But much of the empirical research on organizations casts doubt on this assumption. An earlier generation of researchers concluded that there was a great gap between the formal and the informal organization (e.g., Dalton 1959; Downs 1967; Homans 1950). A related observation is that formal organizations are often loosely coupled (March and Olsen 1976; Weick 1976): structural elements are only loosely linked to each other and to activities, rules are often violated, decisions are often unimplemented, or if implemented have uncertain consequences, technologies are of problematic efficiency, and evaluation and inspection systems are subverted or rendered so vague as to provide little coordination.

Formal organizations are endemic in modern societies. There is need for an explanation of their rise that is partially free from the assumption that, in practice, formal structures actually coordinate and control work. Such an explanation should account for the elaboration of purposes, positions, policies, and procedural rules that characterizes formal organizations, but must do so without supposing that these structural features are implemented in routine work activity.

Institutional Sources of Formal Structure

By focusing on the management of complex relational networks and the exercise of coordination and control, prevailing theories have neglected an alternative Weberian source of formal structure: the legitimacy of rationalized formal structures. In prevailing theories, legitimacy is a given: assertions about bureaucratization rest on the assumption of norms of rationality (Thompson 1967). When norms do play causal roles in theories of bureaucratization, it is because they are thought to be built into modern societies and personalities as very general values, which are thought to facilitate formal organization. But norms of rationality are not simply general values. They exist in much more specific and powerful ways in the rules, understandings, and meanings attached to institutionalized social structures. The causal importance of such institutions in the process of bureaucratization has been neglected.

Formal structures are not only creatures of their relational networks in the social organization. In modern societies, the elements of rationalized formal structure are deeply ingrained in, and reflect, widespread understandings of social reality. Many of the positions, policies, programs, and procedures of modern organizations are enforced by public opinion, by the views of important constituents, by knowledge legitimated through the educational system, by social prestige, by the laws, and by the definitions of negligence and prudence used by the courts. Such elements of formal structure are manifestations of powerful institutional rules which function as highly rationalized myths that are binding on particular organizations.

In modern societies, the myths generating formal organizational structure have two key properties. First, they are rationalized and impersonal prescriptions that identify various social purposes as technical ones and specify in a rulelike way the appropriate means to pursue these technical purposes rationally (Ellul 1964). Second, they are highly institutionalized and thus in some measure beyond the discretion of any individual participant or organization. They must, therefore, be taken for granted as legitimate, apart from evaluations of their impact on work outcomes.

Many elements of formal structure are highly institutionalized and function as myths. Examples include professions, programs, and technologies:

Large numbers of rationalized professions emerge (Wilensky 1965; Bell 1973). These are occupations controlled, not only by direct inspection of work outcomes but also by social rules of licensing, certifying, and schooling. The occupations are rationalized, being understood to control impersonal techniques rather than moral mysteries. Further, they are highly institutionalized: the delegation of activities to the appropriate occupations is socially expected and often legally obligatory over and above any calculations of its efficiency.

Many formalized organizational programs are also institutionalized in society. Ideologies define the functions appropriate to a business—such as sales, production, advertising, or accounting; to a university—such as instruction and research in history, engineering, and literature; and to a hospital—such as surgery, internal medicine, and obstetrics. Such classifications of organizational functions, and the specifications for conducting each function, are prefabricated formulas available for use by any given organization.

Similarly, technologies are institutionalized and become myths binding on organizations. Technical procedures of production, accounting, personnel selection, or data processing become taken-for-granted means to accomplish organizational ends. Quite apart from their possible efficiency, such institutionalized techniques establish an organization as appropriate, rational, and modern. Their use displays responsibility and avoids claims of negligence.

The impact of such rationalized institutional elements on organizations and organizing situations is enormous. These rules define new organizing situations, redefine existing ones, and specify the means for coping rationally with each. They enable, and often require, participants to organize along prescribed lines. And they spread very rapidly in modern society as part of the rise of postindustrial society (Bell 1973). New and extant domains of activity are codified in institutionalized programs, professions, or techniques, and organizations incorporate the packaged codes. For example:

The discipline of psychology creates a rationalized theory of personnel selection and certifies personnel professionals. Personnel departments and functionaries appear in all sorts of extant organizations, and new specialized personnel agencies also appear.

As programs of research and development are created and professionals with expertise in these fields are trained and defined, organizations come under increasing pressure to incorporate R & D units.

As the prerational profession of prostitution is rationalized along medical lines, bureaucratized organizations—sex-therapy clinics, massage parlors, and the like—spring up more easily.

As the issues of safety and environmental pollution arise, and as relevant professions and programs become institutionalized in laws, union ideologies, and public opinion, organizations incorporate these programs and professions.

The growth of rationalized institutional structures in society makes formal organizations more common and more elaborate. Such institutions are myths which make formal organizations both easier to create and more necessary. After all, the building blocks for organizations come to be littered around the societal landscape; it takes only a little entrepreneurial energy to assemble them into a structure. And because these building blocks are considered proper, adequate, rational, and necessary, organizations must incorporate them to avoid illegitimacy. Thus, the myths built into rationalized institutional elements create the necessity, the opportunity, and the impulse to organize rationally, over and above pressures in this direction created by the need to manage proximate relational networks:

Proposition 1. *As rationalized institutional rules arise in given domains of work activity, formal organizations form and expand by incorporating these rules as structural elements.*

Two distinct ideas are implied here: (1*A*) As institutionalized myths define new domains of rationalized activity, formal organizations emerge in these domains. (1*B*) As rationalizing institutional myths arise in existing domains of activity, extant organizations expand their formal structures so as to become isomorphic with these new myths.

To understand the larger historical process it is useful to note that

Proposition 2. *The more modernized the society, the more extended the rationalized institutional structure in given domains and the greater the number of domains containing rationalized institutions.*

Modern institutions, then, are thoroughly rationalized, and these rationalized elements act as myths giving rise to more formal organization. When propositions 1 and 2 are combined, two more specific ideas follow: (2*A*) Formal organizations are more likely to emerge in more modernized societies, even with the complexity of immediate relational networks held constant. (2*B*) Formal organizations in a given domain of activity are likely to have more elaborated structures in more modernized societies, even with the complexity of immediate relational networks held constant.

Combining the ideas above with prevailing organization theory, it becomes clear that modern societies are filled with rationalized bureaucracies for two reasons. First, as the prevailing theories have asserted, relational networks become increasingly complex as societies modernize. Second, modern societies are filled with institutional rules which function as myths depicting various formal structures as rational means to the attainment of desirable ends. Figure 3.1 summarizes these two lines of theory. Both lines suggest that the postindustrial society—the society dominated by rational organization even more than by the forces of production—arises both out of the complexity of the modern social organizational network and, more directly, as an ideological matter. Once institutionalized, rationality becomes a myth with explosive organizing potential, as both Ellul (1964) and Bell (1973)—though with rather different reactions—observe.

The Relation of Organizations to Their Institutional Environments

The observation is not new that organizations are structured by phenomena in their environments and tend to become isomorphic with them. One expla-

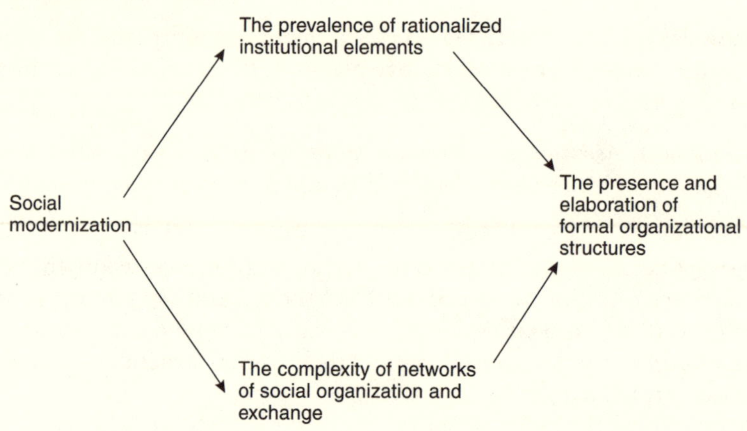

FIGURE 3.1. The origins and elaboration of formal organizational structures

nation of such isomorphism is that formal organizations become matched with their environments by technical and exchange interdependencies. This line of reasoning can be seen in the works of Aiken and Hage (1968), Hawley (1968), and Thompson (1967). This explanation asserts that structural elements diffuse because environments create boundary-spanning exigencies for organizations, and that organizations which incorporate structural elements isomorphic with the environment are able to manage such interdependencies.

A second explanation for the parallelism between organizations and their environments—and the one emphasized here—is that organizations structurally reflect socially constructed reality (Berger and Luckmann 1967). This view is suggested in the work of Parsons (1956) and Udy (1970), who see organizations as greatly conditioned by their general institutional environments and therefore as institutions themselves in part. Emery and Trist (1965) also see organizations as responding directly to environmental structures and distinguish such effects sharply from those that occur through boundary-spanning exchanges. According to the institutional conception as developed here, organizations tend to disappear as distinct and bounded units. Quite beyond the environmental interrelations suggested in open-systems theories, institutional theories in their extreme forms define organizations as dramatic enactments of the rationalized myths pervading modern societies, rather than as units involved in exchange—no matter how complex—with their environments.

The two explanations of environmental isomorphism are not entirely inconsistent. Organizations both deal with their environments at their boundaries and imitate environmental elements in their structures. However, the two lines of explanation have very different implications for internal organizational processes, as will be argued below.

The Origins of Rational Institutional Myths

Bureaucratization is caused in part by the proliferation of rationalized myths in society, and this in turn involves the evolution of the whole modern institutional system. Although the latter topic is beyond the scope of this paper, three specific processes that generate rationalized myths of organizational structure can be noted.

THE ELABORATION OF COMPLEX RELATIONAL NETWORKS

As the relational networks in societies become dense and interconnected, increasing numbers of rationalized myths arise. Some of them are highly generalized: for example, the principles of universalism (Parsons 1971), contracts (Spencer 1897), restitution (Durkheim 1933), and expertise (Weber 1947) are generalized to diverse occupations, organizational programs, and organizational practices. Other myths describe specific structural elements. These myths may originate from narrow contexts and be applied in different ones. For example, in modern societies the relational contexts of business organizations in a single industry are roughly similar from place to place. Under these conditions a particularly effective practice, occupational specialty, or principle of coordination can be codified into mythlike form. The laws, the educational and credentialing systems, and public opinion then make it necessary or advantageous for organizations to incorporate the new structures.

THE DEGREE OF COLLECTIVE ORGANIZATION OF THE ENVIRONMENT

The myths generated by particular organizational practices and diffused through relational networks have legitimacy based on the supposition that they are rationally effective. But many myths also have official legitimacy based on legal mandates. Societies that, through nation building and state formation, have developed rational-legal orders are especially prone to give collective (legal) authority to institutions which legitimate particular organizational structures. The rise of centralized states and integrated nations means that organized agents of society assume jurisdiction over large numbers of activity domains (Swanson 1971). Legislative and judicial authorities create and interpret legal mandates; administrative agencies—such as state and federal governments, port authorities, and school districts—establish rules of practice; and licenses and credentials become necessary in order to practice occupations. The stronger the rational-legal order, the greater the extent to which rationalized rules and procedures and personnel become institutional requirements. New formal organizations emerge and extant organizations acquire new structural elements.

LEADERSHIP EFFORTS OF LOCAL ORGANIZATIONS

The rise of the state and the expansion of collective jurisdiction are often thought to result in domesticated organizations (Carlson 1962) subject to high levels of goal displacement (Clark 1956; Selznick 1949; Zald and Denton 1963). This view is misleading: organizations do often adapt to their institutional contexts, but they often play active roles in shaping those contexts (Dowling and Pfeffer 1975; Parsons 1956; Perrow 1970; Thompson 1967). Many organizations actively seek charters from collective authorities and manage to institutionalize their goals and structures in the rules of such authorities.

Efforts to mold institutional environments proceed along two dimensions. First, powerful organizations force their immediate relational networks to adapt to their structures and relations. For instance, automobile producers help create demands for particular kinds of roads, transportation systems, and fuels that make automobiles virtual necessities; competitive forms of transportation have to adapt to the existing relational context. But second, powerful organizations attempt to build their goals and procedures directly into society as institutional rules. Automobile producers, for instance, attempt to create the standards in public opinion defining desirable cars, to influence legal standards defining satisfactory cars, to affect judicial rules defining cars adequate enough to avoid manufacturer liability, and to force agents of the collectivity to purchase only their cars. Rivals must then compete both in social networks or markets and in contexts of institutional rules which are defined by extant organizations. In this fashion, given organizational forms perpetuate themselves by becoming institutionalized rules. For example:

School administrators who create new curricula or training programs attempt to validate them as legitimate innovations in educational theory and governmental requirements. If they are successful, the new procedures can be perpetuated as authoritatively required or at least satisfactory.

New departments within business enterprises, such as personnel, advertising, or research and development departments, attempt to professionalize by creating rules of practice and personnel certification that are enforced by the schools, prestige systems, and the laws.

Organizations under attack in competitive environments—small farms, passenger railways, or Rolls-Royce—attempt to establish themselves as central to the cultural traditions of their societies in order to receive official protection.

The Impact of Institutional Environments on Organizations

Isomorphism with environmental institutions has some crucial consequences for organizations: (*a*) they incorporate elements which are legitimated externally, rather than in terms of efficiency; (*b*) they employ external or ceremonial assessment criteria to define the value of structural elements; and (*c*) dependence on externally fixed institutions reduces turbulence and maintains stability. As a result, it is argued here, institutional isomorphism promotes the success and survival of organizations. Incorporating externally legitimated formal structures increases the commitment of internal participants and external constituents. And the use of external assessment criteria—that is, moving toward the status in society of a subunit rather than an independent system—can enable an organization to remain successful by social definition, buffering it from failure.

CHANGING FORMAL STRUCTURES

By designing a formal structure that adheres to the prescriptions of myths in the institutional environment, an organization demonstrates that it is acting on collectively valued purposes in a proper and adequate manner (Dowling and Pfeffer 1975; Meyer and Rowan 1975). The incorporation of institutionalized elements provides an account (Scott and Lyman 1968) of its activities that protects the organization from having its conduct questioned. The organization becomes, in a word, legitimate, and it uses its legitimacy to strengthen its support and secure its survival.

From an institutional perspective, then, a most important aspect of isomorphism with environmental institutions is the evolution of organizational language. The labels of the organization chart as well as the vocabulary used to delineate organizational goals, procedures, and policies are analogous to the vocabularies of motive used to account for the activities of individuals (Blum and McHugh 1971; Mills 1940). Just as jealousy, anger, altruism, and love are myths that interpret and explain the actions of individuals, the myths of doctors, of accountants, or of the assembly line explain organizational activities. Thus, some can say that the engineers will solve a specific problem or that the secretaries will perform certain tasks, without knowing who these engineers or secretaries will be or exactly what they will do. Both the speaker and the listeners understand such statements to describe how certain responsibilities will be carried out.

Vocabularies of structure which are isomorphic with institutional rules provide prudent, rational, and legitimate accounts. Organizations described in legitimated vocabularies are assumed to be oriented to collectively defined, and often collectively mandated, ends. The myths of personnel services, for example, not only account for the rationality of employment practices but also indicate that personnel services are valuable to an organization. Employees, applicants, managers, trustees, and governmental agencies are predisposed to trust the hiring practices of organizations that follow legitimated procedures—such as equal opportunity programs, or personality testing—and they are more willing to participate in or to fund such organizations. On the other hand, organizations that omit environmentally legitimated elements of structure or create unique structures lack acceptable legitimated accounts of their activities. Such organizations are more vulnerable to claims that they are negligent, irrational, or unnecessary. Claims of this kind, whether made by internal participants, external constituents, or the government, can cause organizations to incur real costs. For example:

With the rise of modern medical institutions, large organizations that do not arrange medical-care facilities for their workers come to be seen as negligent—by the workers, by management factions, by insurers, by courts which legally define negligence, and often by laws. The costs of illegitimacy in insurance premiums and legal liabilities are very real.

Similarly, environmental safety institutions make it important for organizations to create formal safety rules, safety departments, and safety programs. No Smoking rules and signs, regardless of their enforcement, are necessary to avoid charges of negligence and to avoid the extreme of illegitimation: the closing of buildings by the state.

The rise of professionalized economics makes it useful for organizations to incorporate groups of economists and econometric analyses. Though no one may read, understand, or believe them, econometric analyses help legitimate the organization's plans in the eyes of investors, customers (as with Defense Department contractors), and internal participants. Such analyses can also provide rational accountings after failures occur: managers whose plans have failed can demonstrate to investors, stockholders, and superiors that procedures were prudent and that decisions were made by rational means.

Thus, rationalized institutions create myths of formal structure which shape organizations. Failure to incorporate the proper elements of structure is negligent and irrational; the continued flow of support is threatened and internal dissidents are strengthened. At the same time, these myths present organizations with great opportunities for expansion. Affixing the right labels to activities can change them into valuable services and mobilize the commitments of internal participants and external constituents.

ADOPTING EXTERNAL ASSESSMENT CRITERIA

In institutionally elaborated environments organizations also become sensitive to, and employ, external criteria of worth. Such criteria include, for instance, such ceremonial awards as the Nobel Prize, endorsements by important people, the standard prices of professionals and consultants, or the prestige of programs or personnel in external social circles. For example, the conventions of modern accounting attempt to assign value to particular components of organizations on the basis of their contribution—through the organization's production function—to the goods and services the organization produces. But for many units—service departments, administrative sectors, and others—it is utterly unclear what is being produced that has clear or definable value in terms of its contribution to the organizational product. In these situations, accountants employ shadow prices: they assume that given organizational units are necessary and calculate their value from their prices in the world outside the organization. Thus modern accounting creates ceremonial production functions and maps them onto economic production functions: organizations assign externally defined worth to advertising departments, safety departments, managers, econometricians, and occasionally even sociologists, whether or not these units contribute measurably to the production of outputs. Monetary prices, in postindustrial society, reflect hosts of ceremonial influences, as do economic measures of efficiency, profitability, or net worth (Hirsch 1975).

Ceremonial criteria of worth and ceremonially derived production functions are useful to organizations: they legitimate organizations with internal participants, stockholders, the public, and the state, as with the IRS or the SEC. They demonstrate socially the fitness of an organization. The incorporation of structures with high ceremonial value, such as those reflecting the latest expert thinking or those with the most prestige, makes the credit position of an organization more favorable. Loans, donations, or investments are more easily obtained. Finally, units within the organization use ceremonial assessments as accounts of their productive service to the organization. Their internal power rises with their performance on ceremonial measures (Salancik and Pfeffer 1974).

STABILIZATION

The rise of an elaborate institutional environment stabilizes both external and internal organizational relationships. Centralized states, trade association, unions, professional associations, and coalitions among organizations standardize and stabilize (see the review by Starbuck 1976).

Market conditions, the characteristics of inputs and outputs, and technological procedures are brought under the jurisdiction of institutional meanings and controls. Stabilization also results as a given organization becomes part of the wider collective system. Support is guaranteed by agreements instead of depending entirely on performance. For example, apart from whether schools educate students, or hospitals cure patients, people and governmental agencies remain committed to these organizations, funding and using them almost automatically year after year.

Institutionally controlled environments buffer organizations from turbulence (Emery and Trist 1965; Terreberry 1968). Adaptations occur less rapidly as increased numbers of agreements are enacted. Collectively granted monopolies guarantee clienteles for organizations like schools, hospitals, or professional associations. The taken-for-granted (and legally regulated) quality of institutional rules makes dramatic instabilities in products, techniques, or policies unlikely. And legitimacy as accepted subunits of society protects organizations from immediate sanctions for variations in technical performance:

> Thus, American school districts (like other governmental units) have near monopolies and are very stable. They must conform to wider rules about proper classifications and credentials of teachers and students, and of topics of study. But they are protected by rules which make education as defined by these classifications compulsory. Alternative or private schools are possible, but must conform so closely to the required structures and classifications as to be able to generate little advantage.
>
> Some business organizations obtain very high levels of institutional stabilization. A large defense contractor may be paid for following agreed-on procedures, even if the product is ineffective. In the extreme, such organizations may be so successful as to survive bankruptcy intact—as Lockheed and Penn Central have done—by becoming partially components of the state. More commonly, such firms are guaranteed survival by state-regulated rates which secure profits regardless of costs, as with American public utility firms.
>
> Large automobile firms are a little less stabilized. They exist in an environment that contains enough structures to make automobiles, as conventionally defined, virtual necessities. But still, customers and governments can inspect each automobile and can evaluate and even legally discredit it. Legal action cannot as easily discredit a high school graduate.

ORGANIZATIONAL SUCCESS AND SURVIVAL

Thus, organizational success depends on factors other than efficient coordination and control of productive activities. Independent of their productive efficiency, organizations which exist in highly elaborated institutional environments and succeed in becoming isomorphic with these environments gain the legitimacy and resources needed to survive. In part, this depends on environmental processes and on the capacity of given organizational leadership to mold these processes (Hirsch 1975). In part, it depends on the ability of given organizations to conform to, and become legitimated by, environmental institutions. In institutionally elaborated environments, sagacious conformity is required: leadership (in a university, a hospital, or a business) requires an understanding of changing fashions and governmental programs. But this kind of conformity—and the almost guaranteed survival which may accompany it—is possible only in an environment with a highly institutionalized structure. In such a context an organization can be locked into isomorphism,

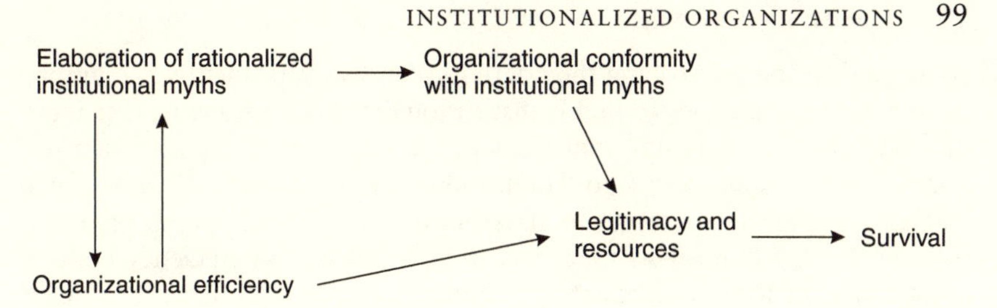

FIGURE 3.2. Organizational survival

ceremonially reflecting the institutional environment in its structure, functionaries, and procedures. Thus, in addition to the conventionally defined sources of organizational success and survival, the following general assertion can be proposed:

> **Proposition 3.** *Organizations that incorporate societally legitimated rationalized elements in their formal structures maximize their legitimacy and increase their resources and survival capabilities.*

This proposition asserts that the long-run survival prospects of organizations increase as state structures elaborate and as organizations respond to institutionalized rules. In the United States, for instance, schools, hospitals, and welfare organizations show considerable ability to survive, precisely because they are matched with—and almost absorbed by—their institutional environments. In the same way, organizations fail when they deviate from the prescriptions of institutionalizing myths: quite apart from technical efficiency, organizations which innovate in important structural ways bear considerable costs in legitimacy.

Figure 3.2 summarizes the general argument of this section, alongside the established view that organizations succeed through efficiency.

Institutionalized Structures and Organizational Activities

Rationalized formal structures arise in two contexts. First, the demands of local relational networks encourage the development of structures that coordinate and control activities. Such structures contribute to the efficiency of organizations and give them competitive advantages over less efficient competitors. Second, the interconnectedness of societal relations, the collective organization of society, and the leadership of organizational elites create a highly institutionalized context. In this context rationalized structures present an acceptable account of organizational activities, and organizations gain legitimacy, stability, and resources.

All organizations, to one degree or another, are embedded in both relational and institutionalized contexts and are therefore concerned both with coordinating and controlling their activities and with prudently accounting for them. Organizations in highly institutionalized environments face internal and boundary-spanning contingencies. Schools, for example, must transport students to and from school under some circumstances and must assign teachers, students, and topics to classrooms. On the other hand, organizations producing in markets that place great emphasis on efficiency build in units whose relation to production is obscure and whose efficiency is determined, not by a true production function, but by ceremonial definition.

Nevertheless, the survival of some organizations depends more on managing the demands of internal and boundary-spanning relations, while the survival of others depends more on the ceremonial demands of highly institutionalized environments. The discussion to follow shows that whether an organization's survival depends primarily on relational or on institutional demands determines the tightness of alignments between structures and activities.

Types of Organizations

Institutionalized myths differ in the completeness with which they describe cause and effect relationships, and in the clarity with which they describe standards that should be used to evaluate outputs (Thompson 1967). Some organizations use routine, clearly defined technologies to produce outputs. When output can be easily evaluated a market often develops, and consumers gain considerable rights of inspection and control. In this context, efficiency often determines success. Organizations must face exigencies of close coordination with their relational networks, and they cope with these exigencies by organizing around immediate technical problems.

But the rise of collectively organized society and the increasing interconnectedness of social relations have eroded many market contexts. Increasingly, such organizations as schools, R & D units, and governmental bureaucracies use variable, ambiguous technologies to produce outputs that are difficult to appraise, and other organizations with clearly defined technologies find themselves unable to adapt to environmental turbulence. The uncertainties of unpredictable technical contingencies or of adapting to environmental change cannot be resolved on the basis of efficiency. Internal participants and external constituents alike call for institutionalized rules that promote trust and confidence in outputs and buffer organizations from failure (Emery and Trist 1965).

Thus, one can conceive of a continuum along which organizations can be ordered. At one end are production organizations under strong output controls (Ouchi and Maguire 1975) whose success depends on the management of relational networks. At the other end are institutionalized organizations whose success depends on the confidence and stability achieved by isomorphism with institutional rules. For two reasons it is important not to assume that an organization's location on this continuum is based on the inherent technical properties of its output and therefore permanent. First, the technical properties of outputs are socially defined and do not exist in some concrete sense that allows them to be empirically discovered. Second, environments and organizations often redefine the nature of products, services, and technologies. Redefinition sometimes clarifies techniques or evaluative standards. But often organizations and environments redefine the nature of techniques and output so that ambiguity is introduced and rights of inspection and control are lowered. For example, American schools have evolved from producing rather specific training that was evaluated according to strict criteria of efficiency to producing ambiguously defined services that are evaluated according to criteria of certification (Callahan 1962; Tyack 1974; Meyer and Rowan 1975).

Structural Inconsistencies in Institutionalized Organizations

Two very general problems face an organization if its success depends primarily on isomorphism with institutionalized rules. First, technical activities and demands for efficiency create conflicts and inconsistencies in an institutionalized organization's efforts to conform to the ceremonial rules of production. Second, because these ceremonial rules are transmitted by myths that may arise from different parts of the environment, the rules may conflict with one another. These inconsistencies make a concern for efficiency and tight coordination and control problematic.

Formal structures that celebrate institutionalized myths differ from structures that act efficiently. Ceremonial activity is significant in relation to categorical rules, not in its concrete effects (Merton 1940; March and Simon 1958). A sick worker must be treated by a doctor using accepted medical procedures; whether the worker is treated effectively is less important. A bus company must service required routes whether or not there are many passengers. A university must maintain appropriate departments independently of the departments' enrollments. Activity, that is, has ritual significance: it maintains appearances and validates an organization.

Categorical rules conflict with the logic of efficiency. Organizations often face the dilemma that activities celebrating institutionalized rules, although they count as virtuous ceremonial expenditures, are pure costs from the point of view of efficiency. For example, hiring a Nobel Prize winner brings great ceremonial benefits to a university. The celebrated name can lead to research grants, brighter students, or reputational gains. But from the point of view of immediate outcomes, the expenditure lowers the instructional return per dollar expended and lowers the university's ability to solve immediate logistical problems. Also, expensive technologies, which bring prestige to hospitals and business firms, may be simply excessive costs from the point of view of immediate production. Similarly, highly professionalized consultants who bring external blessings on an organization are often difficult to justify in terms of improved productivity, yet may be very important in maintaining internal and external legitimacy.

Other conflicts between categorical rules and efficiency arise because institutional rules are couched at high levels of generalization (Durkheim 1933) whereas technical activities vary with specific, unstandardized, and possibly unique conditions. Because standardized ceremonial categories must confront technical variations and anomalies, the generalized rules of the institutional environment are often inappropriate to specific situations. A governmentally mandated curriculum may be inappropriate for the students at hand, a conventional medical treatment may make little sense given the characteristics of a patient, and federal safety inspectors may intolerably delay boundary-spanning exchanges.

Yet another source of conflict between categorical rules and efficiency is the inconsistency among institutionalized elements. Institutional environments are often pluralistic (Udy 1970), and societies promulgate sharply inconsistent myths. As a result, organizations in search of external support and stability incorporate all sorts of incompatible structural elements. Professions are incorporated although they make overlapping jurisdictional claims. Programs are adopted which contend with each other for authority over a given domain. For instance, if one inquires who decides what curricula will be taught in schools, any number of parties from the various governments down to individual teachers may say that they decide.

In institutionalized organizations, then, concern with the efficiency of day-to-day activities creates enormous uncertainties. Specific contexts highlight the inadequacies of the prescriptions of generalized myths, and inconsistent structural elements conflict over jurisdictional rights. Thus the organization must struggle to link the requirements of ceremonial elements to technical activities and to link inconsistent ceremonial elements to each other.

Resolving Inconsistencies

There are four partial solutions to these inconsistencies. First, an organization can resist ceremonial requirements. But an organization that neglects ceremonial requirements and portrays itself as efficient may be unsuccessful in documenting its efficiency. Also, rejecting ceremonial requirements neglects an important source of resources and stability. Second, an organization can maintain rigid conformity to institutionalized prescriptions by cutting off external relations. Although such isolation upholds ceremonial requirements, internal participants and external constituents may soon become disillusioned with their inability to manage boundary-spanning exchanges. Institutionalized organizations must not only conform to myths but must also maintain the appearance that the myths actually work. Third, an organization can cynically acknowledge that its structure is inconsistent with work requirements. But this strategy denies the validity of institutionalized myths and sabotages the legitimacy of the organization. Fourth, an organization can promise reform. People may picture the present as unworkable but the future as filled with promising reforms of both structure and activity. But by defining the organization's valid structure as lying in the future, this strategy makes the organization's current structure illegitimate.

Instead of relying on a partial solution, however, an organization can resolve conflicts between ceremonial rules and efficiency by employing two interrelated devices: decoupling and the logic of confidence.

DECOUPLING

Ideally, organizations built around efficiency attempt to maintain close alignments between structures and activities. Conformity is enforced through inspection, output quality is continually monitored, the efficiency of various units is evaluated, and the various goals are unified and coordinated. But a policy of close alignment in institutionalized organizations merely makes public a record of inefficiency and inconsistency.

Institutionalized organizations protect their formal structures from evaluation on the basis of technical performance: inspection, evaluation, and control of activities are minimized, and coordination, interdependence, and mutual adjustments among structural units are handled informally.

Proposition 4. *Because attempts to control and coordinate activities in institutionalized organizations lead to conflicts and loss of legitimacy, elements of structure are decoupled from activities and from each other.*

Some well-known properties of organizations illustrate the decoupling process:

Activities are performed beyond the purview of managers. In particular, organizations actively encourage professionalism, and activities are delegated to professionals.

Goals are made ambiguous or vacuous, and categorical ends are substituted for technical ends. Hospitals treat, not cure, patients. Schools produce students, not learning. In fact, data on technical performance are eliminated or rendered invisible. Hospitals try to ignore information on cure rates, public services avoid data about effectiveness, and schools de-emphasize measures of achievement.

Integration is avoided, program implementation is neglected, and inspection and evaluation are ceremonialized.

Human relations are made very important. The organization cannot formally coordinate activities because its formal rules, if applied, would generate inconsistencies. Therefore individuals are left to work out technical interdependencies informally. The ability to coordinate things in violation of the rules—that is, to get along with other people—is highly valued.

The advantages of decoupling are clear. The assumption that formal structures are really working is buffered from the inconsistencies and anomalies involved in technical activities. Also, because integration is avoided disputes and conflicts are minimized, and an organization can mobilize support from a broader range of external constituents.

Thus, decoupling enables organizations to maintain standardized, legitimating, formal structures while their activities vary in response to practical considerations. The organizations in an industry tend to be similar in formal structure—reflecting their common institutional origins—but may show much diversity in actual practice.

THE LOGIC OF CONFIDENCE AND GOOD FAITH

Despite the lack of coordination and control, decoupled organizations are not anarchies. Day-to-day activities proceed in an orderly fashion. What legitimates institutionalized organizations, enabling them to appear useful in spite of the lack of technical validation, is the confidence and good faith of their internal participants and their external constituents.

Considerations of face characterize ceremonial management (Goffman 1967). Confidence in structural elements is maintained through three practices—avoidance, discretion, and overlooking (Goffman 1967, 12–18). Avoidance and discretion are encouraged by decoupling autonomous subunits; overlooking anomalies is also quite common. Both internal participants and external constituents cooperate in these practices. Assuring that individual participants maintain face sustains confidence in the organization, and ultimately reinforces confidence in the myths that rationalize the organization's existence.

Delegation, professionalization, goal ambiguity, the elimination of output data, and maintenance of face are all mechanisms for absorbing uncertainty while preserving the formal structure of the organization (March and Simon 1958). They contribute to a general aura of confidence within and outside the organization. Although the literature on informal organization often treats these practices as mechanisms for the achievement of deviant and subgroup purposes (Downs 1967), such treatment ignores a critical feature of organization life: effectively absorbing uncertainty and maintaining confidence requires people to assume that everyone is acting in good faith. The assumption that things are as they seem, that employees and managers are performing their roles properly, allows an organization to perform its daily routines with a decoupled structure.

Decoupling and maintenance of face, in other words, are mechanisms that maintain the assumption that people are acting in good faith. Professionalization is not merely a way of avoiding inspection—it binds both supervisors and subordinates to act in good faith. So in a smaller way does strategic leniency (Blau 1956). And so do the public displays of morale and satisfaction which are characteristic of many organizations. Organizations employ a host of mechanisms to dramatize the ritual commitments which their participants make to basic structural elements. These mechanisms are especially common in organizations which strongly reflect their institutionalized environments.

Proposition 5. *The more an organization's structure is derived from institutionalized myths, the more it maintains elaborate displays of confidence, satisfaction, and good faith, internally and externally.*

The commitments built up by displays of morale and satisfaction are not simply vacuous affirmations of institutionalized myths. Participants not only commit themselves to supporting an organization's ceremonial facade but also commit themselves to making things work out backstage. The committed participants engage in informal coordination that, although often formally inappropriate, keeps technical activities running smoothly and avoids public embarrassments. In this sense the confidence and good faith generated by ceremonial action is in no way fraudulent. It may even be the most reasonable way to get participants to make their best efforts in situations that are made problematic by institutionalized myths that are at odds with immediate technical demands.

CEREMONIAL INSPECTION AND EVALUATION

All organizations, even those maintaining high levels of confidence and good faith, are in environments that have institutionalized the rationalized rituals of inspection and evaluation. And inspection and evaluation can uncover events and deviations that undermine legitimacy. So institutionalized organizations minimize and ceremonialize inspection and evaluation.

In institutionalized organizations, in fact, evaluation accompanies and produces illegitimacy. The interest in evaluation research by the American federal government, for instance, is partly intended to undercut the state, local, and private authorities which have managed social services in the United States. The federal authorities, of course, have usually not evaluated those programs which are completely under federal jurisdiction; they have only evaluated those over which federal controls are incomplete. Similarly, state governments have often insisted on evaluating the special fundings they create in welfare and education but ordinarily do not evaluate the programs which they fund in a routine way.

Evaluation and inspection are public assertions of societal control which violate the assumption that everyone is acting with competence and in good faith. Violating this assumption lowers morale and confidence. Thus, evaluation and inspection undermine the ceremonial aspects of organizations.

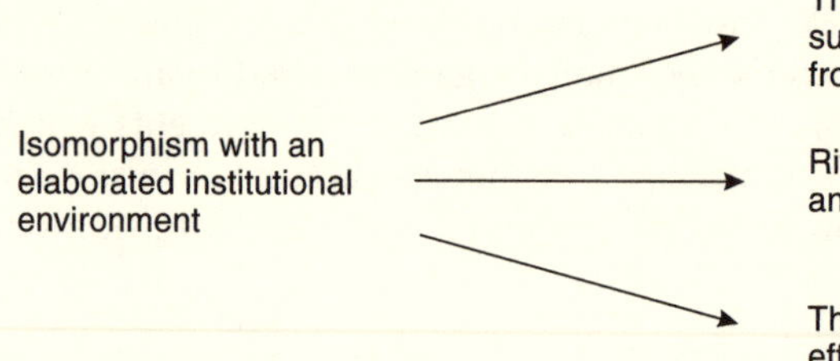

FIGURE 3.3. The effects of institutional isomorphism on organizations

Proposition 6. *Institutionalized organizations seek to minimize inspection and evaluation by both internal managers and external constituents.*

Decoupling and the avoidance of inspection and evaluation are not merely devices used by the organization. External constituents, too, avoid inspecting and controlling institutionalized organizations (Meyer and Rowan 1975). Accrediting agencies, boards of trustees, government agencies, and individuals accept ceremonially at face value the credentials, ambiguous goals, and categorical evaluations that are characteristic of ceremonial organizations. In elaborate institutional environments these external constituents are themselves likely to be corporately organized agents of society. Maintaining categorical relationships with their organizational subunits is more stable and more certain than is relying on inspection and control.

Figure 3.3 summarizes the main arguments of this section of our discussion.

Summary and Research Implications

Organizational structures are created and made more elaborate with the rise of institutionalized myths, and, in highly institutionalized contexts, organizational action must support these myths. But an organization must also attend to practical activity. The two requirements are at odds. A stable solution is to maintain the organization in a loosely coupled state.

No position is taken here on the overall social effectiveness of isomorphic and loosely coupled organizations. To some extent such structures buffer activity from efficiency criteria and produce ineffectiveness. On the other hand, by binding participants to act in good faith, and to adhere to the larger rationalities of the wider structure, they may maximize long-run effectiveness. It should not be assumed that the creation of microscopic rationalities in the daily activity of workers effects social ends more efficiently than commitment to larger institutional claims and purposes.

Research Implications

The argument presented here generates several major theses that have clear research implications.

1. Environments and environmental domains which have institutionalized a greater number of rational myths generate more formal organization. This thesis leads to the research hypothesis that formal organizations rise and become more complex as a result of the rise of the elaborated state and other institutions for collective action. This hypothesis should hold true even when economic and technical development are held constant. Studies could trace the diffusion to formal organizations of specific institutions: professions, clearly labeled programs, and the like. For instance, the effects of the rise of theories and professions of personnel selection on the creation of personnel departments in organizations could be studied. Other studies could follow the diffusion of sales departments or research and development departments. Organizations should be found to adapt to such environmental changes, even if no evidence of their effectiveness exists.

Experimentally, one could study the impact on the decisions of organizational managers, in planning or altering organizational structures, of hypothetical variations in environmental institutionalization. Do managers plan differently if they are informed about the existence of established occupations or programmatic institutions in their environments? Do they plan differently if they are designing organizations for more or less institutionally elaborated environments?

2. Organizations which incorporate institutionalized myths are more legitimate, successful, and likely to survive. Here, research should compare similar organizations in different contexts. For instance, the presence of personnel departments or research and development units should predict success in environments in which they are widely institutionalized. Organizations which have structural elements not institutionalized in their environments should be more likely to fail, as such unauthorized complexity must be justified by claims of efficiency and effectiveness.

More generally, organizations whose claims to support are based on evaluations should be less likely to survive than those which are more highly institutionalized. An implication of this argument is that organizations existing in a highly institutionalized environment are generally more likely to survive.

Experimentally, one could study the size of the loans banks would be willing to provide organizations which vary only in (1) the degree of environmental institutionalization, and (2) the degree to which the organization structurally incorporates environmental institutions. Are banks willing to lend more money to firms whose plans are accompanied by econometric projections? And is this tendency greater in societies in which such projections are more widely institutionalized?

3. Organizational control efforts, especially in highly institutionalized contexts, are devoted to ritual conformity, both internally and externally. Such organizations, that is, decouple structure from activity and structures from each other. The idea here is that the more highly institutionalized the environment, the more time and energy organizational elites devote to managing their organization's public image and status and the less they devote to coordination and to managing particular boundary-spanning relationships. Further, the argument is that in such contexts managers devote more time to articulating internal structures and relationships at an abstract or ritual level, in contrast to managing particular relationships among activities and interdependencies.

Experimentally, the time and energy allocations proposed by managers presented with differently described environments could be studied. Do managers, presented with the description of an elaborately institutionalized environment, propose to spend more energy maintaining ritual isomorphism and less on monitoring internal conformity? Do they tend to become inattentive to evaluation? Do they elaborate doctrines of professionalism and good faith?

The arguments here, in other words, suggest both comparative and experimental studies examining the effects on organizational structure and coordination of variations in the institutional structure of the wider environment. Variations in organizational structure among societies, and within any society across time, are central to this conception of the problem.

References

Aiken, Michael, and Jerald Hage. 1968. "Organizational Interdependence and Intraorganizational Structure." *American Sociological Review* 33:912–30.

Bell, Daniel. 1973. *The Coming of Post-industrial Society.* New York: Basic.

Bendix, Reinhard. 1964. *Nation-Building and Citizenship.* New York: Wiley.

———. 1968. "Bureaucracy." In *International Encyclopedia of the Social Sciences*, ed. David L. Sills. New York: Macmillan.

Berger, Peter L., and Thomas Luckmann. 1967. *The Social Construction of Reality: A Treatise in the Sociology of Knowledge.* New York: Doubleday.

Blau, Peter M. 1956. *Bureaucracy in Modern Society.* New York: Random House.

———. 1970. "A Formal Theory of Differentiation in Organizations." *American Sociological Review* 35:201–18.

Blum, Alan F., and Peter McHugh. 1971. "The Social Ascription of Motives." *American Sociological Review* 36:98–109.

Callahan, Raymond E. 1962. *Education and the Cult of Efficiency.* Chicago: University of Chicago Press.

Carlson, Richard O. 1962. *Executive Succession and Organizational Change.* Chicago: Midwest Administration Center, University of Chicago.

Clark, Burton R. 1956. *Adult Education in Transition.* Berkeley and Los Angeles: University of California Press.

Dalton, Melville. 1959. *Men Who Manage: Fusions of Feeling and Theory in Administration*. New York: Wiley.

Dowling, John, and Jeffrey Pfeffer. 1975. "Organizational Legitimacy: Social Values and Organizational Behavior." *Pacific Sociological Review* 18:122–36.

Downs, Anthony. 1967. *Inside Bureaucracy*. Boston: Little, Brown.

Durkheim, Emile. 1933. *The Division of Labor in Society*. Trans. George Simpson. New York: Macmillan.

Ellul, Jacques. 1964. *The Technological Society*. New York: Knopf.

Emery, Fred L., and Eric L. Trist. 1965. "The Causal Texture of Organizational Environments." *Human Relations* 18:21–32.

Freeman, John Henry. 1973. "Environment, Technology, and Administrative Intensity of Manufacturing Organizations." *American Sociological Review* 38:750–63.

Goffman, Erving. 1967. *Interaction Ritual: Essays in Face-to-Face Behavior*. Garden City, N.Y.: Anchor.

Hawley, Amos H. 1968. "Human Ecology." In *International Encyclopedia of the Social Sciences*, ed. David L. Sills. New York: Macmillan.

Hirsch, Paul M. 1975. "Organizational Effectiveness and the Institutional Environment." *Administrative Science Quarterly* 20:327–44.

Homans, George C. 1950. *The Human Group*. New York: Harcourt, Brace.

March, James G., and Johan P. Olsen. 1976. *Ambiguity and Choice in Organizations*. Bergen: Universitetsforlaget.

March, James G., and Herbert A. Simon. 1958. *Organizations*. New York: Wiley.

Merton, Robert K. 1940. "Bureaucratic Structure and Personality." *Social Forces* 18:560–68.

Meyer, John W., and Brian Rowan. 1975. "Notes on the Structure of Educational Organizations." Paper presented at Annual Meetings of the American Sociological Association, San Francisco.

Mills, C. Wright. 1940. "Situated Actions and Vocabularies of Motive." *American Sociological Review* 5:904–13.

Ouchi, William, and Mary Ann Maguire. 1975. "Organizational Control: Two Functions." *Administrative Science Quarterly* 20: 559–69.

Parsons, Talcott. 1956. "Suggestions for a Sociological Approach to the Theory of Organizations I." *Administrative Science Quarterly* 1:63–85.

———. 1971. *The System of Modern Societies*. Englewood Cliffs, N.J.: Prentice-Hall.

Perrow, Charles. 1970. *Organizational Analysis: A Sociological View*. Belmont, Calif.: Wadsworth.

Salancik, Gerald R., and Jeffrey Pfeffer. 1974. "The Bases and Use of Power in Organizational Decision Making." *Administrative Science Quarterly* 19:453–73.

Scott, Marvin B., and Stanford M. Lyman. 1968. "Accounts." *American Sociological Review* 33:46–62.

Scott, W. Richard. 1975. "Organizational Structure." In *Annual Review of Sociology*, vol. 1, ed. Alex Inkeles. Palo Alto, Calif.: Annual Reviews.

Selznick, Philip. 1949. *TVA and the Grass Roots*. Berkeley and Los Angeles: University of California Press.

Spencer, Herbert. 1897. *Principles of Sociology*. 2 vols. New York: Appleton.

Starbuck, William H. 1976. "Organizations and Their Environments." In *Handbook of Industrial and Organizational Psychology*, ed. Marvin D. Dunnette. New York: Rand McNally.

Swanson, Guy E. 1971. "An Organizational Analysis of Collectivities." *American Sociological Review* 36:607–24.

Terreberry, Shirley. 1968. "The Evolution of Organizational Environments." *Administrative Science Quarterly* 12: 590–613.

Thompson, James D. 1967. *Organizations in Action: Social Science Bases of Administrative Thoery.* New York: McGraw-Hill.

Tyack, David B. 1974. *The One Best System: A History of American Urban Education.* Cambridge: Harvard University Press.

Udy, Stanley H., Jr. 1970. *Work in Traditional and Modern Society.* Englewood Cliffs, N.J.: Prentice-Hall.

Weber, Max. 1930. *The Protestant Ethic and the Spirit of Capitalism.* Trans. Talcott Parsons. New York: Scribner's.

———. 1946. *From Max Weber: Essays in Sociology.* Ed. and trans. Hans H. Goth and C. Wright Mills. Oxford: Oxford University Press.

———. 1947. *The Theory of Social and Economic Organization.* Ed. Talcott Parsons. Trans. A. M. Henderson and Talcott Parsons. Oxford: Oxford University Press.

Weick, Karl E. 1976. "Educational Organizations as Loosely Coupled Systems." *Administrative Science Quarterly* 21: 1–19.

Wilensky, Harold L. 1965. "The Professionalization of Everyone?" *American Journal of Sociology* 70:137–58.

Woodward, Joan. 1965. *Industrial Organization: Theory and Practice.* Oxford: Oxford University Press.

Zald, Mayer N., and Patricia Denton. 1963. "From Evangelism to General Service: The Transformation of the YMCA." *Administrative Science Quarterly* 8:214–34.

Chapter 4

THE IRON CAGE REVISITED: INSTITUTIONAL ISOMORPHISM AND COLLECTIVE RATIONALITY IN ORGANIZATIONAL FIELDS

PAUL J. DIMAGGIO AND WALTER W. POWELL

IN *THE PROTESTANT ETHIC AND THE SPIRIT OF CAPITALISM*, Max Weber warned that the rationalist spirit ushered in by asceticism had achieved a momentum of its own and that, under capitalism, the rationalist order had become an iron cage in which humanity was, save for the possibility of prophetic revival, imprisoned "perhaps until the last ton of fossilized coal is burnt" (Weber 1952, 181–82). In his essay on bureaucracy, Weber returned to this theme, contending that bureaucracy, the rational spirit's organizational manifestation, was so efficient and powerful a means of controlling men and women that, once established, the momentum of bureaucratization was irreversible (Weber 1968).

The imagery of the iron cage has haunted students of society as the tempo of bureaucratization has quickened. But while bureaucracy has spread continuously in the eighty years since Weber wrote, we suggest that the engine of organizational rationalization has shifted. For Weber, bureaucratization resulted from three related causes: competition among capitalist firms in the marketplace; competition among states, increasing rulers' need to control their staff and citizenry; and bourgeois demands for equal protection under the law. Of these three, the most important was the competitive marketplace. "Today," Weber (1968, 974) wrote:

> it is primarily the capitalist market economy which demands that the official business of administration be discharged precisely, unambiguously, continuously, and with as much speed as possible. Normally, the very large, modern capitalist enterprises are themselves unequalled models of strict bureaucratic organization.

We argue that the causes of bureaucratization and rationalization have changed. The bureaucratization of the corporation and the state has been

Paul J. DiMaggio and Walter W. Powell. 1983. "The Iron Cage Revisited: Institutional Isomorphism and Collective Rationality in Organizational Fields." *American Sociological Review.* 48:147–60. Reprinted by kind permission of the American Sociological Association.

achieved. Organizations are still becoming more homogeneous, and bureaucracy remains the common organizational form. Today, however, structural change in organizations seems less and less driven by competition or by the need for efficiency. Instead, we will contend, bureaucratization and other forms of organizational change occur as the result of processes that make organizations more similar without necessarily making them more efficient. Bureaucratization and other forms of homogenization emerge, we argue, out of the structuration (Giddens 1979) of organizational fields. This process, in turn, is effected largely by the state and the professions, which have become the great rationalizers of the second half of the twentieth century. For reasons that we will explain, highly structured organizational fields provide a context in which individual efforts to deal rationally with uncertainty and constraint often lead, in the aggregate, to homogeneity in structure, culture, and output.

Organizational Theory and Organizational Diversity

Much of modern organizational theory posits a diverse and differentiated world of organizations and seeks to explain variation among organizations in structure and behavior (e.g., Woodward 1965; Child and Kieser 1981). Hannan and Freeman begin a major theoretical paper (1977) with the question, "Why are there so many kinds of organizations?" Even our investigatory technologies (for example, those based on least-squares techniques) are geared towards explaining variation rather than its absence.

We ask, instead, why there is such startling homogeneity of organizational forms and practices; and we seek to explain homogeneity, not variation. In the initial stages of their life cycle, organizational fields display considerable diversity in approach and form. Once a field becomes well established, however, there is an inexorable push towards homogenization.

Coser, Kadushin, and Powell (1982) describe the evolution of American college textbook publishing from a period of initial diversity to the current hegemony of only two models, the large bureaucratic generalist and the small specialist. Rothman (1980) describes the winnowing of several competing models of legal education into two dominant approaches. Starr (1980) provides evidence of mimicry in the development of the hospital field; Tyack (1974) and Katz (1975) show a similar process in public schools; Barnouw (1966–68) describes the development of dominant forms in the radio industry; and DiMaggio (1981) depicts the emergence of dominant organizational models for the provision of high culture in the late nineteenth century.

What we see in each of these cases is the emergence and structuration of an organizational field as a result of the activities of a diverse set of organizations; and, second, the homogenization of these organizations, and of new entrants as well, once the field is established.

By organizational field, we mean those organizations that, in the aggregate, constitute a recognized area of institutional life: key suppliers, resource and product consumers, regulatory agencies, and other organizations that produce similar services or products. The virtue of this unit of analysis is that it directs our attention not simply to competing firms, as does the population approach of Hannan and Freeman (1977), or to networks of organizations that actually interact, as does the interorganizational network approach of Laumann, Galaskiewicz, and Marsden (1978), but to the totality of relevant actors. In doing this, the field idea comprehends the importance of both *connectedness* (see Laumann, Galaskiewicz, and Marsden 1978) and *structural equivalence* (White, Boorman, and Breiger 1976).[1]

The structure of an organizational field cannot be determined a priori but must be defined on the basis of empirical investigation. Fields only exist to the extent that they are institutionally defined. The process of institutional definition, or "structuration," consists of four parts: an increase in the extent of interaction among organizations in the field; the emergence of sharply defined interorganizational structures of domination and patterns of coalition; an increase in the information load with which organizations in a field must contend; and the development of a mutual awareness among participants in a set of organizations that they are involved in a common enterprise (DiMaggio 1982).

Once disparate organizations in the same line of business are structured into an actual field (as we shall argue, by competition, the state, or the professions), powerful forces emerge that lead them to become more similar to one another. Organizations may change their goals or develop new practices, and new organizations enter the field. But, in the long run, organizational actors making rational decisions construct around themselves an environment that constrains their ability to change further in later years. Early adopters of organizational innovations are commonly driven by a desire to improve performance. But new practices can become, in Selznick's words (1957, 17), "infused with value beyond the technical requirements of the task at hand." As an innovation spreads, a threshold is reached beyond which adoption provides legitimacy rather than improves performance (Meyer and Rowan 1977). Strategies that are rational for individual organizations may not be rational if adopted by large numbers. Yet the very fact that they are normatively sanctioned increases the likelihood of their adoption. Thus organizations may try to change constantly; but, after a certain point in the structuration of an organizational field, the aggregate effect of individual change is to lessen the extent of diversity within the field.[2] Organizations in a structured field, to paraphrase Schelling (1978, 14), respond to an environment that consists of other organizations responding to their environment, which consists of organizations responding to an environment of organizations' responses.

Zucker and Tolbert's (1981) work on the adoption of civil-service reform in the United States illustrates this process. Early adoption of civil-service reforms was related to internal governmental needs, and strongly predicted by such city characteristics as the size of immigrant population, political reform movements, socioeconomic composition, and city size. Later adoption, however, is not predicted by city characteristics, but is related to institutional definitions of the legitimate structural form for municipal administration.[3] Marshall Meyer's (1981) study of the bureaucratization of urban fiscal agencies has yielded similar findings: strong relationships between city characteristics and organizational attributes at the turn of the century, null relationships in recent years. Carroll and Delacroix's (1982) findings on the birth and death rates of newspapers support the view that selection acts with great force only in the early years of an industry's existence.[4] Freeman (1982, 14) suggests that older, larger organizations reach a point where they can dominate their environments rather than adjust to them.

The concept that best captures the process of homogenization is *isomorphism*. In Hawley's (1968) description, isomorphism is a constraining process that forces one unit in a population to resemble other units that face the same set of environmental conditions. At the population level, such an approach suggests that organizational characteristics are modified in the direction of increasing compatibility with environmental characteristics; the number of organizations in a population is a function of environmental carrying capacity; and the diversity of organizational forms is isomorphic to environmental diversity. Hannan and Freeman (1977) have significantly extended Hawley's ideas. They argue that isomorphism can result because nonoptimal forms are selected out of a population of organizations *or* because organizational decision makers learn appropriate responses and adjust their behavior accordingly. Hannan and Freeman's focus is almost solely on the first process: selection.[5]

Following Meyer (1979) and Fennell (1980), we maintain that there are two types of isomorphism: competitive and institutional. Hannan and Freeman's classic paper (1977), and much of their recent work, deals with competitive isomorphism, assuming a system rationality that emphasizes market competition, niche change, and fitness measures. Such a view, we suggest, is most relevant for those fields in which free and open competition exists. It explains parts of the process of bureaucratization that Weber observed, and may apply to early adoption of innovation, but it does not present a fully adequate picture of the modern world of organizations. For this purpose it must be supplemented by an institutional view of isomorphism of the sort introduced by Kanter (1972, 152–54) in her discussion of the forces pressing communes toward accommodation with the outside world. As Aldrich (1979, 265) has argued, "the major factors that organizations must take into account are other organizations." Organizations compete not just for resources and customers, but for political power and institutional legitimacy, for social as well as economic fitness.[6] The concept of institutional isomorphism is a useful tool for understanding the politics and ceremony that pervade much modern organizational life.

Three Mechanisms of Institutional Isomorphic Change

We identify three mechanisms through which institutional isomorphic change occurs, each with its own antecedents: (1) *coercive* isomorphism that stems from political influence and the problem of legitimacy; (2) *mimetic* isomorphism resulting from standard responses to uncertainty; and (3) *normative* isomorphism, associated with professionalization. This typology is an analytic one: the types are not always empirically distinct. For example, external actors may induce an organization to conform to its peers by requiring it to perform a particular task and specifying the profession responsible for its performance. Or mimetic change may reflect environmentally constructed uncertainties.[7] Yet, while the three types intermingle in empirical setting, they tend to derive from different conditions and may lead to different outcomes.

COERCIVE ISOMORPHISM

Coercive isomorphism results from both formal and informal pressures exerted on organizations by other organizations upon which they are dependent and by cultural expectations in the society within which organizations function. Such pressures may be felt as force, as persuasion, or as invitations to join in collusion. In some circumstances, organizational change is a direct response to government mandate: manufacturers adopt new pollution control technologies to conform to environmental regulations; nonprofits maintain accounts, and hire accountants, in order to meet tax law requirements; and organizations employ affirmative-action officers to fend off allegations of discrimination. Schools mainstream special students and hire special education teachers, cultivate PTAs and administrators who get along with them, and promulgate curricula that conform with state standards (Meyer, Scott, and Deal 1981). The fact that these changes may be largely ceremonial does not mean that they are inconsequential. As Ritti and Goldner (1979) have argued, staff become involved in advocacy for their functions that can alter power relations within organizations over the long run.

The existence of a common legal environment affects many aspects of an organization's behavior and structure. Weber pointed out the profound impact of a complex, rationalized system of contract law that requires the necessary organizational controls to honor legal commitments. Other legal and technical requirements of the state—the vicissitudes of the budget cycle, the ubiquity of certain fiscal years, annual reports, and financial reporting requirements that ensure eligibility for the receipt of federal contracts or funds—also shape organizations in similar ways. Pfeffer and Salancik (1978, 188–224) have discussed how organizations faced with unmanageable interdependence seek to use the greater power of the larger social system and its government to eliminate difficulties or provide for needs. They observe that politically constructed environments have two characteristic features: political decision-makers often do not experience directly the consequences of their actions; and political decisions are applied across the board to entire classes of organizations, thus making such decisions less adaptive and less flexible.

Meyer and Rowan (1977) have argued persuasively that as rationalized states and other large rational organizations expand their dominance over more arenas of social life, organizational structures increasingly come to reflect rules institutionalized and legitimated by and within the state (also see Meyer and Hannan 1979). As a result, organizations are increasingly homogeneous within given domains and increasingly organized around rituals of conformity to wider institutions. At the same time, organizations are decreasingly structurally determined by the constraints posed by technical activities, and decreasingly held together by output controls. Under such circumstances, organizations employ ritualized controls of credentials and group solidarity.

Direct imposition of standard operating procedures and legitimated rules and structures also occurs outside the governmental arena. Michael Sedlak (1981) has documented the ways that United Charities in the 1930s altered and homogenized the structures, methods, and philosophies of the social service agencies that depended upon them for support. As conglomerate corporations increase in size and scope, standard performance criteria are not necessarily imposed on subsidiaries, but it is common for subsidiaries to be subject to standardized reporting mechanisms (Coser, Kadushin, and Dowell 1982). Subsidiaries must adopt accounting practices, performance evaluations, and budgetary plans that are compatible with the policies of the parent corporation. A variety of service infrastructures, often provided by monopolistic firms—for example, telecommunications and transportation—exert common pressures over the organizations that use them. Thus, the expansion of the central state, the centralization of capital, and the coordination of philanthropy all support the homogenization of organizational models through direct authority relationships.

We have so far referred only to the direct and explicit imposition of organizational models on dependent organizations. Coercive isomorphism, however, may be more subtle and less explicit than these examples suggest. Milofsky (1981) has described the ways in which neighborhood organizations in urban communities, many of which are committed to participatory democracy, are driven to developing organizational hierarchies in order to gain support from more hierarchically organized donor organizations. Similarly, Swidler (1979) describes the tensions created in the free schools she studied by the need to have a "principal" to negotiate with the district superintendent and to represent the school to outside agencies. In general, the need to lodge responsibility and managerial authority at least ceremonially in a formally defined role in order to interact with hierarchical organizations is a constant obstacle to the maintenance of egalitarian or collectivist organizational forms (Kanter 1972; Rothschild-Whitt 1979).

MIMETIC PROCESSES

Not all institutional isomorphism, however, derives from coercive authority. Uncertainty is also a powerful force that encourages imitation. When organizational technologies are poorly understood (March and Olsen 1976), when goals are ambiguous, or when the environment creates symbolic uncertainty, organizations may model themselves on other organizations. The advantages of mimetic behavior in the economy of human action are considerable; when an organization faces a problem with ambiguous causes or unclear solutions, problemistic search may yield a viable solution with little expense (Cyert and March 1963).

Modeling, as we use the term, is a response to uncertainty. The modeled organization may be unaware of the modeling or may have no desire to be copied; it merely serves as a convenient source of practices that the borrowing organization may use. Models may be diffused unintentionally, indirectly through employee transfer or turnover, or explicitly by organizations such as consulting firms or industry trade associations. Even innovation can be accounted for by organizational modeling. As Alchian (1950) has observed:

> While there certainly are those who consciously innovate, there are those who, in their imperfect attempts to imitate others, unconsciously innovate by unwittingly acquiring some unexpected or unsought unique attributes which under the prevailing circumstances prove partly responsible for the success. Others, in turn, will attempt to copy the uniqueness, and the innovation-imitation process continues.

One of the most dramatic instances of modeling was the effort of Japan's modernizers in the late nineteenth century to model new governmental initiatives on apparently successful Western prototypes. Thus, the imperial government sent its officers to study the courts, army, and police in France, the navy and postal system in Great Britain, and banking and art education in the United States (see Westney 1987). American corporations are now returning the compliment by implementing (their perceptions of) Japanese models to cope with thorny productivity and personnel problems in their own firms. The rapid proliferation of quality circles and quality-of-work-life issues in American firms is, at least in part, an attempt to model Japanese and European successes. These developments also have a ritual aspect; companies adopt these "innovations" to enhance their legitimacy, to demonstrate they are at least trying to improve working conditions. More generally, the wider the population of personnel employed by, or customers served by, an organization, the stronger the pressure felt by the organization to provide the programs and services offered by other organizations. Thus, either a skilled labor force or a broad customer base may encourage mimetic isomorphism.

Much homogeneity in organizational structures stems from the fact that despite considerable search for diversity there is relatively little variation to be selected from. New organizations are modeled upon old ones throughout the economy, and managers actively seek models upon which to build (Kimberly 1980). Thus, in the arts one can find textbooks on how to organize a community arts council or how to start a symphony women's guild. Large organizations choose from a relatively small set of major consulting firms, which, like Johnny Appleseeds, spread a few organizational models throughout the land. Such models are powerful because structural changes are observable, whereas changes in policy and strategy are less easily noticed. With the advice of a major consulting firm, a large metropolitan public television station switched from a functional design to a multidivisional structure. The stations' executives were skeptical that the new structure was more efficient; in fact, some services were now duplicated across divisions. But they were convinced that the new design would carry a powerful message to the for-profit firms with whom the station regularly dealt. These firms, whether in the role of corporate underwriters or as potential partners in joint ventures, would view the reorganization as a sign that "the sleepy nonprofit station was becoming more business-minded" (Powell, forthcoming). The history of management reform in American government agencies, which are noted for their goal ambiguity, is almost a textbook case of isomorphic modeling, from the PPPB of the McNamara era to the zero-based budgeting of the Carter administration.

Organizations tend to model themselves after similar organizations in their field that they perceive to be more legitimate or successful. The ubiquity of certain kinds of structural arrangements can more likely be credited to the universality of mimetic processes than to any concrete evidence that the adopted models enhance efficiency. John Meyer (1981) contends that it is easy to predict the organization of a newly emerging nation's administration without knowing anything about the nation itself, since "peripheral nations are far more isomorphic—in administrative form and economic pattern—than any theory of the world system of economic division of labor would lead one to expect."

NORMATIVE PRESSURES

A third source of isomorphic organizational change is normative and stems primarily from professionalization. Following Larson (1977) and Collins (1979), we interpret professionalization as the collective struggle of members of an occupation to define the conditions and methods of their work, to control "the production of producers" (Larson 1977, 49–52), and to establish a cognitive base and legitimation for their occupational autonomy. As Larson points out, the professional project is rarely achieved with complete success. Professionals must compromise with nonprofessional clients, bosses, or regulators. The major recent growth in the professions has been among organizational professionals, particularly managers and specialized staff of large organizations. The increased professionalization of workers whose futures are inextricably bound up with the fortunes of the organizations that employ them has rendered obsolescent (if not obsolete) the dichotomy between organizational commitment and professional allegiance that characterized traditional professionals in earlier organizations (Hall 1968). Professions are subject to the same coercive and mimetic pressures as are organizations. Moreover, while various kinds of professionals within an organization may differ from one another, they exhibit much similarity to their professional counterparts in other organizations. In addition, in many cases, professional power is as much assigned by the state as it is created by the activities of the professions.

Two aspects of professionalization are important sources of isomorphism. One is the resting of formal education and of legitimation in a cognitive base produced by university specialists; the second is the growth and elaboration of professional networks that span organizations and across which new models diffuse rapidly. Universities and professional training institutions are important centers for the development of organizational norms among professional managers and their staff. Professional and trace associations are another vehicle for the definition and promulgation of normative rules about organizational and professional behavior. Such mechanisms create a pool of almost interchangeable individuals who occupy similar positions across a range of organizations and possess a similarity of orientation and disposition that may override variations in tradition and control that might otherwise shape organizational behavior (Perrow 1974).

One important mechanism for encouraging normative isomorphism is the filtering of personnel. Within many organizational fields filtering occurs through the hiring of individuals from firms within the same industry; through the recruitment of fast-track staff from a narrow range of training institutions; through common promotion practices, such as always hiring top executives from financial or legal departments; and from skill-level requirements for particular jobs. Many professional career tracks are so closely guarded, both at the entry level and throughout the career progression, that individuals who make it to the top are virtually indistinguishable. March and March (1977) found that individuals who attained the position of school superintendent in Wisconsin were so alike in background and orientation as to make further career advancement random and unpredictable. Hirsch and Whisler (1982) find a similar absence of variation among *Fortune* 500 board members. In addition, individuals in an organizational field undergo anticipatory socialization to common expectations about their personal behavior, appropriate style of dress, organizational vocabularies (Cicourel 1970; Williamson 1975) and standard methods of speaking, joking, or addressing others (Ouchi 1980). Particularly in industries with a service or financial orientation (Collins 1979 argues that the importance of credentials is strongest in these areas), the filtering of personnel approaches what Kanter (1977) refers to as the "homosexual reproduction of management." To the extent managers and key staff are drawn from the same universities and filtered on a common set of attributes, they will tend to view problems in a similar fashion, see the same policies, procedures and structures as normatively sanctioned and legitimated, and approach decisions in much the same way.

Entrants to professional career tracks who somehow escape the filtering process—for example, Jewish naval officers, woman stockbrokers, or black insurance executives—are likely to be subjected to pervasive on-the-job socialization. To the extent that organizations in a field differ and primary socialization occurs on the job, socialization could reinforce, not erode, differences among organizations. But when organizations in a field are similar and occupational socialization is carried out in trade association workshops, in-service educational programs, consultant arrangements, employer-professional school networks, and in the pages of trade magazines, socialization acts as an isomorphic force.

The professionalization of management tends to proceed in tandem with the structuration of organizational fields. The exchange of information among professionals helps contribute to a commonly recognized hierarchy of status, of center and periphery, that becomes a matrix for information flows and personnel movement across organizations. This status ordering occurs through both formal and informal means. The designation of a few large firms in an industry as key bargaining agents in union-management negotiations may make these central firms pivotal in other respects as well. Government recognition of key firms or organizations through the grant or contract process may give these organizations legitimacy and visibility and lead competing firms to copy aspects of their structure or operating procedures in hope of obtaining similar rewards. Professional and trade associations provide other arenas in which center organizations are recognized and their personnel given positions of substantive or ceremonial influence. Managers in highly visible organizations may in turn have their stature reinforced by representation on the boards of other organizations, participation in industry-wide or interindustry councils, and consultation by agencies of government (Useem 1979). In the nonprofit sector, where legal barriers to collusion do not exist, structuration may proceed even more rapidly. Thus executive producers or artistic directors of leading theaters head trade or professional association committees, sit on government and foundation grant-award panels, or consult as government- or foundation-financed management advisors to smaller theaters, or sit on smaller organizations' boards, even as their stature is reinforced and enlarged by the grants their theaters receive from government, corporate, and foundation funding sources (DiMaggio 1982).

Such central organizations serve as both active and passive models; their policies and structures will be copied throughout their fields. Their centrality is reinforced as upwardly mobile managers and staff seek to secure positions in these central organizations in order to further their own careers. Aspiring managers may undergo anticipatory socialization into the norms and mores of the organizations they hope to join. Career paths may also involve movement from entry positions in the center organizations to middle-management positions in peripheral organizations. Personnel flows within an organizational field are further encouraged by structural homogenization, for example the existence of common career titles and paths (such as assistant, associate, and full professor) with meanings that are commonly understood.

It is important to note that each of the institutional isomorphic processes can be expected to proceed in the absence of evidence that they increase internal organizational efficiency. To the extent that organizational effectiveness is enhanced, the reason will often be that organizations are rewarded for being similar to other organizations in their fields. This similarity can make it easier for organizations to transact with other organizations, to attract career-minded staff, to be acknowledged as legitimate and reputable, and to fit into administrative categories that define eligibility for public and private grants and contracts. None of this, however, insures that conformist organizations do what they do more efficiently than do their more deviant peers.

Pressures for competitive efficiency are also mitigated in many fields because the number of organizations is limited and there are strong fiscal and legal barriers to entry and exit. Lee (1971, 51) maintains this is why hospital administrators are less concerned with the efficient use of resources and more concerned with status competition and parity in prestige. Fennell (1980) notes that hospitals are a poor market system because patients lack the needed knowledge of potential exchange partners and prices. She argues that physicians and hospital administrators are the actual consumers. Competition among hospitals is based on "attracting physicians, who, in turn, bring their patients to the hospital." Fennell (505) concludes that

> Hospitals operate according to a norm of social legitimation that frequently conflicts with market considerations of efficiency and system rationality. Apparently, hospitals can increase their range of services not because there is an actual need for a particular service or facility within the patient population, but because they will be defined as fit only if they can offer everything other hospitals in the area offer.

These results suggest a more general pattern. Organizational fields that include a large professionally trained labor force will be driven primarily by status competition. Organizational prestige and resources are key elements in attracting professionals. This process encourages homogenization as organizations seek to ensure that they can provide the same benefits and services as their competitors.

Predictors of Isomorphic Change

It follows from our discussion of the mechanism by which isomorphic change occurs that we should be able to predict empirically which organizational fields will be most homogeneous in structure, process, and behavior. While an empirical test of such predictions is beyond the scope of this paper, the ultimate value of our perspective will lie in its predictive utility. The hypotheses discussed below are not meant to exhaust the universe of predictors, but merely to suggest several hypotheses that may be pursued using data on the characteristics of organizations in a field, either cross-sectionally or, preferably, over time. The hypotheses are implicitly governed by ceteris paribus assumptions, particularly with regard to size, technology, and centralization of external resources.

A. Organizational-Level Predictors

There is variability in the extent to and rate at which organizations in a field change to become more like their peers. Some organizations respond to external pressures quickly; others change only after a long period of resistance. The first two hypotheses derive from our discussion of coercive isomorphism and constraint.

> **Hypothesis A-1:** *The greater the dependence of an organization on another organization, the more similar it will become to that organization in structure, climate, and behavioral focus.*

Following Thompson (1957) and Pfeffer and Salancik (1978), this proposition recognizes the greater ability of organizations to resist the demands of organizations on whom they are not dependent. A position of dependence leads to isomorphic change. Coercive pressures are built into exchange relationships. As Williamson (1979) has shown, exchanges are characterized by transaction-specific investments in both knowledge and equipment. Once an organization chooses a specific supplier or distributor for particular parts or services, the supplier or distributor develops expertise in the performance of the task as well as idiosyncratic knowledge about the exchange relationship. The organization comes to rely on the supplier or distributor, and such transaction-specific investments give the supplier or distributor considerable advantages in any subsequent competition with other suppliers or distributors.

Hypothesis A-2: *The greater the centralization of organization A's resource supply, the greater the extent to which organization A will change isomorphically to resemble the organizations on which it depends for resources.*

As Thompson (1967) notes, organizations that depend on the same sources for funding, personnel, and legitimacy will be more subject to the whims of resource suppliers than will organizations that can play one source of support off against another. In cases where alternative sources are either not readily available or require effort to locate, the stronger party to the transaction can coerce the weaker party to adopt its practices in order to accommodate the stronger party's needs (see Powell 1983).

The third and fourth hypotheses derive from our discussion of mimetic isomorphism, modeling, and uncertainty.

Hypothesis A-3: *The more uncertain the relationship between means and ends the greater the extent to which an organization will model itself after organizations it perceives to be successful.*

The mimetic thought process involved in the search for models is characteristic of change in organizations in which key technologies are only poorly understood (March and Cohen 1974). Here our prediction diverges somewhat from Meyer and Rowan (1977), who argue, as we do, that organizations which lack well-defined technologies will import institutionalized rules and practices. Meyer and Rowan posit a loose coupling between legitimated external practices and internal organizational behavior. From an ecologist's point of view, loosely coupled organizations are more likely to vary internally. In contrast, we expect substantive internal changes in tandem with more ceremonial practices, thus greater homogeneity and less variation and change. Internal consistency of this sort is an important means of interorganizational coordination. It also increases organizational stability.

Hypothesis A-4: *The more ambiguous the goals of an organization, the greater the extent to which the organization will model itself after organizations that it perceives to be successful.*

There are two reasons for this. First, organizations with ambiguous or disputed goals are likely to be highly dependent upon appearances for legitimacy. Such organizations may find it to their advantage to meet the expectations of important constituencies about how they should be designed and run. In contrast to our view, ecologists would argue that organizations that copy other organizations usually have no competitive advantage. We contend that, in most situations, reliance on established, legitimated procedures enhances organizational legitimacy and survival characteristics. A second reason for modeling behavior is found in situations where conflict over organizational goals is repressed in the interest of harmony; thus participants find it easier to mimic other organizations than to make decisions on the basis of systematic analyses of goals since such analyses would prove painful or disruptive.

The fifth and sixth hypotheses are based on our discussion of normative processes found in professional organizations.

Hypothesis A-5: *The greater the reliance on academic credentials in choosing managerial and staff personnel, the greater the extent to which an organization will become like other organizations in its field.*

Applicants with academic credentials have already undergone a socialization process in university programs, and are thus more likely than others to have internalized reigning norms and dominant organizational models.

Hypothesis A-6: *The greater the participation of organizational managers in trade and professional associations, the more likely the organization will be, or will become, like other organizations in its field.*

This hypothesis is parallel to the institutional view that the more elaborate the relational networks among organizations and their members, the greater the collective organization of the environment (Meyer and Rowan 1977).

B. Field-Level Predictors

The following six hypotheses describe the expected effects of several characteristics of organizational fields on the extent of isomorphism in a particular field. Since the effect of institutional isomorphism is homogenization, the best indicator of isomorphic change is a decrease in variation and diversity, which could be measured by lower standard deviations of the values of selected indicators in a set of organizations. The key indicators would vary with the nature of the field and the interests of the investigator. In all cases, however, field-level measures are expected to affect organizations in a field regardless of each organization's scores on related organizational-level measures.

Hypothesis B-1: *The greater the extent to which an organizational field is dependent upon a single (or several similar) source of support for vital resources, the higher the level of isomorphism.*

The centralization of resources within a field both directly causes homogenization by placing organizations under similar pressures from resource suppliers, and interacts with uncertainty and goal ambiguity to increase their impact. This hypothesis is congruent with the ecologists' argument that the number of organizational forms is determined by the distribution of resources in the environment and the terms on which resources are available.

Hypothesis B-2: *The greater the extent to which the organizations in a field transact with agencies of the state, the greater the extent of isomorphism in the field as a whole.*

This follows not just from the previous hypothesis, but from two elements of state/private-sector transactions: their rule-boundedness and formal rationality, and the emphasis of government actors on institutional rules. Moreover, the federal government routinely designates industry standards for an entire field which require adoption by all competing firms. John Meyer (1979) argues convincingly that the aspects of an organization which are affected by state transactions differ to the extent that state participation is unitary or fragmented among several public agencies.

The third and fourth hypotheses follow from our discussion of isomorphic change resulting from uncertainty and modeling.

Hypothesis B-3: *The fewer the number of visible alternative organizational models in a field, the faster the rate of isomorphism in that field.*

The predictions of this hypothesis are less specific than those of others and require further refinement; but our argument is that for any relevant dimension of organizational strategies or structures in an organizational field there will be a threshold level, or a tipping point, beyond which adoption of the dominant form will proceed with increasing speed (Granovetter 1978; Boorman and Levitt 1979).

Hypothesis B-4: *The greater the extent to which technologies are uncertain or goals are ambiguous within a field, the greater the rate of isomorphic change.*

Somewhat counterintuitively, abrupt increases in uncertainty and ambiguity should, after brief periods of ideologically motivated experimentation, lead to rapid isomorphic change. As in the case of A-4, ambiguity and uncertainty may be a function of environmental definition, and, in any case, interact both with centralization of resources (A-1, A-2, B-1, B-2) and with professionalization and structuration (A-5, A-6, B-5, B-6). Moreover, in fields characterized by a high degree of uncertainty, new entrants, which could serve as sources of innovation and variation, will seek to overcome the liability of newness by imitating established practices within the field.

The two final hypotheses in this section follow from our discussion of professional filtering, socialization, and structuration.

Hypothesis B-5: *The greater the extent of professionalization in a field, the greater the amount of institutional isomorphic change.*

Professionalization may be measured by the universality of credential requirements, the robustness of graduate training programs, or the vitality of professional and trade associations.

Hypothesis B-6: *The greater the extent of structuration of a field, the greater the degree of isomorphics.*

Fields that have stable and broadly acknowledged centers, peripheries, and status orders will be more homogeneous both because the diffusion structure for new models and norms is more routine and because the level of interaction among organizations in the field is higher. While structuration may not lend itself to easy measurement, it might be tapped crudely with the use of such familiar measures as concentration ratios, reputational interview studies, or data on network characteristics.

This rather schematic exposition of a dozen hypotheses relating the extent of isomorphism to selected attributes of organizations and of organizational fields does not constitute a complete agenda for empirical assessment of our perspective. We have not discussed the expected nonlinearities and ceiling effects in the relationships that we have posited. Nor have we addressed the issue of the indicators that one must use to measure homogeneity. Organizations in a field may be highly diverse on some dimensions, yet extremely homogeneous on others. While we suspect, in general, that the rate at which the standard deviations of structural or behavioral indicators approach zero will vary with the nature of an organizational field's technology and environment, we will not develop these ideas here. The point of this section is to suggest that the theoretical discussion is susceptible to empirical test, and to lay out a few testable propositions that may guide future analyses.

Implications for Social Theory

A comparison of macrosocial theories of functionalist or Marxist orientation with theoretical and empirical work in the study of organizations yields a paradoxical conclusion. Societies (or elites), so it seems, are smart, while organizations are dumb. Societies comprise institutions that mesh together comfortably in the interests of efficiency (Clark 1962), the dominant value system (Parsons 1951), or, in the Marxist version, capitalists (Domhoff 1967; Althusser 1969). Organizations, by contrast, are either anarchies (Cohen, March, and Olsen 1972), federations of loosely coupled parts (Weick 1976), or autonomy-seeking agents (Gouldner 1954) laboring under such formidable constraints as bounded rationality (March and Simon 1958), uncertain or contested goals (Sills 1957), and unclear technologies (March and Cohen 1974).

Despite the findings of organizational research, the image of society as consisting of tightly and rationally coupled institutions persists throughout much of modern social theory. Rational administration pushes out nonbureaucratic forms, schools assume the structure of the workplace, hospital and university administrations come to resemble the management of for-profit firms, and the modernization of the world economy proceeds unabated. Weberians point to the continuing homogenization of organizational structures as the formal rationality of bureaucracy extends to the limits of contemporary organizational life. Functionalists describe the rational adaptation of the structure of firms, schools, and states to the values and needs of modern society (Chandler 1977; Parsons 1977). Marxists attribute changes in such organizations as welfare agencies (Piven and Cloward 1971) and schools (Bowles and Gintis 1976) to the logic of the accumulation process.

We find it difficult to square the extant literature on organizations with these macrosocial views. How can it be that the confused and contentious bumblers that populate the pages of organizational case studies and theories combine to construct the elaborate and well-proportioned social edifice that macrotheorists describe?

The conventional answer to this paradox has been that some version of natural selection occurs in which selection mechanisms operate to weed out those organizational forms that are less fit. Such arguments, as we have contended, are difficult to mesh with organizational realities. Less efficient organizational forms do persist. In some contexts efficiency or productivity cannot even be measured. In government agencies or in faltering corporations selection may occur on political rather than economic grounds. In other contexts, for example the Metropolitan Opera or the Bohemian Grove, supporters are far more concerned with noneconomic values like aesthetic quality or social status than with efficiency per se. Even in the for-profit sector, where competitive arguments would promise to bear the greatest fruit, Nelson and Winter's work (Winter 1964, 1975; Nelson and Winter 1982) demonstrates that the invisible hand operates with, at best, a light touch.

A second approach to the paradox that we have identified comes from Marxists and theorists who assert that key elites guide and control the social system through their command of crucial positions in major organizations (e.g., the financial institutions that dominate monopoly capitalism). In this view, while organizational actors ordinarily proceed undisturbed through mazes of standard operating procedures, at key turning points capitalist elites get their way by intervening in decisions that set the course of an institution for years to come (Katz 1975).

While evidence suggests that this is, in fact, sometimes the case—Barnouw's account of the early days of broadcasting or Weinstein's (1968) work on the Progressives are good examples—other historians have been less successful in their search for class-conscious elites. In such cases as the development of the New Deal programs (Hawley 1966) or the expansion of the Vietnamese conflict (Halperin 1974), the capitalist class appears to have been muddled and disunited.

Moreover, without constant monitoring, individuals pursuing parochial organizational or subunit interests can quickly undo the work that even the most prescient elites have accomplished. Perrow (1976, 21) has noted that despite superior resources and sanctioning power, organizational elites are often unable to maximize their preferences because "the complexity of modern organizations makes control difficult." Moreover, organizations have increasingly become the vehicle for numerous "gratifications, necessities, and preferences so that many groups within and without the organization seek to use it for ends that restrict the return to masters."

We reject neither the natural-selection nor the elite-control arguments out of hand. Elites do exercise considerable influence over modern life, and aberrant or inefficient organizations sometimes do expire. But we contend that neither of these processes is sufficient to explain the extent to which organizations have become structurally more similar. We argue that a theory of institutional isomorphism may help explain the observations that organizations are becoming more homogeneous, and that elites often get their way, while at the same time enabling us to understand the irrationality, the frustration of power, and the lack of innovation that are so commonplace in organizational life. What is more, our approach is more consonant with the ethnographic and theoretical literature on how organizations work than are either functionalist or elite theories of organizational change.

A focus on institutional isomorphism can also add a much needed perspective on the political struggle for organizational power and survival that is missing from much of population ecology. The institutionalization approach associated with John Meyer and his students posits the importance of myths and ceremony but does not ask how these models arise and whose interests they initially serve. Explicit attention to the genesis of legitimated models and to the definition and elaboration of organizational fields should answer this question. Examination of the diffusion of similar organizational strategies and structures should be a productive means for assessing the influence of elite interests. A consideration of isomorphic processes also leads us to a bifocal view of power and its application in modern politics. To the extent that organizational change is unplanned and goes on largely behind the backs of groups that wish to influence it, our attention should be directed to two forms of power. The first, as March and Simon (1958) and Simon (1957) pointed out years ago, is the power to set premises, to define the norms and standards which shape and channel behavior. The second is the point of critical intervention (Domhoff 1979) at which elites can define appropriate models of organizational structure and policy which then go unquestioned for years to come (see Katz 1975). Such a view is consonant with some of the best recent work on power (see Lukes 1974); research on the structuration of organizational fields and on isomorphic processes may help give it more empirical flesh.

Finally, a more developed theory of organizational isomorphism may have important implications for social policy in those fields in which the state works through private organizations. To the extent that pluralism is a guiding value in public policy deliberations, we need to discover new forms of intersectoral coordination that will encourage diversification rather than hastening homogenization. An understanding of the manner in which fields become more homogeneous would prevent policymakers and analysts from confusing the disappearance of an organizational form with its substantive failure. Current efforts to encourage diversity tend to be conducted in an organizational vacuum. Policymakers concerned with pluralism should consider the impact of their programs on the structure of organizational fields as a whole, and not simply on the programs of individual organizations.

We believe there is much to be gained by attending to similarity as well as to variation among organizations and, in particular, to change in the degree of homogeneity or variation over time. Our approach seeks to study incremental change as well as selection. We take seriously the observations of organizational theorists about the role of change, ambiguity, and constraint and point to the implications of these organizational characteristics for the social structure as a whole. The foci and motive forces of bureaucratization (and, more broadly, homogenization in general) have, as we argued, changed since Weber's time. But the importance of understanding the trends to which he called attention has never been more immediate.

Notes

1. By *connectedness* we mean the existence of transactions tying organizations to one another: such transactions might include formal contractual relationships, participation of personnel in common enterprises such as professional associations, labor unions, or boards of directors, or informal organizational-level ties like personnel flows. A set of organizations that are strongly connected to one another and only weakly connected to other organizations constitutes a *clique*. By *structural equivalence* we refer to similarity of position in a network structure: for example, two organizations are structurally equivalent if they have ties of the same kind to the same set of other organizations, even if they themselves are not connected: here the key structure is the *role* or *block*.

2. By organizational change, we refer to change in formal structure, organizational culture, and goals, program, or mission. Organizational change varies in its responsiveness to technical conditions. In this paper we are most interested in processes that affect organizations in a given field: in most cases these organizations employ similar technical bases; thus we do not attempt to partial out the relative importance of technically functional versus other forms of organizational change. While we shall cite many examples of organizational change as we go along, our purpose here is to identify a widespread class of organizational processes relevant to a broad range of substantive problems, rather than to identify deterministically the causes of specific organizational arrangements.

3. Knoke (1982), in a careful event-history analysis of the spread of municipal reform, refutes the conventional explanations of culture clash or hierarchal diffusion and finds but modest support for modernization theory. His major finding is that regional differences in municipal reform adoption arise not from social compositional differences, "but from some type of imitation or contagion effects as represented by the level of neighboring regional cities previously adopting reform government" (1337).

4. A wide range of factors—interorganizational commitments, elite sponsorship, and government support in form of open-ended contracts, subsidy, tariff barriers and import quotas, or favorable tax laws—reduces selection pressures even in competitive organizational fields. An expanding or a stable, protected market can also mitigate the forces of selection.

5. In contrast to Hannan and Freeman, we emphasize adaptation, but we are not suggesting that managers' actions are necessarily strategic in a long-range sense. Indeed, two of the three forms of isomorphism described below—mimetic and normative—involve managerial behaviors at the level of taken-for-granted assumptions rather than consciously strategic choices. In general, we question the utility of arguments about the motivations of actors that suggest a polarity between the rational and the nonrational. Goal-oriented behavior may be reflexive or prerational in the sense that it reflects deeply embedded predispositions, scripts, schema, or classifications; and behavior oriented to a goal may be reinforced without contributing to the accomplishment of that goal. While isomorphic change may often be mediated by the desires of managers to increase the effectiveness of their organizations, we are more concerned with the menu of possible options that managers consider than with their motives for choosing particular alternatives. In other words, we freely concede that actors' understandings of their own behaviors are interpretable in rational terms. The theory of isomorphism addresses not the psychological states of actors but the structural determinants of the range of choices that actors perceive as rational or prudent.

6. Carroll and Delacroix (1982) clearly recognize this and include political and institutional legitimacy as a major resource. Aldrich (1979) has argued that the population perspective must attend to historical trends and changes in legal and political institutions.

7. This point was suggested by John Meyer.

References

Alchian, Armen. 1950. "Uncertainty, Evolution, and Economic Theory." *Journal of Political Economy* 58:211–21.

Aldrich, Howard. 1979. *Organizations and Environments*. Englewood Cliffs, N.J.: Prentice-Hall.

Althusser, Louis. 1969. *For Marx*. Trans. Ben Brewster. London: Allan Lane.

Barnouw, Erik. 1966–68. *A History of Broadcasting in the United States*. 3 vols. Oxford: Oxford University Press.

Boorman, Scott A., and Paul R. Levitt. 1979. "The Cascade Principle for General Disequilibrium Dynamics." Harvard-Yale Preprints in Mathematical Sociology, no. 15.

Bowles, Samuel, and Herbert Gintis. 1976. *Schooling in Capitalist America*. New York: Basic Books.

Carroll, Glenn R., and Jacques Delacroix. 1982. "Organizational Mortality in the Newspaper Industries of Argentina and Ireland: An Ecological Approach." *Administrative Science Quarterly* 27:169–98.

Chandler, Alfred D. 1977. *The Visible Hand: The Managerial Revolution in American Business*. Cambridge: Harvard University Press.

Child, John, and Alfred Kieser. 1981. "Development of Organizations over Time." In *Handbook of Organizational Design*, ed. Paul C. Nystrom and William H. Starbuck. Oxford: Oxford University Press.

Cicourel, Aaron. 1970. "The Acquisition of Social Structure: Toward a Developmental Sociology of Language." In *Understanding Everyday Life*, ed. Jack D. Douglas. Chicago: Aldine.

Clark, Burton R. 1962. *Educating the Expert Society.* San Francisco: Chandler.

Cohen, Michael D., James G. March, and Johan P. Olsen. 1972. "A Garbage Can Model of Organizational Choice." *Administrative Science Quarterly* 17:1–25.

Collins, Randall. 1979. *The Credential Society.* New York: Academic Press.

Coser, Lewis, Charles Kadushin, and Walter W. Powell. 1982. *Books: The Culture and Commerce of Book Publishing*. New York: Basic Books.

Cyert, Richard M., and James G. March. 1963. *A Behavioral Theory of the Firm.* Englewood Cliffs, N.J.: Prentice-Hall.

DiMaggio, Paul. 1981. "Cultural Entrepreneurship in Nineteenth-Century Boston. Part 1: The Creation of an Organizational Base for High Culture in America." *Media, Culture, and Society* 4:33–50.

1982. "The Structure of Organizational Fields: An Analytical Approach and Policy Implications." Paper prepared for SUNY-Albany Conference on Organizational Theory and Public Policy. April 1 and 2.

Domhoff, J. William. 1967. *Who Rules America*? Englewood Cliffs, N.J.: Prentice-Hall.

1979. *The Powers That Be: Processes of Ruling Class Domination in America.* New York: Random House.

Fennell, Mary L. 1980. "The Effects of Environmental Characteristics on the Structure of Hospital Clusters." *Administrative Science Quarterly* 25:484–510.

Freeman, John H. 1982. "Organizational Life Cycles and Natural Selection Processes." In *Research in Organizational Behavior* ed. Barry M. Staw and Larry L. Cummings, vol. 4, Greenwich, Conn.: JAI.

Giddens, Anthony. 1979. *Central Problems in Social Theory: Action, Structure, and Contradiction in Social Analysis*. Berkeley and Los Angeles: University of California Press.

Gouldner, Alvin W. 1954. *Patterns of Industrial Bureaucracy.* Glencoe, Ill.: Free Press.

Granovetter, Mark. 1978. "Threshold Models of Collective Behavior." *American Journal of Sociology* 83:1420–43.

Hall, Richard. 1968. "Professionalization and Bureaucratization." *American Sociological Review* 33:92–104.

Halperin, Morton H. 1974. *Bureaucratic Politics and Foreign Policy.* Washington, D.C.: Brookings Institution.

Hannan, Michael T., and John H. Freeman. 1977. "The Population Ecology of Organizations." *American Journal of Sociology* 82:929–64.

Hawley, Amos. 1968. "Human Ecology." *International Encyclopedia of the Social Sciences*,ed. David L. Sills. New York: Macmillan.

Hawley, Ellis W. 1966. The *New Deal and the Problem of Monopoly: A Study in Economic Ambivalence*. Princeton: Princeton University Press.

Hirsch, Paul, and Thomas Whisler. 1982. "The View from the Boardroom." Paper presented at Academy of Management Meetings, New York.

Kanter, Rosabeth Moss. 1972. *Commitment and Community: Communes and Utopias in Sociological Perspective*. Cambridge: Harvard University Press.

1977. *Men and Women of the Corporation*. New York: Basic Books.

Katz, Michael B. 1975. *Class, Bureaucracy, and Schools: The Illusion of Educational Change in America*. New York: Praeger.

Kimberly, John. 1980 "Initiation, Innovation, and Institutionalization in the Creation Process." In *The Organizational Life Cycle*, ed. John Kimberly and Robert B. Miles, San Francisco: Jossey-Bass.

Knoke, David. 1982. "The Spread of Municipal Reform: Temporal, Spatial, and Social Dynamics." *American Journal of Sociology* 87:1314–39.

Larson, Magali Sarfatti. 1977. *The Rise of Professionalism: A Sociological Analysis*. Berkeley and Los Angeles: University of California Press.

Laumann, Edward O., Joseph Galaskiewicz, and Peter Marsden. 1978. "Community Structure as Interorganizational Linkage." *Annual Review of Sociology* 4:455–84.

Lee, M. L. 1971. "A Conspicuous Production Theory of Hospital Behavior." *Southern Economic Journal* 38:48–58.

Lukes, Steven. 1974. *Power: A Radical View*. London: Macmillan.

March, James G., and Michael Cohen. 1974. *Leadership and Ambiguity: The American College President*. New York: McGraw-Hill.

March, James C., and James G. March. 1977. "Almost Random Careers: The Wisconsin School Superintendency, 1940–72." *Administrative Science Quarterly* 22:378–409.

March, James G., and Johan P. Olsen. 1976. *Ambiguity and Choice in Organizations*. Bergen, Norway: Universitetsforlaget.

March, James G., and Herbert A. Simon. 1958. *Organizations*. New York: Wiley.

Meyer, John W. 1979. "The Impact of the Centralization of Educational Funding and Control on State and Local Organizational Governance." Institute for Research on Educational Finance and Governance, Stanford University, Program Report no. 79–B20.

———. 1981. Remarks at session "The Present Crisis and the Decline in World Hegemony," Annual Meetings of the American Sociological Association, Toronto.

Meyer, John W. and Michael Hannan. 1979. *National Development and the World System: Educational, Economic, and Political Change*. Chicago: University of Chicago Press.

Meyer, John W. and Brian Rowan. 1977. "Institutionalized Organizations: Formal Structure as Myth and Ceremony." *American Journal of Sociology* 83:340–63.

Meyer, John W., W. Richard Scott, and Terence C. Deal. 1981. "Institutional and Technical Sources of Organizational Structure Explaining the Structure of Educational Organizations." In *Organizations and the Human Services: Cross-Disciplinary Reflections*, ed Herman Stein. Philadelphia: Temple University Press.

Meyer, Marshall. 1981. "Persistence and Change in Bureaucratic Structures." Paper presented at the Annual Meetings of the American Sociological Association, Toronto.

Milofsky, Carl. 1981. "Structure and Process in Community Self-Help Organizations." Yale Program on Non-Profit Organizations, Working Paper no. 17.

Nelson, Richard R. and Sidney Winter. 1982. *An Evolutionary Theory of Economic Change*. Cambridge: Harvard University Press.

Ouchi, William G. 1980. "Markets, Bureaucracies, and Clans." *Administrative Science Quarterly* 25:129–41.
Parsons, Talcott. 1951. *The Social System*. Glencoe, Ill.: Free Press.
———. 1977. *The Evolution of Societies*. Englewood Cliffs, N.J.: Prentice-Hall.
Perrow, Charles. 1974. "Is Business Really Changing?" *Organizational Dynamics* 3:31–44.
———. 1976, "Control in Organizations." Paper presented at the Annual Meetings of the American Sociological Association, New York.
Pfeffer, Jeffrey, and Gerald Salancik. 1978. *The External Control of Organizations: A Resource Dependence Perspective*. New York: Harper and Row.
Piven, Frances Fox, and Richard A. Cloward. 1971. *Regulating the Poor: The Functions of Public Welfare*. New York: Pantheon.
Powell, Walter W. Forthcoming. "The Political Economy of Public Television." New Haven: Program on Non-Profit Organizations.
———. 1983. "New Solutions to Perennial Problems of Bookselling: Whither the Local Bookstore?" *Daedalus*, winter.
Ritti, R. R., and Fred H. Goldner. 1979. "Professional Pluralism in an Industrial Organization." *Management Science* 16:233–46.
Rothman, Mitchell. 1980. "The Evolution of Forms of Legal Education." Department of Sociology, Yale University.
Rothschild-Whitt, Joyce. 1979. "The Collectivist Organization: An Alternative to Rational Bureaucratic Models." *American Sociological Review* 44:509–27.
Schelling, Thomas. 1978. *Micromotives and Macrobehavior*. New York: Norton.
Sedlak, Michael W. 1981. "Youth Policy and Young Women, 1950–1972: The Impact of Private-Sector Programs for Pregnant and Wayward Girls on Public Policy." Paper presented at National Institute for Education Youth Policy Research Conference, Washington, D.C.
Selznick, Philip. 1957. *Leadership in Administration*. New York: Harper and Row.
Sills, David L. 1957. *The Volunteers: Means and Ends in a National Organization*. Glencoe, Ill.: Free Press.
Simon, Herbert A. 1957. *Administrative Behavior*. New York: Free Press.
Starr, Paul. 1980. "Medical Care and the Boundaries of Capitalist Organization." Program on Non-Profit Organizations, Yale University.
Swidler, Ann. 1979. *Organization without Authority: Dilemmas of Social Control of Free Schools*. Cambridge: Harvard University Press.
Thompson, James. 1967. *Organizations in Action*. New York: McGraw-Hill.
Tyack, David. 1974. *The One Best System: A History of American Urban Education*. Cambridge: Harvard University Press.
Useem, Michael. 1979. "The Social Organization of the American Business Elite and Participation of Corporation Directors in the Governance of American Institutions." *American Sociological Review* 44:553–72.
Weber, Max. 1952. *The Protestant Ethic and the Spirit of Capitalism*. Trans. Talcott Parsons. New York: Scribner.
———. 1968. *Economy and Society: An Outline of Interpretive Sociology*. Ed. Guenther Roth and Claus Wittich. Trans. Ephraim Fischoff et al. 3 vols. New York: Bedminster.
Weick, Karl. 1976. "Educational Organizations as loosely coupled systems." *Administrative Science Quarterly* 21:1–19.

Weinstein, James. 1968. *The Corporate Ideal in the Liberal State, 1900–1917*. Boston: Beacon Press.

Westney, D. Eleanor. 1987. *Imitation and Innovation: The Transfer of Western Organizational Patterns to Meiji, Japan*. Cambridge: Harvard University Press.

White, Harrison C., Scott A. Boorman, and Ronald L. Breiger. 1976. "Social Structure from Multiple Networks. I. Blockmodels of Roles and Positions." *American Journal of Sociology* 81:730–80.

Williamson, Oliver E. 1975. *Markets and Hierarchies, Analysis and Antitrust Implications: A Study of the Economics of Internal Organization*. New York: Free Press.

———. 1979. "Transaction-Cost Economies: The Governance of Contractual Relations." *Journal of Law and Economics* 22:233–61.

Winter, Sidney G. 1964. "Economic 'Natural Selection' and the Theory of the Firm." *Yale Economic Essays* 4:224–72.

———. 1975. "Optimization and Evolution in the Theory of the Firm." In *Adaptive Economic Models*, ed. Richard H. Day and Theodore Graves. New York: Academic.

Woodward, John. 1965. *Industrial Organization: Theory and Practice*. Oxford: Oxford University Press.

Zucker, Lynne G., and Pamela S. Tolbert. 1981. "Institutional Sources of Change in the Formal Structure of Organizations: The Diffusion of Civil Service Reform, 1880–1935." Paper presented at the Annual Meetings of the American Sociological Association, Toronto.

Chapter 5

FROM *PRICING THE PRICELESS CHILD: THE CHANGING SOCIAL VALUE OF CHILDREN*

Viviana A. Zelizer

From Useful to Useless: Moral Conflict over Child Labor

Where do we go from here—where?
—We remnants of the throng that started with us
Shall we keep on—
Or drop off on the way, as they have done?
They're earning money now, and make us feel
But useless children in comparison.
Why can't we, too, get into something real?
from "Eighth Grade," by F.B.W., 1923

The 1900 U.S. census reported that one child out of every six between the ages of ten and fifteen was gainfully employed. It was an undercount: The total figure of 1,750,178 excluded many child laborers under ten as well as the children "helping out" their parents in sweatshops and on farms, before or after school hours. Ten years later, the official estimate of working children reached 1,990,225. But by 1930, the economic participation of children had dwindled dramatically. Census figures registered 667,118 laborers under fifteen years of age. The decline was particularly marked among younger children. Between 1900 and 1930, the number of children ten to thirteen years old in nonagricultural occupations alone decreased more than sixfold, from 186,358 to under 30,000.[1]

The exclusion of children from the marketplace involved a difficult and prolonged battle lasting almost fifty years from the 1870s to the 1930s. It was partly an economic confrontation and partly a legal dispute, but it was also a profound "moral revolution."[2] Two groups with sharply conflicting views of childhood struggled to impose their definition of children's proper place in society. For child labor reformers, children's early labor was a viola-

Viviana A. Zelizer. 1987. *Pricing the Priceless Child: The Changing Social Value of Children.* New York: Basic, pp. 56–85, 97–100, 112.

tion of children's sentimental value. As one official of the National Child Labor Committee explained in 1914, a laboring child "is simply a producer, worth so much in dollars and cents, with no standard of value as a human being. . . . How do you calculate your standard of a child's value? . . . as something precious beyond all money standard."[3] On the other hand, opponents of child labor reform were just as vehement in their support of the productive child: "I say it is a tragic thing to contemplate if the Federal Government closes the doors of the factories and you send that little child back, empty-handed; that brave little boy that was looking forward to get money for his mother for something to eat."[4]

The child labor conflict is a key to understanding the profound transformation in the economic and sentimental value of children in the early twentieth century. The price of a useful wage-earning child was directly counterposed to the moral value of an economically useless but emotionally priceless child. In the process, a complex reassessment of children's economic roles took place. It was not just a matter of whether children should work or not. Even the most activist of child labor reformers were unwilling to condemn all types of child work, while their opponents were similarly reluctant to condone all child labor. Instead, their argument centered over conflicting and often ambiguous cultural definitions of what constituted acceptable work for children. New boundaries emerged, differentiating legitimate from illegitimate forms of economic participation by children.

It was not a simple process. As one perplexed contemporary observer noted: "To work or not to work—that is the question. But nobody agrees upon the answer. . . . Who among the controversialists is wrong? And just what is work anyway? When and where does it step across the dead line and become exploitation?"[5] Child work and child money were gradually redefined for the "sacred" twentieth-century child into primarily moral and instructional tools. While child labor laws regulated exclusively working-class children, the new rules for educational child work cut across classes, equally applicable to all "useless" children.

The Useful Child: From Family Asset to Social Problem

In recent studies, economists and historians have documented the vital significance of child labor for working-class families in the late nineteenth century. Using extensive national data from the 1880s and 1890s, Michael Haines concludes that child labor "appears to have been the main source of additional support for the late nineteenth-century urban family under economic stress."[6] In her analysis of U.S. Federal Population Census manuscripts for Philadelphia in 1880, Claudia Goldin found that Irish children contributed between 38 and 46 percent of the total family labor income in two-parent families; German children 33 to 35 percent, and the native-born 28 to 32 percent. Unlike the mid–twentieth century, when married women entered the labor force, in the late nineteenth century a child, not a wife, was likely to become the family's secondary wage earner.

To use children as active participants in the household economy of the working class was not only economically indispensable but also a legitimate social practice. The middle class, with its own children in school, still wistfully admired the moral principle of early labor. As late as 1915, one observer recognized, "There is among us a reaction to be noted from the . . . overindulgence of our children and a realization that perhaps more work and responsibility would do them good."[7] Even children's books and magazines, aimed at an educated middle-class audience, "hymned the joys of usefulness," praising the virtues of work, duty, and discipline to their young readers. The standard villain in these stories was an idle child.[8]

Child labor as a morally righteous institution was not a nineteenth-century invention. American children had always worked. In his classic study of family life in Plymouth Colony, John Demos suggests that by the time children turned six or eight, they were expected to assume the role of "little adults," engaged in useful tasks in their own homes, or apprenticed elsewhere.[9] Laws governing the poor in the seventeenth and eighteenth centuries similarly reflected prevalent Puritan views on the virtue of work by providing employment for dependent children.

Industrial work created different job opportunities for young children in the late eighteenth century. Employers welcomed their nimble "little fingers" for the "gigantic automatons of labor saving machinery."[10] Indeed, the first workers in the American spinning mill set up in Rhode Island by Samuel Slater in 1790 were nine children between the ages of seven and twelve. By 1820, young boys and girls constituted 55 percent of the operatives employed in Rhode Island's textile mills. An enthusiastic writer for *Nile's Register* eagerly anticipated the pecuniary payoffs of child labor for local economies: "If we suppose that before the establishment of these manufactories, there were two hundred children between seven and sixteen years of age, that contributed nothing towards their maintenance and that they are now employed, it makes an immediate difference of $13,500 a year to the value produced in the town!"[11]

Rapid industrialization multiplied job opportunities for children in the late nineteenth century. Official estimates show an increase of over a million child workers between 1870 and 1900. One-third of the workforce in the newly developed southern textile mills, for instance, were children between the ages of ten and thirteen, and many even younger.[12] For working-class families, the employment of children was part of what historian John Modell calls a limited "defensive" mode of family cooperation, "an attempt to pool risks in what was experienced as a very uncertain world."[13] Particularly for nineteenth-century urban families dependent on daily wages, the unemployment, sickness, or death of the main family earner constituted a major threat. The middle-class father could afford to purchase financial protection from life insurance companies; as early as 1851, over $100 million of security was bought. Although cheaper industrial insurance became available to the working class after the 1870s, it only provided limited burial coverage. Mutual aid groups and voluntary associations offered some institutional protection, yet Modell concludes that, for the working class, it was the "individual coresident family that, as budgetary unit, adapted in the face of uncertainty."[14]

The useful child, therefore, provided a unique economic buffer for the working-class family of the late nineteenth century. But by 1900, middle-class reformers began indicting children's economic cooperation as unjustified parental exploitation, and child labor emerged for the first time as a major social problem in the United States. The occasional attempts to regulate the work of children earlier in the century had been largely ineffective and unable to galvanize public opinion. Existing state laws were so lax and vague as to be unenforceable. In fact, they were not even intended to put children out of work. Instead, early child labor legislation was primarily concerned with assuring a minimum of education for working children. The pioneering Massachusetts statute of 1836, for instance, required three months' schooling for young factory laborers. As late as 1905, a *New York Times* editorial contested the "mistaken notion that the advocates for the restriction and regulation of child labor insist that children under fourteen everywhere shall not work at all and shall be compelled to attend school practically all the time." The true aim of the earlier movement was to determine "the amount of labor and the amount of schooling that would be reasonable." In fact, nineteenth-century child welfare organizations were more concerned with idle and vagrant children than with child laborers.[15]

Child labor only gradually achieved national visibility. In 1870, for the first time, the U.S. census provided a separate count of adult and child workers. Bureaus of labor statistics were organized in ten states between 1869 and 1883, producing and distributing data on child workers. Child labor became an issue in the press. *Poole's Index to Periodical Literature* lists only four articles under child labor between 1897 and 1901. Between 1905 and 1909, according to the *Readers' Guide to Periodicals*, over three hundred articles were published on child workers. Child labor rapidly established itself as a priority item in the political agenda of Progressive social reformers. Organizational growth was impressive. The first Child labor Committee was formed in 1901; by 1910 there were twenty-five state and local committees in existence. A National Child Labor Committee was established in 1904. These groups sponsored and indefatigably publicized exposés of child labor conditions. Child labor committees were assisted by the National Consumer's League, the General Federation of Women's Clubs, and the American Federation of Labor. The emerging Socialist Party also directed much attention to the issue of child labor. For instance, in 1903, Mother Jones, the well-known union organizer, led a dramatic "March of the Mill Children," from the Philadelphia area, through New Jersey and into New York, in order to expose the evils of child labor. By 1907, an article in Hearst's influential *Cosmopolitan* assured its readers that child labor would soon take its place "with all the institutions of evil memory—with bull baiting, witch-burning, and all other execrated customs of the past."[16]

Why did twentieth-century child labor lose its nineteenth-century good reputation? What explains the sudden vehemence and urgency to remove all children from the labor market? Most historical interpretations focus on the effect of structural, economic, and technological changes on child labor trends between the 1870s and 1930s. The success of industrial capitalism is assigned primary responsibility for putting children out of work and into schools to satisfy the growing demand for a skilled, educated labor force. Rising real incomes, on the other hand, explains the reduced need for children's wages. As the standard of living steadily improved between the late nineteenth century and the 1920s, child labor declined simply because families could afford to keep their children in school. Particularly important was the institutionalization of the family wage in the first two decades of the twentieth century, by which a male worker was expected to earn enough to forgo the labor of his wife and children. Stricter and better-enforced compulsory education laws further accelerated the unemployment of children.[17]

In his analysis of changes in the youth labor market, Paul Osterman contends that children were "pushed out of industry" not only by the declining demand for unskilled labor but also by a simultaneous increase in its supply. The tide of turn-of-the-century immigrants were children's new competitors. For Osterman, compulsory school legislation was the result, not the cause, of a changing youth labor market: "Since firms no longer required the labor of children and adolescents, those pressing for longer compulsory schooling were able to succeed."[18] Joan Huber similarly points to a conflict of interest between age groups created by the new economic system. In an agrarian economy, as in the early stages of industrialization, the labor of "little work people" was a welcome alternative that freed men for agriculture. But by the turn of the century, the cheap labor of children threatened to depress adult wages.[19]

Demand for child laborers was further undermined by new technology. For example, in late-nineteenth-century department stores, such as Macy's and Marshall Field's, one-third of the labor force was composed of cashgirls or cashboys, young children busily involved in transporting money and goods between sales clerks, the wrapping desk, and the cashier. By 1905, the newly invented pneumatic tube and the adoption of cash registers had usurped most children's jobs.[20]

The issue of child labor, however, cannot be reduced to neat economic equations. If industrial technological developments combined with the increased supply of immigrant unskilled workers inevitably reduced the need for child laborers, why then was their exclusion from the workplace such a complex and controversial process?

The Child Labor Controversy

The history of American child labor legislation is a chronicle of obstacles and defeats. At every step of the battle that lasted some fifty years, the sustained efforts of child labor reformers were blocked by an equally determined, vocal, and highly effective opposition. Until 1938, every major attempt to pass national regulation of child labor was defeated. The two groups were divided by conflicting economic interests and also by opposing legal philosophies. Yet the emotional vigor of their battle revealed an additional, profound cultural schism. Proponents and opponents of child labor legislation became entangled in a moral dispute over the definition of children's economic and sentimental value.

Child labor legislation was first resisted on a state level. Although by 1899 twenty-eight states had some kind of legal protection for child workers, regulations were vague and enforcement lax. The typical child labor law, which only protected children in manufacturing and mining, often contained enough exceptions and loopholes to make it ineffective. For instance, poverty permits allowed young children to work if their earnings were necessary for self-support or to assist their widowed mothers or disabled fathers. As late as 1929, six states retained such an exemption. Legislative progress in the early twentieth century was further undermined by a lack of uniformity in state standards. Progressive states became increasingly reluctant to enact protective legislation that put them at a competitive disadvantage with states where employment of a cheap juvenile force was legal or else minimally regulated.[21]

The struggle for national regulation of child labor began inauspiciously in 1906 with Indiana senator Albert Beveridge's dramatic but unsuccessful attempt in the U.S. Senate to create a federal law to end what he termed "child slavery." The threat of federal regulation only served to consolidate the opposition. In 1916, when Congress finally passed the first federal law banning the products of child labor from interstate and foreign commerce, opponents promptly challenged the new law in court, and two years later the bill was declared unconstitutional. A second federal law was passed in 1919, only to be again dismissed three years later by the Supreme Court as an unconstitutional invasion of state power.

The toughest battle began in 1924 after Congress approved a constitutional amendment introduced by reformers that would authorize Congress to regulate child labor. The campaign against state ratification of the amendment was staggering: "The country was swept with propaganda. It appeared in newspapers and magazine articles, editorials, and advertisements, in enormous quantities of printed leaflets, and in speeches, at meetings, and over the radio. The proposed child labor amendment was one of the most discussed political issues of the year."[22] The opposition effort succeeded; by the summer of 1925, only four states had ratified the amendment and thirty-four had rejected it. Briefly revived in 1933, the amendment again failed to secure sufficient state support. Effective federal regulation of child labor was only obtained after the depression, first with the National Industrial Recovery Act and in 1938 with the Fair Labor Standards Act, which included a section on child labor.

What accounts for this catalog of obstacles? Why weren't child labor reformers able to easily dazzle legislatures or swiftly persuade the public with the justness of their cause? In large part, resistance to legislation was engineered by powerful interest groups. After all, in 1920 over one million children between the ages of ten and fifteen were still at work. From the start, southern cotton mill owners refused to forgo the profitable labor of their many child employees.[23] Child labor reform was often depicted as a dangerous northern conspiracy to destroy the recently expanded southern industry. Mill owners were eventually joined by farmers and other employers of children. Not surprisingly, the National Association of Manufacturers and the American Farm Bureau Federation were two leading forces against the 1924 constitutional amendment. A different type of opposition was based on political and legal principle. In this case, the target was federal regulation. Conservative citizen organizations and even prominent individuals, including the presidents of Columbia University and Hunter College, actively crusaded against the federal child labor amendment because it challenged states' rights.[24]

It would be inaccurate, however, to caricature the child labor dispute simply as a struggle between humane reformers and greedy employers or to reduce it to a technical dispute over the relative merits of state versus federal regulation. The battle involved a much wider range of participants, from clergymen, educators, and journalists to involved citizens, and included as well the parents of child laborers. At issue was a profound cultural uncertainty and dissent over the proper economic roles for children.

In Defense of the Useful Child

In a letter to the editor of the *Chicago News*, a Reverend Dunne of the Guardian Angels' Italian Church bitterly criticized the 1903 Illinois child labor law as a "curse instead of a blessing to those compelled to earn their bread by the sweat of their brow." The priest ridiculed a law that transformed the noble assistance of a working child into an illegal act: "He must not attempt to work; he must not dare to earn his living honestly, because in his case . . . that is against the law."[25] From the early skirmishes in state legislatures to the organized campaign against the 1924 constitutional amendment, opponents of child labor legislation defended the pragmatic and moral legitimacy of a useful child. As a controversial article in the *Saturday Evening Post* asserted: "The work of the world has to be done; and these children have their share . . . why should we . . . place the emphasis on . . . prohibitions, . . . We don't want to rear up a generation of nonworkers, what we want is workers and more workers."[26] From this perspective, regulatory legislation introduced an unwelcome and dangerous "work prohibition": "The discipline, sense of duty and responsibility . . . which come to a boy and girl, in home, on the farm, in workshop, as the result of even hard work . . . is to be . . . prohibited."[27] The consequences would be dire: "If a child is not trained to useful work before the age of eighteen, we shall have a nation of paupers and thieves." Child labor, insisted its supporters, was safer than "child-idleness."[28]

Early labor was also nostalgically defended as the irreplaceable stepping-stone in the life course of American self-made men. The president of the Virginia Farm Bureau, fondly recalling his early years as a child laborer, insisted on the need "to leave to posterity the same chance that I enjoyed under our splendid form of government."[29] Similarly upholding children's "privilege to work," a writer in the *Woman Citizen* speculated if "Lincoln's character could ever have been developed under a system that forced him to do nothing more of drudgery than is necessitated by playing on a ball team after school hours."[30] Overwork, concluded the article, was a preferable alternative to overcoddling. Child work was even occasionally defended with theological arguments: "The Savior has said, 'My Father worketh hitherto, and I work. . . . May not the child follow the footsteps of the Savior . . . ?" If labor redeemed, regulatory laws served the interests of Hell, by making of idle young people the devil's "best workshop."[31]

For working-class families, the usefulness of their children was supported by need and custom. When parents were questioned as to why their children left school early to get to work, it was often "perplexing" for the mother to assign a reason for such an "absolutely natural proceeding—he's of an age to work, why shouldn't he?' " As one mother who employed her young children in homework told an investigator: "Everybody does it. Other people's children help—why not ours?"[32] Studies of immigrant families, in particular, demonstrate that the child was an unquestioned member of the family economic unit. For example, in her study of Canadian workers in the Amoskeag Mills of Manchester, New Hampshire, Tamara Hareven found that the "entire family economy as well as the family's work ethic was built on the assumption that children would contribute to the family's income from the earliest possible age."[33] While generally older boys were more likely to become wage earners, boys under fourteen and girls were still expected to actively assist the family with housework, childcare, and any income obtained from odd jobs.[34]

Government reports occasionally provide glimpses of the legitimacy of child labor: A mother boasting that her baby—a boy of seven—could "make more money than any of them picking shrimp"; or an older sister apologizing for her seven-year-old brother, who was unable to work in a shrimp cannery "because he couldn't reach the car to shuck."[35] Work was a socializer; it kept children busy and out of mischief. As the father of two children who worked at home wiring rosary beads explained: "Keep a kid at home, save shoe leather, make better manners."[36]

Child labor legislation threatened the economic world of the working class. In 1924, one commentator in the *New Republic* predicted the potential disruption of traditional family relationships: "The immemorial right of the parent to train his child in useful tasks . . . is destroyed. The obligation of the child to contribute . . . is destroyed. Parents may still set their children at work; children may still make themselves useful, but it will no longer be by right and obligation, but by default of legislation."[37] Many parents resented and resisted this intrusion. A 1909 investigation of cotton textile mills reported that "fathers and mothers vehemently declare that the State has no right to interfere if they wish to 'put their children to work,' and that it was only fair for the child to 'begin to pay back for its keep.' "[38] In New York canneries, Italian immigrants reportedly took a more aggressive stand. One study reports a quasi riot against a canner who attempted to exclude young children from the sheds: "[He was] besieged by angry Italian women, one of whom bit his finger 'right through.' "[39] Parents routinely sabotaged regulatory legislation simply by lying about their child's age. It was an easy ploy, since until the 1920s many states required only a parental affidavit as proof of a child worker's age. For a small illegal fee, some notary publics were apparently quite willing to produce a false affidavit.[40]

Middle-class critics also opposed child labor legislation in the name of family autonomy. Prominent spokesmen such as Nicholas Murray Butler, president of Columbia University, warned that "No American mother would favor the adoption of a constitutional amendment which would empower Congress to invade the rights of parents and to shape family life to its liking."[41] An assemblyman from Nevada put it more succinctly: "They have taken our women away from us by constitutional amendments; they have taken our liquor from us; and now they want to take our children."[42]

In Defense of the Useless Child

For reformers, the economic participation of children was an illegitimate and inexcusable "commercialization of child life."[43] As one New York City clergyman admonished his parishioners in 1925: "A man who defends the child labor that violates the personalities of children is not a Christian."[44] The world of childhood had to become entirely removed from the world of the market. Already in 1904, Dr. Felix Adler, first chairman of the National Child Labor Committee, insisted that "whatever happens in the sacrifice of workers . . . children shall not be touched . . . childhood shall be sacred . . . commercialism shall not be allowed beyond this point."[45] If the sacred child was "industrially taboo," child labor was a profanation that reduced "the child of God [into] the chattel of Mammon."[46]

The persistence of child labor was attributed in part to a misguided economic system that put "prosperity above . . . the life of sacred childhood."[47] Employers were denounced as "greedy and brutal tyrants," for whom children were little more than a "wage-earning unit," or a profitable dividend.[48] Any professed support of child labor was dismissed as convenient rhetoric: "A prominent businessman who recently remarked that it is good for the children to work in industry is a hypocrite unless he puts his own children there."[49]

Reformers sympathized with the financial hardships of the working class, yet they rarely understood and seldom condoned working-class economic strategies. Instead, parents were depicted as suspect collaborators in the exploitation of their own children. "If fathers and mothers of working children could have their own way, would they be with the child labor reformer or against him?" was a question asked in *The American Child*, a publication of the National Child Labor Committee.[50] Others were more forthright in their indictment: "Those who are fighting for the rights of the children, almost invariably, find their stoutest foes in the fathers and mothers, who coin shameful dollars from the bodies and souls of their own flesh and blood." A child's contribution to the family economy was redefined as the mercenary exploitation of parents "who are determined that their children shall add to the family income, regardless of health, law, or any other consideration."[51] As early as 1873, Jacob Riis had declared that "it requires a character of more disinterestedness . . . than we usually find among the laboring class to be able to forego present profit for the future benefit of the little one."[52] At the root of this harsh indictment was the profound unease of a segment of the middle class with working-class family life. The instrumental orientation toward children was denied all legitimacy: "to permit a parent . . . at his or her will to send a child out to work and repay himself for its maintenance from the earnings of its labor, or perhaps . . . make money out of it seems . . . nothing short of criminal."[53] Child labor, "by urging the duty of the child to its parents," obliterated the "far more binding and important obligation of the parent to the child."[54] This "defective" economic view of children was often attributed to the foreign values of immigrant parents, "who have no civilization, no decency, no anything but covetousness and who would with pleasure immolate their offspring on the shrine of the golden calf."[55] For such "vampire" progenitors, the child became an asset instead of remaining a "blessed incumbrance."[56]

Advocates of child labor legislation were determined to regulate not only factory hours but family feeling. They introduced a new cultural equation: If children were useful and produced money, they were not being properly loved. As a social worker visiting the canneries where Italian mothers worked alongside their children concluded: "Although they love their children, they do not love them in the right way."[57] A National Child Labor Committee leaflet warned that when family relations are materialistic, "It is rare to find a family governed by affection."[58] By excluding children from the "cash nexus," reformers promised to restore proper parental love among working-class families. "It is the new view of the child," wrote Edward T. Devine, editor of *Charities and the Commons*, a leading reform magazine, "that the child is worthy of the parent's sacrifice."[59]

Thus, the conflict over the propriety of child labor between 1870 and 1930 in the United States involved a profound cultural disagreement over the economic and sentimental value of young children. While opponents of child labor legislation hailed the economic usefulness of children, advocates of child labor legislation campaigned for their uselessness. For reformers, true parental love could only exist if the child was defined exclusively as an object of sentiment and not as an agent of production.

From Child Labor to Child Work: Redefining the Economic World of Children

> Ask a dozen persons "What is child labor?" and you will get a dozen answers, most of them in a rather startled and hesitant manner, and in language that may be violent but is likely also to be vague.
>
> Raymond Fuller, "The Truth about Child Labor," 1922

The battle line between proponents and opponents of child labor legislation was confounded by imprecise and ambivalent cultural definitions of child labor. For instance, it was often unclear what specific occupations transformed a child into an exploited laborer, or what determined the legitimacy of some forms of child work. In the early part of the twentieth century this ambiguity frustrated government attempts to reach a precise national accounting of the number of child laborers: "Is a girl at work who merely helps her mother in keeping the house? When a child helps its parents, irregularly, about a little store or a fruit stand, is it working? What of the children who are kept out of school to 'tote dinners'?"[60] Opponents of legislation insisted on children's right to work, yet often categorized certain occupations as illegitimate forms of employment. Reformers' passionate advocacy of the useless child was similarly qualified. Accused of giving work a "black eye," they defensively retorted that the anti–child labor movement was also prowork. Raymond Fuller, at onetime director of research at the National Child Labor Committee and one of the most vocal spokesmen for child labor reform, protested that "Nothing could be farther from the truth than the . . . widespread notion that child labor reform is predicated on the assumption that children should have no work."[61] As the child labor dispute evolved, the relationship of children to work was increasingly examined and reappraised. Gradually, the nineteenth-century utilitarian criteria of labor and wages appropriate for the useful child were replaced by a noneconomic, educational concept of child work and child money better suited to the twentieth-century useless child.

Illegitimate Child Labor or "Good Work"? The Search for New Boundaries

Investigation of why children quit school early suggested that work appealed to them: "The 'call' is one which involves the use of energy in creative work—in accomplishing something useful in the work-a-day world."[62] Yet where could the useless child find useful outlets? Reformers acknowledged the quandary: "The dilemma for the city child seems to be either painful exhaustion and demoralizing work on the one hand, or futile idleness . . . on the other."[63] One observer only half-jokingly proposed the creation of a Society for the Promotion of Useful Work for Children.[64] Raymond Fuller identified the essential difficulty:

> The category of child labor tends to become . . . too broad or too narrow. Some of us are so sure of the badness of child labor that we call bad nearly every activity that takes the aspect of work; and some of . . . us are so sure that work is a good thing for children that we leave out of the category of child labor much that belongs there.[65]

The solution was to devise criteria that would differentiate more clearly between legitimate and illegitimate economic roles for children. Child labor reform would not simply be an absolutist anti–child labor campaign, but instead a pro–"good" child work movement. "To establish children's work," asserted Fuller, "is quite as important as to . . . abolish child labor."[66]

It was a difficult task. As Fuller himself admitted: "There is a dividing line between . . . ordinary, not too numerous, not too heavy tasks, and the tasks that represent an abuse of labor power of children; but it is not a clear, sharp dividing line."[67] At what age, for instance, was the line crossed? By nineteenth-century standards, the employment of a nine- or ten-year-old had been legitimate and for the most part legal. In fact, age was not considered a very important criterion of legitimacy until after the 1860s. Before then, only four states limited the age of employment of children. Nineteenth-century child labor legislation focused primarily on reducing the hours of work and providing some education for child laborers rather than establishing age limits. In 1899, there were still twenty-four states and the District of Columbia without a minimum age requirement for children employed in manufacturing. Child labor reformers met with formidable resistance as they struggled to institute age as a central boundary distinguishing child work from child labor. Critics objected to a legal requirement keeping children useless until twelve and protested even more forcefully against a fourteen-year age limit. Often, parental and legal conceptions of a proper age limit clashed. Enforcement officials complained that many immigrant parents were unable to calculate age in American terms: "I ask a mother the age of her daughter. After the fashion of her particular [Jewish] race, she will shrug her shoulders or turn her head, signifying that she does not know. I insist upon an answer, and she will say 'Tuesday' or 'four o'clock.' "[68] Gradually, age became an accepted measure of legitimacy. Between 1879 and 1909, the number of states with age limit provisions (for any occupation except dangerous employments and mining) increased from seven to forty-four. The legal age limit was first raised from ten to twelve and then to fourteen. After the 1920s, child labor organizations fought to raise the age limit from fourteen to sixteen.[69]

If it was difficult to establish a proper age boundary, it became even more complex to differentiate between types of jobs. Industrial child labor was the most obvious category of illegitimate employment. As one of the most passionate opponents of early labor explained: "Work is what children need. . . . But the bondage and drudgery of these mill-children and factory children and mine-children are not work, but servitude."[70] Accordingly, the earliest child labor laws were almost exclusively designed to regulate the manufacturing and mining industries. Yet even this area of work found its committed supporters. A 1912 book, *The Child That Toileth Not*, provoked a heated debate in the press by asserting that government reports had misled the public by censoring information about the beneficial aspects of child labor in cotton mills. The author, who had investigated child labor conditions in the southern textile industry concluded: "If I were a Carnegie or a Rockefeller seeking to improve the conditions of our poor mountain people, I would build them a cotton mill. I would gather their children in just as they are big enough to doff and spin."[71]

If defending factory work was unusual, farm labor on the other hand was almost blindly and romantically categorized as "good" work. Even though by 1900, 60 percent of all gainfully employed children (ten to fifteen years old) were agricultural workers, their labor was not defined as a social problem. In his pioneering and dramatic exposé of child labor before Congress in 1906, Senator Beveridge of Indiana deliberately excluded agricultural labor: "I do not for a moment pretend that working children on the farm is bad for them . . . there can be no better training."[72] The legitimacy of farmwork was reflected in its legal status. Even as the number of rural child laborers continued to increase, most state laws and the two federal child labor bills focused on industrial child labor, and consistently exempted agriculture from regulation. To be sure, this indemnity was carefully preserved by the powerful farming interests; yet it was also the result of an equally influential cultural consensus. As an officer of the National Child Labor Committee remarked in 1924, "Everybody is against [child labor, but] work on farms . . . is not held to be child labor. The presumption that everything is well with the child in agriculture runs so strong that any inquiry . . . is held by some not only useless but almost improper."[73] As late as 1932, the White House Conference on Child Health and Protection still noted that "the attitude of a large part of the public is not opposed to the employment of children in agriculture."[74]

The idealization of farmwork by child labor reformers wavered as investigations in the 1920s began to uncover some of the hardships experienced by young agricultural laborers. A survey of 845 children in North Dakota, conducted by the U.S. Children's Bureau, found boys and girls under age seventeen engaged in a wide variety of farmwork. Seventy-one percent of the children were under fourteen. Aside from field work, herding cattle was their most common task. Boys and girls, often as young as six years old, were "out on the prairie alone on foot or on horseback for long hours in the heat of the summer without shelter or drink . . . in danger of being thrown from horseback . . . or trampled on by the cattle." Others were involved in the construction of barbed-wire fences, digging or drilling holes for posts as well as assisting with butchering jobs, cleaning seed for the spring planting, and even taking care of farm machinery. Out of the 845 children, almost 750 were also responsible for routine chores and housework. One nine-year-old boy, for instance, "built the fires in the morning, swept the floors of a two-room house, and brought in fuel and water; in addition, before he made a two-mile trip to school, he helped feed stock (5 horse and 12 cows) and chopped wood; in the evening he did the chores and washed dishes."

In the North Dakota study, 20 percent of the children had worked away from home during the preceding year, either for wages or for their board; the majority were under fourteen years of age and had assisted with harvesting chores or as general farm helpers. The Children's Bureau study showed that farm- and homework took children away from their schoolwork. For instance, an examination of the school records of 3,465 children in six rural areas in North Dakota revealed that 42 percent of the 2,776 children under fourteen years of age, and 59 percent of those between ages ten and fourteen, had been kept home for work in defiance of child labor regulations.[75] An earlier investigation of rural children in several North Carolina counties found a similar situation. In a typical mountain county, for instance, a father of eight was asked why he did not buy a corn planter. He responded: "I already have eight." The family's workday often began at six or seven in the morning and ended at sundown, with an hour off for dinner. The report concluded that "although early training in habits of industry is desirable, and . . . a reasonable amount of farm work would scarcely injure a healthy child of sufficient size and strength, children's work on the farm . . . as is described in this report . . . [puts] undue strain upon the strength of the child, the interruption of his schooling . . . the ill effects upon his health."[76]

But the solution was not a wholesale condemnation of farm labor; instead, reformers sought to differentiate better between "good" farmwork and exploitative farm labor. As one writer in the *American Review of Reviews* explained in 1924: "Work on the farm performed by children under parents' direction and without interference with school attendance is not child labor. Work performed by children away from home, for wages, at long hours and under conditions which endanger the child's health, education and morals is child labor."[77] Thus, commercialized agriculture joined the ranks of illegitimate occupations, while the legitimacy of work on the home farm was idyllically preserved.

Between the extremes of industrial child labor and farmwork, there was a variety of other occupations for children of a much more uncertain status and with different claims to legitimacy. Fred Hall, executive secretary of the National Child Labor Committee, identified such occupations as "the borderland or frontier of the child labor program—an area in which the public often assumes that children's work is a valuable preparation for future usefulness."[78] Working as a Senate page, for instance, was a prestigious occupation for children. Working as a cashgirl or cashboy in a department store also promised an attractive and legitimate entry into business life.[79]

Street work and particularly newsboys presented child welfare workers with a unique dilemma. As Raymond Fuller explained in his book *Child Labor and the Constitution:* "Many of us . . . are rather strongly prejudiced in favor of it, finding ourselves obliged to overcome serious difficulties in order to recognize it as child labor."[80] Legislatures similarly hesitated to challenge the legitimacy of street work. While other occupations gradually established fourteen as a minimum age limit, children in street work could legally start work at ten or twelve, and many began as young as six or seven. The White House Conference report of 1932 still considered the regulation of street work as "one of the most difficult problems in the whole field of child labor law."[81] Why, wondered an observer, did people condemn child labor in the factories, yet "tolerate it and even approve of it in the street?" Why did factory work transform a child into a slave, yet street work somehow qualified him as a respectable "little merchant"?[82] As one social worker complained in 1905: "It seems the part of the iconoclast to controvert the public conception of the newsboy."[83]

The legitimacy of newspaper sellers, as well as many child peddlers and bootblacks, was initially determined by nineteenth-century utilitarian values. Unlike factory workers or children in mercantile establishments, street traders were not employees but independent merchants, working for profits and not for wages. It was a glamorous form of entrepreneurship. J. G. Brown, a painter who specialized in nineteenth-century street boys, described them to a reporter: "My boys lived in the open. There wasn't a danger of the streets that they didn't face some time or other during the day. They would take a chance, any time, of being run down by a wagon or a streetcar for the sake of selling a paper or selling a 'shine' . . . they were alert, strong, healthy little chaps."[84] Even twentieth-century reformers were reluctant to put such children out of work. Pioneers in child welfare such as Jacob Riis admiringly referred to the "sturdy independence, love of freedom and absolute self-reliance" of street boys.[85] In 1912, a major study of child labor in the streets marveled at the persistent "widespread delusion that . . . these little 'merchants' of the street are receiving valuable training in business methods and will later develop into leaders in the affairs of men."[86]

As with farm labor, exposés of children working in the streets gradually punctured prevailing myths. A study conducted by the Children's Bureau found children often as young as six and seven selling papers in city streets. As one eleven-year-old newsboy complained, "My little brother sells more . . . because people think he is cute."[87] Newsboys worked late hours, 10 P.M. or sometimes until midnight, especially on Saturday nights, selling the Sunday papers to the theater and restaurant crowds. Street work was found unfit for children, distracting them from school and introducing them into a life of vice and "unnatural desires." After all, if children's games were being pushed off the street, certainly children's street work could not survive much longer. As one expert in the field explained, street work was considerably more hazardous than child play:

> there is a well-known difference in the physical and moral influences surrounding street trading in the downtown district with all the freedom from external control either on the part of city or parent, as compared with . . . street play within the neighborhood . . . where the restrictions of home and friends are able to influence . . . [the child's] conduct.[88]

Once again, the boundaries of legitimacy shifted as reformers distinguished more closely between types of street work. Earlier economic criteria (that is, the distinction between wages and profits) were inadequate: "The effect on the child of work is in no wise determined by the form in which his earnings are calculated."[89] While most street occupations, including the sale of newspapers, were declared to be unfit forms of child labor, the neighborhood carrier who delivered newspapers to the homes of subscribers was gradually singled out for legitimacy. The criteria for "good work," however, were dramatically reversed, converting the previously admired independent role of a newsboy into a liability. Why was the delivery of newspapers acceptable? Precisely because "the delivery boy is in no sense an independent merchant or dealer. He neither buys nor sells . . . and he assumes no responsibility except for his own work. He is an employee."[90] Carrying newspapers, concluded the Children's Bureau investigation, "puts no temptations in the boy's way to stay out of school, nor does it bring him in contact with such influences as many of the street sellers meet." Unlike the newsboy, the carriers' hours were "unobjectionable"; boys delivering evening papers were finished usually before 6 P.M., "their work did not keep them on the streets after dark . . . nor interfere with their family life." It was a perfect occupation for the domesticated child, not real work but a "schoolboy's job."[91] The day messenger service was another form of legitimate street work for young boys. The night messenger service, on the other hand, was harshly condemned for allegedly employing youngsters to deliver telegrams but in fact using them to carry notes, food, liquor, and drugs to prostitutes, pimps, and gamblers.

Child labor in the home raised even more complex and confusing definitional problems. It also involved a different population; while selling newspapers or bootblacking was a boy's job, home occupations were largely, although not exclusively, a girl's domain. Studies suggest that young girls probably constituted from one-half to three-fourths of the children involved with homework, while of the 17,669 children ten to fourteen years of age working as newsboys in 1920, only 168 were girls. Unlike a factory, or a street, or a store, the home was sanctioned by reformers as a proper workplace: "every child needs to be taught to work; but he needs to be taught not in the factory but in the home . . ."[92] Officially, domestic activities were not even considered "real" work. Instructions to census enumerators specified that "children who work for their parents at home merely on general household work, on chores, or at odd times on other work, should be reported as having no occupation."[93]

But what about industrial homework, that is, factory work done at home mostly by mothers with their young children? It usually involved immigrant families or other unskilled low-paid groups living in the tenement districts of large cities. Industrial homework included a wide range of activities, chiefly finishing men's clothing, embroidering, making artificial flowers, and stringing tags. Children helped with the simpler tasks and often delivered the work from the home to the factory. By the late nineteenth century, homework had become one of the most prevalent forms of child labor. Yet many employers claimed that since the "little helpers" worked with their mothers, they were not really employed.[94] Parents themselves praised an occupation that kept their children busy and safely off the streets. Investigators discovered that "In certain streets home work was almost a universal occupation, and when a new family moved into the district the children would take up the work either in imitation of their playmates or at the suggestion of their parents."[95] Homework did not necessarily interfere with schoolwork; children usually worked after school hours, Saturdays, and on vacation days.

The industrialized home forced reformers to reassess the meaning of domestic child labor. Tenement homework was condemned as a "peculiarly vicious" form of child labor.[96] After all, it polluted the one traditionally legitimate workplace. As one critic regretfully remarked: "Truly a noteworthy change from the time when children got a large part . . . of their education in domestic industries to the time when domestic industries must be abolished in order to save the children from exploitation in them!"[97] Yet what distinguished tenement homework from legitimate housework? At what point did work for a parent become exploitation? Parents themselves were considered unreliable judges: "It is obvious many parents know little of the nature of work needed by, or suited to, their children. It is still work because there is work to be done, not because certain selected work is educational."[98] George Hall, secretary of the New York Child Labor Committee, contended that " 'Helping mother' with house-work is all right, for the amount of work to be done is limited and there is little temptation to exploit the child; but 'helping mother' with paid work is another thing. The amount of work is unlimited, and ignorant and selfish parents sacrifice their children."[99]

The solution was not to remove all child work from the home, but to discriminate more intelligently among types of domestic employment. Taking factory work out of the home was only the first step. Equally important was to determine appropriate household tasks for children. As an article, significantly entitled "Ideal Child Labor in the Home," suggested: "The home will understand the educational necessity of work . . . and will allow each child . . . to contribute to the welfare of his family as a group and provide for his best development through the performance of a desirable amount of daily constructive work."[100] Fuller, for example, harshly criticized extreme parental dependence on children to do their housework. Yet he maintained with equal conviction that "Work can be . . . a good thing for children. Little girls helping their mothers with housework . . . sewing and cooking; boys raking leaves . . . these and many other kinds of home occupations are a delight to behold."[101] One progressive Birmingham school even introduced a parent's report card in order "to help the child by recognizing industry and excellence in home occupations."[102] Parents were asked to grade as satisfactory, excellent, fairly good, unsatisfactory, ordinary, or very poor a wide range of domestic activities performed by their children, such as garden work, care of household tools, care of furnace, making fires, care of horse or cow, sweeping and dusting, making beds, and general cooking.

House Chores and a Weekly Allowance: The Economic World of the Useless Child

By 1930, most children under fourteen were out of the labor market and into schools. Yet, significantly, federal regulation of child labor contained some exceptions. The most influential statute in the field of child labor, the Fair Labor Standards Act of 1938, allowed children under fourteen to work in newspaper distribution and in motion pictures and the theater. Except for manufacturing and mining, a child also remained legally entitled to work for her or his parents. Agricultural labor, which still employed the largest number of children, was only semiregulated as children were permitted to work outside of school hours. Similar exceptions were contained in the National Industrial Recovery Act industrial codes passed in 1933 but declared unconstitutional in 1935. The defeat of the Child Labor Amendment in the 1920s and again in the 1930s was partly the result of its failure to recognize any differentiation between children's occupations. By empowering Congress to "limit, regulate, and prohibit the labor of persons under eighteen years of age," the amendment presumably left no room even for legitimate child work.[103]

To be sure, the cultural and legal immunity of certain occupations was partly dictated by the market, in particular, the powerful farming, newspaper, and entertainment industries that had much to lose by a child work prohibition. But it was also based on a radically revised concept of child work. As twentieth-century American children became defined by their sentimental, noneconomic value, child work could no longer remain "real" work; it was only justifiable as a form of education or as sort of game. The useful labor of the nineteenth-century child was replaced by educational work for the useless child. While child labor had served the household economy, child work would benefit primarily the child: "We are interested . . . in work for the sake of the child, and are seeking to find kinds of work best suited to develop his body, mind and character."[104] The legal and cultural differentiation between legitimate and illegitimate occupations for children was thus guided by an entirely new set of criteria suitable for the unemployed "sacred" child. Labor on the home farm, for instance, was condoned "for the unselfishness and the sense of family solidarity it develops." Newspaper work was a legitimate "character-building" occupation. The Children's Bureau investigation in the 1920s found that parents of carriers were "emphatic in their approval of the work . . . because they believed that it provides training in the formation of good habits. . . . It was not the financial reason that stood out in their expressions of approval." Job advertisements for young carriers in the *Ladies' Home Journal* explained that the magazine had solved a problem for "thousands of the brightest boys in America," by providing them with an enjoyable pastime: "They get a lot of fun out of it, earn their own spending money, and get a moral and business training of inestimable value."[105] Acting, claimed its advocates, was not work at all but a liberal education and above all, a joyful child's game. "Work?" queried the *New York Dramatic Mirror*; "most child actors consider it play, and so it is practically that, except that their little minds are being unconsciously developed in a way which would be impossible elsewhere."[106]

As child work shifted from instrumental to instructional, special consideration was given to domestic chores. When an article appearing in *Home Progress* advised parents, "Let your children work," the work referred to "some little household task," not too difficult of course, "for their tender bodies."[107] Already in 1894, popular magazines alerted their middle- and upper-class readers about their children's "eagerness to seize opportunities for sharing the work as well as the play of the home. . . . Shelling peas on Monday because the cook is washing is to him as enchanting as counting pearls on a string."[108] As working-class children left the labor force for the classroom, their mothers were likewise instructed to keep them busy at home: "It is pitiful . . . for a woman to believe that she is 'bettering' her children by . . . allowing them to think that it is degrading for them to help in the housework."[109]

Yet the point was not to assist the mother, but to educate the child. In 1931, the Subcommittee on Housing and Home Management of the White House Conference on Child Health and Protection strongly recommended that "less emphasis . . . be placed on the amount of assistance rendered and more on the educational values [to the child] of the responsibilities involved in the performance of household tasks."[110] It was not always an easy task. As Dr. Amey E. Watson, an expert in household work, acknowledged: "For a busy mother . . . it is far easier to do the job herself than to stop to teach a child to do it; but if she has the long-range point of view and is thinking of the character development of the child, the work should be planned so that . . . the mother . . . can have enough leisure to stop and teach the child."[111]

House chores were therefore not intended to be "real" work, but lessons in helpfulness, order, and unselfishness. Parents were warned to "take great care not to overburden the child with responsibility . . . lest the weight of it should crush him instead of develop a greater strength."[112] Above all, warned *Parents* magazine, one should "never give . . . children cause to suspect us of making use of them to save ourselves work."[113] It was not easy to find such an ideal domestic job. As William Ogburn remarked in 1930, "The household duties are less, and hence the child loses the training and responsibilities that go with these duties."[114] A survey of junior high school students by the 1930 White House conference noted that urban children performed about three-fourths as many household tasks as did the rural child.[115] The "servant-keeping" class was particularly limited in this respect. One well-meaning parent, reported the *Journal of Home Economics*, had tried to teach her young child the "dignity of labor," but the only available job was flower arrangement. In another family, the son simply tipped the butler to do the boy's chores. The problem of unoccupied middle-class children was not new. As Mary Beth Norton notes in a study of eighteenth-century women, "City daughters from well-to-do homes were the only eighteenth-century American women who can accurately be described as leisured."[116] Yet even they did an extensive amount of sewing for their families. The new rules and problems of child work cut across classes, equally applicable to all unemployed children. For instance, in 1915, one observer had noted the extent to which parents of former child laborers were "entirely unprepared to cope with the situation, having little means of home employment for their children." The expanding school system attempted to incorporate "good" work into their curricula. As Edward T. Devine explained, "work which we deny . . . in the factory, for profit, may be demanded in school . . . for education and training."[117]

The transformation of children's economic roles during the first half of the twentieth century illustrates the interaction between economic and noneconomic factors in advanced industrial societies. Children were removed from the market between 1870 and 1930 in large part because it had become more economical and efficient to educate them than to hire them. But cultural guidelines profoundly shaped and directed the process of social change by differentiating legitimate from illegitimate occupations for children and distinguishing licit from illicit forms of child money. As children became increasingly defined as exclusively emotional and moral assets, their economic roles were not eliminated but transformed; child labor was replaced by child work and child wages with a weekly allowance. A child's new job and income were validated more by educational than economic criteria.

Notes

1. For child labor statistics: See *Children in Gainful Occupations at the Fourteenth Census of the United States* (Washington, D.C.: Government Printing Office, 1924); Grace Abbott, *The Child and the State* (Chicago: University of Chicago Press, 1938), 1:259–69; Raymond G. Fuller, "Child Labor," *International Encyclopedia of the Social Sciences* (1930), 412–24.

2. A. J. McKelway, "The Awakening of the South against Child Labor," *Proceedings of the Third Annual Conference on Child Labor* (New York, 1907), 17.

3. Josephine J. Eschenbrenner, *What Is a Child Worth?* National Child Labor Committee, no 236, p. 2.

4. Representative Sumners, cited in *American Child*, July 1924, 3.

5. Elizabeth Fraser, "Children and Work," *Saturday Evening Post*, April 4, 1925, 145.

6. Michael R. Haines, "Poverty, Economic Stress, and the Family in a Late Nineteenth-Century American City: Whites in Philadelphia, 1880," in *Philadelphia*, ed. Theodore Hershberg (Oxford: Oxford University Press, 1981), 265; Claudia Goldin, "Family Strategies and the Family Economy in the Late Nineteenth Century: The Role of Secondary Workers," ibid, in Hershberg, *Philadelphia*, 284.

7. Editorial, *Journal of Home Economics* 7 (August 1915): 371.

8. Daniel T. Rodgers, *The Work Ethic in Industrial America, 1850–1920* (Chicago: University of Chicago Press, 1978), 131.

9. John Demos, *A Little Commonwealth* (Oxford: Oxford University Press, 1972), 140–41. See also Edmund S. Morgan, *The Puritan Family* (New York: Harper and Row, 1966), 66.

10. *Report on Condition of Woman and Child Wage-Earners in the United States* (Washington, D.C., 1910–13), 6:48.

11. *Niles' Register*, October 5, 1816, cited by Edith Abbott, "A Study of the Early History of Child Labor in America," *American Journal of Sociology* 14 (July 1908): 25. See also *Woman and Child Wage-Earners*, 6:49, 52; Stanley Lebergott, *Manpower in Economic Growth* (New York: McGraw-Hill, 1964), 48–51; Robert H. Bremner, ed., *Children and Youth in America* (Cambridge: Harvard University Press, 1971), 1:145–48. On child labor in nineteenth-century England and France, see Lou-

ise A. Tilly and Joan W. Scott, *Women, Work, and Family* (New York: Holt, Rinehart and Winston, 1978). Employment in the early American mills apparently was not restricted to the children of the poor, but included the "children of farmers, mechanics, and manufacturers, in good pecuniary circumstances." Bagnall, *Samuel Slater and the Early Development of the Cotton Manufactures in the United States* (1890), cited by Forest Chester Ensign, "Compulsory School Attendance and Child Labor," Ph.D. diss., Columbia University, 1921.

12. Fuller, "Child Labor," 419; Bremner, *Children and Youth* 2:601.

13. John Modell, "Changing Risks, Changing Adaptations: American Families in the Nineteenth and Twentieth Centuries," in *Kin and Communities: Families in America*, ed. Allan J. Lichtman and John R. Challinor (Washington, D.C.: Smithsonian Institution Press, 1979), 128. On the importance of the family as a work unit in the early stages of industrialization, see Neil J. Smelser, *Social Change and the Industrial Revolution* (Chicago: University of Chicago Press, 1959). Michael Anderson, *Family Structure in Nineteenth-Century Lancashire* (Cambridge: Cambridge University Press, 1971) and Tamara Hareven, *Family Time and Industrial Time* (Cambridge: Cambridge University Press, 1982) demonstrate the survival of the family as a work unit in the nineteenth and even twentieth centuries.

14. Modell, "Changing Risks."

15. See "Child Labor and the Teachers," *New York Times*, July 8, 1905, 7, and Joseph M. Hawes, *Children in Urban Society* (Oxford: York: Oxford University Press, 1971).

16. Edwin Markham, "The Smoke of Sacrifice," *Cosmopolitan* (February 1907), 397. See Philip S. Foner, *Women and the American Labor Movement* (New York: Free Press, 1979), 283–89. For a history of the National Child Labor Committee, see Walter I. Trattner, *Crusade for the Children* (Chicago: Quadrangle Books, 1970), and for an excellent account of child labor reform in New York State, Jeremy Felt, *Hostages of Fortune* (Syracuse, N.Y.: Syracuse University Press, 1965).

17. On the effect of rising real income on the reduction of child labor, see Claudia Goldin, "Household and Market Production of Families in a Late Nineteenth Century American City," *Explorations in Economic History* 16 (1979): 129. On the development of child labor and compulsory school legislation, see Ensign, "Compulsory School Attendance," and Miriam E. Loughran, *The Historical Development of Child-Labor Legislation in the United States* (Washington, D.C.: Catholic University of America, 1921).

18. Paul Osterman, *Getting Started: The Youth Labor Market* (Cambridge: MIT Press, 1980), pp. 60–71. For additional economic explanations of the decline in child labor both in the United States and in nineteenth-century England, see Allen R. Sanderson, "Child Labor Legislation and the Labor Force Participation of Children," *Journal of Economic History* 34 (1974): 298–99, and Clark Nardinelli, "Child Labor and the Factory Acts," *Journal of Economic History* 40 (1980): 739–53.

19. *Niles' Register*, June 7, 1817, 226; Joan Huber, "Toward a Sociotechnological Theory of the Women's Movement," *Social Problems* 23 (1976): 371–88.

20. Osterman, *Getting Started*, 56–59; Selwyn K. Troen, "The Discovery of the Adolescent by American Educational Reformers, 1900–1920," in *Schooling and Society*, ed. Lawrence Stone (Baltimore: Johns Hopkins University Press, 1976), 239–51.

21. On early child labor legislation, see William F. Ogburn, *Progress and Uniformity in Child-Labor Legislation* (New York: Columbia University Press, 1912;

Loughran, *Historical Development Woman and Child Wage-Earners,* vol. 6; Elizabeth H. Davidson, *Child Labor Legislation in the Southern Textile States* (Chapel Hill: University of North Carolina Press, 1939).

22. Elizabeth Sands Johnson, "Child Labor Legislation," in *History of Labor in the United States, 1896–1932*, ed. John R. Commons (New York: Macmillan, 1935), 446. For an excellent interpretation of the legislative aspects of the child labor controversy, see Stephen B. Wood, *Constitutional Politics in the Progressive Era* (Chicago: University of Chicago Press, 1968) and Thomas George Karis, "Congressional Behavior at Constitutional Frontiers," Ph.D. diss., Columbia University, 1951.

23. Davidson, *Child Labor Legislation*, 57.

24. The Child Labor Amendment was also attacked as a Communist plot designed to nationalize American children. See Anne Kruesi Brown, "Opposition to the Child Labor Amendment Found in Trade Journals, Industrial Bulletins, and Other Publications for and By Business Men," M.A. diss., University of Chicago, 1937; Katharine DuPre Lumpkin and Dorothy Wolff Douglass, *Child Workers in America* (New York: Robert McBride, 1937), chap. 12, 13; "The Child Labor Amendment," *University of Texas Bulletin*, August 1, 1925; Tom Ireland, *Child Labor* (New York: G. P. Putnam's Sons, 1937).

25. Reprinted in *Charities* August 8, 1903, 130.

26. Fraser, "Children and Work," 146.

27. Iredell Meares, "Should the Nation Control Child Labor?" *Dearborn Independent*, November 8, 1924, reprinted in "The Child Labor Amendment," 146, 148.

28. Letter to the *New York Chamber of Commerce Bulletin* December 1924, 50, cited in Brown, *Opposition to Amendment*, 35–36.

29. Letter to the *Manufacturers Record*, October 9, 1924, 91 cited in Brown *Opposition to Amendment*, 34.

30. Mrs. William Lowell Putnam, "Why the Amendment Is Dangerous," *Woman Citizen*, December 27, 1924, 12; "The Twentieth Amendment," *Forum* 73 (February 1925): 281.

31. "What the Child Labor Amendment Means," in Abbott, *Child and State* 1:546; Lumpkin and Douglas, *Child Workers in America*, 219.

32. *Woman and Child Wage-Earners*, 7:43; Mary Skinner, *Child Labor in New Jersey*, U.S. Department of Labor, Children's Bureau Publication no. 185 (Washington, D.C., 1928).

33. Tamara K. Hareven, "Family and Work Patterns of Immigrant Laborers in a Planned Industrial Town, 1900–1930," in *Immigrants in Industrial America*, ed. Richard L. Ehrlich (Charlottesville: University Press of Virginia, 1977), 63. On the relative importance of class versus ethnicity in determining the use of child labor, see John Modell, "Patterns of Consumption, Acculturation, and Family Income Strategies in Late Nineteenth-Century America," in *Family and Population in Nineteenth-Century America*, ed. Tamara K. Hareven and Maris A. Vinovskis (Princeton: Princeton University Press, 1978); Goldin, "Household and Market Production"; and Miriam Cohen, "Changing Education Strategies among Immigrant Generations: New York Italians in Comparative Perspective," *Journal of Social History* 15 (1982): 443–66. Until the 1920s, black children were less likely to be employed in the labor market than were immigrant children. See Elizabeth Pleck, "A Mother's Wages: Income Earning among Married Italian and Black Women, 1896–1911," in *The Ameri-*

can Family in Social-Historical Perspective, ed. Michael Gordon, 2d ed. (New York: St. Martin's Press, 1978).

34. *Woman and Child Wage-Earners*, 7:158; Goldin, "Household and Market Production," 118–19.

35. Viola I. Paradise, *Child Labor and the Work of Mothers in Oyster and Shrimp Canning Communities on the Gulf Coast*, U.S. Department of Labor, Children's Bureau Publication no. 98 (Washington, D.C., 1922), 11, 17.

36. *Industrial Home Work of Children*, U.S. Department of Labor, Children's Bureau Publication no. 100 (Washington, D.C., 1924), 23.

37. "Child Labor, the Home, and Liberty," *New Republic*, December 3, 1924, 32.

38. *Woman and Child Wage-Earners*, 1:353.

39. Virginia Yans-McLaughlin, *Family and Community: Italian Immigrants in Buffalo, 1880–1930* (Ithaca, N.Y.: Cornell University Press, 1971), 193.

40. Johnson, "Child Labor Legislation" 429; Felt, *Hostages of Fortune*, 22–23.

41. *New York Times*, December 7, 1924, 19.

42. Cited in *The American Child*, April 1925, 6. Strong Catholic opposition to the Child Labor Amendment was also partly based on the perceived threat to parental authority. See Rev. Vincent A. McQuade, *The American Catholic Attitude on Child Labor since 1891* (Washington, D.C.: Catholic University of America, 1938).

43. J. W. Crabtree, "Dr. Pritchett, Dr. Butler, and Child Labor," *School and Society*, November 8, 1924, 585. Opponents of child labor invoked a variety of different arguments, from the physical and moral hazards of early employment to the economic inefficiency of employing young children. My discussion focuses on those arguments between the 1870s and 1930s, which centered on the changing definition of children's economic and sentimental value.

44. Quoted in *New York Times*, Feruary 2, 1925, 21.

45. Quoted in "The Nation and Child Labor," *New York Times*, April 24, 1904, 6.

46. Felix Adler, "Child Labor in the United States and Its Great Attendant Evils," *Annals of the American Academy of Political and Social Science* 25 (1905); Charles K. Gilbert, "The Church and Child Labor," *American Child* (August 1927), 4.

47. A. J. McKelway, "The Evil of Child Labor," *Outlook* February 16, 1907, 364.

48. Davidson, *Child Labor Legislation*, 65–66; Elinor H. Stoy, "Child-Labor," *Arena* December 1906, 586; "Education, Psychology, and Manufacturers," *American Child*, November 1926, 2.

49. Quoted in *New York Times*, February 2, 1925, 21.

50. "Potters' Clay," *American Child* January 1926, 3.

51. Marion Delcomyn, "Why Children Work," *Forum* 57 March 1917): 324–25.

52. Jacob Riis, "The Little Laborers of New York City," *Harper's New Monthly Magazine* August 1973, 327.

53. Letter to the editor, *New York Times*, November 4, 1910, 8.

54. Alice L. Woodbridge, "Child Labor an Obstacle to Industrial Progress," *Arena*, June 1894, 158.

55. Editorial, *New York Times*, December 17, 1902, 8.

56. Mrs. A. O. Granger, "The Work of the General Federation of Women's Clubs against Child Labor," *Annals of the American Academy of Political and Social Sciences* 25 (May 1905): 104; A. J. McKelway, "The Leadership of the Child," *Annals of the American Academy of Political and Social Science* 32 (July 1908): 21.

57. Quoted in Yans-McLaughlin, *Family and Community*, 190.

58. *The Cost of Child Labor*, National Child Labor Committee, no. 5 (New York, 1905), 35.

59. Edward T. Devine, "The New View of the Child," *Annals of the American Academy of Political and Social Sciences* 32 (1908): 9. Reformers, however, recognized the need to subsidize nonworking children in families that could prove their financial need. In 1905, child labor committees instituted a scholarship system in several cities to compensate needy families who kept a child in school, with a weekly payment equivalent to the child's fore gone income. Apparently, most scholarships went to the children of widowed or deserted women.

60. *Woman and Child Wage-Earners*, 7:15.

61. Raymond G. Fuller, "Child Labor versus Children's Work," *American Child*, February 1922, 281.

62. Theresa Wolfson, "Why, When, and How Children Leave School," *American Child*, May 1919, 61.

63. William Noyes, "Overwork, Idleness, or Industrial Education," *Annals of the American Academy of Political and Social Sciences* 27 (March 1906): 87. There was also a nostalgic recollection of apprenticeship as a lost form of "good" work.

64. Arthur D. Dean, "Child-Labor, or Work for Children," *Craftsman*, March 1914, 515.

65. Raymond G. Fuller, *Child Labor and the Constitution* (New York: Thomas Y. Crowell, 1923), 32.

66. Fuller, "Child Labor versus Children's Work," 281.

67. Fuller, *Child Labor and the Constitution*, 28.

68. *Illiteracy Promoted by Perjury*, National Child Labor Committee pamphlet no. 2 (New York, 1905), 7.

69. See Ogburn, Progress and Uniformity, 90, 103; "Child Labor," *White House Conference on Child Health and Protection* (New York: Century Co., 1932), 27–30; Johnson, "Child Labor Legislation," 413, 428–30.

70. Markham, "The Smoke of Sacrifice," 393.

71. Thomas R. Dawley, *The Child That Toileth Not* (New York: Gracia, 1912), 140. Dawley's argument had some precedent. In 1909, Dr. Charles W. Stiles, an authority in hookworm disease, announced that the health of children from poor farms significantly improved after working in cotton mills. See A. J. McKelway, "The Mill or the Farm?" *Annals of the American Academy of Politial and Social Sciences*, suppl. (March 1910): 52–57.

72. Reprinted in Abbott, *Child and State*, 474.

73. Wiley H. Swift, "Is the Use of Children in Agriculture a Child Welfare Problem?" *Proceedings of the National Conference of Social Work*, 1924, 170.

74. "Child Labor," *White House Conference*, 213. Protected by their rural location, canners of fruits and vegetables sought and often won exemptions from industrial child labor laws.

75. *Child Labor in North Dakota*, U.S. Children's Bureau Publication no. 129 (Washington, D.C., 1923), 21–25, 39.

76. Frances S. Bradley, M.D., and Margaretta A. Williamson, *Rural Children in Selected Counties of North Carolina*, U.S. Children's Bureau Publication no. 33 (Washington, D.C., 1918), 85, 88, 99.

77. E. C. Lindeman, "Child Labor Amendment and the Farmers," reprinted in "The Child Labor Amendment," *University of Texas Bulletin*, August 1, 1925, 87. For an overview of the studies of children employed in agriculture, see *White House Conference*, 222–61.

78. Fred S. Hall, *Forty Years 1902–1942: The Work of the New York Child Labor Committee* (New York: New York Child Labor Committee, 1942), 77.

79. Franklin N. Brewer, "Child Labor in the Department Store," *Annals of the American Academy of Political and Social Sciences* 20 (1902): 167–77.

80. Fuller, *Child Labor and the Constitution*, 76.

81. *White House Conference*, 147. On the regulation of street work, see pp. 164–68.

82. Edward N. Clopper, *Child Labor in City Streets* (1912; reprint New York: Garrett Press, 1970) 6–7.

83. Myron E. Adams, "Children in American Street Trades," *Annals of the American Academy of Political and Social Sciences* 25 (May 1905): 3.

84. *Survey*, June 14, 1913, 380.

85. Jacob A. Riis, *How the Other Half Lives* (1890; reprint New York: Dover, 1971), 153.

86. Clopper, *Child Labor in City Streets*, 7. Besides newspaper selling, other common street occupations for children included peddling, bootblacking, messenger service, delivery service, running errands, and the tending of market stands.

87. Nettie P. McGill, *Child Workers on City Streets*, U.S. Children's Bureau Publication no. 188 (Washington, D.C., 1928), 4.

88. Adams, "Children in American Street Trades," 11, 14.

89. Quoted in Clopper, *Child Labor in City Streets*, 15.

90. "Children in Gainful Occupations," Fourteenth Census (Washington, D.C., 1924), 53.

91. McGill, *Child Workers in City Streets*, 6–7, 36–37.

92. Charles W. Dabney, "Child Labor and the Public Schools," *Annals of the American Academy of Political and Social Sciences* 29 (January 1907): 112. See *White House Conference*, 128–39; "Children in Gainful Occupations," 52, 59. Most street regulations also fixed a higher minimum age for girls than for boys. Domestic and personal services were other predominantly female occupations.

93. "Children in Gainful Occupations," 16.

94. Hall, *Forty Years*, 89. No precise figures of the number of child home workers exist.

95. *Industrial Home Work of Children*, 22.

96. Fuller, *Child Labor and the Constitution*, 87.

97. Noyes, "Overwork."

98. Jessie P. Rich, "Ideal Child Labor in the Home," *Child Labor Bulletin* 3 (May 1914): 7.

99. George A. Hall, "Unrestricted Forms of Child Labor in New York State," *Proceedings of the Twelfth New York State Conference of Charities and Correction* (1911), 104.

100. Rich, "Ideal Child Labor," 8.

101. Fuller, *Child Labor and the Constitution*, 28.

102. *Journal of Education* 78 (October 2, 1913): 325.

103. See Jeremy Felt, "The Child Labor Provisions of the Fair Labor Standards Act," *Labor History* 11 (1970): 467–81; "Second Thought on the Child Labor Amendment," *Massachusetts Law Quarterly* 9 (July 1924): 15–21; "Comments," *Fordham Law Review* 7 (May 1938): 223–25; Brown, "Opposition to Amendment," 46–49.

104. Rich, "Ideal Child Labor," 4. Interestingly, two of the legitimate occupations employed middle-class children. Newspaper carriers, for instance, were likely to come from more prosperous families than city newsboys. Nettie P. McGill, *Children in Street Work*, U.S. Department of Labor, Children's Bureau Publication no. 183 (Washington, D.C., 1928), 38. Although information on the social class of child actors is limited, it appears that particularly in the twentieth century, acting involved middle-class as well as lower-class children. See Everett William Lord, *Children of the Stage* (New York: National Child Labor Committee, 1910); *What of the Stage Child?* (Minneapolis: Women's Cooperative Alliance, 1929).

105. McGill, *Child Workers on City Streets*, 37; "Your Boy's Christmas Money," *Ladies' Home Journal*, November 1, 1910, 1. The newspaper industry gladly encouraged the definition of newspaper work as education and not "real" labor.

106. John Mason, "The Education of the Stage Child," *New York Dramatic Mirror*, March 8, 1911, 5.

107. Lillian Davidson, "Idle Children," *Home Progress*, June 1917, 474.

108. Helen C. Candee, "In the Beginning," *Outlook*, May 5, 1894, 787.

109. Henriette E. Delamare, "Teaching Children to be Helpful at Home," *Home Progress*, November 1913, 115.

110. "The Home and the Child," *White House Conference on Child Health and Protection*, 1931 (New York: Arno Press and New York Times, 1972), 90.

111. Amey E. Watson, "The Reorganization of Household Work," *Annals of the American Academy of Political and Social Sciences* 160 (March 1932): 174.

112. Miriam Finn Scott, "The Perfect Child," *Ladies' Home Journal*, June 1922, 30.

113. Ethel Packard Cook, "All Hands Help," *Parents Magazine*, July 1934, 19.

114. William F. Ogburn, "The Changing Family with Regard to the Child," *Annals of the American Academy of Political and Social Sciences* 151 (September 1930):23.

115. "The Adolescent in the Family," *White House Conference on Child Health and Protection*, 1934 (New York: Arno Press and New York Times, 1972), 37.

116. Mary Beth Norton, *Liberty's Daughters* (Boston: Little, Brown, 1980), 23–24. See Thomas D. Elliot, "Money and the Child's Own Standards of Living," *Journal of Home Economics* 24 (January 1932): 4–5.

117. Devine, "New View," 9. See editorial, *Journal of Home Economics* 7 (August 1915): 372. On the development of industrial education in the early decades of the twentieth century, see Marvin Lazerson and W. Norton Grubb, *American Education and Vocationalism* (New York: Teachers College Press, 1974).

Chapter 6

THE SOCIAL CONSTRUCTION OF ORGANIZATIONS AND MARKETS: THE COMPARATIVE ANALYSIS OF BUSINESS RECIPES

RICHARD WHITLEY

THE SOCIALLY CONSTRUCTED nature of business enterprises as systems of coordination and control of economic activities seems self-evident to most social scientists in the same way that other social institutions and collectivities are socially constituted and variable. However, one corollary of this view, that the nature of firms—or economic actors (Whitley 1987)—and successful ways of managing businesses in market economies vary significantly between societies is less widely accepted. While the socially constructed nature of social phenomena usually implies that their nature and operation depend on conventions and beliefs which often differ significantly between societies, many studies of business structures and practices continue to search for universal rules governing administrative structures and growth.

Some claim, for instance, that there are general relations between dimensions of organizational structure which hold for all successful businesses across all environments (for example, Hickson et al. 1974, 1979) and so are "culture-free" (cf. Child 1987). Others suggest that the patterns of growth and change found among successful large businesses in the United States by Chandler (1962, 1977) reflect general processes of economic development which occur in all industrialized societies, and so should be repeated in other countries, despite considerable evidence to the contrary (for example, Alford 1976; Lane 1989; Lévy-Leboyer 1980). A third group, advocates of the "new institutional economics," hypostatize a universal economic logic which determines the choice of institutional systems for organizing economic transactions, and therefore the existence of large managerial bureaucracies in different industries (for example, Daems 1983; Williamson 1985). All presume that inexorable market pressures generate identical, or very similar, forms of business organization and development across social contexts irrespective of institutional differences.

These assertions of a single economic logic governing the development of effective managerial structures and practices in all situations have, of course, been extensively criticized on both conceptual and empirical grounds (for example, Brossard and Maurice 1976; Granovetter 1985; Sorge 1983). However, some of these criticisms have tended to assume an equally extreme position of cultural relativism, almost implying that since all business systems are social constructions, they are necessarily unique to different societies, which, in turn, suggests they cannot be systematically compared (cf. Rose 1985). While such an extreme culturally determinist view is unsustainable for many of the same reasons that render Winch's (1970) anthropological relativism incoherent (see Bhaskar 1979, 170–79; Gellner 1968), it does highlight the inadequacies of simple generalization of one pattern of business development in one society to all societies, just as reliance on the British industrial revolution as *the* model for industrialization has proved misplaced.

The differences between these views lie as much in the significance they attribute to the socially constructed nature of business organizations as in their acceptance or denial of its validity. While economic rationalists may accept that firms are complex social organizations whose constitution and activities reflect the conceptions and values of owners and/or their agents as well as employees, they consider competitive pressures to be so strong that efficient forms of business organization and "rational" strategic choices quickly dominate all market economies whatever cultural and institutional variations may exist between them. Thus differences between owners' and managers' beliefs and preferences are essentially irrelevant to economic outcomes in this view because all competing firms are constrained to follow the logic of efficient market processes.

Conversely, cultural relativists regard differences in social conventions, rationalities, and moral codes to be so important across societies as to generate highly distinctive forms of business organization and practice which are specific to their context and cannot be readily transferred. Because enterprises are socially constructed, in this view their actions and procedures reflect the beliefs of those in control so that efficient business practices are culturally variable and specific. What constitutes economic efficiency is here seen as being socially determined and contextual.

This contrast of perspectives raises a number of general conceptual issues in the analysis of economic relations and business structures which will now be discussed. They support the general conclusion that variations in economic agents' beliefs and rationalities do necessarily affect economic outcomes. However, the extent to which, and ways in which, dominant social institutions generate sharply distinct forms of business organization vary empirically and there is no overwhelming reason to presume that each "culture" possesses a unique business system.

The Significance of the Social Construction of Business Systems

Considering first the view that there is a single dominant economic rationality which renders differences in beliefs and preferences essentially irrelevant to effective management structures and practices, this fails to take account of the variety of institutional environments which firms have to deal with and manage. These variations affect "efficient" firms' structures and choices. Major differences in the financial systems of European countries, for example, affect relationships between banks and industrial companies and the management of financial risks to the extent that strategic priorities and the significance of financial skills differ considerably between major enterprises in these societies (Lane 1989; Zysman 1983). Thus "efficient" firms in Britain have to adapt to the more active "market for corporate control" (Lawriwsky 1984) and separation of financial institutions from industry (Ingham 1984) in ways that do not apply to firms on the European continent operating within credit-based financial systems. Successful forms of business organization develop interdependently with dominant social institutions and therefore differ significantly where these do. Because business environments vary in many important respects, so too do "efficient" management structures and practices. This means that the contrast between technical and institutional sectors drawn by Meyer and Scott (1983, 140–41) in their analysis of organizational isomorphism is misleading since market efficiency is institutionally constructed (cf. Orru, Biggart, and Hamilton 1988).

Second, the socially constructed nature of firms and markets implies that they are meaningful entities whose nature and operation vary according to differences in meaning systems and dominant rationalities. Thus, the "rules of the game" in competitive markets can and do vary considerably between societal contexts as priorities and dominant conceptions of appropriate forms of economic competition within and between countries differ. Changes in these conceptions and priorities imply changes in market processes, so that what constitutes "rational" economic action also alters, as when the postwar French state sharply changed its role in directing economic development and its attitudes towards international competition. Thus, as institutional views about economic phenomena differ and change, so too do market structures and imperatives. The socially constructed nature of business systems, then, implies that economic rationalities are culturally relative and variable.

Third, since market outcomes are the result of interdependent firms' actions, and since knowledge is always imperfect (Richardson 1960), how major firms make decisions is both economically significant and a matter of judgments and beliefs. The pervasiveness of uncertainty and disequilibrium in market economies means that there is no way of knowing how to make "rational" choices, so economic actors are forced to rely on their necessarily limited and idiosyncratic understanding of market processes. Differences in these understandings generate a variety of economic outcomes since firms' actions are interdependent and so economic efficiency and success can only be discerned *post factum* and are dependent on agents' rationalities. Thus, where dominant managerial beliefs and preferences change, so too will the results of particular strategies and actions. What constitutes a successful strategy and form of business organization varies, then, according to the context and cannot be reduced to a single logic which will "work" in all circumstances.

Fourth, and relatedly, because markets, like all social systems, are essentially "open," they do not generate stable conjunctions of events which are invariant over environmental changes. Open systems in this sense are those in which endogenous changes in the states of system components, and changes in the relations between these components and external phenomena, result in changes in the ways that systems behave (Bhaskar 1979; Sayer 1984). Since people, and collective social entities, learn and change their beliefs, assumptions, and priorities as a result of both internal developments and external changes, social systems do not function as closed deterministic structures. As a result, decisions and practices which were successful in one situation may not be so effective in others, and managerial rationalities which "worked" in one historical period may fail in later ones as participants learn and develop. Thus macroeconomic policies which achieved the desired effect in one situation may generate different outcomes if major economic actors develop different views about their significance and implications, as in the use of interest rates to control inflation.

Together, these points suggest that the socially constructed nature of business systems has significant implications for the analysis of effective managerial structures and practices. In particular, variations in major economic agents' beliefs and rationalities affect economic outcomes and the nature of competitive efficiency. Just as the nature and development of scientific knowledge depend on the institutionalized conventions and practices of those who dominate the research system in our society (Bloor 1976; Whitley 1984), so too the establishment and success of particular forms of business organization depend on the ways in which controllers of economic resources understand and evaluate the world. The lack of any overriding and universally valid epistemological theory of scientific progress which could justify and explain scientists' judgments as necessarily "rational" (Feyerabend 1981) is echoed by the lack of any single economic logic which determines business success. The social construction of business structures and practices means that not only are they the product of collective beliefs, conventions and moral codes which vary between societies, but also the nature of economic success and ways of achieving it are dependent on dominant conceptions of economic practices and rationalities. Where these differ considerably, as they do between many European and East Asian countries, so too do dominant firms' goals and strategic choices (Bauer and Cohen 1981; Kagono et al. 1985; Silin 1976).

For example, many of the contrasts between Japanese and U.S. large firms stem from the quite different logics—or rules of the game—that major economic actors follow in the two societies as a result of considerable differences in their institutional environments, particularly the role of the state (Johnson 1982). In the recent past, the "Japanese logic" seems to be more successful in many international markets, but this does not mean it always will be. Just as the historical success of the large, integrated, and diversified U.S. corporation through much of the twentieth century has been historically specific, so too is that of the Japanese "specialized clan" (Clark 1979). As other logics develop in different societal contexts the overall "rules of the game" of international economic competition will alter, and there is no overriding reason to expect the currently successful Japanese form of business organization to continue to dominate indefinitely. Economic outcomes, like scientific ones, depend on the beliefs, priorities, and actions of economic agents rather than some inexorable universal logic which inevitably leads to "progress." Thus, how particular kinds of economic actors come to control resources, and how they understand "what is going on" (Taylor 1985), affect business practices and economic outcomes to the extent that different groups of resource controllers following different logics and priorities generate different results. The socially constructed nature of economic action, then, implies that the way managers and owners think and act structures not only the organizations and resources they control, but also the nature of competitive processes and their outcomes. What is successful in one particular situation and context may not be in another, different one, and so particular "recipes" for business success which are effective in one context are not necessarily valid across societies or over historical periods.

Once it is agreed that participants' beliefs and practices do have significant consequences for economic outcomes and the nature of economically successful business structures, a number of consequences follow. First, the processes by which different economic rationalities develop and become established in different societies are important influences on business behavior and success. Second, the more these vary and remain distinctive, the more varied will successful forms of business organization be, and the less likely is it that any single pattern will dominate world markets. Third, the more varied and distinct are dominant business structures and practices in different societal contexts, the more difficult will it be to transfer successful techniques and strategies across these contexts. Fourth, as dominant economic rationalities develop and change, so too do market processes and the competitive "rules of the game." Successful business "recipes" therefore may cease to be effective. Indeed, this decline in effectiveness of particular structures and practices may, in part, be the result of their earlier success as other economic actors learn from it and adopt new forms and logics to deal with it. Just as useful social theories and policy instruments can change the reality they purport to explain and influence, and thus alter the grounds of their validity and utility, so too effective ways of organizing and directing economic activities can generate new responses and rationalities which together so alter the system as a whole that they become ineffective (see Taylor 1985).

These consequences in turn suggest that the study of organizations and business systems should focus more on how different ways of organizing economic activities become established and effective in different societal contexts than on searching for universally valid logics of economic action or general structural correlations. The lack of a single dominant logic governing economic outcomes in market systems means that the processes by which particular structures and practices become established and successful in particular societal contexts require analysis, as do the ways in which they change and develop. Once the existence of a universal economic rationality is denied and economic success understood as a contingent, changing phenomenon that varies according to context, it becomes important to explain differences in the relative success of different forms of business organization and sets of practices.

A major part of this analysis and explanation concerns the emergence of distinctive "business recipes" in various institutional environments whose success is linked to particular features of dominant social institutions. These business recipes, or systems, are particular ways of organizing, controlling, and directing business enterprises that become established as the dominant forms of business organization in different societies. They reflect successful patterns of business behavior and understandings of how to achieve economic success that are reproduced and reinforced by crucial institutions. While they vary in the degree to which they differ across institutional environments, and in their internal consistency and integration, the essential point is that business recipes institutionalize different economic rationalities which "work" in particular circumstances.

In suggesting that the comparative analysis of the development, reproduction, and change of business recipes is central to the study of business structures and practices, I am proposing that we should take the social construction of economic phenomena and relations seriously and follow its implications. Thus, acceptance of the economic significance of agents' rationalities—or ways of understanding, evaluating, and acting in the world—requires examination of how such rationalities become established and dominant in different situations, especially between societies. Because they "make a difference" to economic outcomes, and hence to effective managerial systems and practices, these rationalities are important phenomena whose operation and change it is crucial to understand. This is not to say that they constitute homogeneous national recipes which are culturally determined and immune to external influences. The extent to which distinctive business recipes are nationally homogeneous and stable depends on their institutional environments and the distinctive nature of dominant national institutions. It is to emphasize, though, that successful forms of business organization and practices reflect the circumstances in which they developed and cannot be simply transferred to qualitatively different environments. As meaningful social phenomena, business systems exhibit internal relationships with major social institutions such that if these latter change, so too do effective business practices. The comparative analysis of business recipes is therefore concerned with the plurality of effective business practices in different contexts, their establishment, development, and change, as a key component of the social study of business systems in market economies.

This analysis is similar in certain respects to the study of organizational isomorphism developed in the "institutional" school of organizational analysis (for example, DiMaggio and Powell 1983; Meyer and Scott 1983; Scott, 1987; Zucker 1987). In this approach, organizations in the same sector of society are seen as adopting similar forms and practices as a result of institutionalized conventions and "rules of the game." Just as Stinchcombe (1965) suggested that organizations follow the dominant pattern established when an industry first developed, the institutionalists argue that schools, public television stations, hospitals, and other organizations in the United States follow the pattern set by the most successful and legitimate organization in their particular field to demonstrate their correctness and modernity. This mimetic isomorphism is considered especially strong in fields where the standards of organizational success and effectiveness are ambiguous (DiMaggio and Powell 1983), although Fligstein (1985) has discussed the spread of the multidivisional corporate form in similar terms.

Most of the organizations studied by the institutionalists have been non-profit-making, and there has been a tendency to regard isomorphism among privately owned businesses as primarily technical and competitive in nature rather than "institutional" (Meyer and Rowan 1977). This is despite the general assumption that powerful economic agents' beliefs and conceptions affect organization structures and practices (Scott 1987). Indeed, some proponents of the institutionalist approach suggest that the search for institutional legitimacy and imitation of fashionable procedures necessarily lead to technical inefficiency, even though the nature of "efficiency" is clearly institutionally dependent, as argued above (cf. Meyer and Rowan 1977; Zucker 1987).

The comparative analysis of business structures and practices proposed here shares the institutionalists' view that integrated and strong institutional environments encourage isomorphism between organization structures and practices, so that differences between these environments lead to differences in organizational forms. Rather than drawing a distinction between technical and institutional isomorphism, though, it focuses on the ways that different institutional environments generate different kinds of technically efficient business recipes so that equally effective forms of business organization become similar within them but quite different between them. Social institutions, in this view, are key phenomena in the constitution of different competitive orders and should not be counterposed to market efficiency (cf. Orru, Biggart, and Hamilton 1988).

The Nature of Business Recipes

In advocating a comparative analysis of successful ways of organizing economic activities, more than the cross-national study of micro-organizational phenomena is being proposed. In addition to this recognition of the national variability of many attitudinal and similar phenomena, it is important to be aware of the differences in what Richardson (1972) has called the "organization of industry" between institutional contexts. These variations concern patterns of relations between firms and the extent to which they specialize in particular competences and activities. They thus focus on differences in market organization and the relations between markets and hierarchies in different contexts. As Imai and Itami (1984) have emphasized, there are considerable differences between Japanese and U.S. firms in terms of both their internal structures and their interconnections in variously organized markets. These differences arise from the particular institutional environments in which successful firms developed.

Variations in market organization between institutional contexts have important implications for the nature of firms and their internal organization. Differences in the scope and intensity of connections between firms are related to differences in the sorts of activities they coordinate and their competitive strategies. The widespread use of "relational contracting" between Japanese companies, and their common membership of intermarket business groups which exchange information and resources (Clark 1979; Dore 1986; Futatsugi 1986), for example, enable them to specialize in particular activities and competitive capacities at lower risk levels than could firms in Anglo-Saxon societies (see Yoshino and Lifson 1986, 37–50). The nature of firms as authoritative coordinators of economic activities, then, is interdependent with the ways in which they are organized as "industries" and are embedded in reciprocal obligation networks which vary across institutional environments. These variations are also related to differences in authority structures and control systems, as the example of Japanese employment practices and employer-employee commitment indicates (Clark 1979, 221–22). Indeed, the dominant pattern of authoritative coordination and control in different business recipes is not, I suggest, fully comprehensible without considering how firms developed as particular economic decision-making units and their connections with business partners and competitors.

Distinctive business recipes, then, are particular arrangements of hierarchy-market relations which become institutionalized and relatively successful in particular contexts. They combine preferences for particular kinds of activities and skills to be coordinated authoritatively with differences in the discretion of managers from property rights holders and in the ways in which activities are coordinated, and also exhibit variations in the extent and manner in which activities are coordinated between economic actors. Thus the nature of firms as quasi-autonomous economic actors, their internal structures, and their interdependences are all interrelated and differ significantly between institutional contexts.

The comparative study of business recipes therefore involves consideration of how "firms" are constituted as relatively discrete economic actors in different market societies. While all market-based economic systems decentralize control over human and material resources to property rights owners and their agents, the nature of the collective entities that exercise that control, and how they do so, vary considerably, and so what a "firm" is differs across societal contexts. In particular, it is clearly misleading to rely on purely legal definitions of firms' boundaries and activities if we are concerned to explore their role as economic decision-making units. Not only are French industrial groups often much more important than their constituent firms in making strategic choices (Bauer and Cohen 1981), but among the expatriate Chinese it is clear that the key decision unit is the family business rather than the often numerous legally defined "firms" controlled by family heads (Tam 1990; Wong 1985). These differences are important features of distinctive business recipes which are linked to the institutional environments in which they develop and emphasize the contextual nature of "firms" as economic agents.

The variability of economic agents between societies and the different roles of legally defined firms mean that comparisons of business recipes cannot rely on purely formal means of identifying key units of economic action. Similarly, the importance of business groups and networks of relationships between ostensibly independent firms in many countries, especially East Asian ones (Hamilton, Zeile, and Kim 1990), raises questions about how economic agents are to be identified for comparative purposes. If business recipes vary in how they constitute firms as units of economic action, in other words, how are we to compare and contrast them in a systematic way? The critical point here, it should be noted, is not so much what "firms" really are as how we are to conceive of the critical economic agents in market societies so that we can compare them and explain their differences. This obviously depends on our view of how firms and markets function.

Firms are important economic agents in market societies because they, or their controllers, exercise considerable discretion over the acquisition, use, and disposition of human and material resources. They function as economic actors by integrating, coordinating, and controlling resources through an authority system, and it is this authoritative direction of economic activities which is their central characteristic. Authority relations provide the basis for continued and systematic coordination of activities and thus the integrated transformation of resources into productive services (Penrose 1980; 15–25; Whitley 1987). It is through this system that firms "add value" to resources and function as relatively separate units of economic decision-making. Although the degree of central direction of economic activities does, of course, vary, as does the primary basis of authority relations, it is this coordinated control of a varied set of resources which distinguishes firms as distinct economic agents from cooperative networks and ad hoc alliances. Thus, Taiwanese business groups consisting of informal networks between family firms based on kinship connections, joint ventures, financial assistance, and so on, do not constitute the primary units of economic action in this view because they are better regarded as informal coalitions of partnerships than as authoritatively integrated managerial hierarchies (Hamilton and Kao 1990; Hamilton, Zeile, and Kim 1990; Numazaki 1987, 1989). Because each family business retains considerable freedom of action and remains the primary locus of authoritative decision-making and control in Taiwan, it is the family firm that functions as the dominant economic agent there, rather than the business group.

The importance of the highly personal, particularistic, and diffuse ties between family firms in Taiwan, Hong Kong, and other Chinese business communities, as well as the long-term alliances between Japanese companies (Futatsugi 1986; Goto 1982), demonstrate the variable nature of market relationships and the limited generality of the Anglo-Saxon model of firms and markets. It is particularly important to note here that the nature of interfirm connections and market organization is closely linked to the nature of firms as economic actors in these societies and to key features of their "internal" organization and management practices. Distinctive configurations of these interrelated characteristics have become established as separate business recipes in East Asian societies (Whitley 1990). While not all societies institutionalize such different and integrated business recipes, variations in how firms are constituted are usually connected to differences in market organization, and in their authority structures and procedures, to form identifiable and distinct configurations. To illustrate these points, the major distinguishing characteristics of the dominant business recipes in Japan, South Korea, Taiwan, and Hong Kong will now be summarized.

These characteristics can usefully be described under three broad headings derived from the major components of hierarchy-market configurations: the constitution of firms as economic actors, their interconnections in markets, and their internal systems of authoritative coordination and control. First, the nature of the firm as the unit of authoritative coordination of economic activities has two key features. The variety of the activities and skills being coordinated through authority hierarchies, and thus the extent to which firms specialize in their competitive competences and capabilities (see Richardson 1972), differs considerably between East Asian societies. Relatedly, the dominant pattern of strategic choices and growth also varies in terms of firms' willingness to make discontinuous changes in the nature of the activities and resources they control.

The second area concerns market organization. This refers to the importance of long-term connections between firms and preferences for dealing with particular suppliers and customers, as opposed to engaging in impersonal, ad hoc, spot market contracting. It also incorporates the extent to which the activities of firms in different sectors are coordinated through alliances and membership of intermarket business groups or through state agencies. The third area focuses on the coordination and control systems of firms, which can be divided into four major characteristics. Perhaps the most significant in East Asia is the importance of personal ownership and authority. Next, there are considerable differences in the reliance placed on formal coordination and control systems. This, in turn, is related to the dominant managerial style in these firms and, in particular, to whether managers are closely involved in the work of the group and are responsible for maintaining high levels of group morale. Finally, the type and degree of mutual employer-employee commitment and loyalty clearly varies between these business recipes.

The particular configurations of hierarchy-market relations which have become established and successful in Japan, South Korea, Taiwan, and Hong Kong since the Second World War are sufficiently homogeneous within these societies and distinctive between them to be characterized as separate business recipes (Hamilton and Biggart 1988; Hamilton, Zeile, and Kim 1990). In Japan the broad features of the large corporation, or *kaisha*, have been described by Abegglen and Stalk (1985) and Clark (1979) among many others, and it can be termed the specialized clan. In South Korea there is little doubt that the enormous family controlled conglomerates, or *chaebol*, dominate the economy (Amsden 1989; Yoo and Lee 1987). In Taiwan and Hong Kong, the primary unit of economic action in competitive markets is the Chinese family business (CFB), which is also an important form of business organization throughout Southeast Asia (Redding 1990; Silin 1976).

Considering first the nature of firms as economic actors, the variety of economic activities coordinated through authority hierarchies in the Japanese *kaisha* and the CFB is much less than in the Korean *chaebol* (Amsden 1989; Clark 1979, 62–64; Cusumano 1985, 186–93; Tam 1990; Zeile 1989). Japanese and Chinese businesses tend to restrict themselves to activities in which their specialized skills and knowledge provide distinctive capabilities and competitive advantages, and then rely on market contracting to coordinate complementary but dissimilar activities. While most of the Korean *chaebol* are vertically integrated, centrally controlling a variety of functions and activities through managerial hierarchies, Japanese and Chinese firms concentrate on specialized stages of production and are less managerially self-sufficient (Orru et al. 1988). When firms do extend their activities into new industries in Japan, they tend to separate them as distinct entities with their own access to financial resources and enterprise union as soon as they are successful (Clark 1979, 60–62; Dore 1986, 61–63).

Business specialization in Japan is reflected in relatively low rates of unrelated diversification and preferences for evolutionary growth strategies based on existing resources and capabilities rather than discontinuous ones (Kagono et al. 1985, 55–87; Kono 1984, 78–80). The CFB combines growth through the expansion of current activities and capabilities with opportunistic diversification through partnerships and family controlled subsidiaries (Limlingan 1986; Hamilton and Kao 1990). The Korean *chaebol* have grown through vertical integration and state-directed diversification into heavy industry, as well as initiating successful moves into new industries such as construction and financial services (Amsden 1989; Jones and Sakong 1980). While both the Japanese and Chinese tendency to managerial specialization involves the risk of being committed to a declining industry and expertise, their responses to this risk differ. The former rely on high levels of employee commitment and flexibility, together with extensive sharing of risks with subcontractors and members of business groups. The Chinese, on the other hand, limit their commitment to a particular industry by remaining relatively small and relying on elaborate networks of mutual obligations with employees, suppliers, and agents. These obligations are based on personal knowledge and reputations but remain limited and highly flexible (Tam 1990).

Considerable differences also occur in the degree and type of market organization in these countries. High levels of business specialization in Japan, Taiwan, and Hong Kong obviously imply high levels of dependence on purchasing agents, component suppliers, and distributors, but the nature of these contractual linkages vary. They tend to be more stable and involve more extensive sharing of information and skills in Japan than in Taiwan and Hong Kong, reflecting higher levels of trust and, sometimes, reciprocal shareholdings. Generally, Japanese firms are embedded in extensive networks of "relational contracting" (Dore 1986, 77–83), while the CFB tend to be more opportunistic and less exclusively tied to particular business partners, though relying heavily on personal contacts and trust (Numazaki 1986, 1989).

The extent of coordination of economic activities between sectors also varies between these three business recipes. Many large Japanese firms have long-term links with companies in other industries and with banks and insurance companies, which include mutual shareholdings, weekly or monthly "presidents' club" meetings, the exchange of senior managerial personnel, and mutual support when under severe threats (Futatsugi 1986; Goto 1982; Hamilton et al. 1990; Miyazaki 1980). These business groups are not as hierarchically structured or integrated as the prewar *zaibatsu* and appear to function more as informal support groups, pooling information and expertise on an ad hoc basis (Dore 1986, 79–80; Kiyonari and Nakamura 1980). Korean *chaebol* are much less directly interconnected, but are liable to coordination by state agencies and political alliances (Kim 1979). Taiwanese business groups are less significant and less institutionalized than Japanese ones (Hamilton and Kao 1990; Hamilton, Zeile and Kim 1990). Intermarket linkages in the CFB are essentially family, or "family type," connections and so are highly personal and more varied than those between members of Japanese business groups.

Turning now to consider the "internal" authority structures of these firms, large Japanese enterprises manifest less centralization of decision making and initiation of plans than Korean *chaebol* or the CFB (Kagono et al. 1985, 42–43; Liebenberg 1982; Rohlen 1974). This is linked to their less personal and more collective authority system, which in turn is tied to their strong separation of ownership from control (Abegglen and Stalk 1985, 177; Aoki 1987; Dore 1986, 67–72). In contrast, the association of personal authority with ownership is a key characteristic of *chaebol* and the CFB (Orru, Biggart, and Hamilton 1988; Silin 1976). Loyalties and obedience are focused more on the individual owner than on the collective enterprise in the latter two recipes. The importance of personal relations in Korea and Taiwan is highlighted by the extensive use of relatives and others with strong personal ties to the owner in senior management positions (Shin and Chin 1989; Yoo and Lee 1987).

Japanese companies also exhibit considerably greater formalization of procedures and rules (Pugh and Redding 1985), though the existence of elaborate formal rules does not mean they always govern work activities (Lincoln, Harada, and McBride 1986; Rohlen 1974). In general, they appear more formally "bureaucratic" than their Korean and Chinese counterparts, where procedures and formal structures are often bypassed and ignored (Silin 1976). Dominant images of managerial authority and appropriate ways of demonstrating managerial competence also differ in that Japanese managers are not expected to demonstrate omniscience and omnipotence, nor to be remote and aloof from subordinates (Clark 1979; Rohlen 1974; Smith and Misumi 1989). Chinese owner-managers, on the other hand, are expected to reflect Confucian norms of those in authority and demonstrate their moral superiority by being reserved and dignified and by not revealing their emotions (Silin 1976). While Japanese managers are responsible for group morale and facilitating group achievements, Korean and Chinese managers follow a more directive style with little or no attempt to explain decisions, let alone justify them (Liebenberg 1982; Redding and Richardson 1986; Redding and Wong 1986).

All these "recipes" have different employment policies for different groups of workers, and reserve long-term commitments, seniority-linked reward systems, and extensive bonuses for the core group of employees. However, the extent of such long-term commitment and employee loyalty does vary between Japan, Korea, and the CFB, with higher labor turnover being found in Korean companies than in Japan or Taiwan (Amsden 1985; Michell 1988) and loyalties being less "emotional" and intense in large Taiwanese firms than in Japanese ones (Silin 1976, 127–31). As might be expected, given the more personal nature of authority in Korean and Chinese businesses, long-term commitments and employment policies designed to elicit loyalty are less institutionalized in these firms than in successful Japanese ones and are more dependent on the personal choice of the owner. According to Clark (1979, 64–73), movement up the "hierarchy of industry" in Japan is signaled by the adoption of such policies, partly to attract high-quality graduates and partly to advertise success. These differences between the three East Asian business recipes are summarized in table 6.1.

Business Recipes and Institutional Environments

The comparative analysis of business recipes presumes that distinctive ways of organizing economic activities become established and effective because of major differences in key social institutions, such as the state, the financial system, and the education and training system (Maurice, Sorge, and Warner, 1980; Maurice, Sellier, and Silvestre 1986). However, the distinctiveness and homogeneity of successful recipes clearly varies between societies, as does their institutional specificity. Those prevalent in East Asian countries, for instance, seem more different from each other and more homogeneous within each society than those apparent in Western European and North American nations, where variations between industries seem to be significant (Spender 1989). Thus, authority relations and structures within firms differ considerably between Japan, Korea, and Taiwan, while those in most large Western firms share a common reliance on legal-rational norms and bases of legitimacy. Similarly, the prevalence of capital market based financial systems and reliance on "professional" modes of skill development and organization in Anglo-Saxon societies, means that dominant business recipes in Britain and the United States seem to share a preference for financial means of control of operations and subsidiaries, and accord the finance function higher status than many continental European firms (Granick 1972; Horovitz 1980; Lawrence 1980). As a result, some features of particular recipes such as financial control techniques, may be readily transferred between particular contexts, such as Anglo-Saxon societies, while others require substantial modification and "translation."

The distinctiveness of business recipes, then, depends on the integrated and separate nature of the contexts in which they developed. The more that major social institutions, such as the political and financial systems, the organization of labor markets and educational institutions, form distinctive and

TABLE 6.1
East Asian Business Recipes

Characteristics	Japanese Specialized Clan	Korean Chaebol	Chinese Family Business
Nature of firms			
Business specialization	High	Low	High within managerial hierarchies, medium to low across family business groups
Growth patterns	Evolutionary	Opportunistic, discontinuous	Volume expansion and opportunistic diversification
Market Organization			
Relational contracting	High	Low	Medium
Intersector coordination	High, through business groups and state	Low, except through state	Medium, through personal alliances
Authority coordination			
Significance of personal authority and ownership	Low	High	High
Significance of formal procedures	High	Medium	Low
Managerial style	Facilitative	Directive	Didactic
Employee commitment	Emotional	Conditional	Conditional

cohesive configurations, the more dominant business recipes in those social systems will be different and separate. Where distinctive cultural systems and socialization patterns overlap with national boundaries, and state institutions are also distinctive and closely involved in economic development, we would expect successful firms to share major characteristics which differ significantly from those of dominant economic actors in different contexts.

Where, on the other hand, major social institutions are more differentiated and plural in a society, business recipes are likely to be more varied and not so sharply distinct from those elsewhere. Thus, the strong state commitment to the defense industries in Britain and the United States, in contrast to a more laissez-faire attitude to other ones, can be expected to affect attitudes to long-term investments as well as the composition of the dominant coalitions of firms across industries. Similarly, strong regional variations in the pattern of industrialization coupled with considerable local political and financial autonomy can generate quite distinct business recipes within a country, as in the case of Italy. Here, the industrial districts of northeast and central Italy have developed successful systems of subcontracting and highly decentralized production units, which contrast strongly with the predominance of large integrated businesses in northwest Italy (Bamford 1987; Lazerson 1988).

This contrast highlights the variable nature of the relationship between business recipes and national boundaries. Nation-states with relatively homogeneous cultures and institutions generate more distinctive business recipes than do those characterized by greater homogeneity. While East Asian societies appear to have dominant business recipes that are quite dissimilar, for example, many Southeast Asian nations are dominated by the recipe of the same ethnic minority, the Chinese family business (Limlingan 1986; Redding 1990; Yoshihara 1988). These latter countries are often based on colonial boundaries that incorporate a variety of quite distinct cultures and different social institutions. Where political elites have tried to develop a business class drawn from the dominant ethnic group, as in Malaysia, they do not seem to have been successful in generating a viable alternative "national" business recipe (Jesudason 1989).

As well as major ethnic and cultural differences encouraging a variety of distinct business recipes within nation-states, there are of course substantial differences between firm structures and connections across industries, especially in Western Europe and North America. Just as the national distinctiveness and coherence of business recipes depends on the integration and dissimilarity of national institutions, so too the variability of industry-based recipes depends on the differentiation of industrial contexts. However, since many important contextual institutions are common to all industries in each country, such as the financial and political systems, the extent to which industry recipes are sharply distinct and mutually exclusive is limited.

While, then, major differences in capital and energy intensity, in market structure and in the organization of transaction costs may well affect the nature of economic actors and their interrelations between different industries (Daems 1983), they will not generate highly dissimilar business recipes. As Nishida (1990) has shown, different legal and political institutions in Hong Kong encouraged greater vertical integration among Chinese cotton spinners there than in Shanghai. Similarly, Limlingan (1986) has identified distinctive growth patterns and financial strategies in a number of industries dominated by Chinese family businesses in ASEAN (Association of Southeast Asian Nations). Industry differences here seem less crucial than institutional contexts, especially the significance of family identities and affiliations and of trust relations between business partners (Redding 1990; Silin 1976).

The relative importance of industry characteristics, as opposed to more general social institutions in a country, in generating distinctive business recipes depends, then, on the extent to which institutions are homogeneous across industries and dissimilar between societies. The more varied and differentiated are major social institutions—such as the financial, political, and educational systems—the more likely economic actors will differ between industries in certain respects. Thus, societies in which occupational identities are important and distinct, and in which individual rights and duties are more significant than collective ones, are more likely to have a variety of overlapping business recipes than those with more collective and vertical commitments. Anglo-Saxon societies which share a common concern with "professional" identities, market-based wage systems, and commitments to individualism, then, generate greater variations between industries than many continental European and East Asian ones (Child, Glover, and Lawrence, 1983; Dore 1973; Lodge and Vogel 1987).

The dependence of successful business recipes on dominant social institutions additionally implies, of course, that as the latter change, so too will successful recipes. Clearly, if successful ways of organizing and controlling economic activities reflect the nature and operation of major contextual institutions, then as these alter, so too will successful ways of dealing with them. Thus, if the "globalization" of the financial services industry results in the standardization of financial systems on the Anglo-Saxon model—improbable as this may seem—then major Japanese firms are likely to change the ways in which they manage risk and make strategic choices. Similarly, if the British state implemented an education and training policy which resulted in 60 percent of school leavers having certified practical skills, we would expect the employment practices of leading British companies to alter (see Lane 1988; Maurice, Sorge, and Warner 1980).

However, it is important to note that these influences are mutual in that established business practices and structures affect developments in their contexts as well as vice versa. The preference of large Japanese firms for recruiting the graduates of prestigious universities for managerial positions solely on the basis of their success in general competitive examinations, and concentrating on internal training of all staff rather than relying on externally certified skills, has inhibited the development of a public training system comparable to that in Germany (Clark 1979; Dore 1973; Maurice, Sellier, and Silvestre, 1986). Similarly, the extensive family, financial, and other connections between banks, insurance companies, and industrial firms in large French industrial groups (Bauer and Cohen 1981) make it unlikely that Anglo-Saxon types of capital markets with short-term relations between financial institutions and firms will become established in France (see Encaoua and Jacquemin 1982; Lévy-Leboyer 1980). Thus, the development and change of dominant business recipes in a society is a two-way process and their success and growth affect related institutions just as they alter as a result of major contextual changes.

Turning now to consider briefly the major institutions which structure and enable different business recipes to develop and become established, we can distinguish between the more immediate and proximate institutions which affect business behavior relatively directly and in the recent past from those more distant in origin and indirect in impact. In the former category I would place the sorts of phenomena that have been commonly cited as explanations for variations between managerial structures and practices in different countries such as the structure and policies of the state—developmental or regulatory (Johnson 1982)—the nature of the financial system and its role in economic development (Ingham 1984; Zysman 1983), and the education and training system emphasized by the Aix group (Maurice, Sorge, and Warner 1980; Maurice, Sellier, and Silvestre 1986; cf. Lane 1988; Rose 1985). Also included here, of course, are dominant patterns of labor market organization and, in particular, trades union structures and attitudes as well as more general and diffuse attitudes and beliefs about work, material values, and authority relations.

The major institutions in the second category are those which developed during industrialization, and, where this was relatively recent, those which were important in preindustrial periods and influenced the particular patterns of industrialization that occurred. In many countries the dominant political institutions and authority relations reflect those that emerged during or, arguably, that shaped the industrial process. Even where earlier political systems have been discredited by the rise of militarism and defeat in war—as in Germany and Japan—key features of present state structures and policies as well as subordination principles stem from those current at the period of industrialization and, in some cases, earlier patterns of political and economic relationships.

Related significant institutions are family and kinship relations, identities, and authority structures. The significance of family membership and prestige, for instance, varies greatly between cultures and has a considerable influence on conceptions of identity and the role of individual rights and duties as opposed to collective ones. Additionally important are historical patterns of trust and cooperation between kinship groups, which continue to affect trust relations between exchange partners in recently industrialized societies (Redding 1990; Silin 1976). Finally, traditionally cosmologies and beliefs about the natural and social world often structure attitudes towards risk, planning horizons, and preferences about specialization and formalization within authority structures, as Redding (1980; Redding and Wong 1986) has shown in the case of the Chinese family business.

Considering the differences between the East Asian business recipes discussed earlier, the major variations in social institutions which help to explain them are listed in table 6.2. In addition to important differences in the role of state agencies and banks, there are also significant contrasts in the organization of families, trust relations, and vertical authority relations be-

TABLE 6.2
Major Differences in the Institutional Contexts of East Asian Business Systems

	Japan	*Korea*	*Taiwan*	*Hong Kong*
Departmentalist state	Yes	Yes	Yes	No
State coordination of strategies	Medium	High	Medium	Low
Integration of banks with industry	High	High	Medium	Medium
Differentiation of family authority	Considerable	Considerable	Low	Low
Primacy of family	Medium	High	High	High
Particularistic basis of trust and obligation	Medium	High	High	High
Recognition of reciprocity between superiors and subordinates	High	Low	Low	Low
Personal basis of authority	Medium	High	High	High

tween Japan, South Korea, Taiwan, and Hong Kong (Whitley 1991). According to Pye (1985, 75–79), authority in Chinese families is more monolithic and patriarchal than in Korean and Japanese ones. While Japanese fathers feel able to admit to difficulties and involve other members of the family in deciding how to overcome them, Korean and Chinese fathers are commonly expected to be omnicompetent and lose their claim to authority if they admit uncertainty and call upon others for help. Similarly, emotional ties between parents, especially mothers, and children seem to be stronger in Japan. Although family identities and success are more significant in all these societies than in the West, the Japanese family is more outward facing and more willing to engage in cooperation across kinship boundaries than are Korean and Chinese ones. Family loyalties in Japan are also more easily transferred to larger collectives than elsewhere in East Asia (Clark 1979, 38–41; Murayama 1982), and trust between nonkin groups is easier to foster in Japan than in Korean or Chinese societies. In general, trust relations between Japanese are less particularistic and less derived from common ascriptive foundations, such as birthplace, school, or university class, than between Korean and Chinese. Thus, Japanese obligation networks are often formed across ascriptive categories, whereas *guanxi* networks of mutual support amongst Chinese are usually tied to common background characteristics (Pye 1985, 293–98; Wong 1988).

Reciprocal commitments are also stronger between leaders and subordinates in Japanese society, and vertical allegiances are more integrated (Pye 1985, 287–90). Whereas loyalties in Korean and Chinese societies are primarily personal and focused on the family head, faction leader, or head of the clan, they are more organized around particular collective entities in Japan which are, in turn, subordinate to larger ones. Thus reciprocity and recognition of mutual dependence between superiors and subordinates are here combined with strong beliefs in the common commitment to collective goals and the right of individuals to issue commands on the basis of their competence and subservience to common interests (Jacobs 1985; Pye 1985, 163–81; Redding and Wong 1986). The role performance model of filial piety as the exemplary instance of obedience in Chinese society (Hamilton 1984) limits the intensity of vertical loyalties and their mobilization for collective goals beyond the family unit.

Some of these institutional variations stem from the different political and economic systems of preindustrial Japan, Korea, and China and the organizations of agricultural production. In particular, the degree of political and economic pluralism was greater in Japan than in Korea or China, and power was based more on military success than on the presumption of moral worth as manifested through literary examinations (Jacobs 1958; Pye 1985). Both Japan and Korea had a hereditary aristocracy, though under the Confucian Yi dynasty in Korea it was relatively subservient to the ruler. This subservience was enhanced by the principle of equal inheritance of estates, which ensured aristocratic dependence on royal favors (Jacobs 1985, 205). Japanese villages seem to have been more cohesive communities than their Korean and Chinese counterparts, especially with regard to cooperation in agricultural production (Moore 1966, 208; Smith 1959, 50–52), and were more integrated into larger units of political authority with the village headman functioning as the key link between feudal lords and peasants. Collective responsibility for taxation and criminal law, together with the greater interdependence of households, limited open expression of conflicts between families in Japan and ensured that group solidarity was regarded as much more important than individual wishes (Smith 1959, 60–62).

Conclusions

I have suggested in this chapter that the socially constructed nature of economic phenomena and business practices implies that there are a variety of forms of business organization which are effective and that no single economic logic can be regarded as uniquely "rational." The nature of successful managerial actions depends on key social institutions as well as how controllers of major economic resources conceive and evaluate realities and possibilities. Thus, different kinds of hierarchy-market relations develop and become established in different kinds of institutional environments, together with particular conceptions of how business should be structured and developed.

The more integrated and homogeneous are dominant social institutions in a society, the more they generate distinctive business recipes in which firms coordinate and direct certain kinds of economic activities through particular authority relations and manage risk through various quasi-market connections and networks. These business recipes also incorporate developmental strategies and ways of choosing priorities. They thus combine interfirm and intersector modes of organizing economic activities with patterns of strategic choice and "internal" authority structures. Their development, reproduction, and change are central to processes of economic development and change, and their comparative analysis is a key component of the sociology of economic enterprises.

References

Abegglen, James C., and George Stalk. 1985. *Kaisha: The Japanese Corporation.* New York: Basic Books.

Alford, Bernard. 1976. "Strategy and Structure in the UK Tobacco Industry." In *Management Strategy and Business Development*, ed. L. Hannah. London: Macmillan.

Amsden, Alice H. 1985. "The Division of Labour is Limited by the Rate of Growth of the Market: The Taiwan Machine Tool Industry of the 1970s." *Cambridge Journal of Economics* 9:271–84.

———. 1989. *Asia's Next Giant.* Oxford: Oxford University Press.

Aoki, Masahiko. 1987. "The Japanese firm in transition." In *The Political Economy of Japan*, ed. K. Yamamura and Y. Yasuba. Vol. 4, *The Domestic Transformation.* Stanford: Stanford University Press.

Bamford, Julia. 1987. "The Development of Small Firms, the Traditional Family and Agrarian Patterns in Italy." In *Entrepreneurship in Europe*, ed. R. Goffee and R. Scase. London: Croom Helm.

Bauer, M., and E. Cohen. 1981. *Qui gouverne les groupes industriels?* Paris: Seuil.

Bhaskar, Roy. 1979. *The Possibility of Naturalism: A Philosophical Critique of the Contemporary Human Sciences.* Brighton: Harvester.

Bloor, David. 1976. *Knowledge and Social Imagery.* London: Routledge and Kegan Paul.

Brossard, M., and M. Maurice. 1976. "Is There a Universal Model of Organization Structure?" *International Studies of Management and Organization* 6:11–45.

Chandler, Alfred D. 1962. *Strategy and Structure: Chapters in the History of the Industrial Enterprise.* Cambridge: MIT Press.

———. (1977) *The Visible Hand: The Managerial Revolution in American Business.* Cambridge: Harvard University Press.

Child, John. 1987. "Culture, Contingency, and Capitalism in the Cross-National Study of Organisations." *Research in Organizational Behavior* 3:305–56.

Child, John., M. Fores, I. Glover, and P. Lawrence. 1983. "A Price to Pay? Professionalism in Work Organisation in Britain and West Germany." *Sociology* 17:63–78.

Clark, R. 1979. *The Japanese Company.* New Haven: Yale University Press.

Cusumano, Michael A. 1985. *The Japanese Automobile Industry: Technology and Management at Nissan and Toyota.* Cambridge: Harvard University Press.

Daems, H. 1983. "The Determinants of the Hierarchical Organisation of Industry." In *Power, Efficiency, and Institutions*, ed. A. Francis, Jeremy Tuck, and Paul Willman. London: Heinemann.

DiMaggio, Paul J., and Walter W. Powell. 1983. 'The Iron Cage Revisited: Institutional Isomorphism and Collective Rationality in Organizational Fields." *American Sociological Review* 48:147–60.

Dore, Ronald. 1973 *British Factory, Japanese Factory: The Origins of National Diversity in Industrial Relations.* London: Allen and Unwin.

———. 1986. *Flexible Rigidities: Industrial Policy and Structural Adjustment in the Japanese Economy, 1970–80.* Stanford: Stanford University Press.

Encaoua, D., and A. Jacquemin, 1982. "Organizational Efficiency and Monopoly Power: The Case of French Industrial Groups." *European Economic Review* 19:25–51.

Feyerabend, P. K. 1981. "The Methodology of Scientific Research Programmes." In *Problems of Empiricism. Vol. 2 of Philosophical Papers.* Cambridge: Cambridge University Press.

Fligstein, Neil. 1985. "The Spread of the Multidivisional Form among Large Firms, 1919–1979." *American Sociological Review* 50:377–91.

Futatsugi, Yusaku. 1986. *Japanese Enterprise Groups.* Trans. Anthony Kaufmann. Kobe: Kobe University, School of Business Administration.

Gellner, Ernest. 1968. "The New Idealism—Cause and Meaning in the Social Sciences." In *Problems in the Philosophy of Science*, ed. Imre Lakatos and ALan Musgrave. Amsterdam: North Holland.

Goto, A. 1982. "Business Groups in a Market Economy." *European Economic Review* 19:53–70.

Granick, David. 1972. *Managerial Comparisons of Four Developed Countries.* Cambridge: MIT Press.

Granovetter, Mark. 1985. "Economic Action, Social Structure, and Embeddedness," *American Journal of Sociology* 91:481–510.

Hamilton, Gary. 1984. "Patriarchalism in Imperial China and Western Europe." *Theory and Society* 13:393–426.

Hamilton, Gary, and N. W. Biggart. 1988. "Market, Culture, and Authority: A Comparative Analysis of Management and Organization in the Far East." *American Journal of Sociology* 94 (supplement): 552–94.

Hamilton, Gary, and C. S. Kao. 1990. "The Institutional Foundation of Chinese Business: The Family Firm in Taiwan." *Comparative Social Research* 12: 95–112.

Hamilton, Gary, William Zeile, and W. J. Kim. 1990. "The Network Structures of East Asian Economies." In *Capitalism in Contrasting Cultures*, ed. S. Clegg and G. Redding. Berlin: de Gruyter.

Hickson, David, C. R. Hinings, C. J., McMillan, and J. P. Schwitter. 1974. "The Culture-Free Context of Organizational Structure: A Tri-National Comparison." *Sociology* 8:59–80.

Hickson, David, C. J. McMillan, K. Azumi, and D. Horvath. (1979). "Grounds for Comparative Organization Theory: Quicksands or Hard Core?" In *Organizations Alike and Unlike*, ed. C. J. Lammers and D. J. Hickson, London: Routledge and Kegan Paul.

Horovitz, Jacques Henri. 1980. *Top Management Control in Europe*. London: Macmillan.

Imai, K., and H. Itami. 1984. "Interpretation of Organization and Market: Japan's Firm and Market in Comparison with the US." *International Journal of Industrial Organization* 2:285–310.

Ingham, G. 1984. *Capitalism Divided? The City and Industry in British Social Development*. London: Macmillan.

Jacobs, Norman. 1958. *The Origin of Modern Capitalism and Eastern Asia*. Hong Kong: Hong Kong University Press.

———. 1985. *The Korean Road to Modernization and Development*. Urbana: University of Illinois Press.

Jesudason, James V. 1989. *Ethnicity and the Economy: The State, Chinese Business, and Multinationals in Malaysia*. Oxford: Oxford University Press.

Johnson, Chalmers. 1982. *MITI and the Japanese Miracle*. Stanford: Stanford University Press.

Jones, Leroy, and Il SaKong. 1980. *Government, Business, and Entrepreneurship in Economic Development: The Korean Case*. Camabridge: Harvard University Press.

Kagono, Tadao, Ikujiro Alonaka, Kiyonori Sakakibara, and Akihiro Okumara. 1985. *Strategic vs. Evolutionary Management: A U.S.-Japan Comparison of Strategy and Organization*. Amsterdam: North Holland.

Kim, Kyong-Dong. 1979. *Man and Society in Korea's Economic Growth*. Seoul: Seoul National University Press.

Kiyonari, Tadao, and Hideichiro Nakamura. 1980. "The Establishment of the Big Business System." In *Industry and Business in Japan*, ed. K. Sato. New York: M. E. Sharpe.

Kono, Toyohiro. 1984. *Strategy and Structure of Japanese Enterprises*. London: Macmillan.

Lane, Christel. 1988. "Industrial Change in Europe: The Pursuit of Flexible Specialisation in Britain and West Germany." *Work, Employment, and Society* 2: 141–68.

———. 1989. *Management and Labour in Europe*. Aldershot, Hants: Edward Elgar.

Lawrence, Peter. 1980. *Managers and Management in West Germany*. London: Croom-Helm.

Lawriwsky, Michael L. 1984. *Corporate Structure and Performance*. London: Croom-Helm.

Lazerson, M. H. 1988. "Organizational Growth of Small Firms: An Outcome of Markets and Hierarchies." *American Sociological Review* 53:330–42.

Lévy-Leboyer, M. 1980. "The Large Corporation in Modern France." In *Managerial Hierarchies*, ed. A. D. Chandler and H. Daems. Cambridge: Harvard University Press.

Liebenberg, R. D. 1982. " 'Japan Incorporated' and 'The Korean Troops': A Comparative Analysis of Korean Business Organizations." M.A. thesis, Department of Asian Studies, University of Hawaii.

Limlingan, Victor S. 1986. *The Overseas Chinese in ASEAN: Business Strategies and Management Practices*. Pasig, Metro Manila: Vita Development Corporation.

Lincoln, J. R., M. Hanada, and K. McBride. 1986. "Organizational Structures in Japanese and US Manufacturing." *Administrative Science Quarterly* 31:338–64.

Lodge, George C., and Ezra F. Vogel eds. 1987. *Ideology and National Competitiveness: An Analysis of Nine Countries*. Boston: Harvard Business School Press.

Maurice, Marc, François Sellier, and Jean-Jacques Silvestre. 1986. *The Social Bases of Industrial Power*. Cambridge: MIT Press.

Maurice, Marc, Arndt Sorge, and Malcolm Warner. 1980. "Societal Differences in organizing Manufacturing Units." *Organization Studies* 1:59–86.

Meyer, John W., and Brian Rowan. 1977. "Institutionalized Organizations: Formal Structure as Myth and Ceremony." *American Journal of Sociology* 83:440–63.

Meyer, John W., and Richard Scott. 1983. *Organizational Environments*. Beverly Hills: Sage.

Michell, Tony. 1988. *From a Developing to a Newly Industrialized Country: The Republic of Korea, 1961–82*. Geneva: International Labour Organization.

Miyazaki, Yoshikazu. 1980. "Excessive Competition and the Formation of *Keiretsu*." In *Industry and Business in Japan*, ed. K. Sato. New York: M. E. Sharpe.

Moore, Barrington. 1966. *Social Origins of Dictatorship and Democracy*. Boston: Beacon Press.

Murayama, Magoroh. 1982. "Mindscapes, Workers, and Management in Japan and the USA." In *Japanese Management*, eds. Sang M. Lee and Gary Schwendiman. New York: Praeger.

Nishida, Judith. 1990. "The Japanese Influence on the Shanghaiese Textile Industry and Implications for Hong Kong." M.Phil. thesis, University of Hong Kong.

Numazaki, Ichiro. 1986. "Networks of Taiwanese Big Business." *Modern China* 12:487–534.

———. 1987. "Enterprise Groups in Taiwan." *Shoken Keizai* 162 December: 15–23.

———. 1989. "The Role of Personal Networks in the Making of Taiwan's *Guanxiqiye* (Related Enterprises)." Paper presented to the International Conference on Business Groups and Economic Development in East Asia, University of Hong Kong, June 20–22.

Orru, M., Nicole W. Biggart, and Gary Hamilton. 1988. "Organizational Isomorphic in East Asia: Broadening the New Institutionalism," Program in East Asian Culture and Development Research, Institute of Governmental Affairs, University of California, Davis, Working Paper Series no. 10.

Penrose, E. 1980. *The Theory of the Growth of the Firm*. Oxford: Basil Blackwell.

Pugh, Derek S., and Gordon R. Redding. 1985. "The Formal and the Informal: Japanese and Chinese Organization Structures." In *The Enterprise and Management in East Asia*, ed. Stewart R. Clegg, Dexter Dunphy, and S. Gordon Redding. University of Hong Kong: Centre for Asian Studies.

Pye, Lucian W. 1985. *Asian Power and Politics: The Cultural Dimensions of Authority*. Cambridge, MA: Harvard University Press.

Redding, S. Gordon 1980. 'Cognition as an Aspect of Culture and Its Relation to Management Processes: An Exploratory View of the Chinese Case', *Journal of Management Studies*, 17: 127–48.

———. 1990. *The Spirit of Chinese Capitalism*. Berlin: de Gruyter.

Redding, S. Gordon, and S. Richardson. 1986. "Participative Management and Its Varying Relevance in Hong Kong and Singapore." *Asia Pacific Journal of Management* 3:76–98.

Redding, S. Gordon, and Gilbert Y. Y. Wong. 1986. "The Psychology of Chinese Organisational Behaviour." In *The Psychology of the Chinese People*, ed. M. Bond. Oxford: Oxford University Press.

Richardson, George. 1960. *Information and Investment*. Oxford: Oxford University Press.

———. 1972. "The Organization of industry," *Economic Journal* 82:883–96.

Rohlen, Thomas P. 1974. *For Harmony and Strength: Japanese White-Collar Organization in Anthropological Perspective*. Berkeley and Los Angeles: University of California Press.

Rose, Michael. 1985. "Universalism, Culturalism, and the Aix Group: Promise and Problems of a Social Approach to Economic Institutions," *European Sociological Review* 1:65–83.

Sayer, A. 1984. *Method in Social Science*. London: Hutchinson.

Scott, Richard. 1987. "The Adolescence of Institutional Theory," *Administrative Science Quarterly* 33:493–511.

Shin, E. H., and S. W. Chin. 1989. "Social Affinity among Top Managerial Executives of Large Corporations in Korea," *Sociological Forum* 4:3–26.

Silin, R. H. 1976. *Leadership and Values. The Organization of Large Scale Taiwanese Enterprises*. Cambridge: Harvard University Press.

Smith, Peter B., and J. Misumi. 1989. "Japanese Management: A Sun Rising in the West?" In *International Review of Industrial and Organizational Psychology*, ed. C. L. Cooper and I. Robertson. New York: J. Wiley.

Smith, Thomas C. (1959) *The Agrarian Origins of Modern Japan*. Standford: Stanford University Press.

Sorge, Arndt. 1983. "Cultured Organisations." *International Studies of Management and Organization*, 12:106–38.

Spender, J. C. 1989. *Industry Recipes: An Enquiry into the Nature and Sources of Managerial Judgement*. Oxford: Basil Blackwell.

Stinchcombe, A. 1965. "Social Structure and Organizations." In *Handbook of Organizations*, ed. J. G. March. Chicago: Rand McNally.

Tam, Simon. 1990. "Centrifugal versus Centripetal Growth Processes: Contrasting Ideal Types for Conceptualizing the Developmental Patterns of Chinese and Japanese Firms." In *Capitalism in Contrasting Cultures*, ed. Stewart R. Clegg and S. Gordon Redding. Berlin: de Gruyter.

Taylor, C. 1985. "Social Theory as Practice." In *Philosophical Essays*, vol. 2. Cambridge: Cambridge University Press.

Whitley, Richard D. 1984. *The Intellectual and Social Organisation of the Sciences*. Oxford: Oxford University Press.

———. 1987. "Taking Firms Seriously as Economic Actors: Towards a Sociology of Firm Behaviour." *Organization Studies* 8:125–47.

———. 1990. "East Asian Enterprise Structures and the Comparative Analysis of Forms of Business Organization." *Organization Studies* 11:47–74.

———. 1991. "The Social Construction of Business Systems in East Asia," *Organization Studies* 12:1–28.

Williamson, Oliver E. 1985. *The Economic Institutions of Capitalism*. New York: Free Press.

Winch, Peter. 1970. "Understanding a Primitive Society." In *Rationality*, ed. Bryan Wilson. Oxford: Basil Blackwell.

Wong, Siu-Lun. 1985. "The Chinese Family Firm: A Model." *British Journal of Sociology* 36:58–72.

———. 1988. "The Applicability of Asian Family Values to Other Sociocultural Settings." In *In Search of an East Asian Development Model*, ed. P. L. Berger and H.-H. M. Hsiao. New Brunswick, N.J.: Transaction Books.

Yoo, S., and S. M. Lee. 1987. "Management Style and Practice in Korean *Chaebols*." *California Management Review* 29:95–110.

Yoshihara, Kunio. 1988. *The Rise of Ersatz Capitalism in South East Asia*. Oxford: Oxford University Press.

Yoshino, M. Y., and Thomas B. Lifson. 1986. *The Invisible Link: Japan's Sogo Shosha and the Organization of Trade*. Cambridge: MIT Press.

Zeile, William. 1989. "Industrial Policy and Organizational Efficiency: The Korean Chaebol Examined," in East Asian Culture and Development Research, Institute of Governmental Affairs, University of California, Davis, Working Paper no. 30.

Zucker, Lynne G. 1987. "Institutional Theories of Organization." *Annual Review of Sociology* 13:443–64.

Zysman, John. 1983. *Governments, Markets, and Growth: Financial Systems and the Politics of Industrial Change*. Ithaca, N.Y.: Cornell University Press.

Chapter 7

THE DECLINE AND FALL OF THE CONGLOMERATE FIRM IN THE 1980S: THE DEINSTITUTIONALIZATION OF AN ORGANIZATIONAL FORM

GERALD F. DAVIS, KRISTINA A. DIEKMANN,
AND CATHERINE H. TINSLEY

THE DIVERSIFIED corporation became the dominant form of industrial firm in the United States over the course of the twentieth century. During the 1920s, DuPont and General Motors pioneered the use of the multidivisional form (or M-form) to produce and market a number of related products through separate divisions, and this organizational structure subsequently spread (Chandler 1962). The M-form also allowed easy integration of acquired businesses, which enabled firms to grow through acquisition. Following the enactment of the Celler-Kefauver Act in 1950, horizontal and vertical acquisitions (buying competitors, buyers, or suppliers) fell out of regulatory favor, and firms seeking to grow through acquisition were forced to diversify into other industries. This fueled the conglomerate mergers of the late 1960s and 1970s (Fligstein 1991). The strategy of growth through acquiring firms in unrelated lines of business and structuring them as a collection of separate business units reflected an underlying model of appropriate corporate practice—the "firm-as-portfolio" model. By 1980, the triumph of the firm-as-portfolio model seemed complete, as growth through diversification was perhaps the most widely used corporate strategy among large firms (Porter 1987), and fewer than 25 percent of the *Fortune* 500 largest industrial corporations made all their sales within a single broadly defined (two-digit SIC) industry.[1]

During the 1980s, however, a wave of "deconglomeration" restructured American industry and heralded a return to corporate specialization (Bhagat, Shleifer, and Vishny 1990). From an economic perspective, the value of bringing a number of weakly related business operations under a single

Gerald F. Davis, Kristina A. Diekmann, and Catherine H. Tinsley. 1994. "The Decline and Fall of the Conglomerate Firm in the 1980s: The Deinstitutionalization of an Organizational Form." *American Sociological Review* 59: 547–70, by kind permission of the American Sociological Association.

management had long been suspect, as financial orthodoxy insisted that investors should diversify, not firms (Amihud and Lev 1981). Moreover, the construction of a takeover market for large firms in the 1980s, supported by Reagan-era regulatory policy, empowered a mechanism to support this orthodoxy. So-called "bust up" takeovers, where raiders bought conglomerates and financed the deal through the postacquisition sale of their separated parts, became accepted and then commonplace (Lipton and Steinberger 1988), while diversified firms not threatened by takeover voluntarily shed unrelated operations to focus on "core businesses." As prevalent corporate practices changed, revisionist views of conglomerate mergers suggested that it was "almost certainly the biggest collective error ever made by American business," a "colossal mistake" that had left American industry uncompetitive relative to international rivals ("Ebb Tie" 44). As we document in this paper, by the late 1980s only a tiny handful of firms continued to pursue a strategy of unrelated diversification, the prevalence of conglomerates declined substantially, and business rhetoric denounced both the strategy of diversification and the conglomerate form. Thus, over the course of a decade, the firm-as-portfolio model was abandoned on a large scale across the population of the largest American corporations—in a word, corporate conglomerates became "deinstitutionalized."

In retrospect, the "deconglomeration" of American industry in the 1980s can be seen as economically sensible, if not inevitable. The corporate managers who built the conglomerates of 1980 had made a "colossal mistake," either out of self-interest—larger firms pay better, and diversification buffers the employment uncertainty of operating in a single industry (Amihud and Lev 1981)—or out of simple imitation of other firms that had diversified (Fligstein 1991). By the early 1980s, the antitrust regime that had made diversification preferable to buying competitors during the 1960s and 1970s had fallen away (Bhagat, Shleifer, and Vishny 1990), as had the legal impediments that had previously protected large corporations from hostile takeovers (Davis and Stout 1992). Moreover, the stock market undervalued conglomerates relative to sets of "focused" firms operating in the same industries (LeBaron and Speidell 1987) and, at least during the 1980s, punished firms acquiring unrelated businesses with drops in share price (Morck, Shleifer, and Vishny 1990). In hindsight, all these factors indicate that in 1980 the field of the largest American industrial corporations was fundamentally flawed and that an enormous "collective error" had been made. Yet organization theorists provide a cogent argument that it is exceptionally difficult for organizations to make major changes in strategies and structures (Hannan and Freeman 1989), particularly in those structures that have been "institutionalized" and widely adopted across an organizational field (DiMaggio and Powell 1983). Compelling theory and evidence was offered early on that the firm-as-portfolio model was a financial mistake (Levy and Sarnat 1970; Rumelt 1974; Mason and Goudzwaard 1976), and many individual corporations had their own ample evidence that this model was failing, as they divested upwards of three-quarters of the unrelated businesses they had acquired because of their poor postacquisition performances (Porter 1987; Ravenscraft and Scherer 1987). Yet little evidence of either individual or collective learning was evident—bust-up takeovers of conglomerates were unknown during the 1960s (Palmer, et al. 1993) and firms continued to follow the dictates of the firm-as-portfolio model throughout the 1970s, with the vast majority of mergers representing diversification and half the acquired assets being in unrelated industries (Scherer 1980, 124). Thus, the process required to correct the collective error of conglomerate mergers entailed involuntary organizational upheaval on a scale previously unknown in this century.

We believe that the sociology of organizations can benefit from examining the coevolution of corporate strategies and structures and the underlying models of appropriate practice that occurred during the retreat from conglomeration. Recent theoretical approaches in the sociology of organizations have focused on changes in aggregates of organizations, such as populations (Hannan and Freeman 1989) or fields (Powell and DiMaggio 1991), and thus deconglomeration is an appropriate topic of study for both. Yet deconglomeration does not readily fit the explanatory categories of either approach. Ecologists seek "to understand the dynamics of organizational diversity, *how social changes affect the mix of organizations in society*" (Hannan and Freeman 1986, 52), primarily by examining the birth and death rates of relatively inert organizational forms. But organizational births and deaths were unimportant in deconglomeration; rather, the parts of conglomerates were reshuffled as going concerns (through takeovers or restructurings), with most of the same employees continuing to produce the same products in the same industries, suggesting that ecological theory would be of little help in understanding deconglomeration.

Neoinstitutionalists also seek to explain variations in the prevalence of forms and practices in organizational fields, but their focus is more on voluntary shifts, that is, on how models of appropriate action come to be taken for granted, thereby shaping organizational practice. Thus, institutional theory should be more directly relevant to examining deconglomeration as an instance of deinstitutionalization. But as DiMaggio (1988) noted, "[T]he theoretical accomplishments of institutional theory are limited in scope to the diffusion and reproduction of successfully institutionalized organizational forms and practices. . . . Institutional theory tells us [little] about deinstitutionalization: why and how institutionalized forms and practices fall into disuse" (12). Institutionalists have offered two explanations for deinstitutionalization. First, new practices can displace old ones. Peripheral players in a field may introduce practices which come to be seen as preferable to existing arrangements, or conversely core members of a field may adopt a new practice, and other members of the field follow suit (Leblebici et al.

1991; Burns and Wholey 1993). Second, practices can simply be abandoned, either by force, as when federal antitrust regulation in effect ruled out horizontal mergers (Fligstein 1990), or voluntarily, as when hospitals that had adopted a matrix structure subsequently dropped it (Burns and Wholey 1993). These processes are not mutually exclusive; for example, after the Celler-Kefauver Act of 1950 restricted horizontal and vertical mergers, fringe players introduced the practice of unrelated diversification, which subsequently spread widely among established corporations (Fligstein 1991).

The process of deconglomeration does not fit readily into either of these explanations of deinstitutionalization. Bust-up takeovers did not introduce a new organizational structure, but delegitimated an old one—conglomerate firms were taken over and broken up specifically because of their organizational form. The actors responsible for spreading this tactic were often not other organizations—peripheral or core—but simply groups of individuals who saw an opportunity for profit and, implicitly, held alternative views of appropriate corporate structure (Coffee 1988). From the perspective of large corporations, bust-up takeovers were not a voluntary practice, introduced by either fringe or core players; indeed, takeovers were done *to* core players, not *by* them. Further, in contrast to the conglomeration movement of the 1960s, the state did not single-handedly rule out particular practices (such as unrelated acquisitions), but rather deregulated a wide range of practices, allowing the field to evolve on its own. Finally, both explanations of the process of deinstitutionalization described previously take for granted that an organizational field consists of a set of organizations as meaningfully bounded social actors that is relatively stable over time—it is organizations that act, and they adopt and discard practices (organizational strategies and structures) more or less voluntarily (subject to constraints imposed by the state). Yet perhaps the most radical concomitant of the deconglomeration movement was the undermining of the notion of organizations as primordial social units in favor of a radical individualist view in which corporations were simply "financial tinker toys" which could be rearranged at whim, without regard for organizational boundaries (Gordon 1991). Ironically, it was the firm-as-portfolio model itself that made this imagery credible (Espeland and Hirsch 1990). Thus, to accommodate deconglomeration, institutionalist arguments need to be expanded to accommodate contradictions inherent in institutionalized aspects of organizations (Leblebici et al. 1991).

We investigate empirically how the process of deconglomeration occurred and offer an institutionalist interpretation for how corporate practices and rhetoric coevolved during the 1980s. Like most institutional stories, ours is in essence a case study of a single organizational field during a particular time period—the five hundred largest American industrial corporations during the 1980s. As with all case studies, it is difficult to draw strong causal inferences, because there are no comparison cases—say, another field of five hundred large corporations with an alternative regulatory regime.

Thus, while our data comprehensively document the widespread abandonment of practices associated with the firm-as-portfolio model, our interpretation of the cognitive factors underlying the data is of necessity somewhat speculative. Like most singular historical events, deconglomeration was overdetermined. Yet we believe that the shifts in rhetoric that accompanied deconglomeration reflected an institutional shift that was not simply epiphenomenal (Hirsch 1986). Corporate practices reflect underlying models of appropriate action, which in turn are shaped by prior models and practices. Thus, we contend that the move to extreme vertical disintegration in the late 1980s arose in reaction to the firm-as-portfolio model and the subsequent deconglomeration movement.

Institutionalization, Deinstitutionalization, and Organizational Boundaries

Researchers under the banner of the New Institutionalism have documented several episodes of institutionalization (DiMaggio and Powell 1991). The meaning of "institution," however, is somewhat unclear in their work, except that it resembles the notion of "norm" (Scott 1991): Social relations and actions are institutionalized when they come to be taken for granted (Zucker 1983) or associated with situations via rules of appropriateness (March and Olsen 1984); conventions are institutions when they "take on a rulelike status in social thought and action" (Meyer and Rowan 1977, 341); and so on. In short, organizational forms and practices are institutionalized when they are adopted because actors take them for granted, rather than because a rational choice process found them to be best suited for the technical requirements of the task. Judgments of appropriateness are not based solely in individual cognitions, but follow from cognitive structures, such as scripts and schemas, that are more or less shared across societies (DiMaggio and Powell 1991). Moreover, notions of appropriateness impose what is in effect a cognitive viability test on organizational forms and practices: While a variety of social structural arrangements may be possible and technically adequate in principle, to be adopted they must be cognitively "available" to the relevant actors—to both potential adopters and those providing resources. What is available, as well as what is ruled out, follows in part from what has gone before. Thus, imitation and rule-following reduce some of the "cognitive start-up costs" for organizations (DiMaggio and Powell 1991).

In empirical work, institutionalization is typically operationalized by prevalence within a given population of organizations rather than through direct assessments of "taken-for-grantedness" by aggregates of relevant actors. One sign of institutionalization is widespread adoption of a form or practice, independent of evidence that it "works." Thus, Tolbert and Zucker

(1983) found that cities implementing civil service reforms early on tended to have good reasons for doing so, while late adoption of the reforms was not associated with such reasons, indicating that the reforms had become institutionalized. Controlling for the individual characteristics that commonly prompt adoption, Fligstein (1985) showed that firms were more likely to adopt a multidivisional structure when other firms in their industry had done so, and Burns and Wholey (1993) found that hospitals were more likely to adopt a matrix structure when a large proportion of other hospitals in their region had.

But these characterizations of institutionalization offer little sense of when deinstitutionalization can or will occur and imply that institutionalization is a once-and-for-all process. According to this view, absent a disruptive exogenous force, such as the state ruling out a practice that has become common (Fligstein 1990), institutions apparently do not budge: Once a sizable proportion of actors adopts a social structural arrangement, it remains widespread. Unlike most institutionalist writers, however, Douglas (1986) has given an exceptionally clear notion in cognitive terms of what defines institutions and what sustains them; from Douglas we can derive implications regarding when deinstitutionalization is likely to occur. An institution is a convention that has become legitimized. Conventions arise when parties have a common interest in a rule or arrangement that coordinates their actions (e.g., having a speed limit). A convention is legitimized when it is able to withstand challenges based on instrumental grounds. The source of this legitimacy is the "naturalizing analogy," a parallel cognitive structure that sustains the institution by demonstrating its fit with the natural order. When a convention has been institutionalized, it is no longer simply mutual convenience that accounts for why things are done in a particular way, but the convention parallels other aspects of the way the world works and is therefore "natural" (Douglas 1986).

Analogies provide a source of stability for conventions by "scripting" appropriate behavior, and they are a potent rhetorical resource for ordering social arrangements. For example, radio airwaves were initially an unfamiliar medium, and the way that radio frequencies should be allocated by the government was initially unclear. Radio was seen as analogous to a public utility (like the post office) or a "magazine of the air," but eventually an analogy to transportation was settled on—"radio as public waterway"—and appropriate regulatory structures then fell into place (Leblebici et al. 1991).[2] Analogies have their limits, however, and not just any analogy is sufficient to legitimate a practice or structure. Without an authoritative analogy, an institution becomes vulnerable, suggesting a basis for deinstitutionalization and a limit to what institutions can be sustained.

The use of naturalizing analogies to legitimate organizational arrangements has a long history, with the "organization as body" analogy playing a particularly prominent role since before the Middle Ages. Sewell (1980) described the status of corporate actors in France prior to the Revolution, when the king established social groupings, such as guilds, "en corps et communaute"—as a body and community, subsequently considered a single person under the law. The term "corps"—body—implied a set of analogical characteristics:

> All bodies were composed of a variety of organs and members, which were hierarchically arranged and were placed under the command of the head. Each body was distinct from every other, with its own will, its own interests, its own internal order, and its own esprit de corps. Each body was made of a single internally differentiated but interconnected substance, and harm inflicted on any member was felt by the whole. (Sewell 1980, 36–37)

Thus, organizations were sovereign, and members were wholly contained within them, having no separate legal existence. The French Revolution manifested an explicit effort to do away with such bodies, recognizing as sovereign only the individual and the state with no intermediary entities, but the compelling force of the body analogy was not so easily displaced (Sewell 1980). Coleman (1974) documented the origins of the modern corporate form and showed how corporations came to be "juristic persons" with rights and interests that are not simple aggregations of their members' interests. These artificial persons had distinct legal personalities and, unlike their medieval predecessors, did not wholly contain their (voluntary) members. Yet they were still meaningfully referred to as actors. Thus, the legal conceptualization of the corporation relied on and furthered the analogy of the organization as body. Moreover, the perceived rightness and naturalness of the analogy is evident even in theoretical discourse on corporations. Discussions of organizational birth, growth, and death are considered unexceptionable, not transparently metaphorical (Scott 1992).

The body analogy implies a way of thinking about what an organization is—a bounded social structure composed of members—as well as a set of desiderata (e.g., growth and survival) that can guide action and provide a basis for the adoption of organizational practices and forms. Perhaps the most basic aspect of an organizational form is the placement of boundaries—which activities are done inside or outside the organization and which individuals are considered "members" underlie an organization's very identity. Divergent notions about the appropriate placement of organizational boundaries for business corporations have been prevalent in different industries and at different points in history. Transaction cost economists analyze this as the "make or buy" or "efficient boundaries" problem—should an organization buy an input on the market or make the input itself, thus bringing the activity within the organization's boundary. For example, auto manufacturers may have different answers to the question of whether steel should be made or bought. Transaction cost analysis suggests that the appropriate answer turns on asset specificity—in short, the extent to which buyers and sellers make investments that are specific to their relationship and which lose value if the relationship is discontinued (Williamson 1975). When such relationship-specific investments are necessary, Williamson argued, it is more efficient to bring the activity within the boundary of the firm. Against this view, however, Granovetter (1994) pointed out that there is interesting variation across cultures and over time in how economic activities are grouped together, with parts of production processes differentially grouped within firms and firms often grouped into culturally specific supraorganizational structures, such as the *keiretsu* in Japan and the *grupos economicos* in Latin America. The degree of variation across cultures suggests that more than efficiency considerations are governing decisions and that there is an institutional or normative element to the placement of organizational boundaries.

Prevalent ideas about the appropriate placement of organizational boundaries have changed in substantial ways throughout U.S. corporate history (Chandler 1977; Fligstein 1990). A driving principle throughout this history is that bigger is better—that organizational growth (expanding the organization's boundary) is an appropriate end to pursue. Organizations can grow through internal expansion or through acquiring or merging with other organizations. Three merger waves prior to the 1980s manifested each of the following as prevalent means of expanding organizational boundaries: horizontal growth (acquiring competitors) at the turn of the century, vertical growth (acquiring buyers or suppliers) during the 1920s, and diversification (acquiring businesses producing related or unrelated products) during the 1960s (Weston, Chung, and Hoag 1990). The question for institutional analysts is, what was legal and what was appropriate? Because the historical shifts underlying each of these different dominant notions of appropriate organizational growth have been amply documented elsewhere (Chandler 1977; Fligstein 1990), we focus here on only the last model—that of diversification as an organizational growth strategy and on the conglomerate as an organizational form—which we refer to as the "firm-as-portfolio" model.

The Context of Conglomeration

In the United States in 1980, the dominant model of strategy and structure for large corporations was the firm-as-portfolio model (Fligstein 1991). The firm-as-portfolio model implies both a practice (growth through diversification) and a form (the conglomerate). Unrelated diversification entails buying businesses in industries that are neither potential buyers, suppliers, competitors, nor complements to the firm's current business. For example, an appliance manufacturer buying a stock brokerage house is an instance of unrelated diversification. The organizational form that typically results from unrelated diversification is the conglomerate, a corporation with relatively autonomous business units operating in numerous unrelated or weakly related industries and a corporate headquarters acting as an internal capital market, allocating resources among the units. The firm-as-portfolio model was promoted through a range of institutional processes over a period of three decades, including the actions of the state, organizational imitation, the advice of business consultants, and the efficiency rationales of organizational theorists.

The federal government inadvertently promoted corporate diversification through its antitrust policies, which successively eliminated horizontal and vertical growth as viable options for large firms (Bhagat, Shleifer, and Vishny 1990). Unrestrained horizontal growth can lead to an industry being dominated by a monopoly; unrestrained vertical integration where supplies are limited may allow firms to bar their competitors from access. In either event, the effects of such growth were thought to be anticompetitive, and antitrust policy—particularly the Celler-Kefauver Act of 1950—substantially reduced the possibility of horizontal and vertical growth after 1950 (see Weston, Chung, and Hoag 1990, chap. 23 for a concise discussion of U.S. antitrust law). Thus, firms seeking to expand their boundaries were forced to look beyond their primary industry and their buyers' and suppliers' industries for acquisition candidates, and large numbers of firms did this during the 1960s and 1970s, creating the conglomerate merger wave. A handful of highly visible firms—the "acquisitive conglomerates"—experienced dramatic growth through unrelated diversification, prompting other organizations seeking growth to imitate their strategy. The prevalence of this strategy within industries also appears to have been self-reinforcing, as firms were more likely to switch to a strategy of unrelated diversification when others in their industry had previously done so (Fligstein 1991). Corporations rushed to adopt the firm-as-portfolio model, despite the fact that the evidence on conglomerates' profitability was ambiguous at best and disastrous at worst (Black 1992), thus supporting the interpretation that the model was spread more through institutional than market-based processes (Fligstein 1991).

The firm-as-portfolio model was also promoted by management consultants, who spread so-called "portfolio planning" techniques that allowed top corporate managers to deal with the unrelated business units they faced by treating them as analogous to stocks in a portfolio (Haspeslagh 1982). Portfolio planning entailed (1) defining "strategic business units" within the corporation, (2) classifying the units according to their position in their industry and the attractiveness of that industry, and (3) assigning resources across the business units based on a corporate strategy. The Boston Consulting Group, McKinsey, Arthur D. Little, and other consulting firms developed "portfolio grid technologies" for the second part of this process, which reduced what top managers had to know about a business unit to simply the unit's position on an industry grid. Coupled with cash-flow statements, this was virtually all headquarters management needed to manage the corporation as a portfolio. Such techniques spread rapidly during the 1970s, and by 1979, 45 percent of the *Fortune* 500 companies—upwards of 75 percent of the diversified ones—had adopted portfolio planning, with more companies joining the firm-as-portfolio fold every year (Haspeslagh 1982). Operational knowledge about particular industries was no longer required to manage businesses in those industries, in principle allowing organizational boundaries to expand without limit.

Finally, organizational economists provided a theoretical legitimation for the firm-as-portfolio model. From a financial perspective, conglomerates are merely "mutual funds with smokestacks" and redundant headquarters staffs (Espeland and Hirsch 1990, 78). Moreover, unlike individual investors, who can easily change the distribution of holdings in their portfolios, conglomerates are more attached to their divisions and it is more costly to move into and out of businesses as conditions warrant (Porter 1987). The prevalence of the conglomerate form was therefore puzzling to economists with an efficiency orientation. While isolated instances of diversification into unrelated businesses could be dismissed as managerial empire-building, the large number of conglomerates developing in the United States required an efficiency-based explanation. Thus, Williamson (1975, chap. 9) argued that conglomerate acquisitions were a tool for well-run multidivisional form (M-form) corporations to spread their management talents. Conglomerate acquisitions by M-forms did not represent inefficient empire-building by managers, according to Williamson (and contrary to most empirical evidence [Amihud and Lev 1981]); rather, these acquisitions were missionary work meant to rehabilitate poorly run businesses—the M-form's burden. The M-form conglomerate profited by identifying and buying undervalued targets and running them more effectively by implementing appropriate internal financial controls, ultimately benefiting economic efficiency (Williamson 1975).

The result of these processes was the widespread adoption of the firm-as-portfolio model by large corporations. By the early 1980s "almost all of the [one hundred] largest firms [were] significantly diversified and set up in divisions" (Fligstein 1990, 256), and "the concept of corporate strategy most in use [was] portfolio management, which is based primarily on diversification through acquisition" (Porter 1987, 49). Only about 25 percent of the 1980 *Fortune* 500 operated exclusively in a single two-digit SIC industry, while over half operated in three or more. Prevalence of forms and practices is an imperfect proxy for institutionalization, to be sure. Yet all the indicators suggest that the firm-as-portfolio model was widely regarded as an appropriate one for the management of large corporations. To the extent that notions of institutionalization are applicable to large corporations, there is a strong case for regarding the spread of the firm-as-portfolio model—in the absence of good evidence that the model promoted profitability—as an instance of institutionalization.

Changes in the Institutional Climate during the Early 1980s

Despite the widespread adoption of the firm-as-portfolio model by the largest American corporations during the 1960s and 1970s, there was little evidence that it "worked" and mounting evidence that it did not work by one crucial metric: the stock market valuation. According to Black's (1992) review, "The evidence that corporate diversification reduces company value is consistent and collectively damning" (903). Even as early as the 1960s, the financial performance of conglomerates was, on average, inferior to that of randomly selected portfolios of firms operating in the same industries (Mason and Goudzwaard 1976). By the 1980s, the practical implications of this fact had become apparent, and a small industry developed around detecting corporations undervalued by the stock market. For example, LeBaron and Speidell (1987) of Batterymarch Financial Management created a "Chop Shop" valuation model to determine how much a conglomerate would be worth if it were broken up and the parts were sold off. They found that, in general, the sum of the potential stock market value of the parts of a conglomerate was substantially more than the actual stock market value of the whole. Furthermore, this differential increased with the degree of diversification: "The more divisions a company has, the more it is likely to be undervalued" (LeBaron and Speidell 1987, 87). Note that inherent in this valuation model is the idea that activities "inside" the organizational boundary should be subject to the same market tests as those "outside" it (Meyer 1991) and, moreover, that decisions about what activities are appropriate within a particular corporate boundary are not the sole province of those running the corporation, but are revocable by the market.

In addition, the policies that supported the conglomerate form changed substantially during the early Reagan years. The so-called Chicago School of antitrust law and economics gained policy dominance in the early 1980s at the Federal Trade Commission (FTC) (where Chairman James C. Miller III attempted to eliminate the FTC's antitrust arm entirely), and at the Justice Department (where William F. Baxter, assistant attorney general for antitrust, required that any proposed antitrust investigations and cases be cleared with the house economists). Horizontal mergers were no longer scrutinized simply on the basis of the industry concentration that would result; rather, several factors were taken into account before a merger would be considered anticompetitive. In effect, this reduced the barriers to acquisitions in the same industry (Weston et al. 1990). Reduced antitrust barriers meant that in principle the parts of conglomerates could be sold to acquirers in the same industries. Legal barriers to hostile takeovers also fell early in the Reagan years. In the *Edgar v. MITE* (457 U.S. 624 [1982]) decision, the U.S. Supreme Court overturned the laws that made takeovers difficult in most states, and the Reagan administration, relying on the arguments of Chicago

School economists who lauded the efficiency effects of an active market for corporate control, demonstrated a principled resistance against regulations that might make takeovers more difficult (Stearns and Allan 1993).

At roughly the same time as these regulatory changes, innovations in takeover financing emerged that made conglomerates potential targets for "bust-up takeovers" by outside raiders. In a typical bust-up takeover, the raider would identify a conglomerate with readily separable parts and find buyers for some or all of the parts in advance of the takeover attempt. Based on the presale of the separated parts, the raider could secure short-term debt financing through junk bonds or other financial vehicles to complete the takeover, sell the parts, and retire some or all of the debt with the proceeds from the bust-up (see Lipton and Steinberger 1988 for a discussion). One implication of this is that the raider could complete a takeover using very little of his or her own cash—like a mortgage on a house, the value of the property being purchased secured most of the financing. This enabled small firms or even groups of individuals to buy much larger corporations, whereas previously the privilege of acquiring large firms was effectively limited to a pool of even larger corporations (Coffee 1988).

By the early 1980s, then, the model of appropriate corporate practice that had guided the strategies and structures of the largest American corporations had been drastically undermined. The firm-as-portfolio model had weakened corporate financial performance, the regulatory regime that had promoted and sustained the model was gone, and the financial barriers to outside challengers were reduced. Nonetheless, fundamental change in the strategies and structures that prevail across a large organizational field is not a trivial matter, particularly when these practices have been championed by powerful actors. Voluntary change under such circumstances is unlikely, as institutional theorists point out (DiMaggio and Powell 1983). Indeed, by some accounts one of the defining features of an institution is that powerful actors take an active role in its reproduction (Stinchcombe 1968). Firms had continued to make unrelated acquisitions long after they had solid reasons to doubt their profitability, which some have argued indicates that unrelated corporate diversification flowed from managerial discretion (Amihud and Lev 1981). An alternative route to widespread change would entail ousting the individuals who ran the largest American firms and who had assembled the conglomerates in the first place through hostile takeovers. The last time unwanted takeovers had threatened the position of the corporate elite on a large scale, the call for federal protection was swift and effective, culminating in the Williams Act of 1968 (Hirsch 1986), and by some accounts the Reagan administration was uniquely indebted to the corporate elite for its election (Useem 1990). No such protection was forthcoming during the 1980s, however, as Reagan-era policy was guided by a free market stance that ruled out regulation of the so-called "market for corporate control" (Roe 1993). Appeals by the powerful would not be sufficient to save the firm-as-portfolio model.

Perhaps the only remaining barrier to widespread abandonment of the firm-as-portfolio model was its status as an institution, which by definition provides a buffer against challenges that arise out of instrumental or pecuniary concerns alone (Douglas 1986). Institutionalized organizations are, in Selznick's phrase, "infused with value" not reducible to economic measures (Selznick 1957), which helps account for the vigorous efforts put forth by members of chronically underperforming organizations to prevent their (economically sensible) demise (Meyer and Zucker 1989). For external actors to compare parts of organizations to market alternatives and to buy and bust up those that fail the market test is to undermine the notion that corporations as organizations can carry noneconomic value (Meyer 1991). Bust-ups render organizational boundaries provisional at best, meaningless at worst, leaving corporations to be financial Tinkertoys rather than bounded social structures (Gordon 1991). In short, widespread deconglomeration challenges some of the most fundamental aspects of organizations as institutions.

The tensions we have outlined between the firm-as-portfolio model and pressures for market performance drove much of the evolution of the field of the largest U.S. corporations during the 1980s. We now examine four types of evidence regarding changes in these firms' structures and practices: (1) the degree to which diversified firms experienced a greater risk of being taken over, (2) the prevalence of conglomerate (and other) acquisition strategies during the late 1980s, (3) changes in the prevalence of the conglomerate form between 1980 and 1990, and (4) changes in business rhetoric regarding appropriate organizational structures and practices.

The Takeover Risk of Diversified Firms

Bust-up takeovers of diversified firms received a great deal of attention in the media, but despite research documenting the extent to which takeovers were followed by sell-offs (Bhagat, Shleifer, and Vishny 1990; Ravenscraft and Scherer 1987), no previous research has documented whether diversified firms faced a systematically greater risk of takeover than undiversified firms in the 1980s. Our first task, then, is to determine whether this was the case. We examine the effect that a firm's degree of diversification had on its risk for takeover using dynamic analyses covering all takeovers of firms in the 1980 *Fortune* 500 over the course of the 1980s. Based on prior research on the factors that lead to takeover (Palepu 1986; Morck, Shleifer, and Vishny 1989; Davis and Stout 1992), we control for size (sales), performance (market-to-book ratio), age, growth rate, debt structure, ownership by financial institutions, and whether the CEO came from a background in finance.

Data and Variables

Because we were interested in assessing changes affecting large U.S. corporations in general, we focused on an entire population rather than on a sample. Thus, we tracked the 1980 *Fortune* 500 from January 1, 1980, to December 31, 1990. Of interest to us was whether a firm became subject to a takeover attempt, successful or otherwise, during this time period. Because firms can only be taken over if their stock is publicly traded, we excluded any nonpublic firms, such as foreign subsidiaries, joint ventures, and agricultural cooperatives. We were left with an effective sample size of 467 firms before exclusions for missing data.

Under the Williams Act, anyone offering to buy 5 percent or more of a firm's shares is required to immediately disclose the details of the offer by filing Form 14D-1 with the Securities and Exchange Commission. The dates of these filings are available in the *SEC Bulletin* and, for the years after 1985, on *Compact Disclosure*. Using these sources, we determined the date on which any firm in our population was first subject to a takeover bid. Details of the offers, including whether they ultimately ended with a takeover, were compiled using the *Wall Street Journal Index*. In ten cases the first bid was a "friendly" offer initiated by the firm's own management (i.e., a management buyout attempt). These were not considered to be takeover attempts, but rather censoring events which removed the firms from the population at risk for takeover.

Data on diversification were acquired from Standard and Poor's Compustat service for 1980. Firms are required annually to disclose accounting data from operations at the level of the business segment on Form 10-K filed with the SEC. Compustat reports sales and other data by segment as well as classifying segments into industries using up to two four-digit SIC codes for each segment. Using these data, we calculated the entropy measure of diversification for each firm (Jacquemin and Berry 1979). The entropy measure of total diversification (DT) taps the extent to which a firm operates in a number of industries using a weighted average of the proportion of a firm's sales made in each of the industry segments in which it operates:

$$\mathrm{DT} = \sum P_i \ln\,(1/P_i),$$

where P_i is the proportion of the firm's sales made in segment *i*. An advantage of this measure is that it is continuous: Rather than crudely classifying firms as "diversified" or "undiversified," this measure captures the *degree* of diversification, which gives it more subtlety than the categorical measures of diversification popular in the 1970s (see Palepu 1985 for a discussion of the properties and merits of the entropy measure). For firms that operate in only a single industry, ln(1/1) = 0 and therefore DT = 0. Among the 1980 *Fortune* 500, the median firm's level of diversification was DT = 1.0; Minnesota Mining and Manufacturing was the most diversified, with DT = 2.2, followed by Beatrice, AMF, US Industries, and ITT.

Size is measured by sales. *Performance* is measured using the market-to-book ratio, that is, the ratio of the stock market value of the firm's equity to its book (accounting) value. A high market-to-book value indicates that the stock market values the firm more highly than its reported value, and consequently, that the firm cannot be bought at a bargain price. *Age* is the number of years between the year of incorporation and 1980. *Growth rate* is the yearly percentage increase (decrease) in the size of the firm's workforce. *Debt structure* is the ratio of the long-term debt of the firm to its market value. A higher value on this measure implies that the firm is financed more through debt than equity. *Institutional ownership* is measured as the percentage of the firm's equity held by financial institutions (primarily banks, insurance companies, pension funds, and mutual funds). *Finance CEO* is a dummy variable indicating whether the CEO's educational and departmental background was primarily in finance or in another functional area. Annual data on size, performance, growth, and debt for 1979 through 1989 (inclusively) were taken from Standard and Poor's Compustat. Dates of original incorporation were taken from *Standard and Poor's Stock Market Encyclopedia* (various years) and *Moody's Industrial Manual* (various years). Institutional ownership data came from the *Spectrum 3 13(f) Institutional Stockholding Survey* (Computer Directions Advisors, Inc. 1980). CEO functional backgrounds were coded from annual surveys of executive compensation in large corporations published by *Forbes* ("It Ain't Hay" 1980; "How Much" 1981). The *Forbes* sample of firms covered only about three-quarters of the firms in the *Fortune* 500; thus, we ran two sets of models, with and without this indicator.

Method

Because we had data on the exact dates of all takeover attempts for all firms in our population, we were able to use event history techniques to determine the effects of the covariates on the firms' risks of takeover over time. We used a Cox model with time-changing covariates, where a firm's risk of takeover depended on its prior level of diversification, size, and so on (Cox 1972; Tuma and Hannan 1984, Chap. 8). Roughly 30 percent of the firms at risk for takeover (i.e., publicly traded) were subject to a takeover attempt during our time frame. The others were considered censored cases. Firms in these models were deleted after the first takeover attempt; that is, a takeover attempt was considered a fatal event. A second set of models included only successful takeover attempts, that is, nonmanagement tender offers that ended with the firm being acquired. In these models, firms not taken over were considered censored cases.

TABLE 7.1
Event History Analysis of Takeover Bids for 1980 *Fortune* 500 Firms, 1980 to 1990

	All Bids		*All Successful Bids*	
Variable	*Model 1*	*Model 2*	*Model 3*	*Model 4*
Sales	–.0001 (–1.546)	–.0001 (–1.639)	–.0001 (–1.492)	–.0001 (–1.461)
Market/book	–.3178* (–3.639)	–.2968* (–3.302)	–.2837* (–2.883)	–.2725* (–2.653)
Age (log)	.2519 (1.321)	.1685 (.763)	.2019 (.990)	.1256 (.523)
Growth rate	–.0125* (–2.116)	–.0093 (–1.405)	–.0110 (–1.698)	–.0059 (–.797)
Debt structure	–.6553* (–2.677)	–.7209* (–2.430)	–.7587* (–2.634)	–.9256* (–2.497)
Institutional ownership	–.0115 (–1.863)	–.0143 (–1.956)	–.0161* (–2.386)	–.0207* (–2.555)
Diversification	.6545* (3.401)	.6543* (2.890)	.5688* (2.717)	.6453* (2.568)
Finance CEO	—	.5019* (1.987)	—	.2649 (.874)
Number of cases	423	322	423	322
χ^2	43.7*	45.1*	35.7*	34.7*
df	7	8	7	8

Note: Numbers in parentheses are *t*-values.
* $p < .05$ (two-tailed test).

The data were divided into up to eleven spells (firm-years). Firms that were not subject to an outside takeover attempt and did not leave the population for other reasons (such as bankruptcy or a management buyout) had eleven years of data, while those that were taken over or otherwise left the population of publicly traded firms had fewer years of data. Level of diversification, age, institutional ownership, and finance CEO were measured as of 1980: the other measures were updated annually.

Results and Discussion

The results of our analysis are presented in table 7.1. The first two columns present results when the outcome is defined as the initiation of an outside takeover bid (that is, a tender offer not initiated by management). The third and fourth columns present results when the outcome is defined as the initiation of an outside takeover bid that ultimately ended in the firm being acquired (i.e., a "successful" bid). Consistent with previous research, firms with a high market-to-book ratio and firms with substantial debt faced a significantly lower risk of becoming takeover targets in all four models. Firms owned proportionally more by institutional investors were significantly less likely to be subject to successful takeover attempts in models 3 and 4, but this effect was only marginally significant ($p < .10$) when all bids were included (models 1 and 2). Growing firms were less likely to become subject to a takeover attempt (model 1), but this effect was not statistically discernible in model 2 when the Finance CEO variable was included, or in models 3 and 4 when only successful bids were considered. Finally, firms with finance CEOs were significantly more likely to become targets (model 2), but were no more likely to be taken over successfully (model 4).

Controlling for all these other factors, firms faced a significantly greater risk of takeover to the extent that they were diversified in all models ($p < .05$). To interpret the effect of diversification on takeover risk, we exponentiated its estimated coefficient, which gives the multiplier of the rate of takeover that firms in this population experienced. The estimated multiplier effect of diversification is about 1.92 in model 1; thus, firms at the median level of diversification (DT = 1.0) were subject to takeover attempts at a rate 92 percent higher than comparable firms operating in a single industry (DT = 0), while firms at the seventy-fifth percentile of diversification (DT = 1.36) faced 2.6 times the risk of takeover. These results are not dependent on our measure of diversification: identical results were obtained when a simpler measure—the raw number of business segments in which a firm operated—was substituted. Figure 7.1 shows the effect that the number of segments in which a firm operated had on the firm's risk of being successfully taken over using a model that substitutes number of segments for the entropy measure of diversification in the third column of table 7.1. As the figure shows, firms operating in the largest number of business segments in 1980 were taken over at more than four times the rate of firms operating in only one business segment. Thus, net of other variables and using different measures, the more diversified a firm was, the higher the rate at which it was subjected to takeover attempts and the more likely it was to be taken over.

The finding that diversified firms were substantially more likely to be taken over than focused firms differs markedly from the results of a study of takeovers of *Fortune* 500 firms during the previous merger wave in the 1960s. Using similar measures and statistical analyses for a parallel sample over the years 1963 through 1968, Palmer et al. (1993) failed to uncover any significant relation between a firm's level of diversification (measured as the number of two-digit SIC industries in which the firm operated) and its risk of

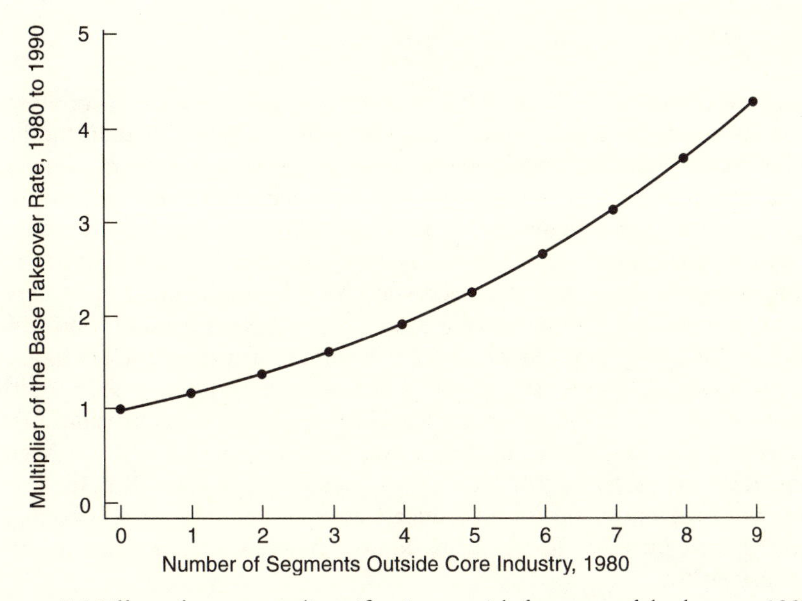

FIGURE 7.1 Effect of corporate diversification on risk for successful takeover: 1980 *Fortune* 500 firms, 1980 to 1990

being taken over. The effect of diversification on takeovers thus appears to have been new in the 1980s.

Although we cannot directly address the subsequent fate of the firms in our sample that were taken over, other researchers have done so for the middle years of our sample period. Bhagat, Shleifer, and Vishny (1990) analyzed the outcomes of all hostile takeover bids between 1984 and 1986 that involved a purchase price of $50 million or more; these data encompass all hostile bids in our sample for those years. Bhagat et al. found that 72 percent of the acquired assets ended up by being owned by corporations in the same businesses. In over one-fourth of the cases, the proceeds from selling off parts of a firm after an acquisition amounted to at least 50 percent of the purchase price. "By and large, then, bustups fit very closely into the picture of strategic acquisitions. Either the original buyer in a hostile takeover keeps the parts it wants, often selling the others to strategic buyers as well; or the company is broken up and sold off largely to strategic buyers" (Bhagat, Shleifer, and Vishny 1990, 51). In combination with our results, this indicates that conglomerates were substantially more likely to be taken over than focused firms and that the individuals or firms which bought them busted them up in whole or in part, keeping the divisions that were in related lines of business and selling the unrelated parts to other related buyers.

Acquisitions in the Late 1980s

It is now clear that the firms that had previously pursued diversification were at a substantially greater risk of takeover during the 1980s than the firms which had shunned conglomerate growth. It is less evident, however, whether the firms that remained independent recognized the implication of this increased risk, or whether the firm-as-portfolio model maintained influence over the growth strategies of large firms. Research on patterns of acquisitions during the 1980s has been somewhat limited, and no prior study has systematically examined the prevalence of different types of acquisitions during this time period. Much of the relevant literature has been in financial economics and has focused on the effects of acquisitions on the acquiring firm's share price, rather than on providing a "census of acquisitions" (e.g., Lewellen, Loderer, and Rosenfeld 1985; Mitchell and Lehn 1990; Morck, Shleifer, and Vishny 1990). Thus, to characterize broad trends in the prevalence of different acquisition practices, we collected data on all significant acquisitions by *Fortune* 500 firms for the five years from 1986 to 1990, inclusively.

Data and Variables

Our population included all firms listed in the 1986 *Fortune* 500. Again, firms were excluded if they were not publicly traded corporations. This left us with an effective sample size of 437 firms, after exclusions for missing data. To allow for the construction of a takeover market to have an effect on firms' acquisition patterns, our time frame began in 1986 and ended in 1990; thus, we had five complete years of data on acquisitions.

For acquisitions prior to 1980, the Federal Trade Commission published data on merger activity in the United States, breaking mergers into horizontal, vertical, product extension, market extension, and pure conglomerate. Unfortunately, this service was discontinued and no replacement has been implemented. Thus, we compiled comparable data for the years of our study by (1) determining all significant acquisitions made by the firms in our sample and (2) coding each acquisition using a scheme comparable to the one used by the FTC. Data on acquisitions were drawn from *Mergers and Acquisitions* (1986–90), which contains compendia widely acknowledged to be the most complete sources of information on merger activity in the United States (Golbe and White 1988). We included only full acquisitions that were large enough to be considered significant. We used a purchase price of $25 million as a minimum cutoff; for comparison purposes, the annual sales of the smallest firm in the 1986 *Fortune* 500 was $424 million. For each acquisition, a four-digit SIC code for the business was assigned from *Standard and Poor's Register of Corporations*. In cases where *Standard and*

Poor's had no data on the acquired business, SIC codes were assigned based on the description of the business in *Mergers and Acquisitions* (1986–90).

We classified acquisitions as horizontal, related, vertical, and conglomerate using a modified version of Ravenscraft and Scherer's (1987) scheme. *Horizontal acquisitions* were those where the acquiring and target firms shared a four-digit SIC code; *related acquisitions* were those where the acquiring and target firms shared a two-digit SIC code, but not a four-digit code; and *vertical acquisitions* were those where the acquiring firm and target firm operated in industries with significant buyer-supplier relationships (that is, where 5 percent or more of the dollar value of the acquiring firm's industry's inputs came from, or outputs went to, the target firm's industry, according to the Bureau of Economic Analysis's [1991] six-digit Industry Input-Output matrix for 1982). *Conglomerate (unrelated) acquisitions* were those that did not fit any of the above categories.

Categorizing mergers posed unique problems, because most firms in this population were already somewhat diversified. Thus, for example, imagine a vertically integrated auto manufacturer that generates 75 percent of its sales in its auto division and 25 percent in its steel division. Acquisition of a steel company could be classified as vertical (for the auto division) or horizontal (for the steel division). We overcame this by using business segment data for the acquiring firm for 1985 from *Standard and Poor's Compustat, Moody's Industrial Manual* (1985), and annual reports. For each business segment we had the percentage of the firm's sales and a primary and secondary four-digit SIC code pertaining to the segment. Firms report financial information on up to ten segments; thus, an acquirer could have up to twenty SIC codes. Using these data, we broke acquisitions into three size classes, pertaining to matches with segments composing 70 percent or more of the acquirer's sales, 20 percent to 70 percent, or below 20 percent. An acquisition's final categorization was determined by the largest of the three classes to which it could be assigned. Thus, in our hypothetical example, the steel company acquisition would be classified as vertical for the first size class and horizontal for the second size class; therefore, we would categorize it as a vertical acquisition.[3]

Results and Discussion

Table 7.2 presents distributions of acquisitions by type. Perhaps most striking is the fact that less than 15 percent of the firms in our population made any conglomerate acquisitions at all, and less than 4 percent made more than one. A small handful were quite active, however. If we define a diversification program as completing three or more unrelated acquisitions within a five-year period, then only four firms among the *Fortune* 500—General Motors, General Electric, Ford, and International Paper—engaged in such a program

TABLE 7.2
Percentage Distribution of Acquisitions by 1986 *Fortune* 500 Firms, 1986 to 1990

	Type of Acquisition			
Number of Acquisitions	*Horizontal*	*Vertical*	*Related*	*Conglomerate*
0	76.1	94.7	75.5	85.1
1	16.7	4.6	17.9	11.5
2	5.3	.7	5.0	2.5
3	.7	.0	.9	.0
4	.5	.0	.7	.5
5	.2	.0	.0	.0
6	.0	.0	.0	.0
7	.2	.0	.0	.5
8	.2	.0	.0	.0
Total[a]	99.9	100.0	100.0	100.1

Note: Number of firms equals 436.
[a] Percentages may not add to 100.0 because of rounding.

during the late 1980s. Put another way, four large firms were responsible for almost one-quarter of the conglomerate acquisitions completed by all *Fortune* 500 firms during the second half of the 1980s. Three of the four most active conglomerate acquirers—GM, Ford, and GE—were, in 1986, also among the four largest industrial firms in the United States in terms of employment levels and were three of the five largest nonoil companies in terms of sales.

The results provide a fairly consistent portrait of corporate acquisitions in the late 1980s. Firms clearly made the best of the lax antitrust enforcement of the 1980s—the incidence of horizontal acquisition increased substantially compared to the 1970s (Scherer 1980), while the vast majority of firms rejected the strategy of growth through unrelated acquisition, and virtually all avoided vertical integration. The results are most striking when put in historical context. Mueller (1980) tracked acquisitions by large U.S. firms from 1962 to 1972, during which time horizontal and vertical mergers were extremely rare and conglomerate acquisitions were most common. He reported that the eight firms responsible for the most acquisitions were Litton, ITT, Teledyne, Beatrice, Gulf+Western, Occidental, Boise Cascade, and TRW—acquisitive conglomerates intent on growth through acquisition. In contrast, during the 1980s the most active conglomerate acquirers were a small number of enormous corporations that had established themselves long before. General Electric, General Motors, and Ford, three of the most active acquirers, each expanded their domain by buying financial and business service firms. GM and GE, the two most active acquirers, had already established a substantial presence in the financial services sectors with General Motors Acceptance Corporation and General Electric Capital Corporation, and GM's purchase of Electronic Data Services in 1984 had established it in the business services sector as well. These acquisitions were part of a larger program of expansion into the service sector by these industrial giants. Ironically, their expansion was occurring at precisely the point when some of the older conglomerates were abandoning the service sector—Ford purchased The Associates, the third-largest independent finance company, from Paramount Communications (formerly Gulf+Western) in 1989, at which point Paramount was moving to spin off unrelated divisions in order to focus on its core movie and publishing businesses.

Although we do not have direct evidence on this point, the findings of Bhagat et al. (1990) indicate that conglomerate acquisitions during the 1980s were often made with the explicit intent of selling off divisions in unrelated industries to buyers in those industries and hanging on to divisions in related industries. That is, when firms in our population made conglomerate acquisitions, it is possible or even likely that they subsequently divested those parts of the acquired firm that were not in their core industries. Where previously conglomerate acquisitions were used to achieve rapid growth by integrating the acquired firm into the acquirer's portfolio, in the 1980s they were used almost exclusively by firms that were already enormous. Ironically, the most active conglomerates all ended the decade with fewer employees than they started it, suggesting that their growth was of a curious type.

Aggregate Changes in Corporate Form

We have demonstrated that diversified firms were taken over at higher rates than focused firms in the 1980s and that during the second half of the decade very few firms pursued conglomerate growth. Next, we assess the impact that the events of the decade had on the overall level of diversification in the population of the largest corporations. Although roughly one-quarter of the 1980 *Fortune* 500 firms disappeared through takeover during the 1980s (largely as a consequence of being diversified), it is possible that the new firms that joined the population of the largest U.S. industrial corporations were themselves highly diversified, as was the case during the 1960s (Fligstein 1990). Conversely, many diversified firms went through deconglomeration programs by selling off divisions and seeking to focus on a "core competence." Thus, changes in aggregate levels of diversification are indeter-

TABLE 7.3
Median Levels of Diversification among *Fortune* 500 Firms: 1980, 1985, and 1990

Variable	*1980*	*1985*	*1990*
Total diversification (four-digit SIC segments)	1.00	.90	.67
Unrelated diversification (two-digit SIC segments)	.63	.59	.35
Number of firms	468	453	448

Note: Level of total diversification is calculated using the entropy measure, $DT = \Sigma P_i \, ln \, (1/P_i)$, where P_i is the proportion of a firm's sales made in industry segment i. Industry segments are defined at the four-digit SIC level. Unrelated diversification is calculated in the same manner, except that segments are defined at the two-digit SIC level; that is, the measure is calculated after first summing sales across two-digit SIC categories. See Palepu 1986 for an explication of this measure and its properties.

minate given the results we have presented. However, we can compare levels of diversification between 1980 and 1990 using data on business segments.

Table 7.3 compares the median level of diversification using the entropy measure (calculated at the four-digit and two-digit SIC industry levels) for the *Fortune* five hundred companies in 1980, 1985, and 1990. Note that the *Fortune* 500 is defined as the 500 U.S. industrial firms with the largest sales in the previous year; thus, although there is a fair degree of overlap among the firms appearing on this list over time, they are not identical. The level of total diversification (i.e., calculated at the four-digit SIC level) among firms in this population dropped from 1.0 in 1980, to .90 in 1985, and to .67 in 1990—a one-third drop over a decade. Even more dramatic is the decline in the level of unrelated diversification (i.e., calculated at the two-digit SIC level), which declined from .63 in 1980, to .59 in 1985, and to .35 in 1990—a 44 percent drop. Figure 7.2 shows the distribution of firms across two-digit industries in 1980 and 1990. Whereas roughly 25 percent of the largest firms in 1980 operated in only a single two-digit industry, 42 percent of the largest firms in 1990 did so.

Thus, there was a marked migration toward more focused organizational forms over the course of the decade—the median large industrial corporation looked quite different in 1990 compared to 1980. The majority (52 percent) of large firms operated in three or more two-digit industries in 1980, while only 30 percent did so in 1990. To the extent that large firms were diversified in 1990, diversification tended to be into closely related industries. Moreover, large firms that started the decade highly diversified overwhelmingly ended the decade more focused: Among the largest firms in 1980 that were not acquired, 76 percent of those that were above the median level of unrelated diversification in 1980 were less diversified in 1990. It is particularly

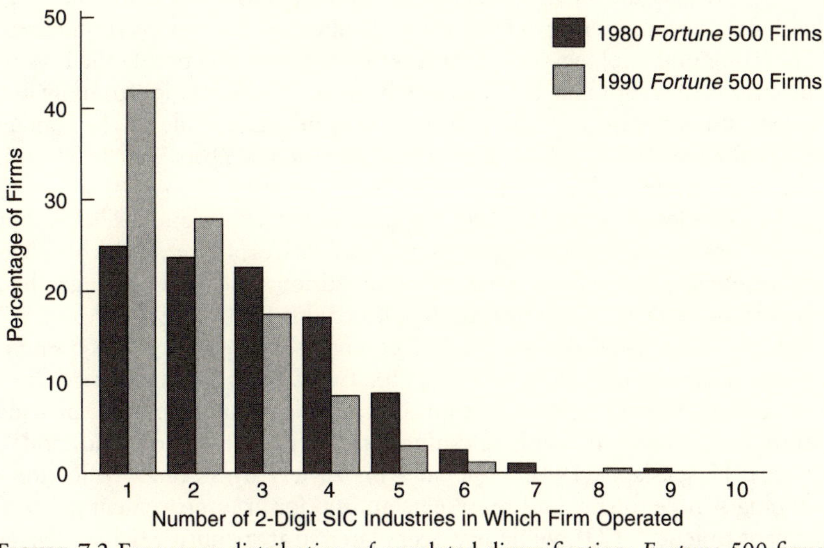

FIGURE 7.2 Frequency distribution of unrelated diversification: *Fortune* 500 firms, 1980 and 1990

instructive to look at the fate of the so-called acquisitive conglomerates of the late 1960s and early 1970s. Of the ten firms Rumelt (1974) classified as acquisitive conglomerates for which data were available in 1980, three (Bangor Punta, Colt Industries, and Lear Siegler) were bought out, and one (Brunswick) fended off a hostile takeover bid. Of the seven firms still operating independently in 1990 (Brunswick, FMC, General Host, W. R. Grace, LTV, Litton Industries, and Whittaker), all but one (FMC) were less diversified.

The results suggest that, in general, highly diversified firms were either taken over or voluntarily restructured to be more focused. The aggregate effect was that the population of the largest firms was considerably more diversified before the 1980s than after.

CHANGES IN BUSINESS RHETORIC DURING THE 1980S

Our analyses show a substantial decline in the prevalence of the form and practice of the firm-as-portfolio model in the United States during the 1980s, but they do not speak directly to the issue of deinstitutionalization as a cognitive phenomenon. Reports in the business press and pronouncements from corporate leaders and Wall Street, however, indicate both a reevaluation of the firm-as-portfolio model and a support for new models of strategy and structure. While there is less agreement about the specifics of a new model, there is virtually universal agreement that the firm-as-portfolio model, and the conglomerate merger movement it facilitated, have been discredited. "The [conglomerate] mergers of the 1960s were almost certainly the biggest collective error ever made by American business. . . . Synergies from diversification did not exist. . . . This was a colossal mistake, made by the managers, for the managers," according to the *Economist* ("Ebb Tide" 1991, 44). This collective error had substantial consequences for the American economy: "[T]he lesson of Britain and America in the 1960s and 1970s is that conglomerates are a short-sighted way out. . . . Corporate America's sluggish response to oil crises, Japanese competition, and other changes had much to do with its conglomerate tangles of the 1960s" ("Mad Mergers" 1992:18). "The 'portfolio' or 'holding company' approach . . . has been increasingly discredited" (Kanter 1991, 69). Two articles in the *Harvard Business Review*, the most prominent quasi-academic business journal, provide a stark comparison of changing evaluations of the firm-as-portfolio model: Philippe Haspeslagh (1982) concludes his review by stating, "[P]ortfolio planning is here to stay and represents an important improvement in management practice" (73), while five years later strategy guru Michael Porter (1987) pronounced, "In most countries, the days when portfolio management was a valid concept of corporate strategy are past" (51).

This changing evaluation of corporate conglomeration influenced the rationales offered by business executives for their strategies. For example, Martin Davis, appointed CEO of venerable conglomerate Gulf+Western in 1983, concluded, "[C]onglomeration is dead. It doesn't make any sense. . . . You can't manage that kind of diversity" (quoted in Morgello 1989, 83). Thus, he reorganized the firm and sold off its financial arm (The Associates, responsible for almost 40 percent of Gulf+Western's earnings) to focus on entertainment and publishing, changing Gulf+Western's name to Paramount Communications in 1988. Textron, an acquisitive conglomerate in the 1960s, reversed course by selling off twenty-four businesses, "from flatware to foundries," between 1985 and 1990. When the firm bought Cessna Aircraft in 1992, however, Textron's CEO felt compelled to argue that Cessna was closely related to its core aerospace businesses in response to critics on Wall Street, who had charged that the repentant conglomerate had fallen off the wagon (Putka 1992).

No clear-cut alternative has arisen to replace the firm-as-portfolio model, but broad outlines indicate that the logic defining what is appropriate to bring within a single organizational boundary has gone from being exceptionally broad (the conglomerate) to strikingly narrow, encompassing ever more specialized components of production processes. In contrast to the firm-as-portfolio model, which supported bringing virtually any type of business within the organization's boundary, rhetoric around appropriate business practices during the late 1980s and early 1990s has suggested extreme specialization and contracting for any aspects of production outside of the firm's "core competence." "Business schools and management consultants preach a unanimous gospel: make it lean, mean and centred on a core business" ("More Baskets" 1989, 75). Under such circumstances, producing complete products often entails forming temporary alliances with several other specialists and results in a network, or "virtual corporation," composed of formally separate entities rather than a single bounded organization. "In a leap of industrial evolution, many companies are shunning vertical integration for a lean, nimble structure centered on what they do best. The idea is to nurture a few core activities . . . and let outside specialists make the parts, handle deliveries, or do the accounting" (Tully 1993, 106). "Today's joint ventures and strategic alliances may be an early glimpse of the business organization of the future: The Virtual Corporation. It's a temporary network of companies that come together to exploit fast-changing opportunities. . . . It will have neither central office nor organization chart. It will have no hierarchy, no vertical integration" (Byrne 1993, 98–99). "Companies are replacing vertical hierarchies with horizontal networks; linking together traditional functions through interfunctional teams; and forming strategic alliances with suppliers, customers, and even competitors. . . . For many executives, a single metaphor has come to embody this managerial challenge and to capture the kind of organization they want to create: the 'corporation without boundaries' " (Hirschhorn and Gilmore 1992, 104).[4] Unfortunately, by their very nature it is difficult to track the prevalence of network forms of organization: Because they do not have stable boundaries and are composed of shifting arrays of specialized elements, they cannot be readily counted in the same manner as bounded actor-organizations. Their prevalence in business rhetoric, however, is clear.

As with the firm-as-portfolio model in the 1970s, academics have provided rationales for the firm-as-network model. Sabel (1991) calls such production structures "Moebius-strip organizations because, as with a looped ribbon twisted once, it is impossible to distinguish their insides from their outsides. . . . [This form of organization] hedges its risks not through portfolio diversification into unrelated activities but by learning to move rapidly from declining markets or market segments into prosperous ones in the same or related industries. [The consequence of this strategy] is the opening of the borders between corporations and between the economy and local society" (25–26) Kanter (1991) heralds the arrival of a "new model of organization structure. . . . A key concept guiding the new corporate ideal . . . is focus: maximizing the core business competence. This contrasts sharply with a tendency to form diversified conglomerates in the period beginning around the 1960s" (66). Two recurring themes in the writings on new organizational forms, both in the business press and in academic discourse, are (1) that organizational boundaries are increasingly blurred or irrelevant and (2) that the appropriate model of the organizational structures that prevail now is not the bounded body, but the (unbounded) network.

Discussion

Conglomerates were prevalent in 1980; many were taken over and broken up; most of those that remained became more focused through voluntary restructuring and sell-offs; and the firms that joined the set of the largest U.S. industrials were less diversified than the ones they replaced, leaving the largest firms in 1990 roughly half as diversified in the aggregate as their predecessors. With few exceptions, firms rejected both vertical integration and growth through conglomerate acquisition. Business rhetoric tracked the trend away from the firm-as-portfolio model. The business press denounced the conglomerate merger movement as a bout of collective madness on the part of American businesses and announced the coming of a firm-as-network model to replace the now-discredited firm-as-portfolio model. Thus, what firms did and how they looked—their practices and structures—as well as how members of the business community talked about corporate practices and structures reflected a mass rejection of the firm-as-portfolio model. In short, the firm-as-portfolio model was deinstitutionalized during the 1980s, and the field of the largest corporations was vastly restructured in a relatively brief period.

Although this characterization of the deconglomeration movement of the 1980s is descriptively accurate, it raises a fundamental question for institutional theory: How was organizational change on such a massive level possible if the firm-as-portfolio model had indeed become institutionalized? Certainly, there was substantial evidence that diversification reduced corporate performance (Black 1992) and that there was money to be made by buying conglomerates and busting them up (LeBaron and Speidell 1987). But not every economically attractive activity is pursued, and not every economically questionable practice is abandoned: Forms and practices (such as bust-ups) must be cognitively available to a number of actors in society for them to achieve prevalence. Bust-up takeovers violated the interests of powerful actors—the individuals running diversified firms, who typically ended up unemployed following successful takeovers. When the prevailing institutional order is threatened, the actors who benefit from that order have compelling reasons to engage in collective action and to seek protection from the state (DiMaggio and Powell 1991). But the threat posed by bust-ups and other takeovers generated little collective action by the corporate elite at the federal level, and while states eventually stepped in to regulate takeovers, it was too late to save the firm-as-portfolio model (Roe 1993). As we have shown, the only firms clearly able to resist the pressures to abandon the portfolio model during the 1980s were a handful of enormous corporations at the core of the intercorporate network that were presumably large enough and powerful enough to evade the pressures of takeovers. Our definition of legitimacy implies the ability of an institutionalized practice or structure to withstand challenges based on purely instrumental grounds (Douglas 1986). But where the firm-as-portfolio model was sustained, it was power, not legitimacy, that supported it.

We suggest that what has been deinstitutionalized is not just the firm-as-portfolio model, but also the very idea of the corporation as a bounded social entity analogous to a sovereign body. Bust-up takeovers were only the most visible manifestation of a more general institutional process in which the ontological status of the corporation as a social structure, including the sovereignty of organizational boundaries, was directly challenged. Growth through acquisition, such as the conglomerate mergers of the 1960s, could be naturalized with reference to analogous processes—the acquired firm becomes a member of (is eaten by) a larger corporate body, and is now inside its boundary rather than outside. But bust-ups undertaken by outsiders are unlike natural processes such as birth, growth, and death—a more gruesome analogy is dismemberment, with body parts being grafted onto other bodies. Bust-up takeovers required the body analogy and the sacrosanct status of the organizational boundary to be jettisoned. Corporations had to be reconceived as voluntary and impermanent social arrangements—as mere conventions, not institutions. This transition had a precedent in the French Revolution, during which the model of the organization as body was replaced, in legal theory if not social reality, with the Enlightenment concept of a social compact among free individuals that was constructed, and could be ended, voluntarily. The architects of this shift sought to rest sovereignty only in individuals and the state and to explicitly disallow efforts to vest sovereignty in an intermediate social structure (Sewell 1980).

We suggest that two factors helped undermine the sovereignty of organizational boundaries and thus allowed bust-ups: the rise to predominance of the nexus-of-contracts theory of the firm and the spread of the conglomerate form. The nexus-of-contracts model maintains that

> most organizations are simply *legal fictions which serve as a nexus for a set of contracting relationships between individuals*. . . . Viewed in this way, it makes little or no sense to try to distinguish those things which are "inside" the firm (or any other organization) from those that are "outside" of it. There is in a very real sense only a multitude of complex relationships (i.e., contracts) between the legal fiction (the firm) and the owners of labor, material and capital inputs and the consumers of output. . . . We seldom fall into the trap of characterizing the wheat or stock market as an individual, but we often make this error by thinking about organizations as if they were persons with motivations and intentions. (Jensen and Meckling 1976, 310–11)

By this account, corporations are not actors but merely "dense patches in networks of relations among economic free agents" (Zukin and DiMaggio 1990, 7). The convention of viewing the organization as a bounded body is simply reification, a cognitive error to be overcome. Notably, the natural attraction of thinking about corporations in these terms is so strong that the analogy requires explicit rejection. The fact that "we often make this error" means that the analogy needs to be exposed as false. To paraphrase Jensen and Meckling (1976), it makes little or no sense to refer to a "corporation without boundaries" unless one starts from the assumption that corporations are otherwise perceived as having an "inside" and "outside" that are separated by a boundary. Not only is the boundary of the organization not sacrosanct, according to this approach; it is nonexistent. Thus, there is no sovereignty to be violated by busting up a nexus of contracts if it fails to produce an adequate return in share price. Beginning in the early 1980s, this approach came to dominate normative discourse on the corporation, particularly in the courts (Easterbrook and Fischel 1991) and Reagan-era regulatory policy. Thus, bust-ups that would have been considered dismemberment under the body analogy were simply the reallocation of assets under the nexus-of-contracts model.

Ironically, by turning the corporation into a portfolio, the spread of the conglomerate form also facilitated the shift away from the notion of the corporation as sovereign bounded entity. Conglomerates strained the body analogy, because they offered no credible basis for a myth of identity. Like a gerrymandered congressional district, the lack of contiguity of the parts rendered the whole suspect—the parts did not *belong* together by any "natural" link. For example, Beatrice Foods counted among its businesses in the late 1970s various packaged foods, dairy products, lunch meats, plumbing supplies, audio equipment, luggage, and travel trailers, among others (see Baker 1992 for a history of Beatrice). Such an agglomeration of businesses bore little resemblance to a unit actor organization; the only apparent principle linking the businesses together was common ownership. Following Douglas's (1986) account, it is clear that the naturalizing analogy of organization as body was strained to the breaking point by organizations such as Beatrice. A few such deviant organizations might not be fatal to the analogy, but when conglomerates became the modal type of large corporation, the analogy could not be sustained. Without an authoritative analogy, conglomerates could not maintain the legitimacy that otherwise might have prevented them from being dismembered simply because money could be made by doing so. Conglomerates may have resulted from strategies for attaining organizational growth, but they inherently undermined the notion of the firm as a bounded actor, capable of growth, and distinct from its environment; and the poor financial performance of conglomerates invited challenges in the form of bust-up takeovers. Moreover, once bust-ups were possible, the sovereignty of any organizational boundary was rendered problematic: Any aspect of what an organization did was a potential candidate for externalization if it failed to meet a market test (Meyer 1991), and actors both inside and outside the organization could render such judgments.

Our interpretation is also consistent with the trend in business rhetoric away from the firm-as-portfolio model and toward the "boundaryless network" model. The repeated reference to the "corporation without boundaries" would be meaningless unless the default model were a corporation *with* boundaries. Once the special status of the organizational boundary was repudiated, a range of new social structural possibilities for regularized economic exchange was opened, including the widespread use of dynamic networks in place of vertical integration (Miles and Snow 1992), temporary employees in place of organizational members (Pfeffer and Baron 1988), and ultimately the "hollow corporation" in which virtually all functions that do not add sufficient value are subcontracted rather than brought within the firm's "boundary" (e.g., Handy 1989). Conglomerates strained the actor analogy; hollow corporations dispense with it entirely. The emerging naturalizing analogy for recurring structures of economic activity would seem to be the network, which makes possible a broad array of new quasi-organizational forms that do not conform to the body analogy, with models emerging from several industries including book publishing, movie production, biotechnology, and construction (Powell 1990). It remains to be seen whether the network model will diffuse as successfully as the firm-as-portfolio model that preceded it.

Conclusion

We have provided the first systematic assessment of organizational changes in the population of the largest American industrial firms in the 1980s, and we have offered an institutional interpretation for a disparate set of findings. Over the course of a decade, the dominant form of corporate organization in the United States, which had taken decades to evolve and attain its normative status (Fligstein 1991), was effectively deinstitutionalized, while new "boundaryless" production structures were advocated as credible quasi-organizational alternatives. This was not a gradual, evolutionary shift in which one type of organizational form died out and was replaced with another. It was an abrupt change, effected through both voluntary and involuntary processes at political, economic, and cognitive levels. We argue that deconglomeration manifests an underlying institutional shift in which the organization-as-body analogy, which sustained the corporate form for centuries (Coleman 1974), was undermined, and that as a result a new range of social structural arrangements for production has emerged to provide alternatives to bounded organizations (Sabel 1991). Our findings and interpretations raise a number of pressing questions for institutional theory and for the sociology of organizations more generally.

It has become a commonplace in social theory that we live in a "society of organizations," created by the spread of corporate forms to all aspects of social life, and that "natural persons" have been eclipsed by corporate persons which stand between individuals and the state (Jepperson and Meyer 1991). But this imagery faces challenges in the form of radical individualist theories about corporations (Jensen and Meckling 1976) and actual corporate practices aimed at creating "corporations without boundaries" (Kanter 1991). Economic theorists of the firm reprise the project of the Enlightenment thinkers who influenced the revolutionaries in late-eighteenth-century France (Sewell 1980)—to remove the social entitivity of the bounded corporate form and rest sovereignty in individuals only. Sovereign individuals may voluntarily enter into contracts with each other, but they cannot in principle form a sovereign corporate body at a level below the state. Sociologists may bristle that such methodological individualism reflects bad social scientific epistemology. Nevertheless, social structures of production increasingly resemble the nexus of contracts described in recent approaches to the firm in economics: individualistic, transient, networklike, with production accomplished by shifting sets of individuals tied through impermanent contracts. As Demsetz (1991) argues, the relevant question now is not the absolute, "When is a nexus-of-contracts *a firm*?" but the relative, "When is a nexus-of-contracts *more firm-like*?" (170). Such "firm-like" arrangements create obvious difficulties for organizational theories that take for granted that the organization is an entity and study analogous processes such as birth, growth, and death, while they create openings for approaches to social structure that take the network as a guiding analogy.

Institutional theory faces these changes from a curious position. On the one hand, the New Institutionalism has focused primarily on sectors, such as schools and mental hospitals, where technical ("market") pressures have traditionally been weak and where the ability to adopt organizational practices and forms is presumably less hampered. The application of such institutional models to business is more problematic, and one might argue that our results demonstrate that eventually the market catches up with institutionalized-but-inefficient organizational practices. On the other hand, business practices are guided to a great degree by analogies and shared norms, as the initial spread of the conglomerate form demonstrates (Fligstein 1991). Moreover, mental models of "what Wall Street wants" have come to have a powerful influence on how top managers of large corporations choose organizational forms and practices, and these models were behind much of the voluntary deconglomeration observed during the 1980s (Useem 1993). "The people who pick stocks find it easier to deal with simpler corporate structures," according to the head of strategic planning at Union Carbide, which helps explain the increase in share price that results from hints that a company will deconglomerate (Fisher 1992, 12). Thus, the New Institutionalism, particularly Douglas's (1986) theory of analogies, may provide crucial theoretical guidance for understanding the production structures that emerge and persist based on their ability to sustain naturalizing analogies.

We have provided initial evidence for how the inability to sustain such an analogy may have led to the deinstitutionalization of the firm-as-portfolio model, and we anticipate that institutional theory will be able to clarify the production structures that come into dominance in the future.

Notes

1. The Standard Industrial Classification (SIC) is a system used by the U.S. Office of Management and Budget as well as other public and private agencies to categorize industries at multiple nested levels of aggregation. Broader categories are denoted by numbers with fewer digits; for example, 28 denotes "Chemicals and allied products"; 281 denotes "Industrial and organic chemicals"; and 2812 denotes "Alkalies and chlorine."

2. Compare this to recent national discussions about the "information superhighway."

3. Details of our classification procedure are available upon request from the authors.

4. Ironically, the rhetoric of the boundaryless corporation has crept into the discourse of the one corporation that continued to operate businesses in a wide array of unrelated industries and to pursue acquisitions of unrelated businesses throughout the 1980s: General Electric's Annual Report for 1989 stated, "Our dream for the 1990s is a boundary-less Company, a Company where we knock down the walls that separate us from each other on the inside and from our key constituencies on the outside," which "will level its *external* walls . . . reaching out to key suppliers to make them part of a single process" (General Electric 1989, 5).

References

Amihud, Yakov, and Baruch Lev. 1981. "Risk Reduction as a Managerial Motive for Conglomerate Mergers." *Bell Journal of Economics* 12:605–17.

Baker, George P. 1992. "Beatrice: A Study in the Creation and Destruction of Value." *Journal of Finance* 47:1081–119.

Bhagat, Sanjai, Andrei Shleifer, and Robert W. Vishny. 1990. "Hostile Takeovers in the 1980s: The Return to Corporate Specialization." In *Brookings Papers on Economic Activity: Microeconomics, 1990*, ed. M. N. Baily and C. Winston. Washington, D.C.: Brookings Institution.

Black, Bernard S. 1992. "The Value of Institutional Investor Monitoring: The Empirical Evidence." *UCLA Law Review* 39:895–939.

Bureau of Economic Analysis. 1991. *1982 Benchmark Six-Digit Input-Output Accounts, Transactions*. Washington, D.C.: Bureau of Economic Analysis, U.S. Department of Commerce.

Burns, Lawton R., and Douglas R. Wholey. 1993. "Adoption and Abandonment of Matrix Management Programs: Effects of Organizational Characteristics and Interorganizational Networks." *Academy of Management Journal* 36:106–38.

Byrne, John A. 1993. "The Virtual Corporation." *Business Week*, February 8, 98–102.

Chandler, Alfred D., Jr. 1962. *Strategy and Structure: Chapters in the History of the American Industrial Enterprise*. Cambridge: MIT Press.

———. 1977. *The Visible Hand: The Managerial Revolution in American Business.* Cambridge: Harvard University Press.

Coffee, John C., Jr. 1988. "Shareholders versus Managers: The Strain in the Corporate Web." In *Knights, Raiders, and Targets: The Impact of the Hostile Takeover*, ed. John C. Coffee Jr., L. Lowenstein, and S. Rose-Ackerman. Oxford: Oxford University Press.

Coleman, James S. 1974. *Power and the Structure of Society.* New York: Norton.

Computer Directions Advisors, Inc. 1980. *Spectrum 3 13(f) Institutional Stock Holdings Survey.* June 30. Silver Spring, Md.: Computer Directions Advisors, Inc.

Cox, D. R. 1972. "Regression Models and Life Tables." *Journal of the Royal Statistical Society* B34:187–220.

Davis, Gerald F., and Suzanne K. Stout. 1992. "Organization Theory and the Market for Corporate Control: A Dynamic Analysis of the Characteristics of Large Takeover Targets, 1980–1990." *Administrative Science Quarterly* 37:605–33.

Demsetz, Harold. 1991. "The Theory of the Firm Revisited." In *The Nature of the Firm: Origins, Evolution, and Development*, ed. by Oliver E. Williamson and S. G. Winter. Oxford: Oxford University Press.

DiMaggio, Paul J. 1988. "Interest and Agency in Institutional Theory." In *Institutional Patterns and Organizations: Culture and Environment*, ed. Lynne G. Zucker. Cambridge, Mass.: Ballinger.

DiMaggio, Paul J., and Walter W. Powell. 1983. "The Iron Cage Revisited: Institutional Isomorphism and Collective Rationality in Organizational Fields." *American Sociological Review* 48:147–60.

———. 1991. Introduction. *The New Institutionalism in Organizational Analysis*, ed. Walter W. Powell and Paul J. DiMaggio. Chicago: University of Chicago Press.

Douglas, Mary. 1986. *How Institutions Think*. Syracuse, N.Y.: Syracuse University Press.

Easterbrook, Frank H., and Daniel R. Fischel. 1991. *The Economic Structure of Corporate Law.* Cambridge: Harvard University Press.

1991. "The Ebb Tide: A Survey of International Finance." *Economist* April 27, special section.

Espeland, Wendy Nelson, and Paul M. Hirsch. 1990. "Ownership Changes, Accounting Practice, and the Redefinition of the Corporation." *Accounting, Organizations, and Society* 15:77–96.

Fisher, Anne B. 1992. "New Way to Go: To Pieces." *Fortune*, April 6, 12.

Fligstein, Neil. 1985. "The Spread of the Multidivisional Form among Large Firms, 1919–1979." *American Sociological Review* 50:377–91.

———. 1990. *The Transformation of Corporate Control.* Cambridge: Harvard University Press.

———. 1991. "The Structural Transformation of American Industry: An Institutional Account of the Causes of Diversification in the Largest Firms, 1919–1979." In *The New Institutionalism in Organizational Analysis*, ed. Walter W. Powell and Paul J. DiMaggio. Chicago: University of Chicago Press.

General Electric Company. 1989. *1989 Annual Report*. Fairfield, Conn.: General Electric.

Golbe, Devra L., and Lawrence J. White. 1988. "A Time-Series Analysis of Mergers and Acquisitions in the U.S. Economy." In *Corporate Takeovers: Causes and Consequences*, ed. A. J. Auerbach. Chicago: University of Chicago Press.

Gordon, Jeffrey N. 1991. "Corporations, Markets, and Courts." *Columbia Law Review* 91:1931–88.

Granovetter, Mark. 1994. "Business Groups." In *Handbook of Economic Sociology*, ed. Neil J. Smelser and Richard Swedberg. Princeton: Princeton University Press.

Handy, Charles. 1989. *The Age of Unreason*. Boston: Harvard Business School Press.

Hannan, Michael T., and John Freeman. 1986. "Where Do Organizational Forms Come From?" *Sociological Forum* 1:50–72.

———. 1989. *Organizational Ecology*. Cambridge: Harvard University Press.

Haspeslagh, Philippe, 1982. "Portfolio Planning: Uses and Limits." *Harvard Business Review* 60, no. 1: 58–73.

Hirsch, Paul M. 1986 "From Ambushes to Golden Parachutes: Corporate Takeovers as an Instance of Cultural Framing and Institutional Integration." *American Journal of Sociology* 91:800–37.

Hirschhorn, Larry, and Thomas Gilmore. 1992, "The New Boundaries of the 'Boundaryless' Company." *Harvard Business Review* 70, no. 3:104–15.

1981. "How Much Does the Boss Make?" *Forbes*. June 8, 114–46.

"It Ain't Hay, but Is It Clover?" 1980. *Forbes*, June 9, 116–48.

Jacquemin, A. P., and C. H. Berry. 1979. "Entropy Measure of Diversification and Corporate Growth." *Journal of Industrial Economics* 27:359–69.

Jensen, Michael C., and William H. Meckling. 1976. "Theory of the Firm: Managerial Behavior, Agency Cost and Ownership Structure." *Journal of Financial Economics* 3:305–60.

Jepperson, Ronald L., and John W. Meyer. 1991. "The Public Order and the Construction of Formal Organizations." In *The New Institutionalism in Organizational Analysis*; ed. Walter W. Powell and Paul J. DiMaggio. Chicago: University of Chicago Press.

Kanter, Rosabeth Moss. 1991. "The Future of Bureaucracy and Hierarchy in Organizational Theory: A Report from the Field." In *Social Theory for a Changing Society*, ed. Pierre Bourdieu and James S. Coleman. Boulder, Colo.: Westview.

LeBaron, Dean, and Lawrence S. Speidell. 1987. "Why Are the Parts Worth More Than the Sum? 'Chop Shop,' a Corporate Valuation Model." In *The Merger Boom*, ed. L. E. Browne and E. S. Rosengren. Boston: Federal Reserve Bank of Boston.

Leblebici, Huseyin, Gerald R. Salancik, Anne Copay, and Tom King. 1991. "Institutional Change and the Transformation of Interorganizational Fields: An Organizational History of the U.S. Radio Broadcasting Industry." *Administrative Science Quarterly* 36:333–63.

Levy, Haim, and Marshall Sarnat. 1970. "Diversification, Portfolio Analysis, and the Uneasy Case for Conglomerate Mergers." *Journal of Finance* 25:795–802.

Lewellen, Wilbur, Claudio Loderer, and Ahron Rosenfeld. 1985. "Merger Decisions and Executive Stock Ownership in Acquiring Firms." *Journal of Accounting and Economics* 7:209–31.

Lipton, Martin, and Erica H. Steinberger. 1988. *Takeovers and Freezeouts*. Vol. 1. New York: Law Journal Seminars.

"Mad Mergers in Europe." 1992. *Economist*, February 1, 18–19.

March, James G., and Johan P. Olsen. 1984. "The New Institutionalism: Organizational Factors in Political Life." *American Political Science Review* 78:734–49.

Mason, R. Hal, and Maurice Goudzwaard. 1976. "Performance of Conglomerate Firms: A Portfolio Approach." *Journal of Finance* 31:39–48.

Mergers and Acquisitions: The Journal of Corporate Venture. 1986–90. Washington, D.C.: Mergers and Acquisitions, Inc.

Meyer, John W., and Brian Rowan. 1977. "Institutionalized Organizations: Formal Structure as Myth and Ceremony." *American Journal of Sociology* 83:340–63.

Meyer, Marshall W. 1991. "The Weberian Tradition in Organizational Research." In *Structures of Power and Constraint: Papers in Honor of Peter M. Blau*, ed. Craig J. Calhoun, Marshall W. Meyer, and W. Richard Scott. Cambridge: Cambridge University Press.

Meyer, Marshall W., and Lynne G. Zucker. 1989. *Permanently Failing Organizations*. Newbury Park, Calif.: Sage.

Miles, Raymond E., and Charles C. Snow. 1992. "Causes of Failure in Network Organizations." *California Management Review* 34, no. 4: 53–72.

Mitchell, Mark L., and Kenneth Lehn. 1990. "Do Bad Bidders Become Good Targets?" *Journal of Political Economy* 98:372–98.

Moody's Investors Service. Various years. *Moody's Industrial Manual*. New York: Moody's Investors Service.

Morck, Randall, Andrei Shleifer, and Robert W. Vishny. 1989. "Alternative Mechanisms for Corporate Control." *American Economic Review* 79:842–52.

———. 1990. "Do Managerial Objectives Drive Bad Acquisitions?" *Journal of Finance* 45:31–48.

"More Baskets, Choicer Eggs." 1989. *Economist*, October 21, 75–76.

Morgello, Clem, 1989. "Martin Davis of Paramount: Restructuring to Create Value." *Institutional Investor* 23, no. 12: 83–84.

Mueller, Dennis C. 1980. "The United States, 1962–1972." In *The Determinants and Effects of Mergers: An International Comparison*, ed. D. C. Mueller. Cambridge, Mass.: Olegeschlager, Gunn, and Hain.

Palepu, Krishna G. 1985. "Diversification Strategy, Profit Performance, and the Entropy Measure." *Strategic Management Journal* 6:239–55.

———. 1986. "Predicting Takeover Targets: A Methodological and Empirical Analysis." *Journal of Accounting and Economics* 8:3–35.

Palmer, Donald, Brad M. Barber, Xueguang Zhou, and Yasemin Soysal. 1993. "The Other Contested Terrain: The Friendly and Predatory Acquisition of Large Corporations in the 1960s." Paper presented at the Annual Meetings of the American Sociological Association, August, Miami, Fla.

Pfeffer, Jeffrey, and James N. Baron. 1988. "Taking the Workers Back Out: Recent Trends in the Structuring of Employment." In *Research in Organizational Behavior*, vol. 10, ed. Barry M. Stan and Larry L. Cummings. Greenwich, Conn.: JAI.

Porter, Michael E. 1987. "From Competitive Advantage to Corporate Strategy." *Harvard Business Review* 65, no. 3: 43–59.

Powell, Walter W. 1990. "Neither Market nor Hierarchy: Network Forms of Organization." In *Research in Organizational Behavior*, vol. 12, ed. Barry M. Stan and Larry L. Cumming. Greenwich, Conn.: JAI.

Powell, Walter W., and Paul J. DiMaggio, eds. 1991. *The New Institutionalism in Organizational Analysis*. Chicago: University of Chicago Press.

Putka, Gary. 1992. "Textron Defends $600 Million Acquisition of Cessna." *Wall Street Journal*, January 23, B6.

Ravenscraft, David J., and F. M. Scherer. 1987. *Mergers, Sell-Offs, and Economic Efficiency*. Washington, D.C.: Brookings Institution.

Roe, Mark J. 1993 "Takeover Politics." In *The Deal Decade: What Takeovers and Leveraged Buyouts Mean for Corporate Governance*, ed. M. M. Blair. Washington, D.C.: Brookings Institution.

Rumelt, Richard. 1974. *Strategy, Structure, and Economic Performance*. Boston: Harvard Business School Press.

Sabel, Charles. 1991. "Moebius-Strip Organizations and Open Labor Markets: Some Consequences of the Reintegration of Conception and Execution in a Volatile Economy." In *Social Theory for a Changing Society*, ed. Pierre Bourdieu and James S. Coleman. Boulder, Colo.: Westview.

Scherer, F. M. 1980. *Industrial Market Structure and Economic Performance*. 2d ed. Boston: Houghton Mifflin.

Scott, W. Richard. 1991: "Unpacking Institutional Arguments." In *The New Institutionalism in Organizational Analysis*, ed. Walter W. Powell and Paul J. DiMaggio. Chicago: University of Chicago Press.

———. 1992. *Organizations: Rational, Natural, and Open Systems*. 3d ed. Englewood Cliffs, N.J.: Prentice-Hall.

Selznick, Philip. 1957, *Leadership in Administration*. New York: Harper and Row.

Sewell, William H., Jr. 1980. *Work and Revolution in France: The Language of Labor from the Old Regime to 1848*. Cambridge: Cambridge University Press.

Standard and Poor's Corporation. Various years *Standard and Poor's Register of Corporations, Directors and Executives*. New York: Standard and Poor's.

———. Various years. *Stock Market Encyclopedia*. New York: Standard and Poor's.

Stearns, Linda Brewster, and Kenneth D. Allan. 1993. "Economic Behavior in an Institutional Setting: The Merger Movement of the 1980s." Paper presented at the Annual Meetings of the American Sociological Association, August, Miami, Fla.

Stinchcombe, Arthur L. 1968. *Constructing Social Theories*. New York: Harcourt Brace and World.

Tolbert, Pamela S., and Lynne G. Zucker. 1983. "Institutional Sources of Change in the Formal Structure of Organizations: The Diffusion of Civil Service Reform, 1880–1935." *Administrative Science Quarterly* 28:22–39.

Tully, Shawn. 1993. "The Modular Corporation." *Fortune*, February 8, 106–14.

Tuma, Nancy Brandon, and Michael T. Hannan. 1984. *Social Dynamics: Models and Methods*. Orlando, Fla.: Academic.

Useem, Michael. 1990. "Business and Politics in the United States and the United Kingdom." In *Structures of Capital: The Social Organization of the Economy*, ed. Sharon Zukin and Paul DiMaggio, Cambridge: Cambridge University Press.

———. 1993. *Executive Defense: Shareholder Power and Corporate Reorganization*. Cambridge: Harvard University Press.

Weston, J. Fred, Kwang S. Chung, and Susan E. Hoag. 1990. *Mergers, Restructuring, and Corporate Control*. Englewood Cliffs, N.J.: Prentice-Hall.

Williamson, Oliver E. 1975. *Markets and Hierarchies: Analysis and Antitrust Implications*. New York: Free Press.

Zucker, Lynne G. 1983. "Organizations as Institutions." In *Research in the Sociology of Organizations*, ed. S. B. Bacharach. Greenwich, Conn.: JAI.

Zukin, Sharon, and Paul J. DiMaggio, eds. 1990. *Structures of Capital: The Social Organization of the Economy*. Cambridge: Cambridge University Press.

NETWORKS

Chapter 8

FROM *THE DIVISION OF LABOR IN SOCIETY*

ÉMILE DURKHEIM

Translated by George Simpson

THE PROBLEM

The division of labor is not of recent origin, but it was only at the end of the eighteenth century that social cognizance was taken of the principle, though, until then, unwitting submission had been rendered to it. To be sure, several thinkers from earliest times saw its importance;[1] but Adam Smith was the first to attempt a theory of it. Moreover, he adopted this phrase that social science later lent to biology.

Nowadays, the phenomenon has developed so generally it is obvious to all. We need have no further illusions about the tendencies of modern industry; it advances steadily towards powerful machines, towards great concentrations of forces and capital, and consequently to the extreme division of labor. Occupations are infinitely separated and specialized, not only inside the factories, but each product is itself a specialty dependent upon others. Adam Smith and John Stuart Mill still hoped that agriculture, at least, would be an exception to the rule, and they saw it as the last resort of small-scale industry. Although one must be careful not to generalize unduly in such matters, nevertheless it is hard to deny today that the principal branches of the agricultural industry are steadily being drawn into the general movement.[2] Finally, business itself is ingeniously following and reflecting in all its shadings the infinite diversity of industrial enterprises; and, while this evolution is realizing itself with unpremeditated spontaneity, the economists, examining its causes and appreciating its results, far from condemning or opposing it, uphold it as necessary. They see in it the supreme law of human societies and the condition of their progress.

But the division of labor is not peculiar to the economic world; we can observe its growing influence in the most varied fields of society. The political, administrative, and judicial functions are growing more and more specialized.

It is the same with the aesthetic and scientific functions. It is long since philosophy reigned as the science unique; it has been broken into a multitude of special disciplines each of which has its object, method, and thought. "Men working in the sciences have become increasingly more specialized."[3]

Before revealing the nature of the studies with which the most illustrious scholars have concerned themselves for two centuries, de Candolle observed that at the time of Leibniz and Newton, it would have been necessary to write "almost always, two or three titles for each scholar; for instance, astronomer and physician, or mathematician, astronomer, and physician, or else to employ only general terms like philosopher or naturalist. Even that would not be enough. The mathematicians and naturalists were sometimes literary men or poets. Even at the end of the eighteenth century, these multiple titles would have been necessary to indicate exactly what such men as Wolff, Haller, Charles Bonnet had done in several categories of the arts and sciences. In the nineteenth century, this difficulty no longer exists, or at least is very rare."[4] Not only has the scholar ceased to take up different sciences simultaneously, but he does not even cover a single science completely any more. The ambit of his researches is restricted to a determined order of problems or even to a single problem. At the same time, the scientific function, formerly always allied with something more lucrative, like that of physician, priest, magistrate, soldier, has become more and more sufficient unto itself. De Candolle even foresees a day when the professions of scholar and teacher, still so intimately united, will finally separate.

The recent speculation in the philosophy of biology has ended by making us see in the division of labor a fact of a very general nature, which the economists, who first proposed it, never suspected. It is general knowledge since the works of Wolff, Von Baer, and Milne-Edwards, that the law of the division of labor applies to organisms as to societies; it can even be said that the more specialized the functions of the organism, the greater its development. This discovery has had the effect of immeasurably extending the scope of the division of labor, placing its origins in an infinitely distant past, since it becomes almost contemporaneous with the coming of life into the world. It is no longer considered only a social institution that has its source in the intelligence and will of men, but is a phenomenon of general biology whose conditions must be sought in the essential properties of organized matter. The division of labor in society appears to be no more than a particular form of this general process; and societies, in conforming to that law, seem to be yielding to a movement that was born before them, and that similarly governs the entire world.

Mechanical Solidarity

Everybody knows that there is a social cohesion whose cause lies in a certain conformity of all particular consciences to a common type which is none other than the psychic type of society. In these conditions, not only are all the members of the group individually attracted to one another because they resemble one another, but also because they are joined to what is the condition of existence of this collective type; that is to say, to the society that they form by their union. Not only do citizens love each other and seek each other out in preference to strangers, but they love their country. They will it as they will themselves, hold to it durably and for prosperity, because, without it, a great part of their psychic lives would function poorly. Inversely, society holds to what they present in the way of fundamental resemblances because that is a condition of its cohesion. There are in us two consciences: one contains states which are personal to each of us and which characterize us, while the states which comprehend the other are common to all society.[5] The first represent only our individual personality and constitute it; the second represent the collective type and, consequently, society, without which it would not exist. When it is one of the elements of this latter which determines our conduct, it is not in view of our personal interest that we act, but we pursue collective ends. Although distinct, these two consciences are linked one to the other, since, in sum, they are only one, having one and the same organic substratum. They are thus solidary. From this results a solidarity sui generis, which, born of resemblances, directly links the individual with society. We shall be better able to show in the next chapter why we propose to call it mechanical. This solidarity does not consist only in a general and indeterminate attachment of the individual to the group, but also makes the detail of his movements harmonious. In short, as these collective movements are always the same, they always produce the same effects. Consequently, each time that they are in play, wills move spontaneously and together in the same sense.

It is this solidarity which repressive law expresses, at least whatever there is vital in it. The acts that it prohibits and qualifies as crimes are of two sorts. Either they directly manifest very violent dissemblance between the agent who accomplishes them and the collective type, or else they offend the organ of the common conscience. In one case as in the other, the force that is offended by the crime and which suppresses it is thus the same. It is a product of the most essential social likenesses, and it has for its effect the maintenance of the social cohesion which results from these likenesses. It is this force which penal law protects against all enfeeblement, both in demanding from each of us a minimum of resemblances without which the individual would be a menace to the unity of the social body, and in imposing upon us the respect for the symbol which expresses and summarizes these resemblances at the same time that it guarantees them.

We thus explain why acts have been so often reputed criminal and punished as such without, in themselves, being evil for society. That is, just as the individual type, the collective type is formed from very diverse causes and even from fortuitous combinations. Produced through historical development, it carries the mark of circumstances of every kind which society has gone through in its history. It would be miraculous, then, if everything that we find there were adjusted to some useful end. But it cannot be that elements more or less numerous were there introduced without having any relation to social utility. Among the inclinations and tendencies that the individual has received from his ancestors, or which he has formed himself, many are certainly of no use, or cost more than they are worth. Of course, the majority are not harmful, for being, under such conditions, does not mean activity. But there are some of them remaining without any use, and those whose services are most incontestable often have an intensity which has no relation to their utility, because it comes to them, in part, from other causes. The case is the same with collective passions. All the acts which offend them are not dangerous in themselves, or, at least, are not as dangerous as they are made out to be. But the reprobation of which these acts are the object still has reason for existing, whatever the origin of the sentiments involved, once they are made part of a collective type; and especially if they are essential elements, everything which contributes to disturb them, at the same time disturbs social cohesion and compromises society. It was not at all useful for them to be born, but once they have endured, it becomes necessary that they persist in spite of their irrationality. That is why it is good, in general, that the acts which offend them be not tolerated. Of course, reasoning in the abstract, we may well show that there is no reason for a society to forbid the eating of such and such a meat, in itself inoffensive. But once the horror of this has become an integral part of the common conscience, it cannot disappear without a social link being broken, and that is what sane consciences obscurely feel.[6]

The case is the same with punishment. Although it proceeds from a quite mechanical reaction, from movements which are passionate and in great part nonreflective, it does play a useful role. Only this role is not where we ordinarily look for it. It does not serve, or else only serves quite secondarily, in correcting the culpable or in intimidating possible followers. From this point of view, its efficacy is justly doubtful and, in any case, mediocre. Its true function is to maintain social cohesion intact, while maintaining all its vitality in the common conscience. Denied so categorically, it would necessarily lose its energy, if an emotional reaction of the community did not come to compensate its loss, and it would result in a breakdown of social solidarity. It is necessary, then, that it be affirmed forcibly at the very moment when it is contradicted, and the only means of affirming it is to express the unanimous aversion which the crime continues to inspire, by an authentic act which can consist only in suffering inflicted upon the agent. Thus, while being the necessary product of the causes which engender it, this suffering is not a gratuitous cruelty. It is the sign which witnesses that collective sentiments are always collective, that the communion of spirits in the same faith rests on a solid foundation, and accordingly, that it is repairing the evil which the crime inflicted upon society. That is why we are right in saying that the criminal must suffer in proportion to his crime, why theories which refuse to punishment any expiatory character appear as so many spirits subversive of the social order. It is because these doctrines could be practiced only in a society where the whole common conscience would be nearly gone. Without this necessary satisfaction, what we call the moral conscience could not be conserved. We can thus say without paradox that punishment is above all designed to act upon upright people, for, since it serves to heal the wounds made upon collective sentiments, it can fill this role only where these sentiments exist, and commensurately with their vivacity. Of course, by warning already disturbed spirits of a new enfeeblement of the collective soul, it can even stop attacks from multiplying, but this result, however useful, is only a particular counterblow. In short, in order to form an exact idea of punishment, we must reconcile the two contradictory theories which deal with it: that which sees it as expiation, and that which makes it a weapon for social defense. It is certain that it functions for the protection of society, but that is because it is expiatory. Moreover, if it must be expiatory, that does not mean that by some mystical virtue pain compensates for the error, but rather that it can produce a socially useful effect only under this condition.[7]

The result of this chapter is this: there exists a social solidarity which comes from a certain number of states of conscience which are common to all the members of the same society. This is what repressive law materially represents, at least insofar as it is essential. The part that it plays in the general integration of society evidently depends upon the greater or lesser extent of the social life which the common conscience embraces and regulates. The greater the diversity of relations wherein the latter makes its action felt, the more also it creates links which attach the individual to the group; the more, consequently, social cohesion derives completely from this source and bears its mark. But the number of these relations is itself proportional to that of the repressive rules. In determining what fraction of the juridical system penal law represents, we, at the same time, measure the relative importance of this solidarity. It is true that in such a procedure we do not take into account certain elements of the collective conscience which, because of their smaller power or their indeterminateness, remain foreign to repressive law while contributing to the assurance of social harmony. These are the ones protected by punishments which are merely diffuse. But the same is the case with other parts of law. There is not one of them which is not complemented by custom, and as there is no reason for supposing that the relation of law and custom is not the same in these different spheres, this elimination is not made at the risk of having to alter the results of our comparison.

Organic Solidarity due to the Division of Labor

The very nature of the restitutive sanction suffices to show that the social solidarity to which this type of law corresponds is of a totally different kind.

What distinguishes this sanction is that it is not expiatory, but consists of a simple *return in state*. Sufferance proportionate to the misdeed is not inflicted on the one who has violated the law or who disregards it; he is simply sentenced to comply with it. If certain things were done, the judge reinstates them as they would have been. He speaks of law; he says nothing of punishment. Damage-interests have no penal character; they are only a means of reviewing the past in order to reinstate it, as far as possible, to its normal form. Tarde, it is true, has tried to find a sort of civil penality in the payment of costs by the defeated party.[8] But, taken in this sense, the word has only a metaphorical value. For punishment to obtain, there would at least have to be some relation between the punishment and the misdeed, and for that it would be necessary for the degree of gravity of the misdeed to be firmly established. In fact, however, he who loses the litigation pays the damages even when his intentions were pure, even when his ignorance alone was his culpability. The reasons for this rule are different from those offered by Tarde: given the fact that justice is not rendered gratuitously, it appears equitable for the damages to be paid by the one who brought them into being. Moreover, it is possible that the prospect of such costs may stop the rash pleader, but that is not sufficient to constitute punishment. The fear of ruin which ordinarily follows indolence or negligence may keep the negotiant active and awake, though ruin is not, in the proper sense of the word, the penal sanction for his misdeeds.

Neglect of these rules is not even punished diffusely. The pleader who has lost in litigation is not disgraced, his honor is not put in question. We can even imagine these rules being other than they are without feeling any repugnance. The idea of tolerating murder arouses us, but we quite easily accept modification of the right of succession, and can even conceive of its possible abolition. It is at least a question which we do not refuse to discuss. Indeed, we admit with impunity that the law of servitudes or that of usufructs may be otherwise organized, that the obligations of vendor and purchaser may be determined in some other manner, that administrative functions may be distributed according to different principles. As these prescriptions do not correspond to any sentiment in us, and as we generally do not scientifically know the reasons for their existence, since this science is not definite, they have no roots in the majority of us. Of course, there are exceptions. We do not tolerate the idea that an engagement contrary to custom or obtained either through violence or fraud can bind the contracting parties. Thus, when public opinion finds itself in the presence of such a case, it shows itself less indifferent than we have just now said, and it increases the legal sanction by its censure. The different domains of the moral life are not radically separated one from another; they are, rather, continuous, and, accordingly, there are among them marginal regions where different characters are found at the same time. However, the preceding proposition remains true in the great majority of cases. It is proof that the rules with a restitutive sanction either do not totally derive from the collective conscience, or are only feeble states of it. Repressive law corresponds to the heart, the center of the common conscience; laws purely moral are a part less central; finally, restitutive law is born in very ex-centric regions whence it spreads further. The more it becomes truly itself, the more removed it is.

This characteristic is, indeed, made manifest by the manner of its functioning. While repressive law tends to remain diffuse within society, restitutive law creates organs which are more and more specialized: consular tribunals, councils of arbitration, administrative tribunals of every sort. Even in its most general part, that which pertains to civil law, it is exercised only through particular functionaries: magistrates, lawyers, etc., who have become apt in this role because of very special training.

But, although these rules are more or less outside the collective conscience, they are not interested solely in individuals. If this were so, restitutive law would have nothing in common with social solidarity, for the relations that it regulates would bind individuals to one another without binding them to society. They would simply be happenings in private life, as friendly relations are. But society is far from having no hand in this sphere of juridical life. It is true that, generally, it does not intervene of itself and through its own movements; it must be solicited by the interested parties. But, in being called forth, its intervention is none the less the essential cog in the machine, since it alone makes it function. It propounds the law through the organ of its representatives.

. . . . .

We shall recognize only two kinds of positive solidarity which are distinguishable by the following qualities:

1. The first binds the individual directly to society without any intermediary. In the second, he depends upon society, because he depends upon the parts of which it is composed.

2. Society is not seen in the same aspect in the two cases. In the first, what we call society is a more or less organized totality of beliefs and sentiments common to all the members of the group: this is the collective type. On the other hand, the society in which we are solidary in the second instance is a system of different, special functions which definite relations unite. These two societies really make up only one. They are two aspects of one and the same reality, but none the less they must be distinguished.

3. From this second difference there arises another which helps us to characterize and name the two kinds of solidarity.

The first [kind of solidarity] can be strong only if the ideas and tendencies common to all the members of the society are greater in number and intensity than those which pertain personally to each member. It is as much stronger as the excess is more considerable. But what makes our personality is how much of our own individual qualities we have, what distinguishes us from others. This solidarity can grow only in inverse ratio to personality. There are in each of us, as we have said, two consciences: one which is common to our group in its entirety, which, consequently, is not ourself, but society living and acting within us; the other, on the contrary, represents that in us which is personal and distinct, that which makes us an individual.[9] Solidarity which comes from likenesses is at its maximum when the collective conscience completely envelops our whole conscience and coincides in all points with it. But, at that moment, our individuality is nil. It can be born only if the community takes smaller toll of us. There are, here, two contrary forces, one centripetal, the other centrifugal, which cannot flourish at the same time. We cannot, at one and the same time, develop ourselves in two opposite senses. If we have a lively desire to think and act for ourselves, we cannot be strongly inclined to think and act as others do. If our ideal is to present a singular and personal appearance, we do not want to resemble everybody else. Moreover, at the moment when this solidarity exercises its force, our personality vanishes, as our definition permits us to say, for we are no longer ourselves, but the collective life.

The social molecules which can be coherent in this way can act together only in the measure that they have no actions of their own, as the molecules of inorganic bodies. That is why we propose to call this type of solidarity mechanical. The term does not signify that it is produced by mechanical and artificial means. We call it that only by analogy to the cohesion which unites the elements of an inanimate body, as opposed to that which makes a unity out of the elements of a living body. What justifies this term is that the link which thus unites the individual to society is wholly analogous to that which attaches a thing to a person. The individual conscience, considered in this light, is a simple dependent upon the collective type and follows all of its movements, as the possessed object follows those of its owner. In societies where this type of solidarity is highly developed, the individual does not appear, as we shall see later. Individuality is something which the society possesses. Thus, in these social types, personal rights are not yet distinguished from real rights.

It is quite otherwise with the solidarity which the division of labor produces. Whereas the previous type implies that individuals resemble each other, this type presumes their difference. The first is possible only insofar as the individual personality is absorbed into the collective personality; the second is possible only if each one has a sphere of action which is peculiar to him; that is, a personality. It is necessary, then, that the collective conscience leave open a part of the individual conscience in order that special functions may be established there, functions which it cannot regulate. The more this region is extended, the stronger is the cohesion which results from this solidarity. In effect, on the one hand, each one depends as much more strictly on society as labor is more divided; and, on the other, the activity of each is as much more personal as it is more specialized. Doubtless, as circumscribed as it is, it is never completely original. Even in the exercise of our occupation, we conform to usages, to practices which are common to our whole professional brotherhood. But, even in this instance, the yoke that we submit to is much less heavy than when society completely controls us, and it leaves much more place open for the free play of our initiative. Here, then, the individuality of all grows at the same time as that of its parts. Society becomes more capable of collective movement, at the same time that each of its elements has more freedom of movement. This solidarity resembles that which we observe among the higher animals. Each organ, in effect, has its special physiognomy, its autonomy. And, moreover, the unity of the organism is as great as the individuation of the parts is more marked. Because of this analogy, we propose to call the solidarity which is due to the division of labor, organic.

Progress of Organic Solidarity

With him [Herbert Spencer], we have said that the place of the individual in society, of no account in its origins, becomes greater with civilization. But this incontestable fact is presented to us under an aspect totally different from that of English philosophy, so that, ultimately, our conclusions are opposed to his more than they are in agreement.

First of all, according to him, this absorption of the individual into the group would be the result of force and of an artificial organization necessitated by the state of war in which lower societies chronically live. It is especially in war that union is necessary to success. A group can defend itself against another group or subject it to itself only by acting together. It is necessary for all the individual forces to be concentrated in a permanent manner in an indissoluble union. But the only means of producing this concentration instantaneously is by instituting a very strong authority to which individuals are absolutely submissive. It is necessary that, as the will of a soldier finds itself suspended in executing the will of his superior, so too does the will of citizens find itself curtailed by that of the government.[10] Thus, it is an organized despotism which would annihilate individuals, and since this organization is essentially military, it is through militarism that Spencer defines these types of society.

We have seen, on the contrary, that this effacement of the individual has as its place of origin a social type which is characterized by a complete absence of all centralization. It is a product of that state of homogeneity which distinguishes primitive societies. If the individual is not distinct from the group, it is because the individual conscience is hardly at all distinguishable from the collective conscience. Spencer and other sociologists with him seem to have interpreted these distant facts in terms of very modern ideas. The very pronounced contemporary sentiment that each of us has of his own individuality has led them to believe that personal rights cannot be restrained to this point except by a coercive organization. We cling to them so firmly that they find it inconceivable for man to have willingly abandoned them. In fact, if in lower societies so small a place is given to individual personality, that is not because it has been restrained or artificially suppressed. It is simply because, at that moment of history, *it did not exist.*

Moreover, Spencer himself realizes that, of these societies, many have a constitution so little military and authoritarian that he qualifies them as democratic.[11] He wishes, however, to see in them the first symptoms of the future which he calls industrial. To that end, it is necessary for him to misconceive the fact that here as in those where there is submission to a despotic government, the individual has no sphere of action proper to him, as the general institution of communism proves. Indeed, the traditions, prejudices, the collective usages of all sorts, are not any the less burdensome to him than would be a constituted authority. Thus, we can term them democratic only by distorting the ordinary sense of the word. Moreover, if they were really impressed with the precocious individualism that is attributed to them, we would come to the strange conclusion that social evolution has tried, from the very first, to produce the most perfect types, since, as he says, no governmental force exists at first except that of the common will expressed in the assembled horde.[12] Would not the movement of history then be circular and would progress consist in anything but a return to the past?

In a general way, it is easy to understand why individuals will not be submissive except to a collective despotism, for the members of a society can be dominated only by a force which is superior to them, and there is only one which has this quality: that is the group. Any personality, as powerful as it might be, would be as nothing against a whole society; the latter can carry on in spite of it. That is why, as we have seen, the force of authoritarian governments does not come from authorities themselves, but from the very constitution of society. If, however, individualism was at this point congenital with humanity, we cannot see how primitive peoples could so easily subject themselves to the despotic authority of a chief, wherever necessary. The ideas, customs, institutions would have opposed such a radical transformation. But all this is explained once we have taken cognizance of the nature of these societies, for then the change is no longer as great as it seems. Individuals, instead of subordinating themselves to the group, were subordinated to that which represented it, and as the collective authority, when it was diffuse, was absolute, that of the chief, who is only its organized incarnation, naturally took on the same character.

Rather than dating the effacement of the individual from the institution of a despotic authority, we must, on the contrary, see in this institution the first step made towards individualism. Chiefs are, in fact, the first personalities who emerge from the social mass. Their exceptional situation, putting them beyond the level of others, gives them a distinct physiognomy and accordingly confers individuality upon them. In dominating society, they are no longer forced to follow all of its movements. Of course, it is from the group that they derive their power, but once power is organized, it becomes autonomous and makes them capable of personal activity. A source of initiative is thus opened which had not existed before then. There is, hereafter, someone who can produce new things and even, in certain measure, deny collective usages. Equilibrium has been broken.[13]

Organic and Contractual Solidarity

Social life comes from a double source, the likeness of consciences and the division of social labor. The individual is socialized in the first case, because, not having any real individuality, he becomes, with those whom he resembles, part of the same collective type; in the second case, because, while having a physiognomy and a personal activity which distinguishes him from others, he depends upon them in the same measure that he is distinguished from them, and consequently upon the society which results from their union.

The similitude of consciences gives rise to juridical rules which, with the threat of repressive measures, impose uniform beliefs and practices upon all. The more pronounced this is, the more completely is social life confounded with religious life, and the nearer to communism are economic institutions.

The division of labor gives rise to juridical rules which determine the nature and the relations of divided functions, but whose violation calls forth only restitutive measures without any expiatory character.

Each of these bodies of juridical rules is, moreover, accompanied by a body of purely moral rules. Where penal law is very voluminous, common morality is very extensive; that is to say, there is a multitude of collective practices placed under the protection of public opinion. Where restitutive law is highly developed, there is an occupational morality for each profession. In the interior of the same group of workers, there exists an opinion, diffuse in the entire extent of this circumscribed aggregate, which, without being furnished with legal sanctions, is rendered obedience. There are usages and customs common to the same order of functionaries which no one of them can break without incurring the censure of the corporation.[14] This morality is distinguished from the preceding by differences analogous to those which separate the two corresponding types of law. It is localized in a limited region of society. Moreover, the repressive character of the sanctions attaching to it is much less accentuated. Professional misdeeds call forth reprobation much more feeble than attacks against public morality.

The rules of occupational morality and justice, however, are as imperative as the others. They force the individual to act in view of ends which are not strictly his own, to make concessions, to consent to compromises, to take into account interests higher than his own. Consequently, even where society relies most completely upon the division of labor, it does not become a jumble of juxtaposed atoms, between which it can establish only external, transient contacts. Rather the members are united by ties which extend deeper and far beyond the short moments during which the exchange is made. Each of the functions that they exercise is, in a fixed way, dependent upon others, and with them forms a solidary system. Accordingly, from the nature of the chosen task permanent duties arise. Because we fill some certain domestic or social function, we are involved in a complex of obligations from which we have no right to free ourselves. There is, above all, an organ upon which we are tending to depend more and more; this is the state. The points at which we are in contact with it multiply as do the occasions when it is entrusted with the duty of reminding us of the sentiment of common solidarity.

Secondary Factors

In a small society, since everyone is clearly placed in the same conditions of existence, the collective environment is essentially concrete. It is made up of beings of all sorts who fill the social horizon. The states of conscience representing it then have the same character. First, they are related to precise objects, as this animal, this tree, this plant, this natural force, etc. Then, as everybody is related to these things in the same way, they affect all consciences in the same way. The whole tribe, if it is not too widely extended, enjoys or suffers the same advantages or inconveniences from the sun, rain, heat, or cold, from this river, or that source, etc. The collective impressions resulting from the fusion of all these individual impressions are then determined in form as well as in object, and, consequently, the common conscience has a defined character. But it changes its nature as societies become more voluminous. Because these societies are spread over a vaster surface, the common conscience is itself obliged to rise above all local diversities, to dominate more space, and consequently to become more abstract. For not many general things can be common to all these diverse environments. It is no longer such an animal, but such a species; not this source, but such sources; not this forest, but forest *in abstracto*.

Moreover, because conditions of life are no longer the same everywhere, these common objects, whatever they may be, can no longer determine perfectly identical sentiments everywhere. The collective resultants then no longer have the same sharpness, and the more so in this respect as their component elements are more unlike. The more differences among individual portraits serving to make a composite portrait, the more indecisive the latter is. True it is that local collective consciences can keep their individuality in the midst of the general collective conscience and that, as they comprise less space, they more easily remain concrete. But we know they slowly tend to vanish from the first, insofar as the social segments to which they correspond are effaced.

The fact which perhaps best manifests this increasing tendency of the common conscience is the parallel transcendence of the most essential of its elements, I mean the idea of divinity. In the beginning, the gods are not distinct from the universe, or rather there are no gods, but only sacred beings, without their sacred character being related to any external entity as their source. The animals or plants of the species which serves as a clan-totem are the objects of worship, but that is not because a principle sui generis comes to communicate their divine nature to them from without. This nature is intrinsic with them; they are divine in and of themselves. But little by little religious forces are detached from the things of which they were first only the attributes, and become hypostatized. Thus is formed the notion of spirits or gods who, while residing here or there as preferred, nevertheless exist outside of the particular objects to which they are more specifically attached.[15] By that very fact they are less concrete. Whether they multiply or have been led back to some certain unity, they are still immanent in the world. If they are in part separated from things, they are always in space. They remain, then, very near us, constantly fused into our life. The Greco-Latin polytheism, which is a more elevated and better organized form of animism, marks new progress in the direction of transcendence. The residence of the gods becomes more sharply distinct from that of men. Set upon the mysterious heights of Olympus or dwelling in the recesses of the earth, they personally intervene in human affairs only in somewhat intermittent fashion. But it is only with Christianity that God takes leave of space; his kingdom is no longer of this world. The dissociation of nature and the divine is so complete that it degenerates into antagonism. At the same time, the concept of divinity becomes more general and more abstract, for it is formed, not of sensations, as originally, but of ideas. The God of humanity necessarily is less concrete than the gods of the city or the clan.

Besides, at the same time as religion, the rules of law become universal, as well as those of morality. Linked at first to local circumstances, to particularities, ethnic, climatic, etc., they free themselves little by little, and with the same stroke become more general. What makes this increase of generality obvious is the uninterrupted decline of formalism. In lower societies, the very external form of conduct is predetermined even to the details. The way in which man must eat, dress in every situation, the gestures he must make, the formulas he must pronounce, are precisely fixed. On the contrary, the further one strays from the point of departure, the more moral and juridical prescriptions lose their sharpness and precision. They rule only the most general forms of conduct, and rule them in a very general manner, saying what must be done, not how it must be done. Now, all that is defined is expressed in a definite form. If collective sentiments had the same determination as formerly, they would not be expressed in a less determined manner. If the concrete details of action and thought were as uniform, they would be as obligatory.

It has often been remarked that civilization has a tendency to become more rational and more logical. The cause is now evident. That alone is rational which is universal. What baffles understanding is the particular and the concrete. Only the general is thought well of. Consequently, the nearer the common conscience is to particular things, the more it bears their imprint, the more unintelligible it also is. That is why primitive civilizations affect us as they do. Being unable to subsume them under logical principles, we succeed in seeing only bizarre and fortuitous combinations of heterogeneous elements. In reality, there is nothing artificial about them. It is necessary only to seek their determining causes in sensations and movements of sensibility, not in concepts. And if this is so, it is because the social environment for which they are made is not sufficiently extended. On the contrary, when civilization is developed over a vaster field of action, when it is applied to more people and things, general ideas necessarily appear and become predominant there. The idea of man, for example, replaces in law, in morality, in religion, that of Roman, which, being more concrete, is more refractory to science. Thus, it is the increase of volume in societies and their greater condensation which explain this great transformation.

But the more general the common conscience becomes, the greater the place it leaves to individual variations. When God is far from things and men, his action is no longer omnipresent, nor ubiquitous. There is nothing fixed save abstract rules which can be freely applied in very different ways. Then they no longer have the same ascendancy nor the same force of resistance. Indeed, if practices and formulas, when they are precise, determine thought and movements with a necessity analogous to that of reflexes, these general principles, on the contrary, can pass into facts only with the aid of intelligence. But, once reflection is awakened, it is not easy to restrain it. When it has taken hold, it develops spontaneously beyond the limits assigned to it. One begins by putting articles of faith beyond discussion; then discussion extends to them. One wishes an explanation of them; one asks their reasons for existing, and, as they submit to this search, they lose a part of their force. For reflective ideas never have the same constraining force as instincts. It is thus that deliberated movements have not the spontaneity of involuntary movements. Because it becomes more rational, the collective conscience becomes less imperative, and for this very reason, it wields less restraint over the free development of individual varieties.

The Causes

Hence, the claim sometimes advanced that in the division of labor lies the fundamental fact of all social life is wrong. Work is not divided among independent and already differentiated individuals who by uniting and associating bring together their different aptitudes. For it would be a miracle if differences thus born through chance circumstance could unite so perfectly as to form a coherent whole. Far from preceding collective life, they derive from it. They can be produced only in the midst of a society, and under the pressure of social sentiments and social needs. That is what makes them essentially harmonious. There is, then, a social life outside the whole division of labor, but which the latter presupposes. That is, indeed, what we have directly established in showing that there are societies whose cohesion is essentially due to a community of beliefs and sentiments, and it is from these societies that those whose unity is assured by the division of labor have emerged. The conclusions of the preceding book and those which we have just reached can then be used to control and mutually confirm each other. The division of physiological labor is itself submitted to this law; it never appears except in the midst of polycellular masses which are already endowed with a certain cohesion.

For a number of theorists, it is a self-evident truth that all society essentially consists of cooperation. Spencer has said that a society in the scientific sense of the word exists only when to the juxtaposition of individuals cooperation is added.[16] We have just seen that this so-called axiom is contrary to the truth. Rather it is evident, as Auguste Comte points out, "that cooperation, far from having produced society, necessarily supposes, as preamble, its spontaneous existence."[17] What bring men together are mechanical causes and impulsive forces, such as affinity of blood, attachment to the same soil, ancestral worship, community of habits, etc. It is only when the group has been formed on these bases that cooperation is organized there.

Further, the only cooperation possible in the beginning is so intermittent and feeble that social life, if it had no other source, would be without force and without continuity. With stronger reason, the complex cooperation resulting from the division of labor is an ulterior and derived phenomenon. It results from internal movements which are developed in the midst of the mass, when the latter is constituted. It is true that once it appears it tightens the social bonds and makes a more perfect individuality of society. But this integration supposes another which it replaces. For social units to be able to be differentiated, they must first be attracted or grouped by virtue of the resemblances they present. This process of formation is observed, not only originally, but in each phase of evolution. We know, indeed, that higher societies result from the union of lower societies of the same type. It is necessary first that these latter be mingled in the midst of the same identical collective conscience for the process of differentiation to begin or recommence. It is thus that more complex organisms are formed by the repetition of more simple, similar organisms which are differentiated only if once associated. In short, association and cooperation are two distinct facts, and if the second, when developed, reacts on the first and transforms it, if human societies steadily become groups of co-operators, the duality of the two phenomena does not vanish for all that.

If this important truth has been disregarded by the utilitarians, it is an error rooted in the manner in which they conceive the genesis of society. They suppose originally isolated and independent individuals, who, consequently, enter into relationships only to cooperate, for they have no other reason to clear the space separating them and to associate. But this theory, so widely held, postulates a veritable *creatio ex nihilo*.

It consists, indeed, in deducing society from the individual. But nothing we know authorizes us to believe in the possibility of such spontaneous generation. According to Spencer, for societies to be formed within this hypothesis, it is necessary that primitive units pass from the state of perfect independence to that of mutual dependence.[18] But what can have determined such a complete transformation in them? Is it the prospect of the advantages presented by social life? But they are counterbalanced, perhaps more than counterbalanced, by the loss of independence, for, among individuals born for a free and solitary life, such a sacrifice is most intolerable. Add to this, that in the first social types social life is as absolute as possible, for nowhere is the individual more completely absorbed in the group. How would man, if he were born an individualist, as is supposed, be able to resign himself to an existence clashing violently with his fundamental inclination? How pale the problematical utility of cooperation must appear to him beside such a fall! With autonomous individualities, as are imagined, nothing can emerge save what is individual, and, consequently, cooperation itself, which is a social fact, submissive to social rules, cannot arise. Thus, the psychologist who starts by restricting himself to the ego cannot emerge to find the non-ego.

Collective life is not born from individual life, but it is, on the contrary, the second which is born from the first. It is on this condition alone that one can explain how the personal individuality of social units has been able to be formed and enlarged without disintegrating society. Indeed, as, in this case, it becomes elaborate in the midst of a preexisting social environment, it necessarily bears its mark. It is made in a manner so as not to ruin this collective order with which it is solidary. It remains adapted to it while detaching itself. It has nothing antisocial about it because it is a product of society. It is not the absolute personality of the monad, which is sufficient unto itself, and could do without the rest of the world, but that of an organ or part of an organ having its determined function, but which cannot, without risking dissolution, separate itself from the rest of the organism. Under these conditions, cooperation becomes not only possible but necessary. Utilitarians thus reverse the natural order of facts, and nothing is more deceiving than this inversion. It is a particular illustration of the general truth that what is first in knowledge is last in reality. Precisely because cooperation is the most recent fact, it strikes sight first. If, then, one clings to appearance, as does common sense, it is inevitable that one see in it the primary fact of moral and social life.

But if it is not all of ethics, it is not necessary to put it outside ethics, as do certain moralists. As the utilitarians, the idealists have it consist exclusively in a system of economic relations, of private arrangements in which egotism is the only active power. In truth, the moral life traverses all the relations which constitute cooperation, since it would not be possible if social sentiments, and, consequently, moral sentiments, did not preside in its elaboration.

Notes

1. Aristotle, *Nicomachean Ethics*, E, 1133a16.
2. *Journal des Economistes*, November 1884, 211.
3. De Candolle, *Histoire des Sciences et des Savants*, 2d ed. (Geneva: H. Georg, 1885), 263.
4. De Candolle, *Histoire des Sciences*, 263.
5. To simplify the exposition, we hold that the individual appears only in one society. In fact, we take part in several groups and there are in us several collective consciences; but this complication changes nothing with regard to the relation that we are now establishing.
6. That does not mean that it is necessary to conserve a penal rule because, at some given moment, it corresponded to some collective sentiment. It has a raison d'être only if this latter is living and energetic. If it has disappeared or been enfeebled, nothing is vainer or worse than trying to keep it alive artificially or by force. It can even be that it was necessary to combat a practice which was common, but is no longer so, and opposes the establishment of new and necessary practices. But we need not enter into this casuistical problem.
7. In saying that punishment, such as it is, has a raison d'être, we do not intend to suggest that it is perfect and incapable of betterment. It is very evident, on the contrary, that having been produced, in great part, by very mechanical causes, it can be but very imperfectly adjusted to its role. The matter is only a question of justification in the large.
8. Gabriel de Tarde, *La Criminalité comparée*, 113.
9. However, these two consciences are not in regions geographically distinct from us, but penetrate from all sides.
10. Herbert Spencer, *The Principles of Sociology*, 2:153.

11. Spencer, *Principles of Sociology*, 2:154–55.

12. Spencer, *Principles of Sociology*, 3:426–27.

13. We find here confirmation of a previously enunciated proposition which makes governmental power an emanation of the inherent life of the collective conscience.

14. This censure, moreover, just as all moral punishment, is translated into external movements (discipline, dismissal of employees, loss of relations, etc.).

15. See Albert Réville, Les *Religions des peuples non civilisés* (Paris: Librairie Fischbacher, 1883), 1:67 ff., 2:230ff.

16. Spencer, *Principles of Sociology*, 3:331.

17. Auguste Comte, *Cours de philosophie positive*, 4:421.

18. Spencer, *Principles of Sociology*, 3:332.

Chapter 9

ECONOMIC ACTION AND SOCIAL STRUCTURE: THE PROBLEM OF EMBEDDEDNESS

MARK GRANOVETTER

INTRODUCTION: THE PROBLEM OF EMBEDDEDNESS

How behavior and institutions are affected by social relations is one of the classic questions of social theory. Since such relations are always present, the situation that would arise in their absence can be imagined only through a thought experiment like Thomas Hobbes's "state of nature" or John Rawls's "original position." Much of the utilitarian tradition, including classical and neoclassical economics, assumes rational, self-interested behavior affected minimally by social relations, thus invoking an idealized state not far from that of these thought experiments. At the other extreme lies what I call the argument of "embeddedness": the argument that the behavior and institutions to be analyzed are so constrained by ongoing social relations that to construe them as independent is a grievous misunderstanding.

This article concerns the embeddedness of economic behavior. It has long been the majority view among sociologists, anthropologists, political scientists, and historians that such behavior was heavily embedded in social relations in premarket societies but became much more autonomous with modernization. This view sees the economy as an increasingly separate, differentiated sphere in modern society, with economic transactions defined no longer by the social or kinship obligations of those transacting but by rational calculations of individual gain. It is sometimes further argued that the traditional situation is reversed: instead of economic life being submerged in social relations, these relations become an epiphenomenon of the market. The embeddedness position is associated with the "substantivist" school in anthropology, identified especially with Karl Polanyi (1944; Polanyi, Arensberg, and Pearson 1957) and with the idea of "moral economy" in history and political science (Thompson 1971; Scott 1976). It has also some obvious relation to Marxist thought.

Mark Granovetter. 1985. "Economic Action and Social Structure: The Problem of Embeddedness." *American Journal of Sociology* 91: 481–510.

Few economists, however, have accepted this conception of a break in embeddedness with modernization; most of them assert instead that embeddedness in earlier societies was not substantially greater than the low level found in modern markets. The tone was set by Adam Smith, who postulated a "certain propensity in human nature . . . to truck, barter and exchange one thing for another" (1979, book 1, chap. 2) and assumed that since labor was the only factor of production in primitive society, goods must have exchanged in proportion to their labor costs—as in the general classical theory of exchange (1979, book 1, chap. 6). From the 1920s on, certain anthropologists took a similar position, which came to be called the "formalist" one: even in tribal societies, economic behavior was sufficiently independent of social relations for standard neoclassical analysis to be useful (Schneider 1974). This position has recently received a new infusion as economists and fellow travelers in history and political science have developed a new interest in the economic analysis of social institutions—much of which falls into what is called the "new institutional economics"—and have argued that behavior and institutions previously interpreted as embedded in earlier societies, as well as in our own, can be better understood as resulting from the pursuit of self-interest by rational, more or less atomized individuals (e.g., North and Thomas 1973; Williamson 1975; Popkin 1979).

My own view diverges from both schools of thought. I assert that the level of embeddedness of economic behavior is lower in nonmarket societies than is claimed by substantivists and development theorists, and it has changed less with "modernization" than they believe; but I argue also that this level has always been and continues to be more substantial than is allowed for by formalists and economists. I do not attempt here to treat the issues posed by nonmarket societies. I proceed instead by a theoretical elaboration of the concept of embeddedness, whose value is then illustrated with a problem from modern society, currently important in the new institutional economics: which transactions in modern capitalist society are carried out in the market, and which subsumed within hierarchically organized firms? This question has been raised to prominence by the "markets and hierarchies" program of research initiated by Oliver Williamson (1975).

Over- and Undersocialized Conceptions of Human Action in Sociology and Economics

I begin by recalling Dennis Wrong's 1961 complaint about an "over-socialized conception of man in modern sociology"—a conception of people as overwhelmingly sensitive to the opinions of others and hence obedient to the dictates of consensually developed systems of norms and values, internalized through socialization, so that obedience is not perceived as a burden. To the extent that such a conception was prominent in 1961, it resulted in large part from Talcott Parsons's recognition of the problem of order as posed by Hobbes and his own attempt to resolve it by transcending the atomized, *undersocialized* conception of man in the utilitarian tradition of which Hobbes was part (Parsons 1937, 89–94). Wrong approved the break with atomized utilitarianism and the emphasis on actors' embeddedness in social context—the crucial factor absent from Hobbes's thinking—but warned of exaggerating the degree of this embeddedness and the extent to which it might eliminate conflict:

> It is frequently the task of the sociologist to call attention to the intensity with which men desire and strive for the good opinion of their immediate associates in a variety of situations, particularly those where received theories or ideologies have unduly emphasized other motives. . . . Thus sociologists have shown that factory workers are more sensitive to the attitudes of their fellow workers than to purely economic incentives. . . . It is certainly not my intention to criticize the findings of such studies. My objection is that . . . [a]lthough sociologists have criticized past efforts to single out one fundamental motive in human conduct, the desire to achieve a favorable self-image by winning approval from others frequently occupies such a position in their own thinking. (1961, 188–89)

Classical and neoclassical economics operates, in contrast, with an atomized, *under*socialized conception of human action, continuing in the utilitarian tradition. The theoretical arguments disallow by hypothesis any impact of social structure and social relations on production, distribution, or consumption. In competitive markets, no producer or consumer noticeably influences aggregate supply or demand or, therefore, prices or other terms of trade. As Albert Hirschman has noted, such idealized markets, involving as they do "large numbers of price-taking anonymous buyers and sellers supplied with perfect information . . . function without any prolonged human or social contact between the parties. Under perfect competition there is no room for bargaining, negotiation, remonstration or mutual adjustment and the various operators that contract together need not enter into recurrent or continuing relationships as a result of which they would get to know each other well" (1982, 1473).

It has long been recognized that the idealized markets of perfect competition have survived intellectual attack in part because self-regulating economic structures are politically attractive to many. Another reason for this survival, less clearly understood, is that the elimination of social relations from economic analysis removes the problem of order from the intellectual agenda, at least in the economic sphere. In Hobbes's argument, disorder arises because conflict-free social and economic transactions depend on trust and the absence of malfeasance. But these are unlikely when individuals are conceived to have neither social relationships nor institutional context—as in the "state of nature." Hobbes contains the difficulty by superimposing a structure of autocratic authority. The solution of classical liberalism, and correspondingly of classical economics, is antithetical: repressive political structures are rendered unnecessary by competitive markets that make force or fraud unavailing. Competition determines the terms of trade in a way that individual traders cannot manipulate. If traders encounter complex or difficult relationships, characterized by mistrust or malfeasance, they can simply move on to the legion of other traders willing to do business on market terms; social relations and their details thus become frictional matters.

In classical and neoclassical economics, therefore, the fact that actors may have social relations with one another has been treated, if at all, as a frictional drag that impedes competitive markets. In a much-quoted line, Adam Smith complained that "people of the same trade seldom meet together, even for merriment and diversion, but the conversation ends in a conspiracy against the public, or in some contrivance to raise prices." His laissez-faire politics allowed few solutions to this problem, but he did suggest repeal of regulations requiring all those in the same trade to sign a public register; the public existence of such information "connects individuals who might never otherwise be known to one another and gives every man of the trade a direction where to find every other man of it." Noteworthy here is not the rather lame policy prescription but the recognition that *social atomization is prerequisite to perfect competition* (Smith 1979, 232–33).

More recent comments by economists on "social influences" construe these as processes in which actors acquire customs, habits, or norms that are followed mechanically and automatically, irrespective of their bearing on rational choice. This view, close to Wrong's "oversocialized conception," is reflected in James Duesenberry's quip that "economics is all about how people make choices; sociology is all about how they don't have any choices to make" (1960, 233) and in E. H. Phelps Brown's description of the "sociologists' approach to pay determination" as deriving from the assumption that people act in "certain ways because to do so is customary, or an obligation, or the 'natural thing to do,' or right and proper, or just and fair" (1977, 17).

But despite the apparent contrast between under- and oversocialized views, we should note an irony of great theoretical importance: both have in common a conception of action and decision carried out by atomized actors. In the undersocialized account, atomization results from narrow utilitarian pursuit of self-interest; in the oversocialized one, from the fact that behavioral patterns have been internalized and ongoing social relations thus have only peripheral effects on behavior. That the internalized rules of behavior are social in origin does not differentiate this argument decisively from a utilitarian one, in which the source of utility functions is left open, leaving room for behavior guided entirely by consensually determined norms and values—as in the oversocialized view. Under- and oversocialized resolutions of the problem of order thus merge in their atomization of actors from immediate social context. This ironic merger is already visible in Hobbes's *Leviathan*, in which the unfortunate denizens of the state of nature, overwhelmed by the disorder consequent to their atomization, cheerfully surrender all their rights to an authoritarian power and subsequently behave in a docile and honorable manner; by the artifice of a social contract, they lurch directly from an undersocialized to an oversocialized state.

When modern economists do attempt to take account of social influences, they typically represent them in the oversocialized manner represented in the quotations above. In so doing, they reverse the judgment that social influences are frictional but sustain the conception of how such influences operate. In the theory of segmented labor markets, for example, Michael Piore has argued that members of each labor market segment are characterized by different styles of decision making and that the making of decisions by rational choice, custom, or command in upper-primary, lower-primary, and secondary labor markets respectively corresponds to the origins of workers in middle-, working-, and lower-class subcultures (Piore 1975). Similarly, Samuel Bowles and Herbert Gintis, in their account of the consequences of American education, argue that different social classes display different cognitive processes because of differences in the education provided to each. Those destined for lower-level jobs are trained to be dependable followers of rules, while those who will be channeled into elite positions attend "elite four-year colleges" that "emphasize social relationships conformable with the higher levels in the production hierarchy. . . . As they 'master' one type of behavioral regulation they are either allowed to progress to the next or are channeled into the corresponding level in the hierarchy of production" (Bowles and Gintis 1975, 132).

But these oversocialized conceptions of how society influences individual behavior are rather mechanical: once we know the individual's social class or labor market sector, everything else in behavior is automatic, since they are so well socialized. Social influence here is an external force that, like the deists' God, sets things in motion and has no further effects—a force that insinuates itself into the minds and bodies of individuals (as in the movie *Invasion of the Body Snatchers*), altering their way of making decisions. Once we know in just what way an individual has been affected, ongoing social relations and structures are irrelevant. Social influences are all contained inside an individual's head, so, in actual decision situations, he or she can be atomized as any *homo economicus*, though perhaps with different rules for decisions. More sophisticated (and thus less oversocialized) analyses of cultural influences (e.g., Fine and Kleinman 1979; Cole 1979, chap. 1) make it clear that culture is not a once-for-all influence but an ongoing process, continuously constructed and reconstructed during interaction. It not only shapes its members but also is shaped by them, in part for their own strategic reasons.

Even when economists do take social relationships seriously, as do such diverse figures as Harvey Leibenstein (1976) and Gary Becker (1976), they invariably abstract away from the history of relations and their position with respect to other relations—what might be called the historical and structural embeddedness of relations. The interpersonal ties described in their arguments are extremely stylized, average, "typical"—devoid of specific content, history, or structural location. Actors' behavior results from their named role positions and role sets; thus we have arguments on how workers and supervisors, husbands and wives, or criminals and law enforcers will interact with one another, but these relations are not assumed to have individualized content beyond that given by the named roles. This procedure is exactly what structural sociologists have criticized in Parsonian sociology—the relegation of the specifics of individual relations to a minor role in the overall conceptual scheme, epiphenomenal in comparison with enduring structures of normative role prescriptions deriving from ultimate value orientations. In economic models, this treatment of social relations has the paradoxical effect of preserving atomized decision making even when decisions are seen to involve more than one individual. Because the analyzed set of individuals—usually dyads, occasionally larger groups—is abstracted out of social context, it is atomized in its behavior from that of other groups and from the history of its own relations. Atomization has not been eliminated, merely transferred to the dyadic or higher level of analysis. Note the use of an oversocialized conception—that of actors behaving exclusively in accord with their prescribed roles—to implement an atomized, undersocialized view.

A fruitful analysis of human action requires us to avoid the atomization implicit in the theoretical extremes of under- and oversocialized conceptions. Actors do not behave or decide as atoms outside a social context, nor do they adhere slavishly to a script written for them by the particular intersection of social categories that they happen to occupy. Their attempts at purposive action are instead embedded in concrete, ongoing systems of social relations. In the remainder of this article I illustrate how this view of embeddedness alters our theoretical and empirical approach to the study of economic behavior. I first narrow the focus to the question of trust and malfeasance in economic life and then use the "markets and hierarchies" problem to illustrate the use of embeddedness ideas in analyzing this question.[1]

Embeddedness, Trust, and Malfeasance in Economic Life

Since about 1970, there has been a flurry of interest among economists in the previously neglected issues of trust and malfeasance. Oliver Williamson has noted that real economic actors engage not merely in the pursuit of self-interest but also in "opportunism"—"self-interest seeking with guile; agents who are skilled at dissembling realize transactional advantages.[2] Economic man . . . is thus a more subtle and devious creature than the usual self-interest seeking assumption reveals" (1975, 255).

But this points out a peculiar assumption of modern economic theory, that one's economic interest is pursued only by comparatively gentlemanly means. The Hobbesian question—how it can be that those who pursue their own interest do not do so mainly by force and fraud—is finessed by this conception. Yet, as Hobbes saw so clearly, there is nothing in the intrinsic meaning of "self-interest" that excludes force or fraud.

In part, this assumption persisted because competitive forces, in a self-regulating market, could be imagined to suppress force and fraud. But the idea is also embedded in the intellectual history of the discipline. In *The Passions and the Interests*, Albert Hirschman (1977) shows that an important strand of intellectual history from the time of *Leviathan* to that of *The Wealth of Nations* consisted of the watering down of Hobbes's problem of order by arguing that certain human motivations kept others under control and that, in particular, the pursuit of economic self-interest was typically not an uncontrollable "passion" but a civilized, gentle activity. The wide though implicit acceptance of such an idea is a powerful example of how under- and oversocialized conceptions complement one another: atomized actors in competitive markets so thoroughly internalize these normative standards of behavior as to guarantee orderly transactions.[3]

What has eroded this confidence in recent years has been increased attention to the micro-level details of imperfectly competitive markets, characterized by small numbers of participants with sunk costs and "specific human capital" investments. In such situations, the alleged discipline of competitive markets cannot be called on to mitigate deceit, so the classical problem of how it can be that daily economic life is not riddled with mistrust and malfeasance has resurfaced.

In the economic literature, I see two fundamental answers to this problem and argue that one is linked to an undersocialized, and the other to an oversocialized, conception of human action. The undersocialized account is found mainly in the new institutional economics—a loosely defined confederation of economists with an interest in explaining social institutions from a neoclassical viewpoint. (See, e.g., Furubotn and Pejovich 1972; Alchian and Demsetz 1973; Lazear 1979; Rosen 1982; Williamson 1975, 1979, 1981; Williamson and Ouchi 1981.) The general story told by members of this school is that social institutions and arrangements previously thought to be the adventitious result of legal, historical, social, or political forces are better viewed as the efficient solution to certain economic problems. The tone is similar to that of structural-functional sociology of the 1940s to the 1960s, and much of the argumentation fails the elementary tests of a sound functional explanation laid down by Robert Merton in 1947. Consider, for example, Schotter's view that to understand any observed economic institution requires only that we "infer the evolutionary problem that must have existed for the institution as we see it to have developed. Every evolutionary economic problem requires a social institution to solve it" (1981, 2).

Malfeasance is here seen to be averted because clever institutional arrangements make it too costly to engage in, and these arrangements—many previously interpreted as serving no economic function—are now seen as having evolved to discourage malfeasance. Note, however, that they do not produce trust but instead are a functional substitute for it. The main such arrangements are elaborate explicit and implicit contracts (Okun 1981), including deferred compensation plans and mandatory retirement—seen to reduce the incentives for "shirking" on the job or absconding with proprietary secrets (Lazear 1979; Pakes and Nitzan 1982)—and authority structures that deflect opportunism by making potentially divisive decisions by fiat (Williamson 1975). These conceptions are undersocialized in that they do not allow for the extent to which concrete personal relations and the obligations inherent in them discourage malfeasance, quite apart from institutional arrangements. *Substituting* these arrangements for trust results actually in a Hobbesian situation, in which any rational individual would be motivated to develop clever ways to evade them; it is then hard to imagine that everyday economic life would not be poisoned by ever more ingenious attempts at deceit.

Other economists have recognized that some degree of trust *must* be assumed to operate, since institutional arrangements alone could not entirely stem force or fraud. But it remains to explain the source of this trust, and appeal is sometimes made to the existence of a "generalized morality." Kenneth Arrow, for example, suggests that societies, "in their evolution have developed implicit agreements to certain kinds of regard for others, agreements which are essential to the survival of the society or at least contribute greatly to the efficiency of its working" (1974, 26; see also Akerlof 1983 on the origins of "honesty").

Now one can hardly doubt the existence of some such generalized morality; without it, you would be afraid to give the gas station attendant a twenty-dollar bill when you had bought only five dollars' worth of gas. But this conception has the oversocialized characteristic of calling on a generalized and automatic response, even though moral action in economic life is hardly automatic or universal (as is well known at gas stations that demand exact change after dark).

Consider a case where generalized morality does indeed seem to be at work: the legendary (I hesitate to say apocryphal) economist who, against all economic rationality, leaves a tip in a roadside restaurant far from home. Note that this transaction has three characteristics that make it somewhat unusual: (1) the transactors are previously unacquainted, (2) they are unlikely to transact again, and (3) information about the activities of either is unlikely to reach others with whom they might transact in the future. I argue that it is only in situations of this kind that the absence of force and fraud can mainly be explained by generalized morality. Even there, one might wonder how effective this morality would be if large costs were incurred.

The embeddedness argument stresses instead the role of concrete personal relations and structures (or "networks") of such relations in generating trust and discouraging malfeasance. The widespread preference for transacting with individuals of known reputation implies that few are actually content to rely on either generalized morality *or* institutional arrangements to guard against trouble. Economists *have* pointed out that one incentive not to cheat is the cost of damage to one's reputation; but this is an undersocialized conception of reputation as a generalized commodity, a ratio of cheating to opportunities for doing so. In practice, we settle for such generalized information when nothing better is available, but ordinarily we seek better information. Better than the statement that someone is known to be reliable is information from a trusted informant that he has dealt with that individual and found him so. Even better is information from one's own past dealings with that person. This is better information for four reasons: (1) it is cheap; (2) one trusts one's own information best—it is richer, more detailed, and known to be accurate; (3) individuals with whom one has a continuing relation have an economic motivation to be trustworthy, so as not to discourage future transactions; and (4) departing from pure economic motives, continuing economic relations often become overlaid with social content that carries strong expectations of trust and abstention from opportunism.

It would never occur to us to doubt this last point in more intimate relations, which make behavior more predictable and thus close off some of the fears that create difficulties among strangers. Consider, for example, why individuals in a burning theater panic and stampede to the door, leading to desperate results. Analysts of collective behavior long considered this to be prototypically irrational behavior, but Roger Brown (1965, chap. 14) points out that the situation is essentially an *n*-person Prisoner's Dilemma: each stampeder is actually being quite rational given the absence of a guarantee that anyone else will walk out calmly, even though all would be better off if everyone did so. Note, however, that in the case of the burning houses featured on the 11:00 P.M. news, we never hear that everyone stampeded out and that family members trampled one another. In the family, there is no Prisoner's Dilemma because each is confident that the others can be counted on.

In business relations the degree of confidence must be more variable, but Prisoner's Dilemmas are nevertheless often obviated by the strength of personal relations, and this strength is a property not of the transactors but of their concrete relations. Standard economic analysis neglects the identity and past relations of individual transactors, but rational individuals know better, relying on their knowledge of these relations. They are less interested in *general* reputations than in whether a particular other may be expected to deal honestly with *them*—mainly a function of whether they or their own contacts have had satisfactory past dealings with the other. One sees this pattern even in situations that appear, at first glance, to approximate the classic higgling of a competitive market, as in the Moroccan bazaar analyzed by Geertz (1979).

Up to this point, I have argued that social relations, rather than institutional arrangements or generalized morality, are mainly responsible for the production of trust in economic life. But I then risk rejecting one kind of optimistic functionalism for another, in which networks of relations, rather than morality or arrangements, are the structure that fulfills the function of sustaining order. There are two ways to reduce this risk. One is to recognize that as a solution to the problem of order, the embeddedness position is less sweeping than either alternative argument, since networks of social relations penetrate irregularly and in differing degrees in different sectors of economic life, thus allowing for what we already know: distrust, opportunism, and disorder are by no means absent.

The second is to insist that while social relations may indeed often be a necessary condition for trust and trustworthy behavior, they are not sufficient to guarantee these and may even provide occasion and means for malfeasance and conflict on a scale larger than in their absence. There are three reasons for this.

1. The trust engendered by personal relations presents, by its very existence, enhanced opportunity for malfeasance. In personal relations it is common knowledge that "you always hurt the one you love"; that person's trust in you results in a position far more vulnerable than that of a stranger. (In the Prisoner's Dilemma, knowledge that one's coconspirator is certain to deny the crime is all the more rational motive to confess, and personal relations that abrogate this dilemma may be less symmetrical than is believed by the party to be deceived.) This elementary fact of social life is the bread and butter of "confidence" rackets that simulate certain relationships, sometimes for long periods, for concealed purposes. In the business world, certain crimes, such as embezzling, are simply impossible for those who have not built up relationships of trust that permit the opportunity to manipulate accounts. The more complete the trust, the greater the potential gain from malfeasance. That such instances are statistically infrequent is a tribute to the force of personal relations and reputation; that they do occur with regularity, however infrequently, shows the limits of this force.

2. Force and fraud are most efficiently pursued by teams, and the structure of these teams requires a level of internal trust—"honor among thieves"—that usually follows preexisting lines of relationship. Elaborate schemes for kickbacks and bid rigging, for example, can hardly be executed by individuals working alone, and when such activity is exposed it is often remarkable that it could have been kept secret given the large numbers involved. Law-enforcement efforts consist of finding an entry point to the network of malfeasance—an individual whose confession implicates others who will, in snowball-sample fashion, "finger" still others until the entire picture is fitted together.

Both enormous trust and enormous malfeasance, then, may follow from personal relations. Yoram Ben-Porath, in the functionalist style of the new institutional economics, emphasizes the positive side, noting that "continuity of relationships can generate behavior on the part of shrewd, self-seeking, or even unscrupulous individuals that could otherwise be interpreted as foolish or purely altruistic. Valuable diamonds change hands on the diamond exchange, and the deals are sealed by a handshake" (1980, 6). I might add, continuing in this positive vein, that this transaction is possible in part because it is not atomized from other transactions but embedded in a close-knit community of diamond merchants who monitor one another's behavior closely. Like other densely knit networks of actors, they generate clearly defined standards of behavior easily policed by the quick spread of information about instances of malfeasance. But the temptations posed by this level of trust are considerable, and the diamond trade has also been the scene of numerous well-publicized "insider job" thefts and of the notorious "CBS murders" of April 1982. In this case, the owner of a diamond company was defrauding a factoring concern by submitting invoices from fictitious sales. The scheme required cooperation from his accounting personnel, one of whom was approached by investigators and turned state's evidence. The owner then contracted for the murder of the disloyal employee and her assistant; three CBS technicians who came to their aid were also gunned down (Shenon 1984).

3. The extent of disorder resulting from force and fraud depends very much on how the network of social relations is structured. Hobbes exaggerated the extent of disorder likely in his atomized state of nature where, in the absence of sustained social relations, one could expect only desultory dyadic conflicts. More extended and large-scale disorder results from coalitions of combatants, impossible without prior relations. We do not generally speak of "war" unless actors have arranged themselves into two sides, as the end result of various coalitions. This occurs only if there are insufficient crosscutting ties, held by actors with enough links to both main potential combatants to have a strong interest in forestalling conflict. The same is true in the business world, where conflicts are relatively tame unless each side can escalate by calling on substantial numbers of allies in other firms, as sometimes happens in attempts to implement or forestall takeovers.

Disorder and malfeasance do of course occur also when social relations are absent. This possibility is already entailed in my earlier claim that the presence of such relations inhibits malfeasance. But the *level* of malfeasance available in a truly atomized social situation is fairly low; instances can only be episodic, unconnected, small scale. The Hobbesian problem is truly a problem, but in transcending it by the smoothing effect of social structure, we also introduce the possibility of disruptions on a larger scale than those available in the "state of nature."

The embeddedness approach to the problem of trust and order in economic life, then, threads its way between the oversocialized approach of generalized morality and the undersocialized one of impersonal, institutional arrangements by following and analyzing concrete patterns of social relations. Unlike either alternative, or the Hobbesian position, it makes no sweeping (and thus unlikely) predictions of universal order or disorder but rather assumes that the details of social structure will determine which is found.

The Problem of Markets and Hierarchies

As a concrete application of the embeddedness approach to economic life, I offer a critique of the influential argument of Oliver Williamson in *Markets and Hierarchies* (1975) and later articles (1979, 1981; Williamson and Ouchi 1981). Williamson asked under what circumstances economic functions are performed within the boundaries of hierarchical firms rather than by market processes that cross these boundaries. His answer, consistent with the general emphasis of the new institutional economics, is that the organizational form observed in any situation is that which deals most efficiently with the cost of economic transactions. Those that are uncertain in outcome, recur frequently, and require substantial "transaction-specific investments"—for example, money, time, or energy that cannot be easily transferred to interaction with others on different matters—are more likely to take place within hierarchically organized firms. Those that are straightforward, nonrepetitive, and require no transaction-specific investment—such as the onetime purchase of standard equipment—will more likely take place between firms, that is, across a market interface.

In this account, the former set of transactions is internalized within hierarchies for two reasons. The first is "bounded rationality," the inability of economic actors to anticipate properly the complex chain of contingencies that might be relevant to long-term contracts. When transactions are internalized, it is unnecessary to anticipate all such contingencies; they can be handled within the firm's "governance structure" instead of leading to complex negotiations. The second reason is "opportunism," the rational pursuit by economic actors of their own advantage, with all means at their command, including guile and deceit. Opportunism is mitigated and constrained by authority relations and by the greater identification with transaction partners that one allegedly has when both are contained within one corporate entity than when they face one another across the chasm of a market boundary.

The appeal to authority relations in order to tame opportunism constitutes a rediscovery of Hobbesian analysis, though confined here to the economic sphere. The Hobbesian flavor of Williamson's argument is suggested by such statements as the following: "Internal organization is not beset with the same kinds of difficulties that autonomous contracting [among independent firms] experiences when disputes arise between the parties. Although interfirm disputes are often settled out of court . . . this resolution is sometimes difficult and interfirm relations are often strained. Costly litigation is sometimes unavoidable. Internal organization, by contrast . . . is able to settle many such disputes by appeal to fiat—an enormously efficient way to settle instrumental differences" (1975, 30). He notes that complex, recurring transactions require long-term relations between identified individuals but that opportunism jeopardizes these relations. The adaptations to changing market circumstances required over the course of a relationship are too complex and unpredictable to be encompassed in some initial contact, and promises of good faith are unenforceable in the absence of an overarching authority:

> A general clause . . . that "I will behave responsibly rather than seek individual advantage when an occasion to adapt arises," would, in the absence of opportunism, suffice. Given, however, the unenforceability of general clauses and the proclivity of human agents to make false and misleading (self-disbelieved) statements, . . . both buyer and seller are strategically situated to bargain over the disposition of any incremental gain whenever a proposal to adapt is made by the other party. . . . Efficient adaptations which would otherwise be made thus result in costly haggling or even go unmentioned, lest the gains be dissipated by costly subgoal pursuit. *Governance structures* which attenuate opportunism and otherwise infuse confidence are evidently needed. (1979, 241–42; emphasis added)

This analysis entails the same mixture of under- and oversocialized assumptions found in *Leviathan*. The efficacy of hierarchical power within the firm is overplayed, as with Hobbes's oversocialized sovereign state.[4] The "market" resembles Hobbes's state of nature. It is the atomized and anonymous market of classical political economy, minus the discipline brought by fully competitive conditions—an undersocialized conception that neglects the role of social relations among individuals in different firms in bringing order to economic life. Williamson does acknowledge that this picture of the market is not always appropriate: "Norms of trustworthy behavior sometimes extend to markets and are enforced, in some degree, by group pressures. . . . Repeated personal contacts across organizational boundaries support some minimum level of courtesy and consideration between the parties. . . . In addition, expectations of repeat business discourage efforts to seek a narrow advantage in any particular transaction. . . . Individual aggressiveness is curbed by the prospect of ostracism among peers, in both trade and social circumstances. The reputation of a firm for fairness is also a business asset not to be dissipated" (1975, 106–8).

A wedge is opened here for analysis of social structural influences on market behavior. But Williamson treats these examples as exceptions and also fails to appreciate the extent to which the dyadic relations he describes are themselves embedded in broader systems of social relations. I argue that the anonymous market of neoclassical models is virtually nonexistent in economic life and that transactions of all kinds are rife with the social connections described. This is not necessarily more the case in transactions between firms than within—it seems plausible, on the contrary, that the network of social relations within the firm might be more dense and long-lasting on the average than that existing between—but all I need show here is that there is sufficient social overlay in economic transactions across firms (in the "market," to use the term as in Williamson's dichotomy) to render dubious the assertion that complex market transactions approximate a Hobbesian state of nature that can only be resolved by internalization within a hierarchical structure.

In a general way, there is evidence all around us of the extent to which business relations are mixed up with social ones. The trade associations deplored by Adam Smith remain of great importance. It is well known that many firms, small and large, are linked by interlocking directorates so that relationships among directors of firms are many and densely knit. That business relations spill over into sociability and vice versa, especially among business elites, is one of the best-documented facts in the sociological study of business (e.g., Domhoff 1971; Useem 1979). In his study of the extent to which litigation was used to settle disputes between firms, Macaulay notes that disputes are "frequently settled without reference to the contract or potential or actual legal sanctions. There is a hesitancy to speak of legal rights or to threaten to sue in these negotiations. . . . Or as one businessman put it, 'You can settle any dispute if you keep the lawyers and accountants out of it. They just do not understand the give-and-take needed in business.' . . . Law suits for breach of contract appear to be rare" (1963, 61). He goes on to explain that the

> top executives of the two firms may know each other. They may sit together on government or trade committees. They may know each other socially and even belong to the same country club. . . . Even where agreement can be reached at the negotiation stage, carefully planned arrangements may create undesirable exchange relationships between business units. Some businessmen object that in such a carefully worked out relationship one gets performance only to the letter of the contract. Such planning indicates a lack of trust and blunts the demands of friendship, turning a cooperative venture into an antagonistic horse trade. . . . Threatening to turn matters over to an attorney may cost no more money than postage or a telephone call; yet few are so skilled in making such a threat that it will not cost some deterioration of the relationship between the firms. (p. 63–64)

It is not only at top levels that firms are connected by networks of personal relations, but at all levels where transactions must take place. It is, for example, a commonplace in the literature on industrial purchasing that buying and selling relationships rarely approximate the spot-market model of classical theory. One source indicates that the "evidence consistently suggests that it takes some kind of 'shock' to jolt the organizational buying out of a pattern of placing repeat orders with a favored supplier or to extend the constrained set of feasible suppliers. A moment's reflection will suggest several reasons for this behavior, including the costs associated with searching for new suppliers and establishing new relationships, the fact that users are likely to prefer sources, the relatively low risk involved in dealing with known vendors, and the likelihood that the buyer has established personal relationships that he values with representatives of the supplying firm" (Webster and Wind 1972, 15).

In a similar vein, Macaulay notes that salesmen "often know purchasing agents well. The same two individuals may have dealt with each other from five to 25 years. Each has something to give the other. Salesmen have gossip about competitors, shortages and price increases to give purchasing agents who treat them well" (1963, 63). Sellers who do not satisfy their customers "become the subject of discussion in the gossip exchanged by purchasing agents and salesmen, at meetings of purchasing agents' associations and trade associations or even at country clubs or social gatherings" (64). Settlement of disputes is eased by this embeddedness of business in social relations: "Even where the parties have a detailed and carefully planned agreement which indicates what is to happen if, say, the seller fails to deliver on time, often they will never refer to the agreement but will negotiate a solution when the problem arises as if there never had been any original contract. One purchasing agent expressed a common business attitude when he said, 'If something comes up, you get the other man on the telephone and deal with the problem. You don't read legalistic contract clauses at each other if you ever want to do business again. One doesn't run to lawyers if he wants to stay in business because one must behave decently' " (Macaulay 1963, 61).

Such patterns may be more easily noted in other countries, where they are supposedly explained by "cultural" peculiarities. Thus, one journalist recently asserted,

> Friendships and longstanding personal connections affect business connections everywhere. But that seems to be especially true in Japan. . . . The after-hours sessions in the bars and nightclubs are where the vital personal contacts are established and nurtured slowly. Once these ties are set, they are not easily undone. . . . The resulting tight-knit nature of Japanese business society has long been a source of frustration to foreign companies trying to sell products in Japan. . . . Chalmers Johnson, a professor at . . . Berkeley, believes that . . . the exclusive dealing within the Japanese industrial groups, buying and selling to and from each other based on decades-old relationships rather than economic competitiveness . . . is . . . a real nontariff barrier [to trade between the United States and Japan]. (Lohr 1982)

The extensive use of subcontracting in many industries also presents opportunities for sustained relationships among firms that are not organized hierarchically within one corporate unit. For example, Eccles cites evidence from many countries that in construction, when projects "are not subject to institutional regulations which require competitive bidding . . . relations between the general contractor and his subcontractors are stable and continuous over fairly long periods of time and only infrequently established through competitive bidding. This type of 'quasi-integration' results in what I call the 'quasifirm.' It is a preferred mode to either pure market transactions or formal vertical integration" (1981, 339–40). Eccles describes this "quasifirm" arrangement of extensive and long-term relationships among contractors and subcontractors as an organizational form logically intermediate between the pure market and the vertically integrated firm. I would argue, however, that it is not *empirically* intermediate, since the former situation is so rare. The case of construction is closer to vertical integration than some other situations where firms interact, such as buying and selling relations, since subcontractors are physically located on the same site as the contractor and are under his general supervision. Furthermore, under the usual fixed-price contracts, there are "obvious incentives for shirking performance requirements" (Eccles 1981, 340).

Yet a hierarchical structure associated with the vertically integrated firm does not arise to meet this "problem." I argue this is because the long-term relations of contractors and subcontractors, as well as the embeddedness of those relations in a community of construction personnel, generate standards of expected behavior that not only obviate the need for but are superior to pure authority relations in discouraging malfeasance. Eccles' own empirical study of residential construction in Massachusetts shows not only that subcontracting relationships are long term in nature but also that it is very rare for a general contractor to employ more than two or three subcontractors in a given trade, whatever number of projects is handled in the course of a year (1981, 349–51). This is true despite the availability of large numbers of alternative subcontractors. This phenomenon can be explained in part in investment terms—through a "continuing association both parties can benefit from the somewhat idiosyncratic investment of learning to work together" (Eccles 1981, 340)—but also must be related to the desire of individuals to derive pleasure from the social interaction that accompanies their daily work, a pleasure that would be considerably blunted by spot-market procedures requiring entirely new and strange work partners each day. As in other parts of economic life, the overlay of social relations on what may begin in purely economic transactions plays a crucial role.

Some comments on labor markets are also relevant here. One advantage that Williamson asserts for hierarchically structured firms over market transactions is the ability to transmit accurate information about employees. "The principal impediment to effective interfirm experience-rating," he argues, "is one of communication. By comparison with the firm, markets lack a rich and common rating language. The language problem is particularly severe where the judgments to be made are highly subjective. The advantages of hierarchy in these circumstances are especially great if those persons who are most familiar with a worker's characteristics, usually his immediate supervisor, also do the experience-rating" (1975, 78). But the notion that good information about the characteristics of an employee can be transmitted only within firms and not between can be sustained only by neglecting the widely variegated social network of interaction that spans firms. Information about employees travels among firms not only because personal relations exist between those in each firm who do business with each other but also, as I have shown in detail (Granovetter 1974), because the relatively high levels of interfirm mobility in the United States guarantee that many workers will be reasonably well known to employees of numerous other firms that might require and solicit their services. Furthermore, the idea that internal information is necessarily accurate and acted on dispassionately by promotion procedures keyed to it seems naive. To say, as Williamson does, that reliance "on internal promotion has affirmative incentive properties because workers can anticipate that differential talent and degrees of cooperativeness will be rewarded" (1975, 78) invokes an ideal type of promotion as reward-for-achievement that can readily be shown to have only limited correspondence to existing internal labor markets (see Granovetter 1983, 40–51, for an extended analysis).

The other side of my critique is to argue that Williamson vastly overestimates the efficacy of hierarchical power ("fiat," in his terminology) within organizations. He asserts, for example, that internal organizations have a great auditing advantage: "An external auditor is typically constrained to review written records. . . . An internal auditor, by contrast, has greater freedom of action. . . . Whereas an internal auditor is not a partisan but regards himself and is regarded by others in mainly instrumental terms, the external auditor is associated with the 'other side' and his motives are regarded suspiciously. The degree of cooperation received by the auditor from the audited party varies accordingly. The external auditor can expect to receive only perfunctory cooperation" (1975, 29–30). The literature on intrafirm audits is sparse, but one thorough account is that of Dalton, in *Men Who Manage*, for a large chemical plant. Audits of parts by the central office were supposed to be conducted on a surprise basis, but warning was typically surreptitiously given. The high level of cooperation shown in these internal audits is suggested by the following account: "Notice that a count of parts was to begin provoked a flurry among the executives to hide certain parts and equipment . . . materials *not* to be counted were moved to: 1) little-known and inaccessible spots; 2) basements and pits that were dirty and therefore unlikely to be examined; 3) departments that had already been inspected and that could be approached circuitously while the counters were en route between official storage areas and 4) places where materials and supplies might be used as a camouflage for parts. . . . As the practice developed, cooperation among the [department] chiefs to use each other's storage areas and available pits became well organized and smoothly functioning" (Dalton 1959, 48–49).

Dalton's work shows brilliantly that cost accounting of all kinds is a highly arbitrary and therefore easily politicized process rather than a technical procedure decided on grounds of efficiency. He details this especially for the relationship between the maintenance department and various production departments in the chemical plant; the department to which maintenance work was charged had less to do with any strict time accounting than with the relative political and social standing of department executives in their relation to maintenance personnel. Furthermore, the more aggressive department heads expedited their maintenance work "by the use of friendships, by bullying and implied threats. As all the heads had the same formal rank, one could say that an inverse relation existed between a given officer's personal influence and his volume of uncompleted repairs" (1959, 34). Questioned about how such practices could escape the attention of auditors, one informant told Dalton, "If Auditing got to snooping around, what the hell could they find out? And if they did find anything, they'd know a damn sight better than to say anything about it. . . . All those guys [department heads] have got lines through Cost Accounting. That's a lot of bunk about Auditing being independent" (32).

Accounts as detailed and perceptive as Dalton's are sadly lacking for a representative sample of firms and so are open to the argument that they are exceptional. But similar points can be made for the problem of transfer pricing—the determination of prices for products traded between divisions of a single firm. Here Williamson argues that though the trading divisions "may have profit-center standing, this is apt to be exercised in a restrained way. . . . Cost-plus pricing rules, and variants thereof, preclude supplier divisions from seeking the monopolistic prices [to] which their sole source supply position might otherwise entitle them. In addition, the managements of the trading divisions are more susceptible to appeals for cooperation" (1975, 29). But in an intensive empirical study of transfer-pricing practices, Eccles, having interviewed nearly 150 managers in thirteen companies, concluded that no cost-based methods could be carried out in a technically neutral way, since there is "no universal criterion for what is cost. . . . Problems often exist with cost-based methods when the buying division does not have access to the information by which the costs are generated. . . . Market prices are especially difficult to determine when internal purchasing is mandated and no external purchases are made of the intermediate good. . . . There is no obvious answer to what is a markup for profit" (1982, 21). The political element in transfer-pricing conflicts strongly affects whose definition of "cost" is accepted: "In general, when transfer pricing practices are seen to enhance one's power and status they will be viewed favorably. When they do not, a countless number of strategic and other sound business reasons will be found to argue for their inadequacy" (1982, 21; see also Eccles 1983, esp. 26–32). Eccles notes the "somewhat ironic fact that many managers consider internal transactions to be more difficult than external ones, even though vertical integration is pursued for presumed advantages" (1983, 28).

Thus, the oversocialized view that orders within a hierarchy elicit easy obedience and that employees internalize the interests of the firm, suppressing any conflict with their own, cannot stand scrutiny against these empirical studies (or, for that matter, against the experience of many of us in actual organizations). Note further that, as shown especially well in Dalton's detailed ethnographic study, resistance to the encroachment of organizational interests on personal or divisional ones requires an extensive network of coalitions. From the viewpoint of management, these coalitions represent malfeasance generated by teams; it could not be managed at all by atomized individuals. Indeed, Dalton asserted that the level of cooperation achieved by divisional chiefs in evading central audits involved joint action "of a kind rarely, if ever, shown in carrying on official activities" (1959, 49).

In addition, the generally lower turnover of personnel characteristic of large hierarchical firms, with their well-defined internal labor markets and elaborate promotion ladders, may make such cooperative evasion more likely. When many employees have long tenures, the conditions are met for a dense and stable network of relations, shared understandings, and political coalitions to be constructed. (See Homans 1950, 1974, for the relevant social psychological discussions; and Pfeffer 1983, for a treatment of the "demography of organizations.") James Lincoln notes, in this connection, that in the ideal-typical Weberian bureaucracy, organizations are "designed to function independently of the collective actions which can be mobilized through [internal] interpersonal networks. Bureaucracy prescribes fixed relationships among positions through which incumbents flow, without, in theory, affecting organizational operations" (1982, 26). He goes on to summarize studies showing, however, that "when turnover is low, relations take on additional contents of an expressive and personal sort which may ultimately transform the network and change the directions of the organization" (26).

To this point I have argued that social relations between firms are more important, and authority within firms less so, in bringing order to economic life than is supposed in the markets and hierarchies line of thought. A balanced and symmetrical argument requires attention to power in "market" relations and social connections within firms. Attention to power relations is needed lest my emphasis on the smoothing role of social relations in the market lead me to neglect the role of these relations in the conduct of conflict. Conflict is an obvious reality, ranging from well-publicized litigation between firms to the occasional cases of "cutthroat competition" gleefully reported by the business press. Since the effective exercise of power between firms will prevent bloody public battles, we can assume that such battles represent only a small proportion of actual conflicts of interest. Conflicts probably become public only when the two sides are fairly equally matched;

recall that this rough equality was precisely one of Hobbes's arguments for a probable "war of all against all" in the "state of nature." But when the power position of one firm is obviously dominant, the other is apt to capitulate early so as to cut its losses. Such capitulation may require not even explicit confrontation but only a clear understanding of what the other side requires (as in the recent Marxist literature on "hegemony" in business life; see, e.g., Mintz and Schwartz 1985).

Though the exact extent to which firms dominate other firms can be debated, the voluminous literature on interlocking directorates, on the role of financial institutions vis-à-vis industrial corporations, and on dual economy surely provides enough evidence to conclude that power relations cannot be neglected. This provides still another reason to doubt that the complexities that arise when formally equal agents negotiate with one another can be resolved only by the subsumption of all parties under a single hierarchy; in fact, many of these complexities are resolved by implicit or explicit power relations *among* firms.

Finally, a brief comment is in order on the webs of social relations that are well known from industrial and organizational sociology to be important within firms. The distinction between the "formal" and the "informal" organization of the firm is one of the oldest in the literature, and it hardly needs repeating that observers who assume firms to be structured in fact by the official organization chart are sociological babes in the woods. The connection of this to the present discussion is that insofar as internalization within firms does result in a better handling of complex and idiosyncratic transactions, it is by no means apparent that hierarchical organization is the best explanation. It may be, instead, that the effect of internalization is to provide a focus (see Feld 1981) for an even denser web of social relations than had occurred between previously independent market entities. Perhaps this web of interaction is mainly what explains the level of efficiency, be it high or low, of the new organizational form.

It is now useful to summarize the differences in explanation and prediction between Williamson's markets and hierarchies approach and the embeddedness view offered here. Williamson explains the inhibition of "opportunism" or malfeasance in economic life and the general existence of cooperation and order by the subsumption of complex economic activity in hierarchically integrated firms. The empirical evidence that I cite shows, rather, that even with complex transactions, a high level of order can often be found in the "market"—that is, across firm boundaries—and a correspondingly high level of disorder within the firm. Whether these occur, instead of what Williamson expects, depends on the nature of personal relations and networks of relations between and within firms. I claim that both order *and* disorder, honesty *and* malfeasance have more to do with structures of such relations than they do with organizational form.

Certain implications follow for the conditions under which one may expect to see vertical integration rather than transactions between firms in a market. Other things being equal, for example, we should expect pressures toward vertical integration in a market where transacting firms lack a network of personal relations that connects them or where such a network eventuates in conflict, disorder, opportunism, or malfeasance. On the other hand, where a stable network of relations mediates complex transactions and generates standards of behavior between firms, such pressures should be absent.

I use the word *pressures* rather than predict that vertical integration will always follow the pattern described in order to avoid the functionalism implicit in Williamson's assumption that whatever organizational form is most efficient will be the one observed. Before we can make this assumption, two further conditions must be satisfied: (1) well-defined and powerful selection pressures toward efficiency must be operating, and (2) some actors must have the ability and resources to "solve" the efficiency problem by constructing a vertically integrated firm.

The selection pressures that guarantee efficient organization of transactions are nowhere clearly described by Williamson. As in much of the new institutional economics, the need to make such matters explicit is obviated by an implicit Darwinian argument that efficient solutions, however they may originate, have a staying power akin to that enforced by natural selection in the biological world. Thus it is granted that not all business executives "accurately perceive their business opportunities and faultlessly respond. Over time, however, those [vertical] integration moves that have better rationality properties (in transaction cost and scale-economy terms) tend to have better survival properties" (Williamson and Ouchi 1981, 389; see also Williamson 1981, 573–74). But Darwinian arguments, invoked in this cavalier fashion, careen toward a Panglossian view of whatever institution is analyzed. The operation of alleged selection pressures is here neither an object of study nor even a falsifiable proposition but rather an article of faith.

Even if one could document selection pressures that made survival of certain organizational forms more likely, it would remain to show how such forms could be implemented. To treat them implicitly as mutations, by analogy to biological evolution, merely evades the issue. As in other functionalist explanations, it cannot be automatically assumed that the solution to some problem is feasible. Among the resources required to implement vertical integration might be some measure of market power, access to capital through retained earnings or capital markets, and appropriate connections to legal or regulatory authorities.

Where selection pressures are weak (especially likely in the imperfect markets claimed by Williamson to produce vertical integration) and resources problematic, the social-structural configurations that I have outlined are still related to the efficiency of transaction costs, but no guarantee can be given that an efficient solution will occur. Motives for integration unrelated to efficiency, such as personal aggrandizement of CEOs in acquiring firms, may in such settings become important.

What the viewpoint proposed here requires is that future research on the markets-hierarchies question pay careful and systematic attention to the actual patterns of personal relations by which economic transactions are carried out. Such attention will not only better sort out the motives for vertical integration but also make it easier to comprehend the various complex intermediate forms between idealized atomized markets and completely integrated firms, such as the quasi firm discussed above for the construction industry. Intermediate forms of this kind are so intimately bound up with networks of personal relations that any perspective that considers these relations peripheral will fail to see clearly what "organizational form" has been effected. Existing empirical studies of industrial organization pay little attention to patterns of relations, in part because relevant data are harder to find than those on technology and market structure but also because the dominant economic framework remains one of atomized actors, so personal relations are perceived as frictional in effect.

Discussion

In this article, I have argued that most behavior is closely embedded in networks of interpersonal relations and that such an argument avoids the extremes of under- and oversocialized views of human action. Though I believe this to be so for all behavior, I concentrate here on economic behavior for two reasons: (1) it is the type-case of behavior inadequately interpreted because those who study it professionally are so strongly committed to atomized theories of action; and (2) with few exceptions, sociologists have refrained from serious study of any subject already claimed by neoclassical economics. They have implicitly accepted the presumption of economists that "market processes" are not suitable objects of sociological study because social relations play only a frictional and disruptive role, not a central one, in modern societies. (Recent exceptions are Baker 1983; Burt 1983; and White 1981.) In those instances in which sociologists study processes where markets are central, they usually still manage to avoid their analysis. Until recently, for example, the large sociological literature on wages was cast in terms of "income attainment," obscuring the labor market context in which wages are set and focusing instead on the background and attainment of individuals (see Granovetter 1981 for an extended critique). Or, as Stearns has pointed out, the literature on who controls corporations has implicitly assumed that analysis must be at the level of political relations and broad assumptions about the nature of capitalism. Even though it is widely admitted that how corporations acquire capital is a major determinant of control, most relevant research "since the turn of the century has eliminated that [capital] market as an objective of investigation" (1982, 5–6). Even in organization theory, where considerable literature implements the limits placed on economic decisions by social structural complexity, little attempt has been made to demonstrate the implications of this for the neoclassical theory of the firm or for a general understanding of production or such macroeconomic outcomes as growth, inflation, and unemployment.

In trying to demonstrate that all market processes are amenable to sociological analysis and that such analysis reveals central, not peripheral, features of these processes, I have narrowed my focus to problems of trust and malfeasance. I have also used the "market and hierarchies" argument of Oliver Williamson as an illustration of how the embeddedness perspective generates different understandings and predictions from that implemented by economists. Williamson's perspective is itself "revisionist" within economics, diverging from the neglect of institutional and transactional considerations typical of neoclassical work. In this sense, it may appear to have more kinship to a sociological perspective than the usual economic arguments. But the main thrust of the "new institutional economists" is to deflect the analysis of institutions from sociological, historical, and legal argumentation and show instead that they arise as the efficient solution to economic problems. This mission and the pervasive functionalism it implies discourage the detailed analysis of social structure that I argue here is the key to understanding how existing institutions arrived at their present state.

Insofar as rational choice arguments are narrowly construed as referring to atomized individuals and economic goals, they are inconsistent with the embeddedness position presented here. In a broader formulation of rational choice, however, the two views have much in common. Much of the revisionist work by economists that I criticize above in my discussion of over- and undersocialized conceptions of action relies on a strategy that might be called "psychological revisionism"—an attempt to reform economic theory by abandoning an absolute assumption of rational decision making. This strategy has led to Leibenstein's "selective rationality" in his arguments on "X-inefficiency" (1976), for example, and to the claims of segmented labor-market theorists that workers in different market segments have different kinds of decision-making rules, rational choice being only for upper-primary (i.e., professional, managerial, technical) workers (Piore 1979).

I suggest, in contrast, that while the assumption of rational action must always be problematic, it is a good working hypothesis that should not easily be abandoned. What looks to the analyst like nonrational behavior may be quite sensible when situational constraints, especially those of embeddedness, are fully appreciated. When the social situation of those in nonprofessional labor markets is fully analyzed, their behavior looks less like the automatic application of "cultural" rules and more like a reasonable response to their present situation (as, e.g., in the discussion of Liebow 1966).

Managers who evade audits and fight over transfer pricing are acting nonrationally in some strict economic sense, in terms of a firm's profit maximization; but when their position and ambitions in intrafirm networks and political coalitions are analyzed, the behavior is easily interpreted.

That such behavior is rational or instrumental is more readily seen, moreover, if we note that it aims not only at economic goals but also at sociability, approval, status, and power. Economists rarely see such goals as rational, in part on account of the arbitrary separation that arose historically, as Albert Hirschman (1977) points out, in the seventeenth and eighteenth centuries, between the "passions" and the "interests," the latter connoting economic motives only. This way of putting the matter has led economists to specialize in analysis of behavior motivated only by "interest" and to assume that other motives occur in separate and nonrationally organized spheres; hence Samuelson's much-quoted comment that "many economists would separate economics from sociology upon the basis of rational or irrational behavior" (1947, 90). The notion that rational choice is derailed by social influences has long discouraged detailed sociological analysis of economic life and led revisionist economists to reform economic theory by focusing on its naive psychology. My claim here is that however naive that psychology may be, this is not where the main difficulty lies—it is rather in the neglect of social structure.

Finally, I should add that the level of causal analysis adopted in the embeddedness argument is a rather proximate one. I have had little to say about what broad historical or macrostructural circumstances have led systems to display the social-structural characteristics they have, so I make no claims for this analysis to answer large-scale questions about the nature of modern society or the sources of economic and political change. But the focus on proximate causes is intentional, for these broader questions cannot be satisfactorily addressed without more detailed understanding of the mechanisms by which sweeping change has its effects. My claim is that one of the most important and least analyzed of such mechanisms is the impact of such change on the social relations in which economic life is embedded. If this is so, no adequate link between macro- and micro-level theories can be established without a much fuller understanding of these relations.

The use of embeddedness analysis in explicating proximate causes of patterns of macro-level interest is well illustrated by the markets and hierarchies question. The extent of vertical integration and the reasons for the persistence of small firms operating through the market are not only narrow concerns of industrial organization; they are of interest to all students of the institutions of advanced capitalism. Similar issues arise in the analysis of "dual economy," dependent development, and the nature of modern corporate elites. But whether small firms are indeed eclipsed by giant corporations is usually analyzed in broad and sweeping macropolitical or macroeconomic terms, with little appreciation of proximate social structural causes.

Analysts of dual economy have often suggested, for example, that the persistence of large numbers of small firms in the "periphery" is explained by large corporations' need to shift the risks of cyclical fluctuations in demand or of uncertain R & D activities; failures of these small units will not adversely affect the larger firms' earnings. I suggest here that small firms in a market setting may persist instead because a dense network of social relations is overlaid on the business relations connecting such firms and reduces pressures for integration. This does not rule out risk shifting as an explanation with a certain face validity. But the embeddedness account may be more useful in explaining the large number of small establishments not characterized by satellite or peripheral status. (For a discussion of the surprising extent of employment in small establishments, see Granovetter 1984.) This account is restricted to proximate causes: it logically leads to but does not answer the questions why, when, and in what sectors does the market display various types of social structure. But those questions, which link to a more macro level of analysis, would themselves not arise without a prior appreciation of the importance of social structure in the market.

The markets and hierarchies analysis, important as it may be, is presented here mainly as an illustration. I believe the embeddedness argument to have very general applicability and to demonstrate not only that there is a place for sociologists in the study of economic life but that their perspective is urgently required there. In avoiding the analysis of phenomena at the center of standard economic theory, sociologists have unnecessarily cut themselves off from a large and important aspect of social life and from the European tradition—stemming especially from Max Weber—in which economic action is seen only as a special, if important, category of social action. I hope to have shown here that this Weberian program is consistent with and furthered by some of the insights of modern structural sociology.

Notes

1. There are many parallels between what are referred to here as the "undersocialized" and "oversocialized" views of action and what Burt (1982, chap. 9) calls the "atomistic" and "normative" approaches. Similarly, the embeddedness approach proposed here as a middle ground between under- and oversocialized views has an obvious family resemblance to Burt's "structural" approach to action. My distinctions and approach also differ from Burt's in many ways that cannot be quickly summarized; these can be best appreciated by comparison of this article with his useful summary (1982, chap. 9) and with the formal models that implement his conception (1982, 1983). Another approach that resembles mine in its emphasis on how social connections affect purposive action is Marsden's extension of James Coleman's theories of collective action and decision to situations where such connections modify results that would occur in a purely atomistic situation (Marsden 1981, 1983).

2. Students of the sociology of sport will note that this proposition had been put forward previously, in slightly different form, by Leo Durocher.

3. I am indebted to an anonymous referee for pointing this out.

4. Williamson's confidence in the efficacy of hierarchy leads him, in discussing Chester Barnard's "zone of indifference"—that realm within which employees obey orders simply because they are indifferent about whether or not they do what is ordered—to speak instead of a "zone of acceptance" (1975, 77), thus undercutting Barnard's emphasis on the problematic nature of obedience. This transformation of Barnard's usage appears to have originated with Herbert Simon, who does not justify it, noting only that he "prefer[s] the term 'acceptance' " (1957, 12).

References

Akerlof, George. 1983. "Loyalty Filters." *American Economic Review* 73: 54–63.

Alchian, Armen, and Harold Demsetz. 1973. "The Property Rights Paradigm." *Journal of Economic History* 33: 16–27.

Arrow, Kenneth. 1974. *The Limits of Organization.* New York: Norton.

Baker, Wayne. 1983. "Floor Trading and Crowd Dynamics." In *Social Dynamics of Financial Markets*, ed. Patricia Adler and Peter Adler. Greenwich, Conn.: JAI.

Becker, Gary. 1976. *The Economic Approach to Human Behavior.* Chicago: University of Chicago Press.

Ben-Porath, Yoram. 1980. "The F-Connection: Families, Friends, and Firms in the Organization of Exchange." *Population and Development Review* 6, no. 1: 1–30.

Bowles, Samuel, and Herbert Gintis. 1975. *Schooling in Capitalist America.* New York: Basic Books.

Brown, Roger. 1965. *Social Psychology.* New York: Free Press.

Burt, Ronald. 1982. *Toward a Structural Theory of Action.* New York: Academic Press.

———. 1983. *Corporate Profits and Cooptation.* New York: Academic Press.

Cole, Robert. 1979. *Work, Mobility, and Participation: A Comparative Study of American and Japanese Industry.* Berkeley and Los Angeles: University of California Press.

Dalton, Melville. 1959. *Men Who Manage: Fusions of Feeling and Theory in Administration.* New York: Wiley.

Domhoff, G. William. 1971. *The Higher Circles: The Governing Class in America.* New York: Random House.

Duesenberry, James. 1960. Comment on "An Economic Analysis of Fertility." In *Demographic and Economic Change in Developed Countries*, ed. Universities—National Bureau Committee for Economic Research. Princeton: Princeton University Press.

Eccles, Robert. 1981. "The Quasifirm in the Construction Industry." *Journal of Economic Behavior and Organization* 2:335–57.

———. 1982. "A Synopsis of *Transfer Pricing: An Analysis and Action Plan.*" Harvard Business School. Photocopy

———. 1983. "Transfer Pricing, Fairness, and Control." Harvard Business School. Working Paper no. HBS 83–167.

Feld, Scott. 1981. "The Focused Organization of Social Ties." *American Journal of Sociology* 86:1015–35.

Fine, Gary, and Sherryl Kleinman. 1979. "Rethinking Subculture: An Interactionist Analysis." *American Journal of Sociology* 85:1–20.

Furubotn, E., and S. Pejovich. 1972. "Property Rights and Economic Theory: A Survey of Recent Literature." *Journal of Economic Literature* 10:1137–62.

Geertz, Clifford. 1979. "Suq: The Bazaar Economy in Sefrou." In *Meaning and Order in Moroccan Society*, ed. Clifford Geertz, Hildred Geertz, and Lawrence Rosen. Cambridge: Cambridge University Press.

Granovetter, Mark. 1974. *Getting a Job: A Study of Contacts and Careers*. Cambridge: Harvard University Press.

———. 1981. "Toward a Sociological Theory of Income Differences." In *Sociological Perspectives on Labor Markets*, ed. Ivar Berg. New York: Academic Press.

———. 1983. "Labor Mobility, Internal Markets, and Job-Matching: A Comparison of the Sociological and Economic Approaches." Photocopy.

———. 1984. "Small Is Bountiful: Labor Markets and Establishment Size." *American Sociological Review* 49:323–34.

Hirschman, Albert. 1977. *The Passions and the Interests*. Princeton: Princeton University Press.

———. 1982. "Rival Interpretations of Market Society: Civilizing, Destructive, or Feeble?" *Journal of Economic Literature* 20: 1463–84.

Homans, George. 1950. *The Human Group*. New York: Harcourt Brace.

———. 1974. *Social Behavior.* New York: Harcourt Brace Jovanovich.

Lazear, Edward. 1979. "Why Is There Mandatory Retirement?" *Journal of Political Economy* 87:1261–84.

Leibenstein, Harvey. 1976. *Beyond Economic Man*. Cambridge: Harvard University Press.

Liebow, Elliot. 1966. *Tally's Corner.* Boston: Little, Brown.

Lincoln, James. 1982. "Intra- (and Inter-) Organizational Networks." In *Research in the Sociology of Organizations*, vol. 1; ed. S. Bacharach. Greenwich, Conn.: JAI.

Lohr, Steve. 1982. "When Money Doesn't Matter in Japan." *New York Times*, December 30.

Macaulay, Stewart. 1963. "Non-contractual Relations in Business: A Preliminary Study." *American Sociological Review* 28:55–67.

Marsden, Peter. 1981. "Introducing Influence Processes into a System of Collective Decisions." *American Journal of Sociology* 86:1203–35.

———. 1983. "Restricted Access in Networks and Models of Power." *American Journal of Sociology* 88:686–17.

Merton, Robert. 1947. "Manifest and Latent Functions." In *Social Theory and Social Structure*. New York: Free Press.

Mintz, Beth, and Michael Schwartz. 1985. *The Power Structure of American Business*. Chicago: University of Chicago Press.

North, Douglass C., and Robert Paul Thomas. 1973. *The Rise of the Western World.* Cambridge: Cambridge University Press.

Okun, Arthur. 1981. *Prices and Quantities: A Macroeconomic Analysis*. Washington, D.C.: Brookings Institution.

Pakes, Ariel, and S. Nitzan. 1982. "Optimum Contracts for Research Personnel, Research Employment and the Establishment of 'Rival' Enterprises." NBER Working Paper no. 871. Cambridge, Mass.: National Bureau of Economic Research.

Parsons, Talcott. 1937. *The Structure of Social Action*. New York: Macmillan.

Pfeffer, Jeffrey. 1983. "Organizational Demography." *In Research in Organizational Behavior*, vol. 5, ed. Larry L. Cummings and Barry M. Staw. Greenwich, Conn.: JAI.

Phelps Brown, Ernest Henry. 1977. *The Inequality of Pay*. Berkeley and Los Angeles: University of California Press.

Piore, Michael. 1975. "Notes for a Theory of Labor Market Stratification." In *Labor Market Segmentation*, ed. R. Edwards, M. Reich, and D. Gordon. Lexington, Mass.: Heath.

———, ed. 1979. *Unemployment and Inflation: Institutionalist and Structuralist Views*. White Plains, N.Y.: M. E. Sharpe.

Polanyi, Karl. 1944. *The Great Transformation*. New York: Holt, Rinehart.

Polanyi, Karl, C. Arensberg, and H. Pearson. 1957. *Trade and Market in the Early Empires*. New York: Free Press.

Popkin, Samuel. 1979. *The Rational Peasant: The Political Economy of Rural Society in Vietnam*. Berkeley and Los Angeles: University of California Press.

Rosen, Sherwin. 1982. "Authority, Control, and the Distribution of Earnings." *Bell Journal of Economics* 13:311–23.

Samuelson, Paul. 1947. *Foundations of Economic Analysis*. Cambridge: Harvard University Press.

Schneider, Harold. 1974. *Economic Man: The Anthropology of Economics*. New York: Free Press.

Schotter, Andrew. 1981. *The Economic Theory of Social Institutions*. Cambridge: Cambridge University Press.

Scott, James. 1976. *The Moral Economy of the Peasant*. New Haven: Yale University Press.

Shenon, Philip. 1984. "Margolies Is Found Guilty of Murdering Two Women." *New York Times*, June 1.

Simon, Herbert. 1957. *Administrative Behavior: A Study of Decision-Making Processes in Administrative Organization*. Glencoe, Ill.; Free Press.

Smith, Adam. 1979. *The Wealth of Nations*. Ed. Andrew Skinner. Baltimore: Penguin.

Stearns, Linda. 1982. "Corporate Dependency and the Structure of the Capital Market: 1880–1980." Ph.D. diss., State University of New York at Stony Brook.

Thompson, E. P. 1971. "The Moral Economy of the English Crowd in the Eighteenth Century." *Past and Present* 50 (February): 76–136.

Useem, Michael. 1979. "The Social Organization of the American Business Elite and Participation of Corporation Directors in the Governance of American Institutions." *American Sociological Review* 44:553–72.

Webster, Frederick, and Yoram Wind. 1972. *Organizational Buying Behavior*. Englewood Cliffs, N.J.: Prentice-Hall.

White, Harrison C. 1981. "Where Do Markets Come From?" *American Journal of Sociology* 87:517–47.

Williamson, Oliver, 1975. *Markets and Hierarchies, Analysis and Antitrust Implications: A Study of the Economics of Internal Organization*. New York: Free Press.

———. 1979. "Transaction-Cost Economics: The Governance of Contractual Relations." *Journal of Law and Economics* 22:233–61.

———. 1981. "The Economics of Organization: The Transaction Cost Approach." *American Journal of Sociology* 87:548–77.

Williamson, Oliver, and William Ouchi. 1981. "The Markets and Hierarchies and Visible Hand Perspectives." In *Perspectives on Organizational Design and Behavior*, ed. Andrew Van de Ven and William Joyce. New York: Wiley.

Wrong, Dennis. 1961. "The Oversocialized Conception of Man in Modern Sociology." *American Sociological Review* 26:183–93.

Chapter 10

EMBEDDEDNESS AND IMMIGRATION: NOTES ON THE SOCIAL DETERMINANTS OF ECONOMIC ACTION

ALEJANDRO PORTES AND JULIA SENSENBRENNER

RECENT WORK in economic sociology represents one of the most exciting developments in the field insofar as it promises to vindicate the heritage of Max Weber in the analysis of economic life and, by the same token, to rescue this vast area from the exclusive sway of the neoclassical perspective. Spearheaded by Mark Granovetter's (1985) critique of a pure "market" approach to economic action, the sociological perspective has been reinforced by the introduction and subsequent use of the concepts of "social capital" (Bourdieu 1979; Bourdieu, Newman, and Wocquant 1991; Coleman 1988), the emphasis on the predictive power of contextual variables in addition to individual characteristics (Wellman and Wortley 1990), and extensive research on the structure and dynamics of social networks (Marsden 1990; Laumann and Knoke 1986; Mintz and Schwartz 1985; White 1970).

Granovetter's treatment of the concept of "embeddedness" represents a veritable manifesto for those whose sociological cast of mind has led them to question individualistic analyses of such phenomena as socioeconomic attainment and the culturalistic arguments that neoclassical economists sometimes invoke when their own perspective can go no further. The concept was originally coined by Karl Polanyi and his associates (Polanyi, Arensberg, and Pearson 1957) in their analysis of trades and markets but, in its more recent formulation, it has sparked renewed interest in what sociology has to say about economic life.

The purpose of this article is to contribute to this emerging perspective by (1) delving into the classical roots of recent theoretical developments so as to refine the concepts invoked by present-day economic sociologists; (2) fleshing out the concepts of embeddedness and, in particular, social capital

Alejandro Portes and Julia Sensenbrenner. 1993. "Embeddedness and Immigration: Notes on the Social Determinants of Economic Action." *American Journal of Sociology* 98: 1320–50.

into more specific components; (3) using the resulting typology as the basis for a series of hypotheses amenable to empirical research; and (4) showing how this theoretical program relates to the recent literature on immigration and ethnicity and can be advanced by it.

As developed so far, the concepts of the new economic sociology represent a broad programmatic statement in need of further specification. Embeddedness, for example, provides a very useful standpoint for criticizing neoclassical models, but when turned around to provide concrete propositions, it suffers from theoretical vagueness. The observation that outcomes are uncertain because they depend on how economic action is embedded does not help us meet the positivistic goals of predictive improvement and theoretical accumulation. To fulfill these goals, we must better specify just how social structure constrains, supports, or derails individual goal-seeking behavior. Our attempt to move in this direction takes two forms.

First, we try to arrive at a more systematic understanding of the different sources of what is, today, called social capital, by tracing the roots of the concept in the sociological classics. Second, we utilize contemporary research on immigration to document the operation of some of these sources and their effects, positive and negative. In keeping with the goal of theoretical specificity, our strategy is to use knowledge about immigrant economic adaptation to generate propositions of more general applicability.

The following analysis focuses on the concept of social capital, introduced in the recent sociological literature by Pierre Bourdieu and developed in English by James Coleman, since we believe it is more suitable to the enterprise of theoretical fleshing out than the more general notion of embeddedness. Coleman (1988, S98) defines social capital as a variety of entities with two characteristics in common: "They all consist of some aspect of social structures, and they facilitate actions within that structure." The facilitational component is highlighted by Coleman, who likens "social" to "material" and "human" capitals as resources available to individuals to attain their ends. The main difference is that social capital is more intangible than the other forms, since it inheres in the structure of relations within which purposive action takes place.

Although insightful, Coleman's contribution suffers from two shortcomings: first, a theoretical indefiniteness that leaves open the question of what those social entities facilitating individual goal attainment are and where they come from; second, a marked instrumentalist orientation that views social structural forces only from a positive perspective. This positive bent sacrifices the insight (present in Granovetter's broader analysis of embeddedness) that social structures can advance as well as constrain individual goal seeking and that they can even redefine the content of such goals. We can respecify at this point the purpose of our own analysis as an attempt to further refine the concept of social capital by (*a*) attempting to identify its different types and sources and (*b*) clarifying conditions under which it can not only promote but also constrain or derail economic goal seeking.

Before plunging into this task, it is important to say a word about the source of the empirical material used in the remainder of this article. This source—immigration studies—has been frequently, albeit haphazardly, mined by writers in the theoretical literature on economic sociology. Coleman (1988), for example, uses Asian immigrant families as an illustration of what he labels "closure" of social relations, and both he and Granovetter (1985) highlight the significance of the immigrant rotating credit association as an example of either embeddedness or social capital. This frequent utilization of immigration research is not surprising, because foreign-born communities represent one of the clearest examples of the bearing contextual factors can have on individual economic action. With skills learned in the home country devalued in the receiving labor market and with a generally poor command of the receiving country's language, immigrants' economic destinies depend heavily on the structures in which they become incorporated and, in particular, on the character of their own communities. Few instances of economic action can be found that are more embedded. The task before us will be to review this empirical literature more systematically with an eye to developing propositions of general applicability.

Social Capital and Its Types

The effervescence of research following the reconceptualization of economic sociology in recent years has somewhat obscured the fact that many of these same ideas have been present all along in the sociological tradition and that they are, in a sense, central to the founding of the discipline. Our purpose here is not historical exegesis but the investigation of classic sources for clues to the various mechanisms through which social structures affect economic action. We begin by redefining social capital as those expectations for action within a collectivity that affect the economic goals and goal-seeking behavior of its members, even if these expectations are not oriented toward the economic sphere.

This definition differs from Coleman's, where the emphasis is on social structures facilitating individual rational pursuits. As we shall see below, this positive emphasis is only half of the story because the same constellation of forces can have the opposite effects. As redefined here, social capital seems sufficiently general to encompass most uses of the term in the recent sociological literature. These include Bourdieu's original formulations, as well as more specific analyses concerning the behavior of various social groups in the marketplace (Light and Bonacich 1988; White 1970; Eccles and White 1988; Bailey and Waldinger 1991). However, by its very generality, the concept encompasses such a plurality of situations as to make its empirical application difficult. Thus we must further specify what those collective expectations are, what their sources are, and how they are likely to affect economic behavior.

It is possible to distinguish four specific types of economically relevant expectations. The first, *value introjection*, takes its cue from Durkheim and a certain interpretation of Weber to emphasize the moral character of economic transactions that are guided by value imperatives learned during the process of socialization (Parsons 1937; Parsons and Smelser 1956). The central role accorded to this process in American functionalist sociology draws its inspiration from passages such as the following, from Weber's analysis of Puritan values: "One's duty in a calling is what is most characteristic of the social ethic of capitalist culture and is, in a sense, the fundamental basis of it. It is an obligation which the individual is supposed to feel and does feel towards the content of his professional activity, no matter in what it consists" (1958, 54).

Similarly, Durkheim's analysis of the "noncontractual elements of contract" provides powerful intellectual justification for a sociological analysis of economic transactions as reflections of an underlying moral order: "The contract is not sufficient by itself, but is only possible because of the regulation of contracts, which is of social origin. This is implicit . . . because the function of the contract is less to create new rules than to diversify preestablished rules in particular cases" (Durkheim 1984, 162).

Value introjection is a first source of social capital because it prompts individuals to behave in ways other than naked greed; such behavior then becomes appropriable by others or by the collectivity as a resource. Although criticized later as an "oversocialized" conception of human action (Wrong 1961), this source remains central to the sociological perspective and figures prominently in contemporary examples of the effects of social structure on economic action (Swedberg 1991). Economists bent on dismissing the "sociological approach" to economic behavior also tend to target their criticism in this first source (Leff 1979; McCloskey and Sandberg 1971; Baker and Faulkner 1991).

The second source of social capital takes its clue from the classic work of Georg Simmel (1955) to focus on the dynamics of group affiliation. As elaborated by exchange theorists, social life consists of a vast series of primary transactions where favors, information, approval, and other valued items are given and received. Social capital arising from *reciprocity transactions* consists of the accumulation of "chits" based on previous good deeds to others, backed by the norm of reciprocity. In contrast to the first type, individuals are not expected to behave according to a higher group morality, but rather to pursue selfish ends. The difference from regular market behavior is that transactions center not on money and material goods, but social intangibles (Gouldner 1960; Blau 1964; Hechter 1987). Nevertheless, the analogy of social capital to money capital is nowhere closer than in these exchange analyses of group life.

The third source of social capital, *bounded solidarity*, focuses on those situational circumstances that can lead to the emergence of principled group-oriented behavior quite apart from any early value introjection. Its classic sources are best exemplified by Marx's analysis of the rise of proletarian consciousness and the transformation of workers into a class-for-itself. The passages of the *Communist Manifesto* where this type of social capital makes its appearance are familiar, but no attempt at paraphrasing can do justice to the original: "With the development of industry the proletariat not only increases in number; it becomes concentrated in greater masses, its strength grows, and it feels that strength more. The various interests and conditions of life within the ranks of the proletariat are more and more equalized. . . . The collisions between individual workmen and individual bourgeois take more and more the character of collisions between two classes" (Marx and Engels 1948, 17–18).

The weapon of the working class in this struggle is precisely its internal solidarity born out of a common awareness of capitalist exploitation. This emergent collective sentiment transforms what had hitherto been individual market encounters between employer and employee into a group affair where subordinates have the advantage of numbers. Starting from an analysis of pure market competition, Marx hence arrives at sociability. It is not, however, the sociability underlying the "noncontractual elements of the contract" or that arising out of Puritan values, but the defensive banding together of the losers in the market struggle. Their individual self-interests are welded together into a higher form of consciousness that, in some passages of Marx's writings, acquires the force for social control that Weber assigned to Puritan values.

As a source of social capital, bounded solidarity does not arise out of the introjection of established values or from individual reciprocity exchanges, but out of the situational reaction of a class of people faced with common adversities. If sufficiently strong, this emergent sentiment will lead to the observance of norms of mutual support, appropriable by individuals as a resource in their own pursuits. The social dynamics at play will be illustrated in greater detail below.

The final source, *enforceable trust*, is captured in Weber's (1947) classic distinction between formal and substantive rationality in market transactions. Formal rationality is associated with transactions based on universalistic norms and open exchange; substantive rationality involves particularistic obligations in monopolies or semimonopolies benefiting a particular group. With substantive rationality, we are, of course, in the realm of embeddedness, because group goals govern economic behavior. The significant point, however, is that individual members subordinate their present desires to collective expectations in anticipation of what Weber designates as "utili-

TABLE 10.1
Social Capital: Types and Characteristics

Sources	*Operating Principle*	*Individual Motivation for Compliance*	*Classical Referents*	*Modern Applications*
Value introjection	Socialization into consensually established beliefs	Principled	Durkheim's (1984) analysis of the social underpinnings of legal contracts	Functionalist economic sociology (Parsons and Smelser 1956)
Reciprocity exchanges	Norm of reciprocity in face-to-face interaction	Instrumental	Simmel's (1955) analysis of exchanges in dyads and trials	Exchange and power in social life (Blau 1964)
Bounded solidarity	Situational reactive sentiments	Principled	Marx and Engels's (1947, 1948) analysis of the emergence of working-class consciousness	Solidarity bonds in immigrant and ethnic communities (Tilly 1990; Yancey et al. 1976)
Enforceable trust	Particularistic rewards and sanctions linked to group membership	Instrumental	Weber's (1947) analysis of substantive rationality in economic transactions	Dynamics of ethnic entrepreneurship (Light 1972; Aldrich and Zimmer 1986)

Note: Social capital is defined as "collective expectations affecting individual economic behavior."

ties," that is long-term market advantages by virtue of group membership. The process and some of the institutional structures underlying it are summarized as follows: "Relationships which are valued as a potential source of present or future disposal over utilities are, however, also objects of economic provision. The opportunities of advantages which are made available by custom, by the constellation of interests, or by conventional or legal order for the purposes of an economic unit, will be called economic advantages" (Weber 1947, 165).

Social capital is generated by individual members' disciplined compliance with group expectations. However, the motivating force in this case is not value convictions, but the anticipation of utilities associated with "good standing" in a particular collectivity. As with reciprocity exchanges, the predominant orientation is utilitarian, except that the actor's behavior is not oriented to a particular other but to the web of social networks of the entire community.

For the sake of clarity, table 10.1 formalizes the typology of social capital elaborated so far. The table summarizes the processes through which individual maximizing behavior is constrained in ways that lead to reliable expectations by others; under certain conditions these expectations can be appropriated as a resource. While the first two types in the table are the core of entire schools of sociological thought, the last two have been less theorized. Both depend on a heightened sense of community and hence have the greatest affinity to the experience of immigrant groups. As the examples below will illustrate, it is the particular circumstance of "foreignness" that often best explains the rise of these types of social capital among immigrants.

The linkage is highlighted in table 10.1, where examples of modern analyses of the last two types are drawn from the literature on immigrant adaptation. The remainder of the article focuses on the processes underlying these two sources of social capital, seeking to formulate propositions of general applicability and to document both the positive and negative consequences of each source. The material presented is not intended to "prove" the formal propositions concluding each section, but rather to demonstrate their plausibility. As indicated at the start, our goal is to flesh out the implications of general concepts rather than to provide a definitive test of these implications.

Bounded Solidarity

The last riot in Miami in 1989 was triggered by the shooting of two black cyclists by a Colombian-born policeman. Officer William B. Lozano was suspended without pay from the Miami police force and found himself facing the wrath of the entire black community. To defend himself against the hostile mood among much of the local population, he hired one of Miami's best criminal attorneys. As the legal bills mounted, the unemployed Lozano found that he had no other recourse but to go to the local Spanish-language radio stations to plead for help from his fellow Colombians and other Latins. Lozano had no means of verifying his claims to innocence and, as a potential felon, he should have received little sympathy from most citizens. However, he counted on the emergent feeling among Colombians that he was being turned into a scapegoat and on the growing sympathy toward that position in the rest of the Latin community. After his first radio broadcast, Lozano collected $150,000 for his legal bills; subsequent appeals have also produced substantial sums.[1]

The mechanism at work in this case is labeled bounded solidarity since it is limited to members of a particular group who find themselves affected by common events in a particular time and place. As in Marx's (1967) description of the rise of class consciousness, this mechanism depends on an emergent sentiment of "we-ness" among those confronting a similar difficult situation. The resulting behaviors are, of course, not well explained by utility-maximizing models of economic action. Instead, forms of altruistic conduct emerge that can be tapped by other group members to obtain privileged access to various resources. The fundamental characteristic of this source of social capital is that it does not depend on its enforceability, but on the moral imperative felt by individuals to behave in a certain way. In this sense, it is akin to value introjection, except that it represents the emergent product of a particular situation.

The confrontation with the host society has created solidary communities among immigrants both today and at the turn of the century. Nee and Nee (1973), Boswell (1986), and Zhou (1992) describe the plight of early Chinese immigrants in New York and San Francisco, who were subjected to all forms of discrimination and lacked the means to return home. Barred from factory employment by nativist prejudice and prevented from bringing wives and other family members by the Chinese Exclusion Act, these hapless seekers of the "Mountain of Gold" had no recourse but to band together in tightly knit communities that were the precursors of today's Chinatowns (Zhou 1992). Solidarity born out of common adversity is reflected in the "clannishness" and "secretiveness" that outsiders were later to attribute to these communities. Such communities also provided the basis for the rapid growth of fledgling immigrant enterprises. Today, Chinese immigrants and their descendants have one of the highest rates of self-employment among all ethnic groups, and their enterprises are, on the average, the largest among both native- and foreign-born minorities (U.S. Bureau of the Census 1991; "Asian-Americans Take Lead" 1991).

The confrontation with the receiving society is capable not only of activating dormant feelings of nationality among immigrants but of creating such feelings where none existed before. In a well-known passage, Glazer refers to the case of Sicilian peasants coming to New York in the early 1900s whose original loyalties did not extend much beyond their local villages. These immigrants learned to think of themselves as Italian and to band together on that basis after the native population began to treat them in the same manner and to apply to them the same derogatory labels. This situation created unexpected outcomes: "Thus the American relatives of Southern Italians (to whom the Ethiopian war meant nothing more than another affliction visited upon them by the alien government to the North) became Italian patriots in America, supporting here the war to which they would have been indifferent at home" (Glazer 1954, 167).

Not all immigrant groups have experienced equal levels of confrontation, which accounts, in part, for the different strength of reactive solidarity. The cultural and linguistic distance between home country and receiving society and the distinctness of immigrants relative to the native-born population govern, to a large extent, the magnitude of the clash. A second factor critical to forging solidarity is the possibility of "exit" from the host society to return home. Immigrants for whom escape from nativist prejudice and discrimination is but a cheap ride away are not likely to develop as high levels of bounded solidarity as those whose return is somehow blocked. Turn-of-the-century Chinese immigrants offer an example of the latter situation and so did Russian Jews who came escaping tsarist persecution at home (Rischin 1962; Dinnerstein 1977). Today, blocked return is characteristic of many political refugees, and higher levels of internal solidarity have indeed been noted among such groups (Gold 1988; Forment 1989; Perez 1986). The dynamics at play can be summarized in this first proposition:

> The more distinct a group is in terms of phenotypical or cultural characteristics from the rest of the population, the greater the level of prejudice associated with these traits, and the lower the probability of exit from this situation, then the stronger the sentiments of in-group solidarity among its members and the higher the appropriable social capital based on this solidarity.

In addition to charitable contributions, like those solicited by Officer Lozano, a more common use of this source of social capital is in the creation and consolidation of small enterprises. A solidary ethnic community represents, simultaneously, a market for culturally defined goods, a pool of reliable low-wage labor, and a potential source for start-up capital. Privileged access to these resources by immigrant entrepreneurs is, of course, not easily explainable on the basis of economic models focused on individual human capital and atomized market competition (Baker and Faulkner 1991). Aldrich and Zimmer (1986, 14) make essentially the same point when they note that "conditions that raise the salience of group boundaries and identity, leading persons to form new social ties and action sets, increase the likelihood of entrepreneurial attempts by persons within that group and raise the probability of success."

However, reaction to cultural differences and outside discrimination alone do not account fully for the observed differences in the strength of bounded solidarity among different immigrant communities. We find such differences among groups subjected to similar levels of discrimination and even among those whose exit is equally blocked. The missing element seems to be the ability of certain minorities to activate a cultural repertoire, brought from the home country, which allows them to construct an autonomous portrayal of their situation that goes beyond a mere adversarial reaction.

German and Russian Jews arriving in the nineteenth century and in the early twentieth represent the paradigmatic example of a group whose situational solidarity, when confronted with widespread native prejudice, was not limited to an adversarial stance, but went well beyond it by taking advantage of a rich cultural heritage. Jewish-American society developed its own autonomous logic governed not so much by what "natives were thinking of us" as by concerns and interests springing from the group's distinct religious and cultural traditions (Howe 1976; Rischin 1962). Chinese-Americans were not far behind. According to Nee and Nee (1973), the "bachelor society" of San Francisco's Chinatown was organized along lines that reproduced in close detail the influence of Kwangtung Province, where most immigrants originated.[2] As in

Kwangtung, the basis of social organization in Chinatown was the kinship group or clan that incorporated males who claimed descent from a common ancestor: "The Wong, Lee, and Chin families were the largest and most powerful clans in Chinatown. Basic everyday needs were dealt with within the framework of the clan unit in which a sense of shared collective responsibility and mutual loyalty were central values" (Nee and Nee 1973, 64).

The reproduction of Chinese practices and values to deal with adverse circumstances continues to our day (Zhou 1992). The opening chapter of Amy Tan's (1989) autobiographical novel tells of the re-creation in San Francisco of a weekly club originating in Kweilin (Guilin) during the Japanese invasion of China. Organized by immigrant women, the Joy Luck Club had the purpose of easing the difficulties of poverty and cultural adjustment by providing an atmosphere of camaraderie through good food and games. A generation later the club was still functioning with its members discussing joint investments in the stock market while they sat around the mah-jong table.

The salience of many cultural practices and their reenactment after immigration do not come about spontaneously, but usually result from the clash with the host society, and they are, in this sense, an emergent product. The fundamental source of solidarity is still situational, since it is the reality of discrimination and minority status that activates dormant home customs (Yancey, Ericksen, and Juliani 1976).

Because of its recency, the Nicaraguan immigrant community of Miami provides an excellent example of the birth of bounded solidarity and the reactivation of a cultural repertoire brought from the home country. In the words of one community leader, Nicaraguan refugees resent that "people think we're all uneducated, poor people without documents" (Branch 1989, 20). To reassert their own identity and distinctness, Nicaraguans have resorted to a variety of practices including the revival of near-forgotten folk items. Ethnic stores, for example, do a brisk business selling Nicaraguan products such as *cotonas* (a cotton shirt usually worn only by Nicaraguan Indians) to well-to-do refugees. As one store owner put it, "The people who always wore American brands and European clothes in Nicaragua now come shopping for a *cotona* to wear to parties" (Veciana-Suarez 1983, 10).

Not all immigrants have the same opportunity to reinforce the emergent solidarity arising out of confrontation with a foreign society with a sense of cultural continuity and autonomous presence. Among groups whose ethnicity was "made in America," such as those described by Glazer, the necessary elements for construction of a collective identity may be missing or may have been forgotten, forcing the minority to borrow them from the very cultural mainstream to which it is reacting. Peasants from southern Italy and the eastern reaches of the Austro-Hungarian Empire recruited to work in American factories and mines had but a faint idea of the nations they left behind. As they clustered together in ethnic communities in America, they often had to accept definitions of their own identity based on host-society stereotypes. Similarly, Polish immigrants arriving in the early years of this century often learned about their nationality in the United States; in Poland, the rural lords were the Poles, the peasants were just peasants (Glazer 1954; Greeley 1971; Sowell 1981).

Although most contemporary immigrants have a clear idea of their national identities, exceptional circumstances still exist that prevent their reenactment in places of reception. Peasant refugees from the remote highlands of Southeast Asia resettled in American cities offer an appropriate example. Unable to reimplement cultural practices from a preindustrial past in such a vastly different environment, they often lapse into despair and various forms of emotional disorder (Rumbaut and Ima 1988). The following statement from a Hmong refugee in southern California illustrates a situation reminiscent of those recorded by Thomas and Znaniecki (1984) among Polish peasant immigrants at the turn of the century: "In our old country, whatever we had was made or brought in by our own hands; we never had any doubts that we would not have enough for our mouth. But from now on to the future, that time is over. So you see, when you think these things over, you don't want to live anymore. . . . Don't know how to read and write, don't know how to speak the language. My life is only to live day by day until the last day I live, and maybe that is the time when my problems will be solved" (Rumbaut 1985, 471–72).

These contrasting experiences lead to the following second proposition:

> Social capital arising out of situational confrontations is strongest when the resulting bounded solidarity is not limited to the actual events but brings about the construction of an alternative definition of the situation based on reenactment of past practices and a common cultural memory.

Enforceable Trust

The fourth source of social capital is also based on the existence of community except that, in this case, it is not sentiments of solidarity based on outward confrontation, but the internal sanctioning capacity of the community itself that plays the central role. In his article, Coleman identifies this mechanism as the difference between open and closed social structures: "Closure of the social structure is important not only for the existence of effective norms but also for another form of social capital: the trustworthiness of social structures that allows the proliferation of obligations and expectations" (1988, S107–S108).

What Coleman refers to as "closure" is, of course, the degree to which a particular collectivity forms a group at all, as opposed to a mere aggregate of individuals. Commonalities in experiences of departure from the home country and conditions at arrival in the United States create bonds among immigrants and give rise to a multiplicity of social networks that frequently coalesce into tightly knit ethnic communities. The social capital emerging from the monitoring capacity of these communities is best referred to as enforceable trust.

As seen above, bounded solidarity shares with the first source of social capital (value introjection) an element of moral obligation. Individuals behave in certain ways because they must—either because they have been socialized in the appropriate values or because they enact emergent sentiments of loyalty toward others like themselves. Such behavior can occur even in the absence of reward or punishment. The final source of social capital discussed here shares with the second (reciprocity exchanges) a strong instrumental orientation. In both cases, individuals behave according to expectations not only because they must, but out of fear of punishment or in anticipation of rewards. The predictability in the behavior of members of a group is in direct proportion to its sanctioning capacity. Hence, the oxymoron: *trust* exists in economic transactions precisely because it is *enforceable* by means that transcend the individuals involved.

The economic-sociology literature has already noted that the rewards and sanctions administered by ethnic communities are generally nonmaterial in character, but that they can have very material consequences in the long run. A key aspect of the latter is access to resources for capitalizing small enterprises. Economic sociology has here one of the prime instances showing the utility of its approach as compared with individualistic accounts of economic attainment. For illustration, however, sociologists seem to have hit on only one example: the rotating credit association. Since Ivan Light (1972) called attention to this form of small-firm capitalization, rotating credit associations have become de rigueur as an illustration of the significance of embeddedness (Granovetter 1985), social capital (Coleman 1988), and "group solidarity" (Hechter 1987, 108). Other network-based mechanisms exist, however, as the following two examples show.

Dominicans in New York City

The Dominican immigrant community in New York City was characterized until recently as a working-class ghetto composed mostly of illegal immigrants working for low wages in sweatshops and menial service occupations. A study conducted under the auspices of the U.S. Congressional Commission for the Study of Immigration contradicts this description and points to the emergence of a budding entrepreneurial enclave among Dominican immigrants (Portes and Guarnizo 1991). The city-within-a-city that one encounters when entering the Washington Heights area of New York with its multiplicity of ethnic restaurants and stores, Spanish-language newspapers, and travel agencies is, to a large extent, a Dominican creation built on the strength of skills brought from the Dominican Republic, ready access to a low-wage labor pool, and the development of informal credit channels.[3]

New York hosts several formally registered Dominican finance agencies (*financieras*), but, in addition, networks of informal loan operations grant credit with little or no paperwork. Capital comes from profits of the drug trade, but also from established ethnic firms and savings of workers who obtain higher interest rates in the ethnic finance networks than in formal banking institutions. These sources are reinforced by flight capital from the Dominican Republic. Money circulates within community networks and is made available for business start-ups because recipients are fully expected to repay. This expectation is based first on the reputation of the recipient and second on swift retribution against those who default. Such punishment may include coercive measures but is more often based on ostracism from ethnic business circles. Outside the immigrant enclave, Dominicans have very few opportunities other than low-wage menial labor.

These patterns can be illustrated by the experiences of a Dominican entrepreneur interviewed in the course of fieldwork in New York. This man whom we shall call Nicolas is thirty-eight years old and already owns five shops in New York City and a *financiera* in the Dominican Republic. He employs a staff of thirty, almost all of whom are Dominican relatives or friends of relatives. For finance, he relies exclusively on the informal system of Washington Heights. Sometimes he acts as an investor and sometimes as a borrower. As an investor, Nicolas has earned a good reputation that enables him to collect several thousand dollars to be invested in his businesses in New York and Santo Domingo. These investments generally come from other immigrants who do not yet have enough capital to initiate businesses themselves. As a borrower, he seems to enjoy ample credit. At the time of the interview, Nicolas had two active loans—one for $125,000 and the other for $200,000—only one of which was accompanied by some signed papers. He was paying a monthly interest of 2.6%.[4]

Cubans in Miami

Conventional accounts of business success among Cuban exiles in south Florida attributed their advance to material capital brought by the earlier arrivals. Subsequent studies have shown the inadequacy of this explanation since few of the businesses that formed the core of the Miami enclave were capitalized in this fashion (Wilson and Portes 1980; Wilson and Martin 1982). The rotating credit association did not exist as a cultural practice in Cuba, so a different type of mechanism had to give rise to the first ethnic firms. By the mid-1960s, a few small banks in Miami were owned by wealthy South American families who began hiring unemployed Cuban exile bankers first as clerks and then as loan officers. Once their own jobs became secure, these bankers started a program of lending small sums—from $10,000 to $30,000—to fellow exiles for business start-ups. These loans were made without collateral and were based exclusively on the personal reputation of the recipient in Cuba.[5]

This source of credit became known as "character" loans. Its effect was to allow penniless refugees who had no standing in the American banking system to gain a foothold in the local economy. A banker who took part in this operation described it as follows:

> At the start, most Cuban enterprises were gas stations; then came grocery shops and restaurants. No American bank would lend to them. By the mid-sixties we started a policy at our bank of making small loans to Cubans who wanted to start their own business, but did not have the capital. These loans of $10,000 or $15,000 were made because the person was known to us by his reputation and integrity. All of them paid back; there were zero losses. With some exceptions they have continued being clients of the bank. People who used to borrow $15,000 on a one-time basis now take $50,000 in a week. In 1973, the policy was discontinued. The reason was that the new refugees coming at that time were unknown to us. (Portes and Stepick 1993)

Character loans made possible the creation of a thick layer of small and midsize firms that are today the core of the Cuban ethnic economy. Bounded solidarity clearly had something to do with the initiative since fellow exiles were preferred to other potential recipients. However, this mechanism was not enough. The contrast between the exiles arriving in the 1960s to whom these loans were available and those who came after 1973 who were ineligible for them marks the boundaries of a prerevolutionary community of businesspeople in which personal reputation and social ties were a precondition for success. Once in Miami, these connections became all the more valuable because penniless refugees had little else on which to rebuild their careers.

The Cuban bankers, therefore, had good reasons for making these loans because they were certain that their clients would pay back. Anyone defaulting or otherwise violating the expectations built into such deals would be excluded from the community and, as it was with the Dominicans in New York, there was precious little else in Miami in the way of economic opportunity. Character loans were backed, therefore, by much more than sentiments of loyalty or a written promise to repay, but by the sanctioning capacity built into the business networks of the enclave. The fact that bounded solidarity did not suffice is demonstrated by the exclusion of Cubans who came after the exodus of the prerevolutionary business elite was complete.[6]

Community Resources

As a source of social capital, enforceable trust varies greatly with the characteristics of the community. Since the relevant behaviors are guided by instrumentalist expectations, the likelihood of their occurrence is conditioned by the extent to which the community is the sole or principal source of certain rewards. When immigrants can draw on a variety of valued resources—from social approval to business opportunities—from their association with outsiders, the power of their ethnic community becomes weaker. Conversely, when outside prejudice denies them access to such rewards, observance of community norms and expectations becomes much more likely. After reviewing studies of business behavior of the overseas Chinese in the Philippines and of Asian Indians in Kenya, Granovetter (in press) arrives essentially at the same conclusion, noting that "the discrimination that minority groups face can actually generate an advantage. . . . Once this discrimination fades, intergenerational continuity in business is harder to sustain." These observations lead to the following third proposition:

> As a source of social capital, enforceable trust is directly proportional to the strength of outside discrimination and inversely proportional to the available options outside the community for securing social honor and economic opportunity.

What happens on the outside must be balanced, however, with the resources available in the ethnic community itself. It may be that a second- or third-generation Chinese-American or Jewish-American faces no great prejudice in contemporary American society, yet she or he may choose to preserve ties to the ethnic community because of the opportunities available through such networks. The durability of institutions created by successful immigrant groups may have less to do with the long-term persistence of outside discrimination than with the ability of these institutions to "compete" effectively with resources and rewards available in the broader society. Conversely, a resource-poor immigrant community will have trouble enforcing normative patterns even if its members continue to face severe outside discrimination.

An ongoing study of second-generation Haitian students in Miami high schools illustrates the point.[7] Like other immigrant groups before them, Haitian parents want their children to preserve their culture and language as they adapt to the American environment. However, Haitian parents lack the means to send their children to private schools, and, in any case, there are none in Miami that teach in French or foster Haitian culture. As a result, many Haitian-American students must attend the same high school that serves the inner-city area known as Liberty City. There Haitian students are socialized in a different set of values, including the futility of trying to advance in life through education. They find their culture denigrated by native-born minority students who often poke fun at Haitians' accents and docility. Since immigrant parents have very little to show for their efforts, and the Haitian community as a whole is poor and politically weak, second-generation students have few incentives to stay within it, and many opt to melt into the mainstream. In this instance, "mainstream" does not mean the white society, but the impoverished black community of Liberty City. As this happens, social capital based on immigrant community networks is dissipated.[8]

Last, the effectiveness of collective sanctions through which enforceable trust is built depends on the group's ability to monitor the behavior of its members and its capacity to publicize the identity of deviants. Sanctioning capacity is increased by the possibility of bestowing public honor or inflicting public shame immediately after certain deeds are committed. Means of communication, in particular the ethnic media, play a crucial role in this regard (Olzak and West 1991). Foreign-language newspapers, radio stations, and television spots exist not only to entertain and inform the respective communities, but also to uphold collective values and highlight their observance or violation (Forment 1989, 63–64). As such, the existence of well-developed media channels within an ethnic community represents a powerful instrument of social control.

These observations can be summarized in a fourth proposition:

> The greater the ability of a community to confer unique rewards on its members, and the more developed its internal means of communication, then the greater the strength of enforceable trust and the higher the level of social capital stemming from it.

By failing to take into account the differential presence of resources giving rise to enforceable trust, orthodox economic models of minority poverty and mobility deprive themselves of a crucial analytical tool. Recent research shows that levels of entrepreneurship vary significantly among ethnic minorities and that such differences are positively associated with average incomes (Fratoe and Meeks 1985; Aldrich and Zimmer 1986; Light and Bonacich 1988; Borjas 1990). Other analyses indicate that neither the origins of ethnic entrepreneurship nor its average higher levels of remuneration are fully explained by human capital differences (Portes and Zhou 1992). Social capital arising from enforceable trust may well account for the remaining differences. These favorable consequences are, of course, congruent with those hypothesized by Coleman (1988). Having concluded the analysis of different types of social capital and the processes giving rise to them, it is appropriate at this point to consider the other side of the matter.

Negative Effects

Coleman's analysis of social capital sounds a note of consistent praise for the various mechanisms that lead people to behave in ways different from naked self-interest. His writing adopts at times a tone of undisguised nostalgia, reminiscent of Tönnies' longing for the times when there was more social closure and when gemeinschaft had the upper hand (Tönnies 1963). Indeed, it is our sociological bias to see good things emerging out of social embeddedness; bad things are more commonly associated with the behavior of *homo economicus*. Many examples could be cited in support of the sociological position in addition to those presented by Coleman (see Hechter 1987; Uehara 1990). To do so, however, would only belabor the point. Instead, this final section considers the other side of the question. When it is put on a par with money capital and human capital, an instrumentalist analysis of social capital is necessarily biased toward emphasizing its positive uses—from capitalizing minority enterprises to cutting down the number of lawyers required for enforcing contracts.

It is important, however, not to lose sight of the fact that the same social mechanisms that give rise to appropriable resources for individual use can also constrain action or even derail it from its original goals. At first glance, the term "social debit" might seem appropriate in order to preserve the parallel with money capital. However, on closer examination, this term is inadequate because the relevant phenomena do not reflect the *absence* of the same forces giving rise to social capital but rather their other, presumably less desirable, manifestations. The following examples illustrate these alternative facets.

Costs of Community Solidarity

The existence of a measure of solidarity and trust in a community represents a precondition for the emergence of a network of successful enterprises. However, the exacerbation of these sentiments and obligations can conspire against exactly such a network. In his study of the rise of commercial enterprises in Bali, Clifford Geertz observed how successful entrepreneurs were constantly assaulted by job- and loan-seeking kinsmen. These claims were buttressed by strong norms enjoining mutual assistance within the extended family and among community members in general. Balinese social life is based on groups called *seka*, and individuals typically belong to several of these. "The value of *seka* loyalty, putting the needs of one's group above one's own is, along with caste pride, a central value of Balinese social life" (Geertz 1963, 84). Although entrepreneurship is highly valued in this community, successful businessmen face the problem of numerous claims on their profits based on the expectation that economic decisions "will lead to a higher level of welfare for the organic community as a whole" (Geertz 1963, 123). The result is to turn promising enterprises into welfare hotels, checking their economic expansion.

Granovetter (in press), who calls attention to this phenomenon, notes that it is the same problem that classic economic development theory identified among traditional enterprises and that modern capitalist firms were designed to overcome. Weber (1963) made the same point when he identified arm's-length transactions guided by the principle of universalism as one of the major reasons for the success of Puritan enterprises. Hence, cozy intergroup relationships of the sort frequently found in solidary communities can give rise to a gigantic free-riding problem. Less diligent group members can enforce on successful members all types of demands backed by the same normative structure that makes the existence of trust possible.

In the indigenous villages surrounding the town of Otavalo in the Ecuadoran Andes, male owners of garment and leather artisan shops are often Protestant (or "Evangelicals" as they are known locally) rather than Catholic. The reason is not that the Protestant ethic spurred them to greater entrepreneurial achievement nor that they found Evangelical doctrine to be more compatible with their own beliefs, but a rather more instrumental one. By shifting religious allegiance, these entrepreneurs remove themselves from the host of social obligations for male family heads associated with the Catholic Church and its local organizations. The Evangelical convert becomes, in a sense, a stranger in his own community, which insulates him from free riding by others who follow Catholic-inspired norms.[9]

Among present-day immigrant communities in the United States scattered instances of this phenomenon appear to be operating. Southeast Asian, and particularly Vietnamese, businesses in California have been affected by a particularly destructive form of collective demands from fellow exiles, including Vietnamese youth and former military officers (Chea 1985; Efron 1990). In the course of fieldwork in Orange County, California, Rubén Rumbaut interviewed a successful Vietnamese electronics manufacturer who employed approximately three hundred workers in his plant. Not one of them was Vietnamese. The owner had anglicized his name and cut most of his ties to the immigrant community. The reason was less a desire for assimilation than fear of the demands of other Vietnamese, especially the private "security services" organized by former members of the Vietnamese police.[10]

Constraints on Freedom

A second manifestation of negative effects consists of the constraints that community norms put on individual action and receptivity to outside culture. This is an expression of the age-old dilemma between community solidarity and individual freedom in the modern metropolis, already analyzed by Simmel (1964). The dilemma becomes acute in the case of tightly knit immigrant communities since they are usually inserted in the core of the metropolis, yet are simultaneously upholding an exotic culture. The city-within-a-city sustained by the operation of solidarity and trust creates unique economic opportunities for immigrants, but often at the cost of fierce regimentation and limited contacts with the outside world. The Spanish-language media, so instrumental in maintaining community controls among Latins in South Florida (Forment 1989), also imposes, in the opinion of many observers, a virtual censorship. Joan Didion reports the views on the matter of a dissident exile banker: "This is Miami. . . . A million Cubans are blackmailed, totally controlled by three radio stations. I feel sorry for the Cuban community in Miami. Because they have imposed on themselves, by way of the right, the same condition that Castro has imposed in Cuba. Total intolerance" (Didion 1987, 113).

Until a few years ago, San Francisco's Chinatown was a tightly knit community where the family clans and the Chinese Six Companies ruled supreme. These powerful associations regulated the business and social life of the community, guaranteeing its normative order and privileged access to resources for its entrepreneurs. Such assets came, however, at the cost of restrictions on most members' scope of action and access to the outside world. In their study of Chinatown, Nee and Nee (1973) report on the continuing power of the clans and the Chinese companies and their strong conservative bent. What put teeth in the clans' demands was their control of land and business opportunities in the Chinese enclave and their willingness to exclude those who violated normative consensus by adopting a "progressive" stance. One of the Nees' informants complained about this conservative stronghold in terms similar to those of the Miami banker above:

> And not only the Moon Family Association, all the family associations, the Six Companies, any young person who wants to make some changes, they call him a communist right away. He's redcapped right away. They use all kinds of tricks to run him out. You see, in old Chinatown, they didn't respect a scholarly person or an intelligent person. . . . They hold on to everything the way it was in China, in Kwangtung. Even though we're in a different society, a different era. (Nee and Nee 1973, 190)

Like Chinatown in San Francisco, the Korean community of New York is undergirded by a number of associations—from traditional extended family groups and various types of *gye* (rotating credit associations) to modern businesses and professional organizations. The role of this associational structure in generating social capital for collective advancement follows closely the pattern of enforceable trust already described. The flip side of this structure takes, however, a peculiar form among Koreans. As described by Illsoo Kim (1981), the South Korean government, represented by its consulate general, has played a very prominent role in the development of the ethnic community. "Partly because Korean immigrants have a strong sense of nationalism and therefore identify with the home government, the Korean Consulate General in New York City . . . has determined the basic tone of community-wide politics" (Kim 1981, 227).

This position has, in the past, enabled the South Korean government to promote its own interests by rewarding "loyal" immigrants with honors and business concessions and by intimidating its opponents. Especially during the government of Park Chung-hee, the Korean CIA (KCIA) was active in the community, rooting out anti-Park elements and silencing them with threats of financial ruin or even physical harm. In an American context, this heavy political hand became excessive, leading other community organizations to mobilize in order to weaken its hold. The consulate remained, however, an integral part of this community and a significant institutional factor.

The solidarity and enforcement capacity that promote ethnic business success also restrict the scope of individual expression and the extent of extra-community contacts. Combined with the first type of negative effect discussed above, these examples can be summarized in the following fifth proposition:

> The greater the social capital produced by bounded solidarity and community controls, then the greater the particularistic demands placed on successful entrepreneurs and the more extensive the restrictions on individual expression.

Leveling Pressures

The first two negative effects above are not intrinsically at odds with economic mobility, but represent its marginal costs, as it were: successful individuals are beset by fellow group members relying on the strength of collective norms, and highly solidary communities restrict the scope of personal action as the cost of privileged access to economic resources. The last form discussed in this section conspires directly against efforts toward individual mobility by exerting leveling pressures to keep members of downtrodden groups in the same situation as their peers. The mechanism at work is the fear that a solidarity born out of common adversity would be undermined by the departure of the more successful members. Each success story saps the morale of a group, if that morale is built precisely on the limited possibilities for ascent under an oppressive social order.

This conflict is experienced by the Haitian-American teenagers discussed above, as they are torn between parental expectations for success through education and an inner-city youth culture that denies that such a thing is possible. Assimilation to American culture for these immigrant children often means giving up the dream of making it in America through individual achievement.[11] The neologism "wannabe," arguably the latest contribution of inner-city youth to the cultural mainstream, captures succinctly the process at hand. Calling someone by this name is a way of ridiculing his or her aspiration to move above his or her present station and of exercising social pressure on the person to remain in it. In his ethnographic research among Puerto Rican crack dealers in the Bronx, Bourgois (1991) calls attention to the local version of the "wannabe" among second-generation Puerto Rican youngsters—the "turnover." He reports the views of one of his informants:

> When you see someone go downtown and get a good job, if they be Puerto Rican, you see them fix up their hair and put some contact lens in their eyes. Then they fit in. And they do it! I have seen it! . . . Look at all the people in that building, they all turn-overs. They people who want to be white. Man, if you call them in Spanish it wind up a problem. I mean like take the name Pedro—I'm just telling you this as an example—Pedro be saying (imitating a whitened accent) "My name is Peter." Where do you get Peter from Pedro? (Bourgois 1991, 32)

In their description of what they label the "hyperghetto" of Chicago's South Side, Wacquant and Wilson (1989) speak of a similar phenomenon in which solidarity cemented on common adversity discourages individuals from seeking or pursuing outside opportunities. Notice that in each such situation, social capital is still present, but its effects are exactly the opposite of those found among other immigrant communities. Whereas among Asian, Middle Eastern, and other foreign groups, social capital based on bounded solidarity is one of the bases for the construction of successful enterprises, in the inner city it has the opposite effect.

This contrast is all the more telling because it often involves groups from the same broad cultural origin. In this regard, the use of Spanish in Miami and in the Bronx is instructive. In the Bronx, shifting to English and anglicizing one's name is a sign that the individual aspires to move up by leaving behind his or her ethnic community. In Miami, the same behavior would bring exclusion from the business networks of the enclave and the unique mobility opportunities that they make available. In both instances, public use of Spanish signals membership in the ethnic community, but the socioeconomic consequences are very different.

Perhaps the most destructive consequence of this negative manifestation of social capital is the wedge that it drives between successful members of the minority and those left behind. To the extent that community solidarity is exclusively based on an adversarial view of the mainstream, those who attempt to make it through conventional means are often compelled to adopt majority opinions antithetical to their own group. Bourgois (1991) illustrates this point with the example of a former Bronx pusher, now a born-again Christian and insurance salesman in the Connecticut suburbs:

> If anything when you look at me you know I'm Hispanic. When I jog down the neighborhood, people get scared. It's not a problem for me because I have self-confidence . . . every once in a while I used to get a crank call in the house, saying "Hey, spic," you know "spic" and other stuff, but I don't worry about that.
>
> In a sense, I've learned to be in their shoes. You see what I mean. Because I've seen what minorities as a group can do to a neighborhood. So I step into their shoes and I understand, I sympathize with them. Cause I've seen great neighborhoods go down. (34–35)

For the lone escapee from the ghetto, "self-confidence" takes the place of group support. Confronting prejudice alone often means accepting some of its premises and turning them against one's own past. The suburban white, perceived from the ghetto as an adversary, is transformed into a sympathetic figure "in whose shoes" one can stand.

It is beyond the scope of this article to explore the contextual forces leading to the widely different outcomes of ethnic solidarity. The existing literature suggests, however, one common strand in every manifestation of this last type of negative effect based on downward leveling norms. Each such instance has been preceded by extensive periods of time, sometimes generations, in which the upward mobility of the group has been blocked (Marks 1989; Barrera 1980; Nelson and Tienda 1985). This has been followed by the emergence of collective solidarity based on opposition to these conditions and an accompanying explanation of the group's social and economic inferiority as caused by outside oppression. Although correct historically, this position frequently produces negative consequences for individual mobility through the operation of the mechanism discussed above. These observations lead to the following sixth and final proposition:

> The longer the economic mobility of a group has been blocked by coercive nonmarket means, then the more likely the emergence of a bounded solidarity that negates the possibility of advancement through fair market competition and that opposes individual efforts in this direction.

The six propositions presented above are summarized in figure 10.1, which attempts to formalize the discussion of antecedents and effects of solidarity and trust. As indicated previously, the propositions have the character of hypotheses that have been drawn from past and ongoing research on immigration, but will be subject to the test of additional evidence. The present state of knowledge does not allow a more refined analysis of the character of relationships between antecedent and consequent factors including, for example, whether they involve additive or interactive effects. Such refinements and possible corrections to the set of hypothesized relationships must await additional work.

Figure 10.1 does not fully resolve the apparent ambiguity in the final proposition, which, at first glance, contradicts earlier ones concerning the positive effects of bounded solidarity. In fact, it supports them: the reactive mechanism giving rise to bounded solidarity in response to outward discrimination is the same as outlined earlier. The crucial difference lies in the extent of discrimination and its duration. Protracted periods of oppression, especially in a no-exit situation, undermine the cultural and linguistic resources available to a group for constructing an alternative definition of the situation (second proposition). A situation of permanent subordination also deprives a collectivity of the resources necessary to reward or punish its members independently (fourth proposition), so that its enforcement capacity is entirely dependent on outside discrimination that forces its members to band together (third proposition). The downward leveling pressures reviewed here are a reaction to the partial breakdown of this last source of sanctioning capacity, as fissures in the barriers confronting the group allow some of its members—"wannabes" or "turnovers"—to escape its hold.

Summary and Conclusion

In this article, we have attempted to contribute to the reemerging field of economic sociology by delving into its classic roots and by using empirical examples from the immigration literature to explore the different forms in which social structures can affect economic action. Social embeddedness provides a suitable conceptual umbrella for this exploration, although, to analyze its specific manifestations, we have focused on the concept of social capital. We have argued that previous analyses of this concept have been too vague concerning its origins and too instrumentalist about its effects. Accordingly, the aim of our analysis has been to identify the various mechanisms leading to the emergence of social capital and to highlight its consequences, positive and negative.

Economic sociology traces its origins not only to Max Weber and other sociological classics, but also to economists such as Joseph Schumpeter who saw in this field a needed corrective to the simplifications of classical economy theory. Schumpeter and other "historical school" economists in Germany, as well as Veblen and later institutionalist economists in the United States, struggled mightily to stem the growing tide to convert individuals into "mere clotheslines on which to hang propositions of economic logic" (Schumpeter 1954, 885–87; Swedberg 1991). The effort to highlight the economic significance of what Schumpeter called "social institutions" collapsed, however, under the relentless expansion of individualism and rational utilitarian models, to the point that these perspectives have begun to make significant inroads into sociology itself.

In this context, the efforts of Granovetter (1985, 1990), Block (1990), and others to reopen space for social structures in the analysis of economic life represent a commendable, but still fragile, venture. In our view, such efforts will not prosper if limited, as in the past, to a critique of neoclassical theories without there being anything proposed to replace them. A viable strategy for filling this gap is not to ground sociological perspective in armchair speculation, but in established bodies of empirical knowledge. The modest but rapidly growing immigration-research literature offers a rich source for such efforts, exemplified but not exhausted by the exercise in these pages.

Notes

1. Officer Lozano was initially convicted by a Miami jury, but an appeals court threw out the conviction on the grounds that he could not get a fair trial in the city.

At the moment of this writing, the case is still pending. The venue of the retrial was first moved to Orlando and later to Tallahassee. Throughout the process, Lozano has continued to make appeals for financial support through the Spanish-language radio stations ("Lozano Gets Seven Years" 1990; "Lozano Wins a Manslaughter Retrial" 1991; fieldwork by authors).

2. Nee and Nee use the Wade-Giles spelling system. In Pinyin, the romanization system now used in China, the province name is spelled Guangdong.

3. According to the Federation of Dominican Industrialists and Merchants of New York, the city hosts some twenty thousand Dominican-owned businesses, including about 70 percent of all Spanish grocery stores, or bodegas, 90 percent of the gypsy cabs in Upper Manhattan, three chains of Spanish supermarkets, and several newspapers and radio stations. Allowing for a measure of prideful exaggeration in these figures, they still point to the diversity of business initiatives in which Dominican immigrants can be found (Guarnizo 1992).

4. From field interviews in New York conducted as part of the same study (Portes and Guarnizo 1991).

5. This material was gathered by the senior author during fieldwork in Miami and will be included in a forthcoming book on that city (Portes and Stepick 1993).

6. For a periodicization of the stages of the Cuban exodus, see Diaz-Briquets and Perez 1981: and Pedraza-Bailey 1985.

7. Study in progress entitled, "Children of Immigrants: The Adaptation Process of the Second-Generation." The material presented herein comes from preliminary fieldwork conducted by the senior author in south Florida during the summer of 1990 (see Portes and Stepick 1993, chap. 8).

8. See n. 7 above. On the condition of Haitians in south Florida, see also Stepick 1982 and Miller 1984.

9. Preliminary results of an ongoing study of indigenous entrepreneurship in the Andes being conducted by the Latin American School of Social Sciences (FLACSO) in Quito. Personal communication with the study director, Dr. Jorge Leon, June 1991.

10. This interview was conducted in June 1985 and is reported in Portes and Rumbaut 1990, 3–4.

11. For a similar situation confronting Mexican and Central American immigrant children in California schools, see Suarez-Orozco 1987.

References

Aldrich, Howard E., and Catharine Zimmer. 1986. "Entrepreneurship through Social Networks." In *The Art and Science of Entrepreneurship*, ed. D. L. Sexton and R. W. Smilor. Cambridge, Mass.: Ballinger.

1991. "Asian-Americans Take Lead in Starting U.S. Businesses." *Wall Street Journal*. Enterprise section, August 21.

Bailey, Thomas, and Roger Waldinger. 1991. "Primary, Secondary, and Enclave Labor Markets: A Training Systems Approach." *American Sociological Review* 56:432–45.

Barrera, Mario. 1980. *Race and Class in the Southwest: A Theory of Racial Inequality*. Notre Dame, Ind.: University of Notre Dame Press.

Baker, Wayne E., and Robert R. Faulkner. 1991. "Role as Resource in the Hollywood Film Industry." *American Journal of Sociology* 97:279–309.

Blau, Peter M. 1964. *Exchange and Power in Social Life*. New York: Wiley.

Block, Fred. 1990. *Postindustrial Possibilities: A Critique of Economic Discourse*. Berkeley and Los Angeles: University of California Press.

Borjas, George. 1990. *Friends or Strangers*. New York: Basic Books.

Boswell, Terry E. 1986. "A Split Labor Market Analysis of Discrimination against Chinese Immigrants, 1850–1882." *American Sociological Review* 52:352–71.

Bourdieu, Pierre. 1979. "Les trois états du capital culturel." *Actes de la Recherche en Sciences Sociales* 30:3–5.

Bourdieu, Pierre, Channa Newman, and Loïc J. D. Wacquant. 1991. "The Peculiar History of Scientific Reason." *Sociological Forum* 6:3–26.

Bourgois, Philippe. 1991. "In Search of Respect: The New Service Economy and the Crack Alternative in Spanish Harlem." Paper presented at the Conference on Poverty, Immigration, and Urban Marginality in Advanced Societies, Maison Suger, Paris, May 10–11.

Branch, Karen. 1989. "Nicaraguan Culture: Alive and Growing in Dade." *Miami Herald*. Neighbors section, 20.

Chea, Chantan S. 1985. "Southeast Asian Refugees in Orange County: An Overview." Report, Southeast Asian Genetics Program, University of California, Irvine, April.

Coleman, James S. 1988. "Social Capital in the Creation of Human Capital." *American Journal of Sociology* 94:S95–S121.

Diaz-Briquets, Sergio, and Lisandro Perez. 1981. "Cuba: The Demography of Revolution." *Population Bulletin* 36:2–41.

Didion, Joan. 1987. *Miami*. New York: Simon and Schuster.

Dinnerstein, Leonard. 1977. "The East European Jewish Migration." In *Uncertain Americans: Readings in Ethnic History*, ed. Leonard Dinnerstein and Frederic C. Jaher. Oxford: Oxford University Press.

Durkheim, Émile. 1984. *The Division of Labor in Society*. Trans. W. D. Halls. New York: Free Press.

Eccles, Robert G., and Harrison C. White. 1988. "Price and Authority in Inter-profit Center Transactions." *American Journal of Sociology* 94:S517–S552.

Efron, Souni. 1990. "Few Viet Exiles Find U.S. Riches." *Los Angeles Times*, April 29.

Forment, Carlos A. 1989, "Political Practice and the Rise of the Ethnic Enclave, the Cuban-American Case, 1959–1979." *Theory and Society* 18:47–81.

Fratoe, Frank A., and Ronald L. Meeks. 1985. "Business Participation Rates of the 50 Largest U.S. Ancestry Groups: Preliminary Reports." Minority Business Development Agency, U.S. Department of Commerce, Washington, D.C.

Geertz, Clifford. 1963. *Peddlers and Princes: Social Change and Economic Modernization in Two Indonesian Towns*. Chicago: University of Chicago Press.

Glazer, Nathan. 1954. "Ethnic Groups in America." In *Freedom and Control in Modern Society*, ed. M. Berger, T. Abel, and C. Page. New York: Van Nostrand.

Gold, Steve. 1988. "Refugees and Small Business: The Case of Soviet Jews and Vietnamese." *Ethnic and Racial Studies* 11:411–38.

Gouldner, Alvin. 1960. "The Norm of Reciprocity: A Preliminary Statement." *American Sociological Review* 25:161–79.

Granovetter, Mark. 1985. "Economic Action and Social Structure: The Problem of Embeddedness." *American Journal of Sociology* 91:481–510.

———. 1990. "The Old and the New Economic Sociology: A History and an Agenda." In *Beyond the Marketplace*, ed. R. Friedland and A. F. Robertson. New York: Aldine de Gruyter.

———. In press. "Entrepreneurship, Development, and the Emergence of Firms." In *Society and Economy: The Social Construction of Economic Institutions*. Cambridge: Harvard University Press.

Greeley, Andrew M. 1971. *Why Can't They Be Like Us? America's White Ethnic Groups*. New York: E. P. Dutton.

Guarnizo, Luis E. 1992. "One Country in Two: Dominican-Owned Firms in New York and in the Dominican Republic." Ph.D. diss. Department of Sociology, Johns Hopkins University.

Hechter, Michael. 1987. *Principles of Group Solidarity*. Berkeley and Los Angeles: University of California Press.

Howe, Irving. 1976. *The Immigrant Jews of New York: 1881 to the Present*. London: Routledge and Kegan Paul.

Kim, Illsoo. 1981. *New Urban Immigrants: The Korean Community in New York*. Princeton: Princeton University Press.

Laumann, Edward O., and David Knoke. 1986. "Social Network Theory." In *Approaches to Social Theory*, ed. Siegwart Linderberg, James S. Coleman, and Stefan Nowak. New York: Russell Sage.

Leff, Nathanael. 1979. "Entrepreneurship and Economic Development: The Problem Revisited." *Journal of Economic Literature* 17:46–64.

Light, Ivan H. 1972. *Ethnic Enterprise in America: Business and Welfare among Chinese, Japanese, and Blacks*. Berkeley and Los Angeles: University of California Press.

Light, Ivan H., and Edna Bonacich. 1988. *Immigrant Entrepreneurs: Koreans in Los Angeles, 1965–1982*. Berkeley and Los Angeles: University of California Press.

"Lozano Gets 7 Years," 1990. *Miami Herald*, January 25.

"Lozano Wins a Manslaughter Retrial." 1991. *Miami Herald*, June 26.

Marks, Carole. 1989. *Farewell—We're Good and Gone: The Great Black Migration*. Bloomington: Indiana University Press.

Marsden, Peter V. 1990. "Network and Data Measurement." *Annual Review of Sociology* 16:435–63.

Marx, Karl. 1967. *Capital*. Vol. 3. New York: International.

Marx, Karl, and Frederick Engels. 1947. *The German Ideology*. New York: International.

———. 1948. *The Communist Manifesto*. New York: International.

McCloskey, Donald, and Lars Sandberg. 1971. "From Damnation to Redemption: Judgments on the Late Victorian Entrepreneur." *Explorations in Economic History* 9:89–108.

Miller, Jake C. 1984. *The Plight of Haitian Refugees*. New York: Praeger.

Mintz, Beth, and Michael Schwartz. 1985. *The Power Structure of American Business*. Chicago: University of Chicago Press.

Nee, Victor, and Brett de Bary Nee. 1973. *Longtime California: A Documentary Study of an American Chinatown*. New York: Pantheon.

Nelson, Candace, and Marta Tienda. 1985. "The Structuring of Hispanic Ethnicity: Historical and Contemporary Perspectives." *Ethnic and Racial Studies* 8:49–74.

Olzak, Susan, and Elizabeth West. 1991. "Ethnic Conflict and the Rise and Fall of Ethnic Newspapers." *American Sociological Review* 56:458–74.

Parsons, Talcott. 1937. *The Structure of Social Action*. New York: McGraw-Hill.

Parsons, Talcott, and Neil J. Smelser. 1956. *Economy and Society: A Study in the Integration of Economic and Social Theory.* New York: Free Press.

Pedraza-Bailey, Silvia. 1985. "Cuba's Exiles: Portrait of a Refugee Migration." *International Migration Review* 19:4–34.

Perez, Lisandro. 1986. "Immigrant Economic Adjustment and Family Orientation: The Cuban Success Story." *International Migration Review* 20:4–20.

Polanyi, Karl, C. Arensberg, and H. Pearson. 1957. *Trade and Markets in the Early Empires*. New York: Free Press.

Portes, Alejandro, and Luis E. Guarnizo. 1991. "Tropical Capitalists: U.S.-Bound Immigration and Small Enterprise Development in the Dominican Republic." In *Migration, Remittances, and Small Business Development, Mexico and Caribbean Basin Countries*, ed. S. Diaz-Briquets and S. Weintraub. Boulder, Colo.: Westview.

Portes, Alejandro, and Rubén G. Rumbaut. 1990. *Immigrant America: A Portrait.* Berkeley and Los Angeles: University of California Press.

Portes, Alejandro, and Alex Stepick. 1993. *City on the Edge: The Transformation of Miami.* Berkeley and Los Angeles: University of California Press.

Portes, Alejandro, and Min Zhou. 1992. "Divergent Destinies: Immigration, Poverty, and Entrepreneurship in the United States." Russell Sage Foundation, Working Paper no. 27.

Rischin, Moses. 1962. *The Promised City: New York Jews, 1870–1914*. Cambridge, Mass.: Harvard University Press.

Rumbaut, Rubén G. 1985. "Mental Health and the Refugee Experience." In *Southeast Asian Mental Health*, edited by T. C. Owan. Rockville, Md.: National Institute of Mental Health.

Rumbaut, Rubén G., and Kenji Ima. 1988. *The Adaptation of Southeast Asian Refugee Youth: A Comparative Study.* Washington, D.C.: Office of Refugee Resettlement.

Schumpeter, Joseph A. 1954. *History of Economic Analysis*. London: Allen and Unwin.

Simmel, Georg. 1955. Conflict and The Web of Group Affiliations. Trans. Kurt H. Wolff and Reinhard Bendix. New York: Free Press.

———. 1964. "The Metropolis and Mental Life" In *The Sociology of Georg Simmel*, ed. and trans. Kurt H. Wolff. New York: Free Press.

Sowell, Thomas. 1981. *Ethnic America: A History.* New York: Basic Books.

Stepick, Alex. 1982. "Haitian Refugees in the U.S." Minority Rights Group, London, Minority Rights Group Report no. 52.

Suarez-Orozco, Marcelo M. 1987. "Towards a Psychosocial Understanding of Hispanic Adaptation to American Schooling." In *Success or Failure? Learning and the Languages of Minority Students*, ed. H. T. Trueba. New York: Newbury House.

Swedberg, Richard. 1991. "Major Traditions of Economic Sociology." *Annual Review of Sociology* 17:251–76.

Tan, Amy. 1989. *The Joy Luck Club*. New York: Putnam's.

Thomas, William I., and Florian Znaniecki. 1984. *The Polish Peasant in Europe and America*. Ed. Eli Zaretsky. Urbana: University of Illinois Press.

Tilly, Charles. 1990. "Transplanted Networks." In *Immigration Reconsidered: History, Sociology, and Politics*, ed. Virginia Yans-McLaughlin. Oxford: Oxford University Press.

Tönnies, Ferdinand. 1963. *Community and Society*. New York: Harper and Row.

Uehara, Edwina. 1990. "Dual Exchange Theory, Social Networks, and Informal Social Support." *American Journal of Sociology* 96:521–57.

U.S. Bureau of the Census. 1991. *Census of Minority-Owned Business Enterprises, Asians*. Washington, D.C.: Government Printing Office.

Veciana-Suarez, Ana. 1983. "Nicaraguan Exiles Begin to Climb the Ladder." *Miami Herald*, Business section, March 28.

Wacquant, Loïc J. D., and William J. Wilson. 1989. "The Cost of Racial and Class Exclusion in the Inner City." *Annals of the American Academy of Political and Social Science* 501:8–26.

Weber, Max. 1958. *The Protestant Ethic and the Spirit of Capitalism*. Trans. Talcott Parsons. New York: Charles Scribner's Sons.

———. 1947. *The Theory of Social and Economic Organization*. Ed. Talcott Parsons. Trans. A. M. Henderson and Talcott Parsons. New York: Free Press.

———. 1963. *The Sociology of Religion*. Trans. Ephraim Fischoff. Boston: Beacon.

Wellman, Barry, and Scott Wortley. 1990. "Different Strokes from Different Folks: Community Ties and Social Support." *American Journal of Sociology* 96: 558–88.

White, Harrison C. 1970. *Chains of Opportunity: System Models of Mobility in Organizations*. Cambridge: Harvard University Press.

Wilson, Kenneth, and W. Allen Martin. 1982. "Ethnic Enclaves: A Comparison of the Cuban and Black Economies in Miami." *American Journal of Sociology* 88:135–60.

Wilson, Kenneth, and Alejandro Portes. 1980. "Immigrant Enclaves: An Analysis of the Labor Market Experiences of Cubans in Miami." *American Journal of Sociology* 86:295–319.

Wrong, Dennis. 1961. "The Oversocialized Conception of Man in Modern Sociology." *American Sociological Review* 26:183–93.

Yancey, William, Eugene P. Ericksen, and Richard N. Juliani. 1976. "Emergent Ethnicity: A Review and Reformulation." *American Sociological Review* 41:391–403.

Zhou, Min. 1992. *Chinatown: The Socioeconomic Potential of an Urban Enclave*. Philadelphia: Temple University Press.

Chapter 11

A STRUCTURAL APPROACH TO MARKETS

ERIC M. LEIFER AND HARRISON C. WHITE

STRUCTURAL ANALYSIS focuses upon the patterns of relationships among social actors. This emphasis rests on the often unspoken postulate that these patterns—independent of the content of the ties—are themselves central to individual action. Moreover, structural analysis posits that the constraints associated with positions in a network of relationships are frequently more important in determining individual action than either the information or attitudes people hold (Berkowitz 1982, 8).

Structural context is represented by patterns of ties of varying content, and the analyst's interest is in how individual behavior serves to reproduce the structural context (Burt1982). The discovery of "self-reproducing" structural contexts has occupied structural analysts in such diverse areas as kinship systems (White 1963), organizational structures (Kanter 1977), world systems (Snyder and Kick 1979; Love 1982; Breiger 1981), and abstract social structures (Lorrain and White 1971). In this endeavor structures are "explained" when their self-reproducing properties—and therefore their continued existence—are analytically understood.[1]

This approach contrasts sharply with information-oriented approaches, which explain the existence and/or continuation of a particular structure by showing how it is more "efficient" (in terms of a set of defined goals) than any available alternative (Williamson 1975). Only efficient structures are likely to be empirically observed, because inefficient structures would perish through natural selection or be made more efficient through the "maximizing" efforts of interested individuals. Structural approaches, on the other hand, identify a self-perpetuating system of structural constraints, without stepping within the kind of information framework needed to assess efficiency.

Structural analysis is often criticized because it excludes maximization and efficiency considerations, and hence lacks a solid basis for explaining how individual actors choose among the alternatives available to them. Though

Eric Leifer and Harrison White. 1987. "A Structural Approach to Markets," in *Intercorporate Relations: The Structural Analysis of Business*. Edited by Mark Mizruchi and Michael Schwartz, pp. 85–108. New York: Cambridge University Press.

some notable efforts have been made to include maximizing considerations (Boorman 1975; Winship 1978; Burt 1982), we will argue that to do so risks violating a basic thematic of structural analysis: *structures exist and reproduce themselves in part because the information needed to pursue maximization and efficiency* is not available. In other words, an individual frequently does not know in advance which option will produce, for example, the highest profits or the lowest costs. In these circumstances, *the only tangible guidance available to the actor is that which can be inferred from the patterns and outcomes which emerge from relations among actors.* That is, the individual makes his or her choice by observing the fate of others who have faced similar, but by no means identical choices. Maximization, if relevant, is defined only within the limited *social* framework of existing outcomes. Other alternatives may not appear or may be left unexplored simply because no useful evidence about them can be generated. Individuals rely on existing outcomes for guidance, and in doing so generate new outcomes to rely on. *Reproducibility*, rather than efficiency, *is the main issue.*

In this chapter, we present a recent model of production markets (see White 1981a, 1981b, 1987; Leifer 1985) that adopts the orientation of structural analysis. It shows how manufacturers of a particular product decide on the volume of their production and the prices they charge in a setting where they have a distinct reputation (i.e. their product is perceived and treated by their potential customers as being different from that of the competition in the market).

The vexing problem manufacturers must resolve is how they "fit into" the market, or, more to the point, how their customers would have them fit in. The producer would, of course, like to know how consumers would respond to volume and price changes, as well as how other producers would respond to such changes.

However, the requisite "demand curves" are almost never available and game-theoretic efforts to second-guess competitors' reactions must rely on implausible assumptions. In the real world businesses cannot know how consumers or competitors will respond to a particular change in volume or price. Our proposed structural model pulls the producer out of the mythical information setting in which everything is known and has the individual entrepreneur seeking guidance purely on the basis of the *observed* outcomes for all the producers in his or her market in the prior production period. The various outcomes are treated as a menu of fates (i.e. roles, or niches), to select from in the coming period. Producers "maximize" within this very limited social framework. They assess future possibilities by observing competitors' past pricing volume strategies, and find their place among the competitors by assessing these possibilities against their own production costs. The parallel action of competitors will influence each producer's fate that is observed in the next production period.

Our concern here is with the circumstances in which a viable market is produced, one where the summation of producers' choices serves to reproduce the role structure from the previous production period, and it is then used in a subsequent period with the same effect. When these circumstances materialize, the producers become locked into a self-fulfilling framework in which their unique fate (role) is perpetuated from period to period.

We begin our exposition with a speculative discussion of how Tony's frozen pizza operation uses its experience (and that of its competitors) to make choices about pricing and volume of production—and, hence, total revenues. We then sketch the formal model that underlies the speculation, moving from the interests of Tony to an interest in the conditions under which markets can function and reproduce themselves. Finally, we shift to the comparative issue, developing a topology of markets to show how inequality of revenue outcomes results from different cost and valuation contexts. We conclude with a discussion contrasting our structural approach with the information approaches found in the economic and business literature.

Tony's Dilemma

Tony produces and distributes frozen pizzas at the national level. Every three months he evaluates the market performance of his frozen pizzas and makes a decision about his volume (y) of production and his suggested retail price[2] for the coming quarter—and hence his projected revenue (W).[3] Tony uses his knowledge of the frozen pizza market to make this decision.

The market for Tony is populated by other frozen pizza producers that Tony knows by name and reputation. A brand name is attached to the frozen pizzas of each producer, and these give the producers distinct public images. Totino's and Jeno's, for example, are high-volume, inexpensive party pizzas. Stouffer's, on the other hand, sports a "French crust" (home-based in Ohio) and finds its way into more intimate gatherings at a higher price and a much lower volume. Celeste implants itself in the middle range, a favorite in middle-class families where neither parent has much time to cook.

These reputations are quite stable and, combined with the distinctive reputation of his own pizza, create a powerful constraint on Tony's choices. At least for the next three months, Tony assumes these reputations are not likely to change. Even in the long run, however, Tony is very uncertain about what would happen if he tried to induce a change in the reputation of his frozen pizza and therefore change his niche; and he is equally uncertain about how he would go about doing this. Tony perceives himself as locked in a structure of distinct "niches" over which he has little control.

The reputation of each frozen pizza brand can be represented in two dimensions: volume and revenue. Market shares are quite stable. The lower "quality" frozen pizzas command a large proportion of the market, while higher "quality" pizzas account for a small percentage. These reputational price differences are sharp and stable. Stouffer's costs more than Totino's, and this difference is an acknowledged feature of the "market" Tony has come to know. Tony accepts the fact that consumers are willing to pay different prices for different brands of frozen pizzas, without needing to understand the dynamics of consumer behavior. In textbook terms, Tony is operating in a "differentiated" market.

Quality differentiation poses a formidable problem for Tony's production and pricing decisions. Tony cannot take "price" as a given, since there is no single price in the market, but a unique price for each brand of goods. He could, of course, simply reuse the price he received in the prior period, but this has some potential drawbacks. First, in doing so he may be ignoring significant changes in the conditions of his market, and this could result in major problems. Second, Tony would be evading the basic question (which he might reflect on, but a researcher would insist on) of why he occupies the particular niche that he occupies. That is, a good businessperson should seek to change niches, if it is possible and profitable to do so. Finally, Tony could not safely assume his current price would be accepted if he changed his production volume (explained below).

Hence, his own production figures for the previous quarter offer Tony only a little guidance concerning the possibilities he faces. Outside of simply repeating his past period decision for both price and volume, no obvious guidelines for action appear present. The uniqueness of Tony's niche and the niches of other frozen pizza producers makes it unclear how Tony can use his own past, or the pasts of others, for guidance for the future.

Fortunately, Tony's knowledge of the "market" goes beyond the mere description of each producer's "niche" and his own production figures. *Tony knows how the niches are tied together.* There is a particular order to them. In Tony's market, low "quality" (that is, price) is tied to high production volumes (though in other markets, like disposable diapers, it may be the opposite). This he takes as a basic fact of the market he is in. This fact is crucial in his production volume and pricing decisions. If Tony successfully increased his market share, his public reputation would undergo a change also. He would become a mass market pizza maker and, in this market, the perceived quality of his product would decline. Thus Tony cannot make his volume decision independent from his price decision. The two are interrelated, as they are both tied to a distinct set of reputations, or niches, that are sustainable in this particular market.

This arrangement—or menu—is not secret; every pizza maker, market analyst, and noncasual observer of the business knows it well. The menu simply consists of the basic prices, sales volume, and—hence—revenues of frozen pizza producers in the prior production period. These figures are published

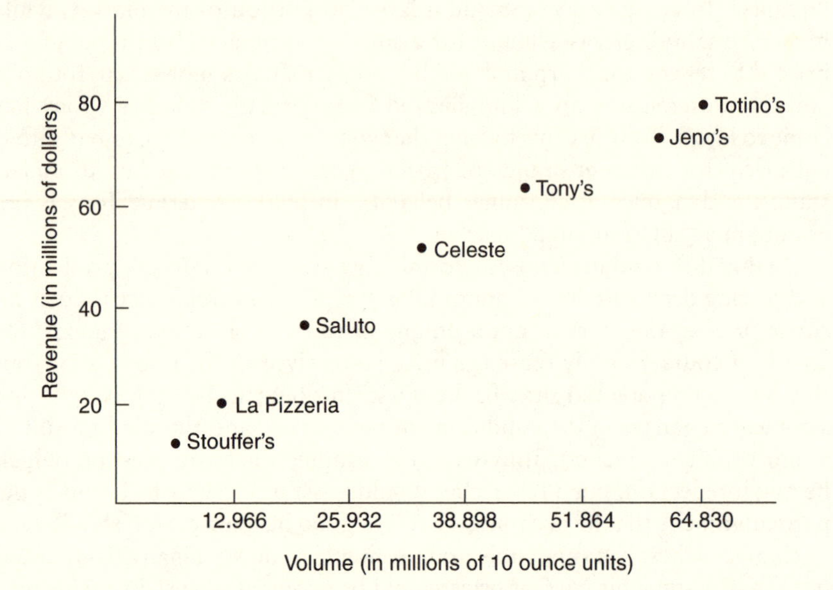

FIGURE 11.1 A menu of fares. The (annual) volume, revenue outcomes for seven frozen pizza producers. The menu defines the possibilities awaiting the producers in the next production period.

routinely in trade publications and business indexes, and reflected locally in retail prices and shelf space allocations. The menu that Tony observes is provided in figure 11.1. The orderliness of this menu is found in the fact that each production volume is associated with a unique revenue (i.e. price), insofar as the producer's outcomes fall on an "orderly" (though not usually linear) curve.

The menu of producer outcomes is the only tangible evidence for the possible niches that are sustainable within the frozen pizza market. To step outside this tangible menu would involve considerations of reputation formation, consumer psychology, and producer reactions that hold few prospects for sure-footed guidance for Tony. Tony uses the observed fates of other frozen pizza producers as his "opportunity set," because his knowledge of the market goes no further.

The rest is simple. Tony has a good idea of his (variable) production costs over a range of volumes. He assesses these costs against the assumed revenue opportunities in the market, and selects the production volume and appropriate asked revenue (price) that maximizes his return (profits). This can be done with a graph and ruler, as illustrated in figure 11.2. In a stable market, with each producer operating like Tony, the individual maximizing decisions lead each producer to choose the same niche as the previous period. The producer therefore reproduces the same opportunity set (menu of possibili-

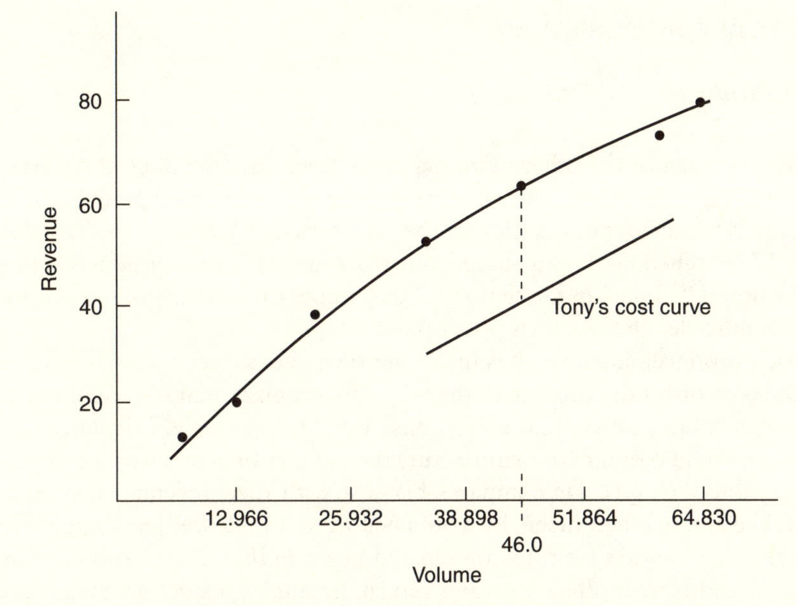

FIGURE 11.2 Tony's optimization problem. Tony assesses his production costs against the volume, revenue opportunities defined by actual outcomes of frozen pizza producers in the prior production period. Tony chooses the production volume, and associated price, which optimizes the difference between revenue and cost (i.e. profit).

ties). This is then used for guidance in the next period, yet this does not arise through mechanically repeating past (y, W) actions; *each enterprise assesses its situation in each cycle and reaffirms that its niche in a structure of niches is where it is best suited.* The frozen pizza producers' belief in the market is self-fulfilling, but it is a useful and reasonable belief, since without it they would lack any tangible guidance in choosing a production-pricing strategy.

The market is a simple affair for Tony, which he can use with no mathematical effort. From Tony's point of view, the reliance on tangible price and volume data—not just his own, but also his competitors—is reassuring. The ease of using these data enhances their appeal, particularly in comparisons to the largely fictional (difficult to utilize) curves of the econometrician. Tony has little incentive to abandon his particular view of the market as long as it seems to work for him—that is, as long as he is making money.

Exploring the conditions under which markets work, in the sense of market behavior reproducing market structure, requires going beyond Tony's simple point of view. The analytic underpinnings of Tony's market must be developed, so we can understand how distinct roles are sustained and orderliness is reproduced. We do this in the next section (for a more thorough treatment, see White 1981a or Leifer 1985).

Reproducing Structures

The Producer

Tony, and each of the other pizza manufacturers, uses the data of observed volume (y), revenue (W) outcomes from the prior production period to construct a schedule of possibilities for the next period. We refer to this schedule as a $W(y)$ schedule. It is a shared construct among all the producers; they are a closed "clique" in the sense that they know each other's outcomes and use them to define their own possibilities.[4]

Each producer, however, has his or her own cost curve. These differences in the cost of production mean that the various pizza makers will come to different volume and revenue decisions. Tony, for example, calculates how much it would cost him to manufacture the number of pizzas that a competitor produces ($C(y)$). He compares his cost with their revenues (assuming that if he entered their niche, he would be forced [or allowed] to charge their price) and computes his total anticipated profit *in that niche*. If some niche other than his own offers a greater return, he must consider a change. The desirability of particular niches will be different for producers with manufacturing costs different from Tony's.

In mathematical form, the volume decision is resolved by solving the maximization problem below:

$$\max_{y} W(y) - C_i(y), \quad (11.1)$$

where $C_i(y)$ = producer i's total production cost for volume y and $W(y)$ = total revenues for volume y ($W(y)$ is not unique to producer i, but rather is a menu shared by all producers). Equation 11.1 is a mathematical representation of the process illustrated in figure 11.2.

We will approximate the cost curves of the different producers as a family of similar and simple shapes. First, all producers experience the same economies of scale where c is a shape parameter that taps economies ($c < 1$) or diseconomies ($c > 1$) of scale, and q is a scale parameter. To account for differences in the scale of costs, we introduce a cost index g_i that is unique for each producer i.[5] The cost curves are given the following form:

$$\text{Costs}_i = C_i = q y^c g_i^d, \quad (11.2)$$

where d allows the range of cost differentiation fixed by the cost indices (g_i) to be stretched or shrunk, and can be positive or negative.[6] The need for this stretching or shrinking of cost differences between producers will become apparent when we show how cost differences have to be related to consumer valuation differences for a stable market to be possible.

Maximizing profits (equation 11.1) is assured when the well-known marginal condition is met:

$$\frac{dW}{dy} = \frac{dC}{dy} \quad (11.3)$$

(in words, when the slope of the cost curve equals the slope of the revenue curve, marginal cost equals marginal revenue; this can be seen in figure 11.2.) along with the second-order condition (ensuring a maximum as opposed to a minimum):

$$\frac{d^2W}{dy^2} < \frac{d^2C}{dy^2}. \quad (11.4)$$

In addition, producers require positive profits to produce. These conditions provide a complete specification of the producer's behavior.[7] In the real world, each manufacturer can (without fancy mathematics) approximate the profit-maximizing solution for his or her cost curve and pursue that niche.

The Consumer

There is another side to markets, the consumer side. There is always some mystery associated with consumer behavior in differentiated markets, because consumers are so often willing to pay substantially higher prices for a product whose superiority cannot be "objectively" established. The producer never looks directly inside the mysterious consumer.[8] Yet consumer behavior in aggregate plays a fundamental role in shaping producer outcomes.

A desirable feature of our model is that producers never have to look past the outcomes of other producers to see the consumer side. The role of the aggregate consumer can be represented as follows. The consumer, for whatever reason, values the different goods (brands) differently, that is, is willing to pay a higher price for some brands than others. As a group, consumers also value different quantities of each good differentially, for example, they may be willing to pay only 50 percent more for two pizzas than for one. This aggregate taste can be expressed mathematically as a collective value consumers receive from the goods of producer i:

$$\text{Value}_i = S_i = ry^a h_i^b. \quad (11.5)$$

Here r is a scale parameter; the exponent a relates quantity (y) to value; h_i is a unique "value" index for the good of producer i; and b is a parameter that determines the spread for these indices across producers (it can only be positive, due to the convention of assigning a higher value index to producers whose products are perceived as more valuable).[9]

The consumer makes comparisons across products, and insists that value received bears some relation to dollars given out for each product. If one producer's total offering has less value for the consumer than another's, then the consumer will insist on paying less for the total output. A product which successfully occupies a niche in a differentiated market must sell for a price appropriate to its (perceived) quality; it must confer the same "value per dollar" as other products. Hence in a stable market, the same ratio (θ) of value per dollar holds across all goods, or

$$\theta = \frac{S_i}{W_i} = \frac{S_j}{W_j} \quad (11.6)$$

for all goods of producers i, j.

The stage is set now for showing how the differences in costs and differences in valuations provide the materials for building a stable market. Tony's cost position vis-à-vis the other producers and the valuation his pizzas receive vis-à-vis other frozen pizzas will "voluntaristically" restrain the niches he can occupy in the market. These positions are set in the g and h indices, respectively.

Tying the Sides Together

We have now given mathematical expression to both the cost and value elements in differentiated markets. In order for an equilibrium $W(y)$ schedule consistent with these elements to exist, the ordering of producers on costs must be the same as the ordering of their goods on value, though these orderings can be stretched and shrunk or even reversed. This means that either (1) the producer whose product commands the highest value has the highest costs, the second highest value has second highest costs, etc., or (2) the producer who commands the highest value has the lowest costs, the second highest has the second lowest, etc.

We call this constraint the *coherence condition*, as the constraint is that the two orderings must cohere. Without this coherence the behavior of the producer and consumer sides could not be tied together in a reproducible market, as we will show below. The fact that the elusive "value" to the consumer must be related to production costs is somewhat reassuring. We see this as a reasonable hypothesis about real-world economics: *a sustainable market cannot be built among a set of products whose valuations are unrelated to their costs.*

Mathematically, we proceed as follows. The abstract property that lies at the basis of both cost and value differentiation can be called quality: Let n_i be the quality index for producer i. The coherence condition insures that

$$n_i = g_i = h_i \quad (11.7)$$

for all i

So let g and h be vectors of indices. The producers insist that (from equations 11.2 and 11.3)

$$\frac{dC}{dy} = cqy^{c-1} g^{d} = \frac{dW}{dy} \quad (11.8)$$

i.e. maximum profit. The consumer insists that

$$S = \theta W = ry^{a}h^{b} \Rightarrow h = (\theta W/ry^{a})^{1/b}$$

$$\frac{dW}{dy} = \frac{cqy^{c-1}(\theta W)_{d/b}}{r^{d/b}y^{ad/b}} = cqy^{((bc-ad)/b)-1}(\theta W/r)^{d/b} \quad (11.9)$$

i.e. competitive value per dollar. Only a market where equations 11.8 and 11.9 hold will satisfy both producers and the consumer. The coherence condition implies that the solution for h in equation 11.9 can be substituted for g in equation 11.8, producing an equation where the abstract quality index disappears. By rearranging the terms in this equation and integrating, a solution can be obtained for W (revenue) in terms of y (volume). The $W(y)$ equation is

$$w = ((cq(b-d)/(bc-ad))(\theta/r)^{d/b}y^{(bc-ad)/b} + K)^{b/(b-d)} \quad (11.10)$$

or $W = (Py^{e} + K)^{f}$ with the appropriate substitution for P, e, and f. Given the context of differentiated costs and valuations (equations 11.2 and 11.5, with 11.7) that characterizes a particular market, the ratio θ, and the historically determined constant of integration K, observed producer outcomes should fall on the $W(y)$ schedule of equation 11.10. Producers, of course, "see" only the discrete outcomes, and not the $W(y)$ equation.

The crucial interdependence between volume and quality sensed by producers like Tony can be derived by solving the following problem:

$$\frac{d(profits)}{dy} = \frac{dW}{dy} - \frac{dC}{dy} = f(Py^{e} + K)^{f-1}Pey^{e-1} - cqy^{c-1}n^{d} = 0$$

to obtain (with substitution for P, e, and f):

$$n^{b-d} = (cq\theta(b-d)/(r(bc-ad))y^{c-a} + K(\theta/r)^{(b-d)/b\,/\,ya(b-d)/b}). \quad (11.11)$$

Given the range of quality indices and contextual parameters, this equation yields the optimal production volumes for producers in a market. (Note that these volumes cannot be obtained through a closed form solution unless K happens to equal zero.)

Interpretation

The alert reader might suppose that equations 11.10 and 11.11 would relieve a producer like Tony from the task of observing outcomes of other producers. This is not the case, however. The quality index "n" will be meaningless to Tony since he is aware of only his own costs, so equation 11.11 cannot be used to find his optimal volume. The $W(y)$ equation (11.10) looks more promising, since "n" does not appear in it. Even assuming Tony knows the cost and value parameters in equations 11.2 and 11.5, however, he could not obtain an analytical solution for his (y, W) decision (with equation 11.3) because there are two indeterminacies K and θ, which require observational data to obtain. These indeterminacies imply that the schedule of niches that emerges in any given market will not be uniquely determined by the cost and value context (equations 11.2 and 11.5). A range of schedules is possible that all "work" in the sense of both satisfying the producer and consumer sides and being reproduced through the behavior of these sides. Tony, or researchers, cannot predict the exact shape or scale of a schedule in a specific market. *No amount of analytical finesse can relieve Tony of his social interdependence on other producers in defining his "opportunity set," or relieve the researcher of a dependence on data.*

The indeterminacies fit neatly with, and strengthen the case for, our portrait of real-world market behavior. In an ongoing market for frozen pizzas (or other products), there are established, discernible niches—for example, a cheap, quick, doughy product may occupy the bottom end of the spectrum, just below the less inexpensive, slightly more time-consuming, very cheesy entry. While it is possible to conceive of an infinity of new products (say a cheaper cheesy pizza), it is impossible to calculate their impact on the current niche structure. It is far simpler to estimate the consequences of invading (or remaining in) an existing niche. That is, producers correctly (from a mathematical *and* practical perspective) rely on the current structure as a frame for decision making, basing future choices on data derived from the current circumstances of themselves and their competitors.

This raises a new substantive and analytic issue. If both Tony and the researcher must look at producer outcomes for guidance and parameter estimates, how should this schedule be interpreted? Only a discrete set of outcomes is observed, yet it represents a continuous $W(y)$ schedule. What is the meaning of such a schedule, above and beyond the discrete producer outcomes it is based upon?

To illustrate this issue mathematically, we note that parameter K in equation 11.10 can take on nonzero values. If the continuous $W(y)$ schedule had a reality independent from the discrete producer outcomes, one would be led to the implausible conclusion that producing nothing ($y = 0$) might yield positive revenue. We are therefore tempted to limit the range of the continuous $W(y)$ schedule to the close vicinity of the actual producer outcomes.

Yet even within a limited range the interpretation of a continuous schedule is not unambiguous. The equation for this schedule (equation 11.10) has parameters b and d, θ and K, and possibly r and q, which depend upon a specific set of producers (ns) for their values. A different set of producers

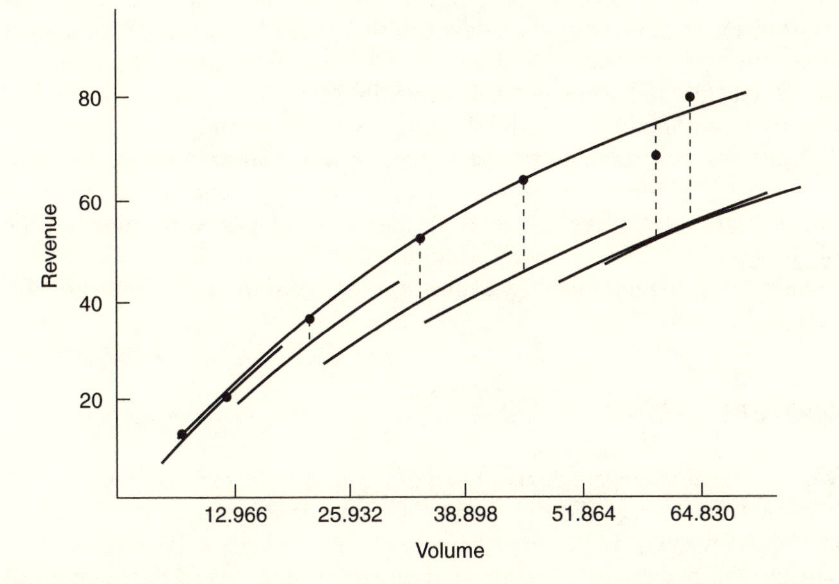

FIGURE 11.3 A self-reproducing market. Each producer uses the shared menu of fares (market outcomes) to select a volume and associated price for the next production period. In a self-reproducing market, their selections will reproduce the menu of fates they used for guidance. That is, they will reselect the niche they occupied in the prior period.

(and thus quality index range) would yield different values for b and d, as well as the other parameters above. Therefore, though producers could assume that any point on the continuous $W(y)$ schedule represents a viable niche, this assumption stands in tension with the dependence of the $W(y)$ schedule on a specific set of producers.

Producers assume they could be anywhere on the $W(y)$ schedule while simultaneously realizing that the schedule itself is built from their own uniqueness. The only situation where these dual beliefs do not stand in contradiction is when the $W(y)$ schedule leads them to reselect their prior niche, and hence reproduce the schedule. We believe that this is a key to understanding the real-world conservatism of producers: they have little tangible motivation to step outside of their niche in a reproducible market.

Tony produces in a market that continually reproduces itself through the actions of Tony and the other producers, and the mysterious consumer. The production has a structural context, which both guides it and is reproduced by it. To illustrate this reproduction process, figure 11.3 shows some partially simulated data from the frozen pizza market. Each producer is producing at an optimum volume, and therefore chooses to remain in the same niche after each production period. The volumes and revenues suggested by this context serve to reproduce the context (assuming reacceptance by the consumer). The reproduced context can then serve for guidance in the next production period, and so on. Tony is locked into this reproducible structure by his self-fulfilling behavior. He has little incentive to step outside this structure into a setting of *ex ante* information and expectations.

A possible new entrant into the market, however, must be concerned with the viability of the untested positions. A continuous schedule implies that any position is viable, yet the schedule itself may have little meaning outside of the set of distinct producers around which it is constituted. To address the issue of *potential* niches, we must look at constraints on aggregate volume and revenue flows.

Aggregating Differentiation

We must treat aggregate demand in a different way from traditional theory, because we accept qualitative distinctions among the various entries in the market. However, the frozen pizza industry (and other similar sectors) does constitute a market in the sense that entries or exits that affect aggregate flows will affect existing producers in the market. It makes sense, therefore, to ignore the uniqueness of each producer's goods, and to speak of an aggregate demand, even if this total demand depends very much on the specific products offered. If, for example, the cheap, quick, doughy pizza were pulled from the market and replaced by an equally cheap and quick cheesy entry, the aggregate demand might change upward or downward. Therefore, we can speak of aggregate demand, but we must be sensitive to its dependence on the particular schedule of products offered.

The aggregate mechanism is expressed in a satiation parameter, γ, which operates on aggregate value in the following way:

$$\text{Total value} = V = (\Sigma_i S\ (y(n_i), n_i))^{\gamma}. \quad (11.12)$$

Hence a γ of less than 1 means the sum of value obtained from separate goods is discounted. This discounting, however, will affect the ratio of value per dollar (θ) through a complex feedback path (see White 1981a). To illustrate the connection between θ and γ, assume that the market is operating at a level where the total value to the consumer is equal to the total revenue flow ($W = \Sigma_i S\ (y\ (n_i))$). The θ_0 associated with this special case is derived in the following manner:

$$V = (\Sigma_i S\ (y(n_i), n_i))^{\gamma}. = (\theta \Sigma_i W(y(n_i)))^{\gamma} = \theta^{\gamma} W^{\gamma} = W$$
$$\Rightarrow \text{breakeven theta} = \theta_O = W^{(1-\gamma)/\gamma} \quad (11.13)$$

Thus while γ is not found in the $W\ (y)$ schedule (equation 11.10), its influence operates through θ and hence can affect the scale of flows in a market.

Entry and exit will be very noticeable events in such markets involving named producers and significant shifts in the market schedule faced by all producers. The ultimate shape of the market is contingent not only on a specific set of unique producers, but also on the aggregate flows they generate. The continuous $W(y)$ schedule that links discrete producers, mathematically given in equation 11.10, is a fragile construct that has a clear interpretation only when it functions so as to reproduce itself across periods. Should the producer be guided to shift niches, or a new producer contemplate entering the market, their acceptance would be dependent upon factors only vaguely understood.[10]

One strength of our model is that it gives considerable leverage over such possible changes. The tools outlined here allow predictions of the consequences of a change in costs or valuations as well as the effects of entry, exit or niche changes. These predictions are illustrated and discussed in Leifer 1985.

A Topology of Reproducible Structures

Our model can also be used to explore the variety of possible reproducible market structures. Markets can vary widely in the degree to which producers are *spread out* in their costs of production (d) or in the value of their goods to consumers (b). They can also vary in the consequences of *shifting* their volumes on production costs (c) or value to consumers (a). Variation on these spread and shift dimensions corresponds to considerable variation in market operation.

There is, therefore, no single type of market, but instead a whole topology of market contexts. Some cost and valuation contexts will not sustain a reproducible market. For example, in some contexts, the perceived comparative value of the products, combined with the cost structures associated with them, lead to an "unraveling" of the $W(y)$ schedule by encouraging producers to seek a corner solution. In these circumstances, we expect that markets do not appear. Conversely, our model predicts reproducible markets where none were thought possible in economic theory, for example in circumstances where it would cost less to produce more—a situation common in real markets. Among reproducible markets, variations will be found in the inequality of outcome (volumes, revenues, profits) between producers, and on basic aspects of market functioning.

In an earlier paper, White (1981a) maps out the cost and valuation contexts that can sustain reproducible markets. Here we focus on a portion of these contexts—those in which it costs more to make higher-quality goods—and explore the possible range of inequalities among producers. Though the analytic results we offer are dependent upon a number of simplifying assumptions and specific functional forms, they provide an intriguing glimpse into the variety of reproducible market structures one should expect to find in comparative studies of markets.

For present purposes, the topology of reproducible market structures can be represented in two dimensions. The first dimension concerns spreads or, more precisely, a ratio of spreads. This ratio (b/d) compares the spread of goods in value to consumers with their spread on costs of production. If the spreads are equal ($b/d = 1$) this means, for example, that if one product costs twice as much to produce as another, consumers perceive it as twice as valuable. A ratio of greater than 1 ($b/d > 1$) means that goods are more differentiated on value to consumers than they are on the manufacturing costs for producers, and a ratio of less than 1 implies the reverse.

In the frozen pizza market, the ratio is greater than 1, since valuation differences are large relative to cost differences. Using a number of guesses in the absence of reliable data, and methods developed elsewhere (Leifer 1985), we have placed the b/d ratio for the frozen pizza market around 2.5. (For example, Stouffer's pizza may cost 1.2 times as much as Jeno's to produce, while conferring 1.5 times the value.)

The second dimension concerns shifts. It too turns out to be a ratio. This ratio (a/c) compares the consequences of shifting production volumes on value to consumers and costs to producers. Stated simply, if overall production were doubled, it might increase production costs by 75 percent (considering economies of scale). If consumer values increased by 90 percent for the doubled output, however, then our ratio is greater than one ($a/c > 1$). If an increase in production volume increases the dollar value to consumers as much as it increases dollar costs to producers, then our ratio (a/c) is 1.

We have placed the ratio for the frozen pizza market around 1.89 with $c = 0.9$ (unit costs would decrease slightly with an increase in production volume) and $a = 1.7$ (value to consumers would increase sharply with an increase in producer volumes).

These two dimensions—the spread ratio (b/d) and the shift ratio (a/c)—define the axes of a topology of market structures. We will focus only on regions that can sustain viable markets in the upper right quadrant. This quadrant is shown in figure 11.4. The frozen pizza market is a solitary point in this quadrant. One can imagine, or discover through comparative efforts, a multitude of diverse markets in different regions of the quadrant. Each market would have its own inequalities and sensitivities, as we will now map out.

We limit our attention to the prime regions for stable markets. These correspond to the "Stable" areas in figure 11.4. In the market region "Unravels" there is a tendency for producers to select corner solutions in their production decisions, and hence "unravel" the volume-revenue schedule as all producers move toward the same "corner." In the market region "Explodes" there is a potential (in certain parameter configurations) for explosive

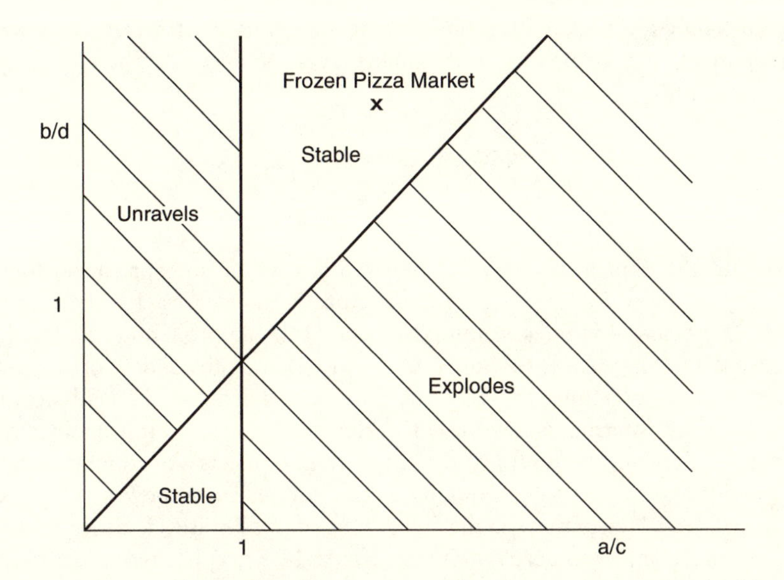

FIGURE 11.4 A topology of market contents. The parameters associated with cost and value contexts define a two-dimensional topology of market contexts. The dimensions are the ratios of spreads on value over spreads on cost between goods, and volume shift consequences on value over volume shift consequences on costs.

growth[11] because companies are monetarily rewarded for increased production. In either instance, though relative niches can be found, there is no stability in the niches sought across production periods. Each company migrates at each decisional juncture. For a more detailed explanation of stable and unstable regions, see White 1981a.

Within the stable market region—where firms are constrained to maintain their niches—it turns out that inequality in market (revenue) share depends primarily on the ratio which we call *g*.

$$g = \frac{(b/c)-1}{(a/c)-1}$$

In the shaded region, *g* is constant across lines passing through (1,1), though it is not defined on (1,1) as here the denominator of *g* is zero. As will become evident, (1,1) is a highly peculiar point in the topology of reproducible markets. It is the point where the spreads and shifts are the same for the producer and consumer sides.

To mathematically explore inequality as a function of *g*, some simplifying assumptions are necessary. We assume that *K* (see equation 11.10) is zero, and that producers are spread uniformly across the entire range of *n* (see equations 11.2, 11.5, and 11.7). With these assumptions, an equation for the Gini index, a widely used measure of inequality, which ranges between 0 (equality), and 1 (maximum inequality), can be derived. The Gini index, G, is equal to

$$\text{Gini} = G = \frac{1}{1 + \frac{2}{(g-1)d}}.$$

Due to the appearance of d in the equation for G, interpretation for inequality in the topology of market structure is the clearest for the limiting cases of 90° and 45° lines running through (1,1). Approaching the 90° line (where $a/c = 1$), g heads toward infinity so G heads toward 1, or maximal inequality. Approaching the 45° line, g heads toward 1 so G heads toward 0, or equality. Intermediate values of G between these two limiting lines will, of course, depend on d, but given a constant d, one gets a gradual transition from maximal inequality to equality as one rotates from the 90° to 45° line through (1,1). Hence there is the full gamut of possibilities for inequality in market share or profits across markets. Figure 11.5 graphs these possibilities, for $d = 1$.[12]

To get some intuitive feel for this measure, consider that inequality in pay in a typical business hierarchy of managers might be about .2, inequality in earned income in a Western society might run about .4, and the Gini for inequality in some major forms of property, say agricultural land in traditional societies or capital ownership in ours, could go as high as .8 or more.

The Gini index for actual revenue outcomes in the frozen pizza market is .283, a considerable but not extreme degree of inequality. Though the assumptions used to derive the analytical Gini index results are not strictly met in the actual frozen pizza market, the analytically derived prediction for inequality is .255, close enough to suggest that the analytic results might be quite robust. The frozen pizza market is demarcated in the sea of possibilities charted in figure 11.5. Each location in figure 11.5 carries with it a distinct reality that is analytically sliced from many angles by interested onlookers and lived in by producers like Tony and others. Figure 11.5, however, is offered as a potent illustration that real-life diversity may share a common underlying processual logic.

In this section, we have moved a long way from Tony and his operating concerns. Tony makes his production decisions in the framework defined by the decisions of other producers, whose products and production options are comparable, but differentiated, from his. Tony and the other frozen pizza producers share a common context of costs and valuations which shapes the way their market will function and respond to exogenous changes, and which shape the inequality in their outcomes. In this section, we have moved to the level of a topology of market contexts in which diverse markets can be placed. The basic structuralist credo holds at this level with equal force:

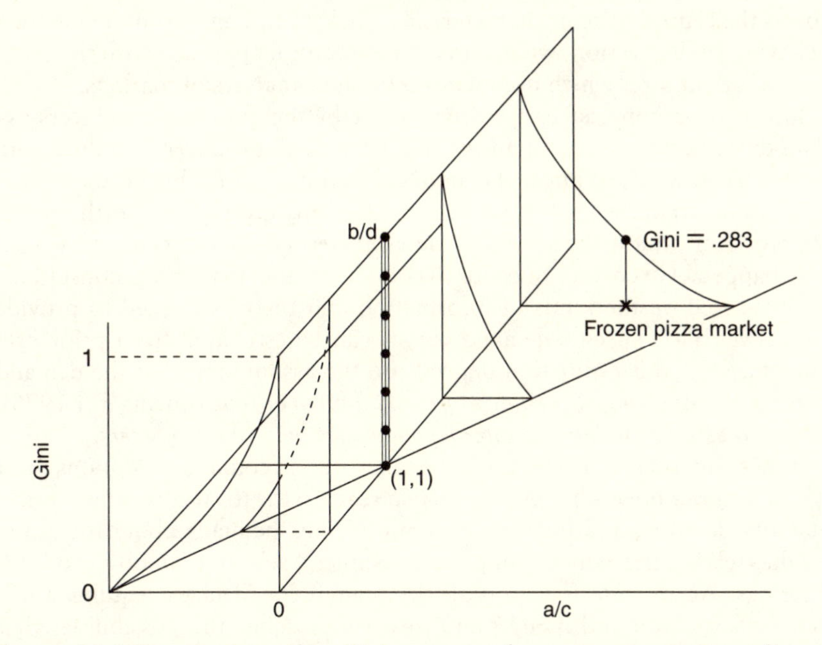

FIGURE 11.5 Outcome inequality. Gini measures of revenue outcome inequality are graphed over the topology of stable market contexts. Inequality approaches 1 along the vertical $a/c = 1$ (though it is not defined over $a/c = 1$). Equality holds where $a/c = b/d$ (i.e. Gini = 0). The point (1, 1) is a "black hole" where the lines of maximal inequality and equality intersect.

position in a topology of market contexts constrains the functioning of a market, just as position in a market constrains ("voluntaristically") the decisions of producers.

DISCUSSION

The model presented here defines the structural context of producers by referring to the relations among producer outcomes. The shape and location of the structural context of market activity are dependent on specific sets of producers, and cannot be defined apart from them. The structural context of a schedule of niches sums up market possibilities and thereby provides a guide for producer behavior. In a viable market, producer behavior is guided in such a way that it functions to reproduce the structural context from which it derives. Our model provides the conceptual and mathematical conditions for self-reproducing structural contexts, and thus delimits the variety of markets which can be empirically observed. Reproducibility therefore becomes the central issue in characterizing markets and understanding market behavior. In this section, we contrast this structural approach with the information orientation which dominates economic analyses of markets.

Information approaches are driven more by the questions producers ask than the way they go about answering them. Each producer, in a differentiated market, wants to know the unique demand curve for his product. That is, he wants to know how much he can sell at any given price. Furthermore, the producer's questions are asked in *ex ante* terms—he wants to know what *will* happen. Given this question, economists and marketing consultants have focused on the kinds of information and theories needed to provide an answer. Firm-specific demand curves can be estimated from prior firm outcomes, yet this estimation depends on the assumption that the demand curve *does not change (or changes predictably) over time* (Intriligator 1978), *and such estimation ignores interdependencies between producers.*

If these interdependencies are to be taken into account, assumptions must be made about how other producers *will* react to the focal companies' price-quantity decision, and further assumptions must be made about the cross-product elasticities which guide the consumers' selection among producer offerings. An *ex ante* focus on all these interdependencies requires much more information and many more theories to define the possibilities that face each producer. An answer to the simple question asked by producers therefore invariably requires invoking a whole series of assumptions which inspire little confidence because they are based on mathematical convenience rather than empirical plausibility. A definitive answer has therefore not been found, and if left to be provided by the theory of games, it does not look like one will be found (see Shubik 1982; Smith 1982).

One might wonder why the producer's simple question is so central if the solution is intractable, or at best dependent on such arbitrary assumptions. Producers, after all, seem to function in the absence of a clear answer, and few would claim that markets must be fully understood (in the form of explicit theory) in order to operate.

A solution to this dilemma comes from recognizing the link between the producer's question and the idea of efficiency. If we view the producer as situated in a visible spectrum of evaluatable alternatives, efficiency can become a relevant concern. The wider the range, the more relevant is the idea of efficiency in rationalizing actions (see Granovetter 1985 for a critique of the centrality of efficiency in economic thought). Answers to the question of what will happen must cover all real-world possibilities for efficiency to be relevant. The producer's ultimate choice must be set against a backdrop of possible, yet less desirable, behaviors. This circumstance simply does not occur in the real world.

The problem with focusing on the hypothetical producer's question is that it stands in the way of discovering any distinct reality associated with a "market." Firm-specific demand curves divert attention from markets altogether.

Yet the producer's reputation, behavior, and possibilities may be defined, as we have claimed, purely from the standpoint of the producer's relation to other producers in a "market." These relations are knowable (observable) only *ex post*, from market structure, or what has worked in past periods. An "orderly" market structure therefore reflects the interdependencies in the market, *ex post.* When the producer is viewed from the standpoint of the market, these "ex post" interdependencies—already observed in the previous production period—replace speculated gaming interdependencies and cross-product elasticities—which are assumed in some a priori manner.

The producer's position and possibilities are defined in terms of these *ex post* interdependencies that make up market structure. This central feature of structural analysis is lost when we lock ourselves inside a hypothetical producer's *ex ante* point of view and attempt to depict *ex ante* possibilities that lie outside of observed *ex post* interdependencies. In our structural approach, producer behavior can be understood only from the point of view of the market. The "market" assumes a distinct reality of its own, and it provides guidance to producers. Rather than being a consequence of solutions to producers' *ex ante* speculations, it is an empirical premise derived from past production periods.

In stepping outside a hypothetical producer's *ex ante* point of view, efficiency ceases to be well defined. A wide range of market structures becomes possible for any particular set of producers, the particular structure that appears being partly determined by historical accident (K) and scale indeterminacies (θ). The varying structures will be associated with varying levels and dispersions of profits across producers. In most cases, producers will make positive profits; and different profit levels will exist across producers as stable features of the market. The "zero profit" criteria for "equilibrium" markets that economists insist upon has no place in the proposed structural approach. The positions of producers in a market, with their distinct profitability implications, must be treated as givens. For this treatment of position to be useful, positions must be stable, else the structural context of interrelated positions could not provide a useful source of guidance.

Reproducibility, not efficiency, is the relevant issue in structural analysis. The range of possibilities is defined by the structures in which position holders operate. It does not extend beyond these *extant* structures, as would be needed to assess the abstract efficiency of a structure. Given the narrow and well-defined range of possibilities that defines a reproducible structure, the behavior of position holders is self-fulfilling. It functions to maintain their position within the structure. Figure 11.4 showed that not all imputed market structures are reproducible in this sense. Clearly if the behavior of "position holders" serves to undermine positions and structure, then the reality of "position" and "structure" as observer constructs must be suspect.

In our model, markets are real structures with definite boundaries. Producers are position holders whose behavior reaffirms their position in the market, marked by a distinct reputation in the "culture" associated with a market. Positive and unequal profits are facts-of-life institutional details for most markets. This treatment of markets as real structures contrasts sharply with the (neoclassical) economist's treatment of markets as a convenient analytical device for drawing inferences about the "economy," or systems of markets. It also contrasts with most applied economics treatments (e.g. Porter 1980), which treat markets as loosely defined arenas for strategic (*ex ante*) ploys. Our model tries to combine some of the analytical rigor of the economist with some of the institutional realism of the business professor. Markets become a realistic device that can be used by concrete producers and studied by researchers.

Notes

1. It should be stressed that, unlike functionalism, structural analysis does not assume that a social arrangement is self-reproducing. Integral structural contradictions can produce ongoing conflict and change—or even destruction—of a social institution. This point is elaborated below.

2. We assume Tony treats the retail customer as the "consumer," as opposed to the distributors and/or retail outlets which buy pizzas directly from him. Tony allows a standard markup for these outlets in arriving at the price he will charge them, and thus absorbs the costs and benefits from market fluctuations. Other arrangements are certainly possible. Defining the "consumer" must involve careful consideration of the distribution channels for a product, with regard to the pricing, packaging, and marketing responsibilities of each concern that handles the product.

3. Since revenues equal price times volume, this is analytically identical to describing the dimensions as volume and price. In our formulation, we use y (volume) and W (revenue).

4. In advocating structural over information approaches, our argument largely rests on the "publicness" of information and not its presence or absence. The advantage of the proposed structural approach is that it assumes actors act on the basis of information that is readily obtainable, through informal communications, trade association publications, marketing reports, and the like. (We do not assume a producer knows the other producers' costs, which are not easy to obtain—and present difficulties for the researcher in estimating parameters for a market.) Information approaches, in adopting an *ex ante* point of view, tend to freely assume the availability of "private" information that has no tangible existence in the producer's operating world.

5. We treat cost differences as exogenously determined. They could result from the use of different production techniques, factors of production, labor rates, locations, etc. If one envisions, however, the formation of a market as a trial-and-error process, where products and images are put before the consumer and either received or rejected, initial cost differences might be related to initial role perceptions of the producers. That is, the producer who perceives he is slipping into a definite market role (e.g. as a high-quality producer) may alter his product or its image (e.g. packaging), and hence its costs, in a way that conforms to the perceived role. Cost differ-

ences, and their relation to valuation differences (see below), cease to be so mysterious when viewed in this light.

6. To get unique estimates for g and d, the range of g_i must be arbitrarily fixed. The interval selected for the lowest and highest g will determine how d is interpreted (e.g. if a "large" interval is selected, then a "small" d may still mean there is some differentiation in cost structures between producers).

7. The second-order condition ensuring maximization (equation 11.4), and the condition that producers require positive profits to produce, correspond to the satisfaction of the two inequalities below:

$$(cd(a-c)/(bc-ad))\ y^{(bc-ad)/b} > -adK/bq(\theta/r)^{d/b}$$

$$(d(a-c)/(bc-ad))\ y^{(bc-ad)/b} > -K/q(\theta/r)^{d/b}.$$

8. This assumption obviously downplays the importance of marketing research in production and pricing decisions within a stable market context. Much marketing research, however, is used for other purposes anyway, like exploring potential market areas or at least legitimating already made decisions to enter new areas. If some routine production and pricing decisions are based on marketing research, the error that might be introduced in ignoring this research (assuming its conclusions differ from those of the unaided producer) is small, we claim, relative to the error and intermediacy we would face in conceding that production and pricing decisions *are* based on marketing research.

9. Value can be viewed as measurable in dollar units. In discussing aggregate value and revenue later, we suggest the assumption that aggregate value equals aggregate revenue provides a convenient calibrating device. Thus if $240 million is spent on frozen pizzas annually, we assume that all the frozen pizzas purchased are "worth" $240 million to the aggregate consumer. The difficulties entailed in actually measuring this "worth" motivated the first author to design techniques for estimating market parameters without directly measuring value (see Leifer 1985). The researcher, however, has to make an assumption about how much valuations differ across products (b) and, without data for multiple production periods, an assumption about the aggregate satiation (γ), a factor discussed later.

10. This imagery stands in sharp contrast to the fluidity of competitive markets in economics (aside from Chamberlain 1933), where only the aggregates matter. The distinct reputations of producers are not "frictional" effects in the $W(y)$ model, but the basic building blocks of markets.

11. This potential is dependent upon a/c being greater than $1/\gamma$. The γ dimension, however, can be suppressed for present purposes.

12. The point (1,1) is a sort of "black hole" in the topology of market structures. It is the point where the lines of maximal inequality and equality intersect, and hence represents a most peculiar situation. Mathematically, a Gini index is not defined at the (1,1) point, and no stable market is possible there either. At the (1,1) point, spreads on cost and value between producer goods are identical for producers and consumers, respectively, as are sensitivities to shifts across production volumes. Why this symmetry in spreads and shift sensitivities between producer and consumers precludes a stable market is a puzzle we must leave to the reader to solve. The solution to this riddle may give insight into the prerequisites for interfaces in general which tie together two distinct sides.

References

Berkowitz, S. D. 1982. *An Introduction to Structural Analysis: The Network Approach to Social Research.* Toronto: Butterworths.

Boorman, S. A. 1975. "A Combinatorial Optimization Model for Transmission of Job Information through Contact Networks." *Bell Journal of Economics* 6: 216–49.

Breiger, Ronald. 1981. "Structures of Economic Interdependence among Nations." In *Continuities in Structural Inquiry*, ed. Peter M. Blau and Robert K. Merton. Beverly Hills: Sage.

Burt, Ronald S. 1982. *Toward a Structural Theory of Action: Network Models of Social Structure, Perception, and Action.* New York: Academic Press.

Chamberlain, Edward H. 1933. *The Theory of Monopolistic Competition.* Cambridge: Harvard University Press.

Granovetter, Mark. 1985. "Economic Action and Social Structure: The Problem of Embeddedness." *American Journal of Sociology* 91:481–510.

Intriligator, Michael D. 1978. *Econometric Models, Techniques, and Applications.* Englewood Cliffs, N.J.: Prentice-Hall.

Kanter, Rosabeth Moss. 1977. *Men and Women of the Corporation.* New York: Basic Books.

Leifer, Eric M. 1985. "Markets as Mechanisms: Using a Role Structure." *Social Forces* 64: 442–72.

Lorrain, F. P., and Harrison C. White. 1971. "Structural Equivalence of Individuals in Social Networks." *Journal of Mathematical Sociology* 1:49–80.

Love, Geoffrey. 1982. "An Investigation of Block-Modeling Techniques Applied to International Trade Flows." Undergraduate thesis, Harvard University.

Porter, Michael E. 1980. *Competitive Strategy.* New York: Academic Press.

Shubik, Martin. 1982. *Game Theory in the Social Sciences.* Cambridge: MIT Press.

Smith, Alasdair. 1982. *A Mathematical Introduction to Economics.* Totowa, N.J.: Barnes and Noble.

Snyder, David, and Edward L. Kick. 1979. "Structural Position in the World System and Economic Growth, 1955–1970: A Multiple Network Analysis of Transnational Interactions." *American Journal of Sociology* 84:1096–126.

White, Harrison C. 1963. *An Anatomy of Kinship.* Englewood Cliffs, N.J.: Prentice-Hall.

———. 1981a. "Production Markets as Induced Role Structures." In *Sociological Methodology*, ed. S. L. Leinhardt. San Francisco: Jossey-Bass.

———.1981b. "Where Do Markets Come From?" *American Journal of Sociology* 87: 517–47.

———. 1987. "Varieties of Markets." In *Structural Sociology*, ed. Barry Wellman and S. D. Berkowitz. Cambridge University Press.

Williamson, Oliver E. 1975. *Markets and Hierarchies: Analysis and Antitrust Implications.* New York: Free Press.

Winship, Christopher. 1978. "Allocation of Time among Individuals." In *Sociological Methodology*, ed. Karl F. Schuessler. San Francisco: Jossey-Bass.

Chapter 12

FROM *STRUCTURAL HOLES: THE SOCIAL STRUCTURE OF COMPETITION*

RONALD S. BURT

A PLAYER BRINGS capital to the competitive arena and walks away with profit determined by the rate of return where the capital was invested. The market production equation predicts profit: invested capital, multiplied by the going rate of return, equals the profit to be expected from the investment. You invest a million dollars. The going rate of return is 10 percent. The profit is one hundred thousand dollars. Investments create an ability to produce a competitive product. For example, capital is invested to build and operate a factory. Rate of return is an opportunity to profit from the investment.

The rate of return is keyed to the social structure of the competitive arena and is the focus here. Each player has a network of contacts in the arena. Something about the structure of the player's network and the location of the player's contacts in the social structure of the arena provides a competitive advantage in getting higher rates of return on investment. This chapter is about that advantage. It is a description of the way in which social structure renders competition imperfect by creating entrepreneurial opportunities for certain players and not for others.[1]

OPPORTUNITY AND CAPITAL

A player brings at least three kinds of capital to the competitive arena. Other distinctions can be made, but three are sufficient here. First, the player has financial capital: cash in hand, reserves in the bank, investments coming due, lines of credit. Second, the player has human capital. Your natural qualities—charm, health, intelligence, and looks—combined with the skills you have acquired in formal education and job experience give you abilities to excel at certain tasks.

Third, the player has social capital: relationships with other players. You have friends, colleagues, and more general contacts through whom you receive opportunities to use your financial and human capital. I refer to opportunities in a broad sense, but I certainly mean to include the obvious examples of job promotions, participation in significant projects, influential access to important decisions, and so on. The social capital of people aggregates into the social capital of organizations. In a firm providing services—for example, advertising, brokerage, or consulting—there are people valued for their ability to deliver a quality product. Then there are "rainmakers," valued for their ability to deliver clients. Those who deliver the product do the work, and the rainmakers make it possible for all to profit from the work. The former represent the financial and human capital of the firm. The latter represent its social capital. More generally, property and human assets define the firm's production capabilities. Relations within and beyond the firm are social capital.

Distinguishing Social Capital

Financial and human capital are distinct from social capital in two ways. First, they are the property of individuals. They are owned in whole or in part by a single individual defined in law as capable of ownership, typically a person or corporation. Second, they concern the investment term in the market production equation. Whether held by a person or the fictive person of a firm, financial and human capital gets invested to create production capabilities. Investments in supplies, facilities, and people serve to build and operate a factory. Investments of money, time, and energy produce a skilled manager. Financial capital is needed for raw materials and production facilities. Human capital is needed to craft the raw materials into a competitive product.

Social capital is different on both counts. First, it is a thing owned jointly by the parties to a relationship. No one player has exclusive ownership rights to social capital. If you or your partner in a relationship withdraws, the connection, with whatever social capital it contained, dissolves. If a firm treats a cluster of customers poorly and they leave, the social capital represented by the firm-cluster relationship is lost. Second, social capital concerns rate of return in the market production equation. Through relations with colleagues, friends, and clients come the opportunities to transform financial and human capital into profit.

Social capital is the final arbiter of competitive success. The capital invested to bring your organization to the point of producing a superb product is as rewarding as the opportunities to sell the product at a profit. The investment to make you a skilled manager is as valuable as the opportunities—the leadership positions—you get to apply your managerial skills. The investment to make you a skilled scientist with state-of-the-art research facilities is as valuable as the opportunities—the projects—you get to apply those skills and facilities.

More accurately, social capital is as important as competition is imperfect and investment capital is abundant. Under perfect competition, social capital is a constant in the production equation. There is a single rate of return because capital moves freely from low-yield to high-yield investments until rates of return are homogeneous across alternative investments. When competition is imperfect, capital is less mobile and plays a more complex role in the production equation. There are financial, social, and legal impediments to moving cash between investments. There are impediments to reallocating human capital, both in terms of changing the people to whom you have a commitment and in terms of replacing them with new people. Rate of return depends on the relations in which capital is invested. Social capital is a critical variable. This is all the more true when financial and human capital are abundant—which in essence reduces the investment term in the production equation to an unproblematic constant.

These conditions are generic to the competitive arena, which makes social capital a factor as routinely critical as financial and human capital. Competition is never perfect. The rules of trade are ambiguous in the aggregate and everywhere negotiable in the particular. The allocation of opportunities is rarely made with respect to a single dimension of abilities needed for a task. Within an acceptable range of needed abilities, there are many people with financial and human capital comparable to your own. Whatever you bring to a production task, there are other people who could do the same job—perhaps not as well in every detail, but probably as well within the tolerances of the people for whom the job is done. Criteria other than financial and human capital are used to narrow the pool down to the individual who gets the opportunity. Those other criteria are social capital. New life is given to the proverb that says success is determined less by what you know than by whom you know. As a senior colleague once remarked (and Cole 1992, chaps. 7–8, makes into an intriguing research program), "Publishing high-quality work is important for getting university resources, but friends are essential." Of those who are equally qualified, only a select few get the most rewarding opportunities. Of the products that are of comparably high quality, only some come to dominate their markets. The question is how.

Who and How

The competitive arena has a social structure: players trusting certain others, obligated to support certain others, dependent on exchange with certain others, and so on. Against this backdrop, each player has a network of contacts—everyone the player now knows, everyone the player has ever known, and all the people who know the player even though he or she doesn't know them. Something about the structure of the player's network and the location of the player's contacts in the social structure of the arena provides a competitive advantage in getting higher rates of return on investment.

WHO

There are two routes into the social capital question. The first describes a network as your access to people with specific resources, which creates a correlation between theirs and yours. This idea has circulated as power, prestige, social resources, and more recently, social capital. Nan Lin and his colleagues provide an exemplar of this line of work, showing how the occupational prestige of a person's job is contingent on the occupational prestige of a personal contact leading to the job (Lin 1982; Lin, Ensel, and Vaughn 1981; Lin and Dumin 1986). Related empirical results appear in Campbell, Marsden, and Hurlbert 1986; De Graaf and Flap 1988; Flap and De Graaf 1989; and Marsden and Hurlbert 1988. Coleman (1988) discusses the transmission of human capital across generations. Flap and Tazelaar (1989) provide a thorough review with special attention to social network analysis.

Empirical questions in this line of work concern the magnitude of association between contact resources and the actor's own resources, and variation in the association across kinds of relationships. Granovetter's (1973) weak-tie metaphor, discussed in detail shortly, is often invoked to distinguish kinds of relationships.[2]

Network analysts will recognize this as an example of social contagion analysis. Network structure is not used to predict attitudes or behaviors directly. It is used to predict similarity between attitudes and behaviors (compare Barber 1978, for a causal analysis). The research tradition is tied to the Columbia Sociology survey studies of social influence conducted during the 1940s and 1950s. In one of the first well-known studies, for example, Lazarsfeld, Berelson, and Gaudet (1944) show how a person's vote is associated with the party affiliations of friends. Persons claiming to have voted for the presidential candidate of a specific political party tend to have friends affiliated with that party. Social capital theory developed from this line of work describes the manner in which resources available to any one person in a population are contingent on the resources available to individuals socially proximate to the person.

Empirical evidence is readily available. People develop relations with people like themselves (for example, Fischer 1982; Marsden 1987; Burt 1990). Wealthy people develop ties with other wealthy people. Educated people develop ties with one another. Young people develop ties with one another. There are reasons for this. Socially similar people, even in the pursuit of independent interests, spend time in the same places. Relationships emerge. Socially similar people have more shared interests. Relationships are maintained. Further, we are sufficiently egocentric to find people with similar tastes attractive. Whatever the etiology for strong relations between socially similar people, it is to be expected that the resources and opinions of any one individual will be correlated with the resources and opinions of his or her close contacts.

HOW

A second line of work describes social structure as capital in its own right. The first line describes the network as a conduit; the second line describes how networks are themselves a form of social capital. This line of work is less developed than the first. Indeed, it is little developed beyond intuitions in empirical research on social capital. Network range, indicated by size, is the primary measure. For example, Boxman, De Graaf, and Flap (1991) show that people with larger contact networks obtain higher-paying positions than people with small networks. A similar finding in social support research shows that persons with larger networks tend to live longer (Berkman and Syme 1979).

Both lines of work are essential to a general definition of social capital. Social capital is at once the resources contacts hold and the structure of contacts in a network. The first term describes whom you reach. The second describes how you reach.

For two reasons, however, I ignore the question of whom to concentrate on how. The first is generality. The question of whom elicits a more idiographic class of answers. Predicting rate of return depends on knowing the resources of a player's contacts. There will be interesting empirical variation from one kind of activity to another, say, job searches versus mobilizing support for a charity, but the empirical generalization is obvious. Doing business with wealthy clients, however wealth is defined, has a higher margin than doing business with poor clients. I want to identify parameters of social capital that generalize beyond the specific individuals connected by a relationship.

The second reason is correlation. The two components in social capital should be so strongly correlated that I can reconstruct much of the phenomenon from whichever component more easily yields a general explanation. To the extent that people play an active role in shaping their relationships, then a player who knows how to structure a network to provide high opportunity knows whom to include in the network. Even if networks are passively inherited, the manner in which a player is connected within social structure says much about contact resources. I will show that players with well-structured networks obtain higher rates of return. Resources accumulate in their hands. People develop relations with people like themselves. Therefore, how a player is connected in social structure indicates the volume of resources held by the player and the volume to which the player is connected.[3]

The nub of the matter is to describe network benefits in the competitive arena in order to be able to describe how certain structures enhance those benefits. The benefits are of two kinds, information and control.

Information

Opportunities spring up everywhere: new institutions and projects that need leadership, new funding initiatives looking for proposals, new jobs for which you know of a good candidate, valuable items entering the market for which you know interested buyers. The information benefits of a network define who knows about these opportunities, when they know, and who gets to participate in them. Players with a network optimally structured to provide these benefits enjoy higher rates of return to their investments, because such players know about, and have a hand in, more rewarding opportunities.

Access, Timing, and Referrals

Information benefits occur in three forms: access, timing, and referrals. Access refers to receiving a valuable piece of information and knowing who can use it. Information does not spread evenly across the competitive arena. It isn't that players are secretive, although that too can be an issue. The issue is that players are unevenly connected with one another, are attentive to the information pertinent to themselves and their friends, and are all overwhelmed by the flow of information. There are limits to the volume of information you can use intelligently. You can only keep up with so many books, articles, memos, and news services. Given a limit to the volume of information that anyone can process, the network becomes an important screening device. It is an army of people processing information who can call your attention to key bits—keeping you up to date on developing opportunities, warning you of impending disasters. This secondhand information is often fuzzy or inaccurate, but it serves to signal something to be looked into more carefully.

Related to knowing about an opportunity is knowing whom to bring into it. Given a limit to the financing and skills that we possess individually, most complex projects will require coordination with other people as staff, colleagues, or clients. The manager asks, "Whom do I know with the skills to do a good job with that part of the project?" The capitalist asks, "Whom do I know who would be interested in acquiring this product or a piece of the project?" The department head asks, "Who are the key players needed to strengthen the department's position?" Add to each of these the more common question, "Whom do I know who is most likely to know the kind of person I need?"

Timing is a significant feature of the information received by network. Beyond making sure that you are informed, personal contacts can make you one of the people who is informed early. It is one thing to find out that the stock market is crashing today. It is another to discover that the price of your stocks will plummet tomorrow. It is one thing to learn the names of the two people referred to the board for the new vice-presidency. It is another to discover that the job will be created and that your credentials could make you a serious candidate for the position. Personal contacts get significant information to you before the average person receives it. That early warning is an opportunity to act on the information yourself or to invest it back into the network by passing it on to a friend who could benefit from it.

These benefits involve information flowing from contacts. There are also benefits in the opposite flow. The network that filters information coming to you also directs, concentrates, and legitimates information about you going to others.

In part, this network does no more than alleviate a logistics problem. You can only be in a limited number of places within a limited amount of time. Personal contacts get your name mentioned at the right time in the right place so that opportunities are presented to you. Their referrals are a positive force for future opportunities. They are the motor expanding the third category of people in your network, the players you do not know who are aware of you. Consider the remark so often heard in recruitment deliberations: "I don't know her personally, but several people whose opinion I trust have spoken well of her."

Beyond logistics, there is the issue of legitimacy. Even if you know about an opportunity and can present a solid case for why you should get it, you are a suspect source of information. The same information has more legitimacy when it comes from someone inside the decision-making process who can speak to your virtues. Candidates offered the university positions with the greatest opportunity, for example, are people who have a strong personal advocate in the decision-making process, a person in touch with the candidate to ensure that both favorable information and responses to any negative information get distributed during the decision.

Benefit-Rich Networks

A player with a network rich in information benefits has contacts (*a*) established in the places where useful bits of information are likely to air, and (*b*) providing a reliable flow of information to and from those places.

SELECTING CONTACTS

The second criterion is as ambiguous as it is critical. It is a matter of trust, of confidence in the information passed and the care with which contacts look out for your interests. Trust is critical precisely because competition is imperfect. The question is not whether to trust, but whom to trust. In a perfectly competitive arena, you can trust the system to provide a fair return on your investments. In the imperfectly competitive arena, you have only your personal contacts. The matter comes down to a question of interpersonal debt. If I do for her, will she for me? There is no general answer. The answer lies in the match between specific people. If a contact feels that he is somehow better than you—a sexist male dealing with a woman, a racist white dealing with a black, an old-money matron dealing with an upwardly mobile ethnic—your investment in the relationship will be taken as proper obeisance to a superior. No debt is incurred. We use whatever cues can be found for a continuing evaluation of the trust in a relation, but we never know a debt is recognized until the trusted person helps us when we need it. With this kind of uncertainty, players are cautious about extending themselves for people whose reputation for honoring interpersonal debt is unknown. The importance of this point is illustrated by the political boundary around senior management discussed in chapter 4. The more general point of trust as people meeting your expectations is illustrated in Barber's (1983) analysis of competence and duty as dimensions of trust relations in diverse institutions in American society.

Theory and research exist to identify trustworthy contacts. Strong relationships and mutual acquaintances tend to develop between people with similar social attributes such as education, income, occupation, and age (for example, Fischer 1982; Burt 1986, 1990; Marsden 1987; and see note 4 below). Both factors are linked to trust. Trust is a component in the strong relationships, and mutual acquaintances are like an insurance policy through which interpersonal debt is enforced such that the other person can be deemed trustworthy (Nohria 1991). Whether egocentrism, cues from presumed shared background and interests, or confidence in mutual acquaintances to enforce interpersonal debt, the operational guide to the formation of close, trusting relations seems to be that a person more like me is less likely to betray me. For the purposes here, I set the whole issue to one side as person-specific and presume that it is resolved by the able player.

SITING CONTACTS

That leaves the first criterion, establishing contacts where useful bits of information are likely to air. Everything else constant, a large, diverse network is the best guarantee of having a contact present where useful information is aired. This is not to say that benefits must increase linearly with size and diversity, a point to which I will return (fig. 12.5), but only that, other things held constant, the information benefits of a large, diverse network are more than the information benefits of a small, homogeneous network.

Size is the more familiar criterion. Bigger is better. Acting on this understanding, people can expand their networks by adding more and more con-

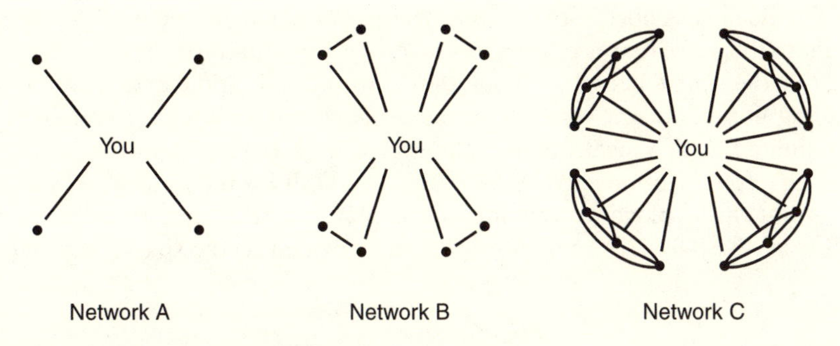

FIGURE 12.1 Network expansion

tacts. They make more cold calls, affiliate with more clubs, attend more social functions. Numerous books and self-help groups can assist them in "networking" their way to success by putting them in contact with a large number of potentially useful, or helpful, or like-minded people. The process is illustrated by the networks in figure 12.1. The four-contact network at the left expands to sixteen contacts at the right. Relations are developed with a friend of each contact in network A, doubling the contacts to eight in network B. Snowballing through friends of friends, there are sixteen contacts in network C, and so on.

Size is a mixed blessing. More contacts can mean more exposure to valuable information, more likely early exposure, and more referrals. But increasing network size without considering diversity can cripple a network in significant ways. What matters is the number of nonredundant contacts. Contacts are redundant to the extent that they lead to the same people, and so provide the same information benefits.

Consider two four-contact networks, one sparse, the other dense. There are no relations between the contacts in the sparse network, and strong relations between every contact in the dense network. Both networks cost whatever time and energy is required to maintain four relationships. The sparse network provides four nonredundant contacts, one for each relationship. No single one of the contacts gets the player to the same people reached by the other contacts. In the dense network, each relationship puts the player in contact with the same people reached through the other relationships. The dense network contains only one nonredundant contact. Any three are redundant with the fourth.

The sparse network provides more information benefits. It reaches information in four separate areas of social activity. The dense network is a virtually worthless monitoring device. Because the relations between people in that network are strong, each person knows what the other people know and all will discover the same opportunities at the same time.

The issue is opportunity costs. At minimum, the dense network is inefficient in the sense that it returns less diverse information for the same cost as that of the sparse network. A solution is to put more time and energy into adding nonredundant contacts to the dense network. But time and energy are limited, which means that inefficiency translates into opportunity costs. If I take four relationships as an illustrative limit on the number of strong relations that a player can maintain, the player in the dense network is cut off from three-fourths of the information provided by the sparse network.

Structural Holes

I use the term *structural hole* for the separation between nonredundant contacts. Nonredundant contacts are connected by a structural hole. A structural hole is a relationship of nonredundancy between two contacts. The hole is a buffer, like an insulator in an electric circuit. As a result of the hole between them, the two contacts provide network benefits that are in some degree additive rather than overlapping.

Empirical Indicators

Nonredundant contacts are disconnected in some way—either directly, in the sense that they have no direct contact with one another, or indirectly, in the sense that one has contacts that exclude the others. The respective empirical conditions that indicate a structural hole are cohesion and structural equivalence. Both conditions define holes by indicating where they are absent.

Under the cohesion criterion, two contacts are redundant to the extent that they are connected by a strong relationship. A strong relationship indicates the absence of a structural hole. Examples are father and son, brother and sister, husband and wife, close friends, people who have been partners for a long time, people who frequently get together for social occasions, and so on. You have easy access to both people if either is a contact. Redundancy by cohesion is illustrated at the top of figure 12.2. The three contacts are connected to one another, and so provide the same network benefits. The presumption here—routine in network analysis since Festinger, Schachter, and Back's (1950) analysis of information flowing through personal relations and Homans's (1950) theory of social groups—is that the likelihood that information will move from one person to another is proportional to the strength of their relationship. Empirically, strength has two independent dimensions: frequent contact and emotional closeness (see Marsden and Hurlbert 1988; Burt 1990).

Structural equivalence is a useful second indicator for detecting structural holes. Two people are structurally equivalent to the extent that they have

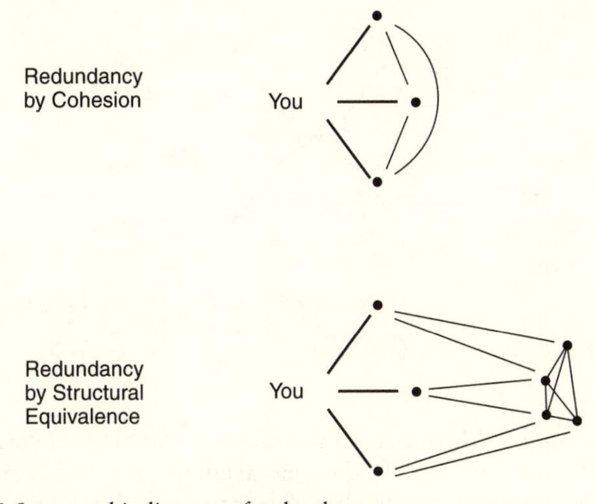

FIGURE 12.2 Structural indicators of redundancy

the same contacts. Regardless of the relation between structurally equivalent people, they lead to the same sources of information and so are redundant. Cohesion concerns direct connection; structural equivalence concerns indirect connection by mutual contact. Redundancy by structural equivalence is illustrated at the bottom of figure 12.2. The three contacts have no direct ties with one another. They are nonredundant by cohesion. But each leads you to the same cluster of more distant players. The information that comes to them, and the people to whom they send information, are redundant. Both networks in figure 12.2 provide one nonredundant contact at a cost of maintaining three.

The indicators are neither absolute nor independent. Relations deemed strong are only strong relative to others. They are our strongest relations. Structural equivalence rarely reaches the extreme of complete equivalence. People are more or less structurally equivalent. In addition, the criteria are correlated. People who spend a lot of time with the same other people often get to know one another. The mutual contacts responsible for structural equivalence set a stage for the direct connection of cohesion. The empirical conditions between two players will be a messy combination of cohesion and structural equivalence, present to varying degrees, at varying levels of correlation.

Cohesion is the more certain indicator. If two people are connected with the same people in a player's network (making them redundant by structural equivalence), they can still be connected with different people beyond the network (making them nonredundant). But if they meet frequently and feel close to one another, then they are likely to communicate and probably have

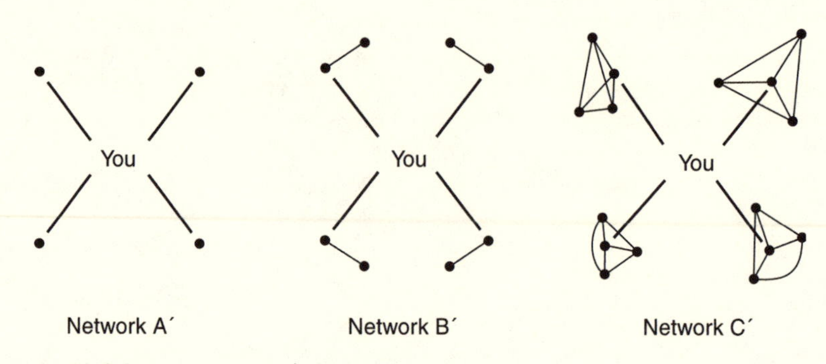

FIGURE 12.3 Strategic network expansion

contacts in common. More generally, and especially for fieldwork informed by attention to network benefits, the general guide is the definition of a structural hole. There is a structural hole between two people who provide nonredundant network benefits. If the cohesion and structural equivalence conditions are considered together, redundancy is most likely between structurally equivalent people connected by a strong relationship. Redundancy is unlikely, indicating a structural hole, between total strangers in distant groups. I will return to this issue again, to discuss the depth of a hole, after control benefits have been introduced.

The Efficient-Effective Network

Balancing network size and diversity is a question of optimizing structural holes. The number of structural holes can be expected to increase with network size, but the holes are the key to information benefits. The optimized network has two design principles.

EFFICIENCY

The first design principle of an optimized network concerns efficiency: Maximize the number of nonredundant contacts in the network to maximize the yield in structural holes per contact. Given two networks of equal size, the one with more nonredundant contacts provides more benefits. There is little gain from a new contact redundant with existing contacts. Time and energy would be better spent cultivating a new contact to unreached people.[4] Maximizing the nonredundancy of contacts maximizes the structural holes obtained per contact.[5]

Efficiency is illustrated by the networks in figure 12.3. These reach the same people reached by the networks in figure 12.1, but in a different way. What expands in figure 12.1 is not the benefits, but the cost of maintaining the network. Network A provides four nonredundant contacts. Network B provides the same number. The information benefits provided by the initial four contacts are redundant with benefits provided by their close friends. All that has changed is the doubled number of relationships maintained in the network. The situation deteriorates even further with the sixteen contacts in network C. There are still only four nonredundant contacts in the network, but their benefits are now obtained at a cost of maintaining sixteen relationships.

With a little network surgery, the sixteen contacts can be maintained at a fourth of the cost. As illustrated in figure 12.3, select one contact in each cluster to be a primary link to the cluster. Concentrate on maintaining the primary contact, and allow direct relationships with others in the cluster to weaken into indirect relations through the primary contact. These players reached indirectly are secondary contacts. Among the redundant contacts in a cluster, the primary contact should be the one most easily maintained and most likely to honor an interpersonal debt to you in particular. The secondary contacts are less easily maintained or less likely to work for you (even if they might work well for someone else). The critical decision obviously lies in selecting the right person to be a primary contact. The importance of trust has already been discussed. With a trustworthy primary contact, there is little loss in information benefits from the cluster and a gain in the reduced effort needed to maintain the cluster in the network.

Repeating this operation for each cluster in the network recovers effort that would otherwise be spent maintaining redundant contacts. By reinvesting that saved time and effort in developing primary contacts to new clusters, the network expands to include an exponentially larger number of contacts while expanding contact diversity. The sixteen contacts in network C of figure 12.1, for example, are maintained at a cost of four primary contacts in network C' of figure 12.3. Some portion of the time spent maintaining the redundant other twelve contacts can be reallocated to expanding the network to include new clusters.

EFFECTIVENESS

The second design principle of an optimized network requires a further shift in perspective: Distinguish primary from secondary contacts in order to focus resources on preserving the primary contacts. Here contacts are not people on the other end of your relations; they are ports of access to clusters of people beyond. Guided by the first principle, these ports should be nonredundant so as to reach separate, and therefore more diverse, social worlds of network benefits. Instead of maintaining relations with all contacts, the task of maintaining the total network is delegated to primary contacts. The player at the center of the network is then free to focus on properly supporting relations with primary contacts and expanding the network to include new clusters. The first principle concerns the average number of people

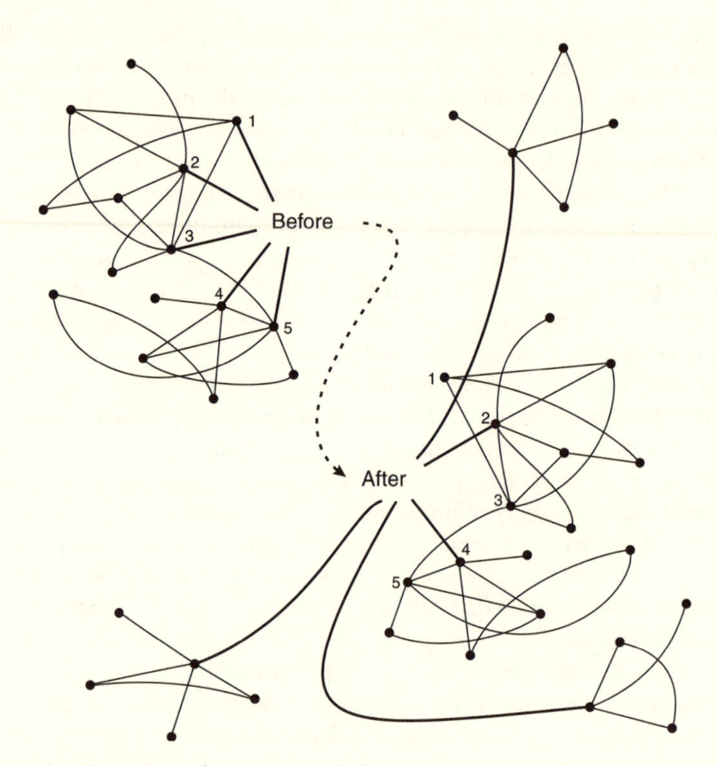

FIGURE 12.4 Optimizing for structural holes

reached with a primary contact; the second concerns the total number of people reached with all primary contacts. The first principle concerns the yield per primary contact. The second concerns the total yield of the network. More concretely, the first principle moves from the networks in figure 12.1 to the corresponding networks in figure 12.3. The second principle moves from left to right in figure 12.3. The target is network C' in figure 12.3: a network of few primary contacts, each a port of access to a cluster of many secondary contacts.

Figure 12.4 illustrates some complexities in unpacking a network to maximize structural holes. The "before" network contains five primary contacts and reaches a total of fifteen people. However, there are only two clusters of nonredundant contacts in the network. Contacts 2 and 3 are redundant in the sense of being connected with each other and reaching the same people (cohesion and structural equivalence criteria). The same is true of contacts 4 and 5. Contact 1 is not connected directly to contact 2, but he reaches the same secondary contacts; thus contacts 1 and 2 provide redundant network benefits (structural equivalence criterion). Illustrating the other extreme, contacts 3 and 5 are connected directly, but they are nonredundant because they reach separate clusters of secondary contacts (structural equivalence criterion). In the "after" network, contact 2 is used to reach the first cluster in the "before" network, and contact 4 is used to reach the second cluster. The time and energy saved by withdrawing from relations with the other three primary contacts is reallocated to primary contacts in new clusters. The "before" and "after" networks are both maintained at a cost of five primary relationships, but the "after" network is dramatically richer in structural holes, and so network benefits.

Network benefits are enhanced in several ways. There is a higher volume of benefits, because more contacts are included in the network. Beyond volume, diversity enhances the quality of benefits. Nonredundant contacts ensure exposure to diverse sources of information. Each cluster of contacts is an independent source of information. One cluster, no matter how numerous its members, is only one source of information, because people connected to one another tend to know about the same things at about the same time. The information screen provided by multiple clusters of contacts is broader, providing better assurance that you, the player, will be informed of opportunities and impending disasters. Further, because nonredundant contacts are only linked through the central player, you are assured of being the first to see new opportunities created by needs in one group that could be served by skills in another group. You become the person who first brings people together, which gives you the opportunity to coordinate their activities. These benefits are compounded by the fact that having a network that yields such benefits makes you even more attractive as a network contact to other people, thus easing your task of expanding the network to best serve your interests.

GROWTH PATTERNS

A more general sense of efficiency and effectiveness is illustrated with network growth. In figure 12.5, the number of contacts in a player's network increases from left to right on the horizontal axis. The number who are nonredundant increases up the vertical axis. Observed network size increases on the horizontal, effective size up the vertical. Networks can be anywhere in the gray area. The maximum efficiency line describes networks in which each new contact is completely nonredundant with other contacts. Effective size equals actual size. Efficient-effective networks are in the upper right of the graph. The minimum efficiency line describes networks in which each new contact is completely redundant with other contacts; effective size equals one, regardless of multiple contacts in the network.

The two lines between the extremes illustrate more probable growth patterns. The decreasing efficiency line shows players building good information benefits into their initial network, then relaxing to allow increasing redundancy as the network gets large. Friends of friends begin to be included.

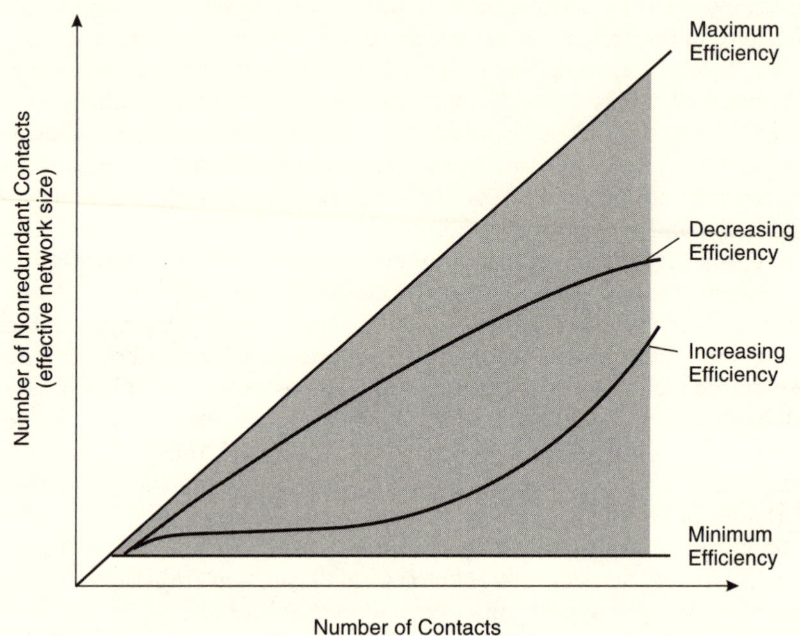

FIGURE 12.5 Efficiency and effectiveness

Comparisons across networks of different sizes suggest that this is the growth pattern among managers (see figure 12.15), though controls for time would be necessary to make the suggestion an inference.

The increasing efficiency line illustrates a different growth pattern. Initial contacts are redundant with one another. A foundation is established with multiple contacts in the same cluster. After the foundation is established, the player's network expands to include contacts in other clusters and effective size begins to increase. There are two kinds of clusters in which optimizing for saturation is wiser than optimizing for efficiency. The first is obvious. Leisure and domestic clusters are a congenial environment of low-maintenance, redundant contacts. Efficiency mixes poorly with friendship. Judging friends on the basis of efficiency is an interpersonal flatulence from which friends will flee. The second exception is a cluster of contacts where resources are dense. For the CEO, the board of directors is such a cluster. The university provost is similarly tied to the board of trustees. For the more typical manager, the immediate work group is such a cluster, especially with respect to funding authority within the group. These clusters are so important to the vitality of the rest of the network that it is worth treating each person in them as a primary contact, regardless of redundancy. Saturation minimizes the risk of losing effective contact with the cluster and minimizes the risk of missing an important opportunity anywhere in the cluster.

The more general point is that the probability of receiving network benefits from a cluster has two components, the probability that a contact will transmit information to you and the probability that it will be transmitted to the contact. I count on dense ties within a cluster to set the second probability to one. The probability of having a benefit transmitted to you therefore depends only on the strength of your relationship with a contact in the cluster. However, where the density of ties in an opportunity-rich cluster lowers the probability that your contact will know about an opportunity, there is value in increasing the number, and thus the redundancy, of contacts in the cluster so that total coverage of the cluster compensates for imperfect transmission within it.

Structural Holes and Weak Ties

Discontinuities in social structure have long been a subject of study in sociology. Fitting the structural hole argument into the history of sociological thought is not the task of this book, but one piece of contemporary history adds value to the argument here. Mark Granovetter's weak-tie argument provides an illuminating aside on the information benefits of structural holes.

HISTORY

In the late 1960s and early 1970s at Harvard University, Harrison White, with a cluster of exceptional sociology graduate students, was engaged in studying the importance of gaps, as opposed to the ties, in social structure. First came his celebrated work on chains of mobility (White 1970), and later his work with colleagues, most notably Ronald Breiger and Scott Boorman, on concrete network models—blockmodels—of social structure (White, Boorman, and Breiger 1976; see Burt 1982, 63–69, for review). The usual analysis of mobility describes patterns of mobility, or careers, created by people moving between positions in a social structure. White (1970) shifted perspective to focus on the hole, or opportunity, created when a person leaves a position. As people move up the hierarchy, they create opportunities for people below them. Chains of promotion move up a hierarchy. Chains of opportunity move down. Looking at social structure more generally, White, Boorman, and Breiger (1976, esp. 732n, 737–40) stressed the structural hole metaphor as a substantive motivation for their network blockmodels. They focused on "zeroblocks" as an especially significant component in the relation pattern defining a position in social structure. It is clear from their analysis that they meant structural holes to be important for understanding network contingent action as well as the task they addressed of clustering network elements into blocks (for example, see 763ff. on the low rate of change in zeroblocks).

One of the students, Mark Granovetter, found a troubling result in his dissertation research. Hoping to link network structure to job searches, he interviewed men about how they found their current jobs and included sociometric items asking for the names of close contacts. The troubling result was that the men almost never found work through close contacts. When information on a job opportunity came through a personal contact, the contact was often distant, such as a high school acquaintance met by accident at a recent social event. He developed the point in a widely cited article, "The Strength of Weak Ties" (Granovetter 1973), and in a book, *Getting a Job* (Granovetter 1974).

CONNECTING THE TWO ARGUMENTS

The weak-tie argument is elegantly simple. The stage is set with results familiar from the social psychology of Festinger and Homans circa 1950, discussed above with respect to cohesion indicators of structural holes. People live in a cluster of others with whom they have strong relations. Information circulates at a high velocity within these clusters. Each person tends to know what the other people know. The spread of information on new ideas and opportunities, therefore, must come through the weak ties that connect people in separate clusters. The weak ties so often ignored by social scientists are in fact a critical element of social structure. Hence the strength of weak ties. Weak ties are essential to the flow of information that integrates otherwise disconnected social clusters into a broader society.

The idea and its connection with structural holes is illustrated in figure 12.6. There are three clusters of players. Strong ties, indicated by solid lines, connect players within clusters. Dashed lines indicate two weak ties between players in separate clusters. One of the players, you, has a unique pattern of four ties: two strong ties within your cluster and a weak tie to a contact in each in the other clusters. There are three classes of structural holes in your network: (*a*) holes between the cluster around contact A and everyone in your own cluster, for example, the hole between contacts A and C; (*b*) holes between the cluster around contact B and everyone in your own cluster, for example, the hole between contacts B and C; and (*c*) the hole between contacts A and B.

Weak ties and structural holes seem to describe the same phenomenon. In figure 12.6, for example, they predict the same ranking of information benefits. You are best positioned for information benefits, contacts A and B are next, followed by everyone else. You have two weak ties, contacts A and B have one each, and everyone else has none. You have the largest volume of structural holes between your contacts, contacts A and B have fewer, and everyone else has few or none.

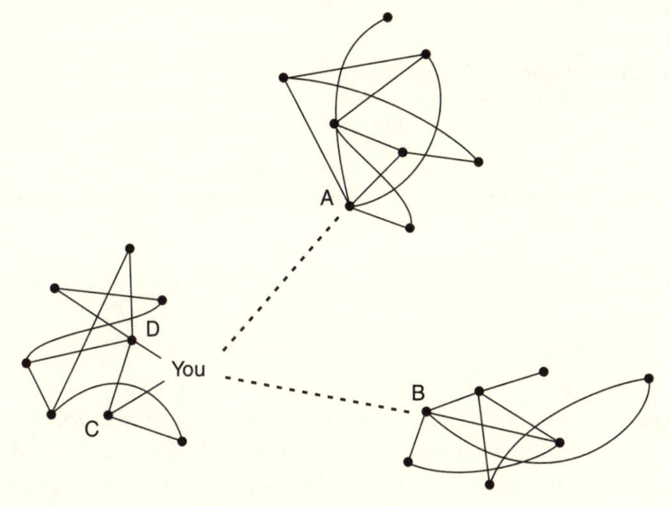

FIGURE 12.6 Structural holes and weak ties

THE STRENGTH OF STRUCTURAL HOLES

The weak-tie argument is simpler and already well known. Why complicate the situation with the structural hole argument? There are two reasons.

First, the causal agent in the phenomenon is not the weakness of a tie but the structural hole it spans. Tie weakness is a correlate, not a cause. The structural hole argument captures the causal agent directly and thus provides a stronger foundation for theory and a clearer guide for empirical research. Second, by shifting attention away from the structural hole responsible for information benefits, to the strength of the tie providing them, the weak-tie argument obscures the control benefits of structural holes. Control benefits augment and in some ways are more important than the information benefits of structural holes. Building both benefits into the argument speaks more clearly to the generality of the phenomenon under study. I will elaborate the first point, then move to the second in the next section.

The weak-tie argument is about the strength of relationships at the same time that it is about their location. The two dashed lines in figure 12.6 are bridges. They are the only connection between two otherwise separate clusters of strongly interconnected players (compare Granovetter 1973, 1365, on weak ties as bridges). A bridge is at once two things. It is a chasm spanned and the span itself. By title and subsequent application, the weak-tie argument is about the strength of relationships that span the chasm between two social clusters. The structural hole argument is about the chasm spanned. It is the latter that generates information benefits. Whether a relationship is strong or weak, it generates information benefits when it is a bridge over a structural hole.

TABLE 12.1
The Natural Distribution of Relationships

	Location in Social Structure		
Strength	*Redundant Tie within Cluster*	*Nonredundant Tie beyond Cluster*	*Total*
Weak tie	many	some	More
Strong tie	some	rare	Less
Total	More	Less	

Consider a cross-tabulation of ties by their strength and location. Your relationships can be sorted into two categories of strength. Strong ties are your most frequent and close contacts. Weak ties are your less frequent, less close contacts. Between these two categories, you have a few strong ties and many weak ties.

Now sort, by location, redundant ties within your social cluster versus nonredundant ties to people in other clusters. The nonredundant ties are your bridges to other clusters. From what we know about the natural etiology of relationships, bridges are less likely to develop than ties within clusters. The category of redundant ties includes your strong ties to close friends and colleagues, whom you see often, but it also includes their friends, and friends of friends, whom you meet only occasionally if at all. As you expand your inventory from your closest, most frequent contacts to your more distant, contacts tend to be people like yourself before you reach a sufficiently low level of relationship to include people from completely separate social worlds. This tendency varies from one person to the next, but it is in the aggregate the substance of the well-documented tendency already discussed for relations to develop between socially similar people. In figure 12.6, you are one of nine people in your social cluster. You have strong ties to two people. Through those two, you have weak ties to the other six people in the cluster. To keep the sociogram simple, I deleted the dashed lines for those ties and their equivalent inside the other clusters. The other six people in your cluster are friends of friends whom you know and sometimes meet but do not have the time or energy to include among your closest contacts. The cluster is clearly held together by strong ties. Everyone has two to five strong ties to others within the cluster. All nine people are likely to know about the same opportunities as expected in a cohesive cluster. Of the thirty-six possible connections among the nine people in the cluster, however, only twelve are solid line strong ties. The remaining two-thirds are weak ties between redundant friends of friends.

Now cross-tabulate the two classifications and take expected values. The result is given in table 12.1. Information benefits vary across the columns of the table and are higher through nonredundant ties. This is accurately represented in both the weak-tie and the structural hole argument. But a quick reading of the weak-tie argument, with its emphasis on the strength of a relationship, has led some to test the idea that information benefits covary inversely with the strength of ties. This is a correlation between the rows and columns of table 12.1, which is no correlation at all. In fact, the typical tie in table 12.1 is weak and provides redundant information. The correlation in a study population depends on the distribution of ties in the table, but there is no theoretical reason to expect a strong correlation between the strength of a relationship and the information benefits it provides.

The weak-tie argument is about the two cells in the second column of the table. It predicts that nonredundant ties, the bridges that provide information benefits, are more likely weak than strong. In the second column of table 12.1, weak-tie bridges are more likely than strong-tie bridges. To simplify his argument, Granovetter makes this tendency absolute by ruling out strong-tie bridges (the "rare" cell in table 12.1, the "forbidden triad" in Granovetter's argument, 1973, 1363). He says, "A strong tie can be a bridge, therefore, only if neither party to it has any other strong ties, unlikely in a social network of any size (though possible in a small group). Weak ties suffer no such restriction, though they are certainly not automatically bridges. What is important, rather, is that all bridges are weak ties" (1973, 1364).

Bridge strength is an aside in the structural hole argument. Information benefits are expected to travel over all bridges, strong or weak. Benefits vary between redundant and nonredundant ties, the columns of table 12.1. Thus structural holes capture the condition directly responsible for the information benefits. The task for a strategic player building an efficient-effective network is to focus resources on the maintenance of bridge ties. Otherwise, and this is the correlative substance of the weak-tie argument, bridges will fall into their natural state of being weak ties.

Notes

1. I refer to people and organizations in the competitive arena as "players." Richard Swedberg has commented that I use the term to denote a very active actor, seeking out contacts and opportunities. He gently suggested that the term had a touch of frivolity that I might do well to eliminate with a more neutral term such as "actor." I have used the more neutral term in more general discussion (Burt 1982), but for the topic of competition, I prefer the term "player." It better fits my felt-reality of the phenomenon. More than implying activity, it is a term of peer recognition: "Yes, he's a player." He's a presence in the game. If you have the motivation, resources, and skills to compete, you're a player; otherwise, you're scenery. Everyone is a player in some arenas, scenery in most. This chapter is about the social structural conditions that give certain players a competitive advantage.

2. Coleman's (1988, S105–S108, S109–S116) argument for the importance of network closure in the transmission of human capital between generations is an illustrative alternative to Granovetter's weak-tie metaphor. The weak-tie metaphor is that weaker ties are most important to transmission. The work spawned by Lazarsfeld focuses on strong ties. Coleman emphasizes the importance of strong ties reinforced by other ties. Although the argument is not grounded in network models of Simmel's conflicting group-affiliation metaphor, the resemblance is obvious. For example, parents are presumed to prefer that their children obtain at least the minimal education required to graduate from high school. Relying on attribute data, Coleman (1988, S114–S115) shows that children in Catholic high schools—where parents are presumed to be closely connected with one another and other parents, and so constrain the choices of their children—have lower dropout rates than do children in public high schools. Network analysis improves the power of such arguments, by providing: (*a*) concrete measures of the extent to which parents (versus others, such as peers) are structurally positioned to constrain the choices of specific children, and (*b*) formal theory creating more precise, testable understandings of how constraint operates. These points are both illustrated in the forthcoming argument.

3. Network contagion measures of social capital will always be a valuable addition to the application of the general definition to the situation of a specific individual. For example, a person with a poorly structured network that includes just one well-placed contact can do well through that contact's sponsorship regardless of how well the person's network as a whole is structured. We will see some evidence of this in the analysis of managers in chapter 4 [not included in this anthology]. We will also see the downside. Being known as someone's minion, dependent on their sponsorship, limits the minion's attractiveness as a social capital addition in other networks. Relations require an investment of time and trust that in this case depend entirely on the sponsor's support. The minion is not a serious player independently shaping the course of events in the arena. This makes the minion role adhesive. It holds the player with dependence on the sponsor's support. It cauterizes the development of relations with other players through which the dependence could be made more negotiable.

4. This point is significant because it contradicts the natural growth of contact networks. Left to the normal course of events, a network will accumulate redundant contacts. Friends introduce you to their friends and expect you to like them. Business contacts introduce you to their colleagues. You will like the people you meet in this way. The factors that make your friends attractive make their friends attractive because like seeks out like. Your network grows to include more and more people. These relations come easily, they are comfortable, and they are easy to maintain. But these easily accumulated contacts do not expand the network so much as they fatten it, weakening its efficiency and effectiveness by increasing contact redundancy and tying up time. The process is amplified by spending time in a single place: in your family, or neighborhood, or in the office. The more time you spend with any specific primary contact, the more likely you will be introduced to their friends. Evidence of these processes can be found in studies of balance and transitivity in social relations (see Burt 1982, 55–60, for review) and in studies of the tendency for redundant relations to develop among physically proximate people (for example, the suggestively detailed work of Festinger, Schachter, and Back 1950; or the work with more definitive data by Fischer 1982, on social contexts, and Feld 1981, 1982, on social foci). Here I ignore the many day-to-day tactical issues critical to maintaining a network.

5. The number of structural holes is not increased directly, but is likely to increase. The presumption through all this is that the time and energy to maintain relationships is limited and that the constant pressure to include new contacts will use all the time and energy available (as in the preceding note). Although structural holes are not increased directly by maximizing nonredundant contacts, they can be expected to increase indirectly through the reallocation of time and energy from maintaining redundant contacts to acquiring new nonredundant contacts (as illustrated in figure 12.4).

References

Barber, Bernard. 1978. "Inequality and Occupation Prestige: Theory, Research, and Social Policy." *Sociological Inquiry* 48:75–88.

———. 1986. *Logic and Limits of Trust.* New Brunswick, N.J.: Rutgers University Press.

Berkman, Lisa F., and S. Leonard Syme. 1979. "Social Networks, Host Resistance, and Mortality: A Nine-Year Follow-up Study of Alameda County Residents." *American Journal of Epidemiology* 109:186–204.

Boxman, Ed A. W., Paul M. De Graaf, and Hendrik D. Flap. 1991. "The Impact of Social and Human Capital on the Income Attainment of Dutch Managers." *Social Networks* 13:51–73.

Burt, Ronald S. 1982. *Toward a Structural Theory of Action.* New York: Academic Press.

———. 1986. "A Note on Sociometric Order in the General Social Survey Network Data." *Social Networks* 8:149–74.

———. 1990. "Kinds of Relations in American Discussion Networks." *In Structures of Power and Constraint: Papers in Honor of Peter M. Blau*, ed. Craig J. Calhoun, Marshall W. Meyer, and W. Richard Scott. Cambridge: Cambridge University Press.

Campbell, Karen E., Peter V. Marsden, and Jeanne S. Hurlbert. 1986. "Social Resources and Socioeconomic Status." *Social Networks* 8:97–117.

Cole, Stephen. 1992. *Making Science.* Cambridge: Harvard University Press.

Coleman, James S. 1988. "Social Capital in the Creation of Human Capital." *American Journal of Sociology* 94:S95–S120.

De Graaf, Nan D., and Hendrik D. Flap. 1988. "With a Little Help from My Friends." *Social Forces* 67:453–72.

Feld, Scott L. 1981. "The Focused Organization of Social Ties." *American Journal of Sociology.* 86:1015–35.

———. "Structural Determinants of Similarity among Associates." *American Sociological Review* 47:797–801.

Festinger, Leon, Stanley Schachter, and Kurt W. Back. 1950. *Social Pressures in Informal Groups.* Stanford: Stanford University Press.

Fischer, Claude S. 1982. *To Dwell among Friends.* Chicago: University of Chicago Press.

Flap, Hendrik D., and Nan D. De Graaf. 1989. "Social Capital and Attained Occupational Status." *Netherlands Journal of Sociology* 22:145–61.

Flap, Hendrik D., and F. Tazelaar. 1989. "The Role of Informal Social Networks on the Labor Market: Flexibilization and Closure." In *Flexibilization of the Labor Market*, ed. Hendrik D. Flap. Utrecht: ISOR, University of Utrecht.

Granovetter, Mark S. 1973. "The Strength of Weak Ties." *American Journal of Sociology* 78:1360–80.

———. 1974. *Getting a Job: A Study of Contacts and Careers*. Cambridge: Harvard University Press.

Homans, George C. 1950. *The Human Group*. New York: Harcourt, Brace and World.

Lazarfeld, Paul F., Bernard Berelson, and Hazel Gaudet. 1944. *The People's Choice: How the Voter Makes Up His Mind in a Presidential Campaign*. New York: Columbia University Press.

Lin, Nan. 1982. "Social Resources and Instrumental Action." In *Social Structure and Network Analysis*, ed. P. V. Marsden and Nan Lin. Beverly Hills, Calif.: Sage.

Lin, Nan, and Mary Dumin. 1986. "Access to Occupations through Social Ties." *Social Networks* 8:365–85.

Lin, Nan, Walter M. Ensel, and John C. Vaughn. 1981. "Social Resources and Strength of Ties." *American Sociological Review* 46:393–405.

Marsden, Peter V. 1987. "Core Discussion Networks of Americans." *American Sociological Review* 52:122–31.

Marsden, Peter V., and Jeanne S. Hurlbert. 1988. "Social Resources and Mobility Outcomes: A Replication and Extension." *Social Forces* 67:1038–59.

Nohria, Nitin. 1991. "Structural Equivalence as an Occasion for the Production of Trust." Paper presented at the Euro-American conference "Boundaries and Units."

White, Harrison C. 1970. *Chains of Opportunity*. Cambridge: Harvard University Press.

White, Harrison C., Scott Boorman, and Ronald L. Breiger. 1976. "Social Structure from Multiple Networks. I. Blockmodels of Roles and Positions." *American Journal of Sociology* 81:730–80.

Chapter 13

EMBEDDEDNESS IN THE MAKING OF FINANCIAL CAPITAL: HOW SOCIAL RELATIONS AND NETWORKS BENEFIT FIRMS SEEKING FINANCING

BRIAN UZZI

WHICH FIRMS get capital and at what cost? The answer can determine the life chances of firms, the growth of economies, and how markets stratify firms and persons through the rationing and pricing of credit. In financial theory, any firm with a positive economic net present value should obtain credit at a competitive price (Petersen and Rajan 1994). Sociological theory does not necessarily reject this axiom, yet argues that banking transactions are embedded in social relations that uniquely shape credit access and costs in ways that are inadequately incorporated into financial theory (Baker 1990; Mintz and Schwartz 1985; Mizruchi and Stearns 1994b; Podolny 1993; Uzzi and Gillespie 1999). Bankers and entrepreneurs echo this observation and complain that financial models often do not appreciate the value of bank-client relationships. This suggests that there is a growing demand for sociological theory on finance (Abolafia 1997; Arrow 1998; Haunschild 1994; Mizruchi and Stearns 1994b).

Most sociological research on lending has not focused on the availability and pricing of capital. Rather, classical writings take a philosophical approach to analyzing money economies, and most contemporary work concentrates on how bank-firm ties, coarsely defined as the incidence of a director interlock, affect the politics and level of a firm's borrowing (Baker 1990; Mintz and Schwartz 1985; Mizruchi and Stearns 1994a). These approaches, while productive for certain problems, leave unexplored how the embeddedness of commercial transactions in social attachments and networks affects personal and corporate financial dealings (DiMaggio and Louch 1998; Uzzi 1997). Finance research similarly concludes that while bank-firm ties are more critical to lending markets than classical theory suggests, inconsistencies in financial theory also signify a need for more research on how social

Brian Uzzi. 1999. "Embeddedness in the Making of Financial Capital: How Social Relations and Networks Benefit Firms Seeking Financing." *American Sociological Review* 64: 481–505, by kind permission of the American Sociological Association.

relationships and networks affect who gets capital and at what cost (Arrow 1998; Petersen and Rajan 1994).

I examine how bank-borrower relationships and networks affect a firm's acquisition and cost of capital using a social embeddedness approach (Granovetter 1985). The social embeddedness approach aims to explain why economic transactions become embedded in social relations that differentially affect the allocation and valuation of resources. Social embeddedness is defined as the degree to which commercial transactions take place through social relations and networks of relations that use exchange protocols associated with social, noncommercial attachments to govern business dealings (Marsden 1981; Uzzi 1997). I argue that embedding commercial transactions in social attachments benefits firms that are seeking financing by promoting distinctive governance mechanisms and the transfer of private information—factors that motivate banks and firms to find integrative solutions to financing problems beyond those possible through market relations, which possess different benefits.

In developing my arguments, I analyze how both social relationships and networks affect lending. At the level of relationships, I draw on research that examines how properties of embedded ties and arm's-length ties promote different kinds of access and governance benefits in market exchanges. At the level of the network, I elaborate on the finding that networks incorporating a mix of embedded ties and market ties provide premium benefits because they enable a firm to synthesize the advantages of partnering via embedded ties with the advantages of brokerage offered by arm's-length ties. I argue that firms are more likely to secure loans and receive lower interest rates if they are tied to their lenders through embedded ties and if their networks of bank ties have a mix of embedded ties and arm's-length ties.

My study aims to enhance sociological theory on finance in several ways. First, I examine the setting of interest rates, the touchstone market mechanism by which value is created, thereby extending sociological research on markets to price formation (Fligstein 1996; Podolny 1993). Second, since financial capital is a substitutable commodity and banks can write nearly complete contracts by holding collateral, this study reveals how social embeddedness operates in the presence of market "efficiency" conditions thought to supplant it (Carruthers 1996). Third, I focus on what bankers dub "the midmarket"—a sector of the economy that has been neglected in research yet deserves closer analysis (Fama 1985). The midmarket is composed of firms with fewer than five hundred employees or less than $500 million in annual sales and is bountiful in its social and economic effects. The midmarket accounts for more than one-half of the U.S. gross domestic product (GDP), has twice the innovations per employee as large firms, and since 1970 has created two-thirds of the jobs in the United States. In the 1980s, it emerged as a seedbed for entrepreneurship and a source of sixteen million of the twenty million new jobs created in that decade.

Before proceeding, it is worth noting the unique qualitative and quantitative materials used in this analysis. Because the effect of embeddedness in financial markets is contested and remains "in need of greater theoretical specification" (Smelser and Swedberg 1994, 18), I strengthen my analysis using a triangulation of theory, fieldwork, and statistical analysis (King, Keohane, and Verba 1994). I use original field data on bank-borrower ties to help explicate and illustrate the mechanisms by which embeddedness produces outcomes and actors construct markets. I then use a national random sample of 2,400 companies to test the validity and generalizability of my theory.

Theory

The social embeddedness framework is one of several sociological accounts for how social structure affects financial markets (Granovetter 1985; Portes and Sensenbrenner 1993; Romo and Schwartz 1995, Uzzi 1996, 1997). Research has focused on the types of social relations and social networks that exist and their economic effects. Following this literature, I treat social embeddedness as a variable and focus on how the quality of relationships and the configuration of ties in a network influence a firm's ability to obtain loans and to lower the cost of borrowing.

Relationships vary between arm's-length and embedded (Baker 1990; Lie 1997; Powell 1990; Uzzi 1996, 1997). *Arm's-length ties* are characterized by lean and sporadic transactions and "function without any prolonged human or social contact between parties . . . [who] need not enter into recurrent or continuing relations as a result of which they would get to know each other well" (Hirschman 1982, 1473). Weber (1946) characterized them as lacking social distinction and having an expressive nature that "knows nothing of honor" (192). The main proposition related to arm's-length ties is that they determine the degree to which an actor can access heterogeneous information in a market, even if that information is publicly available through advertising or publicity, because actors use network ties to search for opportunities and investments. For example, Granovetter (1973) found that job-seekers tend to search for and learn about new job openings through acquaintances, even when the jobs were publicly advertised. Davis (1991) found that firms adopted "poison pills" chiefly through interlock ties, despite the takeover defense's public notoriety and marketing by many legal firms. Burt (1992) developed this formulation's most trenchant propositions. He argued that the strategic expansion of networks through the use of arm's-length ties offers the highest possible returns to firms and persons by linking them to diverse pools of market information, which they broker among less informed actors who reside in cloistered networks of relations that hinder their autonomy.

In contrast, there is less theory and empirical justification for expecting that socially embedded ties generate exchange benefits in markets. Recent research on interfirm networks suggests that embedding economic exchanges in social attachments can both *create* unique value and motivate exchange partners to *share* the value for their mutual benefit. Embedded ties promote these outcomes through the transfer of private resources and self-enforcing governance (Portes and Sensenbrenner 1993; Uzzi 1997). Private resources and private information are distinctive in that they identify where an actor's expertise and dependencies reside. They might include, for example, unpublished capabilities in products, the need to source a particular material, the strategic blueprints for an executive succession, investment plans, failed solutions, the rollout date of a new product, or critical resource dependencies. In essence, private information differs from public market information, such as financial statements or job listings, in that it is not "information for the asking," but information that must be voluntarily transferred in an exchange. In fact, because private knowledge can be misappropriated, it is commonly inaccessible through arm's-length ties and is shared only within a set of trustworthy exchange partners.

The transfer of private knowledge promotes value creation in exchanges by revealing to exchange partners the unique possibilities they possess for matching their competencies and resources. In contrast, public information such as ask-and-bid prices can be a source of value creation, but is less so in competitive markets because it is less restricted and unique than private knowledge and resources. Hence, the solutions prompted by the transfer of private knowledge are valuable not only because they are distinctive, but also because they are hard for competitors without private knowledge to imitate. Consistent with this argument, Eccles and Crane (1988) found that investment bankers were able to customize deals and create innovative risk-reducing financial instruments for their clients when they possessed information and resources beyond what firms made publicly available. Mark Twain Bancshares, a lucrative midmarket bank, gained recognition by using private information to tailor their bank products and loan structures to the distinctive and often confidential capabilities of their customers (Baker 1994).

The embedding of commercial transactions in social attachments promotes the benefits discussed above by enacting expectations of trust and reciprocal obligation that actors espouse as the right and proper protocols for governing exchange with persons they come to know well (Blau 1964; DiMaggio and Louch 1998; Portes and Sensenbrenner 1993).[1] These expectations reduce fears of misappropriation because transactors anticipate that others will not voluntarily engage in opportunistic behavior. Instead, exchange partners share the belief that these motives, coupled with access to private information, can enlarge the pool of potentially beneficial transactions that are not available through market means. Moreover, because the protocols of embedded ties are borrowed from the protocols of social attachments, which are learned from preexisting structures, they are serviceable in business dealings not just as "good faith conformity" norms, but as clear expectations for a "meeting of the minds" (Macneil 2000). Potentially this can save on the costs of organizing other governance arrangements, freeing resources for future productive prospects (Fukuyama 1995). In this way, embedding transactions in social ties does not foreordain cooperative outcomes. Rather, it provides an essential *priming mechanism* that promotes initial offers of trust and reciprocity that, if accepted and returned, solidify through reciprocal investments and self-enforcement. In contrast, the expectation of avaricious actions that is anticipated in arm's-length ties is likely to prompt distrust, even if action is credible, except for discrete cases in which economic incentives are aligned or third parties enforce fairness (Kollock 1994).[2]

Extending the above arguments to lending relationships suggests that the availability and costs of a firm's capital should vary with the degree to which its commercial transactions with a bank are embedded in social attachments. Embedded ties furnish governance and access to private information benefits that can channel resources and motivate attempts at integrative solutions to lending problems that are not available through market ties. Building on these arguments for how embeddedness affects dyadic exchange also suggests that an actor's network of ties is pertinent to the financing process. Previous research has argued that a large network of arm's-length ties to banks expands the firm's pool of potential loan offers and the firm's ability to play banks off against one another (Baker 1990; Eccles and Crane 1988). While I agree in part with this logic, my analysis of lending suggests that "shopping the market" for potential offers is an incomplete picture of the lending process. Firms secure loans and lower their borrowing costs by shopping the market for what's available *and* through collaborative problem-solving over terms with specific lenders. This suggests that firms embedded in networks that enable them to gather information about the range of loan deals available in a market *and* to access the private resources of particular lenders gain premium benefits from social structure because their ability to "broker and partner" on loan deals is enhanced.

Ethnographic Fieldwork

I conducted field research to help formulate my embeddedness framework. Given the scarcity of research on midmarket banking, field research furnished an empirical basis for describing the pertinent actors, resources, and relationships. It also enabled a more refined analysis of bank-borrower ties than would have been possible using coarser methodological tools, although the small sample size moderated generalizability. Field research also permitted a triangulation of theory, ethnography, and statistical analysis on lending.[3]

I conducted field research at eleven midmarket banks in the Chicago area, a highly competitive banking market. Table 13.1 describes the demographic and organizational backgrounds of my twenty-six interviewees and their eleven banks. My sample of interviewees typified the racial, gender, and educational profiles of bankers, who are largely white, male, and college-educated. I principally interviewed "Relationship Managers" (hereafter RMs), the bank personnel who make lending decisions and interface with clients. I also interviewed two bank CEOs and two bad-debt collectors (who deal with fraudulent clients) to understand and cross-examine the viewpoints of other types of lending officers. I focused on RMs because they make the judgments about a client's loan eligibility and consequently can reveal how social and network ties affect *their* lending decisions. I also reviewed Federal Reserve Bank Opinion Surveys on lending to corroborate RMs' accounts. Appendix A describes these sources and the fieldwork methodology in greater detail.

The Social Embeddedness of Lending Relationships

The fieldwork revealed that bankers segment the market into three strata: new corporate, midmarket, and entry-level firms. Table 13.2 summarizes the segments, lending practices, and bank-firm relationships in these markets. While important distinctions exist between the new corporate segment and the other two segments, RMs rarely distinguish between midmarket and entry-market clients and typically maintain ties to both types of firms in their portfolios. Thus, I treat midmarket and entry-market firms similarly in my fieldwork and control for possible differences due to organizational size in my statistical analysis.

Consistent with previous research, I found that in the new corporate segment, public and certified financial statements provide banks with ready access to pertinent information about a firm's creditworthiness (Mizruchi and Stearns 1994b). Similarly, firms use their large treasury departments to identify the lowest cost loans or to gain bargaining position vis-à-vis banks by borrowing directly from money markets.[4] Thus, lending ties between big firms and banks are transactional, with banks chasing customers who treat loans and banks as commodities (Davis and Mizruchi 1999).

The social structure of the midmarket differs from the new corporate segment in ways that have important theoretical and substantive implications. Firms experience ambiguity in evaluating banks because they lack sophisticated financial expertise and are too small to borrow from money markets. Thus, they depend on banks for financial advice and credit, yet they lack the clout and financial wherewithal to ensure a bank's probity, increasing their reluctance to share private information with the bank's RMs. For example, one RM observed.

TABLE 13.1
Characteristics of Interviewees in the Field Research: Relationship Managers (RMs) at Chicago Banks, 1988

		RM's Profile			
Bank	*Bank Deposits*[a] *(in $1,000s)*	*Sex/Race*	*Number of Years in Industry*	*Number of Firms in Portfolio*	*Interview Time (in Minutes)*
Entry-Level					
First Bank of Evanston	104,181	Male/white	17	21	60
		Female/white	2	9	30
First National Bank of La Grange	125,475	Male/white	40+	50	120
		Male/white	8	17	120
		Male/white	3	6	120
First Midwest Bank	178,825	Male/white	35	—	60
		Male/white	4	17	45
Midmarket					
Bank One–Chicago	1,156,874	Male/white	15	50	45
		Male/black	3	12	50
		Female/white	6	26	30
Cole Taylor	1,327,893	Male/white	20	54	45
		Male/white	5	13	50
BankAmerica	3,887,571	Female/white	19	—	60
		Male/white	7	15	45
		Female/white	9	35	30
		Male/white	19	50	75
American National Bank	4,357,509	Male/white	9	25	50
Northern Trust	6,301,607	Male/white	25	27	120
		Male/white	7	—	60
		Male/white	5	8	30
		Male/white	15	19	70
Midmarket and New Corporate					
Harris Bank	8,653,638	Male/white	7	21	60
		Female/white	9	18	55
		Male/white	12	14	45
LaSalle National Bank	9,761,356	Male/white	12	25	50
First National Bank of Chicago	17,961,480	Male/white	25	50	35

Note: A total of 26 RMs were interviewed at 11 different Chicago banks. Interviews were conducted on site between February 1 and May 1, 1988. Interview time totaled 26 hours.

[a] Bank deposits came from the *Bank and Thrift Branch office Data Book* (FDIC 1998).

TABLE 13.2
Characteristics of Banks by Market Segment

	Market Segment		
Characteristic	*New Corporate*	*Midmarket*	*Entry Level*
Sales segmentation and market range	500 million or more Multimarket Multiproduct	10 to 500 million Single market Single or multiproduct	Up to 10 million Single market Single product
Financial market intermediation	Firms debt rated Certified financial statements	Firms rarely debt rated Unreliable or no certified financial statements	Firms rarely debt rated Unreliable or no certified financial statements
Firm's financial decision structure	Treasury department Separation of CEO and CFO positions	Limited or no financial staff CEO is owner-manager No CFO	No financial staff CEO is owner-manager No CFO
Firm's capital dependence on banks	Firms have multiple sources of external financing Firms have multiple sources of internal financing	Banks are major source of external financing for firms Limited or no internal financing for firms	Banks are major source of external financing for firms Limited or no internal financing for firms
Role of relationship manager in making deals	Solicits requests for financing from corporate treasury departments Makes bids on corporate offerings	Assesses financial and managerial credit-worthiness Makes loan decision Seeks loan approval from bank	Assesses financial and managerial credit-worthiness Makes loan decision Seeks loan approval from bank

Sources: Ettin 1994; Berger, Kashyap, and Scalise 1995; Gorton and Rosen 1995; Federal Reserve bulletins on bank changes (November 1996); Federal Reserve Board senior loan officer opinion surveys; and original field research.

> If it's company money it might be in the right pocket, if it's personal money it might be in their left pocket, but it's all in the same pair of pants. It's all their money. It's very personal to them. . . . A lot of them will feel like, "We're just a small guy, they're from a big bank."

Although banks control the flow of capital, they also experience ambiguity in evaluating midmarket firms, which are typically not debt rated or certified. In particular, the bundling of the business and private lives of the firm's managers is viewed as a key source of performance ambiguity. Because the firm's capital and the entrepreneur's capital are often intertwined, banks' RMs need to assess how a client's private life affects the firm's economic performance. These social preconditions importantly affect economic exchange in this market and, in the course of everyday business dealings, also encourage discussions of private matters normally had with social attachments, deepening the embeddedness of commercial transactions between firms and banks in social attachments and networks. An RM explained,

> It's something you wouldn't think . . . has to do with major business, but . . . [e]very social issue is played out in economic form. They [CEOs] have children of unequal talents: the CEO is less talented than the children. Somebody doesn't want to give up stock. Somebody does. . . . Can't see that on a balance sheet or P & L [profit and loss statement]. You need to understand what's going on around the individual. . . . and that plays out in "situations." That's the dynamic.
>
> So information is not efficient, and with that comes the need for the bank to interpret. . . . [I]mperfect information and [the firm's] imperfect awareness of alternatives means that most conversations are negotiations because there needs to be a meeting of the minds. . . . You also will develop, as a byproduct of that attention, a relationship.

In a fashion analogous to how financial markets govern exchanges and certify the validity of publicly available information, the embedding of commercial transactions in social attachments and networks creates a mechanism by which to govern exchanges of private resources (Abolafia 1997). RMs refer to this process as "market making," a phrase that denotes their view of how social ties furnish governance arrangements and promote transfers of private resources, which in turn make deals that would not arise in their absence. A lead RM summarized these essential conditions:

> If anybody tells you a story, it reflects their view of the world, which doesn't mean that they're lying but it's impossible to separate out the storyteller from their objectives. . . . [Y]ou couldn't just say. "Oh the truth is in the financial statements." Take a company, and based on different accounting treatments you have different-looking balance sheets. If all you did was look at the numbers, you would make different decisions on the same company! I'll ask questions about financial statements or projections or the business but getting answers is not enough. So, we need this interactive process, . . . which is this digging in and re-creating of something so that you understand the components. . . . That's a relationship . . . a market being made.

Also consistent with embeddedness theory, I found that the degree to which interviewees embed their transactions in social structure varies. The more that commercial transactions are embedded in social attachments, the more expectations of trust govern exchanges. One RM expressed it this way:

> [A] relationship [means] that you know a person like his family and you feel on a level with him—not pure friends—but that he trusts what you say. That you're taking care of him. . . . [So] the more I know a person, the more he understands why I'm asking these questions. He doesn't feel so defensive. Otherwise, with market ties it's a battle.

Another RM said,

> A relationship on a social basis tends to break a lot of ice and develop a multidimensional relationship that's more than cold facts, interest rates, and products. It's an emotion-based bond . . . that's so important to have . . . [because] the customer will let us know about problems early, so we can correct them.

Other RMs noted that reciprocity characterizes embedded ties, an outcome that is bolstered by expectations of trust. As another RM explained,

> On the golf course, at a ball game, or the theater, they'll let their guard down more often. We exchange information—not like a marriage—more like dating. I share information about me as a person. I let them see me and share with them our company's struggles. As I share that information, I get information back. It's kind of a quid pro quo.

A distinctive aspect of the embedding of commercial transactions in this market is that they often have properties of *extended closure* that promote the creation of a common set of inferences among the members of a network. These properties of closure arise when RMs and entrepreneurs form direct relations with third persons, such as spouses and children, which entrepreneurs and RMs confidentially rely on for perceptions of character and trustworthiness in their business dealings with others. By enclosing private and public information flows in a matrix of social ties, shared expectations and regularized behavior arises not through the enforcement by a third party, such as the courts, but through unanimity of inference. This unanimity of inference is important for undertaking risky actions, such as estimating credit eligibility or long-term returns on loans, because it reduces the perceived uncertainty associated with estimating an actor's most likely behavior. In its application and consequences, this property combines the consequences of network closure typically found within common social groupings (Coleman 1988) with the purposeful multivocal strategies used by the Medici to interlock the economic and personal fates of Florentine merchants and bankers (Padgett and Ansell 1993). A key difference is that the Medici constructed this closure through formal marriages and contracts, whereas modern-day bankers achieve similar governance outcomes by organizing informal social events that promote relationship-building among RMs, entrepreneurs, and their significant others. Tom, a lead RM at a large midmarket bank, described the process of enclosing social ties so that they crisscrossed the personal and business networks of entrepreneurs, increasing the embeddedness of the tie between the banker and entrepreneur and the uniformity of inference about the banker's credibility. Here Tom refers to his client, Jim, Jim's spouse, Ellen, and the consequences for governance of this type of embedding:

> For Ellen to tell Jim, "You know, that Tom. I really like him and I trust him a lot," has more impact on his view of me than if his controller told him that. It's sort of the old Nancy Reagan "pillow talk" thing with Ron. They're integral to their spouses' decisions. Getting to know them and having them get to know you, bridges those personal things that you talk about and know about them. And the web gets woven deeper in terms of the personal side.

While these results illustrate the prevalence and material consequences of embedded ties, my fieldwork revealed that embedded relations retain "passions" that are uncharacteristic of the antipathy of arm's-length transacting (Hirschman 1977). Even if embedding is initiated for governance and access benefits, the resulting intimacy imbues the relationship with expressive value that is separate from purely material stipulations, even if it impinges upon them. For example, one RM declared,

> [Y]ou have to maintain that professional distance because you never know when you're going to have to make that tough call [i.e., risk losing the attachment over a business difference]. But having said that, . . . I have clients that I'm very close with, and in most circumstances it helps. I know their kids' names and when their kids have the flu. I go out socially with my wife and with them and their spouses.

Another RM explained how embedding spontaneously infuses a business tie with social values and attitudes that would be irrelevant in the market model:

> After he [the entrepreneur] becomes a friend, you want to see your friend succeed and that goes along many lines. If I can be a part of helping them do that, it's a real good feeling and I'm providing a service not only to them but their employees. . . . So there's a lot of things that you kind of from a moral standpoint take into effect. . . . That is kind of a side effect of your relationship.

By contrast, arm's-length ties lack the expectations of trust and reciprocity needed for knowledge transfer and collaboration, resulting in different economic consequences. For example, one RM described how arm's-length ties might be effective at governing price data across different banks but are poor governance arrangements for imbuing information with credibility or transferring private information. He said,

> Firms got to get comparative information. . . . [But] oftentimes entrepreneurs will negotiate with you and they'll tell you they've got a deal from somebody else and they don't. That's part of where that honesty and integrity and being able to trust the people that you're dealing with becomes very important.

Another RM stated that arm's-length ties put

> a relationship out for bidding. Every opportunity a customer has to get credit they'll shop your deal. [They will say,] "I've talked to a couple other banks and they're willing to give me this." . . . It's price oriented. . . . [If] I ask questions about performance, the client is aggressive and that's not fun.

Relational Embeddedness and Loan Acquisition and Costs

How do these properties of embeddedness affect an organization's cost and acquisition of capital? I argue that embedded ties both create value in the dyad and motivate exchange partners to share that value. Focusing on the mechanisms by which value is created and shared from the firm's perspective, the two most relevant processes have to do with the *creation of contingent contracts* and the *leveraging of social capital* from one RM to another RM on behalf of the firm.[5] The high level of trust in the relationship enables firms and banks to negotiate contingent loan agreements. A contingent loan agreement converts a loan with a homogeneous price structure into a loan that has separate components and a tiered price structure. A gradient of prices and terms in a contingent agreement enables a firm to start with and maintain low capital costs and few loan restrictions so long as it sustains a preset level of performance, thereby enhancing its credit eligibility and reducing its borrowing costs relative to one-cost, one-structure loans. By contrast, loans negotiated through arm's-length ties often have homogeneous structures because there is no basis of trustworthiness on which to estimate how credit risks can be assessed relative to the firm's promises to repay. A case often recounted by RMs concerned attempts to structure loans in ways that gave firms the benefit of the doubt contingent on the interpretation of ambiguous performance data that would otherwise result in loan denial, an unfavorable rate, or tight restrictions. Using a contingent agreement, RMs might offer, for instance, a low interest rate the first year that would rise in subsequent years only if the firm failed to maintain its projected performance level. Remarkably, this specification of the contingent ordering of the risk inherent in the loan deal was often predicated on the level of trust and reciprocity in the relationship rather than on comparative information that appeared in public financial statements. In particular, the trust and reciprocity of embedded ties enhanced the transfer and credibility of the private information that was essential to the creation of a unique contingent loan agreement for the firm. A lead RM explained how his embedded tie to an entrepreneur motivated an integrative solution to the firm's credit request through the design of a specialized contingent contract, which resulted in better access and lower costs than arm's-length relations could have provided:

> [B]ecause we knew this guy [I said,] . . . "Tell you what we'll do: We'll give you a price of X today. We'll base our pricing as if those expenses were not in your financial statements. . . . But after 12 months, . . . if it's all flushed through, you will continue on in this price level. If you don't, boom, your pricing will go up." So, because of the relationship, because we knew the guy and we really believed in him and trusted him, we gave him the benefit of the doubt on the pricing for the first year. He has to continue to perform or it goes up. So, that's a way we would sort of marry the two, the objective and the subjective, if you will.

Embedded ties also benefit firms by motivating bankers to leverage their personal social capital at the bank on the firm's behalf. Unlike the advantages described above, these outcomes are not necessarily attempts to affect the loan's tangible features. Rather, RMs use aspects of their social capital *within* the bank, such as their reputation or social ties to other RMs, to influence the expectations of other relevant bank decision makers regarding a firm's creditworthiness. I observed a similar phenomenon (Uzzi 1996) when I found that the expectations of trust and reciprocity between two economic actors could be "rolled over" to a new third party, thereby establishing trust and reciprocal obligations between two parties that lacked a prior history of exchange. In an analogous process, RMs seeking to act on a firm's behalf primed first-time introductions between other RMs and the firm's managers with expectations of trust—extending the web of shared beliefs about the firm's creditworthiness to other relevant bank decision makers. One RM described how these factors can play out for a firm in a deal in which its creditworthiness is indefinite. In particular, she noted how her reciprocal obligee to the entrepreneur and the entrepreneur's personal expression of need induced her to pledge her social capital at the bank on the firm's behalf, despite the performance ambiguity reported in the firm's financial statements:

> [T]he deal on paper is a tough deal. And he [the CEO] said, "I'm fucking scared." I said. "Okay, as long as I know where you stand." . . . Well, obviously that's a long way from I'm fucking scared to there's a deal here. [So,] I go to my president and we go through the credit risks. I said, "All the credit risks are blatantly obvious. . . . He said, "Well, how do you overcome it?" [I said,] "We've got to go see the business and meet the people." And he agreed and said, "Then I want to see the business and meet the people." Now, I can't control what his "gut" is going to be. But I know the principals of the firm, a regional credit officer who's chairing up a loan committee, my president and senior lender. [So,] it's got to be a real bad credit for them to say no, especially when I have a 40 percent growth markup.

These arguments and findings illustrate patterns of relational embeddedness and how it operates even in well-developed financial markets by positively affecting a firm's ability to acquire capital and lower its cost of capital. Embedded ties generate surplus value for the firm by promoting private information and resource transfers that create value and motivate banks to share the value created in the relationship with the firm. Therefore, based on my framework and fieldwork, I expect statistical analysis to support the following hypotheses:

Hypothesis 1: The more a firm's commercial exchanges with a bank are embedded in social attachments, the more likely the firm is to *acquire* financing at that bank.

Hypothesis 2: The more a firm's commercial exchanges with a bank are embedded in social attachments, the lower the firm's *cost* of financing at that bank.

Structural Embeddedness and Loan Acquisition and Costs

My argument has focused on the properties and consequences of dyadic bank-firm social attachments, yet dyadic exchanges reside within a larger network of ties that amplifies or diminishes their benefits. Some finance and organization theories hold that firms with expansive networks of arm's-length ties to banks optimize their bargaining power and provide access to a large pool of price and loan possibilities, thereby increasing their chances at getting corporate financing (Mintz and Schwartz 1985; Petersen and Rajan 1994). My argument about network structure partly agrees with these theories, but focuses on the organization rather than on network size as the operative mechanism. Although an expansive network of arm's-length ties can enable a firm to effectively scan the market for deals and help broker information among banks, it lacks the embedded ties that facilitate partnering. Conversely, while embedded ties promote collaboration, a network composed only of embedded ties could induce overattentiveness to local resources and historical conventions, limiting a firm's access to market information and new ideas. This suggests that a network composed of both embedded ties and arm's-length ties can moderate the shortcomings of each type of tie while preserving their strengths, optimizing the firm's range of available action.

Building on prior research (Baker 1990; Uzzi 1996, 1997), I refer to a network's ability to synthesize the benefits of different types of ties as *network complementarity.* Networks high in complementarity produce premium outcomes because the features of different ties reinforce one another's advantages while mitigating their disadvantages. Thus, while I argue that embedded ties provide special informational and governance benefits with a specific lender, I acknowledge that a firm that maintains a network composed only of embedded ties risks suboptimal network-level outcomes by not capitalizing on the properties of network complementarity.[6]

Heterogeneity in the market for loans suggests that networks high in complementarity should enhance a firm's ability to get financing and lower its financing costs. Access to capital grows with a firm's ability to (*a*) shop the market for a loan structure that is compatible with its credit profile and (*b*) partner with a bank on the customization of a loan structure that fits its credit profile. Thus, high network complementarity should enhance a firm's access to capital by promoting both brokerage and partnering benefits. In my fieldwork, the dual benefits of networks high in complementarity were manifested in several ways. Bankers noted that firms with networks high in complementarity used their arm's-length ties to scan the market for differences in loan prices and structures. That information was then transferred to their close lender through an embedded tie, which imbued market data and unfamiliar loan stipulations with credibility and motivated the lender to use novel market data to the mutual benefit of the firm and bank. In this way, firms with networks of embedded ties and arm's-length ties combined the partnering benefits of embedded ties with the brokering benefits of arm's-length ties.

In an example of this process, an RM recounted the dynamics of a recent deal in which his bank was one of the arm's-length ties in the network of a firm seeking corporate financing. He noted how the entrepreneur used an arm's-length tie to his bank to access information about his bank's loan prices and structures. The entrepreneur then disclosed that information to his close lender, which customized a deal for the firm using the bank's distinctive capabilities and resources *and* the novel loan ideas of other banks that the entrepreneur had accumulated through its arm's-length ties. What's more, the RM observed that the embedded tie between the entrepreneur and his bank was the main source of both the trust and reciprocal obligations needed to customize deals that benefit from a synthesis of market information and exclusive private resources. The RM reported:

> Three banks were pitching on the same deal, and the company said to me, "Give us a creative idea on how you would structure this financing." We provided a very creative idea with term loans and revolving credit [factors affecting price and structure]. They said, "We really like this structure, but X has been our bank for fifty years and we don't want to pull the agency from them." When the term sheet came back from X bank, X bank had basically our term sheet with their name on it. Later, the CFO said to me, . . . "Look, you guys came up with the idea. So, we'd like to give you the first shot at our trust business or the private banking of the owners" [a conciliation prize for providing valuable ideas]. So, we gave the banking insight on the marketplace to the firm [but lost the deal].

The above argument and data suggest that networks high in complementary produce premium benefits by preserving the strengths and diminishing the weaknesses of different types of ties. In the context of corporate financing, complementarity increases a firm's ability to broker market information and instigate partnering around custom deals by drawing on both the novel information that is dispersed among players in a heterogeneous market and the private resources obtained through relationships. Thus, based on my framework and the fieldwork data, I expect statistical analysis to support the following hypotheses:

> **Hypothesis 3**: A firm's likelihood of *acquiring* financing increases when it has a network with an integrated mix of embedded ties and arm's-length ties and decreases when it has a network that tends toward either solely embedded ties or solely arm's-length ties.

> **Hypothesis 4**: A firm's *cost* of financing decreases when it has a network with an integrated mix of embedded and arm's-length ties and increases when it has a network that tends toward either solely embedded ties or solely arm's-length ties.

Data and Methods

I tested my hypotheses using data from the National Survey of Small Business Finances, a survey administered by the Federal Reserve Bank to investigate how market and organizational characteristics affect capital costs and availability. This in-person survey collected data on firms' lending ties, sources of financing, loans, and organizational and financial characteristics. The random sample consisted of 1,875 corporations and 1,529 partnerships/sole proprietorships with up to 500 employees and $154 million in assets, operating in 1989 in the U.S. nonagricultural sector. Depending on the item, the response rate was 70 to 80 percent, reducing the sample size to about 2,300 cases. Nearly 90 percent of the businesses were owner-managed: 12 percent were owned by women and 7 percent were minority-owned.

Dependent Variables

The two dependent variables I examined correspond to the first and second stages of the corporate financing process. The first stage concerns whether a firm acquires capital (i.e., a loan). The standard assumption in lending research is that small- to medium-sized firms constantly need credit. Consequently, the lack of a loan suggests that a firm was denied credit or offered unattractive loan agreements, which in effect informally counsel applicants to withdraw their requests, making self-restricted consumption tantamount to denial of a loan (Lummer and McConnell 1989; Munnell et al. 1992). Given these complexities, most research cannot fully determine whether a lack of a loan is due to credit rationing by the bank or to the firm's self-restricted consumption. Hence, research generally adopts the convention that if a firm's need for credit is controlled for, firms without loans were probably denied credit (Cole and Wolken 1995; Hawley and Fujii 1991). Given that my data coincide with previous research in this area, I followed the above convention, defining a firm as *credit accessed* (coded 1) if it obtained a loan between 1987 and 1989 (coded 0 if not). This approach allowed me to extend prior research, even if a judicious interpretation of this stage of the model's results was called for. Stage 2 estimates the *cost of capital*, which I defined as the interest rate on the firm's loan—the typical measure used in research and practice on lending (Petersen and Rajan 1994).

Independent Variables

A methodological issue concerns how to create valid quantitative measures that capture the dimensions of the ethnographic findings and yet are parsimonious and amenable to statistical analysis. Using Miles and Huberman's (1994) and Bollen and Paxton's (1998) methods, I applied techniques that look for convergence among theory, face validity, and discriminant validity. In these methods, validity increases if independent sources of theory and evidence converge on a consistent pattern and discriminate among other concepts.[7]

Prior research holds that embedding increases with the duration of the relationship and the multiplexity of the relationship (Blau 1964; Gulati 1994; Lazerson 1995; Larson 1992; Lin, Ensel, and Vaughn 1981; Marsden and Campbell 1984; Seabright, Levinthal, and Fichmen 1992). Time in a relationship permits network partners to learn about and share private information, incur debits and credits in the relationship, form bonds of trust, and exploit opportunities for reciprocity. Seabright, Levinthal, and Fichmen (1992) operationalize a social attachment between an auditor and a CEO as "the length of time the individual engages in activities associated with the relationship . . . [the strength of the social attachment] is likely to increase with the years of tenure that have elapsed since the formation of the interorganizational relationships" (133–34). They also operationalize attachment strength between an auditor and a CEO as the multiplexity of overlapping roles they interfaced around (CEO, CFO, or CAO).

I looked for convergence between my theory, prior operationalizations, and the accounts of RMs (i.e., face validity) by asking RMs about how embedded ties could be operationalized and distinguished from other quantitative measures of the bank-firm relationship (i.e., discriminant validity). For instance, I probed RMs with inquiries such as, "If you want to determine if your colleague has a close tie with a client like the one we have been discussing, what quantitative information would you use or look for?" Consistent with research, RMs independently stated that sound measures of embedded ties included (*a*) the duration of the relationship and (*b*) the multiplexity of the relationship between the lender and the firm. Thus, I defined the *duration of the relationship* in years and the *multiplexity of the relationship* as the number of business services (e.g., cash box services, wire transfers) *and* personal bank services (e.g., personal bank accounts, wills, estate planning) used by the entrepreneur. Business and personal services included brokerage, capital leases, cash management services, credit card receipt processing, letters of credit, night depository, pension funds, personal estate planning, trusts, retirement planning, revolving credit arrangements, money/coins for operations, and wire transfers. Finally, I performed discriminant validity checks by inquiring if these indicators might also measure lower loan production costs. RMs said these factors lowered transaction costs and increased retention, but they did not directly lower the costs of administering a loan. One RM stated, "It doesn't make it less expensive to manage a tie the longer it's around because some long-term clients want to see the banker every month or utilize the bank's services where that gets expensive."

I used the same method to construct my measure of network complementarity, which operationalizes the degree to which a firm uses arm's-length ties, embedded ties, or a mix of ties to transact with the banks in its network. (Here, the term *network* refers to the egocentric network of direct ties between a firm and all its banks, not just the lending bank.) Baker (1990) shows that a Herfindahl index, a relative of the Gibbs-Martin index of social heterogeneity (Blau and Schwartz 1984), parsimoniously measures the mix of different types of ties in a firm's network. The index varies between greater than 0 and less than or equal to 1. As the index nears 0, a firm disperses its transactions among many banks through arm's-length ties; as it nears 1, a firm consolidates its transactions with one or few embedded ties. At intermediate values, a firm has an integrated mix of embedded ties and arm's-length ties. In the analysis, I used a linear and quadratic term to capture these curvilinear effects. The measure is defined as $\Sigma(P_j^2)$, where j varies from 1 to N banks, and P_j is the proportion of the firm's banking business that is dedicated to bank j. I defined P_j as the sum of three fundamental accounts—savings, checking, and line-of-credit accounts—that RMs used to indicate the intensity of exchange between a firm and a bank. For example, if a firm used three banks and apportions 70 percent of its business to bank 1, 20 percent to bank 2, and the remaining 10 percent to bank 3, then its network structure score is equal to $(.70)^2 + (.20)^2 + (.10)^2 = .54$. One potential shortcoming of this measure is that it is difficult to compare across cases if the sizes of the firms' banking networks vary widely. Because midmarket firms vary but not excessively in the size of their banking networks, I directly controlled for network size in the regressions.

Consistent with the assumptions of my measure of network complementarity, interviewees stated that firms that consolidated their banking with one bank tended to embed their commercial transactions in social attachments. In contrast, interviewees revealed that firms that dispersed their banking transactions tended to have arm's-length ties and that at least occasional arm's-length business at the bank was a prerequisite for them to respond to clients' requests for information on loan pricing or structures. (RMs rarely supplied similar information to customers without at least an arm's-length tie, such as cold-callers, that RMs considered to be nonrelationships.) Finally, to examine the discriminant validity of this measure with measures of resource dependence, I asked bankers whether their willingness to collaborate was motivated by reciprocal obligations and trust or dependence on a firm's business. They declared that banks rarely feel dependent on any one firm's business, particularly in this banking market segment where banks are larger than firms. Thus, this measure has the advantage of summarizing the level of the embeddedness of a firm's ego-network in one measure that has high face validity and precedent in studies of banking.

Control Variables

I controlled for the organizational, market, and loan characteristics known to affect corporate financing using the standard measures applied in prior research (Cole and Wolken 1995; Mizruchi and Stearns 1994a). Organizational controls included *number of employees, organization age, log of sales change* (current year minus previous year), *corporate status* (1 = yes), and *cash on hand*, which controlled for the firm's need for credit. I controlled for the firm's ability to convert assets into cash and to carry debt using the firm's *acid ratio* ([current assets—inventory]/current liabilities) and *debt ratio* (total liabilities/total assets), respectively. To control for gender and racial discrepancies in credit decisions (Arrow 1998), I defined a firm as *women-owned* (1 = yes) or *minority-owned* (1 = yes) if it had 51 percent or more ownership by women or minorities (the survey did not collect the exact percentage). To control for the size of a firm's ego-network for banking, I created *network size*, a count of the number of financial institutions a firm uses for financial services. This variable is highly correlated with more complex indices of network structure, thus furnishing a reasonable proxy for size and degree measures of network structure that my data did not allow me to construct (Borgatti 1997).

To control for the loan characteristics that affect lending, I measured the *prime rate* (the interest rate to which loans are pegged) at the month and year the loan was granted. *Term structure spread* was defined as the yield on a government bond of the same maturity of the loan less the Treasury bill yield and accounts for interest rate differences that vary with the loan's maturity (Petersen and Rajan 1994, 13). Two indicator variables, *collateral* (1 = yes) and *fixed-rate loan* (1 = yes) controlled for systematic differences in interest rates for loans that require collateral or that have fixed rather than variable rates. *Bank competition* in the firm's locale was measured using the Federal Reserve's bank concentration index (1 = high concentration, 2 = moderate concentration, and 3 = low concentration). In the analysis, I reversed the scale of this variable so that higher values correspond to greater bank competition. This measure captures both the market pressures on banks to offer favorable interest rates and the range of interest rates in a market (Petersen and Rajan 1995). Differences in interest rates in the Northeast, North Central, South, and West were controlled for with four *regional indicators*; industry differences were controlled for with seven industry indicators using two-digit SIC codes (lowest level of disaggregation in the data). Table 13.3 reports the correlations and descriptive statistics for the variables used in the analysis.

Statistical Model

I modeled the effect of social ties and networks on the acquisition and cost of capital with a Heckman two-stage selection model (Heckman 1976). This model is used when one dependent variable (e.g., the cost of capital) depends on another dependent variable (e.g., having a loan). The first stage is a probit regression that models whether the firm accessed credit. The second stage is an OLS regression that uses the estimated Mills ratio from the first stage to account for selection bias in estimating the interest rate on the outstanding loan. If regressions were run on the firms with loans, it could produce biased results if access to capital was not random. Fitting variables that correlate with access to credit but not with the interest rate helps solve the problem. Thus, I chose variables for each stage based on previous research and on my fieldwork (Mizruchi and Stearns 1994b; Petersen and Rajan 1994).[8]

Results

Table 13.4 presents the results of the selection model, which examines the correlates of the acquisition (model 1) and cost of corporate financing (model 2). The control variable effects are noteworthy because they establish a baseline for gauging the effects of social structure and the appropriateness

TABLE 13.3

Correlation Coefficients between Variables Used in the Analysis: U.S. Nonagricultural Firms, 1989

Variable	*(1)*	*(2)*	*(3)*	*(4)*	*(5)*	*(6)*	*(7)*	*(8)*	*(9)*	*(10)*	*(11)*	*(12)*	*(13)*	*(14)*	*(15)*	*(16)*	*(17)*	*(18)*	*(19)*	*(20)*
(1) Interest rate	1.00																			
(2) Duration of bank-firm relationship	–.12	1.00																		
(3) Multiplexity of bank-firm relationship	–.14	.09	1.00																	
(4) Network complementarity	–.08	–.00	–.02	1.00																
(5) Network complementarity squared	–.03	–.03	–.05	.97	1.00															
(6) Network size	–.06	.05	.21	–.12	–.20	1.00														
(7) Women-managed firm	.02	–.08	–.03	–.04	–.02	–.01	1.00													
(8) Minority-managed firm	.03	–.04	–.05	.00	.00	–.04	.03	1.00												
(9) Number of employees	–.04	.03	.11	.00	–.01	.15	.00	–.00	1.00											
(10) Age of firm	–.12	.44	.09	.05	.02	.12	–.10	–.09	.10	1.00										
(11) Corporation	–.17	.08	.11	.07	.03	.17	–.05	–.06	.08	.12	1.00									
(12) Cash in retained earnings	–.25	.10	.17	.46	.34	.21	–.07	.00	.12	.12	.31	1.00								
(13) Sales change (log)	–.11	–.00	.05	.06	.04	.10	–.00	–.00	.10	.00	.08	.17	1.00							
(14) Acid ratio	.04	.02	–.06	.04	.04	–.12	–.00	.03	–.03	.05	–.11	.03	–.00	1.00						
(15) Debt ratio	.02	–.09	.03	–.09	–.08	.13	.04	–.03	.00	–.14	.12	–.15	–.05	–.34	1.00					
(16) Prime rate	.04	–.01	.02	.00	.00	.02	–.02	.00	.02	–.07	.08	.06	.04	–.02	.03	1.00				
(17) Term structure spread	.14	–.06	–.14	–.05	–.03	.04	.04	.01	–.04	–.07	–.01	–.07	–.00	.01	.00	.00	1.00			
(18) Collateral on loan	–.03	–.06	–.00	.01	.03	.04	.00	–.02	–.01	–.06	.08	–.00	.05	–.06	.04	.00	.25	1.00		
(19) Fixed-rate loan	.20	–.06	–.18	–.06	–.04	–.00	.05	.01	–.08	–.05	–.09	–.14	–.02	.08	–.06	.00	.75	.15	1.00	
(20) Bank competition	.08	.04	–.03	–.06	–.04	–.03	.01	–.07	.04	–.02	–.07	–.16	.00	–.06	.02	–.06	–.00	–.00	.00	1.00
Mean	10.97	12.98	2.68	.80	.77	2.23	.12	.07	25.6	14.08	.55	8.55	4.06	6.79	.52	9.14	.89	.79	.53	2.51
Standard deviation	2.60	12.77	3.56	.35	.38	1.54	—	—	54.9	12.52	—	3.54	8.84	40.64	.75	1.97	1.07	—	—	.65

Note: Means are expressed as percentages: $N = 2,226$.

TABLE 13.4
Coefficients from the Heckman Selection Regression of Access to Credit and Interest Rate Loan on Selected Independent Variable: U.S. Nonagricultural Firms, 1989

	Model 1 (Credit Accessed)		*Model 2 (Cost of Capital)*	
Independent Variable	*Coefficient*	*S.E.*	*Coefficient*	*S.E.*
Constant	1.164**	(.184)	11.233**	(1.155)
Embeddedness				
Duration of bank-firm relationship	–.001	(.002)	–.013*	(.005)
Multiplexity of bank-firm relationship	.005	(.008)	–.042*	(.018)
Complementarity of firm's bank network	1.772*	(.547)	–6.275**	(1.134)
(Complementarity of firm's bank network)^2	–1.119*	(.461)	5.030**	(.960)
Size of firm's bank network	.133**	(.020)	.039	(.053)
Organizational characteristics				
Women-managed firm	–.189*	(.086)	.020	(.221)
Minority-managed firm	–.180	(.107)	.371	(.288)
Number of employees	.001	(.001)	–.002*	(.001)
Age of firm	–.007**	(.002)	—	—
Corporation	–.132*	(.063)	—	—
Cash in retained earnings	–.023	(.013)	—	—
Sales change (log)	.005	(.003)	–.022**	(.007)
Acid ratio	–.025**	(.004)	.028*	(.015)
Debt ratio	.004	(.038)	.070	(.150)
Loan characteristics				
Prime rate	—	—	.155	(.096)
Term structure spread	—	—	–.020	(.106)
Collateral on loan	—	—	–.393*	(.175)
Fixed-rate loan	—	—	.709**	(.207)
Region and industry indicators				
Bank competition	–.140**	(.043)	.193	(.111)
Northeast	.264**	(.082)	—	—
North Central	.211**	(.085)	—	—
South	.138*	(.081)	—	—
Mining	.257	(.316)	—	—
Construction	.104	(.093)	—	—
Manufacturing	–.063	(.097)	—	—
Transportation, communication, public utilities	.124	(.164)	—	—
Wholesale trade	–.004	(.070)	—	—
Retail trade	.178	(.141)	—	—
Wald χ^2 (df = 16)		131.31**		
Log-likelihood		–3363.2		
Rho		–.352		

Note: N = 2,226.
$^*p < .05$ $^{**}p < .01$. (Two-tailed tests.)

of the model's specification. Consistent with previous research, model 1 shows that organizations are more likely to access credit if they are younger, have liquidity, have a noncorporate form, and are located in regions with low bank competition or low credit costs; model 2 shows that large firms and firms with increasing sales, variable rate loans, or loans with collateral have lower costs of capital (Petersen and Rajan 1994).

In model 2, however, it is somewhat surprising that prime rate and term structure spread had null effects. In a post hoc analysis, I dropped the fixed-rate loan variable from the regression equation to see if it was capturing the effects of these variables. As expected, prime rate had a positive effect and term structure spread had a negative effect on the cost of capital when this fixed effect was removed from the equation. Also of substantive importance is the finding that women-owned, and to a lesser degree minority-owned firms (significant at the $p < .05$ level in a one-tailed test), are less likely to access credit than firms managed by white males. The discrepancy among these social categories is significant because access to capital may be more critical than its cost, particularly to liquidity-sensitive small firms. Taken together, these results suggest that the models are adequately specified and that the embeddedness measures capture net effects not explained by current financial theory.

Hypotheses 1 and 2 predicted that relationship duration and relationship multiplexity increase a firm's probability of access to credit and lower its cost of capital. Consistent with hypothesis 2, model 2 shows that the duration of the relationship and multiplexity of the relationship have large and significant effects on reducing the cost of capital net of standard market, firm, and loan control variables. Furthermore, the consistent effects of both independent variables suggest that they capture a similar underlying construct net of each other's effects. In real terms, the coefficients in model 2 indicate that an additional year in a relationship lowers a firm's interest rate by 1.3 basis points (.013 percentage points), while an additional dimension (service) of multiplexity lowers a firm's interest rate by 4.2 basis points (.042 percentage points). In this market, such interest rate reductions are significant and underscore the importance of relational embeddedness relative to conventional financial and organizational factors that affect interest rates.

Inconsistent with hypothesis 1, neither duration of the relationship nor multiplexity of the relationship affects the probability of accessing credit. These null effects indicate that while the quality of a relationship can influence the competitiveness of a rate, it is unrelated to whether or not a firm "passes the bar" for credit eligibility. This suggests that relationships influence market allocation *once* a firm has been deemed creditworthy but do not independently influence whether a firm is categorized as credit eligible. This inference fits with my interview data, which indicated that there is a level of risk at which banks deny loans, even if they are close to the client, because no level of confidence in the client's competency can offset the credit-carrying shortfalls that emanate from other business factors. Thus, it appears that long-term and multiplex ties influence the "pricing" decision only if creditworthiness has been established by other factors, some of which are financial and others of which are sociological.

Consistent with hypotheses 3 and 4, network complementarity improves a firm's access to credit and its cost of capital. In model 1, the linear coefficient is positive and the squared coefficient is negative. Conversely, in model 2 the linear coefficient is negative and the squared coefficient is positive. Thus, as hypothesized, networks composed of an integrated mix of embedded ties and arm's-length ties increase access to capital and reduce capital costs relative to networks composed predominantly of arm's-length ties or embedded ties. These results suggest that the complementarity of different types of ties in a network produces optimal benefits relative to networks that lack complementarity.

This conclusion is strengthened by the effects of network size on credit access and credit costs. In model 1, network size increases the propensity for credit accessibility. This is consistent with my argument and field data that indicate that arm's-length ties increase a firm's knowledge of market innovations and the availability of different loans and pricing. Taken at face value, a larger network is better than a smaller network for access to credit. However, *if price is a factor*, the null effect for network size in model 2 indicates that network size does not reduce pricing. This suggests that increases in the number of arm's-length ties to banks can help firms shop the market for loan availability but appear to ineffectively motivate banks to incorporate rivals' prices or to cut prices on a loan. Consistent with this inference, several RMs recounted situations in which a firm linked to them by an arm's-length tie applied for a loan, and because of the RMs' desire to be competitive with the firm's other banks they offered a loan but at a high, unattractive price (Uzzi 1999). Another effect that supports this line of inference emerged from a post hoc analysis of the employment sizes of firms with networks high in complementarity. The analysis showed that firms with integrated networks were larger than firms with embedded networks, but did not differ in size from firms with large arm's-length networks. This further suggests that the effect of network structure is not a proxy for firm size, but is an effect of the social organization of the ties in the firm's network. I infer that large networks of arm's-length ties effectively garner public market data but are comparatively less effective than embedded ties at promoting the trust and reciprocity that facilitate deal-making and innovation. Thus, networks high in complementarity seem to provide premium benefits by providing a bridge for integrating the public information found in markets with the private resources of particular relationships.

Figure 13.1 illustrates the combined effects of embeddedness in a three-dimensional surface plot that was generated holding the other significant variables in model 2 at their means. The plot shows the interplay between

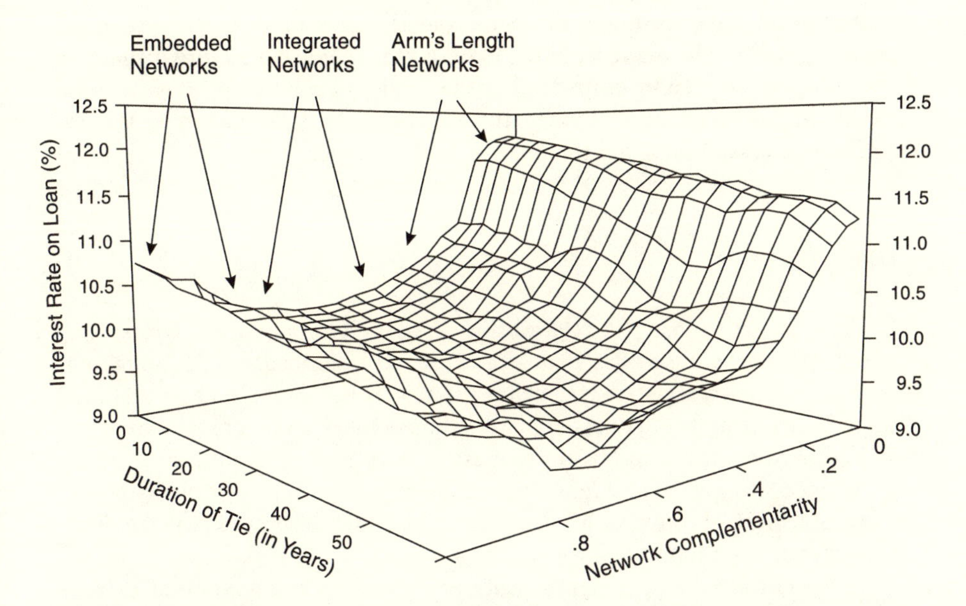

FIGURE 13.1 Social embeddedness and the firm's cost of financial capital: U.S. nonagricultural firms, 1989

relational embeddedness, structural embeddedness, and the magnitudes of three effects related to the cost of capital. First, firms that maintain integrated mixed-mode networks (the trough of the curve area) lower their cost of capital, an effect that increases linearly as the duration of the relationship between the bank and firm increases. Moreover, a proper level of network complementarity lowers the cost of capital below that of either embedded-tie networks or arm's-length networks by up to 3.0 percentage points, or 300 basis points (the difference between the U-shaped curve's right-hand tails and the trough). In terms of dollars and cents, this difference is substantial: a $100,000 loan at 8.5 percent interest and a ten-year maturity has a final cost of $226,098. In contrast, the same loan with an interest rate of 11.5 percent has a final cost of $296,994. Thus, a 3 percent or 300-basis-point difference in the interest rate results in savings of $70,896 over the life of the loan. Second, consistent with my argument, the difference in the right and left tails of the U-shaped curve indicates that while neither an embedded-tie network nor an arm's-length network is as beneficial as a mixed-mode network, an embedded network is better than an arms-length network, at least for small firms. Third, the estimated interest rate does not fall below about 9.1 percent, yet the average prime rate over this period is 8.5 percent. This suggests that banks and clients share the benefits created by social attachments and social networks, yet on average this does *not* result in loan costs below prime—the bank's cost of capital. Rather, the results suggest that embeddedness prompts the bank and the firm to share the potential profits that could be made from the loan. A reasonable conjecture is that the social capital created by embeddedness in modern capitalist markets is both closely aligned with performance and less particularistic than typically assumed in classical financial theory.

Discussion

Bankers have an adage, "A relationship is worth a basis point." This saying reflects their belief that value is measured the old-fashioned and unambiguous way—at the cash register—yet belies the real value they credit to relationships. Using an embeddedness approach, I have found that commercial transactions between firms and banks that are embedded in relationships *increase* firms' access to capital and *lower* their borrowing costs net of other determinants of lending. Ethnographic and statistical evidence showed that the more commercial transactions between a firm and the bank it borrows from are embedded in social attachments, the more expectations of trust and reciprocity shape transacting, thereby promoting governance benefits and transfers of private resources that are inaccessible through market ties. The governance benefits of embedded ties make investments in unique solutions to lending problems more predictable to banks and firms, while the high level of private resource transfer provides the substantive material for creating distinctive solutions to a firm's financing needs. These findings are important because most studies of financial market behavior focus on access to public information and the use of formal governance mechanisms such as written contracts. Embeddedness is therefore a conduit to resources and governance arrangements that are difficult to emulate through other exchange mechanisms.

These benefits of embeddedness are also enhanced when the firm's network of ties to all its banks—those banks from which it borrows and those at which it conducts other banking business—consists of a complementary mix of embedded ties and arm's-length ties. Firms that have networks composed of a complementary mix of ties optimize the benefits of embeddedness because the characteristics of different types of ties offset each other's weaknesses while preserving their strengths. In networks high in complementarity, arm's-length ties effectively search for and broker differences in loan structures among banks, while embedded ties facilitate the partnering that is needed to successfully synthesize diverse market information and unique private resources into innovative, low-cost loan structures. In contrast, networks of only arm's-length ties can effectively broker market differences but lack arrangements that facilitate partnering, while networks of only embedded ties promote partnering yet have limited facilities for brokering resources between disconnected actors. I refer to this portfolio-like property of a network as *network complementarity* and view it as one way network structure optimizes an actor's brokering *and* partnering benefits vis-à-vis other actors.

Apart from the substantive ramifications of the findings, implications for the sociology of markets and organizations are also evident. In economic sociology, there are two general theories for understanding how social relations and networks create economic and social benefits. The weak-tie approach argues that a large, nonredundant network of arm's-length ties is most advantageous; the strong-tie approach argues that a closed, tightly knit network of embedded ties is most advantageous (Sandefur and Laumann 1998). How can these opposing approaches to tie quality (weak versus strong) and network structure ("holely" versus dense) be reconciled? My analysis of arm's-length ties supports the weak-tie thesis, demonstrating that weak ties are superior at "shopping" the market for publicly available information. Similarly, my analysis of embedded ties supports the strong-tie approach by showing that embedded ties are superior at "plugging" actors into the unique collective resources of dense network clusters. Thus, I suggest that embedded ties and arm's-length ties are complementary rather than cannibalistic when they are combined within the same network, because one type of tie helps overcome the limitations of the other type while enlarging information and governance benefits. While I have addressed these portfolio-like properties of network complementarity, the concept should be further developed and fully confirmed. Future research should be directed at accumulating additional evidence along the lines of this study on network complementarity and build on current work that includes studies of research productivity, learning, industrial change, and direct sales marketing (Etzkowitz, Kemelgor, and Uzzi 2000; Gabbay 1997; Talmud and Mesch 1997; Uzzi 1996).

The results also suggest that the theoretical distinction between instrumental versus expressive interests may be moot because embeddedness changes actors' motives rather than treats them as immutable. While RMs may build networks to gain access to private information, enacting a relationship also attenuates the narrow aims that may have motivated it originally because such ties tend to create expectations that normally accompany noneconomic attachments. As my data show, even in a business culture that uses the yardstick of money to gauge value, bankers and clients develop expressive bonds that affect their economic decisions. Consequently, there is no tradeoff between selfish interests and an exchange partner's interests because valuing an exchange partner's interest is appropriate for roles that are linked through embedded ties.

A class of theoretical implications concern the similarities and differences between the embeddedness approach and other approaches to transacting across organizational boundaries, particularly transaction cost economics, which also conceptualizes exchange in terms of information access and governance (Granovetter 1985; Uzzi 1996, 1997). In this paper, I have presented three factors that distinguish the ways in which information and governance problems are treated in the embeddedness and transaction cost economic approaches. Two differences concern the mechanisms by which information and governance problems are resolved (i.e., private information transfer and networks) and one difference concerns the motivations of actors (i.e., an embedded logic of exchange).

First, the embeddedness and transaction cost approaches differ in their emphases on the degree to which private information or asset specificity—the main explanatory variable of the transaction cost approach (also see Blau 1964, 160 for an early treatment of asset-specificity's effect on exchange)—affects the value of relationships. While the concepts of private information and asset specificity are not necessarily in conflict with one another, private information and asset specificity are not synonymous. I have shown how private information is unlike asset-specific information in that private information need not be relationship-specific or decrease in value if redeployed in another transaction. Rather, it provides value through *relationships* and therefore does not necessarily lose value when redeployed in a new relationship or when used in several exchange relationships simultaneously. In this sense, private information shares with relationship specific investments the quality of value creation, but it has fewer restrictions on how widely it can be used.

Second, noncontractual social relationships and network structure also play a key role in embeddedness by regulating an actor's ability to broker and partner in exchanges—features of social structure that are given short shrift in the transaction cost economics focus on dyads.

Third, transaction cost economics holds that trust muddies the waters of individual calculativeness because "the only reliable human motive is avariciousness" (Williamson 1996, 50). As such, the transaction cost model focuses on the use of formal governance mechanisms such as contracts, franchise agreements, or hostage-taking. In contrast, I have presented numerous examples and statistical findings that showed how social trust can offer distinctive governance benefits that translate into lower costs of capital and improved access to capital. Another important consequence of this distinction is that the governance arrangements of social embeddedness appear to come before, rather than follow from, the attributes of transactions. In this way, embeddedness inverts the logic of transaction costs by showing how self-enforcing governance arrangements pave the way for the transfer of private information and integrative bargaining rather than follow the attributes of transactions as purported in transaction cost economics.

While the triangulation of methods and independent data sources provides more robust inferences than does a single source of data, the cross-sectional properties of these materials suggest that the framework's confirmation requires longitudinal study of the origin, change, and scope of embeddedness in markets (Uzzi 1999). A specific provisional finding of this study is that women-managed and minority-managed firms are less likely than other firms to access credit. One reason for these discrepancies may be that the "scripts" that white male RMs use to forge ties with white male entrepreneurs are "coded" differently by minorities and women (e.g., an evening of dinner and the theater becomes comparable to a "date") because relationship-building involves contextually defined activities. These differences may therefore unintentionally hamper the formation of embedded ties between groups that use alternative scripts. Thus, one tentative conclusion is that prejudices against an out-group may explain only part of the discrepancies in lending because collaboration among in-group members improves access for in-group members, *even if* out-group bias does not exist. Thus, if these provisos are correct they suggest that in-group effects may be as important as out-group effects in explaining market stratification. They also suggest that the systems lenders use to select and train RMs in relational practices can improve minorities' access to credit, as well as lenders' ability to attract the business of undervalued firms.

In summary, my key substantive conclusion is that social structure stratifies market outcomes by influencing both who gets credit and what that credit costs. My broad finding is that the ability to meet financial selection criteria is a product of a firm's characteristics *as well as* the socially arranged opportunity structures within which it is embedded. Firms with embedded relations and high network complementarity are more likely to be deemed credit eligible and to receive lower-cost financing. While it has recently been recognized that particular networks can benefit firms in competitive environments, *less attention has been paid* to a second, commensurately important outcome of networks: that social and network relations also can encourage a firm to put forth extra effort, increasing its future performance beyond what it would have been had it been embedded in a more limiting set of relations. In this sense, embeddedness can promote both individual and social welfare in markets in the same way that advantaged social positions, independent of personal attributes, help actors get ahead and also motivate them to achieve. Conversely, disadvantaged positions stall mobility and reduce aspiration and motivation. Thus, market making—or the creation of exchanges for mutual benefit—depends on social relations and networks, which are themselves likely to generate premium benefits for firms and economies when they provide a bridge for integrating the public resources of markets with the private resources of relationships.

Appendix: Fieldwork Methodology

I obtained interviewees' names from each bank's CEO. The CEO's name was acquired through the Banking Resource Center, a research institute on banking located within the Kellogg Graduate School of Management. Banks sampled ranged in size from small community banks (assets < $100 million) to high-end midmarket banks (assets < $225 billion).

At each bank, I interviewed "relationship managers," a widely used title that displaced the former title of "lending officer" in the early 1980s. The title "relationship manager" (RM) is sociologically interesting in that it connotes the social nature and identity of this role in banks and the manner in which it is enacted with corporate clients. RMs normally attain the rank of vice president, a status that reflects seniority, success, and decision-making power. Of the twenty-four interviewees, nineteen were RMs, three were CEOs actively involved in lending, and two were bad-debt collectors. Bad-debt collectors are presumably more skeptical of social ties than RMs given that their typical interactions are with persons and firms that default and defraud on loan agreements. Total interview time amounted to twenty-six hours, and the average number of years of experience of interviewees was about ten years. The average number of firms that each interviewee managed ranged from nine to fifty. The gender and race demographics of the RM sample approximate the population demographics of the banking industry; five were women and one was an African American male.

I used Miles and Huberman's (1994) data collection and analysis methods. I recorded all interviews on tape and then transcribed them to create a behavioral record for each interviewee. In some cases, long narrative passages were broken into stanzas, which consisted of an uninterrupted series of sentences on a single topic (e.g., transactions, trust, market-making). In these cases and when narratives were reported in their entirety, the lack of fluency that is typical of spoken English was edited to increase comprehension. Questions were open-ended and moderately directive. Questions focused on the nature of the credit decision—especially access to capital (who qualifies) and the cost of capital. Follow-up questions focused on the nature, function, and dynamics of bank-client ties. Thus, there was an active attempt to use the interviews to discover interesting and surprising relationships, rather than to use them as a proxy for survey data. For example, some typical questions were: "How does the bank assess the creditworthiness of a corporate borrower?" "What types of things do you discuss with a client in order to assess their creditworthiness?" "What do you typically do when you meet clients?" "What is the basis of a good relationship with a client?" "How do relationships between you and the client develop?" To probe sensitive issues and avoid directiveness, responses were postscripted with phrases such as: "Can you tell me more about that? I am interested in those kinds of details," "Is there anything else?" "Would you consider this typical or atypical?"

Data analysis was a two-step procedure. First, I formed an understanding of the patterns in the data. This task centered on a content analysis and frequency count of the interviewees' data in which their responses were compiled into different factors that decomposed the range of responses (i.e., the variance) into its major components. Second, I worked back and forth between theory and the emerging framework. In this step, evidence was added, dropped, or revised as my working formulation took shape. My purpose was to explain how social structure influences economic behavior, which in this context considers how relationships and network ties condition a firm's access to capital and the cost of capital. Like psychometric and econometric models, this formulation aims to accurately illustrate the sources of variation in the data rather than explain all the variance.

Notes

1. The literature on attachments distinguishes between ties between persons and ties between organizations (Baker, Faulkner, and Fisher 1998; Blau 1964; Levinthal and Fichman 1988; Seabright, Levinthal, and Fichman 1992) and views social attachments as personal ties (which constitute ties between the individuals' firms, even if the reverse does not hold). A social attachment is an affiliation of shared interests and fidelity that develops when behavior that is culturally associated with familiar and noncommercial transactions is enacted as part of the commercial exchange (Iacobucci and Ostrom 1996). In this study, such social behaviors include wedding invitations, parties, dining, sports competitions, shows, or other social events that both friends and businesspersons can and do commonly enact through time and that are valued in that persons share these behaviors in proprietary ways with select others.

2. While my objective is to propose and investigate these processes rather than to assert their validity, much social psychological research on decision making supports these processes. Montgomery (1998) showed how transactors who assume the identity of "friend" are likely to cooperate, while transactors who assume the identity of "businessperson" are unlikely to cooperate (even if commitments are credible) because there is no priming mechanism for trust. The logic of appropriateness, first identified by March (1994), suggests that decision makers choose actions by asking, "Who am I and what is the appropriate action for my role?" rather than basing these actions on situation-free personal preferences. Cognitive dissonance research also finds that attitudes and interests are aligned with role behavior (Kunda 1990, 484). This suggests that motives to create and share value are supported by psychological processes that are set in motion by embedding processes.

3. Lending decisions are made in two stages. In stage 1, a bank decides whether to offer a loan to an applicant. Loan denial reflects cases in which the bank will not raise the interest rate to make up for a bad credit risk. In stage 2, the bank decides what cost of credit to charge applicants who were deemed creditworthy in stage 1.

4. Money markets sell capital directly to firms at the same rate as banks. London InterBank Offer Rate is the current money market standard for lending rates and reflects the interest rate paid on deposits among banks in the Eurodollar market.

5. Embeddedness creates value for banks by enhancing their ability to reduce the costs of writing loan contracts, to retain clients, and to decommodify financial capital. These processes and their effects on the bank's profit spread and contractual restrictions on a loan are explored in Uzzi (1999).

6. My concept of network complementarity builds on portfolio theory, which argues that assets in a portfolio have a contingent value that depends on the other assets in the portfolio, not just the properties of the individual asset. In a similar manner, a tie's value is greatest when other types of ties complement its strengths, while the

entire portfolio's value rises if the benefits of the different types of ties that compose the portfolio do not coincide. In this context, a network refers to the firm's ego network of direct ties to banks, not the aggregation of all bank-firm networks in an arbitrary region or industry boundary. Previous research has also referred metaphorically to ego networks as portfolios (Powell, Koput, and Smith-Doerr 1996, 120).

7. Triangulation determines the validity of constructs by looking for convergence in the outcomes of different methods. As with some other psychometric methods (e.g., factor analysis), no formal statistical tests are involved. Triangulation works by demonstrating that a measure accurately represents the construct even if some nuances are omitted in the same way that econometric models do not explain all the variance. Moreover, the weaknesses of this method are not unique, but are part of a class of statistical problems that introduce measurement error into network variables. Thus, since measurement error normally attenuates estimates, tests of hypotheses are conservative (McPherson, Popielarz, and Drobnic 1992).

8. I checked my model specifications by estimating the interest rate and an interest rate deviation score (firm's interest rate minus the prime rate) with nested OLS regressions. While OLS does not handle selection error, it allows subsets of variables to be entered separately—a nested procedure that tends to bias the Heckman model, which is sensitive to specification error. I also examined possible distributional artifacts. I truncated the duration variable at its ninety-fifth percentile to test for sensitivity to distributional extremes. I ran separate models with multiplexity dichotomized (no services versus one service versus multiple services). I ran models on the subset of data where network complementarity was not equal to 1 to investigate whether the effects were sensitive to observations where network complementarity is equal to network size because the firm uses just one bank. The results were substantively identical to those reported in models 1 and 2, supporting my specifications.

References

Abolafia, Mitchell Y. 1997. *Making Markets: Opportunism and Restraint on Wall Street*. Cambridge: Harvard University Press.

Arrow, Kenneth J. 1998. "What Has Economics to Say about Racial Discrimination." *Journal of Economic Perspectives* 12:91–100.

Baker, Wayne E. 1990. "Market Networks and Corporate Behavior." *American Journal of Sociology* 6:589–625.

———. 1994. *Networking Smart: How to Build Relationships for Personal and Organizational Success*. New York: McGraw-Hill.

Baker, Wayne E., Robert R. Faulkner, and Gene A. Fisher. 1998. "Hazards of the Market: The Continuity and Dissolution of Interorganizational Market Relationships." *American Sociological Review* 63:147–77.

Berger, Allen N., Anil K. Kashyap, and Joseph M. Scalise. 1995. "The Transformation of the U.S. Banking Industry: What a Long Strange Trip It's Been." *Brookings Papers on Economic Activity* 1:55–218.

Blau, Peter M. 1964. *Exchange and Power in Social Life*. New York: Wiley.

Blau, Peter M., and Joseph E. Schwartz. 1984. *Crosscutting Social Circles*, New York: Academic Press.

Bollen, Kenneth A., and Pamela Paxton. 1998. "Detection and Determinants of Bias in Subjective Measures." *American Sociological Review* 63:465–78.

Borgatti, Stephan P. 1997. "Structural Holes: Unpacking Burt's Redundancy Measures." *Connections* 20:35–38.

Burt, Ronald S. 1992. *Structural Holes: The Social Structure of Competition.* Cambridge: Harvard University Press.

Carruthers, Bruce G. 1996. *City of Capital: Politics and Markets in the English Financial Revolution.* Princeton: Princeton University Press.

Cole, Rebel A., and John D. Wolken. 1995. "Financial Services Used by Small Businesses: Evidence from the 1993 National Survey of Small Business Finances." *Federal Reserve Bulletin* 81:629–67.

Coleman, James S. 1988. "Social Capital in the Creation of Human Capital." *American Journal of Sociology* 94 (suppl.): S95–S120.

Davis, Gerald F. 1991. "Agents without Principles: The Spread of the Poison Pill through the Intercorporate Network." *Administrative Science Quarterly* 36:583–613.

Davis, Gerald F., and Mark S. Mizruchi. 1999. "The Money Center Cannot Hold: Commercial Banks in the U.S. System of Corporate Governance." *Administrative Science Quarterly* 44:215–39.

DiMaggio, Paul, and Hugh Louch. 1998. "Socially Embedded Consumer Transactions: For What Kinds of Purchases Do People Most Often Use Networks?" *American Sociological Review* 63:619–37.

Eccles, Robert G., and Dwight B. Crane. 1988. *Doing Deals: Investment Banks at Work.* Boston: Harvard Business School Press.

Ettin, Edward C. 1994. "The Evolution of the North American Banking System." Prepared for the Experts' Meeting on Structural Changes in Financial Markets: Trends and Practices, Organization for Economic Cooperation and Development, Paris.

Etzkowitz, Henry, Carol Kemelgor, and Brian Uzzi. 2000. *Athena Unbound: The Advancement of Women in Science and Technology.* Cambridge: Cambridge University Press.

Fama, Eugene. 1985. "What's Different about Banks?" *Journal of Monetary Economics* 15:29–36.

Federal Deposit Insurance Corporation (FDIC). 1998. *1998 Bank and Thrift Branch Office Data Book: Office Deposits and Addresses of FDIC Insured Institutions—Summary of Deposits Central Region.* Washington, D.C.: Federal Deposit Insurance Corporation.

Fligstein, Neil. 1996. "Markets as Politics: A Political-Cultural Approach to Market Institutions." *American Sociological Review* 61:656–73.

Fukuyama, Francis. 1995. *Trust, Social Virtues, and the Creation of Prosperity.* New York: Free Press.

Gabbay, Shaul. 1997. *Social Capital in the Creation of Financial Capital: The Case of Network Marketing.* Champaign, Ill.: Stipes.

Gorton, Gary, and Richard Rosen. 1995. "Corporate Control, Portfolio Choice, and the Decline of Banking." *Journal of Finance* 50:1377–420.

Granovetter, Mark. 1973. "The Strength of Weak Ties." *American Journal of Sociology* 78:1360–80.

Granovetter, Mark. 1985. "Economic Action and Social Structure: The Problem of Embeddedness." *American Journal of Sociology* 91:481–510.

Gulati, Ranjay. 1994. "Does Familiarity Breed Trust? The Implications of Repeated Ties for Contractual Choice in Alliances." *Academy of Management Journal* 38, no. 4: 85–112.

Haunschild, Pamela R. 1994. "How Much Is That Company Worth? Interorganizational Relationships, Uncertainly, and Acquisition Premiums." *Administrative Science Quarterly* 39:391–411.

Hawley, Clifford B., and Edwin T. Fujii. 1991. "Discrimination in Consumer Credit Markets." *Eastern Economic Journal* 17, no. 1: 21–30.

Heckman, James. 1976. "The Common Structure of Statistical Models of Truncation, Sample Selection, and Limited Dependent Variables and a Simple Estimator for Such Models." *Annals of Economic and Social Measurement* 5:475–92.

Hirschman, Albert O. 1977. *The Passions and the Interests: Political Arguments for Capitalism before Its Triumph*. Princeton: Princeton University Press.

———. 1982. "Rival Interpretations of Market Society: Civilizing, Destructive, or Feeble?" *Journal of Economic Literature* 20:1463–84.

Iacobucci, Dawn, and Amy Ostrom. 1996. "Commercial and Interpersonal Relationships: Using the Structure of Interpersonal Relationships to Understand Individual-to-Individual, Individual-to-Firm, and Firm-to-Firm Relationships in Commerce." *International Journal of Research in Marketing* 13:53–72.

King, Gary, Robert O. Keohane, and Sidney Verba. 1994. *Designing Social Inquiry: Scientific Inference in Qualitative Research*. Princeton: Princeton University Press.

Kollock, Peter. 1994. "The Emergence of Exchange Structures: An Experimental Study of Uncertainty, Commitment, and Trust." *American Journal of Sociology* 100:313–45.

Kunda, Ziva. 1990. "The Case for Motivated Reasoning." *Psychological Bulletin* 108:480–98.

Larson, Andrea. 1992. "Network Dyads in Entrepreneurial Settings: A Study of the Governance of Exchange Processes." *Administrative Science Quarterly* 37:76–104.

Lazerson, Mark. 1995. "A New Phoenix: Modern Putting-Out in the Modena Knitwear Industry." *Administrative Science Quarterly* 40:34–59.

Levinthal, Daniel A., and Mark Fichman. 1988. "Dynamics of Interorganizational Attachments: Auditor-Client Relationships." *Administrative Science Quarterly* 33:345–69.

Lie, John. 1997. "Sociology of Markets." *Annual Review of Sociology* 23:341–60.

Lin, Nan, Walter Ensel, and Jan Vaughn. 1981. "Social Resources and Strength of Ties: Structural Factors in Occupational Status Attainment." *American Sociological Review* 46:393–405.

Lummer, Scott, and John McConnell. 1989. "Further Evidence on the Bank Lending Process and the Capital Market Response to Bank Loan Agreements." *Journal of Financial Economics* 25:99–112.

Macneil, Ian. 2000. "Relational Contract Theory: Challenges and Queries." *Northwestern University Law Review* 94: 877–905.

March, James G. 1994. *A Primer on Decision Making: How Decisions Happen*. New York: Free Press.

Marsden, Peter V. 1981. "Introducing Influence Processes into a System of Collective Decisions." *American Journal of Sociology* 86:1203–35.

Marsden, Peter V., and Karen E. Campbell. 1984. "Measuring Tie Strength." *Social Forces* 63:482–501.

McPherson, Miller J., Pamela A. Popielarz, and Sonja Drobnic. 1992. "Social Networks and Organizational Dynamics." *American Sociological Review* 57:153–70.

Miles, Matthew B., and Michael Huberman. 1994. *Qualitative Data Analysis*. Newbury Park, Calif.: Sage.

Mintz, Beth, and Michael Schwartz. 1985. *The Power Structure of American Business*. Chicago: University of Chicago Press.

Mizruchi, Mark S., and Linda B. Stearns. 1994a. "A Longitudinal Study of Borrowing by Large American Corporations." *Administrative Science Quarterly* 39:118–40.

———. 1994b. "Money, Banking, and Financial Markets." In *Handbook of Economic Sociology*, ed. Neil J. Smelser and Richard Swedberg. Princeton: Princeton University Press.

Montgomery, James D. 1998. "Toward a Role-Theoretic Conception of Embeddedness." *American Journal of Sociology* 104:92–125.

Munnell, Alicia H., Lynn E. Browne, James McEneaney, and Geoffrey M. B. Tootell. 1992. "Mortgage Lending in Boston: Interpreting HMDA Data." Federal Reserve Bank of Boston, Working Paper 92–7.

Padgett, John F., and Christopher K. Ansell. 1993. "Robust Action and the Rise of the Medici, 1400–1434." *American Journal of Sociology* 98:1259–319.

Petersen, Mitchell A., and Raghuram G. Rajan. 1994. "The Benefits of Lending Relationships: Evidence from Small Business Data." *Journal of Finance* 49:3–37.

———. 1995. "The Effect of Credit Market Competition on Lending Relationships." *Quarterly Journal of Economics* 110:407–43.

Podolny, Joel M. 1993. "A Status-Based Model of Market Competition." *American Journal of Sociology* 98:829–72.

Portes, Alejandro, and Julia Sensenbrenner. 1993. "Embeddedness and Immigration: Notes on the Social Determinants of Economic Action." *American Journal of Sociology* 98:1320–50.

Powell, Walter W. 1990. "Neither Market nor Hierarchy: Network Forms of Organization." In *Research in Organizational Behavior*, vol. 5, ed. Barry M. Staw and Larry L. Cummings. Greenwich, Conn.: JAI.

Powell, Walter W., Kenneth W. Koput, and Laurel Smith-Doerr. 1996. "Interorganizational Collaboration and the Locus of Innovation: Networks of Learning in Biotechnology." *Administrative Science Quarterly* 41:116–45.

Romo, Frank P., and Michael Schwartz. 1995. "Structural Embeddedness of Business Decisions: A Sociological Assessment of the Migration Behavior of Plants in New York State between 1960 and 1985." *American Sociological Review* 60:874–907.

Sandefur, Rebecca L., and Edward O. Laumann. 1998. "A Paradigm for Social Capital." *Rationality and Society* 10:481–501.

Seabright, Mark A., Daniel A. Levinthal, and Mark Fichman. 1992. "Role of Individual Attachments in the Dissolution of Interorganizational Relationships." *Academy of Management Journal* 35, no. 1: 122–60.

Smelser, Neil J., and Richard Swedberg. 1994. "The Sociological Perspective on the Economy." In *The Handbook of Economic Sociology*, edited by Neil J. Smelser and Richard Swedberg. Princeton: Princeton University Press.

Talmud, Ilan, and Gustavo Mesch. 1997. "Market Embeddedness and Corporate Instability: The Econology of Inter-industrial Networks." *Social Science Research* 26:419–41.

Uzzi, Brian. 1996. "The Sources and Consequences of Embeddedness for the Economic Performance of Organizations." *American Sociological Review* 61:674–8.

———. 1997. "Social Structure and Competition in Interfirm Networks: The Paradox of Embeddedness." *Administrative Science Quarterly* 42:35–67.

———. 1999. "Governance Benefits through Embedded Ties and Network Complementarity: The Case of Banks Making Corporate Loans." Institute for Policy Analysis, Northwestern University, Working Paper 99–15.

Uzzi, Brian, and James J. Gillespie. 1999. "Inter-firm Ties and the Organization of the Firm's Capital Structure in the Middle Financial Market." In *Research in the Sociology of Organizations*, ed. D. Knoke and S. Andrews. Stanford, Conn.: JAI Press.

Weber, Max. 1946. "Class Status and Party." In *From Max Weber: Essays in Sociology*, ed. and trans. Hans H. Gerth and C. Wright Mills. Oxford: Oxford University Press.

Williamson, Oliver C. 1996. "Economic Organization: The Case for Candor." *Academy of Management Review* 21, no.1: 48–57.

POWER

Chapter 14

FROM *THE GERMAN IDEOLOGY*

KARL MARX

Translated by S. Ryazanskaya

THE PREMISES from which we begin are not arbitrary ones, not dogmas, but real premises from which abstraction can only be made in the imagination. They are the real individuals, their activity and the material conditions under which they live, both those which they find already existing and those produced by their activity. These premises can thus be verified in a purely empirical way.

The first premise of all human history is, of course, the existence of living human individuals. Thus the first fact to be established is the physical organization of these individuals and their consequent relation to the rest of nature. Of course, we cannot here go either into the actual physical nature of man, or into the natural conditions in which man finds himself—geological, orohydrographical, climatic, and so on. The writing of history must always set out from these natural bases and their modification in the course of history through the action of men.

Men can be distinguished from animals by consciousness, by religion, or anything else you like. They themselves begin to distinguish themselves from animals as soon as they begin to *produce* their means of subsistence, a step which is conditioned by their physical organization. By producing their means of subsistence men are indirectly producing their actual material life.

The way in which men produce their means of subsistence depends first of all on the nature of the actual means of subsistence they find in existence and have to reproduce. This mode of production must not be considered simply as being the reproduction of the physical existence of the individuals. Rather it is a definite form of activity of these individuals, a definite form of expressing their life, a definite *mode of life* on their part. As individuals express their life, so they are. What they are, therefore, coincides with their production, both with *what* they produce and with *how* they produce. The nature of individuals thus depends on the material conditions determining their production.

This production only makes its appearance with the *increase of population.* In its turn this presupposes the *intercourse* [*Verkehr*] of individuals with one another. The form of this intercourse is again determined by production.

The relations of different nations among themselves depend upon the extent to which each has developed its productive forces, the division of labor, and internal intercourse. This statement is generally recognized. But not only the relation of one nation to others, but also the whole internal structure of the nation itself depends on the stage of development reached by its production and its internal and external intercourse. How far the productive forces of a nation are developed is shown most manifestly by the degree to which the division of labor has been carried. Each new productive force, insofar as it is not merely a quantitative extension of productive forces already known (for instance the bringing into cultivation of fresh land), causes a further development of the division of labor.

The division of labor inside a nation leads at first to the separation of industrial and commercial from agricultural labor, and hence to the separation of *town* and *country* and to the conflict of their interests. Its further development leads to the separation of commercial from industrial labor. At the same time through the division of labor inside these various branches there develop various divisions among the individuals cooperating in definite kinds of labor. The relative position of these individual groups is determined by the methods employed in agriculture, industry, and commerce (patriarchalism, slavery, estates, classes). These same conditions are to be seen (given a more developed intercourse) in the relations of different nations to one another.

The various stages of development in the division of labor are just so many different forms of ownership, i.e., the existing stage in the division of labor determines also the relations of individuals to one another with reference to the material, instrument, and product of labor.

The first form of ownership is tribal [*Stammeigentum*] ownership. It corresponds to the undeveloped stage of production, at which a people lives by hunting and fishing, by the rearing of beasts or, in the highest stage, agriculture. In the latter case it presupposes a great mass of uncultivated stretches of land. The division of labor is at this stage still very elementary and is confined to a further extension of the natural division of labor existing in the family. The social structure is, therefore, limited to an extension of the family; patriarchal family chieftains, below them the members of the tribe, finally slaves. The slavery latent in the family only develops gradually with the increase of population, the growth of wants, and with the extension of external relations, both of war and of barter.

The second form is the ancient communal and state ownership which proceeds especially from the union of several tribes into a *city* by agreement or by conquest, and which is still accompanied by slavery. Beside communal ownership we already find movable, and later also immovable, private property developing, but as an abnormal form subordinate to communal ownership. The citizens hold power over their laboring slaves only in their community, and on this account alone, therefore, they are bound to the form of communal ownership. It is the communal private property which compels the active citizens to remain in this spontaneously derived form of association over against their slaves. For this reason the whole structure of society based on this communal ownership, and with it the power of the people, decays in the same measure as, in particular, immovable private property evolves. The division of labor is already more developed. We already find the antagonism of town and country; later the antagonism between those states which represent town interests and those which represent country interests, and inside the towns themselves the antagonism between industry and maritime commerce. The class relation between citizens and slaves is now completely developed.

This whole interpretation of history appears to be contradicted by the fact of conquest. Up till now violence, war, pillage, murder and robbery, etc., have been accepted as the driving force of history. Here we must limit ourselves to the chief points and take, therefore, only the most striking example—the destruction of an old civilization by a barbarous people and the resulting formation of an entirely new organization of society. (Rome and the barbarians; feudalism and Gaul; the Byzantine Empire and the Turks.) With the conquering barbarian people war itself is still, as indicated above, a regular form of intercourse, which is the more eagerly exploited as the increase in population together with the traditional and, for it, the only possible, crude mode of production gives rise to the need for new means of production. In Italy, on the other hand, the concentration of landed property (caused not only by buying-up and indebtedness but also by inheritance, since loose living being rife and marriage rare, the old families gradually died out and their possessions fell into the hands of a few) and its conversion into grazing-land (caused not only by the usual economic forces still operative today but by the importation of plundered and tribute corn and the resultant lack of demand for Italian corn) brought about the almost total disappearance of the free population. The very slaves died out again and again, and had constantly to be replaced by new ones. Slavery remained the basis of the whole productive system. The plebeians, midway between freemen and slaves, never succeeded in becoming more than a proletarian rabble. Rome indeed never became more than a city; its connection with the provinces was almost exclusively political and could, therefore, easily be broken again by political events.

With the development of private property, we find here for the first time the same conditions which we shall find again, only on a more extensive scale, with modern private property. On the one hand, the concentration of private property, which began very early in Rome (as the Licinian agrarian law proves) and proceeded very rapidly from the time of the civil wars and especially under the emperors; on the other hand, coupled with this, the transformation of the plebeian small peasantry into a proletariat, which, however, owing to its intermediate position between propertied citizens and slaves, never achieved an independent development.

The third form of ownership is feudal or estate property. If antiquity started out from the town and its little territory, the Middle Ages started out from the *country*. This different starting point was determined by the sparseness of the population at that time, which was scattered over a large area and which received no large increase from the conquerors. In contrast to Greece and Rome, feudal development at the outset, therefore, extends over a much wider territory, prepared by the Roman conquests and the spread of agriculture at first associated with them. The last centuries of the declining Roman Empire and its conquest by the barbarians destroyed a number of productive forces; agriculture had declined, industry had decayed for want of a market, trade had died out or been violently suspended, the rural and urban population had decreased. From these conditions and the mode of organization of the conquest determined by them, feudal property developed under the influence of the Germanic military constitution. Like tribal and communal ownership, it is based again on a community; but the directly producing class standing over against it is not, as in the case of the ancient community, the slaves, but the enserfed small peasantry. As soon as feudalism is fully developed, there also arises antagonism to the towns. The hierarchical structure of landownership, and the armed bodies of retainers associated with it, gave the nobility power over the serfs. This feudal organization was, just as much as the ancient communal ownership, an association against a subjected producing class; but the form of association and the relation to the direct producers were different because of the different conditions of production.

This feudal system of landownership had its counterpart in the *towns* in the shape of corporative property, the feudal organization of trades. Here property consisted chiefly in the labor of each individual person. The necessity for association against the organized robber nobility, the need for communal covered markets in an age when the industrialist was at the same time a merchant, the growing competition of the escaped serfs swarming into the rising towns, the feudal structure of the whole country: these combined to bring about the *guilds*. The gradually accumulated small capital of individual craftsmen and their stable numbers, as against the growing population, evolved the relation of journeyman and apprentice, which brought into being in the towns a hierarchy similar to that in the country.

Thus the chief form of property during the feudal epoch consisted on the one hand of landed property with serf labor chained to it, and on the other of the labor of the individual with small capital commanding the labor of journeymen. The organization of both was determined by the restricted conditions of production—the small-scale and primitive cultivation of the land, and the craft type of industry. There was little division of labor in the heyday of feudalism. Each country bore in itself the antithesis of town and country; the division into estates was certainly strongly marked; but apart from the differentiation of princes, nobility, clergy, and peasants in the country, and masters, journeymen, apprentices and soon also the rabble of casual laborers in the towns, no division of importance took place. In agriculture it was rendered difficult by the strip-system, beside which the cottage industry of the peasants themselves emerged. In industry there was no division of labor at all in the individual trades themselves, and very little between them. The separation of industry and commerce was found already in existence in older towns; in the newer it only developed later, when the towns entered into mutual relations.

The grouping of larger territories into feudal kingdoms was a necessity for the landed nobility as for the towns. The organization of the ruling class, the nobility, had, therefore, everywhere a monarch at its head.

The fact is, therefore, that definite individuals who are productively active in a definite way enter into these definite social and political relations. Empirical observation must in each separate instance bring out empirically, and without any mystification and speculation, the connection of the social and political structure with production. The social structure and the state are continually evolving out of the life process of definite individuals, but of individuals, not as they may appear in their own or other people's imagination, but as they *really* are; i.e., as they operate, produce materially, and hence as they work under definite material limits, presuppositions, and conditions independent of their will.

The production of ideas, of conceptions, of consciousness, is at first directly interwoven with the material activity and the material intercourse of men, the language of real life. Conceiving, thinking, the mental intercourse of men, appear at this stage as the direct efflux of their material behavior. The same applies to mental production as expressed in the language of politics, laws, morality, religion, metaphysics, etc., of a people. Men are the producers of their conceptions, ideas, etc.—real, active men, as they are conditioned by a definite development of their productive forces and of the intercourse corresponding to these, up to its furthest forms. Consciousness can never be anything else than conscious existence, and the existence of men is their actual life-process. If in all ideology men and their circumstances appear upside down as in a camera obscura, this phenomenon arises just as much from their historical life-process as the inversion of objects on the retina does from their physical life-process.

In direct contrast to German philosophy, which descends from heaven to earth, here we ascend from earth to heaven. That is to say, we do not set out from what men say, imagine, conceive, nor from men as narrated, thought of, imagined, conceived, in order to arrive at men in the flesh. We set out from real, active men, and on the basis of their real life-process we demonstrate the development of the ideological reflexes and echoes of this life-process. The phantoms formed in the human brain are also, necessarily, sublimates of their material life-process, which is empirically verifiable and bound to material premises. Morality, religion, metaphysics, all the rest of ideology and their corresponding forms of consciousness, thus no longer retain the semblance of independence. They have no history, no development; but men, developing their material production and their material intercourse, alter, along with this their real existence, their thinking and the products of their thinking. Life is not determined by consciousness, but consciousness by life. In the first method of approach the starting point is consciousness taken as the living individual; in the second method, which conforms to real life, it is the real living individuals themselves, and consciousness is considered solely as *their* consciousness.

This method of approach is not devoid of premises. It starts out from the real premises and does not abandon them for a moment. Its premises are men, not in any fantastic isolation and rigidity, but in their actual, empirically perceptible process of development under definite conditions. As soon as this active life-process is described, history ceases to be a collection of dead facts, as it is with the empiricists (themselves still abstract), or an imagined activity of imagined subjects, as with the idealists.

Concerning the Production of Consciousness

History is nothing but the succession of the separate generations, each of which exploits the materials, the capital funds, the productive forces handed down to it by all preceding generations, and thus, on the one hand, continues the traditional activity in completely changed circumstances and, on the other, modifies the old circumstances with a completely changed activity. This can be speculatively distorted so that later history is made the goal of earlier history, e.g., the goal ascribed to the discovery of America is to further the eruption of the French Revolution. Thereby history receives its own special aims and becomes "a person ranking with other persons" (to wit: "Self-Consciousness, Criticism, the Unique," etc.), while what is designated with the words *destiny*, *goal*, *germ*, or *ideal* of earlier history is nothing more than an abstraction formed from later history, from the active influence which earlier history exercises on later history.

The further the separate spheres, which act on one another, extend in the course of this development, the more the original isolation of the separate nationalities is destroyed by the developed mode of production and intercourse and the division of labor between various nations naturally brought forth by these, the more history becomes world history. Thus, for instance, if in England a machine is invented, which deprives countless workers of bread in India and China, and overturns the whole form of existence of these empires, this invention becomes a world-historical fact. Or again, take the case of sugar and coffee, which have proved their world-historical importance in the nineteenth century by the fact that the lack of these products, occasioned by the Napoleonic continental system, caused the Germans to rise against Napoleon, and thus became the real basis of the glorious Wars of Liberation of 1813. From this it follows that this transformation of history into world history is not indeed a mere abstract act on the part of the "self-consciousness," the world spirit, or of any other metaphysical specter, but a quite material, empirically verifiable act, an act the proof of which every individual furnishes as he comes and goes, eats, drinks, and clothes himself.

The ideas of the ruling class are in every epoch the ruling ideas: i.e., the class which is the ruling *material* force of society, is at the same time its ruling *intellectual* force. The class which has the means of material production at its disposal, has control at the same time over the means of mental production, so that thereby, generally speaking, the ideas of those who lack the means of mental production are subject to it. The ruling ideas are nothing more than the ideal expression of the dominant material relationships, the dominant material relationships grasped as ideas; hence of the relationships which make the one class the ruling one, therefore, the ideas of its dominance. The individuals composing the ruling class possess among other things consciousness, and therefore think. Insofar, therefore, as they rule as a class and determine the extent and compass of an epoch, it is self-evident that they do this in its whole range, hence among other things rule also as thinkers, as producers of ideas, and regulate the production and distribution of the ideas of their age: thus their ideas are the ruling ideas of the epoch. For instance, in an age and in a country where royal power, aristocracy, and bourgeoisie are contending for mastery and where, therefore, mastery is shared, the doctrine of the separation of powers proves to be the dominant idea and is expressed as an "eternal law."

The division of labor, which we have already seen above as one of the chief forces of history up till now, manifests itself also in the ruling class as the division of mental and material labor, so that inside this class one part appears as the thinkers of the class (its active, conceptive ideologists, who make the perfecting of the illusion of the class about itself their chief source of livelihood), while the others' attitude to these ideas and illusions is more passive and receptive, because they are in reality the active members of this class and have less time to make up illusions and ideas about themselves. Within this class this cleavage can even develop into a certain opposition and hostility between the two parts, which, however, in the case of a practical collision, in which the class itself is endangered, automatically comes to nothing, in which case there also vanishes the semblance that the ruling ideas were not the ideas of the ruling class and had a power distinct from the power of this class. The existence of revolutionary ideas in a particular period presupposes the existence of a revolutionary class; about the premises for the latter sufficient has already been said above.

If now in considering the course of history we detach the ideas of the ruling class from the ruling class itself and attribute to them an independent existence, if we confine ourselves to saying that these or those ideas were dominant at a given time, without bothering ourselves about the conditions of production and the producers of these ideas, if we thus ignore the individuals and world conditions which are the source of the ideas, we can say, for instance, that during the time that the aristocracy was dominant, the concepts honor, loyalty, etc., were dominant, during the dominance of the bourgeoisie the concepts freedom, equality, etc. The ruling class itself on the whole imagines this to be so. This conception of history, which is common to all historians, particularly since the eighteenth century, will necessarily come up against the phenomenon that increasingly abstract ideas hold sway, i.e., ideas which increasingly take on the form of universality. For each new class which puts itself in the place of one ruling before it, is compelled, merely in order to carry through its aim, to represent its interest as the common interest of all the members of society, that is, expressed in ideal form: it has to give its ideas the form of universality, and represent them as the only rational, universally valid ones.

Intercourse and Productive Forces

The greatest division of material and mental labor is the separation of town and country. The antagonism between town and country begins with the transition from barbarism to civilization, from tribe to state, from locality to nation, and runs through the whole history of civilization to the present day (the Anti–Corn Law League).

The existence of the town implies, at the same time, the necessity of administration, police, taxes, etc., in short, of the municipality, and thus of politics in general. Here first became manifest the division of the population into two great classes, which is directly based on the division of labor and on the instruments of production. The town already is in actual fact the concentration of the population, of the instruments of production, of capital, of pleasures, of needs, while the country demonstrates just the opposite fact, isolation and separation. The antagonism between town and country can only exist within the framework of private property. It is the most crass expression of the subjection of the individual under the division of labor, under a definite activity forced upon him—a subjection which makes one man into a restricted town-animal, the other into a restricted country-animal, and daily creates anew the conflict between their interests. Labor is here again the chief thing, power *over* individuals, and as long as the latter exists, private property must exist. The abolition of the antagonism between town and country is one of the first conditions of communal life, a condition which again depends on a mass of material premises and which cannot be fulfilled by the mere will, as anyone can see at the first glance. (These conditions have still to be enumerated.) The separation of town and country can also be understood as the separation of capital and landed property, as the beginning of the existence and development of capital independent of landed property—the beginning of property having its basis only in labor and exchange.

In the towns which, in the Middle Ages, did not derive ready-made from an earlier period but were formed anew by the serfs who had become free, each man's own particular labor was his only property apart from the small capital he brought with him, consisting almost solely of the most necessary tools of his craft. The competition of serfs constantly escaping into the town, the constant war of the country against the towns and thus the necessity of an organized municipal military force, the bond of common ownership in a particular kind of labor, the necessity of common buildings for sale of their wares at a time when craftsmen were also traders, and the consequent exclusion of the unauthorized from these buildings, the conflict among the interests of the various crafts, the necessity of protecting their laboriously acquired skill, and the feudal organization of the whole of the country: these were the causes of the union of the workers of each craft in guilds. We have not at this point to go further into the manifold modifications of the guild system, which arise through later historical developments. The flight of the serfs into the towns went on without interruption right through the Middle Ages. These serfs, persecuted by their lords in the country, came separately into the towns, where they found an organized community, against which they were powerless and in which they had to subject themselves to the station assigned to them by the demand for their labor and the interest of their organized urban competitors. These workers, entering separately, were never able to attain to any power, since, if their labor was of the guild type which had to be learned, the guild masters bent them to their will and organized them according to their interest; or if their labor was not such as had to be learned, and therefore not of the guild type, they became day laborers and never managed to organize, remaining an unorganized rabble. The need for day laborers in the towns created the rabble.

These towns were true "associations," called forth by the direct need, the care of providing for the protection of property, and of multiplying the means of production and defense of the separate members. The rabble of these towns was devoid of any power, composed as it was of individuals strange to one another who had entered separately, and who stood unorganized over against an organized power, armed for war, and jealously watching over them. The journeymen and apprentices were organized in each craft as it best suited the interest of the masters. The patriarchal relationship existing between them and their masters gave the latter a double power—on the one hand because of their influence on the whole life of the journeymen, and on the other because, for the journeymen who worked with the same master, it was a real bond which held them together against the journeymen of other masters and separated them from these. And finally, the journeymen were bound to the existing order by their simple interest in becoming masters themselves. While, therefore, the rabble at least carried out revolts against the whole municipal order, revolts which remained completely ineffective because of their powerlessness, the journeymen never got further than small acts of insubordination within separate guilds, such as belong to the very nature of the guild system. The great risings of the Middle Ages all radiated from the country, but equally remained totally ineffective because of the isolation and consequent crudity of the peasants.

In the towns, the division of labor between the individual guilds was as yet [quite naturally derived] and, in the guilds themselves, not at all developed between the individual workers. Every workman had to be versed in a whole round of tasks, had to be able to make everything that was to be made with his tools. The limited commerce and the scanty communication between the individual towns, the lack of population and the narrow needs did not allow of a higher division of labor, and therefore every man who wished to become a master had to be proficient in the whole of his craft. Thus there is found with medieval craftsmen an interest in their special work and in proficiency in it, which was capable of rising to a narrow artistic sense. For this very reason, however, every medieval craftsman was completely absorbed in his work, to which he had a contented, slavish relationship, and to which he was subjected to a far greater extent than the modern worker, whose work is a matter of indifference to him.

Capital in these towns was a naturally derived capital, consisting of a house, the tools of the craft, and the natural, hereditary customers; and not being realizable, on account of the backwardness of commerce and the lack of circulation, it descended from father to son. Unlike modern capital, which can be assessed in money and which may be indifferently invested in this thing or that, this capital was directly connected with the particular work of the owner, inseparable from it and to this extent *estate* capital.

The next extension of the division of labor was the separation of production and commerce, the formation of a special class of merchants; a separation which, in the towns bequeathed by a former period, had been handed down (among other things with the Jews) and which very soon appeared in the newly formed ones. With this there was given the possibility of commercial communications transcending the immediate neighborhood, a possibility, the realization of which depended on the existing means of communication, the state of public safety in the countryside, which was determined by political conditions (during the whole of the Middle Ages, as is well known, the merchants traveled in armed caravans), and on the cruder or more advanced needs (determined by the stage of culture attained) of the region accessible to intercourse.

With commerce the prerogative of a particular class, with the extension of trade through the merchants beyond the immediate surroundings of the town, there immediately appears a reciprocal action between production and commerce. The towns enter into relations *with one another*, new tools are brought from one town into the other, and the separation between production and commerce soon calls forth a new division of production between the individual towns, each of which is soon exploiting a predominant branch of industry. The local restrictions of earlier times begin gradually to be broken down.

In the Middle Ages the citizens in each town were compelled to unite against the landed nobility to save their skins. The extension of trade, the establishment of communications, led the separate towns to get to know other towns, which had asserted the same interests in the struggle with the same antagonist. Out of the many local corporations of burghers there arose only gradually the burgher *class*. The conditions of life of the individual burghers became, on account of their contradiction to the existing relationships and of the mode of labor determined by these, conditions which were common to them all and independent of each individual. The burghers had created the conditions insofar as they had torn themselves free from feudal ties, and were created by them insofar as they were determined by their antagonism to the feudal system which they found in existence. When the individual towns began to enter into associations, these common conditions developed into class conditions. The same conditions, the same contradiction, the same interests necessarily called forth on the whole similar customs everywhere. The bourgeoisie itself, with its conditions, develops only gradually, splits according to the division of labor into various fractions and finally absorbs all propertied classes it finds in existence[1] (while it develops the majority of the earlier propertyless and a part of the hitherto propertied classes into a new class, the proletariat) in the measure to which all property found in existence is transformed into industrial or commercial capital. The separate individuals form a class only insofar as they have to carry on a common battle against another class; otherwise they are on hostile terms with each other as competitors. On the other hand, the class in its turn achieves an independent existence over against the individuals, so that the latter find their conditions of existence predestined, and hence have their position in life and their personal development assigned to them by their class, become subsumed under it. This is the same phenomenon as the subjection of the separate individuals to the division of labor and can only be removed by the abolition of private property and of labor itself. We have already indicated several times how this subsuming of individuals under the class brings with it their subjection to all kinds of ideas, etc.

It depends purely on the extension of commerce whether the productive forces achieved in a locality, especially inventions, are lost for later development or not. As long as there exists no commerce transcending the immediate neighborhood, every invention must be made separately in each locality, and mere chances such as irruptions of barbaric peoples, even ordinary wars, are sufficient to cause a country with advanced productive forces and needs to have to start right over again from the beginning. In primitive history every invention had to be made daily anew and in each locality independently. How little highly developed productive forces are safe from complete destruction, given even a relatively very extensive commerce, is proved by the Phoenicians,[2] whose inventions were for the most part lost for a long time to come through the ousting of this nation from commerce, its conquest by Alexander and its consequent decline: Likewise, for instance, glass-painting in the Middle Ages. Only when commerce has become world commerce and has as its basis large-scale industry, when all nations are drawn into the competitive struggle, is the permanence of the acquired productive forces assured.

The immediate consequence of the division of labor between the various towns was the rise of manufactures, branches of production which had outgrown the guild system. Manufactures first flourished, in Italy and later in Flanders, under the historical premise of commerce with foreign nations. In other countries, England and France for example, manufactures were at first confined to the home market. Besides the premises already mentioned manufactures depend on an already advanced concentration of population, particularly in the countryside, and of capital, which began to accumulate in the hands of individuals, partly in the guilds in spite of the guild regulations, partly among the merchants.

That labor which from the first presupposed a machine, even of the crudest sort, soon showed itself the most capable of development. Weaving, earlier carried on in the country by the peasants as a secondary occupation to procure their clothing, was the first labor to receive an impetus and a further development through the extension of commerce. Weaving was the first and remained the principal manufacture. The rising demand for clothing materials, consequent on the growth of population, the growing accumulation and mobilization of natural capital through accelerated circulation, the demand for luxuries called forth by the latter and favored generally by the gradual extension of commerce, gave weaving a quantitative and qualitative stimulus, which wrenched it out of the form of production hitherto existing. Alongside the peasants weaving for their own use, who continued, and still continue, with this sort of work, there emerged a new class of weavers in the towns, whose fabrics were destined for the whole home market and usually for foreign markets too.

Weaving, an occupation demanding in most cases little skill and soon splitting up into countless branches, by its whole nature resisted the trammels of the guild. Weaving was, therefore, carried on mostly in villages and market centers without guild organisation, which gradually became towns, and indeed the most flourishing towns in each land.

With guild-free manufacture, property relations also quickly changed. The first advance beyond naturally derived estate capital was provided by the rise of merchants whose capital was from the beginning movable, capital in the modern sense as far as one can speak of it, given the circumstances of those times. The second advance came with manufacture, which again made mobile a mass of natural capital, and altogether increased the mass of movable capital as against that of natural capital.

At the same time, manufacture became a refuge of the peasants from the guilds which excluded them or paid them badly, just as earlier the guild towns had [served] as a refuge for the peasants from [the oppressive landed nobility].

Simultaneously with the beginning of manufactures there was a period of vagabondage caused by the abolition of the feudal bodies of retainers, the disbanding of the swollen armies which had flocked to serve the kings against their vassals, the improvement of agriculture, and the transformation of great strips of tillage into pastureland. From this alone it is clear how this vagabondage is strictly connected with the disintegration of the feudal system. As early as the thirteenth century we find isolated epochs of this kind, but only at the end of the fifteenth and beginning of the sixteenth does this vagabondage make a general and permanent appearance. These vagabonds, who were so numerous that, for instance, Henry VIII of England had 72,000 of them hanged, were only prevailed upon to work with the greatest difficulty and through the most extreme necessity, and then only after long resistance. The rapid rise of manufactures, particularly in England, absorbed them gradually.

With the advent of manufactures, the various nations entered into a competitive relationship, the struggle for trade, which was fought out in wars, protective duties, and prohibitions, whereas earlier the nations, insofar as they were connected at all, had carried on an inoffensive exchange with each other. Trade had from now on a political significance.

With the advent of manufacture the relationship between worker and employer changed. In the guilds the patriarchal relationship between journeyman and master continued to exist; in manufacture its place was taken by the monetary relation between worker and capitalist—a relationship which in the countryside and in small towns retained a patriarchal tinge, but in the larger, the real manufacturing towns, quite early lost almost all patriarchal complexion.

Manufacture and the movement of production in general received an enormous impetus through the extension of commerce which came with the discovery of America and the sea route to the East Indies. The new products imported thence, particularly the masses of gold and silver which came into circulation and totally changed the position of the classes towards one another, dealing a hard blow to feudal landed property and to the workers; the expeditions of adventurers, colonization; and above all the extension of markets into a world market, which had now become possible and was daily becoming more and more a fact, called forth a new phase of historical development, into which in general we cannot here enter further. Through the colonization of the newly discovered countries the commercial struggle of the nations among one another was given new fuel and accordingly greater extension and animosity.

The expansion of trade and manufacture accelerated the accumulation of movable capital, while in the guilds, which were not stimulated to extend their production, natural capital remained stationary or even declined. Trade and manufacture created the big bourgeoisie; in the guilds was concentrated the petty bourgeoisie, which no longer was dominant in the towns as formerly, but had to bow to the might of the great merchants and manufacturers.[3] Hence the decline of the guilds, as soon as they came into contact with manufacture.

The intercourse of nations took on, in the epoch of which we have been speaking, two different forms. At first the small quantity of gold and silver in circulation involved the ban on the export of these metals; and industry, for the most part imported from abroad and made necessary by the need for employing the growing urban population, could not do without those privileges which could be granted not only, of course, against home competition, but chiefly against foreign. The local guild privilege was in these original prohibitions extended over the whole nation. Customs duties originated from the tributes which the feudal lords exacted as protective levies against robbery from merchants passing through their territories, tributes later imposed likewise by the towns, and which, with the rise of the modern states, were the Treasury's most obvious means of raising money.

The appearance of American gold and silver on the European markets, the gradual development of industry, the rapid expansion of trade and the consequent rise of the nonguild bourgeoisie and of money, gave these measures another significance. The state, which was daily less and less able to do without money, now retained the ban on the export of gold and silver out of fiscal considerations; the bourgeois, for whom these masses of money which were hurled onto the market became the chief object of speculative buying, were thoroughly content with this; privileges established earlier became a source of income for the government and were sold for money; in the customs legislation there appeared the export duty, which, since it only [placed] a hindrance in the way of industry, had a purely fiscal aim.

The second period began in the middle of the seventeenth century and lasted almost to the end of the eighteenth. Commerce and navigation had expanded more rapidly than manufacture, which played a secondary role; the colonies were becoming considerable consumers; and after long struggles the separate nations shared out the opening world market among themselves. This period begins with the Navigation Laws and colonial monopolies. The competition of the nations among themselves was excluded as far as possible by tariffs, prohibitions, and treaties; and in the last resort the competitive struggle was carried on and decided by wars (especially naval wars). The mightiest maritime nation, the English, retained preponderance in trade and manufacture. Here, already, we find concentration in one country.

Manufacture was all the time sheltered by protective duties in the home market, by monopolies in the colonial market, and abroad as much as possible by differential duties. The working-up of home-produced material was encouraged (wool and linen in England, silk in France), the export of home-produced raw material forbidden (wool in England), and the [working-up] of imported material neglected or suppressed (cotton in England). The nation dominant in sea trade and colonial power naturally secured for itself also the greatest quantitative and qualitative expansion of manufacture. Manufacture could not be carried on without protection, since, if the slightest change takes place in other countries, it can lose its market and be ruined; under reasonably favorable conditions it may easily be introduced into a country, but for this very reason can easily be destroyed. At the same time through the mode in which it is carried on, particularly in the eighteenth century, in the countryside, it is to such an extent interwoven with the vital relationships of a great mass of individuals, that no country dare jeopardize its existence by permitting free competition. Insofar as it manages to export, it therefore depends entirely on the extension or restriction of commerce, and exercises a relatively very small reaction [on the latter]. Hence its secondary [importance] and the influence of [the merchants] in the eighteenth century. It was the merchants and especially the shippers who more than anybody else pressed for state protection and monopolies; the manufacturers also demanded and indeed received protection, but all the time were inferior in political importance to the merchants. The commercial towns, particularly the maritime towns, became to some extent civilized and acquired the outlook of the big bourgeoisie, but in the factory towns an extreme petite-bourgeois outlook persisted. Cf. Aiken, etc. The eighteenth century was the century of trade. Pinto says this expressly: "Le commerce fait la marotte du siècle";[4] and: "Depuis quelque temps il n'est plus question que de commerce, de navigation et de marine."[5]

This period is also characterized by the cessation of the bans on the export of gold and silver and the beginning of the trade in money; by banks, national debts, paper money; by speculation in stocks and shares and stockjobbing in all articles; by the development of finance in general. Again capital lost a great part of the natural character which had still clung to it.

The concentration of trade and manufacture in one country, England, developing irresistibly in the seventeenth century, gradually created for this country a relative world market, and thus a demand for the manufactured products of this country, which could no longer be met by the industrial productive forces hitherto existing. This demand, outgrowing the productive forces, was the motive power which, by producing big industry—the application of elemental forces to industrial ends, machinery, and the most complex division of labor—called into existence the third period of private ownership since the Middle Ages. There already existed in England the other preconditions of this new phase: freedom of competition inside the nation, the development of theoretical mechanics, etc. (Indeed, the science of mechanics perfected by Newton was altogether the most popular science in France and England in the eighteenth century.) (Free competition inside the nation itself had everywhere to be conquered by a revolution—1640 and 1688 in England, 1789 in France.) Competition soon compelled every country that wished to retain its historical role to protect its manufactures by renewed customs regulations (the old duties were no longer any good against big industry) and soon after to introduce big industry under protective duties. Big industry universalized competition in spite of these protective measures (it is practical free trade; the protective duty is only a palliative, a measure of defense *within* free trade), established means of communication and the modern world market, subordinated trade to itself, transformed all capital into industrial capital, and thus produced the rapid circulation (development of the financial system) and the centralization of capital. By universal competition it forced all individuals to strain their energy to the utmost. It destroyed as far as possible ideology, religion, morality, etc., and where it could not do this, made them into a palpable lie. It produced world history for the first time, insofar as it made all civilized nations and every individual member of them dependent for the satisfaction of their wants on the whole world, thus destroying the former natural exclusiveness of separate nations. It made natural science subservient to capital and took from the division of labor the last semblance of its natural character. It destroyed natural growth in general, as far as this is possible while labor exists, and resolved all natural relationships into money relationships. In the place of naturally grown towns it created the modern, large industrial cities which have sprung up overnight. Wherever it penetrated, it destroyed the crafts and all earlier stages of industry. It completed the victory of the commercial town over the countryside. [Its first premise] was the automatic system. [Its development] produced a mass of productive forces, for which private [property] became just as much a fetter as the guild had been for manufacture and the small, rural workshop for the developing craft. These productive forces received under the system of private property a one-sided development only, and became for the majority destructive forces; moreover, a great multitude of such forces could find no application at all within this system. Generally speaking, big industry created everywhere the same relations between the classes of society, and thus destroyed the peculiar individuality of the various nationalities. And finally, while the bourgeoisie of each nation still retained separate national interests, big industry created a class, which in all nations has the same interest and with which nationality is already dead; a class which is really rid of all the old world and at the same time stands pitted against it. Big industry makes for the worker not only the relation to the capitalist, but labor itself, unbearable.

It is evident that big industry does not reach the same level of development in all districts of a country. This does not, however, retard the class movement of the proletariat, because the proletarians created by big industry assume leadership of this movement and carry the whole mass along with them, and because the workers excluded from big industry are placed by it in a still worse situation than the workers in big industry itself. The countries in which big industry is developed act in a similar manner upon the more or less nonindustrial countries, insofar as the latter are swept by universal commerce into the universal competitive struggle.[6]

These different forms are just so many forms of the organization of labor, and hence of property. In each period a unification of the existing productive forces takes place, insofar as this has been rendered necessary by needs.

The Relation of State and Law to Property

The first form of property, in the ancient world as in the Middle Ages, is tribal property, determined with the Romans chiefly by war, with the Germans by the rearing of cattle. In the case of the ancient peoples, since several tribes live together in one town, the tribal property appears as state property, and the right of the individual to it as mere "possession" which, however, like tribal property as a whole, is confined to landed property only. Real private property began with the ancients, as with modern nations, with movable property—(slavery and community) (*dominium ex jure Quiritum.*)[7] In the case of the nations which grew out of the Middle Ages, tribal property evolved through various stages—feudal landed property, corporative movable property, capital invested in manufacture—to modern capital, determined by big industry and universal competition, i.e., pure private property, which has cast off all semblance of a communal institution and has shut out the state from any influence on the development of property. To this modern private property corresponds the modern state, which, purchased gradually by the owners of property by means of taxation, has fallen entirely into their hands through the national debt, and its existence has become wholly dependent on the commercial credit which the owners of property, the bourgeois, extend to it, as reflected in the rise and fall of state funds on the stock exchange. By the mere fact that it is a *class* and no longer an *estate*, the bourgeoisie is forced to organize itself no longer locally, but nationally, and to give a general form to its mean average interest. Through the emancipation of private property from the community, the state has become a separate entity, beside and outside civil society; but it is nothing more than the form of organization which the bourgeois necessarily adopt both for internal and external purposes, for the mutual guarantee of their property and interests. The independence of the state is only found nowadays in those countries where the estates have not yet completely developed into classes, where the estates, done away with in more advanced countries, still have a part to play, and where there exists a mixture; countries, that is to say, in which no one section of the population can achieve dominance over the others. This is the case particularly in Germany. The most perfect example of the modern state is North America. The modern French, English, and American writers all express the opinion that the state exists only for the sake of private property, so that this fact has penetrated into the consciousness of the normal man.

Since the state is the form in which the individuals of a ruling class assert their common interests, and in which the whole civil society of an epoch is epitomized, it follows that the state mediates in the formation of all common institutions and that the institutions receive a political form. Hence the illusion that law is based on the will, and indeed on the will divorced from its real basis—on *free* will. Similarly, justice is in its turn reduced to the actual laws.

Civil law develops simultaneously with private property out of the disintegration of the natural community. With the Romans the development of private property and civil law had no further industrial and commercial consequences, because their whole mode of production did not alter.[8] With modern peoples, where the feudal community was disintegrated by industry and trade, there began with the rise of private property and civil law a new phase, which was capable of further development. The very first town which carried on an extensive maritime trade in the Middle Ages, Amalfi, also developed maritime law. As soon as industry and trade developed private property further, first in Italy and later in other countries, the highly developed Roman civil law was immediately adopted again and raised to authority. When later the bourgeoisie had acquired so much power that the princes took up its interests in order to overthrow the feudal nobility by means of the bourgeoisie, there began in all countries—in France in the sixteenth century—the real development of law, which in all countries except England proceeded on the basis of the Roman Codex. In England, too, Roman legal principles had to be introduced to further the development of civil law (especially in the case of movable property). (It must not be forgotten that law has just as little an independent history as religion.)

In civil law the existing property relationships are declared to be the result of the general will. The *jus utendi et abutendi*[9] itself asserts on the one hand the fact that private property has become entirely independent of the community, and on the other the illusion that private property itself is based solely on the private will, the arbitrary disposal of the thing. In practice, the *abuti*[10] has very definite economic limitations for the owner of private property, if he does not wish to see his property and hence his *jus abutendi* pass into other hands, since actually the thing, considered merely with reference to his will, is not a thing at all, but only becomes a thing, true property in intercourse, and independently of the law (a *relationship*, which the philosophers call an idea.)[11] This juridical illusion, which reduces law to the mere will, necessarily leads, in the further development of property relationships, to the position that a man may have a legal title to a thing without really having the thing. If, for instance, the income from a piece of land is lost owing to competition, then the proprietor has certainly his legal title to it along with the *jus utendi et abutendi*. But he can do nothing with it: he owns nothing as a landed proprietor if in addition he has not enough capital to cultivate his ground. This illusion of the jurists also explains the fact that for them, as for every code, it is altogether fortuitous that individuals enter into relationships among themselves (e.g., contracts); it explains why they consider that these relationships [can] be entered into or not at will, and that their content rests purely on the individual [free] will of the contracting parties.

Whenever, through the development of industry and commerce, new forms of intercourse have been evolved (e.g., insurance companies, etc.), the law has always been compelled to admit them among the modes of acquiring property.

Notes

1. Marginal note by Marx: "To begin with it absorbs the branches of labor directly belonging to the state and then all ± [more or less] ideological estates."
2. Marginal note by Marx: "and the manufacture of glass in the Middle Ages."
3. Marginal note by Marx: "Petty bourgeoisie—middle class—big bourgeoisie."
4. "Commerce is the rage of the century."
5. "For some time now people have been talking only about commerce, navigation, and the navy." [The movement of capital, although considerably accelerated, still remained, however, relatively slow. The splitting-up of the world market into separate parts, each of which was exploited by a particular nation, the exclusion of competition among themselves on the part of the nations, the clumsiness of production itself, and the fact that finance was only evolving from its early stages, greatly impeded circulation. The consequence of this was a haggling, mean, and niggardly spirit which still clung to all merchants and to the whole mode of carrying on trade. Compared with the manufacturers, and above all with the craftsmen, they were certainly big bourgeois; compared with the merchants and industrialists of the next period they remain petty bourgeois. Cf. Adam Smith.—*Marx*]
6. Competition separates individuals from one another, not only the bourgeois but still more the workers, in spite of the fact that it brings them together. Hence it is a long time before these individuals can unite, apart from the fact that for the purposes of this union—if it is not to be merely local—the necessary means, the great industrial cities and cheap and quick communications, have first to be produced by big industry. Hence every organized power standing over against these isolated individuals, who live in relationships daily reproducing this isolation, can only be overcome after long struggles. To demand the opposite would be tantamount to demanding that competition should not exist in this definite epoch of history, or that

the individuals should banish from their minds relationships over which in their isolation they have no control. [*Marx*]

7. Ownership in accordance with the law applying to full Roman citizens.

8. Marginal note by Engels: "(Usury)"

9. The right of using and consuming (also: abusing), i.e., of disposing of a thing at will.

10. Consuming or abusing.

11. Marginal note by Marx: "*For the philosophers relationship = idea.* They only know the relation of 'Man' to himself and hence for them all real relations become ideas."

Chapter 15

FROM *THE TRANSFORMATION OF CORPORATE CONTROL*

NEIL FLIGSTEIN

MY CENTRAL THESIS is that the viability of the large industrial enterprise in the United States is most related to the long-term shifts in the conception of how the largest firms should operate to preserve their growth and profitability. These shifts have occurred in response to a complex set of interactions between the largest firms, those who have risen to control those firms, and the government. They originated with managers and entrepreneurs who sought more control over their internal and external environments. When one solution was blocked by the actions of the government, new solutions were created and diffused. The result was a shift to a new conception of the large corporation and hence a new set of strategies and structures.

These changes were not the product of profit-maximizing actors in efficient firms working to become more efficient. Managers and entrepreneurs were not optimizers or satisficers. Instead, they constructed new courses of action based on their analyses of the problems of control they faced. The new conceptions and the strategies and structures that resulted were successful to the degree they allowed firms to survive and grow.

Consider, for example, the finance conception of the firm: the purpose of the firm is to increase short-run profits by manipulating assets in order to produce growth through mergers and diversification. This conception has come to dominate the world of the largest firms and for those firms has generated a successful strategy for growth. Indeed, between 1947 and 1985, the asset concentration of the five hundred largest manufacturing companies increased from 42 percent to 76 percent. Most of this increase occurred through diversified mergers. This conception, however, has had the ironic effect of promoting the health and growth of the largest firms, while impeding expansion of manufacturing facilities. For those who control the largest firms, their actions have been profitable and sensible. For the economy as a whole, the effects have been less positive.

The current system has come about in a complex, yet explicable way. It emerged under a certain set of rules and as those rules changed, the system changed. These changes were driven by managers and entrepreneurs seeking tactics for survival in the face of economic crisis, instability in their relations with competitors, and the restrictions of antitrust laws. The finance conception of the large corporation, consequently, is the historical product of a dynamic system.

In the scholarly literature, there exist two opposing images of the large, modern corporation. The first stresses the success of the corporate form as a vehicle that deploys capital efficiently to maximize returns. The heroes of this version of the corporation are the top managers who maintain control through decentralized administration and detailed financial reporting. These tools allow top managers to assess problems and react quickly to shifts in markets, technology, and consumer preferences.

The second version focuses on the failure of the modern firm as inefficient with low-quality production leading to an inability to compete in world markets. Managers, rather than being heroes, rule over bloated bureaucracies that do not produce sufficiently high returns on investment to stockholders. Instead, these managers concentrate on their personal aggrandizement by surrounding themselves with large staffs and perquisites. This poor performance is measured by the fall of a firm's stock price below the book value of its assets.

These descriptions evaluate the firm primarily in financial terms. Both accounts place too much responsibility for the success or failure of the corporation on managers. While managers have played a central role in the transformation of the large corporation, they have done so in ways that are much more subtle and constrained than either point of view would acknowledge. Neither version theorizes the context of production or allows for the interaction between managers' ideas about appropriate corporate behavior, how the firms actually work, and what is occurring in the organizations surrounding the firm. In any given moment, there exists a conventional wisdom that guides action, and managers face pressures to conform to that view. The internal strategy and structure of existing firms reflect organized power and interests. Managers, as part of those organized interests, behave to preserve what is. The organizations that surround the firm provide constant clues as to what is occurring in the firm's product markets. This information is filtered and interpreted and greatly affects what actions are possible.

Neither point of view considers the state's effect on corporations. For instance, corporate charters were granted by the various levels of government, and the rights and privileges of the corporate form have depended on legislatures and courts. The state also drew the boundaries of appropriate corporate behavior in defining how markets were to be constructed. The antitrust laws defined the limits of competitive behavior and had a great effect on possible courses of action. In these ways, the worlds of top managers have always been highly structured and their actions shaped by social and political contexts.

Finally, neither point of view takes the problem of constructing managerial courses of action seriously enough; the motives of managers are taken to be somewhat obvious. In the first description, managers act as maximizers for the benefit of the stockholders, and in the second they act against those interests and narrowly for their own. The problem is that courses of action are constructed not with reference to the manager and the issue of self-interest (whether it be that of the shareholder or the manager), but rather in terms of the social context in which managers operate. The existence of conceptions of the firm and the strategies and structures they imply, the example of competitors' behavior, and the actual experiences of the managers in the firm make plotting a course of action depend on what is viewed as appropriate or normative in their worlds. Managers may seek profits, but the ways they choose to do so will tend to be consistent with the existing distribution of power in their organization and similar organizations.

Courses of action are determined by a legal framework and a self-conscious version of the world that make both old and new courses of action possible and desirable. Like everyone else, managers tend to see the world in a certain way and the framing of action often takes place in a context where the action taken was the only and obvious one. New courses of action require risk takers with alternative conceptions of the world. Some succeed and others fail, but if the winners outnumber the losers the course of action will spread through the business community and become the new obvious tactic. Given the high cost of failure, it should not be surprising that there have been relatively few conceptions of the corporation and few accepted courses of action.

In the neoclassical theory of the firm, the motives and actions of managers and entrepreneurs presume that firms must maximize profits. What I will examine is how they have chosen to do so. I claim that the central goal of managers in the past hundred years has been to make sure their firms survived. To promote survival they proposed various forms of control, both inside and outside the firm. Internally, control was oriented to ensuring that organizational resources were deployed so that top management could be confident that their directives were being executed. Externally, this control was oriented toward establishing stable relations between competitors to promote the survival of their organizations. This search for control had other constituencies: boards of directors, labor, and middle management on the inside and the state on the outside. It was difficult to construct courses of action leading to stability. Once in place, these conceptions tended to remain stable for relatively long periods of time. Nevertheless, the concern with survival and control did not produce one solution that held sway forever.

Indeed, shocks to stable structures meant that managers and entrepreneurs had to analyze their problems differently at various points in time and then construct new solutions.

Organizational Theory

In my organizational history of the large modern corporation over the past hundred years I use a distinctly sociological framework that originates in current organizational theory. To support the arguments I also use the tools of both the historian and the economist.

Organizational theory focuses on three relevant institutional contexts in which the transformation of organizations takes place.[1] First, organizations are embedded in larger groups of organizations which are called organizational fields that may be defined in terms of product line, industry, or firm size. The other organizations are most frequently competitors, although sometimes they are suppliers, distributors, or owners. Second, the state sets the rules that define what organizations can do and what the limits of legal behavior are. Third, organizations have in place a set of strategies, structures, technologies, and physical limits that shape and constrain their patterns of growth and change.

The existence of organizational fields is established by the mutual recognition of actors in different firms of their interdependence. These actors share a similar conception of legitimate action and the place of each organization in that field. The function of organizational fields is, first and foremost, to promote stability. They are the basic mechanism of control of the external environment available to managers and entrepreneurs.

Organizational fields are not generally benign and cooperative arrangements held in place by a sense of duty or honor, although the rhetoric and ideology of their proponents might lead one to think so. Instead, they are set up to benefit their most powerful members. These firms have often organized the rules and have the power to enforce them. The most important determinants of that power are the size of the firms and the ability of actors in them to prevent other organizations from entering their fields. Large size implies they have resources to undercut possible competitors. The most common barriers to entry are patents, technologies, and large initial investments.

From the point of view of actors in less powerful organizations in the field, the reasons to support the dominant organizations all revolve around survival. Direct challenges to the leading firms may result in persecution of the smaller or weaker firms. The conditions that promote the stability of the organizational field also lead to stability for the less powerful members of those fields. Being a member of the field, albeit a dependent one, is one way to survive. While competition continues to exist, it is no longer predatory.

For these reasons, once stable organizational fields come into existence, it is in the interest of all organizations in the field not to upset them.

The actual formation of organizational fields requires a high level of social organization. Managers or entrepreneurs in leading firms must articulate a set of rules to control the field and be willing and able to enforce those rules. In order to do this, actors in one firm must have the ability to observe their competitors. For these reasons, organizational fields are more likely to form where the number of leading organizations is small or where some form of trade association exists. Through observation of one another managers construct courses of action and find market niches for themselves. The problem is deciding whom to watch and how to interpret their actions.

There have been many extensively constructed organizational fields. The first were built around single products, but as time went on and large firms diversified, reference groups changed. By the 1930s managers in the largest firms viewed their organizational fields as industries, not just product lines. In the past twenty-five years managers of the largest firms have come to define their organizational fields in terms of the group of the largest firms, as well as entire industries. Many of the largest firms are highly diversified and the firms their managers watch are naturally those whom they most wish to resemble. This means that the dominant conception of the large corporation is generally held by all of the largest firms.

The largest firms have the most influence on the stability of their organizational fields. They also provide examples of success to the constituent members. Actors in organizations exist in murky worlds where the consequence of any given action is unclear and the definition of any given situation is open to interpretation. Because of this they mimic what they perceive as successful strategies and organizational innovations in their fields. The dependency on and the example of successful large organizations cause actors in less powerful organizations to conform to the patterns and expectations of their more powerful neighbors. Fields define normative behavior, but they depend on the relative power of the largest, most successful firms to enforce those norms.

Organizational fields can be destabilized by a number of forces. Most frequently, organizations from outside the field upset the status quo and create new rules. Often, innovative behavior occurs in newly emerging organizational fields, fields whose structures and rules have yet to coalesce. If their behavior is observed as producing relatively successful results, it can spread to neighboring fields. Macroeconomic and political shocks can produce crises that destabilize the power structure of an already existing field. In such a situation, actors in leading organizations within a field can respond to internal or external crises by changing their behavior and thereby altering the rules. This kind of transformation is somewhat rare, as it involves great risks and potential undermining of their control.

The state is made up of the organizations, institutions, and practices that constitute the political function of any given society. The organizations each have agendas that are determined by the political actors that control them and the economic and social forces that lurk behind the political process. The organizations of the state are driven by actors who have interests shaped by different, and often conflicting, purposes.

The state is an important force in the economy in several ways. It defines the rules by which actions in the economy are carried out. It is one thing to say you are in favor of free markets, and quite another to actually define what a free market is. That definition has shifted over time and the dispute has primarily been between firms and the state. Laws regarding incorporation, antitrust, and the regulation of various industries are important aspects of state definitions. The state also affects the economy by consuming products, intervening in the business cycle, and providing for the redistribution of income through taxation and social expenditures.

State actions can have both intended and unintended consequences. A state action may be to limit the power of the large firm, the intended consequence. For example, if the state decides to outlaw monopolies, and its actions are effective, no monopolies will exist. However, the state's actions may have unintended consequences. By foreclosing the possibility for monopoly and collusion between firms in a single market, the state opens other possibilities for firms. In the United States, for example, two alternative courses of action emerged when monopolies were outlawed: oligopoly conditions in a number of industries where one or several firms shared a large portion of a given market and maintained stable prices, and product diversification, where firms achieved stability by spreading their risks across products. Neither of these results was intended by the state. But by eliminating possibilities, the state encourages organizations in society to innovate. It places limits on legal behavior so that firms must find new courses of action given those limits. Once new tactics are taken by firms, actors in the state have to decide on what subsequent course of action to take. This sets the cycle in motion again.

Perhaps the most pressing theoretical issue in political sociology today is the relative autonomy of the state. This issue basically turns on the question of how and in whose interests policy is made. Marxists view the state as controlled by the interests of capital while pluralists see the state as the arena where political conflict between groups is adjudicated. Max Weber proposed that the state is a structure controlled by actors with their own interests in organizing society. In this sense, the state can be viewed as a set of organizations that act autonomously from the economy.

The relationship between the state and large firms generally has been to serve the interests of the firms. At times, state agencies have been captured by corporate interests, and policies are made for their benefit. The state can, however, act as a mediator between interests and in its own interests, and the problem of deciding what is occurring is an empirical question. For instance, antitrust laws and their enforcement are deep-rooted issues concerning the legitimacy of the entire system. It is not surprising that firms resist their implementation, while the electorate generally favors them. Antitrust efforts have a bureaucratic constituency in the Justice Department and the Federal Trade Commission. The concern over the issue has waxed and waned in both the legislative and executive branches, however, depending on who has held power in them.

The internal structuring of the organization is the final arena to consider. As it turns out, there have not been many organizational innovations in the past hundred years. This reflects the fact that managers in organizations are generally highly constrained and that to change the course of the large firm requires taking huge risks. Equally important, managers and entrepreneurs have a stake in what exists. They have an organizational story about what the organization does and how it does it. Those who are in control generally base that control on existing organizational strategy and structure. This illustrates one of the central insights of organizational theory: organizations tend not to change what they are doing because of deep-seated interests to continue business as usual. Only when those interests can be changed do organizations strike out on new courses of action.

The major impetus toward such change can be generated internally or externally. In either case it will rely on a perceived crisis. The crisis can be that the company is losing money, or only that actors in the company want to achieve more growth or profits. Either way, certain actors in key organizations must interpret their organization's problems and propose a solution, which can follow practices of other organizations in their field or be novel. But in order for the solution to be carried out, the actors must have the power to act. Organizational innovation will often occur in new organizations where there is not an established set of practices or power relations between key actors or in organizational fields where rules are not firmly established.

All large organizations have an internal power struggle over the goals and resources of the organization. Those who control the resources use them to force their view of appropriate organizational behavior. In the largest firms, there are two bases of control: formal ownership and authority. Those who own the firm control by virtue of ownership. Authority relations embedded in the organizational structure legitimate how managers can control organizations. In the large modern corporation, the set of managers who control the organization has changed over the past one hundred years. Structural position is determined by observing the subunit in the organization from which the president or chief executive officer (CEO) originates. Aside from entrepreneurs, the subunits of power represented are manufacturing, sales and marketing, and finance. The basis for claims on organizational power concern the ability of executives in these three functional subunits to propose solutions to organizational crises.

Actors who control organizations, be they in the employ of the state or firms, must interpret their organizational fields and then make policy based on their reading of those fields. This policy, by necessity, will be bounded by the internal logic of their organizations, what those actors know, how they perceive the world, and what they define as appropriate organizational behavior. The perspective that managers and entrepreneurs develop can be called a conception of control. This term refers to the fact that these actors want to control their internal and external environments. The way in which they try to achieve and exercise control is dependent upon their perspective of what constitutes appropriate behavior. Conceptions of control are totalizing worldviews that cause actors to interpret every situation from a given perspective. They are forms of analysis used by actors to find solutions to the current problems of the organization. At the center of conceptions of control are simplifying assumptions about how the world is to be analyzed.

A distinction can be made between a conception of appropriate organizational action and organizational strategy. The conception of control refers to a totalizing worldview of managers or entrepreneurs that causes them to filter the problems of the world in a certain way. This means that two individuals with different conceptions will perceive a given organizational crisis differently and indeed one of them may see no crisis whatsoever. It also means their analysis may lead them to propose different solutions to the problem. An organizational strategy refers to the actual goals of the organization and the policies put in place to reach those goals. The conception of control refers to why managers view those strategies as appropriate for what the firm ought to do. Differing conceptions generally imply a small set of strategies which will be consistent with the orientation of each conception. Different conceptions of control may implement the same strategy, but they will interpret the efficacy of that strategy in their own terms.

To illustrate this distinction, diversification is one organizational strategy. It reflects a policy of the organization concerning its product mix. But the conceptions of control that support diversification give different reasons for pursuing that course of action. For example, a sales and marketing executive may diversify product lines in order to have a full line of goods to sell customers. A finance executive will view the same diversification as a way to spread risk for the firm. The strategy of increasing the number of products is the same for both executives, but the meaning each attaches to the action is quite different.

Managers' and entrepreneurs' conceptions create different views about how control is to be achieved. Their actions will be justified as ways to extend their control over the situation at hand. These conceptions are not static, but depend on interaction with the world. The model of action proposed is not to be mistaken for either the rational or bounded rational actors of economic theory. Actors are assumed to construct *rationales* for their behavior on the basis of how they view the world. Their goals and strategies result from those views and are not the product of an abstract rationality. The construction of courses of action depends greatly on the position of actors within the structure of the organization, which forms the interests and identities of actors.

Setting the Stage

In my study I concentrate on the one thousand largest industrial enterprises in the United States *since 1880*. Since membership in this group has been fluid (indeed, it would be hard to identify the one thousand largest corporations in 1880), my goal is to understand how the group was transformed in terms of conception, identity, strategy, and structure. Most of the quantitative data presented actually refer to a much smaller group, the one hundred or five hundred largest firms. The manufacturing and mining sector of the economy is my central focus, although I also discuss firms engaged in retail and entertainment. I do not consider the financial sector, however. My emphasis instead is on the goods-producing and goods-distributing sectors of the economy.

I use a number of key constructs throughout this book. These terms reflect the theoretical arguments just made, but apply more precisely to the large modern corporation. My analysis revolves around six key notions. *Conception of control* is a perspective on how firms ought to solve their competitive problems and is collectively held and reflected in their organizational fields. Constructs that concern the internal organization of the firm are its *strategy*, *structure*, and *subunit power base*. The *state* and the *organizational field* constitute the firm's external environment.

The primary question is how the *conceptions of control* in the largest U.S. firms have been transformed in the past one hundred years. The strategies, structures, and organizational fields that have emerged embody these different conceptions. Once in place as control perspectives, they are widely shared ways of reducing the complexity of the world. They come into existence in a piecemeal fashion and are articulated by representatives of the largest, most successful firms. They are propagated by the business press and informal links between organizations and then are supported by those organizations and their organizational fields.

Since 1880 there have been only four conceptions of control used by the leaders of the largest firms: direct control of competitors, manufacturing control, sales and marketing control, and finance control. These conceptions are not disembodied, idealist constructs. They emerged from the interaction among leaders of large firms and are conditioned by the state. They become successful by helping create organizational fields and by being accepted as principles to guide action within those fields. Once they prove successful, they disseminate across organizational fields. Each conception of control makes use of a small number of consistent actions, or strategies. *Strategy* implies an explicit understanding of the goals of the organization and the construction of appropriate courses of action for reaching those goals.

The conception of the firm that emphasizes direct *control of one's competitors* became dominant in the late nineteenth century. At the time there were no rules governing behavior among competitors and there were no stable organizational fields. The intent of the conception of the firm that emerged under these chaotic conditions was to lessen competition. Managers and entrepreneurs, in an effort to achieve stability for their firms, attacked their most important competitors. Since there were few laws or rules guiding behavior, almost anything was acceptable. There were only two ways to protect one's firm: attack others before they attacked you or if this failed unite with your competitors to stop competition. Often firms moved from confrontation to cooperation. Within the direct control conception of the firm, three strategies were evident: predatory trade practices, cartelization, and monopolization.

The first strategy consisted of engaging in different forms of predatory competition. These included price competition, making it difficult for competitors to obtain raw materials for their production processes, and disrupting competitors' sales through legal and illegal means. Patents were another way to control competitors. Another tactic was secretly to purchase a competitor's stock and continue to operate the firm as a separate entity. An extension of this was for firms under common ownership to form what were called "communities of interest" to control competition. A large proportion of the antitrust suits in the early part of the twentieth century were directed toward these predatory trade practices.

The second strategy to directly control competitors was cartelization. Cartels involved elaborate written agreements to divide territory, assign production quotas, or set prices. Trade associations were often the vehicle for making these arrangements. Cartels were always defined around product lines and represented the first step toward establishing stable organizational fields.

The third control strategy was to try and create monopolies. Managers and entrepreneurs reasoned that if all of the productive forces of a given product line could be concentrated under a single ownership, then production and prices would stabilize. The merger movement at the turn of the century reflected the desire of managers and entrepreneurs to organize holding companies that would control a substantial portion of product lines.

The problem of controlling competition persisted well into the twentieth century. The manufacturing conception of control then attempted to solve it by stabilizing the production process and creating oligopolistic pricing conditions in organizational fields. The central goal was to manufacture a product without interference from competitors by controlling inputs and outputs through the vertical and horizontal integration of production. These defensive measures tended to make the production process operate more effectively and lessen costs. Another part of this conception was to protect the firm by making it larger than its competitors. Once this control was achieved, then competitors would have less incentive for direct confrontation because they did not want to risk becoming engaged in a price war that would threaten everyone. From the manufacturing perspective, a firm's best way to control was stable, reliable, and cost-effective production.

The strategies pursued to achieve this control were backwards and forwards integration of production, mergers to increase market share, and the creation of oligopolistic product markets. Vertical integration meant that managers and entrepreneurs extended their control by absorbing suppliers and marketing functions into their organization. This protected them from the predatory acts of their competitors who would attempt to disrupt their suppliers or customers. It also lowered the overall cost of production and allowed firms to compete only with other large firms. A large market share obtained through mergers protected the production process of the firm by making it able to threaten competitors who might engage in price wars. Once a small number of large vertically integrated producers existed in a given organizational field, they used their market power to set up oligopolistic price structures. They would publicize their prices for a given commodity and because of their influence most of their competitors followed suit.

The sales and marketing conception of the firm began with the marketing revolution of the 1920s and came to dominate the largest firms in the post–World War II era. This conception of control emphasized that the key problem for firms was the selling of goods, and therefore the solution was to expand sales. The sales and marketing conception focused the firm's attention on finding, creating, and keeping markets. The strategies that this conception inspired were oriented toward growth by nonpredatory competition. The view of what the corporation should be was radically altered from one focused on the destruction or control of competitors, to one concerned with its continuous expansion.

The sales and marketing perspective created a number of strategies: differentiation from competitors in terms of product quality and price; more advertising to increase market share; new products to stimulate growth; and expanded markets for existing goods, particularly overseas. Advertising was the major way in which firms were able to differentiate products from competitors and guarantee market share. Advertising also meant that price competition lessened as qualitative differences between products became important to their success. Expanding markets nationally and internationally allowed firms to continuously grow without cannibalizing their competitor's market share. The diversification of firms provided some security that when one product line faltered, another would emerge to take its place and produce growth. The organizational fields of the largest firms shifted from those based on products to those based on whole industries as firms diversified their product lines.

The finance conception of the modern corporation, which currently dominates, emphasizes control through the use of financial tools which measure performance according to profit rates. Product lines are evaluated on their short-run profitability, and important management decisions are based on the potential profitability of each line. Firms are viewed as collections of assets earning differing rates of return, not as producers of given goods. The firm is not seen as being a member of only one industry. Consequently if the prospect of an industry in which it participates declines, the firm disinvests. The problem for management from this perspective is to maximize short-run rates of return by altering product mix, thereby increasing shareholder equity and keeping the stock price high.

The key strategies are diversification through mergers and divestments (as opposed to internal expansion); financial ploys to increase the stock price, indebtedness, and ability to absorb other firms; and the use of financial controls to make decisions about the internal allocation of capital. The product mix of firms is less important in the finance conception because each of the firm's businesses is no longer a product line, but a profit center. Since the goal is to increase assets and profits, the organizational fields of the finance-driven firms are no longer industrial based. Once large firms began to pay more attention to one another than to industries or products, strategic innovations that reflected the finance conception of control spread more rapidly across the population of the large firms. Currently, leveraged buyouts, stock repurchases, and corporate restructuring, which all reflect the finance conception, have disseminated throughout the largest firms as appropriate strategies for growth and profits.

The successive conceptions contain elements of their immediate predecessors: each was built on the insights and successes of what came before. The search for price stability was the central motivation of those who tried direct controls. Firms with the manufacturing perspective tried to achieve that price stability through the internal control of the production process and the creation of organizational fields based on oligopolistic pricing. The sales and marketing conception led to the realization that without sales, production ground to a halt. But the sales and marketing perspective was predicated on the ability to produce goods consistently and reliably for a mass market. The sales and marketing conception provided the impetus for developing the multiproduct, multidivisional firm. The basic insight of the finance conception was that such a firm could be more tightly controlled by strict accounting. This progression does not imply, however, that one conception of control caused the emergence of its successor. New conceptions of control evolved out of key interactions among firms and between firms and the state.

Structure refers to the design of the organization and the lines of authority that link the divisions of the organization and the divisions with the central office. In order to execute strategies, it is necessary in the large corporation to have a sound structure. To the degree that a given structure helps implement the strategies, it will vindicate and strengthen those strategies.

Five structures have been utilized for the large modern corporation: the trust, the holding company, and the unitary, functional, and multidivisional forms. The trust existed for only a few years in the late nineteenth century and represented a loose confederation of corporations. A holding company owns the stock of many companies which are operated from a small central office. The constituent firms often maintain their identities and are generally independent of one another. The unitary and functional forms are quite similar in design. The functional form organized production into departments that reflected the sequential movement of products through production stages. An oil company might contain drilling, shipping, refining, and sales departments, with a central office for financial matters. The unitary form is a simpler version of the functional form. It contains manufacturing, sales and marketing, and finance departments.

The multidivisional form organizes the large firm into product divisions. Each division is responsible for its manufacturing, sales, and financial performance. The central office monitors the divisions through financial controls and makes long-term decisions on investment for the firm. The multidivisional form attempts to distribute day-to-day decision making to executives who are close to production, while holding those same executives accountable for their performance. Almost all large modern corporations are organized into some version of the multidivisional form.

The power struggle within the firm determines which conception of control will dominate and how that conception will be translated into concrete strategies. The winners of this struggle will push the organization in a certain direction and maintain that direction as long as their strategies bring positive results. I use the term *subunit power base* to refer to the group in the organization that currently has claim on its strategy and structure. The power struggle in an organization over its goals takes place within the existing structure. A key position in the structure supplies actors in the struggle with a number of resources, the most important of which is authority. To the degree that owners and managers control their subordinates and can use their subordinates to deliver valuable goods, they can influence higher levels of the organization.

A powerful position in the structure provides actors with access to resources and continued input into the strategies of the organization. When the power relations are stable, then the structure and existing strategies will remain the same. When actors in key positions mobilize themselves and others, they can force strategies and structures to change.

Powerful positions can be characterized not just in terms of structure but also in terms of ideology and function. Actors in different subunits in the organization will think about the world differently. Their formal schooling and on-the-job training will make them see the organization and its problems in a particular way. Managers in charge of production will tend to see the problems of the firm as problems of production, while those in charge of sales will emphasize selling instead. These experiences will shape what organizational goals will be supported by subunit members and define in any given power struggle how members will act. Not surprisingly, the subunit in control will tend to pursue goals consistent with its view of the organization's critical problems.

Three significant subunits of any company involve its manufacturing, sales and marketing, and finance functions. Representatives of each subunit will organize criteria of success that will allow them to claim that a course of action did or did not achieve success. Their ability to take power will depend on how their conception of control operates as a convincing analysis of the firm's problems. That in turn will depend on what is occurring in the firm's organizational field and in its relations to the state. Once in power a subunit will implement strategies and structures consistent with their perspective. Fundamental change in a firm's direction will generally require a new resolution of the internal power struggle, as those in established positions will not want to take actions that would undermine the status quo.

These three ways of analyzing the corporate world imply radically different courses of action. Indeed, executives with these different points of view will analyze any given situation in quite different terms. Since this suggests different interpretations of reality, the problem of deciding when a strategy is working or whether a competitor's strategy is superior is always going to be difficult. I use the term *successful* or *efficient* in this book to signify when actors perceive that a course of action produces superior results over some alternative course of action. Success is a qualitative construct that actors must come to agree about. In the world of managers, there are no profit-maximizing or even satisfying actions. This is because such success is impossible to define strictly from the actor's point of view. Criteria of success are always relative to the organization and its field.

When managers pursue strategies which in the end are not profitable, it is because those actors with power have a limited view of the world. For example, the conglomerate strategy of merging unrelated firms to achieve growth spread quickly through the population of the largest firms. Yet most economic studies show that conglomerates did not earn higher profits than samples of similar size firms that were not pursuing that strategy.

The strategy spread and persisted for two reasons. First, conglomerate mergers produced spectacular rates of growth for firms. Executives in sales and marketing and finance pursued growth for its own sake, as that appeared to increase the stability and status of the firm. As long as profits were at acceptable levels and the stock price remained high, managers pursued growth. Competitors observed this and decided to emulate those actions. Second, once this view of mergers for growth became established, it became an institutionalized myth and accepted as one appropriate way to do business. While disinvestment occurred in the 1970s and early 1980s of many firms that pursued the conglomerate strategy, the largest firms have remained highly diversified despite the lack of evidence their performance was superior.

Organizational fields have shifted in definition from those based on product lines to industry to the population of the largest firms. These shifts have coincided with the shifts in the conception of the largest firms. Organizational fields depend on the actions of the largest firms for their stability. They also allow firms to monitor competitor's actions. They present like firms with evidence of appropriate strategies and structures and define acceptable courses of action for them. Managers may switch organizational fields in order to supply themselves with a new reference group, one that embodies a new strategy or structure and new possibilities for growth. When firms invade existing organizational fields or a firm in a given field develops a new strategy or structure that produces positive results, then executives in other firms follow those examples. One way to determine the existence and boundaries of organizational fields is to assess the limits of the spread of given conceptions, strategies, and structures.

The *state* has been the central arbiter of legal and illegal market behavior on the part of firms. The American government has influenced the American economy in a unique way. The practices that emerged in the largest firms were a response to the state's perception of a need to control markets. These practices reflect only one way of responding to the situation and, as such, are not provided by an a priori reading of the logic of markets. Rather, they are best viewed as a result of the strategic interaction between actors in the state and actors in firms. In this sense, markets in the abstract do not suggest anything about how to organize production. That organization is an outcome of social processes whereby firms interact with one another and the state to produce what can be called a market.

Periodization of Strategies, Structures, and the State

In order to see the historical changes that occur, one cannot begin by claiming that those changes have produced the best, that is, most efficient, organizational forms. This is an extremely teleological way to view history and one that would require comparative historical analysis to sustain. Given the state of our economy today, it would be hard to argue that the large diversified American firm is the most competitive organization in the world. Hence, to argue that the most efficient is what survived is to misunderstand the actual historical process by which the large firms emerged.

An organizational and institutional history reads history forward, not backward. In this book I will attempt to analyze developments from the point of view of the actors involved. By pursuing this strategy and using the organizational theory of the state and firms just proposed, we can recover a nonfunctionalist history of the large modern corporation.

New conceptions of control emerged where stable organizational fields had not existed. A new conception proved its worth by providing stability and profits for its leading practitioners. Once established, new fields remained in existence for long periods of time. Their construction was the solution to the problem of control and helped create norms that guided action in their fields and neighboring ones.

The preconditions for a new conception of control to emerge were twofold. Some form of economic crisis often provided a stimulus for innovation. In the case of unstable organizational fields, that condition was chronic. The economic depressions of the late nineteenth century proved pivotal in the emergence of direct control. Similarly, the depression of the 1930s proved the worth of the sales and marketing conception. The transition from manufacturing control to sales and marketing control resulted when firms were relatively more successful with diversified product strategies.

The state provided the second precondition for the construction of a new course of action. This worked in two ways. First, the state had to decide whether or not the conception of control was legal. Second, the state often took actions that blunted the course of a given conception and thereby opened up the possibility for a new course of action. The state was crucial in the shift from direct control to manufacturing control and the shift from sales and marketing control to finance control. In the first case, it ruled that all forms of direct control were illegal. In the second, the state encouraged mergers for diversification indirectly by banning vertical and horizontal mergers.

The conception of control through direct means had its origins in the post–Civil War era. In this period there were no established organizational fields, no rules to guide trade practices, and no established way to do business. The economy of the period was characterized by periods of growth, followed by inevitable decline because of too much competition. With a rapid expansion of markets and relatively high profit margins, the quantity of goods available increased dramatically. But markets quickly became saturated and there was downward pressure on prices. Many firms were caught with too many goods, too few buyers, and too low prices. Bankruptcies occurred, firms started laying off workers, and demand fell. This situation produced three substantial depressions between 1870 and 1895.

Economic theory predicts that a firm will produce until it no longer can make a profit. Unfortunately, in the nineteenth-century world, firms continued to produce well beyond the point of zero profitability. This was because entrepreneurs incurred substantial costs in shutting down their plants. An idle plant meant their investment was worthless. If they had borrowed money to open the plant, then they were pressured by creditors to keep the plant running to prevent bankruptcy. As long as production continued, the firm might lose money, but it might outlast its competitors and eventually begin to make money again.

Leading executives of the time all decried the cutthroat competition. What they desired was price stability and a fair return on their investments. But there was no way to achieve such goals. There were no rules governing competitive behavior, so firms engaged in many ruthless practices to destroy their competition. Aggressive trade tactics failed as frequently as they succeeded, which forced managers and entrepreneurs to consider cooperative forms of organization. The formation of trade associations or cartels to divide market share, assign production quotas, and set prices were the first attempts at cooperation.

The impetus toward direct forms of control was most strongly felt in the rapidly expanding sectors of the economy where capital investment was the greatest: railroads, steel, oil, and the emerging chemical and electrical machinery industries. The effort to directly control one's competitors was felt most acutely where there was the most to lose. For instance, cartels formed in capital intensive industries where profits were falling. But cartel arrangements were inherently unstable. They were not enforceable by law; hence, there was no legislated consequence for cheating on the agreement. Further, firms who were not party to the agreement could choose to enter the market and undersell the members of the cartel.

While managers and entrepreneurs were trying to regulate competition, the politicians and judges who controlled the state and federal governments consistently opposed such arrangements. This was despite the fact that the state and federal governments generally favored economic development and passed laws granting railroads, merchants, and capitalists great latitude, including creating the limited liability joint stock corporation which was already common by 1870.

The relationship between the state and the emerging large corporations, however, was complicated by a number of factors. The fragmented character of the political system granted the federal government authority to regulate interstate commerce and gave the states power only over intrastate commerce. Firms had to conform to the rules of the state where they did business and that state had the right to grant them corporate charters. Corporate activities could be strictly limited by state actions, which would appear to have given the states a great deal of power over corporations. But as interstate commerce expanded, states lost their ability to control corporations from a different state. They could not interfere with interstate commerce and the courts consistently ruled against the states and for interstate corporations. Since the states did not have uniform incorporation acts, it was advantageous for firms to incorporate in states with the most favorable policy. Managers and entrepreneurs of the largest interstate firms became capable of dictating the rules by which they did business.

Managers and entrepreneurs never got the upper hand when it came to directly interfering with the operation of competitive markets. There was a long tradition in Anglo-American law to make restraints of trade illegal. Almost every state had laws preventing agreements between parties to restrict production or control prices. Firms formed cartels in spite of these laws, as they were willing to do anything to control competition. The longstanding stricture against cartels was formalized in the Sherman Antitrust Act of 1890. The act was most successfully used against arrangements that involved a "conspiracy in restraint of trade."

In Europe during the nineteenth century the governments were generally more favorable toward collusive behavior. Laws existed that made cartel agreements enforceable contracts. As a result they became the major strategy for coping with competition. Representatives of large firms would gather and divide markets by product and region. These cartels had the effect of providing a market for everyone and made even the smallest firms viable. Firms would be sanctioned by other firms for breaking cartel shares by either being denied raw materials or having their markets taken over by other cartel members. Since the cartel agreements were legal, firms had great incentives to comply with them.

Given that cartels were unenforceable contracts in the United States and therefore inherently unstable, there were three alternative strategies of control over competition and prices. First, firms continued to engage in predatory trade practices to destroy their competitors through any means possible. Second, firms tried to have the federal government regulate industries in order to stabilize prices and profits. In the nineteenth century only the railroads tested the strategy and only in the twentieth century did it succeed. Third, firms could end competition by combining the assets in a given product line.

The issue of how to control one's competitors legally was paramount in the late nineteenth century. The trust was formed in the late 1880s as an attempt to avoid the laws that prohibited cartels. Managers and entrepreneurs gave ownership in their firms to a collectively held trust, which was administered by a board of trustees, who most often were the same people who operated the constituent parts of the trust. In return they received shares in the trust equal to the assets they brought to it. The trust was short-lived, however, because state government officials used existing statutes to sanction them. The courts ruled that corporations that formed trusts were restraining trade and that continued participation in the trust would nullify their corporate charters. In the face of these problems the trust form disappeared and was replaced by the holding company.

The holding company was a financial device whereby individual firms were bought by one company with controlling stock in each of them. The firms ran semiautonomously with only financial control emanating from the central office. Since holding companies incorporated in states that allowed corporations to hold stock in other corporations, there was little that state governments could do to prevent their existence. Cases against violators of the Sherman Act in the middle- and late 1890s upheld the right of holding companies to produce near monopolies, yet cartels were ruled to be illegal.

The legality of the holding company and the desire of managers and entrepreneurs to control competition produced the merger movement at the turn of the century. Since cartels were illegal and holding companies were not, firms jumped on the merger bandwagon. Between 1895 and 1905, 35 percent of the assets of American manufacturers were involved in mergers. Industries that had tried cartels were now most likely to engage in consolidation.

The attempt to create monopolies did not end the problem of competition, however. By 1919, about 60 percent of the large mergers had failed. Businesses achieved no economies of scale by consolidating into large corporations. In fact, production costs often increased because firms were difficult or impossible to manage. Many of the industries were easy for other firms to enter and using predatory trade practices to stop them could prove grounds for an antitrust suit.

In the late nineteenth century state governments protected competition in the American economy. But during the first twenty years of this century the federal government assumed this role. The Progressive Era in American politics can be interpreted in two ways: as a liberal era when middle-class reformers adopted populist ideology and attempted to ameliorate some of the worst qualities of the emerging industrial order, or as the triumph of big business. Both interpretations have merit. On the one hand, liberal reformers were not trying to destroy the large firm. On the other hand, legislation such as the Federal Reserve Act furthered the interests of one fraction of capital. The major pieces of legislation to regulate firm relations were the Clayton Act and the Federal Trade Commission Act.

The Clayton Act was an attempt to outlaw specific types of competitive behavior that were thought to lead to monopoly conditions. These included purchasing a competitor's stock to control its actions, tying agreements to force customers to buy nonessential materials in order to get essential materials, and predatory pricing behavior. The authors of the Clayton Act had no intention of attacking already existing corporate concentration, but were oriented toward preventing unfair advantages of one firm over another. The Federal Trade Commission (FTC) was set up to control unfair trade practices, especially price fixing. Its actions were consistent with an economic ideology that defined anticompetitive behavior as collusive direct control of prices. Both acts were consistent with the theory of "restraints of trade" and neither was meant to undermine the power of large firms.

The Sherman Act was also used to great effect during the Progressive Era. Starting with the Northern Securities decision in 1904, enforcers pursued the firms that most closely approached predatory monopolies. The Supreme

Court forced Standard Oil, DuPont, and American Tobacco to divest a substantial portion of their businesses. The laws against price fixing, cartels, monopolization, or other forms of direct control were enforced consistently. The problem of competition for the large firm, therefore, persisted well into the twentieth century. Without collusive arrangements, prices, profits, and market shares were always threatened. Indeed, before World War I the economy continually drifted in and out of recession. The war then provided a market for goods and caused wages, prices, and profits to rise. After the war, prices and wages remained high and that fueled a great period of growth in the 1920s.

The only stable solution to the problem of competition was the manufacturing conception, which emerged when all of the more direct strategies of control were made illegal. The manufacturing conception of control developed in fields of single products or industries, and those tended to be the highly capital-intensive industries, that is, steel, oil, and electrical machinery. The key managers in this endeavor were those engaged in manufacturing the product, since they had the most knowledge of the production process.

Two features of these fields worked together to bring them stability: large firms that were willing to be price leaders and a successful organizational structure, that is, the unitary and functional forms. Large market share gave the leading firm sufficient influence to set prices, and the integrated production apparatus gave it the ability to enforce them by undercutting competitors. The holding company had not been able to coordinate the day-to-day activities of a large number of plants because the central office could not effectively regulate the flow of products. Indeed, single plants could often adapt more easily to changes in supply or demand. Hence, the functional and unitary forms solved the problem by controlling the flow of production.

This tactic of controlling prices was not illegal because there was no direct collusion. One of the leading advocates of the new manufacturing conception was the U.S. Steel Company, which had been formed during the merger movement. Indeed, the antitrust suit against U.S. Steel was decided in its favor: the firm had not intentionally used its large size to damage its competitors. Once it became evident that large vertically integrated firms could control prices legally as oligopolists, the manufacturing conception began to spread. The peak for the manufacturing conception of control was reached during the merger movement of the 1920s.

There were two major reasons why the second merger movement occurred. Mergers were profitable in key industries such as steel, oil, electrical equipment, and chemicals; and the federal government was lax in enforcing the antitrust laws. The Clayton Act, for instance, was interpreted in a very narrow fashion by the Supreme Court, thereby nullifying any effect it might have had on the merger movement. Managers and entrepreneurs, therefore, took this opportunity to increase their market share and stabilize their industry, like the steel industry twenty years earlier, without opposition from the antitrust authorities.

Section 7 of the Clayton Act outlawed the purchase of competitors' stock when doing so would lessen competition. The intent of the law was at least partially to impede the development of monopolies. Four Supreme Court cases were heard in the 1920s which tested this law. Three of the cases involved firms that had purchased the assets and then stock of other firms. One of the cases was against a firm that had purchased the stock first and then the assets. In all four cases the Supreme Court decided for the purchasing firms even though there was evidence the mergers would have anticompetitive effects. Their defense had been that the Clayton Act forbade purchase of stock not assets and therefore the mergers were perfectly legal. When stock was purchased first, but assets were acquired subsequently, the Supreme Court decided there was no case. On the basis of this interpretation of the Clayton Act, any attempts at slowing the merger movement through litigation were eliminated.

The manufacturing solution to competition was successful but placed limits on growth because it was a defensive tactic. In economic downturns, vertically integrated firms faced rapidly declining markets. Since collusion was disallowed, those firms with large investments in fixed capital stock were still vulnerable. The largest firms continued their efforts to control competition through the 1920s and expanded them during the 1930s. Their managers and owners favored some form of legalized price fixing before the depression.

The National Industrial Recovery Act gave firms the right to set reasonable prices and workers the right to unionize. The philosophy of the act was to increase profits by increasing prices, thereby expanding business. Unions would guarantee higher wages and job security and workers would have more money, thereby increasing consumption. The effect of the act, however, was to raise prices but not production and consumption. It failed to produce industrial recovery as promised and would have disappeared had it not been declared unconstitutional in 1935. The Roosevelt administration's economic policy drifted for the next several years, trying only government spending to stimulate consumption. In 1937, Roosevelt shifted his policy to vigorous enforcement of the antitrust laws.

At the same time, the sales and marketing conception was emerging in organizational fields where oligopolies did not exist and rules of competition of the manufacturing conception had not yet triumphed. These firms tended to be in consumer product industries such as food, drugs, chemicals, automobiles, and other durables. The marketing revolution had begun during the 1920s when managers and entrepreneurs realized that products had life cycles. This meant that firms needed to have a mix of products, some new and some mature, to insure continued growth in the firm.

As firms began to produce related products, a shift occurred in the organizational fields of the large firms. Managers and entrepreneurs began to define their fields in broader terms. They participated in many markets with different competitors depending on the product. Marketing departments gained power because they knew how to sell the products and how to find new markets. The sales and marketing conception began when one firm in an industry pursued product diversification and spread when others followed.

This new conception of the firm required a new structure. The multidivisional form became the accepted organizational structure for the large corporation between 1920 and 1970, with the greatest diffusion after World War II. For many of the firms the marketing function within each division became quite powerful by dictating the schedules, innovation, and introduction of products. The central office monitored their progress and overall contribution to the firm's growth and profits, and also approved large-scale development projects.

During the depression diversified firms outperformed nondiversified firms. When most of the vertically integrated firms were seeking government aid in raising prices, sales-and-marketing-oriented firms introduced new products at a high rate, indeed higher than during the 1920s. Managers and entrepreneurs realized they needed to sell products to survive, and if traditional markets declined then the firm had to enter new markets.

Because the government had a narrow definition of monopoly, diversification did not seem threatening at this time. Consequently by 1950 it was the primary strategy of big business in America. Several events between 1940 and 1960 reinforced this trend. One was increased antitrust activity in the 1940s. Beginning in 1937, Roosevelt encouraged Thurman Arnold, head of the Antitrust Division, to make creative use of the antitrust laws. After World War II, antitrust prosecution reached an all-time peak. The largest firms were constantly being threatened by the federal government and by 1950 about half of the one hundred largest firms had an antitrust suit pending against them.

In the late 1930s several people throughout the federal government wanted to use the antitrust laws to increase competition in the American economy. Thurman Arnold headed the Antitrust Division, a modern, professional corps of lawyers who worked toward that end. In the Congress, Senator Joseph O'Mahoney and Representatives Estes Kefauver and Emmanuel Celler became interested in the issue. The federal trade commissioners also became more active in studying and prosecuting violations of the antitrust laws. These people were brought together by the formation of the Temporary National Economic Commission (TNEC) in 1937. The commission concluded that the central problem in the economy was the existence of large firms which tended to create monopolies or oligopolies in key markets. While the commission had little immediate legislative or policy impact, it set the stage for more vigorous antitrust enforcement in the postwar era.

The TNEC recommended altering Section 7 of the Clayton Act to outlaw anticompetitive mergers through the purchase of assets, thereby closing the loophole in the act. The antitrust community, with the FTC in the lead, began to push for that legislation after World War II because they argued that mergers were increasing. Kefauver and Celler guided the legislation through Congress. They introduced bills to amend the Clayton Act in every session of Congress from 1945 on. The final bill passed in 1950 when Democrats controlled both the House and the Senate.

The Celler-Kefauver Act was intended to slow the growth of monopoly by preventing firms from increasing their product concentration. While the act was also intended to prevent mergers among firms that were producing related or unrelated products, it rarely succeeded. The Celler-Kefauver Act was most often applied to horizontal and vertical mergers. The dominant theory of antitrust at the time was that concentration within product lines restricted competition. The unintended consequence of the Celler-Kefauver Act was that it set up the preconditions for the third large merger movement. But the mergers of the late 1950s and 1960s did not produce monopolies or oligopolies. Instead they produced conglomerates and the large modern diversified multinational firm.

The finance conception of the firm, the most recent, developed for two reasons. In order to grow, large firms needed to diversify. The sales and marketing conception had continued to prove profitable, but lacked a way to direct diversification. Those who controlled the firm lacked the expertise to evaluate new products on their own merits. As a result, investments began to be made only on a financial basis. The implementation of financial controls and advanced accounting systems, therefore, shifted power in the large firms to those who could judge whether a product made money. Firms then paid more attention to short-run objectives. Instead of building a new plant which might take years to show a profit, it was easier to buy an existing company.

The second impetus for the finance conception was the antitrust environment, which was hostile toward large firms in general and horizontal and vertical mergers in particular. The first Supreme Court decisions after the passing of the Celler-Kefauver Act made mergers illegal between relatively small firms with moderate market shares. The large firms quickly responded and stopped merging for market share. Instead, they turned their attention to product-related and -unrelated mergers as a strategy for growth.

From 1945 to 1969 the largest firms rapidly diversified mostly through mergers. The business community had one important example of the pure financial strategy: the acquisitive conglomerate. The acquisitive conglomerates were built by people on the edges of the American corporate sector, often outside New York, where most of the large firms were located. Many of the original conglomerates had been in declining industries and then their founders removed them from their established organizational fields. Using financial ploys, these executives parlayed the smaller firms into larger firms through mergers and the floating of debt. By 1955 the conglomerate strategy of buying disparate firms and creating a large highly diversified corporation was already well known. The emergence of Textron, Ling-Temco-Vought (LTV), International Telephone and Telegraph (ITT), Litton Industries, and Gulf and Western in the early 1960s, encouraged other firms to try instant growth through mergers.

The finance conception remade the organizational fields of the largest firms. Managers saw that the acquisitive conglomerates merged their way into the ranks of the largest industrial enterprises in a short period of time. This caused managers in otherwise stable organizational fields that were defined by industry to shift their attention from their position in the industry to their position in the hierarchy of large American corporations. While the acquisitive conglomerate garnered much attention, the most important phenomenon in the economy was the spread of product-related diversification strategies to firms such as Rockwell International, W. R. Grace, Thompson-Ramo-Wooldridge (TRW), and Minnesota Mining and Manufacturing (3M). It eventually also spread to firms in the staid oil and steel industries. The finance conception rose to prominence and today still dominates the actions of the largest U.S. firms.

The merger movement of the 1960s, however, ended for two reasons. First, when the stock market crashed in 1969, money for mergers got tighter. Equally important was the antitrust policy of the Nixon administration. John Mitchell, then attorney general, announced in 1969 that all mergers of large corporations would be pursued under the amended Clayton Act. Richard McLaren, the head of the Justice Department Antitrust Division, prepared highly publicized cases against ITT, LTV, and other acquisitive conglomerates. Soon thereafter mergers slowed considerably.

The Mitchell-McLaren antitrust policy was abandoned in 1972. The Supreme Court no longer accepted the government's arguments regarding Section 7 of the Clayton Act. Antitrust cases had been built mostly on the potential, not the actual, anticompetitive effects of increased product concentration. In order to apply those laws to product related and unrelated mergers, those arguments had to extend to show how those mergers were potentially anticompetitive. Consequently some scholars and people in the private antitrust community began to question whether or not mergers in fact restricted competition. Most thought that mergers were probably creating more efficient organizations. The core of their counterargument was that the government's cases needed to concentrate not only on the structural effects of mergers on an industry, but on the performance of firms in that industry.

The Nixon appointees to the Supreme Court were more sympathetic to their perspective. In 1973 and 1974 the Supreme Court limited the use of the Celler-Kefauver Act for product-related and -unrelated mergers and even limited its applicability in horizontal and vertical mergers. The Antitrust Division under Ronald Reagan basically abandoned its enforcement, and mergers have greatly accelerated in recent years, initiating the fourth large merger movement.

By 1979 finance presidents were the single largest group of presidents of the one hundred largest firms. Finance-oriented executives are not committed to any given industry and no longer identify their firms in market terms. Instead, the population of the largest firms is now the reference group for these managers. Nonetheless, because many of the firms are in one or two major industries, they must continue to monitor competition in those industries.

The current vogue is to argue that the economy should be left alone. Investment decisions, merger decisions, and industrial policy should be placed in the hands of the largest firms who are most influential in the marketplace. But this argument ignores the fact that over time firms have operated under different conceptions which resulted from the dynamic interaction of the economic environment, the political environment, and the internal organization of the firm. The structures that are in place now are not the products of some pure process of competition. Nor has competition been weakened by the actions of government. Instead, what has come into existence is the result of a social and political process that defines and redefines markets. If left to their own devices, the managers of the largest firms would continue to do what they are doing. Eliminating government regulation and antitrust enforcement will not automatically produce a more competitive corporate world. The finance conception remains in effect and the incentives that produced it continue.

To view the economy and its development outside of the current conceptions of the actors dominating major institutions means one will not understand the actions of those institutions. One is also not likely to be able to anticipate what any political action oriented toward the economy is going to have. To argue that current conceptions somehow reflect the best of all possible worlds is neither historically informed nor scientific, but ideological. Instead, what has emerged is the product of large-scale social organization over a substantial period of time.

Notes

1. The following discussion owes a great debt to A. D. Chandler Jr., *Strategy and Structure* (Cambridge: MIT Press, 1962), and *The Visible Hand* (Cambridge: Harvard University Press, 1977); P. DiMaggio and W. Powell, "Institutional Isomorphism," *American Sociological Review* 48 (1983): 147–60; M. Hannan and J. Freeman, "The Population Ecology of Organizations," *American Journal of Sociology* 82 (1977): 929–66, and "Structural Inertia and Organizational Change," *American Sociological Review* 49 (1984): 149–64; J. Meyer and B. Rowan, "Institutionalized

Organizations: Formal Structure as Myth and Ceremony," *American Journal of Sociology* 83 (1977): 340–63; J. Meyer and W. R. Scott, *Organizational Environments* (Beverly Hills: Sage, 1983); C. Perrow, "Departmental Power and Perspectives in Industrial Firms," in *Power in Organizations*, ed. M. Zald (Nashville: Vanderbilt University Press, 1970); J. Pfeffer, *Power in Organizations* (Marshfield, Mass.: Pitman, 1981); and H. White, "Where Do Markets Come From?" *American Journal of Sociology* 87 (1981): 517–47; and to my earlier papers, N. Fligstein, "The Spread of the Multidivisional Form," *American Sociological Review* 50 (1985); 377–91, "The Intraorganizational Power Struggle: The Rise of Finance Presidents in Large Corporations, 1919–1979," *American Sociological Review* 52 (1987): 44–58, "The Structural Transformation of American Industry," in *The New Institutionalism in Organizational Theory*, ed. W. Powell and P. DiMaggio (Chicago: University of Chicago Press, 1990), "Organizational, Demographic, and economic Determinants of the Growth Patterns of Large Firms," in *Research on Organizations*, ed. C. Calhoun (Greenwich, Conn.: JAI Press, 1990); and N. Fligstein and K. Dauber, "Changes in Corporate Organization," in *Annual Review of Sociology*, ed. W. R. Scott (Palo Alto: Annual Reviews 1989).

Chapter 16

FROM *SOCIALIZING CAPITAL: THE RISE OF THE LARGE INDUSTRIAL CORPORATION IN AMERICA*

WILLIAM G. ROY

INTRODUCTION

In the first year of this century, a group of bankers led by the venerable J. P. Morgan and a group of steel men created the U.S. Steel Corporation, America's first billion-dollar corporation. Built around the core of the former Carnegie Steel Company, U.S. Steel merged nearly all major producers of iron, steel, and coke. Public opinion at the time focused on its mammoth size and its potential monopoly power. Looking back, we recognize it as a symbol of a broader movement that we now metaphorically but appropriately call the "corporate revolution." As in political revolutions, the economic changes that came to a head in these years were cataclysmic and far reaching. Like the transformations in France, Russia, or China, the corporate revolution had been brewing from slower, evolutionary changes, but was triggered by a set of events unanticipated by most of the participants. The nature of this revolution, its causes and consequences, have been energetically debated in both academic and popular circles, often with thinly veiled ideological overtones. But all agree that the corporate revolution was a major watershed in American history. The period at the turn of the twentieth century marked the transformation from one way of life to another, from a society based on rural, agrarian, local, small-scale, individual relations to one based on urban, industrial, national, large-scale, and organizational relations. At the heart of this was the rise of the large industrial corporation, which has continued to cast its shadow over all society ever since.

Americans recognized U.S. Steel as a milestone even if they did not realize all its historical ramifications. Only twenty years earlier, an entity like U.S. Steel would have been implausible. Although the institutional structure of corporate capitalism, including the stock market, investment banks, brokerage houses, and the financial press had been operating for decades, it was confined almost entirely to government bonds, transportation, and communication. The large, publicly traded *manufacturing* corporation was rare.

The large manufacturing corporation, unusual before 1890, became the dominant mode of business organization in two major steps. The first was the creation of the large private business corporate institution itself, its origins as a quasi-government agency and its metamorphosis into private property. The historical question is how an organizational form constituted as an extension of state power to accomplish publicly useful projects was transformed into a sanctuary from state power as the institutional basis of private accumulation. This was achieved in the 1870s. But until the century's end, the corporate institutional structure was confined to those arenas of economic life that Western governments have generally claimed special jurisdiction over, namely, infrastructural sectors of transportation, communication, and finance.

The second step was the extension of the corporate institutional structure into manufacturing. As late as 1890, fewer than ten manufacturing securities were traded on the major stock exchanges, and most of those, like Pullman's Palace Car Company were closely associated with the railroad (*Manual of Statistics* 1890). The world of manufacturing and the world of finance capital were institutionally distinct. Investors considered manufacturing companies too risky and industrialists resisted surrendering control to outsiders (Navin and Sears 1955; Carosso 1970). To be sure, there were large corporations. The hundred-million-dollar Pennsylvania Railroad was the largest company in the world. And there were large manufacturing companies. Carnegie Steel Company, an unincorporated limited partnership, was the largest manufacturing operation in the world (Wall 1989). The institutional structures of those two giants, however, were distinct from each other. Industrialists created firms through personal funds, reinvested mercantile capital, and internal growth. Andrew Carnegie started his steel company from personal profits amassed speculating in railroads and built it by selling steel to railroad and locomotive companies. He had close personal relations with railroad leaders, but few institutional relations outside of market transactions (Wall 1989). As in most industrial firms, ownership was personal and confined to one or a few individuals.

Wall Street, in contrast, operated as a distinct institutional structure, following the dynamics of a speculative securities market, only indirectly related to the world of manufacturing. The stocks and bonds traded there financed railroads, telegraph, municipalities, and governments. The railroad companies which laced the country with steel rails were considered virtual money machines for local elites, who were convinced that their city would become the next St. Louis, the archetypical boomtown; for the deep-pocketed foreign investors, who hoped to capture their profits from America's Manifest Destiny; and for the investment bankers and stockbrokers, who enjoyed commissions from others' investments as well as reaping the profits of their own.

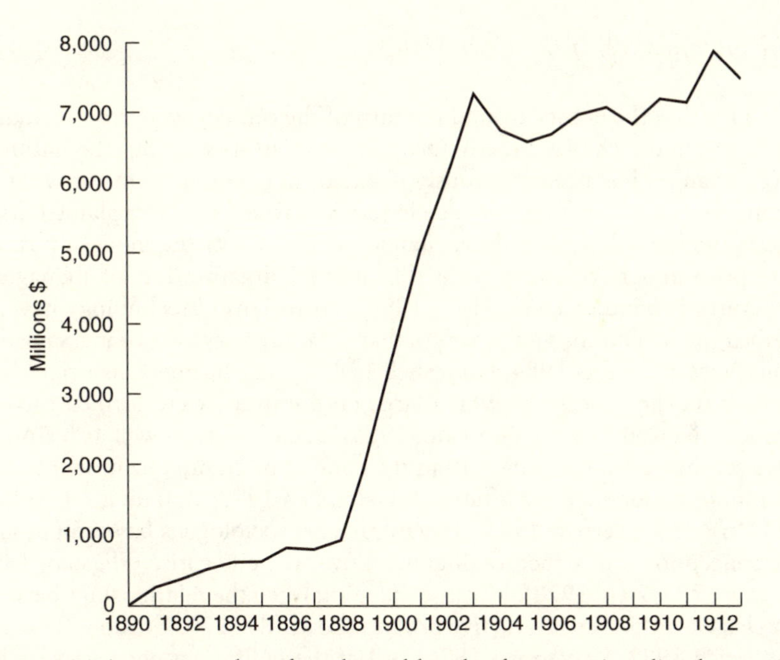

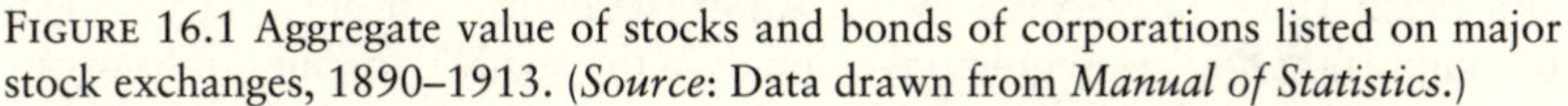

FIGURE 16.1 Aggregate value of stocks and bonds of corporations listed on major stock exchanges, 1890–1913. (*Source*: Data drawn from *Manual of Statistics*.)

In the years around the turn of the century, these two institutions, the industrial world of manufacturing and the financial world of stocks and bonds, merged together in what we now call the corporate revolution, a remarkably abrupt proliferation of large manufacturing corporations from virtually nothing to economic domination. Starting from 1890, the aggregate amount of capital in publicly traded manufacturing companies crept up until 1893, when the depression stalled economic expansion, then jumped from $33 million in 1890 to $260 million the following year (see figure 16.1). But these figures were small compared with the multi-billion-dollar totals after the turn of the century. In 1901 the food industry alone totaled $210 million in common stocks (*Manual of Statistics* 1901). The major expansion began after 1897, and in 1898 almost reached a billion dollars. It doubled in 1899 to over two billion, and doubled again over the subsequent two years, and hit over seven billion dollars in 1903. It then fluctuated around the six- to seven-billion-dollar mark until the outbreak of World War I. These figures from the years 1898 to 1903 trace a major change from one economic system to another, a new corporate order in manufacturing. The total par value of manufacturing stocks and bonds listed on the major exchanges in 1904 was $6.8 billion, more than half the $11.6 billion book value of all manufacturing capital enumerated in the 1904 census (U.S. Bureau of the Census 1975, 684).[1]

The Significance of the Corporation

All agree that the events around the turn of the century were transformative and profoundly changed the nature of American society. But the nature of those changes has been vigorously debated, not only in terms of what explains the transformation, but also in terms of what is to be explained. Managerialists have described these changes as the rise of the modern business enterprise and have emphasized the internal organization of managerial structures (Chandler 1969, 1977, 1990). Historians of technology have described the inventions and practices that created the system of mass production (Piore and Sabel 1984; Hounshell 1984). Some business historians have focused on the process by which large corporations were formed through mergers (Nelson 1959; Lamoreaux 1985). Sociologists as well as historians have set the new large firms within the context of an organizational revolution in all major social institutions (Galambos 1970; Boulding 1953; Lash and Urry 1987; Perrow 1991). Organizational sociologists have emphasized the conception and structure of control over the enterprise (Fligstein 1990; Perrow 1986; Zald 1978). Marxists have analyzed the relationships between the classes within the productive process (Edwards 1979; Gordon, Edwards, and Reich 1982; Braverman 1974). All of these different perspectives identify important and consequential changes in the social dynamics of how our society creates and distributes material resources. Despite the different emphases, they address the same agenda in two ways: first, they all agree that the appearance of U.S. Steel, General Electric, American Tobacco, and similar entities marked a major transformation in the American social structure. Second, they have all participated in a major underlying debate over the extent to which the economy operates according to an economic logic based on efficiency or operates according to a social logic based on institutional arrangements, including power.

This book makes two simple claims. First, I argue that one of the most fundamental and dynamic facets of the transformation underlying the rise of entities like U.S. Steel was a shift in the form and organization of property, as constituted in major political and economic institutions. The large publicly traded corporation transformed the organization of ownership so that economic entities were each owned by many individuals rather than a few, and many individuals owned pieces of many units. This transformation socialized property, altering the basic relationships among owners, workers, managers, suppliers, and consumers. That is not to say that managerial structures, technologies, mergers, or systems of control were unimportant. Each of them had major autonomous effects, but their effects were refracted through the institutional relations of property. Second, I will argue that efficiency theory, the prevailing explanation of change in the organization of the economy, is inadequate to explain the rise of the large publicly traded industrial corporation.

Property, Power, and Institutions

While others have framed the rise of the large corporation in terms of managerial hierarchies, technological developments, mergers of smaller firms, the general growth of large organizations, the conception of internal control, and the conflict between classes, I examine major corporations as a form of property set within a broader institutional structure shaped by the dynamics of power at least as much as by efficiency. The major, publicly traded large-scale corporation constituted a new type of property, socialized property (Zeitlin 1989). Socialized property means that instead of each firm being owned by one or a few individuals, each firm became owned by many individuals, and individual owners in turn typically owned pieces of many firms.[2] In the process the social nature of property itself was transformed. The consideration of property implies a degree of inequality, that the social processes determining the shape of the economy are explainable by power, not just efficiency. Moreover, the social relations of property and the underlying dynamics of power are set within the interorganizational frameworks we know as institutions. This section sketches how the concepts of property, power, and institution shape the analysis of the corporate revolution and concludes that they intersect at the concept of social class.

PROPERTY

Property can be defined as the set of politically enforced rights, entitlements, and obligations that people have in relationship to objects and in relationship to other individuals (owners and nonowners). Rights include such things as authority to make decisions about what products to produce or whom to hire as labor, and how to dispose of a completed product. The conventional conception of property rights emphasizes that property rights limit government intrusion in the same sense that the right of free speech or religion limits the government's powers over individuals (Ryan 1987). Entitlements involve matters such as profits from the use of objects. Capitalism makes no distinction between the entitlement of using objects for oneself and regulating how others may use objects that one owns. A factory or leased land is legally equivalent to one's clothes or residence. Obligations are a matter of accountability concerning objects, especially liability for injuries suffered while using objects or debts incurred while using them. Although courts, especially in this century, have tightened the liability that owners have concerning injury related to their property, the corporation's limited liability has shielded owners from any risk greater than their invested capital. I want to emphasize three points about this definition: the fact that the specific rights, entitlements, and obligations are variable rather than fixed; the social nature of property relations; and the active role of the state in enforcing property rights.

First, the specific rights, entitlements, and obligations are quite variable. Contrary to classic liberalism, there are no inherent or natural "property rights." The conception of inalienable or natural property rights existing prior to society or history may have been an effective ideology for creating capitalism, but it has clouded the historical analysis of what specific rights, entitlements, and obligations govern economic relations. Rather, the content of property relations is historically constructed and must be explained, not taken for granted. The rise of the corporation fundamentally changed the nature of the rights, entitlements, and obligations bundled with ownership of productive enterprise (Berle and Means 1932; Horwitz 1977; Sklar 1988; Creighton 1990; Lindberg and Campbell 1991). The nominal owners effectively lost many of their rights, entitlements, and obligations. Whereas previously the right to determine what products to produce or whom to hire and the entitlement to profits and the obligation to pay debts had been bundled together with ownership, the corporation separated them.[3] Courts and legislatures increasingly treated the corporation as an entity in itself, legally distinct from the individuals who owned it, and increasingly treated management, not stockholders, as its representative. For example, prior to the 1880s, when a railroad entered receivership, judges ordinarily appointed a committee of owners, bondholders, and debtors to reorganize it. But the practice changed abruptly when judges began to appoint managers. Given that receivership was one of the primary means of altering the distribution of entitlements, stockholders were substantially disenfranchised (Berk 1994).

The second point to emphasize about this definition is that property is a social relationship; it involves rights, entitlements, and obligations not only in relation to an object itself but also in relationship to other individuals (Hurst 1978; Horwitz 1977; Renner 1949). The owner of a factory not only has the right to decide what to use his or her factory for, a relationship of the owner to the object, but also the right of authority over others participating in using the factory, the right to distribute the value created in the factory (an entitlement), and obligations to pay debts incurred in production. The social relationship among owners, managers, suppliers, workers, and customers was radically altered by the corporation. No particular owner retained any authority over any particular worker, but all authority was mediated through the board of directors and management. Rather than freeing those who run enterprise to become "soulful," managers are constrained to maximize profits for those to whom they are ultimately accountable.

Third, this definition of property emphasizes that property is a relationship enforced by the state (Sklar 1988; Weber 1978; Zald 1978; Fligstein 1990; Lindberg and Campbell 1991; Campbell and Lindberg 1991; Scheiber 1975). Although the American state has developed a relatively small apparatus to regulate markets and oversee production, even at its most laissez-faire, it defined and enforced the rights, entitlements, and obligations of property. Even the freest of markets requires specific government actions and policies to enforce contracts, punish cheaters, regulate money, and ensure stability. There is no such thing as nonintervention (Polanyi 1957). The corporation is a creation of the law, a "legal fiction." Natural individuals are automatically recognized by the law and have a basic right to own property, sign contracts with others concerning that property, and sell that property without explicit recognition by the state. But a corporation exists only when chartered by the state. A group of natural individuals can constitute themselves as an organization, and can sign individual contracts defining their economic relationship to one another and the rights and obligations they have to the organization, but the organization itself cannot exercise property rights, sign enforceable contracts, or sell property unless it is explicitly granted that right by the state. Thus, explaining the rise of the large industrial corporation requires analysis of the legal changes underlying corporate property. Although most treatments of the American state have focused on the federal government, it was the individual states that were constitutionally and practically responsible for defining and enforcing property rights. There was considerable variation among the states in the particular rights, entitlements, and obligations that came with incorporation, and these differences affected the form and location of corporations. At the one extreme, by the end of the century New Jersey allowed corporations to own other corporations, making it the overwhelming choice of huge mergers, while at the other, Ohio continued to uphold double liability; by which owners were liable not only for their invested capital but for an additional amount equal to it.

I will argue that corporate rights and entitlements and the new social relations enforced by the state did not dissolve the class nature of property as much as they changed it by socializing it throughout the class and by creating an organizational mediation among the classes and class segments (Zeitlin 1980, 1989).[4] By mediation, I mean that the underlying class relationship became redefined in terms of not just one's relationship to legal ownership but one's social relationship to corporate property. The relationships that class describes, such as hiring people to labor, exercising authority over decisions about what to produce or what technologies to adopt, determining how products are sold, are now mediated by the corporation. One is no longer hired by individuals, but hired by a corporation; one can no longer sue owners, but only the corporation. In contemporary America, one's relationship to corporations is now the most important determinant of wealth. Whether one works for a corporation, manages a corporation, owns stock in a corporation, or lends money to a corporation differentiates the wealthy from the rest. To assert that the large corporation did not dissolve the capitalist class does not mean that I claim that class dynamics by themselves explain the rise of the corporation, nor does it indicate that the capitalist class acted as an organized, coherent, or conscious group throughout these events. The extent to which class interests are at stake, that is, the extent to which people objectively gain or lose from historical events, the extent to which people with common class interests act in concert, and the extent to which they are aware that they share interests with others are empirical questions, not articles of faith. But such issues of class do belong on the agenda for explaining how economic relationships change. When class interests (or the interests of class segments) are at stake, such as when manufacturers were resisting corporate takeover, the outcome will be determined in large part by the extent to which people with common class interests act in common. For example, the antitrust legal actions corroded class solidarity among small and medium-sized manufacturers, making it easier for corporate capitalists, who were knitted together by shared ownership and common investment institutions, to prevail both economically and legally.

POWER

The conventional sociological definition of power is taken from Weber (1978): the ability of one actor to impose his or her will on another despite resistance. I broaden that to define power as the extent to which the behavior of one person is explained in terms of the behavior of another. Like Weber's, this definition characterizes a relationship rather than a single person. It incorporates Weber's definition as one dimension of power, "behavioral power," which refers to the visible overt behavior of the power wielder in the form of a command, request, or suggestion. But Weber's definition does not go far enough to cover all the ways that behavior is affected by others. There is a second dimension of power, "structural power," the ability to determine the context within which decisions are made by affecting the consequences of one alternative over another. For example, an employer that hires sociology majors rather than economics majors structures the consequences of choosing a major and is exercising power over students deciding on a major.[5]

This second dimension of power, structural power, allows us to include rational action within a theory of power. The concept of structural power permits a variety of motives for behavior, including rationality. The fact that an actor rationally decides to maximize his or her utility does not mean that power is irrelevant to an explanation of behavior; power operates in setting up the choices the actor faces and the consequences of any particular action. For example, most of the new manufacturing corporations formed at the turn of the century were mergers of many entrepreneurially owned companies. Many proud, hardworking manufacturers sold their family legacy for stock certificates and a demotion from owner to manager. Why? Efficiency theory posits that economies of scale and productive technologies led to ruinous competition and the necessary amalgamation into managerial hierarchies. Such accounts are devoid of actors except for the rationalizing managers creating a more efficient division of labor. But we also need to know what alternatives the owners of merged firms faced and who determined the consequences of their choices. If an owner had to choose between competing against a corporation selling products below cost or joining a merger and enjoying continuing profits, it is understandable that he or she chose the latter. The choices the manufacturers faced in 1899 were radically different from those of just a decade earlier, and to understand why manufacturers incorporated we must also understand how financiers, government officials, and other industrialists affected the consequences of reorganizing enterprise within the corporate system, in other words, the institutional structure.

In this perspective rationality becomes an empirical question, not an a priori assumption. Compared with efficiency theory, power theory thus proposes a very different agenda for research: Who made the decisions that created large industrial corporations? What were the alternative choices they faced? To what extent did rationality, social influence, or other decision-making logics shape their decisions? Who set the alternative choices and the consequences of each alternative they faced? How did their choices shape the alternatives and payoffs for other actors? One of the reasons these questions are often difficult to answer is that the alternative choices and the payoffs are embedded within institutions whose genesis has been forgotten or obscured.

INSTITUTIONS

As a system of property relations shaped by the dynamics of power, corporations operated within and helped constitute a social institution (Meyer and Rowan 1977; DiMaggio and Powell 1983; Zucker 1988; Powell and DiMaggio 1991). To understand how the corporation operates requires more than knowing how it works internally, the people who operate it, its goals and strategies, or its division of labor and hierarchy. By social institution I mean the matrix of organizations, taken-for-granted categories, and the agreed-upon modes of relationship among those organizations that administer a major social task. The concept includes three analytically distinct aspects: (1) Institutions use a set of categories and practices that are understood to be the "way things are done" (Meyer and Rowan 1977). Corporations develop a standard division of authority among the owners, directors, managers, and workers; particular accounting practices to measure performance and validate strategies; customary separation of white-collar and blue-collar occupations; and characteristic bureaucratic structures that codify procedures. Institutional practices include such practices as issuing stock, speculation, hiring and promotion of workers and managers, and measurement of success in terms of balance sheets. (2) Institutions include a matrix of organizations, or an organizational field, that in the aggregate constitutes a recognized area of institutional life (DiMaggio and Powell 1983). Just as the medical institution includes hospitals as well as laboratories or medical schools, the institution of corporate capitalism includes factories and railroads as well as the stock markets, investment banks, brokerage houses, and news organizations. Thus when I speak of major public corporations I mean much more than those companies that happen to be incorporated. I mean companies that are legally incorporated and that operate within the institutional structures of corporate capitalism by publicly offering their securities to the securities market, raising capital through investment banks, recruiting directors from the community of corporate directors, and socializing ownership through widespread ownership. It was the transformation of manufacturing enterprise into this institutional structure that exploded at the end of the nineteenth century in the corporate revolution. (3) Institutions describe cultural categories, a sense of reality, a "thing" (Zucker 1977, 1983). All members of society recognize that medicine, education, politics, and mass media are institutions. They are "real." The institutionalization of the entities that do things is more than just a codification of existing practices; the process selects from among competing alternative forms by designating one form as "real" or "established" while marginalizing other forms as "experimental," "fledgling," "novel," "alternative," or "artificial." This process was very important in the institutionalization of the corporation in the late nineteenth century, when writers from a variety of ideological perspectives, speaking to many different types of audiences, declared that good or bad, the corporation was here to stay. Although in retrospect it may appear that things could have been different, the nearly universal feeling that large corporations were inevitable was an important part of their institutionalization, a cause as well as a result of how large corporations became the standard way of doing business.

What is the relationship among property, power, and institutions? All three are interwoven together throughout this analysis, but three propositions succinctly capture their relationship.

Power institutionalizes property. The specific rights, entitlements, and obligations that the state enforces relative to objects are determined by the operation of power and embedded within institutions. Corporate lawyers were able to persuade the New Jersey legislature to change its corporate law to allow corporations to own stock in other corporations, a right that had been previously denied to both partnerships and corporations and that, once granted, created the legal basis for the corporate revolution at the end of the century. The New Jersey legislature was more compliant than other states because that state had long enjoyed a profitable relationship with railroad corporations. The choices it faced and the relative payoff of each differed from the situation faced by other states. The relationship among power, institution, and property was very reflexive and historical: early exercise of power institutionalized a set of property relationships that became the context within which power was exercised to embed new property relations within the institutional relations of corporate capital.

Property institutionalizes power. The specific rights, entitlements, and obligations that are embedded within institutions shape the context within which people make decisions. Those who want to benefit from how a system operates do not need to constantly impose their will, but institutions reproduce power relationships. Berle and Means (1932) describe how in the late nineteenth and early twentieth centuries, such new legal features of the corporations as proxy voting and no par stock[6] disenfranchised stockholders. New property relations were the means by which small stockholders lost power.

Power and property shape institutions. Just as Starr (1982) describes how physicians prevailed to shape modern medicine or Logan and Molotch (1988) demonstrate how property relations shape modern urban relations, a major theme of this book is how power and property, more than efficiency, shaped the corporate institution.

The Story

When applied to the rise of the American industrial corporation these analytical concepts yield a story very different from that found in efficiency studies. Instead of rational managers making pragmatic organizational innovations adapting to new technologies and growing markets, the story depicts a series of political and financial developments redistributing power into new institutional structures and eventually resulting in a new property regime. The lead players in the story are the state; the corporate institutional structure, including investment banks, stock exchanges, brokers, and others; newly privatized railroads; and finally manufacturers themselves. It is the larger structures that best explain why the corporation became the dominant form. These actors and the roles they played are summarized in table 16.1.

The story spans three eras. In the late eighteenth and early nineteenth centuries, business corporations were only one type of corporation created by governments to perform public functions like education, urban services, churches, charities, and infrastructure. Because they were performing a task considered critical for the public, they were given such privileges as monopoly rights, eminent domain, and an exemption on liability. Because they were quasi-government agencies, they were financed by institutional structures we now call Wall Street, which then functioned mainly to circulate government securities. In the middle of the nineteenth century, they fully privatized within the mature corporate infrastructure but remained separate from manufacturing. By allowing incorporation through the simple acts of filing papers and paying a fee rather than requiring a legislative act, states made incorporation a right accessible to all rather than a privilege. Railroad corpo-

TABLE 16.1
Historical Account of the Rise of the Large Corporation

	Era and Role of Corporation		
Actors	*Early Nineteenth Century: corporation as Quasi-Government Agency*	*Mid-Nineteenth Century: Corporation Private but Separate from Manufacturing*	*Late Nineteenth–Early twentieth century: merger of Corporate Institution with Manufacturing*
State	Actively forms corporations Mobilizes resources Holds corporations publicly accountable	Passes general incorporation laws Defines new rights, entitlements, and obligations Treats corporation as legal individual	Prohibits industry governance Enforces relations of corporate property
Corporate institutional structure	Arises to administer public finance Spreads to private corporations Remained distinct from manufacturing	Develops into modern structure Excludes manufacturing	Brings manufacturing in
Railroads	Arise as semipublic agency	Privatize Grow to unprecedented size Amass corporate wealth for reinvestment	Experience declining profitability Merge with manufacturing capital
Manufacturing capital	Exists apart from corporate capital Governs itself by local and regional suprafirm relations	Develops national markets Destabilizes suprafirm relations	Merge with corporate capital

rations grew to unprecedented size and scope; the institutions of Wall Street congealed into their present form, but still remained distinct from manufacturing. Finally the corporate revolution at the turn of the century absorbed manufacturing and fully established the corporate system as we have it today. The corporate revolution was precipitated by government actions that prevented manufacturing industries from governing themselves except through merger, by the saturation and financial collapse of the railroad system, and by an ideological acceptance that the large socially capitalized manufacturing corporation was inevitable.

By 1890 the corporate revolution in manufacturing was probably inevitable in some form, although exactly what form was not entirely clear. The resources concentrated in the corporate institutions were vast and the opportunities to profit from railroad and related sectors diminishing, so investors were looking for new outlets. The legal foundation, insofar as it was based on the railroad as a profit-making company rather than a common carrier accountable to the public, could easily be borrowed by manufacturing. And manufacturers' opposition to corporate takeover was already weakened by the frequent declaration that big business was inevitable, by the temptations of monopolistic profits, and by the trauma inflicted by the great depression of 1893. Belief in the corporate revolution's inevitability has led to its treatment as fairly unproblematic in most conventional accounts, which tell how in the 1880s industrialists like John D. Rockefeller in oil and Henry O. Havemeyer in sugar, after failing to control competition through pools, formed trusts, whereby each constituent firm incorporated for the purpose of exchanging corporate stock for trust certificates, allowing a central board to control entire industries. After the trusts were declared illegal, industries reorganized in holding companies like Standard Oil or the American Sugar Refining Company. At the end of the 1890s hundreds of such corporations were founded primarily through mergers by financiers like J. P. Morgan, who organized General Electric, International Harvester, and U.S. Steel. But such accounts too often neglect how the nature and definition of property, the organization and distribution of wealth, and the institutional practices and definitions were all socially constructed and far from inevitable. My account focuses on explaining these broader factors, emphasizing that they were determined less by the exigencies of economic efficiency or managerial rationality than by the very political dynamics of power.

The Corporation as Public and Private Enterprise

In the twentieth century the corporation has been the preeminent institutional form of the system of private enterprise that we call capitalism. When we think of who wields private power, such corporations as Exxon, AT&T, General Electric, or USX (U.S. Steel) quickly come to mind. Even though capitalist states have, until the last decade or so, regularly intensified their intervention into the economy, the very language we use to describe this process assumes a fundamental distinction between public and private spheres. Most U.S. observers assume that production and distribution are naturally private, best administered by the enlightened self-interest of owners and managers, with government protecting the public from business excesses. The corporation's most fundamental deterrents against government interference have been its right to privacy and the belief of policymakers that as many functions as possible should be left to private rather than public decisions.

The corporation, however, has not always been a private institution. Corporations were originally chartered by governments to accomplish public tasks, to build roads, construct canals, explore and settle new lands, conduct banking, and complete other tasks governments felt could not or should not be conducted privately. Contrary to the notion that corporations autonomously developed because they competed more efficiently or effectively in the market, governments created the corporate form to do things that rational businessmen would not do because they were too risky, too expensive, too unprofitable, or too public, that is, to perform tasks that would not have gotten done if left to the efficient operation of markets. Corporations were developed to undertake jobs that were not rational or not appropriate from the perspective of the individual businessman.

This chapter will describe how the large corporation shifted from a quasi-public agency—in principle accountable to all, embedded within an institutional structure that served the public sector—into a private agency, protected from government accountability by individual rights and legally accountable to no one but its owners. My goal is to demonstrate that the corporation grew into its modern form less by efficiently adapting to the demands of technological development and the growth of markets, than politically, by the exercise of power. The state not only defined what the corporation was and the particular rights, entitlements, and responsibilities that owners, managers, workers, consumers, and citizens could legally exercise relative to the corporation, it actively established and capitalized corporations.

. . . . .

The division of power between public and private sectors is important because it frames the structure of authority, accountability, and power (Horwitz 1977). In the public arena all citizens theoretically have a right to make claims and be taken into account when important decisions are contemplated. Organizations can be held accountable to the collective interest of citizens. In the private sphere, people have a right to influence activities only to the extent that they have vested rights. Vested rights can take the form of membership in voluntary organizations or economic resources in market-based organizations. Marx and Weber both recognized that the most powerful vested rights are those constituted in property. These lines of accountability determine for whose benefit activity is conducted. Is a canal, turnpike, or railroad built to serve the interests of the public at large, or is it built to serve the interests of the stockholders? This is the fundamental difference between public and private property. Public property, of course, does not guarantee that activity is conducted in the public interest, but merely places it in a structure with potential lines of accountability to the public. Private property does not mean there can be no benefit to the public, but only that those making decisions are free to weigh their own interests however they choose.

The division between public and private is itself a historical construct. Economic and political categories are not natural and inevitable, nor is the division of labor between them. What the state does and what others do is historically constructed, constituted in the way that states and other institutions develop. Many of the activities that states routinely conduct have been—and some continue to be—handled privately. Private groups have built roads, supplied water, adjudicated disputes, protected people from enemies, disposed of sewage, educated children, and issued currency. States have in contrast performed such "private" tasks as producing consumer goods, trading commodities, speculating in land, and investing in enterprise. The boundaries that separate modern polities and economies could have been very different. The corporation could have continued as a kind of state agency, an organizational means of mobilizing private resources to serve collective or state interests. For example, the financial market institutions developed in tandem with the federal treasury (Ardent 1975). Rather than sell securities through private brokers, the state could have sold, and at times attempted to sell, securities directly. These boundaries must be explicitly explained, not simply taken as natural.

Thus the private sphere is not the natural home for corporations, which arose after public and private spheres had been not only constructed, but radically redefined and the distinction between them deepened. The organizational features, the social relations constituted among directors, owners, managers, workers, and customers, were all socially constructed. When corporations were public, they were accountable to the government and, in principle, to the people, so profit was only one organizational goal. In order to have the privilege of limited liability, gain access to the bountiful supply of Wall Street capital, and achieve the right to act as legal individuals, the incorporating individuals had to pledge fealty to the state. They had to be accomplishing something for the public good, at least as legislators defined it. Those who pursued private profits for personal gain were on their own. They had to risk their own assets, as business norms dictated responsible individuals should. Even when they supplemented their own resources with those of other similarly liable individuals, the law treated them as their own natural person without the shield of a corporate entity. But they owed nothing to any larger authority or broader public. Profit could be pursued for the sake of profit—private enterprise for private ends.

To say that states and other institutional structures are built, not discovered, is not to say that historical development is entirely accidental or that there are no general principles that help explain the particular structures that did develop. This chapter will show that the corporation arose as a quasi-state activity and became privatized as the result of concrete political conflicts over the nature of the state. The debate was not about whether corporations should be located in preexisting public and private sectors. Rather, the conflict over the corporation coincided with a broader movement for a new definition of appropriate state powers, one that would construct a private sphere that was eventually understood as though it were separate. Within this broad process of socially constructing the boundaries between state and economy, my focus is on the large corporation and the political movements and conflicts that shaped it.

The Corporation as a Public Institution

In 1772, George Washington led a movement in the Virginia legislature to create a company to make the Potomac River navigable. After the American Revolution and some interstate squabbles delayed the project, the Potomac Company was created in 1785, with Washington as president and Thomas Jefferson as one of the directors. By 1801, despite numerous problems and setbacks, 338 miles of river were open for navigation at a total cost of about half a million dollars. Maryland and Virginia had supplied over half the capital, and foreign (Dutch) investors were also involved (Davis 1917; Littlefield 1984). What made this project unusual was its interstate nature and the prominence of its organizers. For Washington, an owner of considerable Virginia land, private interest conveniently coincided with public interest, another common feature of early corporations. Ultimately the Potomac project was a financial disappointment and technical failure. One historian concludes that "indeed its significance lies primarily in its demonstration that joint-stock companies were poorly equipped to carry out major internal improvements without massive and reliable government aid, especially during the first few decades after independence" (Littlefield 1984, 565).[7]

Before the liberal revolutions of the eighteenth and nineteenth centuries, European governments extended sovereignlike legal status to many corporate bodies (Sewell 1992). Guilds, municipalities, associations, and corporations were granted particular rights and the authority to enforce their own law. Each individual was subject to the law of the corporate bodies to which he or she belonged, often without recourse to adjudication to a higher authority. It was against this system that the founders of liberalism professed that all men are created equal, meaning that all men should be under the sovereignty of a single authority, that some should not be privileged with special rights or responsibilities. The corporation, that most "modern" of economic organizations, thus is the continuation of a premodern system. Its legally binding by-laws are a delegation of state sovereignty, a vestige of its public origins. Why the business corporation (along with municipalities, churches, and universities) was able to escape the sword of liberalizing egalitarianism is something that needs to be explained. The taint of privilege and monopoly continued to be the basis of considerable anticorporate mobilization, as we shall see below. Corporations were opposed both by those who advocated the elimination of corporate rights and privileges because they usurped legitimate public power and by those who wanted to extend corporate rights to all. The latter group won; the government extended the rights and entitlements of collective ownership to all who could afford it, and retreated from demanding the responsibilities it once had. The corporation survived, but as a private rather than as a public organization.

As it turned out, the corporation came to be legally constituted in a way that conformed to the liberal doctrine of equal rights for all while maintaining many of the rights and privileges that made corporate property different from individual property. The key to the meaning of privatization is that corporate property could be legally created by the state while being protected from the state by constitutional rights; it could be legally democratic and private. Privatization was achieved by a sociologically naive legal redefinition: treating the corporation as though it were an individual legally separate from the individuals who participated in it. This feature conflicts with a basic tenet of the common law of property: it clouds the distinction between personal rights (in personam) and rights in property (in rem) (Creighton 1990). Traditionally, to redress an injustice or a debt, one could sue not property, but only people. Ownership carried the privileges of profiting from property but also the liability of being responsible for it, a responsibility that extended beyond the value of the property itself to the other assets of the owner. If a horse throws you because the owner failed to shoe him properly, you may sue for more than the value of the horse itself. The owner's possessions can also be taken. In contrast, the corporation embodies a legal entity between the property and the owners. It owns the corporate property, and the stockholders own pieces of it. Because of the common-law distinction between in personam and in rem, private individuals lack the prerogative to create a property-owning corporate entity, but can hold property only as individuals. However, the state can create a new legal entity, an extension of itself and its powers. It is only as a delegation of state powers that states would allow corporations to exist independently of the individuals they comprised. As it turned out historically, states defined the relationship between the groups and their members as a relationship of property, thereby undermining accountability to the public and framing political discourse over the corporation within the language of privacy rights versus state interference. But it need not have been so. Considering all the rights, entitlements, and responsibilities of property, it is curious that states defined the members as owners. States could have created commissions with citizens who served as directors. Such organizations could have raised capital through financial instruments, like bonds, or the powers of taxation, like municipal corporations. Mayors and city council members do not own the city but exercise binding authority within it. Business corporations, however, typically required financial resources from a small number of wealthy individuals who demanded control. Since organizations are inclined to use existing institutionalized forms rather than create entirely new relations, states defined the relations between members and the new organizations as property rights, but transformed the meaning of property by legally divorcing the rights in personam and the rights in rem. The "owners" originally had the rights of ownership but not all the responsibilities. At first this new definition of property was negotiated, because the state had to depend on external resources. And it was for the convenience of the state that such entities were created. Thus the earliest forms of corporations in the United States were those that had the clearest public purpose—churches, schools, and cities. Over time, the institution was used for public needs with clear economic benefits—canals, banks, bridges, and turnpikes. It was last used for explicitly private enterprise in manufacturing and later retail activities.

The boundaries between the personhood of rulers, the state apparatus, and the citizenry have always been fluid and contested. Modern states have created many instruments other than official government agencies to perform tasks. Armies have been composed primarily of mercenaries hired by contracting with professional soldier/entrepreneurs with their own militia. Venality and tax farming were used to allocate jobs and raise funds; justices of the peace and parliaments did so elsewhere. States have created academies of science to develop and certify technical expertise needed for economic and political power. In the United States between 1800 and 1860, especially at the state level, governments extensively built penitentiaries, reformatories, and institutions for the aged, mentally unfit, and disabled. They gave aid to schools and colleges and subsidized county and state agricultural societies (Scheiber 1975; Studenski and Krooss 1963). They financed and regulated banks, insurance companies, and transportation. As will be detailed later, internal improvements were among the most ambitious and most consequential projects they undertook.

Among the various alternatives that American governments had with which to accomplish tasks, it was the corporation they turned to for projects that required more resources than they could raise from taxes. While fledgling American governments were limited by both the low level of commercialization and the strong antitax sentiment that had helped fuel rebellion against colonial rule, the corporate form gave them access to the resources of the world of finance capitalism, especially from abroad. As public entities, corporations were created by what is now known as a special charter, an act of a legislature (or monarch, in some nations) to create a corporation. By the time general incorporation replaced special incorporation, most legislatures were acting pro forma, routinely passing charters without debate. But in the eighteenth century, when corporations were considered public entities, legislatures would conscientiously consider requests for incorporation in committee, hold hearings, and openly debate the merits of each charter. New England towns often collectively supported or opposed proposed water or highway companies (Davis 1917). Failure to serve a public need was sufficient grounds for denying a charter. For example, in 1833 the Pennsylvania legislature vigorously debated a coal company charter, the opposition maintaining that the industry had become sufficiently developed that it could attract private capital and had no need for a charter (Hartz 1968). Both sides assumed that charters were appropriate only for public needs. In New Jersey and Pennsylvania until well into the nineteenth century, legislatures allowed highway companies to be created according to specified procedures, but the corporate charter would be granted only by the governor after the company proved itself. As public entities, corporations had both privileges and responsibilities. Seavoy (1982) explains that the device of the charter "assumed that corporations were legally privileged organizations that had to be closely scrutinized by the legislature because their purposes had to be made consistent with public welfare" (5). By the end of the eighteenth century many states had general incorporation laws for religions, academies, and libraries, but not business corporations. By early in the nineteenth century states were developing laws to regulate all corporations of a particular type, such as canals, turnpikes, banks, or manufacturing.

A charter would be created granting a monopoly over some function if individuals would share in the financing and operation of the new organization. Whether initiated by citizens or officials, the corporate form was used for tasks that served the public, but which neither the government nor the citizens were willing to do on their own—universities (like America's oldest corporation, chartered in 1688, Harvard University), banks, churches, canals, municipalities, and roads.

. . . . .

While some representatives of efficiency theory recognize that the corporate form was a creation of government, they generally attribute the corporation's privatization to the general inefficiency of government ownership, the inevitable failures that plague enterprise not disciplined by the market. The account here interprets the problems of canal companies as the result of such contingent events as heavy investment when virtually no one could have foreseen how quickly railroads would render canals uncompetitive, the first depression of international finance, and the political ascendancy of Jacksonian democracy with its antistate brand of anticorporatism. I have emphasized these contingent events, which suggest an explanatory logic of power rather than efficiency. In this perspective, actors' actions are explained in terms of their relationships with other social actors. The various alternatives they have to choose from and the costs and benefits resulting from the alternatives are determined by some social actors much more than others. Whether or not the resulting structures tend to increase efficiency is thus very contingent and not at all built into the system.

This chapter also illustrates what I mean by a logic of power rather than a logic of efficiency. Whereas efficiency theory was challenged in the previous chapter on empirical grounds, here I offer an alternative formulation. Efficiency theory identifies a pattern or structure such as the modern corporation and seeks to identify ways in which the pattern or structure more efficiently fulfilled important functions. Chandler (1977, 1990), for example, argues that modern business enterprise increased throughput of production and more effectively got products to the customer through extensive sales facilities. Power theory, in contrast, asks who was contending or cooperating to develop a pattern or structure and how the winners were able to prevail. This chapter shows how some actors were able to define unprofitable state ventures in canal building as proof of the folly of government involvement. When decisions are made, the efficiency model asks what the consequences of each alternative are and how the best choice is made to maximize consensually agreed-upon goals. Industrialists at the end of the century are described as facing a choice between the anarchy of ruinous competition or the stability of mergers. A power logic asks how the choices that people face are set by the actions of others. Power does not necessarily involve one actor giving commands, but more typically takes the form of determining the consequences for choices another actor might take. State governments under pressure from merchants to build infrastructures so that trade could more easily flow between cities and frontiers had the "choice" of raising taxes or issuing bonds to finance corporations. Rather than focusing on why the decision to sell bonds was more rational than raising taxes, a power perspective asks why the opponents of taxes and the marketers of bonds prevailed over those who feared that government-financed corporations would compromise government autonomy. Thus, with a logic of power, there is greater emphasis on who is involved and why some actors win while others lose.

Efficiency theory is problematic not only because it neglects the dynamics of power, but also because it attends only to short-term change. By focusing on the events at the end of the nineteenth century, the immediate unfolding of the corporate revolution, it is easy to miss the critical role that government played in the corporation's long-term development. Later chapters will focus more on government's later role, but this chapter has emphasized that a long-term perspective is necessary. The context in which decisions were made at the end of the century was very much structured by the events early in the century. The fact that the corporation arose in the form that it did, the particular powers and features that it embodied, the nature of the class that controlled it, and perhaps most important, the institutional structures in which it was embedded and through which capital became socialized were all shaped by its development as a quasi-government agency. It must be remembered that when American manufacturing wedded the corporate infrastructure at the end of the century, the latter never would have been there if only efficiency had shaped the economy.

Notes

1. These figures do not mean that half the economy was in large corporations; the value of securities was often grossly inflated relative to the value of capital assets.

2. Socialization does not necessarily mean government ownership, but is the opposite of individualization. It only requires that some institution act to synthesize input from individuals and distribute output to individuals. Private health insurance is a form of socialized medicine. All persons pay premiums whether or not they are ill and draw benefits regardless of how much they have paid in.

3. To note that ownership was legally separated from control does not necessarily endorse a managerial perspective. Managerialism assumes that the legal separation from ownership and control (administration of daily affairs) means that managers became autonomous from capital and free to be even "soulful." While most owners lost authority over administration and strategic planning, managers, especially those without a major ownership share, remained beholden to capital and the class that controlled it. The fact that small holders were generally disenfranchised does not mean that large holders or bondholders were enfeebled. Zeitlin (1974) has labeled the separation of ownership and control a "psuedofact" which he disputes by showing how few-late twentieth-century corporations were truly management controlled.

4. The contested implication of this statement is the managerialist contention that only owners and workers are classes, and that insofar as authority passes to managers, class dynamics are extinguished, as managers are seen to exercise authority as they see fit, as likely to be "soulful" as to maximize profits (Berle and Means 1932; Drucker 1946; Chandler 1977). My point here is that the relationship of managers and owners to workers is not fundamentally changed by the rise of the corporation. The degree to which that relationship is exploitative is beyond the scope of this work.

5. One might argue that behavioral power can be reduced to structural power, since making a command is a way of setting alternatives. The subordinate has a choice of obeying or not and will face different consequences depending on his or her choice. However, the dynamics of exercising by command and by merely setting consequences are different enough to warrant this basic distinction.

6. The law specifies the circumstances under which new stock can be issued, setting a limit on "authorized" capital. Issuing stock beyond that authorized requires the approval of some percentage of the voting stock (the percentage varies from state to state). If stock has no par value, there is no way to calculate authorized stock, which means that directors can issue as much stock as they wish without accountability to stockholders.

7. Littlefield's account, however, does not demonstrate that anyone assumed that major public works projects could be completed except with major government support. Most of his account concerns efforts to mobilize support from the bordering states and federal government, all of whom passed the buck to other jurisdictions.

References

Ardent, Gabriel. 1975. "Financial Policy and Economic Infrastructure of Modern States and Nations." In *The Formation of National States in Western Europe*, ed. Charles Tilly. Princeton: Princeton University Press.

Berk, Gerald. 1994. *Alternative Tracks: The Constitution of American Industrial Order, 1865–1917*. Baltimore: Johns Hopkins University Press.

Berle, Adolf A., and Gardiner C. Means. 1932. *The Modern Corporation and Private Property*. New York: Macmillan.

Boulding, Kenneth E. 1953. *The Organizational Revolution*. New York: Harper and Bros.

Braverman, Harry. 1974. *Labor and Monopoly Capital: The Degradation of Work in the Twentieth Century*. New York: Monthly Review Press.

Campbell, John L., and Leon N. Lindberg. 1991. "The Evolution of Governance Regimes." In *Governance of the American Economy*, ed. John L. Campbell, J. Rogers Hollingsworth, and Leon N. Lindberg. Cambridge: Cambridge University Press.

Carosso, Vincent P. 1970. *Investment Banking in America: A History*. Cambridge: Harvard University Press.

———. 1987. *The Morgans: Private International Bankers, 1854–1913*. Cambridge: Harvard University Press.

Chamberlin, Emerson. 1969. "The Loan Market." In *The New York Stock Exchange: Its History, Its Contribution to National Prosperity, and Its Relation to American Finance at the Outset of the Twentieth Century*, ed. Edmund C. Stedman. New York: Greenwood Press.

Chandler, Alfred D. Jr., 1969. "The Structure of American Industry in the Twentieth Century: A Historical Overview." *Business History Review* 43:255–81.

———. 1977. *The Visible Hand: The Managerial Revolution in American Business*. Cambridge: Harvard University Press.

———. 1990. *Scale and Scope: The Dynamics of Industrial Capitalism*. Cambridge: Harvard University Press.

Creighton, Andrew L. 1990. "The Emergence of Incorporation as a Legal Form for Organizations." Ph.D. diss., Stanford University.

Davis, Joseph S. 1917. *Essays in the Earlier History of American Corporations*. Cambridge: Harvard University Press.

DiMaggio, Paul J., and Walter W. Powell. 1983. "The Iron Cage Revisited: Institutional Isomorphism and Collective Rationality in Organizational Fields." *American Sociological Review* 48:147–60.

Drucker, Peter F. 1946. *The Concept of the Corporation*. New York: John Day.

Edwards, Richard C. 1979. *Contested Terrain: The Transformation of the Workplace in America*. New York: Basic Books.

Fligstein, Neil. 1990. *The Transformation of Corporate Control*. Cambridge: Harvard University Press.

Galambos, Louis. 1970. "The Emerging Organizational Synthesis in American History." *Business History Review* 44:279–90.

Gordon, David M., Richard Edwards, and Michael Reich. 1982. *Segmented Work, Divided Workers: The Historical Transformation of Labor in the United States*. Cambridge: Cambridge University Press.

Hartz, Louis. 1968. *Economic Policy and Democratic Thought, 1776–1860.* Chicago: Quadrangle Books.
Horwitz, Morton J. 1977. *The Transformation of American Law, 1780–1960.* Cambridge: Harvard University Press.
Hounshell, David A. 1984. *From the American System to Mass Production, 1900–1932: The Development of Manufacturing Technology in the United States.* Baltimore: Johns Hopkins University Press.
Hurst, J. Willard. 1978. "The Release of Energy." In *American Law and the Constitutional Order*, ed. Lawrence M. Friedman and Harry N. Schieber. Cambridge: Harvard University Press.
Lamoreaux, Naomi. 1985. *The Great Merger Movement in American Business, 1899–1904.* Cambridge: Cambridge University Press.
Lash, Scott, and John Urry. 1987. *The End of Organized Capitalism.* Madison: University of Wisconsin Press.
Lindberg, Leon N., and John L. Campbell. 1991. "The State and the Organization of Economic Activity." In *Governance of the American Economy*, ed. John L. Campbell, J. Rogers Hollingsworth, and Leon N. Lindberg. Cambridge: Cambridge University Press.
Littlefield, Douglas R. 1984. "The Potomac Company: A Misadventure in Financing an Early American Internal Improvement Project." *Business History Review* 58:562–85.
Logan, John R., and Harvey L. Molotch. 1988. *Urban Fortunes: The Political Economy of Place.* Berkeley and Los Angeles: University of California Press.
Manual of Statistics. 1890, 1901. New York: Manual of Statistics Co.
Meyer, John W., and Brian Rowan. 1977. "Institutionalized Organization: Formal Structure as Myth and Ceremony." *American Journal of Sociology* 83:340–63.
Navin, Thomas R., and Marian V. Sears. 1955. "The Rise of a Market for Industrial Securities, 1887–1902." *Business History Review* 29:105–38.
Nelson, Ralph L. 1959. *Merger Movements in American History.* Princeton: Princeton University Press.
Perlo, Victor. 1957. *The Empire of High Finance.* New York: International Publishers.
Perrow, Charles. 1986. "Economic Theories of Organization." *Theory and Society* 15:11–45.
———. 1991. "A Society of Organizations." *Theory and Society* 20:725–62.
Piore, Michael, and Charles Sabel. 1984. *The Second Industrial Divide: Possibilities for Prosperity.* New York: Basic Books.
Polanyi, Karl. 1957. *The Great Transformation.* Boston: Beacon.
Powell, Walter W., and Paul J. DiMaggio. 1991. *The New Institutionalism in Organizational Analysis.* Chicago: University of Chicago Press.
Renner, K. 1949. *The Institutions of Private Law and Their Social Function.* London: Routledge and Kegan Paul.
Ryan, Alan. 1987. *Property.* Minneapolis: University of Minnesota Press.
Scheiber, Harry N. 1975. "Federalism and the American Economic Order, 1789–1910." *Law and Society Review* 10:51–111.
Seavoy, Ronald E. 1982. *The Origins of the American Business Corporation, 1784–1855: Broadening the Concept of Public Service during Industrialization.* Westport, Conn.: Greenwood Press.

Sewell, William H. 1992. "A Theory of Structure: Duality, Agency, and Transformation." *American Journal of Sociology* 98:1–29.

Sklar, Martin. 1988. *The Corporate Reconstruction of American Capitalism, 1890–1916: The Market, the Law, and Politics*. Cambridge: Cambridge University Press.

Starr, Paul. 1982. *The Social Transformation of American Medicine*. New York: Basic Books.

Studenski, Paul, and Herman E. Krooss. 1963. *Financial History of the United States: Fiscal, Monetary, Banking, and Tariff, Including Financial Administration and State and Local Finance*. New York: Random House.

U.S. Bureau of the Census. 1975. *Historical Statistics of the United States: Colonial Times to 1970*. Washington, D.C.: Government Printing Office.

Wall, Joseph Frazier. 1989. *Andrew Carnegie*. Pittsburgh: University of Pittsburgh Press.

Weber, Max. 1978. *Economy and Society: An Outline of Interpretive Sociology*. Ed. Guenther Roth and Claus Wittich. Trans. Ephraim Fischoff et al. 2 vols. Berkeley and Los Angeles: University of California Press.

Zald, Mayer N. 1978. "On the Social Control of Industries." *Social Forces* 57:79–102.

Zeitlin, Maurice. 1974. "Corporate Ownership and Control: The Large Corporation and the Capitalist Class." *American Journal of Sociology* 79:1073–119.

———. 1980. "On Classes, Class Conflict, and the State: An Introductory Note." In *Classes, Class Conflict, and the State*, ed. Maurice Zeitlin. Cambridge, Mass.: Winthrop.

———. 1989. *The Large Corporation and Contemporary Classes*. Cambridge: Polity.

Zucker, Lynne G. 1977. "The Role of Institutionalization in Cultural Persistence." *American Sociological Review* 42:726–42.

———. 1983. "Organizations as Institutions." In *Perspectives in Organizational Sociology: Theory and Research*, ed. Samuel B. Bacharach. Greenwich, Conn.: JAI Press.

———, ed. 1988. *Institutional Patterns and Organizations: Culture and Environment*. Cambridge, Mass.: Ballinger.

Chapter 17

FROM *CITY OF CAPITAL: POLITICS AND MARKETS IN THE ENGLISH FINANCIAL REVOLUTION*

BRUCE G. CARRUTHERS

INTRODUCTION

Joint-Stock Companies in Political Context

The connections among politics, public finance, and the stock market can be traced on two levels. At the institutional level, political parties were centrally involved in the establishment of the three major joint-stock companies (the Bank of England, the New East India Company, and the South Sea Company), and the attempted (but unsuccessful) founding of the Land Bank. The shares of these companies constituted the majority of all shares traded, and so they dominated the London stock market. The same companies also extended large long-term loans to the government and thereby played an important role in public finance. They embodied, in effect, the connection between the private capital market and public finance.

Contemporaries generally regarded debtor-creditor relationships as one-sided, with creditors enjoying the balance of power. Many believed that as a crucial source of much-needed money, joint-stock companies had leverage over the government. By the end of the War of the Spanish Succession in 1713, the government had borrowed in excess of sixteen million pounds from these three companies, more than from any other source. It also borrowed substantial sums from individual investors in the form of annuities and lottery loans, but that money came from a large number of dispersed creditors who could not act in a politically organized fashion, even if they wanted to. If Parliament's control over public purse strings gave it a voice in government policy, then the companies' control over loans also granted them some influence, or so many thought. For political parties whose goal it was to determine policy, this created a powerful incentive to try to seize the joint-stock companies and exploit the political leverage they possessed.

In addition, such control brought financial rewards. With government spending at wartime levels, public finance provided many profitable opportunities for those with the right connections. Investment in government debt was an attractive alternative to overseas trade, which even in peacetime was a risky investment, and to landed property, which at the end of the seventeenth century was burdened by a heavy land tax and high interest rates.[1] Control over joint-stock companies conferred both political and economic advantages to the party that could seize it.

Political Trading

Individual market behavior also reflected the influence of politics. Participation in a stock market involves buying and selling a financial commodity. Ordinarily, we suppose that the point of the buying and selling is to make money or assemble an optimal investment portfolio. Those who become distracted by other goals are eventually bankrupted by those who keep their eyes on the bottom line. Using data on stock transfers, derived from the stock ledgers of the Bank and East India Company, I study patterns of share ownership and share trading for the East India Company and Bank of England in 1712.[2]

How would one know that a particular trade in a market was politically, as opposed to economically, motivated? Can we tell if a trader was more concerned about partisanship than about pounds, shillings, and pence? There are several things to consider before answering in the affirmative. First, it must be clear that there *could be* some kind of political goal that a trader might have pursued through the market. If there was no plausible political end to be served this way, then one can hardly suppose that people in the market were intentionally behaving "politically." Second, one must have a clear idea of what it meant to be apolitical in the market. That is, one must understand what pattern of behavior would arise if people were uninterested in politics or did not let it influence their trading decisions.

Control over joint-stock companies brought with it the opportunity to influence government policy and provide financial rewards to the party faithful. Political ends could be served in the stock market because decisions about share trading ultimately influenced who controlled the company. Voting and economic rights were both in the bundle of property rights that constituted a company share. A shareholder had claims on profits (in the form of dividends) but he or she also had a right to vote for company directors, and thus could help choose company management. If Whig and Tory parties were struggling for control over the joint-stock companies, then their best strategy was to buy blocks of shares (and avoid selling them to the other party) and use their voting rights to elect Whig or Tory company directors. Thus, political goals could be pursued through the buying and selling of shares.

Apolitical traders will focus upon their economic goals and ignore extraneous concerns and distractions. Traders such as these behave rationally in an economically self-interested way and are the familiar inhabitants of economics textbooks. In competitive markets with secure property rights and homogeneous goods, economically rational traders behave in accordance with the Law of Indifference, enunciated by W. Stanley Jevons (1931). Markets populated by rational traders are anonymous and impersonal. Traders focus on the price and quantity of goods but are indifferent to the social characteristics of the people they deal with. So long as the other person's "money is green," a rational trader will trade with anyone. Early-eighteenth-century London had the kind of capital market to which this law applies. Indeed, historians have noted a number of "marriages of convenience" between kings and their financiers which strongly suggest that political differences could be set aside in the pursuit of mutual economic interests.[3]

The Law of Indifference predicts patterns of trading in which social boundaries are regularly transgressed. Indifferent traders ignore differences in status, gender, class, nationality, race, religion, ethnicity, political allegiances, or whatever other social characteristic one can think of. The pursuit of self-interest compels them to trade across all these lines, and the market such traders create does not respect traditional social distinctions. Under certain circumstances, however, it may be economically rational to pay attention to the social identity of a trading partner. But with secure property rights and homogeneous goods in a competitive market, these circumstances do not apply.

To discriminate is, in economic terms, not to be indifferent.[4] It means treating different categories of people differently. Discriminatory economic behavior occurs, for example, when a buyer or seller responds to some economically irrelevant social characteristic of a potential supplier, client, trading partner, or customer. Gender and race are two common bases for economic discrimination. Refusing to sell goods to someone from another racial group, or refusing to hire a woman (even though she is as qualified for the job as a man) are instances of discrimination. Together, discriminating buyers and sellers reproduce social boundaries in the market.

Although it may seem irrational to discriminate, some explanations have been offered to show how and when discrimination can be economically rational. If social features can be used to indicate other hard-to-measure characteristics, then it may be sensible to discriminate. This is what economists call "statistical discrimination." If gender, for example, could be used to estimate job commitment, then employers might rationally discriminate against women on the grounds that they tended to be less committed to their work than men.[5] Or it may be that because of a faulty legal system, it is important that trading partners be trustworthy. If people cannot trust contract law to enforce their agreements, it would be rational to look for other means of enforcement. People will prefer to trade with others they find trustworthy, and this often means trading with people who are members of the same social group. Common group membership provides the basis for informal sanctions that compensate for the absence of formal legal sanctions.[6]

Such explanations suggest that discrimination in a market (trading that reproduces group boundaries) could be economically rational. In the case of the London stock market, if the Law of Indifference is violated because of political discrimination, it is necessary to be sure that such discrimination was not just solving an economic problem (minimizing transaction costs, providing informal sanctions to compensate for faulty contract law, etc.) before concluding that traders were trying to achieve political goals. But after considering this alternative explanation, I will show how domestic political allegiances and international political commitments influenced patterns of share trading.

My general point is that more than just economic behavior takes place in a market. Although it is considered the primary locus for the single-minded pursuit of profits, a market can be a setting in which to pursue other kinds of ends and enact other kinds of social relationships. People bring to markets a rich set of economic and noneconomic motivations. Markets are not populated solely by *homines economici*, and so to understand the structure and dynamics of the market one must look outside to the social context.

In taking up this line of reasoning, I am extending arguments made by Mark Granovetter (1985, 1992, 1993) and others. Granovetter points out that economic relationships are *embedded* in social relationships, and that one cannot understand economic behavior outside of its social context. His programmatic declaration (1985) left unresolved *how* and *why* economic behavior was embedded in social relations, or in *which* social relations it was embedded. But by tracing out the connections that joined partisan conflict over public policy, the use of the national debt to fund the war, company loans to the government, control over joint-stock companies, votes in directors' elections, and trading in company stock, I will answer these how, why, and which questions for the case of the London stock market.

Trading on the London Stock Market

The most common approach supposes that people behave rationally in markets. They are profit maximizers who evaluate their alternatives and choose the best one. Such *homines economici* are not distracted in their decision making by irrelevant details and they focus on only a few key economic variables like price and quantity. They are indifferent about whom they trade with, ceteris paribus.

The economist W. Stanley Jevons elaborated this view in his Law of Indifference. Jevons considered exchange under ideal market conditions: the goods were perfectly homogeneous, the institutional framework provided enforceable contracts and property rights, and traders were knowledgeable profit-maximizers. When these conditions obtain, people buying and selling are indifferent about which specific commodities they purchase or sell, or with whom they transact (Jevons 1931, 90–92). Economically rational traders pay attention only to quantity and price and do not respond to any other traits.[7] Such traders are indifferent about whom they trade with, so all traders are equally likely to be involved in any given transaction.[8] Trading is done anonymously and pairs of transactors form at random. Thus, social group boundaries are ignored and consequently transgressed. In an active market, randomly joined pairs will gather into a single interconnected network.[9] The Law of Indifference leads to a single interconnected network with no subcliques.

Real markets seldom comply with this theoretical ideal, although some come closer than others. Alfred Marshall stressed that goods have varying degrees of homogeneity and the more homogeneous the good, the more likely it was that traders would be indifferent. The best example of a market with homogeneous goods was the stock exchange, for "Any one share or bond of a public company, or any bond of a government is of exactly the same value as any other of the same issue: it can make no difference to any purchaser which of the two he buys" (Marshall 1938, 326–27).[10] This suggests that the Law of Indifference applies particularly to trading in financial securities. In a modern restatement of Jevons, Telser and Higinbotham argue that

> in an organized market the participants trade a standardized contract such that each unit of the contract is a perfect substitute for any other unit. The identities of the parties in any mutually agreeable transaction do not affect the terms of exchange. The organized market itself or some other institution deliberately creates a homogeneous good that can be traded anonymously by the participants or their agents. (Telser and Higinbotham 1977, 997)

Sociologists like Granovetter reject the image of markets as anonymous institutions. Embeddedness means that the social characteristics of traders influence their behavior. How this occurs depends upon which social characteristics are relevant and also upon the ongoing social relations into which traders are entered. In general, "the pursuit of economic goals is normally accompanied by that of such non-economic ones as sociability, approval, status and power" (Granovetter 1992, 4). The plurality of goals is not something that an economist like Gary Becker would find objectionable in principle, although there would be disagreement over how easily actors could pursue noneconomic goals in a competitive market. But the socially situated character of economic action is something that can only be understood in light of the particular context.[11] An embeddedness argument implies that politics could affect trading, depending on how much people in general cared about politics, and how politicized joint-stock companies were.

To determine the actual role of politics in the stock market, it will be necessary to step away from these theoretical approaches and reconsider the three factors mentioned above: the institutional setting of the market, the characteristics of the financial commodities traded in the market, and the preferences of market participants.

The Financial Sector

In early modern England, a variety of financial instruments could be used to complete a transaction. They developed because of the almost permanent shortage of coin and included things like bills of exchange, promissory notes, sealed bills, exchequer bills, and running-cash notes.[12] Bills of exchange were especially important for trade because they were used for international remittances and formed the core of a complex system of international payments.[13] Other instruments were used mostly for domestic payments. How well these functioned as near-monies depended on their negotiability, which was problematic.[14] Nevertheless, because of these alternatives, specie was not always necessary for trade.

If near-monies were useful for transactions, they were hardly appropriate for long-term investment. In the seventeenth century, investors had a range of alternatives.[15] Land was the oldest, most secure investment, and brought with it considerable social and political benefits. Ownership of a landed estate was a sine qua non for elite social status and conferred influence in both national and local politics.[16] As a purely economic investment, however, its rate of return compared unfavorably with most of the other alternatives.[17] Furthermore, land was difficult to convey and hence was a relatively illiquid asset.

Loans secured by land were another type of investment.[18] Mortgages brought a higher rate of return than land per se, and were riskier, but were still relatively safe as compared to other alternatives. Mortgages were also illiquid because of legal complexities and the lack of a national land registry.[19] Scriveners played an important role in the mortgage market.[20]

Investors could also deposit their money and earn interest. Before the Bank of England there were two places to make deposits: goldsmith-bankers and on a more limited scale, scriveners. Goldsmith-bankers were based mostly in London and took in deposits on a large scale. Before 1672, as the Stop of the Exchequer made clear, a large proportion of these deposits were loaned out to the government, but the goldsmith-bankers also issued "running-cash notes" against their deposits, on a crude fractional-reserve system.[21] In addition, they made a variety of other loans. Bankers' deposits were a relatively liquid investment since they could be withdrawn on short notice. As depositors discovered in 1672, however, they were also risky.[22]

Trade and commerce provided opportunities for both passive and active investment. Active investment meant becoming personally involved in trade.

A large proportion of the active merchant's capital would get absorbed by trade credit (i.e., "circulating," as opposed to "fixed," capital), and without connections and experience it was easy to lose money.[23] For passive investment in trade, people could invest in shipping or in loans secured by ships and their cargo (bottomry loans).[24] The growth in overseas trade provided more opportunities for this kind of investment but it was always very risky.[25]

People could also become involved in trade indirectly. This meant investing in the shares or bonds of joint-stock companies that undertook foreign trade: the East India Company, the South Seas Company, the Royal Africa Company, or the Hudson's Bay Company. The development of this kind of investment was a very important part of the growth of the London stock market.

Social Patterns of Share Ownership and Trading

Transactions are the elementary form of market life, involving the exchange of one commodity for another or for money. An empirical analysis of the stock market must, therefore, focus on transactions. The major practical issue is how to "measure" transactions and where to obtain data.

For several reasons, I have selected 1712 as the best year from this period to gather data. Unlike 1710, 1715, or 1720, there were no economic or financial crises to distort the market.[26] The War of the Spanish Succession was winding down and although it was not yet over, its fiscal demands were diminishing. Furthermore, 1712 was not a year with national parliamentary elections (unlike 1708, 1710, and 1713), so there was no general election to inflame partisan feelings. The year 1712 came after the establishment of the South Sea Company (which occurred in 1711) and after the merger of the two East India companies, so there were three major joint-stock companies, each with a different relationship to extant political forces. Comparisons among the three companies can provide important analytical leverage. The year 1712 also preceded the accession of George I (1715), a regnal transition which resulted in a sea change in political forces as the Tory party was consigned to political near-oblivion. Most important, however, 1712 was sufficiently late that one could say the stock market was "up and running." Data from the 1690s and early 1700s would be open to the objection that the market was still too undeveloped to provide a fair test of theories of economic action. From both the perspective of economics and politics, market trading in 1712 was not unduly influenced by national electioneering, financial disasters, company mergers, or the immaturity of the market.

Table 17.1 describes shareholdings and transactions (both purchases and sales) for the Bank of England and East India Company. From the numbers of shareholders, it is clear just how much bigger the market for Bank shares was as compared to East India shares (4,419 vs. 2,261). This difference car-

TABLE 17.1
Shareholdings and Transactions in Bank of England, and United East India Company Stock, 1712

	Shares Owned	*Number of Transactions*
Bank of England		
Mean	1,239.62	1.39
SD	2,762.91	6.72
Median	500.00	0.00
Sum	5,458,055	3,077
N (no. of shareholders) = 4,419		
East India Company		
Mean	1,414.49	1.62
SD	3,497.61	5.40
Median	500.00	0.00
Sum	3,126,016	1,826
N = 2,261		

ried over into the number of market transactions, which totaled around 3,000 for the Bank and 1,800 for the East India Company, and the number of shares (5.5 million for the Bank and 3.1 million for the East India Company).

The variation in holdings among East India Company shareholders was considerably greater than among Bank shareholders. Although median shareholdings were the same (£500 worth), the mean for the East India Company (£1,414.5) was higher than the Bank mean (£1,239.6) because of a relatively large group of very wealthy shareholders.[27] The difference exists at the other end of the shareholding spectrum as well: 25 percent of Bank shareholders held less than £126 worth, while the twenty-fifth percentile for the East India Company was £160. At the time, the Bank was considered to be a more conservative investment, and hence more attractive to small-time investors.

There were more trades in Bank stock but in terms of *relative* activity it appears that the East India Company takes precedence. The average number of transactions for East India Company shareholders was 1.62, while for the Bank it was 1.39. The ninety-ninth percentile for East India transactions was 22, in contrast to only 12 for the Bank. These differences must be taken in context, however, for most shareholders were inactive. Median transactions for both companies was 0. The majority of shareholders simply hung on to their investments, although there was a greater tendency for East India shareholders to play the market.[28]

Shares of both the Bank of England and the East India Company were traded on the London stock market but they were distinct securities, particularly in terms of risk. It is valuable to know the degree of overlap between the two "submarkets," and because active traders dominated the total volume of trades, it is sufficient to consider the active traders. Defined as those making seven or more trades, these traders comprised only 3 percent of the Bank shareholders, and 4.5 percent of East India Company shareholders, yet as buyers or sellers (or both) they accounted for 40 percent and 50 percent, respectively, of all trades. If we shift the threshold down to five or more trades, active traders still constituted only 5 percent of Bank shareholders and 7 percent of East India shareholders but accounted for 47 percent and 58 percent, respectively, of total trades.

Among active traders, Whigs outnumbered the Tories between three and four to one. They comprised only men, and included no persons living abroad. Naturalized, Huguenot, Quaker, or Jewish individuals constituted a significant proportion (about 20 percent for the East India Company, and 30 percent for the Bank). There were no peers in this group, and only two baronets, so England's traditional landed elites were essentially absent.

Bank and East India Company active traders overlapped considerably. Of 192 individuals, more than one-fifth were active traders in both stocks, and these 43 men accounted for a substantial proportion of all trades. There may have been "submarkets" for Bank and East India Company shares but much of the trading in both was accounted for by a single group of individuals. Active traders were a small group that met face-to-face in the same small location, Exchange Alley. They accounted for the bulk of trading in both securities, although some of them specialized in either Bank or East India shares. The overlap between the two groups of active traders is consistent with the analysis of price movements. Social overlap led to common price changes.

In the previous chapter, we analyzed the Bank and East India Company shareholders in terms of gender, social background, social status, and political affiliations. It was clear that shareholders were a diverse group but with a strong tendency to favor men, merchants, nongentry, and Whigs. There was also a small number of prominent traders who were members of ethnic or religious minority groups. Party differences among shareholders are particularly interesting because of their connection to larger political and economic struggles. The contrast between the numbers of Whigs and Tories is especially striking because the primary sources of political information, the two London poll books, are biased in favor of the Tories. Whig dominance is probably underestimated.

The Whig-Tory distinction loomed large in the composition of the stock market. Whigs dominated, although they did not monopolize, the market.

TABLE 17.2
Party Trading in United East India Company Shares, and Log-Linear Analysis

	Tories	*Whigs*	*Unknown*
Tories	39		
Whigs	221	565	
Unknown	134	610	228
Model		*Degrees of Freedom*	G^2
1. No effects		5	1,071.20
2. Quasi independence		3	15.78
3. Endogamy		2	2.14

The Whig-Tory distinction was also salient at the level of company directors and the political struggle for control over joint-stock companies. Did compositional differences among shareholders generate behavioral differences, or to put it differently, did political differences at the institutional level produce political differences in the market? When shareholders transacted, did it matter that potential trading partners were Whigs or Tories, Jews or non-Jews, Huguenots or non-Huguenots? Theoretically, our expectations about trading behavior are set by the arguments reviewed earlier. If this is an efficient market for a homogeneous good, then the Law of Indifference ought to hold. Characterizations like Defoe's only reinforce the impression that politics didn't matter in the stock market.

The top part of table 17.2 sets out trading among Tories, Whigs, and political unknowns in East India Company shares and describes the political characteristics of pairs of traders.[29] No distinction is made between buying and selling; we are concerned here only with trading per se. There are six combinations (Whig trading with Whig, Whig with Tory, Whig with Unknown, Tory with Tory, etc.). The upper right of the table is not filled in since it is just the mirror image of the lower left. The table shows that the two most frequent combinations are Whig trading with Whig, and Whig with Unknown. This is to be expected given that Whigs were more numerous and active than the others.[30] To address the predictions for market trading, however, we need more than just raw numbers.

Table 17.2 can be analyzed using log-linear techniques.[31] What makes these methods useful is that one can operationalize Law of Indifference predictions about market trading. The lower panel of table 17.2 presents the results of fitting three different log-linear models. The no-effects model is a baseline model and predicts equal counts in every cell by estimating a single "propensity to trade" parameter across all political pairings. The likelihood-ratio statistic G^2, which measures how well the model fits the data, is very large, meaning that the model fits poorly. Model 2, the "quasi-independence" model, is the Law of Indifference model.[32] It assumes that each group of traders has a different "propensity to trade" and that they select their trading partners at random, without consideration of politics. It provides a much better fit than the no-effects model, but the predicted and actual counts still diverge considerably.[33] Examination of residuals (not presented here) shows that the Law of Indifference model consistently *underestimates* how much people trade with members of the same party, and *overestimates* how much people from different parties trade with each other.[34] The model most underestimates Tories trading with Tories.

The third model I call the endogamy model because not only does each group have a different "propensity to trade," but there is a parameter measuring the extent to which members of a political group favor trading with other people from the same group. This model uses up another degree of freedom but provides a much better fit than the quasi-independence model. The G^2 statistic drops from 15.78 down to 2.14, a substantial improvement, and there does not appear to be any systematic misfitting of the model. For East India Company stock, there was a strong tendency for party members to favor trading with people from the same party. Contrary to the Law of Indifference (and Daniel Defoe), people did not trade at random: they discriminated on the basis of politics. Whigs traded disproportionately with Whigs, and Tories with Tories.[35]

One can try to explain this pattern, which I term *political endogamy*, in a number of ways. Endogamy might be spurious, it might be a rational response to transaction costs (following Homogeneous Middleman Group theory), or it might be a genuinely political phenomenon. The most obvious explanation, that strong political cleavages made it difficult as a practical matter to trade across party lines, is clearly wrong. Trading of shares, occurred in the coffee shops of Exchange Alley, and there were no separate Whig and Tory stock markets. To begin to explain endogamy, however, it is necessary to understand more about it.

One important dimension is that of number of trades, and splitting the table this way distinguishes market specialists from other traders. The distribution of trades is highly skewed, with a small number of traders accounting for a large number of trades. The explanation of financial endogamy depends on which subtable(s) it persists in. If the small number of active traders traded endogamously, there could have been a conscious arrangement (a "conspiracy") at work. One can imagine something like a price cartel, where instead of trying to raise prices, the conspirators restricted between-group trades. If endogamy existed among the large number of inactive traders, however, a conspiracy seems unlikely and endogamy would have to be the result of a sentiment or condition general enough to influence a large number of persons.[36]

TABLE 17.3
Party Trading in United East India Company Shares Involving Active Traders

	Tories	*Whigs*	*Unknown*
Tories	26		
Whigs	178	496	
Unknown	77	445	93
Model		*Degrees of Freedom*	G^2
1. No effects		5	1,031.10
2. Quasi independence		3	4.48
3. Endogamy		2	4.32

Table 17.3 shows trades in East India stock that involved the active traders (anyone trading seven or more times). This group included the professional traders, those who earned their living and sometimes great notoriety on the London stock market (e.g., Moses Hart and John "Vulture" Hopkins). By this criterion, the number of active traders was very small in relation to the total number of East India Company shareholders: only 102 out of 2,261 (roughly 4.5 percent). It was an extremely wealthy and active group, for on average they owned £5,015 worth of East India shares and traded eighteen times. These individuals were responsible for a disproportionate share of all transactions in East India stock, but it turns out they accounted for virtually none of the endogamy pattern.

Unlike the market as a whole, among active traders the endogamy model performs no better than the quasi-independence model (the G^2 statistics for the two models are virtually the same). The quasi-independence model does a reasonable job fitting the data and there is no systematic underprediction of within-party trades, or overprediction of between-party trades. As far as politics was concerned, the professional brokers at the core of the market did not discriminate, and endogamy cannot be understood as the result of coordinated action on the part of this small group.

If we consider the other subtable, trades that involved only "small," inactive traders, we find endogamy. Table 17.4 presents the trades and the results of the log-linear analysis.

An examination of the fitted values and residuals shows that among inactive traders, there is more within-group trading than one would expect if trading partners were chosen at random. The drop in the G^2 statistic shows the endogamy model to be an improvement over the quasi-independence model. It seems that whatever caused political endogamy was general enough to influence the behavior of a large number of persons.

TABLE 17.4
Party Trading in United East India Company Shares Involving Inactive Traders

	Tories	*Whigs*	*Unknown*
Tories	13		
Whigs	43	69	
Unknown	57	165	135
Model		*Degrees of Freedom*	G^2
1. No effects		5	240,00
2. Quasi independence		3	5.53
3. Endogamy		2	1.15

Another important dimension is wealth, measured here by the size of shareholding. Table 17.5 shows the distribution of trades after splitting the sample into trades which involved wealthy shareholders (defined as a shareholding greater than £5,477) and those which did not.[37]

This log-linear analysis shows that the endogamy pattern persisted among the wealthy shareholders but not among the "poorer" shareholders. The quasi-independence model underpredicts within-group trading and overpredicts between-group trading, and according to the G^2 statistic, the endogamy model fits the data much better.

Separating traders according to activity and wealth shows that political endogamy was not a universal phenomenon. Some traders in East India Company stock discriminated politically while others did not. In particular, endogamy centered around the wealthy shareholders and those who were inactive traders. This was a group that largely *excluded* the market professionals.

The Politics of Endogamy

In an era characterized by the "rage of party," political affiliations were a defining social characteristic. How people voted was usually public knowledge, and consequently the connection between the joint-stock companies and political parties influenced trading in East India Company stock.[38] Company shares conferred both economic and "political" rights since owners enjoyed a claim on profits and a right to vote. A party's voting base in the directors' elections comprised the shares owned by party members. When party members sold shares, that voting base would be eroded if they were sold to a supporter of the other party, or conserved, if sold to a fellow mem-

TABLE 17.5
Party Trading in United East India Company Shares That Involved Wealthy Shareholders

	Tories	*Whigs*	*Unknown*
Tories	10		
Whigs	62	185	
Unknown	27	65	27
Model		*Degrees of Freedom*	G^2
1. No effects		5	367.70
2. Quasi independence		3	26.76
3. Endogamy		2	5.03

ber. Given the intense contest for control of the East India Company, it seems that traders were choosing the latter option. Whig shareholders were not simply selling shares, they were selling Whig shares and so preferred to sell them to other Whigs. Of course, Whigs would prefer to sell to other Whigs (and conserve the voting base of the party) but would also like to buy from Tories (and expand the base). But for a Whig to buy from a Tory, the Tory must sell, which went against the Tory's political interests. Freely negotiated transactions generally occurred only when in the (perceived) mutual interests of both buyer and seller. Self-interest in this context included political and economic components.

Politically, within-party transactions were mutually beneficial. Between-party transactions, in contrast, enlarged the base of one party and diminished that of the other. Since it was not in the interests of both parties, such a transaction was less likely to occur. Of course, cross-party transactions did happen, as can be seen from the tables analyzed above. This could be the result of variation in the strength of partisanship (e.g., lukewarm Tories would be more willing to sell to Whigs than would hard-line Tories) but also because of trade-offs between political and economic interests. A Whig could more easily purchase shares from a Tory if he offered a higher price. The Tory would then face a trade-off between his political interests (which would reject the deal) and his economic interests (which would mean acceptance).[39]

It was only in the East India Company that partisan considerations noticeably influenced trading patterns. This is consistent with Mirowski's finding that only in the case of the East India Company did "share prices have no statistically significant relation to profitability" (Mirowski 1981, 575). Evidently, something besides profits drove the market for these shares.[40] What distinguished the East India Company from the Bank (and the South Sea

Company) was that it was heavily contested. Neither party had firm control over the court of directors and so every trade potentially could shift the political balance from one side to the other.[41]

According to Gary Becker's model of discrimination, if the stock market was perfectly competitive, the party pattern of trading would have involved only a small economic concession to political interest. One would see the "segregation" of shareholdings into Whig and Tory camps but with no significant price differences. To sell shares to a fellow Whig would be easy if the alternative was to sell at the same price to a Tory, the political equivalent of a "free lunch." But in a less than perfect market, a trader who restricted himself to fellow party members was forgoing whatever economic opportunities might be presented by dealing with the other party. Just as a racially discriminating employer hurts him or herself by not hiring qualified minorities, so does a politically discriminating Whig who forgoes dealing with a Tory.

To see how this might happen, consider that a trader wishing to buy shares would be interested in paying the lowest price. He or she would survey the market and collect offer prices, looking for the lowest one. Price dispersion is typical in markets and so the potential buyer will get a range of offers.[42] In general, the larger the sample of sale prices, the lower the expected value of the lowest price.[43] In other words, the more offers the buyer collects, the lower the price he or she will have to pay for the shares. By restricting trading partners to fellow party members, a trader reduced the sample of sale prices and so was likely to pay more for the shares he bought. A similar opportunity cost would be paid by someone looking to sell at the highest price.

Even if this opportunity cost argument were false, and the stock market was perfect and endogamous trading was costless, it would be hard to explain the pattern of political endogamy without concluding that it involved some kind of economic price. If political discrimination were costless, all traders could freely indulge their political whims with no financial penalty. In fact, however, actively trading Whigs and Tories did not let partisanship influence their trades, although many others did. This important difference makes sense if endogamy had a price: active traders were professionals whose livelihood involved trading on the stock market, and so they could not afford to let partisanship interfere with profits.[44] Given their level of activity, even a modest cost would mount up when added across multiple trades.

It seems that the indifference of active traders was predicated on political discrimination among the more numerous inactive traders.[45] With politically defined "submarkets," in which political allies traded with each other, indifferent professional traders could make money by trading or arbitraging between them. Opportunities to exploit price differences between the submarkets would be forgone by discriminating traders, but not by the indifferent. However, without politically discriminating traders, there would be no opportunities for the indifferent to exploit.[46]

TABLE 17.6
East India Company Shareholder Same-Party Partisanship by Political Status

Political Status	*Proportion of All Trades with Same Party*	*Number of Cases*
Politically active	0.2854	110
Politically inactive	0.1179	990
All shareholders	0.1346	1,100

It is telling that the East India Company Tories were more endogamous than the Whigs. In the log-linear analysis, even the endogamy model (which assumes that groups are equally endogamous) underestimates the extent to which the Tories traded among themselves. As the minority in a politically hostile environment, Tories were especially likely to seek out other Tories even though the opportunity cost of endogamy was highest for them (by refusing to trade with Whigs, they were ignoring most of the potential trading partners).

As further evidence of politically motivated trades, consider individual-level trading patterns among East India Company shareholders. By focusing on individuals rather than pairs, we lose the dyadic quality of transactions but gain further insight into the political texture of the market. If political considerations led to politicized trading, then we might expect that politically active traders would be more likely to trade along partisan lines. Table 17.6 takes all the people who traded East India Company shares and constructs for each an index of how frequently they traded with fellow party members (a person trading only with fellow members would score 1). Using this index, the overall proportion of within-party trades for all 1,100 traders is low (0.1346) because of the large numbers of political unknowns and the frequency of trade between party members and unknowns. That aside, however, there is a striking difference between those who were politically active and those who were not.[47] Politically active traders were much more likely to trade with members of the same party than those who were politically inactive.

The results in table 17.6 are dampened by the large numbers of political unknowns. If we remove them, and consider outright partisanship, another strong pattern emerges. Table 17.7 includes only trades by East India Company shareholders who were either Whigs or Tories.

Both Whig and Tory partisans tended to trade with Whigs. Among the 530 shareholders in table 17.7, the overall proportion of trades with Tories was 0.31, while that for Whigs was 0.69. This is an unsurprising consequence of the fact that there were many more Whigs than Tories in the market, and the Whigs were more active. If we divide shareholders into Whig

TABLE 17.7
East India Company Shareholder Partisanship by Party Support

Partisanship	*Proportion of Party Trades with Tories*	*Proportion of Party Trades with Whigs*	*Number of Cases*
Tory supporters	0.4304	0.5696	136
Whig supporters	0.2690	0.7310	394
All shareholders	0.3103	0.6897	530

and Tory supporters, and consider their propensity to trade with other Whigs or Tories, there is a consistent pattern of partisanship. Tory supporters were more likely to trade with Tories than Whig supporters, and Whig supporters were more likely to trade with Whigs than Tory supporters.

Evidence of politics in the stock market is found primarily among patterns of behavior. To be sure, there is much to suggest why political concerns mattered in the market: strident conflict in the society at large, the political salience of joint-stock companies, and the connection between the voting rights attached to share-ownership and the political composition of company directorships. There is, alas, very little evidence that directly documents the subjective motivations and intentions of those who traded shares. Merchants and financiers were not given to recorded introspection, and the documents they left behind chronicled debits and credits much more than designs and concerns.[48] In the absence of such evidence, it may still seem implausible to some that traders in a competitive financial market could have been politically motivated, and some readers might be tempted to return to an economic explanation of party endogamy. Yet the significance of political motivations is not so improbable as it may seem at first.

There are clear instances of investors who were motivated by politics. Sarah, duchess of Marlborough, for example, was a notorious Whig sympathizer, and even though she could not vote in parliamentary elections, her social stature and friendship with Queen Anne made her a powerful political figure. The duchess consistently favored the Whigs in both her public and private undertakings, including her investments. Thus she invested in the Bank of England and in 1712 held in her own name £5,750 worth of stock. Furthermore, despite her penchant for financial investments, the duchess refused to have anything to do with the South Sea Company. Its Tory connections were strong enough to earn her disapproval. Only after the South Sea Company joined the Hanoverian interest in 1714 did she begin to buy South Sea stock. With her enormous wealth the duchess had a substantial economic incentive to invest in a variety of financial securities, but chose not to do so for political reasons.[49]

There are other examples of political investment, including Dr. William Stratford of Christ Church, Oxford, who wrote in a letter of November 1712:

> I am glad to perceive that South Sea rises, I had that faith in my Lord Treasurer [Oxford, the Tory] as to venture all the little ready money that I have in it, I hope it will be at par before the Parliament meets. I expect some strange turn, for the worse I am afraid in my own soul, now I am got into the funds, which I never was before in my life. (Historical Manuscripts Commission, p. 112)

Stratford was just the kind of neophyte investor who would let his Tory loyalties lead him into a new and unfamiliar financial venture. Many other Tories bought Bank stock in 1710 so that they could vote in the directors' elections, not because they had all suddenly decided that the Bank was a good investment. Among Whigs, Anne Clavering wrote to her father in 1710 that "Mr. Lamberts' other bill becomes due when I must return to town. He remitts mony for the new [Tory] Treasury so I will not putt to much confidence in a Tory" (Dickinson 1967, 97). Clavering recognized the political loyalties of financiers, and shaped her dealings with them accordingly.

The variegated nature of endogamous trading suggests that different groups had different concerns. In 1712, professional traders were much more likely to conform to the Law of Indifference than others. Whatever their politics, they would leave partisanship at the entrance to Exchange Alley. In a related context, Rabb (1967) noted that early-seventeenth-century investors in English joint-stock companies also had varied motives for investment. While professional merchants used profitability as their criterion for investment, the gentry were more easily swayed by political considerations and the chance to pursue national glory. Colonies and dramatic explorations were more attractive to the investing squirearchy and aristocracy than to merchants.[50] Not surprisingly, gentry investors were more likely to lose their money. Furthermore, Brenner (1993) points out the importance of Puritanism as a motivation for certain of the colonial projects undertaken during the 1620s. As he put it: "the raison d'être of these ventures [e.g., the Massachusetts Bay Company] was primarily religious and political" (Brenner 1993, 272).[51] Nor was the intrusion of politics into business symptomatic of an immature capitalist spirit, for such things happened in the eighteenth century as well. During the Jacobite uprising of 1745, for example, London merchants signing a declaration stating that they would accept Bank bills were taken to be Whigs.[52] Economic action during the financial crisis was interpreted politically.

Credit relationships were ubiquitous because of the shortage of ready money, and many were constructed without the benefit of formal contracts or debt instruments. Merchants typically bought and sold on credit, and settled accounts at the year's end.[53] Credit relationships would seem to provide a perfect opportunity to witness *homo economicus* unbound, for debtors and creditors could easily gauge their economic interests and act accordingly. When discussed by contemporaries, however, credit relations were interpreted through an ethos of neighborliness, and framed by a language of moral obligation.[54] Such an ethos was more likely to emerge in smaller communities, but it nevertheless shows how noneconomic concerns could enter the early modern market.

These indications are only suggestive, of course, but when joined with economic behavior that is patterned along political lines, the case for political motives in the market becomes much stronger. Even in a competitive market, people were not single-mindedly devoted to profits. They recognized that share-ownership had political and economic consequences.

Notes

1. Earle points out that the return on investment in land "compared unfavourably with almost any other form of investment" (1989, 152).

2. There are no surviving South Sea Company financial records for this period.

3. For example: "Money as always was mobile and its exchange transcended political frontiers even during the big European wars. Huguenot money was lent to Louis XIV by Protestant bankers based in Amsterdam and Geneva, notwithstanding the impecunious Sun King's persecution of their coreligionists who had remained in France. Similarly, the British government probably did not deem it politic to examine the religious beliefs or political backgrounds of bankers prepared to lend it money and enable it to use their credit facilities on the European continent" (Murphy 1986, 26).

4. As I am using the term, discrimination does not mean "price discrimination."

5. See Goldin 1990, 88–89, 214.

6. See Landa 1981; and Cooter and Landa 1984.

7. Jevons was not the first to suggest that rational traders are willing to overlook a lot in the pursuit of profit. As the Roman poet Juvenal expressed it in his *Satires*: "The smell of profit is clean / And sweet, whatever the source."

8. See Cooter and Landa 1984, 15; and Landa 1981, 351.

9. This follows from Friedkin 1981, 44; and Baker 1990, 595.

10. See also Walras 1954, 83–84.

11. Studies have shown the importance of social factors for economic behavior. Podolny (1993) notes the role that status rankings played in competition among American investment banks. Biggart (1989) shows how gender and family relations shape the marketing strategies of direct selling organizations. How culture influenced market prices is Zelizer's focus in her study of insurance (1979). Even money, the primary agent of abstract, rational calculation, is imbued with social meaning (Zelizer 1989, 1994). See also Child 1964.

12. See Anderson 1970, 98.

13. Sperling 1962.

14. See Kerridge 1988, 40–41.

15. By the end of the century, the alternatives also included public lotteries, annuities, tallies, and Exchequer bills.

16. Coleman 1951, 224; and Stone and Stone 1984, 11.

17. Earle 1989, 152; and Grassby 1969, 739.

18. There were a number of different ways in which to configure a mortgage. For a discussion of their legal evolution, see Anderson 1969, 12.

19. See Jones 1988, 281.

20. Their traditional job involved drawing up legal documents (often for the mortgaging or conveyancing of land), but they branched out as brokers for mortgages. Some scriveners even took deposits and acted as bankers, although most confined their financial activities to mortgages. See Melton 1986, 9, 33; and Coleman 1951; 221.

21. For a discussion of these bankers' notes, see Richards 1929, 40–43.

22. Horsefield 1977, 121.

23. In a sample of business inventories, Earle found that the median proportion of liabilities to total assets was about 25 percent. This is likely to be an underestimate, but it shows how much businessmen depended upon credit (Earle 1989, table 4.4).

24. Ships were usually owned by partnerships, not single owners. To minimize risks, the partnerships usually consisted of between ten and twenty partners (Davis 1962, 82, 87).

25. See Davis 1954, 150. Investment in shipping was especially risky during war. Witness the fate of the Turkey Fleet, and all those with a financial interest in it, when it was attacked in 1693 by the French navy. Total losses were estimated at around £600,000 (Jones 1972, 320).

26. See Hoppit 1986.

27. This discrepancy continued further out into the tails of the distribution of shareholdings. The ninety-fifth percentile for the East India Company was £5,478, while for the Bank it was £4,592. The ninety-ninth percentile for the East India Company was £18,217, while for the Bank it was only £12,161.

28. This is consistent with the fact that price-volatility was greater for East India shares than for Bank shares. Changing prices encourage more buying and selling.

29. The stock ledgers distinguished between regular share transfers and those which occurred after a shareholder died, as his or her estate was divided among the heirs. Inheritance practices did not produce the pattern of share transfers among Whigs, Tories, and Unknowns.

30. Since the most frequent combination involves Whigs and Unknowns, it is worth considering who got classified in the latter category. Given the available documentary sources, it is highly likely that many party supporters could not be tracked down. In other words, "unknowns" includes many Whigs and Tories, as well as those who were truly apolitical.

31. For advice on data analysis, I thank Stephen Stigler, Peter McCullagh, David Wallace, and Per Myklund, from the Department of Statistics, University of Chicago.

32. "Quasi-independence" (Goodman 1984, appendix A) refers to independence models of triangular contingency tables. For more details on the statistical models used here, see Carruthers 1991, chap. 7.

33. I have not done formal significance tests of these results for three reasons. All transactions in Bank and East India Company stock are in the data set, so the data represent a population, not a sample, and thus sampling theory is not very relevant. Second, the improvements in fit are so substantial that no test is necessary to see the differences between models. For instance, the G^2 statistic drops from 15.78 to 2.14

between the quasi-independence and endogamy models. For nested models, this difference is chi-square distributed with one degree of freedom and is significant at the 0.0005 level. Third, these data probably violate the assumption of independence since the likelihood that person A trades with person B could well be affected by whether or not A traded with person C.

34. Residuals are simply the difference between the actual counts in the table and the values predicted by particular models. Large residuals mean a poor fitting model and a high value for the G^2.

35. Analysis of two-by-two tables of trades excluding the political Unknowns gives the same result: a strong tendency for trading to occur within parties.

36. Cartels become harder to organize and maintain the larger the number of conspirators.

37. This particular cutoff point corresponded to the ninety-fifth percentile for shareholdings. There were 110 shareholders owning more than £5,477 of East India Company shares.

38. Endogamous trading may also have been a way to affirm political allegiances or bolster party solidarity.

39. Unfortunately, existing price data are daily prices, and are not transaction specific. Companies recorded share transfers, but not the price paid by the buyer. Thus for a given share and fixed time one cannot measure the price differences between a Tory sale to another Tory, and a Tory sale to a Whig.

40. Lease, McConnell, and Mikkelson (1983) show in a modern setting how the value of shareholder voting rights is reflected in share prices.

41. Although the proportion of Whig-to-Tory shareholders was about the same in the two companies, the proportions for directors were quite different.

42. See, e.g., Ashenfelter 1989; Isard 1977; Marvel 1976; Rothschild 1973; and Telser 1973. Maynes et al. (1984) found that even for homogeneous commodities in the same urban area at the same time, the ratio of highest to lowest price sometimes exceeded four-to-one. That is, some sellers were offering goods at a price four times higher than other sellers of the very same good.

43. If sale prices are randomly distributed, then a buyer will be interested in the first-order statistic of the sample of prices drawn from the market (i.e., the lowest price). The distribution of order statistics, and their expected values, is well understood, and in general the larger the sample, the lower the expectation of the first-order statistic (Stigler 1968; David 1970; see the tables in Harter 1969). Similarly, a seller would want to get the highest price, i.e., the n-th order statistic of the sample of n offer prices received from the market. The larger the sample n, the higher the expectation of the n-th order statistic. In other words, to get on average a lower purchase price, or a higher offer price, a trader needs a bigger sample. Thus, someone who refuses to buy from half of the sellers in the market can expect to pay a higher price, even if the buyer picks the lowest price from the subsample. Likewise, someone who refuses to sell to half of the buyers in the market can expect to sell at a lower price.

44. This is why Defoe is partly right in his characterization of the stock market: politics did not affect the trades of the most active traders.

45. Thanks to Ken Dauber for raising this issue.

46. There appear to be two distinct groups in the stock market: fully rational arbitrageurs, and (financially) irrational traders. Recent "noisy trader" models of

financial markets (Grossman and Stiglitz 1980; De Long et al. 1990; and Shleifer and Summers 1990) posit a similar distinction in which the market is populated by a small number of rational traders and a large number of traders who do not respond to the underlying fundamentals of the securities they trade, and there is a suggestive congruence between the models and the results presented here. These newer financial models differ from older ones by showing that the "rational" traders need not drive the "irrational" ones out of the market, and so their coexistence is not a temporary aberration. Early-eighteenth-century noisy traders may have been irrational from an economic standpoint, but may have had very good reasons, albeit noneconomic ones, for doing what they did.

47. By my definition, traders who sat in the Commons or the House of Lords, or who were company directors, were politically active.

48. There is another reason why such evidence may be scarce, and this has to do with the idiom of motivation. When people reflect on why they have done something and record or communicate their thoughts in a form accessible to later generations, they usually draw upon socially constituted idioms. Such reflections on motive are in part rationalizations, and are done with an eye to casting actions in a reasonable or legitimate light. In the early eighteenth century, there was one good reason to avoid framing motives in political terms, and there may have been another recommending economic motives. Although parties were real facts of political life, they were very new and not fully legitimate. Parties were denounced as factions, as representing particular interests rather than the general interest. The idea of institutionalized political conflict had not yet taken hold. All this meant that it was not entirely legitimate to openly embrace political parties. One could not comfortably cast one's motives in a partisan mold. This would make people hesitant to represent their motives as partisan motives, even if that were true (if anything, people were likely to label the motives of their political opponents as partisan). There may have been another reason why economic motives for economic behavior would be stressed. Although the stock market was new, markets in general were not, and the profit motive was widely recognized. To appear reasonable in their financial dealings, people might have preferred to stress their economic motives. This would be particularly true among the mercantile and commercial groups who dominated the stock market.

49. See Harris 1991; 115–16, 227.

50. See Rabb 1967; 31, 36, 41, 69.

51. See also Brenner 1993; 149, 153.

52. See Sutherland 1962; 2.

53. Legal records provide ample evidence of the importance of credit relationships, as Muldrew (1993b) shows.

54. See Muldrew 1993a; 163, 177–81; and Tittler 1994.

References

Anderson, B. L. 1969. "Provincial Aspects of the Financial Revolution of the Eighteenth Century." *Business History* 11, no. 1:11–22.

———. 1970. "Money and the Structure of Credit in the Eighteenth Century." *Business History* 12, no. 2:85–101.

Ashenfelter, Orley. 1989. "How Auctions Work for Wine and Art." *Journal of Economic Perspectives* 3:23–36.

Baker, Wayne E. 1990. "Market Networks and Corporate Behavior." *American Journal of Sociology* 96:589–625.

Biggart, Nicole Woolsey. 1989. *Charismatic Capitalism: Direct Selling Organizations in America.* Chicago: University of Chicago Press.

Brenner, Robert. 1993. *Merchants and Revolution: Commercial Change, Political Conflict, and London's Overseas Traders, 1550–1653.* Princeton: Princeton University Press.

Carruthers, Bruce G. 1991. "State-Building and Market-Making: The Politics of Public Debt in the English Financial Revolution, 1672–1712." Ph.D. diss., University of Chicago.

Coleman, D. C. 1951. "London Scriveners and the Estate Market in the Later Seventeenth Century." *Economic History Review* 4:221–30.

Cooter, Robert, and Janet T. Landa. 1984. "Personal versus Impersonal Trade: The Size of Trading Groups and Contract Law." *International Review of Law and Economics* 4:15–22.

David, H. A. 1970. *Order Statistics.* New York: Wiley.

Davis, Ralph. 1954. "English Foreign Trade, 1660–1700." *Economic History Review* 7:150–66.

———. 1962. *The Rise of the English Shipping Industry in the Seventeenth and Eighteenth Centuries.* Newton Abbot: David and Charles.

De Long, J. Bradford, Andrei Shleifer, Lawrence H. Summers, and Robert J. Waldmann. 1990. "Noise Trader Risk in Financial Markets." *Journal of Political Economy* 98:703–38.

Dickinson, H. T., ed. 1967. *The Correspondence of Sir James Clavering.* Surtees Society Publication, vol. 178.

Earle, Peter. 1989. *The Making of the English Middle Class.* Berkeley and Los Angeles: University of California Press.

Friedkin, Noah E. 1981. "The Development of Structure in Random Networks." *Social Networks* 3:41–52.

Goldin, Claudia. 1990. *Understanding the Gender Gap: An Economic History of American Women.* Oxford: Oxford University Press.

Goodman, Leo A. 1984. *The Analysis of Cross-Classified Data Having Ordered Categories.* Cambridge: Harvard University Press.

Granovetter, Mark. 1985. "Economic Action, Social Structure, and Embeddedness." *American Journal of Sociology* 91:481–510.

———. 1992. "Economic Institutions as Social Constructions." *Acta Sociologica* 35:3–11.

———. 1993. "The Nature of Economic Relationships." In *Explorations in Economic Sociology,* ed. Richard Swedberg. New York: Russell Sage.

Grassby, Richard. 1969. "The Rate of Profit in Seventeenth-Century England," *English Historical Review* 84:721–51.

Grossman, Sanford J., and Joseph E. Stiglitz. 1980. "On the Impossibility of Informationally Efficient Markets." *American Economic Review* 70:393–408.

Harris, Frances. 1991. *A Passion for Government: The Life of Sarah, Duchess of Marlborough.* Oxford: Clarendon Press.

Harter, H. Leon. 1969. *Order Statistics and Their Use in Testing and Estimation.* Vol. 2. Washington, D.C.: Aerospace Research Laboratories, United States Air Force.

Historical Manuscripts Commission. *The Manuscripts of the Duke of Portland.* Vol. 7. London: H.M.S.O.

Hoppit, Julian. 1986. "Financial Crises in Eighteenth-century England." *Economic History Review* 39:39–58.

Horsefield, J. Keith. 1977. "The Beginnings of Paper Money in England." *Journal of European Economic History* 6:117–32.

Isard, Peter. 1977. "How Far Can We Push the 'Law of One Price'?" *American Economic Review* 67:942–48.

Jevons, W. Stanley. 1931. *The Theory of Political Economy.* 4th ed. London: Macmillan.

Jones, D. W. 1972. "London Merchants and the Crisis of the 1690s." In *Crisis and Order in English Towns, 1500–1700*, ed. Peter Clark and Paul Slack. Toronto: University of Toronto Press.

———. 1988. *War and Economy in the Age of William III and Marlborough.* Oxford: Basil Blackwell.

Kerridge, Eric. 1988. *Trade and Banking in Early Modern England.* Manchester: Manchester University Press.

Landa, Janet T. 1981. "A Theory of the Ethnically Homogeneous Middleman Group: An Institutional Alternative to Contract Law." *Journal of Legal Studies* 10:349–62.

Lease, Ronald C., John J. McConnell, and Wayne H. Mikkelson. 1983. "The Market Value of Control in Publicly-Traded Corporations." *Journal of Financial Economics* 11:439–71.

Marshall, Alfred. 1938. *Principles of Economics.* 8th ed. London: Macmillan.

Marvel, Howard P. 1976. "The Economics of Information and Retail Gasoline Price Behavior: An Empirical Analysis," *Journal of Political Economy* 84:1033–60.

Maynes, E. Scott, Robin A. Douthitt, Greg J. Duncan, and Loren V. Geistfeld. 1984. "Informationally Imperfect Markets." In *The Collection and Analysis of Economic and Consumer Behavior Data*, ed. Seymour Sudman and Mary A. Spaeth. Urbana: University of Illinois Press.

Melton, Frank T. 1986. *Sir Robert Clayton and the Origins of English Deposit Banking, 1658–1685.* Cambridge: Cambridge University Press.

Mirowski, Philip. 1981. "The Rise (and Retreat) of a Market: English Joint Stock Shares in the Eighteenth Century." *Journal of Economic History* 41:559–77.

Muldrew, Craig. 1993a. "Interpreting the Market: The Ethics of Credit and Community Relations in Early Modern England," *Social History* 18:163–83.

———. 1993b. "Credit and the Courts: Debt Litigation in a Seventeenth-Century Urban Community," *Economic History Review* 46:3–38.

Murphy, Antoin E. 1986. *Richard Cantillon: Entrepreneur and Economist.* Oxford: Clarendon Press.

Podolny, Joel. 1993. "A Status-Based Model of Market Competition." *American Journal of Sociology* 98:829–72.

Rabb, Theodore K. 1967. *Enterprise and Empire: Merchant and Gentry Investment in the Expansion of England, 1575–1630.* Cambridge: Harvard University Press.

Richards, R. D. 1929. *The Early History of Banking in England.* Westminster: P. S. King and Son.

Rothschild, Michael. 1973. "Models of Market Organization with Imperfect Information." *Journal of Political Economy* 81:1283–1308.

Shleifer, Andrei, and Lawrence H. Summers. 1990. "The Noise Trader Approach to Finance." *Journal of Economic Perspectives* 4:19–33.

Sperling, John G. 1962. "The International Payments Mechanism in the Seventeenth and Eighteenth Centuries." *Economic History Review* 14:446–68.

Stigler, George J. 1968. *The Organization of Industry.* Homewood, Ill.: Richard Irwin.

Stone, Lawrence, and Jeanne C. Fawtier Stone. 1984. *An Open Elite? England, 1540–1880.* Oxford: Clarendon Press.

Sutherland, L. S. 1962. *A London Merchant, 1695–1774.* New York: Barnes and Noble.

Telser, Lester G. 1973. "Searching for the Lowest Price," *American Economic Review* 63(2): 40–49.

———. 1981. "Why There Are Organized Futures Markets," *Journal of Law and Economics* 24: 1–22.

Telser, Lester G., and Harlow N. Higinbotham. 1977. "Organized Futures Markets: Costs and Benefits." *Journal of Political Economy* 85: 969–1000.

Tittler, Robert. 1994. "Money-Lending in the West Midlands: the Activities of Joyce Jefferies, 1638–49," *Historical Research* 67: 249–63.

Walras, Léon. 1954. *Elements of Pure Economics.* William Jaffé, trans. Homewood, Ill.: Richard Irwin.

Zelizer, Viviana A. 1979. *Morals and Markets: The Development of Life Insurance in the United States.* New York: Columbia University Press.

COGNITION

Chapter 18

FROM *THE ELEMENTARY FORMS OF THE RELIGIOUS LIFE*

Émile Durkheim

Translated by Joseph Ward Swain

The totem is before all a symbol, a material expression of something else.[1] But of what?

From the analysis to which we have been giving our attention, it is evident that it expresses and symbolizes two different sorts of things. In the first place, it is the outward and visible form of what we have called the totemic principle or god. But it is also the symbol of the determined society called the clan. It is its flag, it is the sign by which each clan distinguishes itself from the others, the visible mark of its personality, a mark borne by everything which is a part of the clan under any title whatsoever, men, beasts, or things. So if it is at once the symbol of the god and of the society, is that not because the god and the society are only one? How could the emblem of the group have been able to become the figure of this quasi divinity, if the group and the divinity were two distinct realities? The god of the clan, the totemic principle, can therefore be nothing else than the clan itself personified and represented to the imagination under the visible form of the animal or vegetable which serves as totem.

But how has this apotheosis been possible, and how did it happen to take place in this fashion?

. . . . .

The first religious conceptions have often been attributed to feelings of weakness and dependence, of fear and anguish which seized men when they came into contact with the world. Being the victims of nightmares of which they were themselves the creators, they believed themselves surrounded by hostile and redoubtable powers which their rites sought to appease. We have now shown that the first religions were of a wholly different origin. The famous formula *Primus in orbe does fecit timor* is in no way justified by the facts. The primitive does not regard his gods as foreigners, enemies, or thoroughly and necessarily malevolent beings whose favors he must acquire at any price; quite on the contrary, they are rather friends, kindred, or natural protectors for him. Are these not the names he gives to the beings of the totemic species? The power to which the cult is addressed is not represented as soaring high above him and overwhelming him by its superiority; on the contrary, it is very near to him and confers upon him very useful powers which he could never acquire by himself. Perhaps the deity has never been nearer to men than at this period of history, when it is present in the things filling their immediate environment and is, in part, imminent in himself. In fine, the sentiments at the root of totemism are those of happy confidence rather than of terror and compression. If we set aside the funeral rites—the sober side of every religion—we find the totemic cult celebrated in the midst of songs, dances, and dramatic representations. As we shall see, cruel expiations are relatively rare; even the painful and obligatory mutilations of the initiations are not of this character. The terrible and jealous gods appear but slowly in the religious evolution. This is because primitive societies are not those huge Leviathans which overwhelm a man by the enormity of their power and place him under a severe discipline;[2] he gives himself up to them spontaneously and without resistance. As the social soul is then made up of only a small number of ideas and sentiments, it easily becomes wholly incarnate in each individual consciousness. The individual carries it all inside of him; it is a part of him and consequently, when he gives himself up to the impulses inspired by it, he does not feel that he is giving way before compulsion, but that he is going where his nature calls him.[3]

This way of understanding the origins of religious thought escapes the objections raised against the most accredited classical theories.

We have seen how the naturists and animists pretend to construct the idea of sacred beings out of the sensations evoked in us by different phenomena of the physical or biological order, and we have shown how this enterprise is impossible and even self-contradictory. Nothing is worth nothing. The impressions produced in us by the physical world can, by definition, contain nothing that surpasses this world. Out of the visible, only the visible can be made; out of that which is heard, we cannot make something not heard. Then to explain how the idea of sacredness has been able to take form under these conditions, the majority of the theorists have been obliged to admit that men have superimposed upon reality, such as it is given by observation, an unreal world, constructed entirely out of the fantastic images which agitate his mind during a dream, or else out of the frequently monstrous aberrations produced by the mythological imagination under the bewitching but deceiving influence of language. But it remained incomprehensible that humanity should have remained obstinate in these errors through the ages, for experience should have very quickly proven them false.

But from our point of view, these difficulties disappear. Religion ceases to be an inexplicable hallucination and takes a foothold in reality. In fact, we can say that the believer is not deceived when he believes in the existence of a moral power upon which he depends and from which he receives all that is best in himself: this power exists, it is society. When the Australian is carried outside himself and feels a new life flowing within him whose intensity surprises him, he is not the dupe of an illusion; this exaltation is real and is really the effect of forces outside of and superior to the individual. It is true that he is wrong in thinking that this increase of vitality is the work of a power in the form of some animal or plant. But this error is merely in regard to the letter of the symbol by which this being is represented to the mind and the external appearance which the imagination has given it, and not in regard to the fact of its existence. Behind these figures and metaphors, be they gross or refined, there is a concrete and living reality. Thus religion acquires a meaning and a reasonableness that the most intransigent rationalist cannot misunderstand. Its primary object is not to give men a representation of the physical world; for if that were its essential task, we could not understand how it has been able to survive, for, on this side, it is scarcely more than a fabric of errors. Before all, it is a system of ideas with which the individuals represent to themselves the society of which they are members, and the obscure but intimate relations which they have with it. This is its primary function; and though metaphorical and symbolic, this representation is not unfaithful. Quite on the contrary, it translates everything essential in the relations which are to be explained: for it is an eternal truth that outside of us there exists something greater than us, with which we enter into communion.

That is why we can rest assured in advance that the practices of the cult, whatever they may be, are something more than movements without importance and gestures without efficacy. By the mere fact that their apparent function is to strengthen the bonds attaching the believer to his god, they at the same time really strengthen the bonds attaching the individual to the society of which he is a member, since the god is only a figurative expression of the society. We are even able to understand how the fundamental truth thus contained in religion has been able to compensate for the secondary errors which it almost necessarily implies, and how believers have consequently been restrained from tearing themselves off from it, in spite of the misunderstandings which must result from these errors. It is undeniably true that the recipes which it recommends that men use to act upon things are generally found to be ineffective.

. . . . .

Collective representations very frequently attribute to the things to which they are attached qualities which do not exist under any form or to any degree. Out of the commonest object, they can make a most powerful sacred being.

Yet the powers which are thus conferred, though purely ideal, act as though they were real; they determine the conduct of men with the same degree of necessity as physical forces. The Arunta who has been rubbed with his churinga feels himself stronger; he is stronger. If he has eaten the flesh of an animal which, though perfectly healthy, is forbidden to him, he will feel himself sick, and may die of it. Surely the soldier who falls while defending his flag does not believe that he sacrifices himself for a bit of cloth. This is all because social thought, owing to the imperative authority that is in it, has an efficacy that individual thought could never have; by the power which it has over our minds, it can make us see things in whatever light it pleases; it adds to reality or deducts from it according to the circumstances. Thus there is one division of nature where the formula of idealism is applicable almost to the letter: this is the social kingdom. Here more than anywhere else, the idea is the reality. Even in this case, of course, idealism is not true without modification. We can never escape the duality of our nature and free ourselves completely from physical necessities: in order to express our own ideas to ourselves, it is necessary, as has been shown above, that we fix them upon material things which symbolize them. But here the part of matter is reduced to a minimum. The object serving as support for the idea is not much in comparison with the ideal superstructure, beneath which it disappears, and also, it counts for nothing in the superstructure. This is what that pseudodelirium consists in, which we find at the bottom of so many collective representations: it is only a form of this essential idealism.[4] So it is not properly called a delirium, for the ideas thus objectified are well founded, not in the nature of the material things upon which they settle themselves, but in the nature of society.

We are now able to understand how the totemic principle, and in general, every religious force, comes to be outside of the object in which it resides.[5] It is because the idea of it is in no way made up of the impressions directly produced by this thing upon our senses or minds. Religious force is only the sentiment inspired by the group in its members, but projected outside of the consciousnesses that experience them, and objectified. To be objectified, they are fixed upon some object which thus becomes sacred; but any object might fulfill this function. In principle, there are none whose nature predestines them to it to the exclusion of all others; but also there are none that are necessarily impossible.[6] Everything depends upon the circumstances which lead the sentiment creating religious ideas to establish itself here or there, upon this point or upon that one. Therefore, the sacred character assumed by an object is not implied in the intrinsic properties of this latter: *it is added to them.* The world of religious things is not one particular aspect of empirical nature; *it is superimposed upon it.*

. . . . .

We have seen how the Arunta place at the beginning of time a mythical society whose organization exactly reproduces that which still exists today; it includes the same clans and phratries, it is under the same matrimonial rules and it practices the same rites. But the personages who compose it are ideal beings, gifted with powers and virtues to which common mortals cannot pretend. Their nature is not only higher, but it is different, since it is at once animal and human. The evil powers there undergo a similar metamorphosis: evil itself is, as it were, made sublime and idealized. The question now raises itself of whence this idealization comes.

Some reply that men have a natural faculty for idealizing, that is to say, of substituting for the real world another different one, to which they transport themselves by thought. But that is merely changing the terms of the problem; it is not resolving it or even advancing it. This systematic idealization is an essential characteristic of religions. Explaining them by an innate power of idealization is simply replacing one word by another which is the equivalent of the first; it is as if they said that men have made religions because they have a religious nature. Animals know only one world, the one which they perceive by experience, internal as well as external. Men alone have the faculty of conceiving the ideal, of adding something to the real. Now where does this singular privilege come from? Before making it an initial fact or a mysterious virtue which escapes science, we must be sure that it does not depend upon empirically determinable conditions.

The explanation of religion which we have proposed has precisely this advantage, that it gives an answer to this question. For our definition of the sacred is that it is something added to and above the real: now the ideal answers to this same definition; we cannot explain one without explaining the other. In fact, we have seen that if collective life awakens religious thought on reaching a certain degree of intensity, it is because it brings about a state of effervescence which changes the conditions of psychic activity. Vital energies are overexcited, passions more active, sensations stronger; there are even some which are produced only at this moment. A man does not recognize himself; he feels himself transformed and consequently he transforms the environment which surrounds him. In order to account for the very particular impressions which he receives, he attributes to the things with which he is in most direct contact properties which they have not, exceptional powers and virtues which the objects of everyday experience do not possess. In a word, above the real world where his profane life passes he has placed another which, in one sense, does not exist except in thought, but to which he attributes a higher sort of dignity than to the first. Thus, from a double point of view it is an ideal world.

The formation of the ideal world is therefore not an irreducible fact which escapes science; it depends upon conditions which observation can touch; it is a natural product of social life. For a society to become conscious of itself and maintain at the necessary degree of intensity the sentiments which it thus attains, it must assemble and concentrate itself. Now this concentration brings about an exaltation of the mental life which takes form in a group of ideal conceptions where is portrayed the new life thus awakened; they correspond to this new set of psychical forces which is added to those which we have at our disposition for the daily tasks of existence. A society can neither create itself nor re-create itself without at the same time creating an ideal. This creation is not a sort of work of supererogation for it, by which it would complete itself, being already formed; it is the act by which it is periodically made and remade. Therefore when some oppose the ideal society to the real society, like two antagonists which would lead us in opposite directions, they materialize and oppose abstractions. The ideal society is not outside of the real society; it is a part of it. Far from being divided between them as between two poles which mutually repel each other, we cannot hold to one without holding to the other. For a society is not made up merely of the mass of individuals who compose it, the ground which they occupy, the things which they use and the movements which they perform, but above all is the idea which it forms of itself. It is undoubtedly true that it hesitates over the manner in which it ought to conceive itself; it feels itself drawn in divergent directions. But these conflicts which break forth are not between the ideal and reality, but between two different ideals, that of yesterday and that of today, that which has the authority of tradition and that which has the hope of the future. There is surely a place for investigating whence these ideals evolve; but whatever solution may be given to this problem, it still remains that all passes in the world of the ideal.

Thus the collective ideal which religion expresses is far from being due to a vague innate power of the individual, but it is rather at the school of collective life that the individual has learned to idealize. It is in assimilating the ideals elaborated by society that he has become capable of conceiving the ideal. It is society which, by leading him within its sphere of action, has made him acquire the need of raising himself above the world of experience and has at the same time furnished him with the means of conceiving another. For society has constructed this new world in constructing itself, since it is society which this expresses. Thus both with the individual and in the group, the faculty of idealizing has nothing mysterious about it. It is not a sort of luxury which a man could get along without, but a condition of his very existence. He could not be a social being, that is to say, he could not be a man, if he had not acquired it. It is true that in incarnating themselves in individuals, collective ideals tend to individualize themselves. Each understands them after his own fashion and marks them with his own stamp; he suppresses certain elements and adds others. Thus the personal ideal disengages itself from the social ideal in proportion as the individual personality develops itself and becomes an autonomous source of action. But if we wish to understand this aptitude, so singular in appearance, of living outside of reality, it is enough to connect it with the social conditions upon which it depends.

Therefore it is necessary to avoid seeing in this theory of religion a simple restatement of historical materialism: that would be misunderstanding our thought to an extreme degree. In showing that religion is something essentially social, we do not mean to say that it confines itself to translating into another language the material forms of society and its immediate vital necessities. It is true that we take it as evident that social life depends upon its material foundation and bears its mark, just as the mental life of an individual depends upon his nervous system and in fact his whole organism. But collective consciousness is something more than a mere epiphenomenon of its morphological basis, just as individual consciousness is something more than a simple efflorescence of the nervous system. In order that the former may appear, a synthesis sui generis of particular consciousnesses is required. Now this synthesis has the effect of disengaging a whole world of sentiments, ideas, and images which, once born, obey laws all their own. They attract each other, repel each other, unite, divide themselves, and multiply, though these combinations are not commanded and necessitated by the condition of the underlying reality. The life thus brought into being even enjoys so great an independence that it sometimes indulges in manifestations with no purpose or utility of any sort, for the mere pleasure of affirming itself. We have shown that this is often precisely the case with ritual activity and mythological thought.[7]

In a general way, a collective sentiment can become conscious of itself only by being fixed upon some material object; but by this very fact, it participates in the nature of this object, and reciprocally, the object participates in its nature. So it was social necessity which brought about the fusion of notions appearing distinct at first, and social life has facilitated this fusion by the great mental effervescences it determines.[8] This is one more proof that logical understanding is a function of society, for it takes the forms and attitudes that this latter presses upon it.

It is true that this logic is disconcerting for us. Yet we must be careful not to depreciate it: howsoever crude it may appear to us, it has been an aid of the greatest importance in the intellectual evolution of humanity. In fact, it is through it that the first explanation of the world has been made possible. Of course the mental habits it implies prevented men from seeing reality as their senses show it to them; but as they show it, it has the grave inconvenience of allowing of no explanation. For to explain is to attach things to each other and to establish relations between them which make them appear to us as functions of each other and as vibrating sympathetically according to an internal law founded in their nature. But sensations, which see nothing except from the outside, could never make them disclose these relations and internal bonds; the intellect alone can create the notion of them. When I learn that A regularly precedes B, my knowledge is increased by a new fact; but my intelligence is not at all satisfied with a statement which does not show its reason. I commence to *understand* only if it is possible for me to conceive B in a way that makes it appear to me as something that is not foreign to A, and as united to A by some relation of kinship. The great service that religions have rendered to thought is that they have constructed a first representation of what these relations of kinship between things may be. In the circumstances under which it was attempted, the enterprise could obviously attain only precarious results. But then, does it ever attain any that are definite, and is it not always necessary to reconsider them? And also, it is less important to succeed than to try. The essential thing was not to leave the mind enslaved to visible appearances, but to teach it to dominate them and to connect what the senses separated; for from the moment when men have an idea that there are internal connections between things, science and philosophy become possible. Religion opened up the way for them. But if it has been able to play this part, it is only because it is a social affair. In order to make a law for the impressions of the senses and to substitute a new way of representing reality for them, thought of a new sort had to be founded: this is collective thought. If this alone has had this efficacy, it is because of the fact that to create a world of ideals through which the world of experienced realities would appear transfigured, a superexcitation of the intellectual forces was necessary, which is possible only in and through society.

So it is far from true that this mentality has no connection with ours. Our logic was born of this logic. The explanations of contemporary science are surer of being objective because they are more methodical and because they rest on more carefully controlled observations, but they do not differ in nature from those which satisfy primitive thought. Today, as formerly, to explain is to show how one thing participates in one or several others. It has been said that the participations of this sort implied by the mythologies violate the principle of contradiction and that they are by that opposed to those implied by scientific explanations.[9] Is not the statement that a man is a kangaroo or the sun a bird, equal to identifying the two with each other? But our manner of thought is not different when we say of heat that it is a movement, or of light that it is a vibration of the ether, etc. Every time that we unite heterogeneous terms by an internal bond, we forcibly identify contraries. Of course the terms we unite are not those which the Australian brings together; we choose them according to different criteria and for different reasons; but the processes by which the mind puts them in connection do not differ essentially.

It is true that if primitive thought had that sort of general and systematic indifference to contradictions which has been attributed to it,[10] it would be in open contradiction on this point with modern thought, which is always careful to remain consistent with itself. But we do not believe that it is possible to characterize the mentality of inferior societies by a single and exclusive inclination for indistinction. If the primitive confounds things which we distinguish, he also distinguishes things which we connect together, and he even conceives these distinctions in the form of sharp and clear-cut oppositions. Between two things which are classified in two different phratries, there is not only separation, but even antagonism. For this reason, the same Australian who confounds the sun and the white cockatoo, opposes this latter to the black cockatoo as to its contrary. The two seem to him to belong to two separate classes between which there is nothing in common. A still more marked opposition is that existing between sacred things and profane things. They repel and contradict each other with so much force that the mind refuses to think of them at the same time. They mutually expel each other from the consciousness.

Thus between the logic of religious thought and that of scientific thought there is no abyss. The two are made up of the same elements, though inequally and differently developed. The special characteristic of the former seems to be its natural taste for immoderate confusions as well as sharp contrasts. It is voluntarily excessive in each direction. When it connects, it confounds; when it distinguishes, it opposes. It knows no shades and measures; it seeks extremes; it consequently employs logical mechanisms with a certain awkwardness, but it ignores none of them.

. . . . .

It is not at all true that between science on the one hand, and morals and religion on the other, there exists that sort of antinomy which has so frequently been admitted, for the two forms of human activity really come from one and the same source. Kant understood this very well, and therefore he made the speculative reason and the practical reason two different aspects of the same faculty. According to him, what makes their unity is the fact that the two are directed towards the universal. Rational thinking is thinking according to the laws which are imposed upon all reasonable beings; acting morally is conducting one's self according to those maxims which can be extended without contradiction to all wills. In other words, science and morals imply that the individual is capable of raising himself above his own peculiar point of view and of living an impersonal life. In fact, it cannot be doubted that this is a trait common to all the higher forms of thought and action. What Kant's system does not explain, however, is the origin of this sort of contradiction which is realized in man. Why is he forced to do violence to himself by leaving his individuality, and, inversely, why is the impersonal law obliged to be dissipated by incarnating itself in individuals? Is it answered that there are two antagonistic worlds in which we participate equally, the world of matter and sense on the one hand, and the world of pure and impersonal reason on the other? That is merely repeating the question in slightly different terms, for what we are trying to find out is why we must lead these two existences at the same time. Why do these two worlds, which seem to contradict each other, not remain outside of each other, and why must they mutually penetrate one another in spite of their antagonism? The only explanation which has ever been given of this singular necessity is the hypothesis of the Fall, with all the difficulties which it implies, and which need not be repeated here. On the other hand, all mystery disappears the moment that it is recognized that impersonal reason is only another name given to collective thought. For this is possible only through a group of individuals; it supposes them, and in their turn, they suppose it, for they can continue to exist only by grouping themselves together. The kingdom of ends and impersonal truths can realize itself only by the cooperation of particular wills, and the reasons for which these participate in it are the same as those for which they cooperate. In a word, there is something impersonal in us because there is something social in all of us, and since social life embraces at once both representations and practices, this impersonality naturally extends to ideas as well as to acts.

Perhaps some will be surprised to see us connect the most elevated forms of thought with society: the cause appears quite humble, in consideration of the value which we attribute to the effect. Between the world of the senses and appetites on the one hand, and that of reason and morals on the other, the distance is so considerable that the second would seem to have been able to add itself to the first only by a creative act. But attributing to society this preponderating role in the genesis of our nature is not denying this creation; for society has a creative power which no other observable being can equal. In fact, all creation, if not a mystical operation which escapes science and knowledge, is the product of a synthesis. Now if the synthesis of particular conceptions which takes place in each individual consciousness is already and of itself productive of novelties, how much more efficacious these vast synthesis of complete consciousnesses which make society must be! A society is the most powerful combination of physical and moral forces of which nature offers us an example. Nowhere else is an equal richness of different materials, carried to such a degree of concentration, to be found. Then it is not surprising that a higher life disengages itself which, by reacting upon the elements of which it is the product, raises them to a higher plane of existence and transforms them.

Thus sociology appears destined to open a new way to the science of man. Up to the present, thinkers were placed before this double alternative: either explain the superior and specific faculties of men by connecting them to the inferior forms of his being, the reason to the senses, or the mind to matter, which is equivalent to denying their uniqueness; or else attach them to some superexperimental reality which was postulated, but whose existence could be established by no observation. What put them in this difficulty was the fact that the individual passed as being the *finis naturae*—the ultimate creation of nature; it seemed that there was nothing beyond him, or at least nothing that science could touch. But from the moment when it is recognized that above the individual there is society, and that this is not a nominal being created by reason, but a system of active forces, a new manner of explaining men becomes possible. To conserve his distinctive traits it is no longer necessary to put them outside experience. At least, before going to this last extremity, it would be well to see if that which surpasses the individual, though it is within him, does not come from this superindividual reality which we experience in society. To be sure, it cannot be said at present to what point these explanations may be able to reach, and whether or not they are of a nature to resolve all the problems. But it is equally impossible to mark in advance a limit beyond which they cannot go. What must be done is to try the hypothesis and submit it as methodically as possible to the control of facts. This is what we have tried to do.

Notes

1. We say that this derivation is sometimes indirect on account of the industrial methods which, in a large number of cases, seem to be derived from religion through the intermediacy of magic (see H. Hubert and M. Mauss, "Esquisse d'une Théorie Générale de la Magie," Année Sociologique, 7 (1902–3): 144ff.); for, as we believe, magic forces are only a special form of religious forces. We shall have occasion to return to this point several times.

2. At least after he is once adult and fully initiated, for the initiation rites, introducing the young man to the social life, are a severe discipline in themselves.

3. Upon this particular aspect of primitive societies, see our *Division du travail social*, 3d ed., 123, 149, 173ff.

4. Cf. Mauss, "Essai sur les variations saisonnières des sociétés Eskimos" in *Année socialogique* 9 (1904–5): 127.

5. Thus we see how erroneous those theories are which, like the geographical materialism of Ratzel (see especially his *Politische Geographie*), seek to derive all social life from its material foundation (either economic or territorial). They commit an error precisely similar to the one committed by Maudsley in individual psychology. Just as this latter reduced all the psychical life of the individual to a mere epiphenomenon of his physiological basis, they seek to reduce the whole psychical life of the group to its physical basis. But they forget that ideas are realities and forces, and that collective representations are forces even more powerful and active than individual representations. On this point, see our "Représentations individuelles et représentations collectives," in the *Revue de Métaphysique et de Morale*, May 1898.

6. Even the *excreta* have a religious character. See Konrad Preuss, "Der Ursprung der Religion und Kunst," especially chap. 2, entitled "Der Zauber der Defäkation, *Globus* 86 (1904):325ff.

7. On this same question, see our article "Represéntations individuelles et represéntations collectives."

8. Another cause has contributed much to this fusion; this is the extreme contagiousness of religious forces. They seize upon every object within their reach, whatever it may be. Thus a single religious force may animate the most diverse things which, by that very fact, become closely connected and classified within a single group. We shall return again to this contagiousness, when we shall show that it comes from the social origins of the idea of sacredness (bk. 3, chap. 1 *in fine*).

9. Lévy-Bruhl, *Les functions mentales dans les societés inférieures* (Paris: Alea, 1910). 77ff.

10. Ibid., 79.

Chapter 19

FROM *THE SOCIAL CONSTRUCTION OF REALITY: A TREATISE IN THE SOCIOLOGY OF KNOWLEDGE*

PETER L. BERGER AND THOMAS LUCKMANN

INTRODUCTION: THE PROBLEM OF THE SOCIOLOGY OF KNOWLEDGE

The basic contentions of the argument of this book are implicit in its title and subtitle, namely, that reality is socially constructed and that the sociology of knowledge must analyze the processes in which this occurs. The key terms in these contentions are "reality" and "knowledge," terms that are not only current in everyday speech, but that have behind them a long history of philosophical inquiry. We need not enter here into a discussion of the semantic intricacies of either the everyday or the philosophical usage of these terms. It will be enough, for our purposes, to define "reality" as a quality appertaining to phenomena that we recognize as having a being independent of our own volition (we cannot "wish them away"), and to define "knowledge" as the certainty that phenomena are real and that they possess specific characteristics. It is in this (admittedly simplistic) sense that the terms have relevance both to the man in the street and to the philosopher. The man in the street inhabits a world that is "real" to him, albeit in different degrees, and he "knows," with different degrees of confidence, that this world possesses such and such characteristics.

Sociological interest in questions of "reality" and "knowledge" is thus initially justified by the fact of their social relativity. What is "real" to a Tibetan monk may not be "real" to an American businessman. The "knowledge" of the criminal differs from the "knowledge" of the criminologist. It follows that specific agglomerations of "reality" and "knowledge" pertain to specific social contexts, and that these relationships will have to be included in an adequate sociological analysis of these contexts. The need for a "sociology of knowledge" is thus already given with the observable differences between societies in terms of what is taken for granted as "knowledge" in them. Beyond this, however, a discipline calling itself by this name will have to concern itself with the general ways by which "realities" are taken as "known" in human societies. In other words, a "sociology of knowledge" will have to deal not only with the empirical variety of "knowledge" in human societies, but also with the processes by which *any* body of "knowledge" comes to be socially established *as* "reality."

It is our contention, then, that the sociology of knowledge must concern itself with whatever passes for "knowledge" in a society, regardless of the ultimate validity or invalidity (by whatever criteria) of such "knowledge." And insofar as all human "knowledge" is developed, transmitted, and maintained in social situations, the sociology of knowledge must seek to understand the processes by which this is done in such a way that a taken-for-granted "reality" congeals for the man in the street. In other words, we contend that *the sociology of knowledge is concerned with the analysis of the social construction of reality.*

The Foundations of Knowledge in Everyday Life

Since our purpose in this treatise is a sociological analysis of the reality of everyday life, more precisely, of knowledge that guides conduct in everyday life, and we are only tangentially interested in how this reality may appear in various theoretical perspectives to intellectuals, we must begin by a clarification of that reality as it is available to the commonsense of the ordinary members of society. How that common sense reality may be influenced by the theoretical constructions of intellectuals and other merchants of ideas is a further question. Ours is thus an enterprise that, although theoretical in character, is geared to the understanding of a reality that forms the subject matter of the empirical science of sociology, that is, the world of everyday life.

It should be evident, then, that our purpose is *not* to engage in philosophy. All the same, if the reality of everyday life is to be understood, account must be taken of its intrinsic character before we can proceed with sociological analysis proper. Everyday life presents itself as a reality interpreted by men and subjectively meaningful to them as a coherent world. As sociologists we take this reality as the object of our analyses. Within the frame of reference of sociology as an empirical science it is possible to take this reality as given, to take as data particular phenomena arising within it, without further inquiring about the foundations of this reality, which is a philosophical task. However, given the particular purpose of the present treatise, we cannot completely bypass the philosophical problem. The world of everyday life is not only taken for granted as reality by the ordinary members of society in the subjectively meaningful conduct of their lives. It is a world that originates in their thoughts and actions, and is maintained as real by these. Before turning to our main task we must, therefore, attempt to clarify the foundations of knowledge in everyday life, to wit, the objectivations of subjective processes (and meanings) by which the *inter*subjective commonsense world is constructed.

For the purpose at hand, this is a preliminary task, and we can do no more than sketch the main features of what we believe to be an adequate solution to the philosophical problem—adequate, let us hasten to add, only in the sense that it can serve as a starting point for sociological analysis. The considerations immediately following are, therefore, of the nature of philosophical prolegomena and, in themselves, presociological. The method we consider best suited to clarify the foundations of knowledge in everyday life is that of phenomenological analysis, a purely descriptive method and, as such, "empirical" but not "scientific"—as we understand the nature of the empirical sciences.[1]

The phenomenological analysis of everyday life, or rather of the subjective experience of everyday life, refrains from any causal or genetic hypotheses, as well as from assertions about the ontological status of the phenomena analyzed. It is important to remember this. Commonsense contains innumerable pre- and quasi-scientific interpretations about everyday reality, which it takes for granted. If we are to describe the reality of common sense we must refer to these interpretations, just as we must take account of its taken-for-granted character—but we do so within phenomenological brackets.

Consciousness is always intentional; it always intends or is directed toward objects. We can never apprehend some putative substratum of consciousness as such, only consciousness of something or other. This is so regardless of whether the object of consciousness is experienced as belonging to an external physical world or apprehended as an element of an inward subjective reality. Whether I (the first-person singular, here as in the following illustrations, standing for ordinary self-consciousness in everyday life) am viewing the panorama of New York City or whether I become conscious of an inner anxiety, the processes of consciousness involved are intentional in both instances. The point need not be belabored that the consciousness of the Empire State Building differs from the awareness of anxiety. A detailed phenomenological analysis would uncover the various layers of experience, and the different structures of meaning involved in, say, being bitten by a dog, remembering having been bitten by a dog, having a phobia about all dogs, and so forth. What interests us here is the common intentional character of all consciousness.

Different objects present themselves to consciousness as constituents of different spheres of reality. I recognize the fellow men I must deal with in the course of everyday life as pertaining to a reality quite different from the disembodied figures that appear in my dreams. The two sets of objects introduce quite different tensions into my consciousness and I am attentive to them in quite different ways. My consciousness, then, is capable of moving through different spheres of reality. Put differently, I am conscious of the world as consisting of multiple realities. As I move from one reality to another, I experience the transition as a kind of shock. This shock is to be understood as caused by the shift in attentiveness that the transition entails. Waking up from a dream illustrates this shift most simply.

Among the multiple realities there is one that presents itself as the reality par excellence. This is the reality of everyday life. Its privileged position entitles it to the designation of paramount reality. The tension of consciousness is highest in everyday life, that is, the latter imposes itself upon consciousness in the most massive, urgent, and intense manner. It is impossible to ignore, difficult even to weaken in its imperative presence. Consequently, it forces me to be attentive to it in the fullest way. I experience everyday life in the state of being wide awake. This wide awake state of existing in and apprehending the reality of everyday life is taken by me to be normal and self-evident, that is, it constitutes my natural attitude.

I apprehend the reality of everyday life as an ordered reality. Its phenomena are prearranged in patterns that seem to be independent of my apprehension of them and that impose themselves upon the latter. The reality of everyday life appears already objectified, that is, constituted by an order of objects that have been designated *as* objects before my appearance on the scene. The language used in everyday life continuously provides me with the necessary objectifications and posits the order within which these make sense and within which everyday life has meaning for me. I live in a place that is geographically designated; I employ tools, from can openers to sports cars, which are designated in the technical vocabulary of my society; I live within a web of human relationships, from my chess club to the United States of America, which are also ordered by means of vocabulary. In this manner language marks the coordinates of my life in society and fills that life with meaningful objects.

The reality of everyday life is organized around the "here" of my body and the "now" of my present. This "here and now" is the focus of my attention to the reality of everyday life. What is "here and now" presented to me in everyday life is the *realissimum* of my consciousness. The reality of everyday life is not, however, exhausted by these immediate presences, but embraces phenomena that are not present "here and now." This means that I experience everyday life in terms of differing degrees of closeness and remoteness, both spatially and temporally. Closest to me is the zone of everyday life that is directly accessible to my bodily manipulation. This zone contains the world within my reach, the world in which I act so as to modify its reality, or the world in which I work. In this world of working my consciousness is dominated by the pragmatic motive, that is, my attention to this world is mainly determined by what I am doing, have done or plan to do in it. In this way it is *my* world par excellence. I know, of course, that the reality of everyday life contains zones that are not accessible to me in this manner. But either I have no pragmatic interest in these zones or my interest in them is indirect insofar as they may be, potentially, manipulative zones for me. Typically, my interest in the far zones is less intense and certainly less urgent.

I am intensely interested in the cluster of objects involved in my daily occupation—say, the world of the garage, if I am a mechanic. I am interested, though less directly, in what goes on in the testing laboratories of the automobile industry in Detroit—I am unlikely ever to be in one of these laboratories, but the work done there will eventually affect my everyday life. I may also be interested in what goes on at Cape Kennedy or in outer space, but this interest is a matter of private, "leisure time" choice rather than an urgent necessity of my everyday life.

The reality of everyday life further presents itself to me as an intersubjective world, a world that I share with others. This intersubjectivity sharply differentiates everyday life from other realities of which I am conscious. I am alone in the world of my dreams, but I know that the world of everyday life is as real to others as it is to myself. Indeed, I cannot exist in everyday life without continually interacting and communicating with others. I know that my natural attitude to this world corresponds to the natural attitude of others, that they also comprehend the objectifications by which this world is ordered, that they also organize this world around the "here and now" of *their* being in it and have projects for working in it. I also know, of course, that the others have a perspective on this common world that is not identical with mine. My "here" is their "there." My "now" does not fully overlap with theirs. My projects differ from and may even conflict with theirs. All the same, I know that I live with them in a common world. Most importantly, I know that there is an ongoing correspondence between *my* meanings and *their* meanings in this world, that we share a common sense about its reality. The natural attitude is the attitude of commonsense consciousness precisely because it refers to a world that is common to many men. Commonsense knowledge is the knowledge I share with others in the normal, self-evident routines of everyday life.

The reality of everyday life is taken for granted *as* reality. It does not require additional verification over and beyond its simple presence. It is simply *there*, as self-evident and compelling facticity. I *know* that it is real. While I am capable of engaging in doubt about its reality, I am obliged to suspend such doubt as I routinely exist in everyday life. This suspension of doubt is so firm that to abandon it, as I might want to do, say, in theoretical or religious contemplation, I have to make an extreme transition. The world of everyday life proclaims itself and, when I want to challenge the proclamation, I must engage in a deliberate, by no means easy effort. The transition from the natural attitude to the theoretical attitude of the philosopher or scientist illustrates this point. But not all aspects of this reality are equally unproblematic. Everyday life is divided into sectors that are apprehended routinely, and others that present me with problems of one kind or another. Suppose that I am an automobile mechanic who is highly knowledgeable about all American-made cars. Everything that pertains to the latter is a routine, unproblematic facet of my everyday life. But one day someone appears in the garage and asks me to repair his Volkswagen. I am now compelled to enter the problematic world of foreign-made cars. I may do so reluctantly or with professional curiosity, but in either case I am now faced with problems that I have not yet routinized. At the same time, of course, I do not leave the reality of everyday life. Indeed, the latter becomes enriched as I begin to incorporate into it the knowledge and skills required for the repair of foreign-made cars. The reality of everyday life encompasses both kinds of sectors, as long as what appears as a problem does not pertain to a different reality altogether (say, the reality of theoretical physics, or of nightmares). As long as the routines of everyday life continue without interruption they are apprehended as unproblematic.

But even the unproblematic sector of everyday reality is so only until further notice, that is, until its continuity is interrupted by the appearance of a problem. When this happens, the reality of everyday life seeks to integrate the problematic sector into what is already unproblematic. Commonsense knowledge contains a variety of instructions as to how this is to be done. For instance, the others with whom I work are unproblematic to me as long as they perform their familiar, taken-for-granted routinessay, typing away at desks next to mine in my office. They become problematic if they interrupt these routines—say, huddling together in a corner and talking in whispers. As I inquire about the meaning of this unusual activity, there is a variety of possibilities that my commonsense knowledge is capable of reintegrating into the unproblematic routines of everyday life: they may be consulting on how to fix a broken typewriter, or one of them may have some urgent instructions from the boss, and so on. On the other hand, I may find that they are discussing a union directive to go on strike, something as yet outside my experience but still well within the range of problems with which my commonsense knowledge can deal. It will deal with it, though, *as* a problem, rather than simply reintegrating it into the unproblematic sector of everyday life. If, however, I come to the conclusion that my colleagues have gone collectively mad, the problem that presents itself is of yet another kind. I am now faced with a problem that transcends the boundaries of the reality of everyday life and points to an altogether different reality. Indeed, my conclusion that my colleagues have gone mad implies ipso facto that they have gone off into a world that is no longer the common world of everyday life.

Society as Objective Reality

Origins of Institutionalization

All human activity is subject to habitualization. Any action that is repeated frequently becomes cast into a pattern, which can then be reproduced with an economy of effort and which, ipso facto, is apprehended by its performer *as* that pattern. Habitualization further implies that the action in question may be performed again in the future in the same manner and with the same economical effort. This is true of nonsocial as well as of social activity. Even the solitary individual on the proverbial desert island habitualizes his activity. When he wakes up in the morning and resumes his attempts to construct a canoe out of matchsticks, he may mumble to himself, "There I go again," as he starts on step 1 of an operating procedure consisting of, say, ten steps. In other words, even solitary man has at least the company of his operating procedures.

Habitualized actions, of course, retain their meaningful character for the individual although the meanings involved become embedded as routines in his general stock of knowledge, taken for granted by him and at hand for his projects into the future.[2] Habitualization carries with it the important psychological gain that choices are narrowed. While in theory there may be a hundred ways to go about the project of building a canoe out of matchsticks, habitualization narrows these down to one. This frees the individual from the burden of "all those decisions," providing a psychological relief that has its basis in man's undirected instinctual structure. Habitualization provides the direction and the specialization of activity that is lacking in man's biological equipment, thus relieving the accumulation of tensions that result from undirected drives.[3] And by providing a stable background in which human activity may proceed with a minimum of decision making most of the time, it frees energy for such decisions as may be necessary on certain occasions. In other words, the background of habitualized activity opens up a foreground for deliberation and innovation.[4]

In terms of the meanings bestowed by man upon his activity, habitualization makes it unnecessary for each situation to be defined anew, step by step.[5] A large variety of situations may be subsumed under its predefinitions. The activity to be undertaken in these situations can then be anticipated. Even alternatives of conduct can be assigned standard weights.

These processes of habitualization precede any institutionalization, indeed can be made to apply to a hypothetical solitary individual detached from any social interaction. The fact that even such a solitary individual, assuming that he has been formed as a self (as we would have to assume in the case of our matchstick-canoe builder), will habitualize his activity in accordance with biographical experience of a world of social institutions preceding his solitude need not concern us at the moment. Empirically, the more important part of the habitualization of human activity is coextensive with the latter's institutionalization. The question then becomes how do institutions arise.

Institutionalization occurs whenever there is a reciprocal typification of habitualized actions by types of actors. Put differently, any such typification is an institution.[6] What must be stressed is the reciprocity of institutional typifications and the typicality of not only the actions but also the actors in institutions. The typifications of habitualized actions that constitute institutions are always shared ones. They are *available* to all the members of the particular social group in question, and the institution itself typifies individual actors as well as individual actions. The institution posits that actions of type X will be performed by actors of type X. For example, the institution of the law posits that heads shall be chopped off in specific ways under specific circumstances, and that specific types of individuals shall do the chopping (executioners, say, or members of an impure caste, or virgins under a certain age, or those who have been designated by an oracle).

Institutions further imply historicity and control. Reciprocal typifications of actions are built up in the course of a shared history. They cannot be created instantaneously. Institutions always have a history, of which they are the products. It is impossible to understand an institution adequately without an understanding of the historical process in which it was produced. Institutions also, by the very fact of their existence, control human conduct by setting up predefined patterns of conduct, which channel it in one direction as against the many other directions that would theoretically be possible. It is important to stress that this controlling character is inherent in institutionalization as such, prior to or apart from any mechanisms of sanctions specifically set up to support an institution. These mechanisms (the sum of which constitute what is generally called a system of social control) do, of course, exist in many institutions and in all the agglomerations of institutions that we call societies. Their controlling efficacy, however, is of a secondary or supplementary kind. As we shall see again later, the primary social control is given in the existence of an institution as such. To say that a segment of human activity has been institutionalized is already to say that this segment of human activity has been subsumed under social control. Additional control mechanisms are required only insofar as the processes of institutionalization are less than completely successful. Thus, for instance, the law may provide that anyone who breaks the incest taboo will have his head chopped off. This provision may be necessary because there have been cases when individuals offended against the taboo. It is unlikely that this sanction will have to be invoked continuously (unless the institution delineated by the incest taboo is itself in the course of disintegration, a special case that we need not elaborate here). It makes little sense, therefore, to say that human sexuality is socially controlled by beheading certain individuals. Rather, human sexuality is socially controlled by its institutionalization in the course of the particular history in question. One may add, of course, that the incest taboo itself is nothing but the negative side of an assemblage of typifications, which define in the first place which sexual conduct is incestuous and which is not.

In actual experience institutions generally manifest themselves in collectivities containing considerable numbers of people. It is theoretically important, however, to emphasize that the institutionalizing process of reciprocal typification would occur even if two individuals began to interact de novo. Institutionalization is incipient in every social situation continuing in time. Let us assume that two persons from entirely different social worlds begin to interact. By saying "persons" we presuppose that the two individuals have formed selves, something that could, of course, have occurred only in a social process. We are thus for the moment excluding the cases of Adam and Eve, or of two "feral" children meeting in a clearing of a primeval jungle. But we are assuming that the two individuals arrive at their meeting place from social worlds that have been historically produced in segregation from each other, and that the interaction therefore takes place in a situation that has not been institutionally defined for either of the participants. It may be possible to imagine a Man Friday joining our matchstick-canoe builder on his desert island, and to imagine the former as a Papuan and the latter as an American. In that case, however, it is likely that the American will have read or at least have heard about the story of Robinson Crusoe, which will introduce a measure of predefinition of the situation at least for him. Let us, then, simply call our two persons A and B.

As A and B interact, in whatever manner, typifications will be produced quite quickly. A watches B perform. He attributes motives to B's actions and, seeing the actions recur, typifies the motives as recurrent. As B goes on performing, A is soon able to say to himself, "Aha, there he goes again." At the same time, A may assume that B is doing the same thing with regard to him. From the beginning, both A and B assume this reciprocity of typification. In the course of their interaction these typifications will be expressed in specific patterns of conduct. That is, A and B will begin to play roles vis-à-vis each other. This will occur even if each continues to perform actions different from those of the other. The possibility of taking the role of the other will appear with regard to the same actions performed by both. That is, A will inwardly appropriate B's reiterated roles and make them the models for his own role-playing. For example, B's role in the activity of preparing food is not only typified as such by A, but enters as a constitutive element into A's own food-preparation role. Thus a collection of reciprocally typified actions will emerge, habitualized for each in roles, some of which will be performed separately and some in common.[7] While this reciprocal typification is not yet institutionalization (since, there only being two individuals, there is no possibility of a typology of actors), it is clear that institutionalization is already present in *nucleo*.

At this stage one may ask what gains accrue to the two individuals from this development. The most important gain is that each will be able to predict the other's actions. Concomitantly, the interaction of both becomes predictable. The "There he goes again" becomes a "There *we* go again." This relieves both individuals of a considerable amount of tension. They save time and effort, not only in whatever external tasks they might be engaged in separately or jointly, but in terms of their respective psychological economies. Their life together is now defined by a widening sphere of taken-for-granted routines. Many actions are possible on a low level of attention. Each action of one is no longer a source of astonishment and potential danger to the other. Instead, much of what goes on takes on the triviality of what, to both, will be everyday life. This means that the two individuals are constructing a background, in the sense discussed before, which will serve to stabilize both their separate actions and their interaction. The construction of this background of routine in turn makes possible a division of labor between them, opening the way for innovations, which demand a higher level of attention. The division of labor and the innovations will lead to new habitualizations, further widening the background common to both individuals. In other words, a social world will be in process of construction, containing within it the roots of an expanding institutional order.

Generally, all actions repeated once or more tend to be habitualized to some degree, just as all actions observed by another necessarily involve some typification on his part. However, for the kind of reciprocal typification just described to occur there must be a continuing social situation in which the habitualized actions of two or more individuals interlock. Which actions are likely to be reciprocally typified in this manner?

The general answer is, those actions that are relevant to both A and B within their common situation. The areas likely to be relevant in this way will, of course, vary in different situations. Some will be those facing A and B in terms of their previous biographies, others may be the result of the natural, presocial circumstances of the situation. What will in all cases have to be habitualized is the communication process between A and B. Labor, sexuality, and territoriality are other likely foci of typification and habitualization. In these various areas the situation of A and B is paradigmatic of the institutionalization occurring in larger societies.

Let us push our paradigm one step further and imagine that A and B have children. At this point the situation changes qualitatively. The appearance of a third party changes the character of the ongoing social interaction between A and B, and it will change even further as additional individuals continue to be added.[8] The institutional world, which existed *in statu nascendi* in the original situation of A and B, is now passed on to others. In this process institutionalization perfects itself. The habitualizations and typifications undertaken in the common life of A and B, formations that until this point still had the quality of ad hoc conceptions of two individuals, now become historical institutions. With the acquisition of historicity, these formations also acquire another crucial quality, or, more accurately, perfect a quality that was incipient as soon as A and B began the reciprocal typification of their conduct: this quality is objectivity. This means that the institutions that have now been crystallized (for instance, the institution of paternity as it is encountered by the children) are experienced as existing over and beyond the individuals who "happen to" embody them at the moment. In other words, the institutions are now experienced as possessing a reality of their own, a reality that confronts the individual as an external and coercive fact.[9]

As long as the nascent institutions are constructed and maintained only in the interaction of A and B, their objectivity remains tenuous, easily changeable, almost playful, even while they attain a measure of objectivity by the mere fact of their formation. To put this a little differently, the routinized background of A's and B's activity remains fairly accessible to deliberate intervention by A and B. Although the routines, once established, carry within them a tendency to persist, the possibility of changing them or even abolishing them remains at hand in consciousness. A and B alone are responsible for having constructed this world. A and B remain capable of changing or abolishing it. What is more, since they themselves have shaped this world in the course of a shared biography which they can remember, the world thus shaped appears fully transparent to them. They understand the world that they themselves have made. All this changes in the process of transmission to the new generation. The objectivity of the institutional world "thickens" and "hardens," not only for the children, but (by a mirror effect) for the parents as well. The "There we go again" now becomes "This is how these things are done." A world so regarded attains a firmness in consciousness; it becomes real in an ever more massive way and it can no longer be changed so readily. For the children, especially in the early phase of their socialization into it, it becomes *the* world. For the parents, it loses its playful quality and becomes "serious." For the children, the parentally transmitted world is not fully transparent. Since they had no part in shaping it, it confronts them as a given reality that, like nature, is opaque in places at least.

Only at this point does it become possible to speak of a social world at all, in the sense of a comprehensive and given reality confronting the individual in a manner analogous to the reality of the natural world. Only in this way, *as* an objective world, can the social formations be transmitted to a new generation. In the early phases of socialization the child is quite incapable of distinguishing between the objectivity of natural phenomena and the objectivity of the social formations.[10] To take the most important item of socialization, language appears to the child as inherent in the nature of things, and he cannot grasp the notion of its conventionality. A thing *is* what it is called, and it could not be called anything else. All institutions appear in the same way, as given, unalterable, and self-evident. Even in our empirically unlikely example of parents having constructed an institutional world de novo, the objectivity of this world would be increased for them by the socialization of their children, because the objectivity experienced by the children would reflect back upon their own experience of this world. Empirically, of course, the institutional world transmitted by most parents already has the character of historical and objective reality. The process of transmission simply strengthens the parents' sense of reality, if only because, to put it crudely, if one says, "This is how these things are done," often enough one believes it oneself.[11]

An institutional world, then, is experienced as an objective reality. It has a history that antedates the individual's birth and is not accessible to his biographical recollection. It was there before he was born, and it will be there after his death. This history itself, as the tradition of the existing institutions, has the character of objectivity. The individual's biography is apprehended as an episode located within the objective history of the society. The institutions, as historical and objective facticities, confront the individual as undeniable facts. The institutions are *there*, external to him, persistent in their reality, whether he likes it or not. He cannot wish them away. They resist his attempts to change or evade them. They have coercive power over him, both in themselves, by the sheer force of their facticity, and through the control mechanisms that are usually attached to the most important of them. The objective reality of institutions is not diminished if the individual does not understand their purpose or their mode of operation. He may experience large sectors of the social world as incomprehensible, perhaps oppressive in their opaqueness, but real nonetheless. Since institutions exist as external reality, the individual cannot understand them by introspection. He must "go out" and learn about them, just as he must to learn about nature. This remains true even though the social world, as a humanly produced reality, is potentially understandable in a way not possible in the case of the natural world.[12]

It is important to keep in mind that the objectivity of the institutional world, however massive it may appear to the individual, is a humanly produced, constructed objectivity. The process by which the externalized products of human activity attain the character of objectivity is objectivation.[13] The institutional world is objectivated human activity, and so is every single institution. In other words, despite the objectivity that marks the social world in human experience, it does not thereby acquire an ontological status apart from the human activity that produced it. The paradox that man is capable of producing a world that he then experiences as something other than a human product will concern us later on. At the moment, it is important to emphasize that the relationship between man, the producer, and the social world, his product, is and remains a dialectical one. That is, man (not, of course, in isolation but in his collectivities) and his social world interact with each other. The product acts back upon the producer. Externalization and objectivation are moments in a continuing dialectical process. The third moment in this process, which is internalization (by which the objectivated social world is retrojected into consciousness in the course of socialization), will occupy us in considerable detail later on. It is already possible, however, to see the fundamental relationship of these three dialectical moments in social reality. Each of them corresponds to an essential characterization of the social world. Society is a human product. Society is an objective reality. Man is a social product. It may also already be evident that an analysis of the social world that leaves out any one of these three moments will be distortive.[14] One may further add that only with the transmission of the social world to a new generation (that is, internalization as effectuated in socialization) does the fundamental social dialectic appear in its totality. To repeat, only with the appearance of a new generation can one properly speak of a social world.

At the same point, the institutional world requires legitimation, that is, ways by which it can be "explained" and justified. This is not because it appears less real. As we have seen, the reality of the social world gains in massivity in the course of its transmission. This reality, however, is a historical one, which comes to the new generation as a tradition rather than as a biographical memory. In our paradigmatic example, A and B, the original creators of the social world, can always reconstruct the circumstances under which their world and any part of it was established. That is, they can arrive at the meaning of an institution by exercising their powers of recollection. A and B's children are in an altogether different situation. Their knowledge of the institutional history is by way of "hearsay." The original meaning of the institutions is inaccessible to them in terms of memory. It, therefore, becomes necessary to interpret this meaning to them in various legitimating formulas. These will have to be consistent and comprehensive in terms of the institutional order, if they are to carry conviction to the new generation. The same story, so to speak, must be told to all the children. It follows that the expanding institutional order develops a corresponding canopy of legitimations, stretching over it a protective cover of both cognitive and normative interpretation. These legitimations are learned by the new generation during the same process that socializes them into the institutional order. This, again, will occupy us in greater detail further on.

The development of specific mechanisms of social controls also becomes necessary with the historicization and objectivation of institutions. Deviance from the institutionally "programmed" courses of action becomes likely once the institutions have become realities divorced from their original relevance in the concrete social processes from which they arose. To put this more simply, it is more likely that one will deviate from programs set up for one by others than from programs that one has helped establish oneself. The new generation posits a problem of compliance, and its socialization into the institutional order requires the establishment of sanctions. The institutions must and do claim authority over the individual, independently of the subjective meanings he may attach to any particular situation. The priority of the institutional definitions of situations must be consistently maintained over individual temptations at redefinition. The children must be "taught to behave" and, once taught, must be "kept in line." So, of course, must the adults. The more conduct is institutionalized, the more predictable and thus the more controlled it becomes. If socialization into the institutions has been effective, outright coercive measures can be applied economically and selectively. Most of the time, conduct will occur "spontaneously" within the institutionally set channels. The more, on the level of meaning, conduct is taken for granted, the more possible alternatives to the institutional "programs" will recede, and the more predictable and controlled conduct will be.

In principle, institutionalization may take place in any area of collectively relevant conduct. In actual fact, sets of institutionalization processes take place concurrently. There is no a priori reason for assuming that these processes will necessarily "hang together" functionally, let alone as a logically consistent system. To return once more to our paradigmatic example, slightly changing the fictitious situation, let us assume this time, not a budding family of parents and children, but a piquant triangle of a male A, a bisexual female B, and a lesbian C. We need not belabor the point that the sexual relevances of these three individuals will not coincide. Relevance A-B is not shared by C. The habitualizations engendered as a result of relevance A-B need bear no relationship to those engendered by relevances B-C and C-A. There is, after all, no reason why two processes of erotic habitualization, one heterosexual and one lesbian, cannot take place side by side without functionally integrating with each other or with a third habitualization based on a shared interest in, say, the growing of flowers (or whatever other enterprise might be jointly relevant to an active heterosexual male and an active lesbian). In other words, three processes of habitualization or incipient institutionalization may occur without their being functionally or logically integrated as social phenomena. The same reasoning holds if A, B, and C are posited as collectivities rather than individuals, regardless of what content their relevances might have. Also, functional or logical integration cannot be assumed a priori when habitualization or institutionalization processes are limited to the same individuals or collectivities, rather than to the discrete ones assumed in our example.

Nevertheless, the empirical fact remains that institutions do tend to "hang together." If this phenomenon is not to be taken for granted, it must be explained. How can this be done? First, one may argue that *some* relevances will be common to all members of a collectivity. On the other hand, many areas of conduct will be relevant only to certain types. The latter involves an incipient differentiation, at least in the way in which these types are assigned some relatively stable meaning. This assignment may be based on presocial differences, such as sex, or on differences brought about in the course of social interaction, such as those engendered by the division of labor. For example, only women may be concerned with fertility magic and only hunters may engage in cave painting. Or, only the old men may perform the rain ceremonial and only weapon makers may sleep with their maternal cousins. In terms of their external social functionality, these several areas of conduct need not be integrated into *one* cohesive system. They can continue to coexist on the basis of segregated performances. But while performances can be segregated, meanings tend toward at least minimal consistency. As the individual reflects about the successive moments of his experience, he tries to fit their meanings into a consistent biographical framework. This tendency increases as the individual shares with others his meanings and their biographical integration. It is possible that this tendency to integrate meanings is based on a psychological need, which may in turn be physiologically grounded (that is, that there may be a built-in "need" for cohesion in the psycho-physiological constitution of man). Our argument, however, does not rest on such anthropological assumptions, but rather on the analysis of meaningful reciprocity in processes of institutionalization.

It follows that great care is required in any statements one makes about the "logic" of institutions. The logic does not reside in the institutions and their external functionalities, but in the way these are treated in reflection about them. Put differently, reflective consciousness superimposes the quality of logic on the institutional order.[15]

Language provides the fundamental superimposition of logic on the objectivated social world. The edifice of legitimations is built upon language and uses language as its principal instrumentality. The "logic" thus attributed to the institutional order is part of the socially available stock of knowledge and taken for granted as such. Since the well-socialized individual "knows" that his social world is a consistent whole, he will be constrained to explain both its functioning and malfunctioning in terms of this "knowledge." It is very easy, as a result, for the observer of any society to assume that its institutions do indeed function and integrate as they are "supposed to."[16]

De facto, then, institutions *are* integrated. But their integration is not a functional imperative for the social processes that produce them; it is rather brought about in a derivative fashion. Individuals perform discrete institutionalized actions within the context of their biography. This biography is a reflected-upon whole in which the discrete actions are thought of not as isolated events, but as related parts in a subjectively meaningful universe whose meanings are not specific to the individual, but socially articulated and shared. Only by way of this detour of socially shared universes of meaning do we arrive at the need for institutional integration.

This has far-reaching implications for any analysis of social phenomena. If the integration of an institutional order can be understood only in terms of the "knowledge" that its members have of it, it follows that the analysis of such "knowledge" will be essential for an analysis of the institutional order in question. It is important to stress that this does not exclusively or even primarily involve a preoccupation with complex theoretical systems serving as legitimations for the institutional order. Theories also have to be taken into account, of course. But theoretical knowledge is only a small and by no means the most important part of what passes for knowledge in a society. Theoretically sophisticated legitimations appear at particular moments of an institutional history. The primary knowledge about the institutional order is knowledge on the pretheoretical level. It is the sum total of "what everybody knows" about a social world, an assemblage of maxims, morals, proverbial nuggets of wisdom, values and beliefs, myths, and so forth, the theoretical integration of which requires considerable intellectual fortitude in itself, as the long line of heroic integrators from Homer to the latest sociological system-builders testifies. On the pretheoretical level, however, every institution has a body of transmitted recipe knowledge, that is, knowledge that supplies the institutionally appropriate rules of conduct.[17]

Such knowledge constitutes the motivating dynamics of institutionalized conduct. It defines the institutionalized areas of conduct and designates all situations falling within them. It defines and constructs the roles to be played in the context of the institutions in question. Ipso facto, it controls and predicts all such conduct. Since this knowledge is socially objectivated *as* knowledge, that is, as a body of generally valid truths about reality, any radical deviance from the institutional order appears as a departure from reality. Such deviance may be designated as moral depravity, mental disease, or just plain ignorance. While these fine distinctions will have obvious consequences for the treatment of the deviant, they all share an inferior cognitive status within the particular social world. In this way, the particular social world becomes the world tout court. What is taken for granted as knowledge in the society comes to be coextensive with the knowable, or at any rate provides the framework within which anything not yet known will come to be known in the future. This is the knowledge that is learned in the course of socialization and that mediates the internalization within individual consciousness of the objectivated structures of the social world. Knowledge, in this sense, is at the heart of the fundamental dialectic of society. It "programs" the channels in which externalization produces an objective world. It objectifies this world through language and the cognitive apparatus based on language, that is, it orders it into objects to be apprehended as reality.[18] It is internalized again *as* objectively valid truth in the course of socialization. Knowledge about society is thus a *realization* in the double sense of the word, in the sense of apprehending the objectivated social reality, and in the sense of ongoingly producing this reality.

For example, in the course of the division of labor a body of knowledge is developed that refers to the particular activities involved. In its linguistic basis, this knowledge is already indispensable to the institutional "programming" of these economic activities. There will be, say, a vocabulary designating the various modes of hunting, the weapons to be employed, the animals that serve as prey, and so on. There will further be a collection of recipes that must be learned if one is to hunt correctly. This knowledge serves as a channeling, controlling force in itself, an indispensable ingredient of the institutionalization of this area of conduct. As the institution of hunting is crystallized and persists in time, the same body of knowledge serves as an objective (and, incidentally, empirically verifiable) description of it. A whole segment of the social world is objectified by this knowledge. There will be an objective "science" of hunting, corresponding to the objective reality of the hunting economy. The point need not be belabored that here "empirical verification" and "science" are not understood in the sense of modern scientific canons, but rather in the sense of knowledge that may be borne out in experience and that can subsequently become systematically organized as a body of knowledge.

Again, the same body of knowledge is transmitted to the next generation. It is learned as objective truth in the course of socialization and thus internalized as subjective reality. This reality in turn has power to shape the individual. It will produce a specific type of person, namely the hunter, whose identity and biography *as* a hunter have meaning only in a universe constituted by the aforementioned body of knowledge as a whole (say, in a hunters' society) or in part (say, in our own society, in which hunters come together in a subuniverse of their own). In other words, no part of the institutionalization of hunting can exist without the particular knowledge that has been socially produced and objectivated with reference to this activity. To hunt and to be a hunter implies existence in a social world defined and controlled by this body of knowledge. Mutatis mutandis, the same applies to any area of institutionalized conduct.

Conceptual Machineries of Universe Maintenance

It would be obviously absurd to attempt here a detailed discussion of the different conceptual machineries of universe maintenance that are historically available to us.[19] But a few remarks about some conspicuous types of conceptual machineries are in order—mythology, theology, philosophy, and science. Without proposing an evolutionary scheme for such types, it is safe to say that mythology represents the most archaic form of universe-maintenance, as indeed it represents the most archaic form of legitimation generally.[20] Very likely mythology is a necessary phase in the development of human thought as such.[21] In any case, the oldest universe-maintaining conceptualizations available to us are mythological in form. For our purposes, it is sufficient to define mythology as a conception of reality that posits the ongoing penetration of the world of everyday experience by sacred forces.[22] Such a conception naturally entails a high degree of continuity between social and cosmic order, and between all their respective legitimations;[23] all reality appears as made of one cloth.

Mythology as a conceptual machinery is closest to the naive level of the symbolic universe—the level on which there is the least necessity for theoretical universe-maintenance beyond the actual positing of the universe in question as an objective reality. This explains the historically recurrent phenomenon of inconsistent mythological traditions continuing to exist side by side without theoretical integration. Typically, the inconsistency is felt only *after* the traditions have become problematic and some sort of integration has already taken place. The "discovery" of such inconsistency (or, if one prefers, its ex post facto assumption) is usually made by the specialists in the tradition, who are also the most common integrators of the discrete traditional themes. Once the need for integration is felt, the consequent mythological reconstructions may have considerable theoretical sophistication. The example of Homer may suffice to make this point.

Mythology is also close to the naive level in that, although there are specialists in the mythological tradition, their knowledge is not far removed from what is generally known. Initiation into the tradition administered by these specialists may be difficult in extrinsic ways. It may be limited to select candidates, to special occasions or times, and it may involve arduous ritual preparation. It is, however, rarely difficult in terms of the intrinsic qualities of the body of knowledge itself, which is not difficult to acquire. To safeguard the specialists' monopolistic claim the nonaccessibility of their lore must be institutionally established. That is, a "secret" is posited, and an intrinsically exoteric body of knowledge is institutionally defined in esoteric terms. A brief look at the "public relations" of contemporary coteries of theoreticians will reveal that this ancient legerdemain is far from dead today. All the same, there are important sociological differences between societies in which all universe-maintaining conceptualizations are mythological and societies in which they are not.

More elaborate mythological systems strive to eliminate inconsistencies and maintain the mythological universe in theoretically integrated terms. Such "canonical" mythologies, as it were, go over into theological conceptualization proper. For our present purposes, theological thought may be distinguished from its mythological predecessor simply in terms of its greater degree of theoretical systematization. Theological concepts are further removed from the naive level. The cosmos may still be conceived of in terms of the sacred forces or beings of the old mythology, but these sacred entities have been removed to a greater distance. Mythological thought operates within the continuity between the human world and the world of the gods. Theological thought serves to mediate between these two worlds, precisely because their original continuity now appears broken. With the transition from mythology to theology, everyday life appears less ongoingly penetrated by sacred forces. The body of theological knowledge is, consequently, further removed from the general stock of knowledge of the society and thus becomes *intrinsically* more difficult to acquire. Even where it is not deliberately institutionalized as esoteric, it remains "secret" by virtue of its unintelligibility to the general populace. This has the further consequence that the populace may remain relatively unaffected by the sophisticated universe-maintaining theories concocted by the theological specialists. The coexistence of naive mythology among the masses and a sophisticated theology among an elite of theoreticians, *both* serving to maintain the same symbolic universe, is a frequent historical phenomenon. Only with this phenomenon in mind, for example, is it possible to call traditional societies of the Far East "Buddhist," or, for that matter, to call medieval society "Christian."

Theology is paradigmatic for the later philosophical and scientific conceptualizations of the cosmos. While theology may be closer to mythology in the religious contents of its definitions of reality, it is closer to the later secularized conceptualizations in its social location. Unlike mythology, the other three historically dominant forms of conceptual machinery became the property of specialist elites, whose bodies of knowledge were increasingly removed from the common knowledge of the society at large. Modern science is an extreme step in this development, and in the secularization and sophistication of universe maintenance. Science not only completes the removal of the sacred from the world of everyday life, but removes universe-maintaining knowledge as such from that world. Everyday life becomes bereft of both sacred legitimation and the sort of theoretical intelligibility that would link it with the symbolic universe in its intended totality. Put more simply, the "lay" member of society no longer knows how his universe is to be conceptually maintained, although, of course, he still knows who the specialists of universe maintenance are presumed to be. The interesting problems posed by this situation belong to an empirical sociology of knowledge of contemporary society and cannot be further pursued in this context.

Social Organization for Universe Maintenance

Because they are historical products of human activity, all socially constructed universes change, and the change is brought about by the concrete actions of human beings. If one gets absorbed in the intricacies of the conceptual machineries by which any specific universe is maintained, one may forget this fundamental sociological fact. Reality is socially defined. But the definitions are always *embodied*, that is, concrete individuals and groups of individuals serve as definers of reality. To understand the state of the socially constructed universe at any given time, or its change over time, one must understand the social organization that permits the definers to do their defining. Put a little crudely, it is essential to keep pushing questions about the historically available conceptualizations of reality from the abstract "What?" to the sociologically concrete "Says who?"[24]

As we have seen, the specialization of knowledge and the concomitant organization of personnel for the administration of the specialized bodies of knowledge develop as a result of the division of labor. It is possible to conceive of an early stage of this development in which there is no competition between the different experts. Each area of expertise is defined by the pragmatic facts of the division of labor. The hunting expert will not claim fishing expertise and will thus have no ground for competing with the one who does.

As more complex forms of knowledge emerge and an economic surplus is built up, experts devote themselves full time to the subjects of their expertise, which, with the development of conceptual machineries, may become increasingly removed from the pragmatic necessities of everyday life. Experts in these rarefied bodies of knowledge lay claim to a novel status. They are not only experts in this or that sector of the societal stock of knowledge, they claim ultimate jurisdiction over that stock of knowledge in its totality. They are, literally, universal experts. This does *not* mean that they claim to know everything, but rather that they claim to know the ultimate significance of what everybody knows and does. Other men may continue to stake out particular sectors of reality, but they claim expertise in the ultimate definitions of reality as such.

This stage in the development of knowledge has a number of consequences. The first, which we have already discussed, is the emergence of pure theory. Because the universal experts operate on a level of considerable abstraction from the vicissitudes of everyday life, both others and they themselves may conclude that their theories have no relation whatever to the ongoing life of the society, but exist in a sort of Platonic heaven of ahistorical and asocial ideation. This is, of course, an illusion, but it can have great sociohistorical potency, by virtue of the relationship between the reality-defining and reality-producing processes.

A second consequence is a strengthening of traditionalism in the institutionalized actions thus legitimated, that is, a strengthening of the inherent tendency of institutionalization toward inertia.[25] Habitualization and institutionalization in themselves limit the flexibility of human actions. Institutions tend to persist unless they become "problematic." Ultimate legitimations inevitably strengthen this tendency. The more abstract the legitimations are, the less likely they are to be modified in accordance with changing pragmatic exigencies. If there is a tendency to go on as before anyway, the tendency is obviously strengthened by having excellent reasons for doing so. This means that institutions may persist even when, to an outside observer, they have lost their original functionality or practicality. One does certain things not because they *work*, but because they *are right*—right, that is, in terms of the ultimate definitions of reality promulgated by the universal experts.[26]

Notes

1. This entire section of our treatise is based on Alfred Schutz and Thomas Luckmann, *Die Strukturen der Lebenswelt*, now being prepared for publication. In view of this, we have refrained from providing individual references to the places in Schutz's published work where the same problems are discussed. Our argument here is based on Schutz, as developed by Luckmann in the aforementioned work, in toto. The reader wishing to acquaint himself with Schutz's work published to date may

consult Alfred Schutz, *Der sinnhafte Aufbau der sozialen Welt* (Vienna: Springer, 1960), and *Collected Papers*, ed. Maurice Natanson, vols. 1 and 2 (The Hague: Martinus Nijhoff, 1962, 1964). The reader interested in Schutz's adaptation of the phenomenological method to the analysis of the social world may consult especially his *Collected Papers*, 1:99ff., and Maurice Natanson, ed., *Philosophy of the Social Sciences* (New York, Random House, 1963), 183ff.

2. The term "stock of knowledge" is taken from Schutz.

3. Arnold Gehlen refers to this point in his concepts of *Triebüberschuss* and *Entlastung*.

4. Gehlen refers to this point in his concept of *Hintergrundserfüllung*.

5. The concept of the definition of the situation was formed by W. I. Thomas and developed throughout his sociological work.

6. We are aware of the fact that this concept of institution is broader than the prevailing one in contemporary sociology. We think that such a broader concept is useful for a comprehensive analysis of basic social processes. On social control, cf. Friedrich Tenbruck, "Soziale Kontrolle," *Staatslexikon der Goerres-Gesellschaft* (1962), and Heinrich Popitz, "Soziale Normen," *European Journal of Sociology.*

7. The term "taking the role of the other" is taken from George Herbert Mead. We are here taking Mead's paradigm of socialization and applying it to the broader problem of institutionalization. The argument combines key features of both Mead's and Gehlen's approaches.

8. Simmel's analysis of the expansion from the dyad to the triad is important in this connection. The following argument combines Simmel's and Durkheim's conceptions of the objectivity of social reality.

9. In Durkheim's terms this means that, with the expansion of the dyad into a triad and beyond, the original formations become genuine "social facts," that is, they attain *choséité*.

10. Jean Piaget's concept of infantile "realism" may be compared here.

11. For an analysis of this process in the contemporary family, cf. Peter L. Berger and Hansfried Kellner, "Marriage and the Construction of Reality," *Diogenes* 46 (1964): 1ff.

12. The preceding description closely follows Durkheim's analysis of social reality. This does *not* contradict the Weberian conception of the meaningful character of society. Since social reality always originates in meaningful human actions, it continues to carry meaning even if it is opaque to the individual at a given time. The original may be *reconstructed*, precisely by means of what Weber called *Verstehen*.

13. The term "objectivation" is derived from the Hegelian/Marxian *Versachlichung*.

14. Contemporary American sociology tends towards leaving out the first moment. Its perspective on society thus tends to be what Marx called a reification (*Verdinglichung*), that is, an undialectical distortion of social reality that obscures the latter's character as an ongoing human production, viewing it instead in thinglike categories appropriate only to the world of nature. That the dehumanization implicit in this is mitigated by values deriving from the larger tradition of the society is, presumably, morally fortunate, but is irrelevant theoretically.

15. Pareto's analysis of the "logic" of institutions is relevant here. A point similar to ours is made by Friedrich Tenbruck, "Soziale Kontroller." He too insists that the "strain towards consistency" is rooted in the meaningful character of human action.

16. This, of course, is the fundamental weakness of any functionalistically oriented sociology. For an excellent critique of this, cf. the discussion of Bororo society in Claude Lévi-Strauss, *Tristes tropiques*, trans. John Russell (New York: Atheneum, 1964), 183ff.

17. The term "recipe knowledge" is taken from Schutz.

18. The term "objectification" is derived from the Hegelian *Vergegenständlichung*.

19. Pareto comes closest to the writing of a history of thought in sociological terms, which makes Pareto important for the sociology of knowledge regardless of reservations one may have about his theoretical frame of reference. Cf. Brigitte Berger, "Vilfredo Pareto and the Sociology of Knowledge, Ph.D., New School for Social Research, 1964.

20. This may be reminiscent of Auguste Comte's "law of the three stages." We cannot accept this, of course, but it may still be useful in suggesting that consciousness develops in historically recognizable stages, though they cannot be conceived of in Comte's manner. Our own understanding of this is closer to the Hegelian/Marxian approach to the historicity of human thought.

21. Both Lévy-Bruhl and Piaget suggest that mythology constitutes a necessary stage in the development of thought. For a suggestive discussion of the biological roots of mythological/magical thought, *cf.* Arnold Gehlen, *Studien zur Anthropologie und Soziologie* (Berlin: Luchterhand, 1963), 79ff.

22. Our conception of mythology here is influenced by the work of Gerardus van der Leeuw, Mircea Eliade, and Rudolf Bultmann.

23. On the continuity between social and cosmic orders in mythological consciousness, compare again the work of Eliade, and Voegelin.

24. It will be clear from our theoretical presuppositions that we cannot here go in any detail into the questions of the "sociology of intellectuals." In addition to Mannheim's important work in this area (to be found especially in *Ideology and Utopia* and *Essays on the Sociology of Culture*), cf. Florian Znaniecki, *The Social Role of the Man of Knowledge* (New York: Columbia University Press, 1940); Theodor Geiger, *Aufgaben und Stellung der Intelligenz in der Gesellschaft* (Stuttgart: F. Enke 1949); Raymond Aron, *L'opium des intellectuels* (Paris: Calman-Lévy, 1955); George B. de Huszar, ed., *The Intellectuals* (New York: Free Press of Glencoe, 1960).

25. On ultimate legitimations strengthening institutional "inertia" (Simmel's "faithfulness"), compare both Durkheim and Pareto.

26. It is precisely at this point that any functionalist interpretation of institutions is weakest, tending to look for practicalities that are not in fact existing.

Chapter 20

FROM *ORGANIZATIONS:* *COGNITIVE LIMITS ON RATIONALITY*

JAMES G. MARCH AND HERBERT A. SIMON
With the Collaboration of Harold Guetzkow

THE CONCEPT OF RATIONALITY

How does the rationality of "administrative man" compare with that of classical "economic man" or with the rational man of modern statistical decision theory? The rational man of economics and statistical decision theory makes "optimal" choices in a highly specified and clearly defined environment:

1. When we first encounter him in the decision-making situation, he already has laid out before him the whole set of alternatives from which he will choose his action. This set of alternatives is simply "given"; the theory does not tell how it is obtained.
2. To each alternative is attached a set of consequences—the events that will ensue if that particular alternative is chosen. Here the existing theories fall into three categories:

a. *Certainty*: theories that assume the decision maker has complete and accurate knowledge of the consequences that will follow on each alternative.
b. *Risk*: theories that assume accurate knowledge of a probability distribution of the consequences of each alternative.
c. *Uncertainty*: theories that assume that the consequences of each alternative belong to some subset of all possible consequences, but that the decision maker cannot assign definite probabilities to the occurrence of particular consequences.

3. At the outset, the decision maker has a "utility function" or a "preference ordering" that ranks all sets of consequences from the most preferred to the least preferred.
4. The decision maker selects the alternative leading to the preferred set of consequences.

James March, and Herbert Simon. 1993. *Organizations*. 2nd ed., pp. 158–63, 172–79, 190–92. Oxford: Blackwell Publishing, reprinted by kind permission of the publisher.

In the case of *certainty*, the choice is unambiguous. In the case of *risk*, rationality is usually defined as the choice of that alternative for which the expected utility is greatest. Expected utility is defined here as the average, weighted by the probabilities of occurrence, of the utilities attached to all possible consequences. In the case of *uncertainty*, the definition of rationality becomes problematic. One proposal that has had wide currency is the rule of "minimax risk": consider the worst set of consequences that may follow from each alternative, then select the alternative whose "worst set of consequences" is preferred to the worst sets attached to other alternatives. There are other proposals (e.g., the rule of "minimax regret"), but we shall not discuss them here.

Some Difficulties in the Classical Theory

There are difficulties with this model of rational man. In the first place, only in the case of certainty does it agree well with commonsense notions of rationality. In the case of uncertainty, especially, there is little agreement, even among exponents of statistical decision theory, as to the "correct" definition, or whether, indeed, the term "correct" has any meaning here (Marschak 1950).

A second difficulty with existing models of rational man is that they make three exceedingly important demands upon the choice-making mechanism. They assume (1) that all the alternatives of choice are "given"; (2) that all the consequences attached to each alternative are known (in one of the three senses corresponding to certainty, risk, and uncertainty respectively); (3) that the rational man has a complete utility-ordering (or cardinal function) for all possible sets of consequences.

One can hardly take exception to these requirements in a normative model—a model that tells people how they *ought* to choose. For if the rational man lacked information, he might have chosen differently "if only he had known." At best, he is "subjectively" rational, not "objectively" rational. But the notion of objective rationality assumes there is some objective reality in which the "real" alternatives, the "real" consequences, and the "real" utilities exist. If this is so, it is not even clear why the cases of choice under risk and under uncertainty are admitted as rational. If it is not so, it is not clear why only limitations upon knowledge of consequences are considered, and why limitations upon knowledge of alternatives and utilities are ignored in the model of rationality.

From a phenomenological viewpoint we can only speak of rationality relative to a frame of reference; and this frame of reference will be determined by the limitations on the rational man's knowledge. We can, of course, introduce the notion of a person observing the choices of a subject, and can speak of the rationality of the subject relative to the frame of reference of the observer. If the subject is a rat and the observer is a man (especially if he is the man who designed the experimental situation), we may regard the man's perception of the situation as objective and the rat's as subjective. (We leave out of account the specific difficulty that the rat presumably knows his own utility function better than the man does.) If, however, both subject and observer are men—and particularly if the situation is a natural one not constructed for experimental purposes by the observer—then it becomes difficult to specify the objective situation. It will be safest, in such situations, to speak of rationality only relative to some specified frame of reference.

The classical organization theory described in chapter 2, like classical economic theory, failed to make explicit this subjective and relative character of rationality, and in so doing, failed to examine some of its own crucial premises. The organizational and social environment in which the decision maker finds himself determines what consequences he will anticipate, what ones he will not; what alternatives he will consider, what ones he will ignore. In a theory of organization these variables cannot be treated as unexplained independent factors, but must themselves be determined and predicted by the theory.

Routinized and Problem-Solving Responses

The theory of rational choice put forth here incorporates two fundamental characteristics: (1) Choice is always exercised with respect to a limited, approximate, simplified "model" of the real situation. We call the chooser's model his "definition of the situation." (2) The elements of the definition of the situation are not "given"—that is, we do not take these as data of our theory—but are themselves the outcome of psychological and sociological processes, including the chooser's own activities and the activities of others in his environment (Simon 1947, 1955; March 1955; Cyert and March 1955, 1956; Newell, Shaw, and Simon 1958).

Activity (individual or organizational) can usually be traced back to an environmental stimulus of some sort, e.g., a customer order or a fire gong. The responses to stimuli are of various kinds. At one extreme, a stimulus evokes a response—sometimes very elaborate—that has been developed and learned at some previous time as an appropriate response for a stimulus of this class. This is the "routinized" end of the continuum, where a stimulus calls forth a performance program almost instantaneously.

At the other extreme, a stimulus evokes a larger or smaller amount of problem-solving activity directed toward finding performance activities with which to complete the response. Such activity is distinguished by the fact that it can be dispensed with once the performance program has been learned. Problem-solving activities can generally be identified by the extent to which they involve *search*; search aimed at discovering alternatives of action or consequences of action. "Discovering" alternatives may involve inventing and elaborating whole performance programs where these are not already available in the problem solver's repertory (Katona 1951).

When a stimulus is of a kind that has been experienced repeatedly in the past, the response will ordinarily be highly routinized. The stimulus will evoke, with a minimum of problem-solving or other computational activity, a well-structured definition of the situation that will include a repertory of response programs, and programs for selecting an appropriate specific response from the repertory. When a stimulus is relatively novel, it will evoke problem-solving activity aimed initially at constructing a definition of the situation and then at developing one or more appropriate performance programs.

Psychologists (e.g., Wertheimer, Duncker, de Groot, Maier) and observant laymen (e.g., Poincaré, Hadamard) who have studied creative thinking and problem solving have been unanimous in ascribing a large role in these phenomena to search processes. Search is partly random, but in effective problem-solving it is not blind. The design of the search process is itself often an object of rational decision. Thus, we may distinguish substantive planning—developing new performance programs—from procedural planning—developing programs for the problem-solving process itself. The response to a particular stimulus may involve more than performance—the stimulus may evoke a spate of problem-solving activity—but the problem-solving activity may itself be routinized to a greater or lesser degree. For example, search processes may be systematized by the use of check lists.

Satisfactory versus Optimal Standards

What kinds of search and other problem-solving activity are needed to discover an adequate range of alternatives and consequences for choice depends on the criterion applied to the choice. In particular, finding the optimal alternative is a radically different problem from finding a satisfactory alternative. An alternative is *optimal* if

1. there exists a set of criteria that permits all alternatives to be compared, and
2. the alternative in question is preferred, by these criteria, to all other alternatives.

An alternative is *satisfactory* if

1. there exists a set of criteria that describes minimally satisfactory alternatives, and
2. the alternative in question meets or exceeds all these criteria.

Most human decision-making, whether individual or organizational, is concerned with the discovery and selection of satisfactory alternatives; only in exceptional cases is it concerned with the discovery and selection of optimal alternatives. To optimize requires processes several orders of magnitude more complex than those required to satisfice. An example is the difference between searching a haystack to find the sharpest needle in it and searching the haystack to find a needle sharp enough to sew with.

In making choices that meet satisfactory standards, the standards themselves are part of the definition of the situation. Hence, we need not regard these as given—any more than the other elements of the definition of the situation—but may include in the theory the processes through which these standards are set and modified. The standard-setting process may itself meet standards of rationality: for example, an "optimizing" rule would be to set the standard at the level where the marginal improvement in alternatives obtainable by raising it would be just balanced by the marginal cost of searching for alternatives meeting the higher standard. Of course, in practice the "marginal improvement" and the "marginal cost" are seldom measured in comparable units, or with much accuracy. Nevertheless, a similar result would be automatically attained if the standards were raised whenever alternatives proved easy to discover, and lowered whenever they were difficult to discover. Under these circumstances, the alternatives chosen would not be far from the optima, if the cost of search were taken into consideration. Since human standards tend to have this characteristic under many conditions, some theorists have sought to maintain the optimizing model by introducing cost-of-search considerations. Although we doubt whether this will be a fruitful alternative to the model we are proposing in very many situations, neither model has been used for predictive purposes often enough to allow a final judgment.

Performance Programs

We have seen that under certain circumstances the search and choice processes are very much abridged. At the limit, an environmental stimulus may evoke immediately from the organization a highly complex and organized set of responses. Such a set of responses we call a performance program, or simply a program. For example, the sounding of the alarm gong in a fire station initiates such a program. So does the appearance of a relief applicant at a social worker's desk. So does the appearance of an automobile chassis in front of the work station of a worker on the assembly line.

Situations in which a relatively simple stimulus sets off an elaborate program of activity without any apparent interval of search, problem solving, or choice are not rare. They account for a very large part of the behavior of all persons, and for almost all of the behavior of persons in relatively routine positions. Most behavior, and particularly most behavior in organizations, is governed by performance programs.

The term *program* is not intended to connote complete rigidity. The content of the program may be adaptive to a large number of characteristics of the stimulus that initiates it. Even in the simple case of the fire gong, the response depends on the location of the alarm, as indicated by the number of strokes. The program may also be conditional on data that are independent of the initiating stimuli. It is then more properly called a performance strategy. For example, when inventory records show that the quantity on hand of a commodity has decreased to the point where it should be reordered, the decision rule that governs the behavior of the purchasing agent may call upon him to determine the amount to be ordered on the basis of a formula into which he inserts the quantity that has been sold over the past twelve months. In this case, search has been eliminated from the problem, but choice—of a very routinized kind, to be sure—remains.

We will regard a set of activities as routinized, then, to the degree that choice has been simplified by the development of a fixed response to defined stimuli. If search has been eliminated, but a choice remains in the form of a clearly defined and systematic computing routine, we will still say that the activities are routinized. We will regard activities as unroutinized to the extent that they have to be preceded by program-developing activities of a problem-solving kind.

Perception and Identifications

We have seen that humans, whether inside or outside administrative organizations, behave rationally, if at all, only relative to some set of "given" characteristics of the situation. These "givens" include knowledge or assumptions about future events or probability distributions of future events, knowledge of alternatives available for action, knowledge of consequences attached to alternatives—knowledge that may be more or less complete—and rules or principles for ordering consequences or alternatives according to preference.

These four sets of givens define the situation as it appears to the rational actor. In predicting his behavior, we need this specification and not merely a specification of the situation as it "really" is, or, more precisely, as it appears to an outside observer.

The steps that lead, for an actor, to his defining the situation in a particular way involve a complex interweaving of affective and cognitive processes. What a person wants and likes influences what he sees; what he sees influences what he wants and likes.

In the three previous chapters we have examined primarily motivational and affective factors. We have considered the relation between individual goals and organizational goals, the ways in which goals are acquired from reference groups, and the motivational bases for conformity with group goals. Cognition enters into the definition of the situation in connection with goal attainment—determining what means will reach desired ends. But cognition enters into the goal-formation process also, because the goals used as criteria for choice seldom represent "final" or "ultimate" values. Instead, they too reflect the perceived relations of means to ends and hence are modified by changing beliefs about these relations. Since goals provide the principal bridge between motivations and cognition, we will begin our consideration of cognitive elements in the definition of the situation with the topic of subgoal formation.

Cognitive Aspects of Subgoal Formation

An individual can attend to only a limited number of things at a time. The basic reason why the actor's definition of the situation differs greatly from the objective situation is that the latter is far too complex to be handled in all its detail. Rational behavior involves substituting for the complex reality a model of reality that is sufficiently simple to be handled by problem-solving processes.

In organizations where various aspects of the whole complex problem are being handled by different individuals and different groups of individuals, a fundamental technique for simplifying the problem is to factor it into a number of nearly independent parts, so that each organizational unit handles one of these parts and can omit the others from its definition of the situation. This technique is also prominent in individual and small-group behavior. A large complex task is broken down into a sequence of smaller tasks, the conjunction of which adds up to the accomplishment of the larger. The factorization of a large task into parts can be more elaborate for an organization than for an individual, but the underlying reason is the same: the definition of the situation at any one moment must be sufficiently simple to be encompassed by a human mind.

The principal way to factor a problem is to construct a means-end analysis. The means that are specified in this way become subgoals which may be assigned to individual organizational units. This kind of jurisdictional assignment is often called "organization by purpose" or "departmentalization by purpose."

The motivational aspect of this particular process of subgoal formation is rather simple. Whatever will motivate individuals and groups to accept the task assigned them through the legitimate (formal and informal) processes of the organization will provide motivation for subgoals. For the subgoals are implicit or explicit in the definition of the situation as it is incorporated in the task assignment.

When tasks have been allocated to an organizational unit in terms of a subgoal, other subgoals and other aspects of the goals of the larger organization tend to be ignored in the decisions of the subunit. In part, this bias in decision making can be attributed to shifts in the *focus of attention*. The definition of the situation that the subunit employs is simplified by omitting some criteria and paying particular attention to others. In particular, we expect the focus of attention to be a function of the *differentiation of subgoals* and the *persistence of subgoals*.

The tendency of members of an organizational unit to evaluate action only in terms of subgoals, even when these are in conflict with the goals of the larger organization, is reinforced by at least three cognitive mechanisms. The first of these is located within the individual decision maker, the second within the organizational unit, and the third in the environment of the organizational unit.

In the individual there is reinforcement through selective perception and rationalization. That is, the persistence of subgoals is furthered by the focus of attention it helps to generate. The propensity of individuals to see those things that are consistent with their established frame of reference is well established in individual psychology. Perceptions that are discordant with the frame of reference are filtered out before they reach consciousness, or are reinterpreted or "rationalized" so as to remove the discrepancy. The frame of reference serves just as much to validate perceptions as the perceptions do to validate the frame of reference.

Within the organizational unit there is reinforcement through the *content of in-group communication*. Such communication affects the *focus of information*, and thereby increases subgoal persistence. The vast bulk of our knowledge of fact is not gained through direct perception but through the secondhand, thirdhand, and *n*th-hand reports of the perceptions of others, transmitted through the channels of social communication. Since these perceptions have already been filtered by one or more communicators, most of whom have frames of reference similar to our own, the reports are generally consonant with the filtered reports of our own perceptions, and serve to reinforce the latter. In organizations, two principal types of in-groups are of significance in filtering: in-groups with members in a particular organizational unit, and in-groups with members in a common profession. Hence, we may distinguish *organizational* identifications and *professional* identifications. There are others, of course, but empirically these appear to be the most significant.

Finally, there is reinforcement through selective exposure to environmental stimuli. The *division of labor in the organization* affects the information that various members receive. This differentiation of information contributes to the differentiation of subgoals. Thus perceptions of the environment are biased even before they experience the filtering action of the frame of reference of the perceiver. Salesmen live in an environment of customers; company treasurers in an environment of bankers; each sees a quite distinct part of the world (Dearborn and Simon 1958).

There is one important distinction between this source of reinforcement and the two mentioned previously. Reinforcement through selective perception and rationalization and reinforcement through in-group communication serve to explain how a particular definition of the situation, once it becomes established in an individual or group, maintains itself with great stability and tenacity. These mechanisms do not explain, however, what particular definitions of the situation will *become* established in particular environments—they explain behavior persistence and not the origins of behavior. In order to predict what particular subgoals we are likely to find in particular parts of an organization, we must take as our starting point (*a*) the system of subgoal assignment that has resulted from analysis of the organization's goals, and (*b*) the kinds of stimuli to which each organizational unit is exposed in carrying out its assignments. Under the last heading we must include the selective feedback to organizational units of those consequences of action that relate to their particular subgoals.

Through these mechanisms of subgoal formation and subgoal perception, there is selective attention to particular consequences of proposed alternatives, and selective inattention to others. The magnitude of these effects depends in part on variations in the "capacity" of the individual participants in the organization. The smaller the *span of attention*, the narrower the focus of attention and the more critical the screening mechanisms cited above. One variable of particular importance in determining the span of attention is, of course, the *time pressure* involved. In general, we would expect selective perception to be most acute where time is shortest. The relations among these variables are indicated in figure 20.1.

Other Cognitive Aspects of the Definition of the Situation

All the statements of the last section apply, mutatis mutandis, to the other elements of the definition of the situation besides goals and values. That is to say, the definition of the situation represents a simplified, screened, and biased model of the objective situation, and filtering affects all of the "givens" that enter into the decision process: knowledge or assumptions about future events; knowledge of sets of alternatives available for action; knowledge of consequences attached to alternatives; goals and values (Levin 1956; Gore 1956).

Consider just knowledge and assumptions about future and present events—"stipulated facts," "absorption of uncertainty." What the sales of the ABC Company are going to be in 1961 is a question of fact. But this matter of fact may become a matter of organizational stipulation—all action within the organization to which the 1961 sales figure is relevant being based upon an "official" sales forecast. Organizational techniques for dealing with uncertain future and present facts will be discussed in a later section of this chapter.

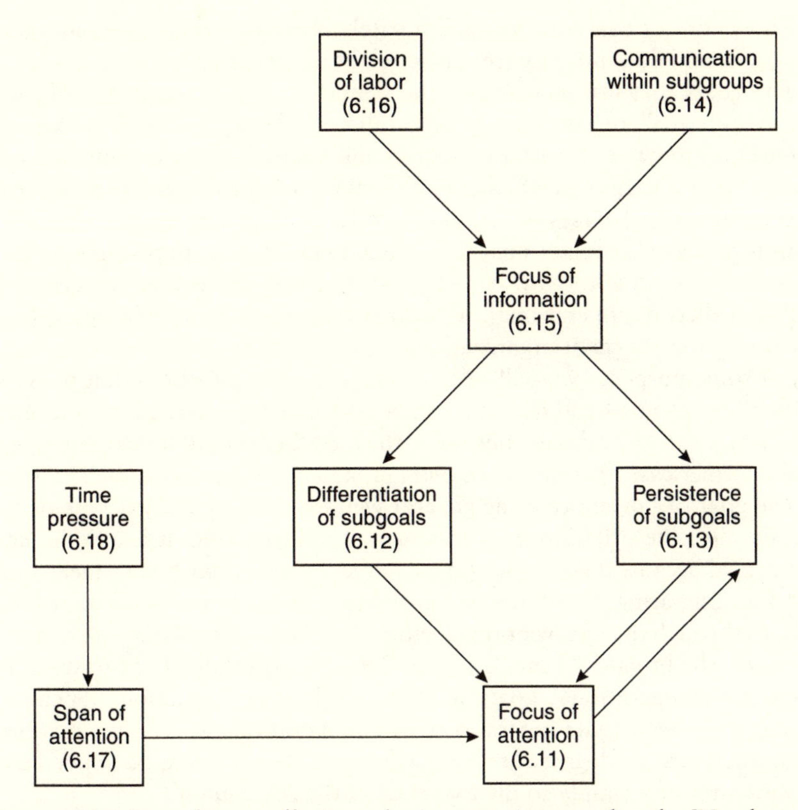

FIGURE 20.1 Some factors affecting selective attention to subgoals. [Numbers, in parentheses refer to sections of chapter as originally published—EDITOR'S NOTE.]

A related phenomenon is the summarizing of raw information to communicate it further in the organization. The weatherman makes observations of temperature, humidity, barometric pressure, but may communicate only his conclusions in the form of a weather forecast. In organizational communication, evidence is replaced with conclusions drawn from that evidence, and these conclusions then become the "facts" on which the rest of the organization acts. One particular form or summarization is classification. When a particular thing has been classified as belonging to a species, all the attributes of the species can be ascribed to the individual instance of it. Priority systems are an example of an important kind of formal classification device.

Similarly, individuals and organizations develop repertories of programs of action suited to different situations. These are frequently combined with classification systems so that once a situation has been assigned to a particular class the appropriate action program can be applied to it. Such repertories of performance programs, and the requisite habits and skills for their use, appear to make up the largest part of professional and vocational training.

Knowledge of consequences is intimately related to selective attention to subgoals, and does not require further elaboration here.

The goals that are included in the definition of the situation influence choice only if there are some means, valid or illusory, for determining the connections between alternative actions and goal satisfaction—only if it can somehow be determined whether and to what extent these goals will be realized if particular courses of action are chosen. When a means of testing actions is perceived to relate a particular goal or criterion with possible courses of action, the criterion will be called *operational*. Otherwise the criterion will be called nonoperational. This distinction has already been made in discussing the effects of organizational reward systems.

For some purposes we will need to make the further distinction between cases where means—end relations can be evaluated prior to action, and those where they can be evaluated only after the fact. We will call operational goals in the former case *operational ex ante*, in the latter case *operational ex post*.

The goal of "promoting the general welfare" is frequently a part of the definition of the situation in governmental policymaking. It is a nonoperational goal because it does not provide (either *ex ante* or *ex post*) a measuring rod for comparing alternative policies, but can only be related to specific actions through the intervention of subgoals. These subgoals, whose connection with the broader "general welfare" goal is postulated but not testable, become the operational goals in the actual choice situation. (Speaking strictly, whether a goal is operational or nonoperational is not a yes-no question. There are all degrees of "operationality." It will often be convenient, however, to refer simply to the two ends of the continuum.)

An important circumstance causing the substitution of subgoals for more general goals as criteria of decision is that the former are perceived as operational, the latter as nonoperational. For example, a business firm may understand to some degree how its specific actions affect its share of market, but may understand less surely how its actions affect long-range profits. Then the subgoal of maintaining a particular share of market may become the effective criterion of action—the operational goal.

The distinction between operational and nonoperational goals, combined with the generalization that behavior in organizations is intendedly rational, leads to the consideration of two qualitatively different decision-making processes associated with these two kinds of goals. When a number of persons are participating in a decision-making process, and these individuals have the same operational goals, differences in opinion about the course of action will be resolved by predominately analytic processes, i.e., by the analysis of the expected consequences of courses of action for realization of the shared goals. When either of the postulated conditions is absent from the situation (when goals are not shared, or when the shared goals are not operational and the operational subgoals are not shared), the decision will be reached by predominately bargaining processes. These are, of course, a distinction and prediction made in chapter 5 [not reproduced here] and lead to a proposition previously suggested: Rational, analytic processes take precedence over bargaining processes to the extent that the former are feasible. The condition of feasibility is that there be shared operational goals. The proposition, while it has not been much tested, is eminently testable. The goal structure of participants in a decision-making process can be determined by observation of their interaction or by interviewing or opinion-polling techniques. Their understanding of the means-end connections, and of possible methods for testing these connections, can be ascertained in the same way. It is not difficult to code their actual interaction in such a way as to detect the amount of bargaining.

The distinction between operational and nonoperational goals has been made the basis for the distinction between unitary and federal organization units (Simon, Smithburg, and Thompson 1950, 268–72).

The distinction between operational and nonoperational goals also serves to explain why a theory of public expenditures has never developed a richness comparable to that of the theory of public revenues. The economic approach to a theory of public expenditures would postulate some kind of "utility" or "welfare" function. A rational expenditure pattern would be one in which the marginal dollar of expenditure in each direction would make an equal marginal contribution to welfare. Although statements of this kind are encountered often enough in the literature of public finance, they are infrequently developed. The reason is that, in the absence of any basis for making the welfare maximization goal operational (because of the absence of an operational common denominator among the subgoals of governmental service), the general statement leads neither to description nor to prescription of behavior (Simon 1943).

In the literature on organizations, identification with subgoals has generally been attributed to motivation. Hence, in an analysis of conflict among organizational units, the affective aspects of the conflict have been stressed. In the present section, we have seen that cognitive processes are extremely important in producing and reinforcing subgoal identification. Subgoals may replace broader goals as a part of the whole process of replacing a complex reality with a simplified model of reality for purposes of decision and action (Blau 1955).

What difference does it make whether subgoal identification is motivationally or cognitively produced—whether the attachment to the subgoal has been internalized or is only indirect, through a cognitive link to some other goal? It may make very little or no difference in the short run; indeed, it may be difficult to find evidence from short-run behavior that would distinguish between these mechanisms. But it may make a great deal of difference in the processes for changing identifications. The greater *the dependence of the identification on cognitive links* to other goals, the greater the *effectiveness of attention-directing stimuli in changing goal emphasis*. By the same token, where identification depends on cognitive links, the invention of new techniques for evaluating the means-ends connections between action alternatives and goals will transform bargaining processes into processes of rational analysis. These hypotheses can be tested empirically.

Organization Structure and the Boundaries of Rationality

It has been the central theme of this chapter that the basic features of organization structure and function derive from the characteristics of human problem-solving processes and rational human choice. Because of the limits of human intellective capacities in comparison with the complexities of the problems that individuals and organizations face, rational behavior calls for simplified models that capture the main features of a problem without capturing all its complexities.

The simplifications have a number of characteristic features:

1. Optimizing is replaced by satisficing—the requirement that satisfactory levels of the criterion variables be attained.
2. Alternatives of action and consequences of action are discovered sequentially through search processes.
3. Repertories of action programs are developed by organizations and individuals, and these serve as the alternatives of choice in recurrent situations.
4. Each specific action program deals with a restricted range of situations and a restricted range of consequences.
5. Each action program is capable of being executed in semi-independence of the others—they are only loosely coupled together.

Action is goal-oriented and adaptive. But because of its approximating and fragmented character, only a few elements of the system are adaptive at any one time; the remainder are, at least in the short run, "givens." So, for example, an individual or organization may attend to improving a particular program, or to selecting an appropriate program from the existing repertory to meet a particular situation. Seldom can both be attended to simultaneously.

The notion that rational behavior deals with a few components at a time was first developed extensively in connection with economic behavior by John R. Commons (1951), who spoke of "limiting factors" that become the foci of attention and adaptation. Commons's theory was further developed by Chester I. Barnard (1938), who preferred the term "strategic factor."

This "one-thing-at-a-time" or "ceteris paribus" approach to adaptive behavior is fundamental to the very existence of something we can call *organization structure*. Organization structure consists simply of those aspects of the pattern of behavior in the organization that are relatively stable and that change only slowly. If behavior in organizations is "intendedly rational," we will expect aspects of the behavior to be relatively stable that either (*a*) represent adaptations to relatively stable elements in the environment, or (*b*) are the learning programs that govern the process of adaptation.

An organization is confronted with a problem like that of Archimedes: in order for an organization to behave adaptively, it needs some stable regulations and procedures that it can employ in carrying out its adaptive practices. Thus, at any given time an organization's programs for performing its tasks are part of its structure, but the least stable part. Slightly more stable are the switching rules that determine when it will apply one program, and when another. Still more stable are the procedures it uses for developing, elaborating, instituting, and revising programs.

The matter may be stated differently. If an organization has a repertory of programs, then it is adaptive in the short run insofar as it has procedures for selecting from this repertory a program appropriate to each specific situation that arises. The process used to select an appropriate program is the "fulcrum" on which short-run adaptiveness rests. If, now, the organization has processes for adding to its repertory of programs or for modifying programs in the repertory, these processes become still more basic fulcrums for accomplishing longer-run adaptiveness. Short-run adaptiveness corresponds to what we ordinarily call problem solving, long-run adaptiveness to learning.

There is no reason, of course, why this hierarchy of mechanisms should have only three levels—or any specified number. In fact, the adaptive mechanisms need not be arranged hierarchically. Mechanism A may include mechanism B within its domain of action, and vice versa. However, in general there is much asymmetry in the ordering, so that certain elements in the process that do not often become strategic factors (the "boundaries of rationality") form the stable core of the organization structure.

We can now see the relation between Commons's and Barnard's theories of the "limiting" or "strategic" factor and organization structure. Organization will have structure, as we have defined the term here, insofar as there are boundaries of rationality—insofar as there are elements of the situation that must be or are in fact taken as givens, and that do not enter into rational calculations as potential strategic factors. If there were not boundaries to rationality, or if the boundaries varied in a rapid and unpredictable manner, there could be no stable organization structure. Some aspects of structure will be more easily modified than others, and hence we may need to distinguish short-run and long-run structure.

References

Barnard, C. I. 1938. *The Functions of the Executive*. Cambridge: Harvard University Press.

Blau, P. M. 1955. *The Dynamics of Bureaucracy*. Chicago: University of Chicago Press.

Commons, J. R. 1951. *The Economics of Collective Action*. London: Macmillan.

Cyert, R. M., and J. G. March. 1955. "Organizational Structure and Pricing Behavior in an Oligopolistic Market." *American Economic Review* 45: 129–39.

Dearborn, D. C., and H. A. Simon. 1958. "Selective Perception: A Note on the Departmental Identifications of Executives." *Sociometry* 21: 140–44.

Gore, W. G. 1956. "Administrative Decision-Making in Federal Field Offices." *Public Administration Review* 16:281–91.

Katona, G. 1951. *Psychological Analysis of Economic Behavior*. New York: McGraw-Hill.

Levin, H. S. 1956. *Office Work and Automation*. New York: Wiley.

March, J. G. 1955. "An Introduction to the Theory and Measurement of Influence." *American Political Science Review* 49:431–51.

Marschak, J. 1950. "Rational Behavior, Uncertain Prospects, and Measurable Utility." *Econometrica* 18:111–41.

Newell, A., J. C. Shaw, and H. A. Simon. 1958. "Elements of a Theory of Human Problem Solving." *Psychological Review* 65:151–66.

Simon, H. A. 1943. *Fiscal Aspects of Metropolitan Consolidation*. Berkeley: Bureau of Public Administration, University of California.

———. 1947. *Administrative Behavior: A Study of Decision-Making Processes in Administrative Organization*. London: Macmillan.

———. 1955. "A Behavioral Model of Rational Choice." *Quarterly Journal of Economics* 69:99–118.

Simon, H. A., D. W. Smithburg, and V. A. Thompson. 1950. *Public Administration*. New York: Knopf.

Chapter 21

FROM *SENSEMAKING IN ORGANIZATIONS*

Karl E. Weick

The Nature of Sensemaking

Sensemaking is tested to the extreme when people encounter an event whose occurrence is so implausible that they hesitate to report it for fear they will not be believed. In essence, these people think to themselves, it can't be, therefore, it isn't. Just such an event is the battered child syndrome.

"The battered child syndrome consists of a pattern of injuries (usually to the head, arms, legs, and ribs) to a child, often a very young one, which the medical 'history' offered by the parents is inadequate to explain. The pattern of injuries is the result of assaults by parents who then either do not report the injuries as having occurred or pretend that they are the result of an accident" (Westrum 1982, 386). The injuries often can be seen only in x-rays, which explains, in part, why it took so long for this syndrome to be recognized by the medical community and eventually outlawed by every legislature in the union.

The battered child syndrome (BCS) was first suggested in 1946 by John Caffey, a pediatric radiologist, in an article based on six cases where parents gave "histories" that were silent about how the injuries, seen in x-ray photographs, had occurred. Some cases in the article were reported eight years after they had first been observed. The author speculated that the accidents may have been due to parents not fully appreciating the seriousness of the injuries or "intentional ill treatment." The article was published in a radiology journal rather than a pediatric journal, and nothing more happened until the mid-1950s. Articles appeared in 1953 (three cases reported by Silverman), 1955 (twelve cases reported by Wooley and Evans), and in 1957 (again by Caffey), but the medical profession remained unconcerned about this "professional blind spot."

Awareness did not change until October 1961, when Frederick Silverman chaired a panel, "The Battered Child Syndrome," at the American Academy of Pediatrics. What made this event significant is that data from a national survey of seventy-seven district attorneys and seventy-one hospitals were reported, and in this report 749 cases were identified. The results and an editorial were then published in the *Journal of the American Medical Association* under the title "The Battered-Child Syndrome."

Public reaction was prompt, and within a few years, laws in all fifty states required that suspected cases of BCS had to be reported. By 1967, when better reporting channels had been established, it was estimated that there were seven thousand cases. This estimate climbed to sixty thousand by 1972 and to five hundred thousand by 1976 (Westrum 1982, 392).

What makes this an instance of sensemaking? First, someone notices something, in an ongoing flow of events, something in the form of a surprise, a discrepant set of cues, something that does not fit. Second, the discrepant cues are spotted when someone looks back over elapsed experience. The act of looking is retrospective. Third, plausible speculations (e.g., parents fail to realize severity of injuries) are offered to explain the cues and their relative rarity. Fourth, the person making the speculations publishes them in a tangible journal article that becomes part of the environment of the medical community for others. He or she creates an object that was not "out there" to begin with but now is there for the noticing. Fifth, the speculations do not generate widespread attention right away because, as Westrum noted, the observations originated with radiologists who have infrequent social contact with pediatricians and families of children. Such contacts are crucial in the construction and perception of problems. And sixth, this example is about sensemaking because issues of identity and reputation are involved. As Westrum puts it, passive social intelligence about hidden events is often slow to develop because there are barriers to reporting the events. Experts overestimate the likelihood that they would surely know about the phenomenon if it actually were taking place. He calls this "the fallacy of centrality": because I don't know about this event, it must not be going on. As Westrum (1982) puts it, "this fallacy is all the more damaging in that it not only discourages curiosity on the part of the person making it but also frequently creates in him/her an antagonistic stance toward the events in question. One might well argue that part of the resistance of pediatricians to a diagnosis of parent-caused trauma was an inability to believe that their own evaluation of parents' dangerousness could be seriously in error" (393). Thus BCS is an instance of sensemaking because it involves identity, retrospect, enactment, social contact, ongoing events, cues, and plausibility.

There remains the question, what makes these events organizational sensemaking? Although a fuller answer will begin to emerge starting with chapter 3 [not reproduced here], its rough outline can be suggested. The setting in which the BCS syndrome was discovered is organizational in several ways. Pediatricians and radiologists, working through interlocking routines that are tied together in relatively formal "nets of collective action" (Czarniawska-Joerges 1992, 32), perform specialized tasks intended to preserve the health of children. Medical personnel have shared understandings of their roles, expertise, and stature, but they also act as shifting coalitions of interest groups. The prevalence of routines, generic understandings, and roles enables personnel to be interchanged.

Although all of this organizing facilitates coordinated action, it also imposes an "invisible hand" on sensemaking. This was clear in Westrum's fallacy of centrality, which is a direct by-product of nets of collective action. If we extend Westrum's observation, it is conceivable that heavily networked organizations might find their dense connections an unexpected liability, if this density encourages the fallacy of centrality. "News" might be discounted if people hear it late and conclude that it is not credible because, if it were, they would have heard it sooner. This dynamic bears watching because it suggests a means by which *perceptions* of information technology might undermine the ability of that technology to facilitate sensemaking. The more advanced the technology is thought to be, the more likely are people to discredit anything that does not come through it. Because of the fallacy of centrality, the better the information system, the less sensitive it is to novel events.

Organizations stay tied together by means of controls in the form of incentives and measures. This suggests that incentives for reporting anomalies, or penalties for nonreporting, should affect sensemaking. More frequent reporting of what Westrum (1982) calls "uncorrected observations and experience" (384) should intensify ambiguity in the short run, until others begin to report similar experiences. As anomalies become shared, sensibleness should become stronger.

Organizations also have their own languages and symbols that have important effects on sensemaking. The relevance of that to the BCS example is the striking difference between the phrase "intentional ill treatment" and the phrase "battered child." The latter phrase evokes a graphic picture of parents beating and killing their children. That image can mobilize outrage and action. The more general point is that vivid words draw attention to new possibilities (Pondy 1978), suggesting that organizations with access to more varied images will engage in sensemaking that is more adaptive than will organizations with more limited vocabularies.

BCS has elements of both sensemaking in general and organizational sensemaking. I turn now to a fuller investigation of each.

The Concept of Sensemaking

The concept of sensemaking is well named because, literally, it means the making of sense. Active agents construct sensible, sensable (Huber and Daft 1987, 154) events. They "structure the unknown" (Waterman 1990, 41). How they construct what they construct, why, and with what effects are the central questions for people interested in sensemaking. Investigators who study sensemaking define it in quite different ways. Many investigators (e.g., Dunbar 1981; Goleman 1985, 197–217) imply what Starbuck and Milliken (1988) make explicit, namely, that sensemaking involves placing stimuli into some kind of framework (51). The well-known phrase *frame of reference* has traditionally meant a generalized point of view that directs interpretations (Cantril 1941, 20). When people put stimuli into frameworks, this enables them "to comprehend, understand, explain, attribute, extrapolate, and predict" (Starbuck and Milliken 1988, 51). For example, people use strategy as a framework that "involves procurement, production, synthesis, manipulation, and diffusion of information in such a way as to give meaning, purpose and direction to the organization" (Westley 1990, 337).

A related conceptualization, grounded in newcomer socialization rather than in strategy, is found in the work of Meryl Louis (1980). She views sensemaking as a thinking process that uses retrospective accounts to explain surprises. "Sense making can be viewed as a recurring cycle comprised of a sequence of events occurring over time. The cycle begins as individuals form unconscious and conscious anticipations and assumptions, which serve as predictions about future events. Subsequently, individuals experience events that may be discrepant from predictions. Discrepant events, or surprises, trigger a need for explanation, or post-diction, and, correspondingly, for a process through which interpretations of discrepancies are developed. Interpretation, or meaning, is attributed to surprises. . . . It is crucial to note that meaning is assigned to surprise as an output of the sense-making process, rather than arising concurrently with the perception or detection of differences" (Louis 1980, 241).

Louis suggests that the activity of placing stimuli into frameworks is most visible when predictions break down, which suggests that sensemaking is partially under the control of expectations. Whenever an expectation is disconfirmed, some kind of ongoing activity is interrupted. Thus, to understand sensemaking is also to understand how people cope with interruptions. The joint influence of expectations and interruptions suggests that sensemaking will be more or less of an issue in organizations, depending on the adequacy of the scripts, routines, and recipes already in place. For example, an organization that expects change may find itself puzzled when something does not.

The activities of sensemaking mentioned by Starbuck, Milliken, Westley, and Louis focus on the placement of stimuli into frameworks, but other investigators include more activities than simply those of placement. Thomas, Clark, and Gioia (1993), for example, describe sensemaking as "the reciprocal interaction of information seeking, meaning ascription, and action" (240), which means that environmental scanning, interpretation, and "associated responses" all are included. Sackman (1991) talks about sensemaking *mechanisms* that organizational members use to attribute meaning to events, mechanisms that "include the standards and rules for perceiving, interpreting, believing, and acting that are typically used in a given cultural setting" (33). Feldman (1989) talks about sensemaking as an interpretive process that is necessary "for organizational members to understand and to share understandings about such features of the organization as what it is about, what it does well and poorly, what the problems it faces are, and how it should resolve them" (19). Whereas both Thomas et al. and Sackman mention "action" in conjunction with sensemaking, Feldman (1989) insists that sensemaking often

> does not result in action. It may result in an understanding that action should not be taken or that a better understanding of the event or situation is needed. It may simply result in members of the organization having more and different information about the ambiguous issue. (20)

Some investigators (e.g., Gioia and Chittipeddi 1991, 444) view sensemaking as a more private, more singular activity. Ring and Rands (1989), for example, define sensemaking as "a process in which individuals develop cognitive maps of their environment" (342). Having made sensemaking an individual activity, they use the term *understanding* to refer to mutual activity, a distinction that is clearly easier to propose than to implement:

> We decided that whenever the written material or responses from individuals reflected an intention on their part to simply enhance their own perspective on a subject, then such actions were indicative of a sensemaking process. . . . On the other hand, when these kinds of activities were pursued in activities that reflected reciprocity, we classified them as understanding. This is, of course, the grey area. The same activity may reflect, at once, sensemaking and understanding processes. (344)

Sensemaking is grounded in both individual and social activity, and whether the two are even separable will be a recurrent issue in this book, because it has been a durable tension in the human condition. Witness this description from Emily Dickinson:

> Much Madness is divinest Sense—
> To a discerning Eye—
> Much Sense—the starkest Madness—
> 'Tis the Majority
> In this, as All, prevail—
> Assent—and you are sane—
> Demur—you're straightaway dangerous—
> And handled with a Chain—
>
> (Cited in Mailloux 1990, 126)

Sense may be in the eye of the beholder, but beholders vote and the majority rules.

The Uniqueness of Sensemaking

My fascination with this topic dates back to conversations in the early 1960s with Harold Garfinkel and Harold Pepinsky. The context was Garfinkel's study of decision making in juries (published in Garfinkel 1967, 104–15; see Maynard and Manzo 1993, for an updating of Garfinkel's study). What I found intriguing was Garfinkel's insistence that jurors did not seem to first decide the harm and its extent, and then allocate blame, and then finally choose a remedy. Instead, they first decided a remedy and then decided the "facts," from among alternative claims, that justified the remedy. Jurors essentially created a sequence that was meaningfully consistent and then treated it as if it were the thing that actually occurred. "If the interpretation makes good sense, then that's what happened" (Garfinkel 1967, 106).

Facts were made sensible retrospectively to support the jurors' choice of verdict. Garfinkel (1967) summarized decision making in commonsense situations of choice this way:

> In place of the view that decisions are made as the occasions require, an alternative formulation needs to be entertained. It consists of the possibility that the person defines retrospectively the decisions that have been made. *The outcome comes before the decision.* In the material reported here, jurors did not actually have an understanding of the conditions that defined a correct decision until after the decision had been made. Only in retrospect did they decide what they did that made their decisions correct ones. When the outcome was in hand they went back to find the "why," the things that led up to the outcome. . . . If the above description is accurate, decision making in daily life would thereby have, as a critical feature, *the decision maker's task of justifying a course of action.* . . . [Decision making in daily life] may be much more preoccupied with the problem of assigning outcomes their legitimate history than with questions of deciding before the actual occasion of choice the conditions under which one, among a set of alternative possible courses of action, will be elected. (114–15)

A crucial property of sensemaking is that human situations are progressively clarified, but this clarification often works in reverse. It is less often the case that an outcome fulfills some prior definition of the situation, and more often the case that an outcome *develops* that prior definition. As Garfinkel (1967) puts it, actors "*in the course of a career of actions*, discover the nature of the situations in which they are acting. . . . [T]he actor's own actions are first order determinants of the sense that situations have, in which, literally speaking, actors *find* themselves" (115).

A similar emphasis on the idea that outcomes develop prior definitions of the situation is found in cognitive dissonance theory (Festinger 1957). Dissonance theory focuses on *post*decisional efforts to revise the meaning of decisions that have negative consequences (Cooper and Fazio 1984; Scher and Cooper 1989; Thibodeau and Aronson 1992). If, for example, people choose between alternatives with nonoverlapping attractions, they forgo the attractions of the nonchosen alternatives and gain the negative features of the chosen alternative. After making such a choice, people may feel anxious and agitated (dissonance). To reduce dissonance, people "spread" the alternatives by enhancing the positive features of the chosen alternative and the negative features of the unchosen alternatives. These operations retrospectively alter the meaning of the decision, the nature of the alternatives, and the "history" of the decision in a manner reminiscent of Garfinkel's jurors. In both cases, people start with an outcome in hand—a verdict, a choice—and then render that outcome sensible by constructing a plausible story that produced it (in Garfinkel's words, "the interpretation makes good sense").

A considerable body of work in organizational studies shows the legacy of cognitive dissonance, including the ideas of enactment (Abolafia Kilduff 1988; Weick 1977), commitment (O'Reilly and Caldwell 1981; Salancik 1977), rationality and rationalization (Staw 1980), escalation (Staw 1981), attribution (Calder 1977; Staw 1975), justification (Staw, McKechnie, and Puffer 1983), and motivation (Staw 1977). What is shared by these diverse ideas is a common set of emphases that can be traced back to dissonance theory. These include the following:

1. Sensemaking by justification, an idea that reflects an earlier emphasis on dissonance reduction by increasing the number of cognitive elements that are consistent with the decision;
2. Choice as the event that focuses sensemaking and justification, an idea that retains the emphasis on postdecision behavior;
3. Sensemaking by retrospect, an idea that retains dissonance theory's emphasis that postdecision outcomes are used to reconstruct predecisional histories;
4. Discrepancy as the occasion for sensemaking, an idea that restates dissonance theory's starting point, namely, action that follows from the obverse of cognitions held by the actor;
5. Social construction of justification, an idea that reflects dissonance reduction by means of social support and proselytizing;
6. Action shapes cognition, an idea that is a composite of items 2, 3, and 4 above.

All six of these strands can be found in dissonance theory, in more recent ideas such as commitment, escalation, and enactment, and there are hints of these strands in ethnomethodological accounts of decision making in everyday life (e.g., Handel 1982; Heap 1975; Gephart 1993). Most important for our purposes, all six are important in any account of sensemaking.

To see this, think about the wonderfully compact account of sensemaking mentioned by Graham Wallas. "The little girl had the making of a poet in her who, being told to be sure of her meaning before she spoke, said: 'How can I know what I think till I see what I say?' " (Wallas 1926, 106). This recipe, which is central in organizational sensemaking (Weick 1979, 133), retains several elements of dissonance theory. The recipe is about justification (my thoughts justify my earlier words), choice (I choose which words to focus on and which thoughts will explain them), retrospective sensemaking (I look back at what I said earlier from a later point in time when the talking has stopped), discrepancies (I feel a need to see what I say when something doesn't make sense), social construction of justification (I invoke the thoughts I have been socialized to label as acceptable), and action as the occasion for sensemaking (my act of speaking starts the sensemaking process).

Sensemaking to social psychologists meant making sense of actions that did not follow from beliefs and self-concepts, whereas to ethnomethodologists it meant reasoning in ways that differed from those rational practices associated with scientific thinking. Sensemaking, because it was influenced by dissonance theory, also meant a focus on conflict, affect, motivation, and instability as antecedents of change, rather than the current, more austere focus in cognitive studies on cool formation processing (Markus and Zajonc 1985, 207).

What makes current thinking about sensemaking robust is that both ethnomethodology (Czarniawska-Joerges 1992, chap. 5; Gephart 1993) and dissonance theory (Chatman, Bell, and Staw 1986; Weick 1993) still inform some of the core ideas. Furthermore, both perspectives share common ideas. The emphasis in ethnomethodology on accounting for what one does in the presence of other people to prove social competence and the rationality of actions is very much like the self-justification of dissonance theory, which is also directed at real or imagined auditors. What is unusual about the topic of sensemaking is that it is grounded as much in deductions from well-articulated theories as it is in inductions from specific cases of struggles to reduce ambiguity. This is a decided advantage for investigators because there is a core set of ideas that holds this perspective together and has held it together for some time. One purpose of this book is to make those ideas explicit.

Although the next chapter will describe important characteristics of sensemaking in more detail, I can now at least summarize how sensemaking differs from interpretation, with which it is often confused. The key distinction is that sensemaking is about the ways people generate what they interpret. Jury deliberations, for example, result in a verdict. Once jurors have that verdict in hand, they look back to construct a plausible account of how they got there. During their deliberations they do the same thing, albeit in miniature. Deliberating primarily develops the meaning of prior deliberating rather than subsequent deliberating. Jurors literally deliberate to discover what they are talking about and what constitutes evidence. They look for meaningful consistencies in what has been said, and then revise those consistencies. Authoring and interpretation are interwoven. The concept of sensemaking highlights the action, activity, and creating that lays down the traces that are interpreted and then reinterpreted.

Sensemaking, therefore, differs from interpretation in ways such as these. Sensemaking is clearly about an activity or a process, whereas interpretation can be a process but is just as likely to describe a product. It is common to hear that someone made "an interpretation." But we seldom hear that someone made "a sensemaking." We hear, instead, that people make sense of something, but even then, the activity rather than the outcome is in the foreground. A focus on sensemaking induces a mind-set to focus on process, whereas this is less true with interpretation.

Even when interpretation is treated as a process, the implied nature of the process is different. The act of interpreting implies that something is there, a text in the world, waiting to be discovered or approximated (see Daft and Weick 1984). Sensemaking, however, is less about discovery than it is about invention. To engage in sensemaking is to construct, filter, frame, create facticity (Turner 1987), and render the subjective into something more tangible.

The contrast between discovery and invention is implicit in the word *sense*. To sense something sounds like an act of discovery. But to sense something, there must be something there to create the sensation. And sensemaking suggests the construction of that which then becomes sensible. Sensemaking might even be described as an ongoing effort to create a world in which object perception, rather than interpersonal perception, would be more appropriate (Swann 1984), although it never succeeds in doing so. As Morgan, Frost, and Pondy (1983) put it, "Individuals are not seen as living in, and acting out their lives in relation *to*, a wider reality, so much as creating and sustaining images of a wider reality, in part to rationalize what they are doing. They realize their reality by 'reading into' their situation patterns of significant meaning" (24).

Thus, the concept of sensemaking is valuable because it highlights the invention that precedes interpretation. It is also valuable because it implies a higher level of engagement by the actor. Interpretation connotes an activity that is more detached and passive than the activity of sensemaking. Sensemaking matters. A failure in sensemaking is consequential as well as existential. It throws into question the nature of self and the world. As Frost and Morgan (1983) suggest, when people make sense of things, they "read into things the meanings they wish to see; they vest objects, utterances, actions and so forth with subjective meaning which helps make their world intelligible to themselves" (207). The stakes are seldom as high when interpretations fail. Interpretations can be added and dropped with less effect on one's self-perceptions, which is not true of efforts to replace one sense of the world with another. And whenever sense is lost, the loss is deeply troubling (e.g., Asch 1952; Garfinkel 1963; Milgram 1963), whereas the loss of an interpretation is more like a nuisance.

It is also important to separate sensemaking from interpretation because sensemaking seems to address incipient puzzles at an earlier, more tentative stage than does interpretation. When people discuss interpretation, it is usually assumed that an interpretation is necessary and that the object to be interpreted is evident. No such presumptions are implied by sensemaking. Instead, sensemaking begins with the basic question, is it still possible to take things for granted? And if the answer is no, if it has become impossible to continue with automatic information processing, then the question becomes, why is this so? And, what next? Several questions arise and have to be dealt with before interpretation even comes into play. The way these earlier questions of sensemaking are resolved determines which interpretations are possible and plausible.

The early emergence of sensemaking is also what sets it apart from decision making, as Drucker (1974) made clear:

> The Westerner and the Japanese man mean something different when they talk of "making a decision." In the West, all the emphasis is on the *answer* to the question. Indeed, our books on decision making try to develop systematic approaches to giving an answer. To the Japanese, however, the important element in decision making is *defining the question*. The important and crucial steps are to decide whether there is a need for a decision and what the decision is about. And it is in that step that the Japanese aim at attaining consensus. Indeed, it is this step that, to the Japanese, is the essence of decision. The answer to the question (what the West considers the decision) follows from its definition. During the process that precedes the decision, no mention is made of what the answer might be. . . . Thus the whole process is focused on finding out what the decision is really about, not what the decision should be. (466–67)

To talk about sensemaking is to talk about reality as an ongoing accomplishment that takes form when people make retrospective sense of the situations in which they find themselves and their creations. There is a strong reflexive quality to this processes. People make sense of things by seeing a world on which they already imposed what they believe. People discover their own inventions, which is why sensemaking understood as invention, and interpretation understood as discovery, can be complementary ideas. If sensemaking is viewed as an act of invention, then it is also possible to argue that the artifacts it produces include language games and texts.

But to argue that the bulk of organizational life is captured by the metaphor of reading texts is to ignore most of the living that goes into that life. I agree with Czarniawska-Joerges's (1992, 253–54) assessment that the text metaphor represents the activity of social construction as a static result, implies that meaning already exists and is waiting to be found rather than that it awaits construction that might not happen or might go awry, and suggests a unity that is untenable when there are subuniverses of meaning. "Organizations are not texts, but a text is a common form of interpretation that we deal with" (Czarniawska-Joerges 1992, 123).

Finally, what sensemaking is *not* is a metaphor. I say this because Morgan, Frost and Pondy (1983) describe sensemaking as one of three metaphors (the other two are language game and text) that are used by people who favor an interpretive approach to organizational studies. They argue that all three positions are "concerned with understanding the genesis of meaningful action, how individuals make sense [*sic*] of their situations, and thus come to define and share realities which may become objectified in fairly routinized ways. In short, to understand how the objective, taken for granted aspects of everyday life are constituted and made real through the medium of symbolic process" (Morgan, Frost, and Pondy 1983, 22).

Although texts and language games are metaphors for interpretation, sensemaking is not. Sensemaking is what it says it is, namely, making something sensible. Sensemaking is to be understood literally, not metaphorically. Notice that Morgan, Frost and Pondy inadvertently acknowledge this when they describe the "metaphor" of sensemaking as "how individuals make sense of their situations." This error of logical typing (Bateson 1972) can be avoided if sensemaking is separated from the class of interpretive activities it names and set above this class as a higher-level abstraction that includes them. Although the word *sensemaking* may have an informal, poetic flavor, that should not mask the fact that it is literally just what it says it is.

The Social Property of Sensemaking

The word *sensemaking* tempts people to think in terms of an individual level of analysis, which induces a blind spot we need to catch early on. When discussing sensemaking, it is easy to forget that "human thinking and social functioning . . . [are] essential aspects of one another" (Resnick, Levine, and Teasley 1991, 3). Many scholars of organizations are mindful of the intertwining of the cognitive and the social, as in this informative definition proposed by Walsh and Ungson (1991): An organization is "a network of intersubjectively shared meanings that are sustained through the development and use of a common language and everyday social interaction" (60). This definition is social several times over in its references to "network," "intersubjectively shared meanings," "common language," and "social interaction."

Those who forget that sensemaking is a social process miss a constant substrate that shapes interpretations and interpreting. Conduct is contingent on the conduct of others, whether those others are imagined or physically present. The contingent quality of sensemaking is found in Allport's (1985) description of social psychology as "an attempt to understand and explain how the thought, feeling, and behavior of individuals are influenced by the actual, *imagined, or implied* presence of others" (3; emphasis added). Burns and Stalker (1961), focusing on organizations, say essentially the same thing:

> In working organizations decisions are made either in the presence of others *or with the knowledge that they will have to be implemented, or understood, or approved by others*. The set of considerations called into relevance on any decision-making occasion has therefore to be one shared with others or acceptable to them. (118; emphasis added)

The caution implicit in both quotations is that imagined presence can be overdone and create a specious social quality. This is the problem with much of so-called social cognition.

> The emphasis of the work on social cognition is that internal constructions of knowledge or logic affect our understanding of social interactions; however, these internal constructions are developed independent of other people. . . . [An alternative view is that] our intentions and feelings do not grow within us but between us. . . . [A]n individual creates novel thoughts in the context of interactions with others, and then communicates them to the larger community. If viable, the larger community generalizes these ideas such that they become part of the culture. (Kahlbaugh 1993, 80, 99)

When people overlook the social substrate, they manufacture theoretical obstacles that can be distracting. For example, Ring and Rands (1989), in their investigation of negotiations between 3M and NASA, equate sensemaking with individual action, and understanding with group action. In doing so, they create obstacles like this: "There also appears to be a definitional question related to sensemaking and understanding processes: What is the relationship between one-way and two-way communication processes and sensemaking and understanding? Clearly, sensemaking can involve one-way communication links. A person tells me something, and it aids in the development of my cognitive map of some phenomenon. I need not respond, but if I do, is the response associated with processes of sensemaking, understanding, or both?" (364).

This forced separation of individual and social contributions to sensemaking leads them to focus most of their attention on a face-to-face interaction where joint understanding was furthered (i.e., a five-day lab tour of NASA facilities involving 3M and NASA personnel, p. 351) and to downplay the importance of the pretour sensemaking built around each anticipating how the other would react to proposals and proposed identities. But it was these anticipations, these attempts to make sense using the implied, imagined presence of the others, that enabled people to make sense during the face-to-face tour. For example, Smith, the NASA representative, learned during the tour that 3M's dollar commitment to the space project was less than expected. But Smith did not suddenly begin to impose the idea of financial commitment on the face-to-face meetings. Instead, what happened on the tour fine-tuned the rehearsing that preceded it. And that rehearsing is just as interactive as the tour itself. Said differently, social influences on sensemaking do not arise solely from physical presence. That is the whole point of the phrase *symbolic* interaction (Blumer 1969).

Sensemaking is never solitary because what a person does internally is contingent on others. Even monologues and one-way communications presume an audience. And the monologue changes as the audience changes.

> Human beings in interacting with one another have to take account of what each other is doing or is about to do; they are forced to direct their own conduct or handle their situation in terms of what they take into account. Thus, the activities of others enter as positive factors in the formation of their own conduct; in the face of the actions of others one may abandon an intention or purpose, revise it, check or suspend it, intensify it, or replace it. The actions of others enter to set what one plans to do, may oppose or prevent such plans, and may demand a very different set of such plans. One has to *fit* one's own line of activity in some manner to the actions of others. The actions of others have to be taken into account and cannot be regarded as merely an arena for the expression of what one is disposed to do or sets out to do. (Blumer 1969, 8)

Several tactics in scholarship on sensemaking themselves make more sense if they are seen as attempts to keep socially conditioned activity in the foreground. For example, socialization is often the setting in which sensemaking is explored, as we saw in work of Louis (1980). More recent discussions (Lave and Wenger 1991) of socialization as a process resembling an apprenticeship retain this focus on a social setting. In general, socialization studies represent a variant of Schutz's (1964) analysis of the stranger, which suggests that newcomers need to learn both how to interpret and how to express themselves in the natives' vernacular.

Investigators who talk about sensemaking often invoke imagery associated with symbolic interactionism (Fine 1993), not so much because this is the unofficial theory of sensemaking but because the theory keeps in play a crucial set of elements, including self, action, interaction, interpretation, meaning, and joint action. As we have already seen, these elements are crucial in the determination of sensemaking, whether one chooses to combine them the way a symbolic interactionist does or not. Because symbolic interactionism derives from the work of Mead, and because Mead was adamant that mind and self arise and develop within the social process, to use the images of symbolic interactionism is to insure that one remains alert to the ways in which people actively shape each other's meanings and sensemaking processes.

People who study sensemaking pay a lot of attention to talk, discourse, and conversation because that is how a great deal of social contact is mediated. Gronn (1983) describes "talk as the work" in educational organizations. March and Olsen (1976) describe organizations as a "set of procedures for argumentation and interpretation" (25). Shotter (1993), in describing the manager as author, cautions that he does not mean that the manager writes texts, but rather that the manager is "a 'practical-ethical author,' a 'conversational author,' able to argue persuasively for a 'landscape' of next possible actions, upon which the 'positions' of all who must take part are clear" (157). And Weick (1985) argues that a significant portion of the organizational environment

> consists of nothing more than talk, symbols, promises, lies, interest, attention, threats, agreements, expectations, memories, rumors, indicators, supporters, detractors, faith, suspicion, trust, appearances, loyalties, and commitments. . . . Words induce stable connections, establish stable entities to which people can orient (e.g., "gender gap"), bind people's time to projects ("Al, I'd like you to spend some time on this one"), and signify important information. Agreement on a label that sticks is as constant a connection as is likely to be found in organizations. (128)

Although it is important to conceptualize sensemaking as a social activity, it is also important to maintain a differentiated view of the forms social influence may take. This sounds obvious, but it is striking how often people discuss "shared meaning" or "social construction," as if that exhausts what there is to say about social sensemaking. However, sensemaking is also social when people coordinate their actions on grounds other than shared meanings, as when joint actions are coordinated by equivalent meanings (Donnellon, Gray, and Bougon 1986), distributed meanings (Rasmussen, Brehmer, and Leplat 1991), overlapping views of ambiguous events (Eisenberg 1984), or nondisclosive intimacy (Eisenberg 1990). Czarniawska-Joerges (1992) argues that shared meaning is not what is crucial for collective action, but rather it is the experience of the collective action that is shared. She cites this example:

> My two colleagues went to hear a speech given by a well-known businessman. One "participated in a most exciting encounter between the wisdom of practice and curiosity of theory," whereas the other "took part in an extremely boring meeting with an elderly gentleman who told old jokes." They are each, nevertheless, members of the same organization, and what was common for them was that they went to the same room at the same hour, sharing only the idea that their bosses expected it. (33)

To understand sensemaking is to pay more attention to sufficient cues for coordination such as a generalized other, prototypes, stereotypes, and roles, especially considering that organizations seem to drift toward an "architecture of simplicity" (Miller 1993). People who make sense are just as likely to satisfice as are people who make decisions. Turner's (1971) analyses of organizational talk revealed that "reasons of expediency, or pragmatic considerations, seem to be the most important rule of naming or defining. Other things being equal . . . a good name was not necessarily the most accurate, but one that allowed action. It makes sense. 'Tree' or 'stone' is enough to decide whether to use a saw or a hammer; 'fir' or 'amethyst,' albeit more accurate, do not improve the pragmatic advantage and may prove more costly in social terms (what if another person at the saw thought it was a pine and wanted to engage in debate?). Naming seems to be a satisfying process, like any decision-making" (quoted in Czarniawska-Joerges 1992, 178–79).

Blumer (1969, 76) summarizes well the reasons to be cautious about overestimating the extent to which social sensemaking means simply shared understanding. He notes that investigators often argue that common values are the "glue" that holds society together, whereas conflicting values destabilize. Blumer (1969) goes on to observe that this

> conception of human society becomes subject to great modification if we think of society as consisting of the fitting together of acts to form joint action. Such alignment may take place for any number of reasons, depending on the situations calling for joint action, and need not involve, or spring from, the sharing of common values. The participants may fit their acts to one another in orderly joint actions on the basis of compromise, out of duress, because they may use one another in achieving their respective ends, because it is the sensible thing to do, or out of sheer necessity. . . . In very large measure, society becomes the formation of *workable* relations. (76; emphasis added)

Alignment is no less social than is sharing. But it does suggest a more varied set of inputs and practices in sensemaking than does sharing. And it keeps lines of action in clear view, which, as we just saw in the discussion of enactment, is crucial.

Summary

The recipe "how can I know what I think until I see what I say?" can be parsed to show how each of the seven properties of sensemaking are built into it.

1. Identity: The recipe is a question about who I am as indicated by discovery of how and what I think.
2. Retrospect: To learn what I think, I look back over what I said earlier.
3. Enactment: I create the object to be seen and inspected when I say or do something.
4. Social: What I say and single out and conclude are determined by who socialized me and how I was socialized, as well as by the audience I anticipate will audit the conclusions I reach.
5. Ongoing: My talking is spread across time, competes for attention with other ongoing projects, and is reflected on after it is finished, which means my interests may already have changed.

6. Extracted cues: The "what" that I single out and embellish as the content of the thought is only a small portion of the utterance that becomes salient because of context and personal dispositions.

7. Plausibility: I need to know enough about what I think to get on with my projects, but no more, which means sufficiency and plausibility take precedence over accuracy.

The close fit between the recipe and the seven properties remains if one or more of the pronouns in the recipe is changed to reflect a collective actor (e.g., how can we know what we think until I see what we say?).

References

Abolafia, M. Y., and M. Kilduff. 1988. "Enacting Market Crisis: The Social Construction of a Speculative Bubble." *Administrative Science Quarterly* 33: 177–93.

Allport, G. W. 1985. "The Historical Background of Social Psychology." In *Handbook of Social Psychology*, ed. G. Lindzey and E. Aronson, vol. 1. 3d ed. New York: Random House.

Asch, S. E. 1952. *Social Psychology.* Englewood Cliffs, N.J.: Prentice-Hall.

Bateson, G. 1972. *Steps to an Ecology of Mind.* New York: Chandler.

Blumer, H. 1969. *Symbolic Interactionism: Perspective and Method.* Englewood Cliffs, N.J.: Prentice-Hall.

Burns, T., & Stalker, G. M. (1961). *The management of innovation.* London: Tavistock.

Calder, B. J. 1977. "An Attribution Theory of Leadership." In *New Directions in Organizational Behavior*, ed. B. M. Staw and G. R. Salancik. Chicago: St. Clair.

Cantril, H. 1941. *The Psychology of Social Movements.* New York: John Wiley.

Chatman, J. A., N. E. Bell, and B. M. Staw. 1986. "The Managed Thought: The Role of Self-Justification and Impression Management in Organizational Settings." In *The Thinking Organization*, ed. H. P. Sims Jr. and D. A. Gioia. San Francisco: Jossey-Bass.

Cooper, J., and R. H. Fazio. 1984. "A New Look at Dissonance Theory." In (Ed.), *Advances in Experimental Social Psychology*, ed. L Berkowitz, vol. 17. Orlando: Academic Press.

Czarniawska-Joerges, B. 1992. *Exploring Complex Organizations: A Cultural Perspective.* Newbury Park, Calif.: Sage.

Daft, R. L., and K. E. Weick. 1984. "Toward a Model of Organizations as Interpretation Systems." *Academy of Management Review* 9:284–95.

Donnellon, A., B. Gray, and M. G. Bougon. 1986. "Communication, Meaning, and Organizational Action." *Administrative Science Quarterly* 31:43–55.

Drucker, P. E. 1974. *Management: Tasks, Responsibilities, Practices.* New York: Harper and Row.

Dunbar, R.L.M. (1981). Designs for organizational control. In P. C. Nystrom & W. H. Starbuck (Eds.), *Handbook of Organizational Design* (Vol. 2, pp. 85–115). New York: Oxford University Press.

Eisenberg, E. M. 1984. "Ambiguity as Strategy in Organizational Communication." *Communication Monographs* 51:227–42.

———. 1990. "Jamming: Transcendence through Organizing." *Communication Research* 17:139–64.

Feldman, M. S. 1989. *Order without Design*. Stanford: Stanford University Press.

Festinger, L. 1954. "A Theory of Social Comparison Processes." *Human Relations* 7:117–40.

———. 1957. *A Theory of Cognitive Dissonance*. Stanford: Stanford University Press.

Fine, G. A. 1993. "The Sad Demise, Mysterious Disappearance, and Glorious Triumph of Symbolic Interactionism." *Annual Review of Sociology* 19:61–87.

Frost, P. J., and G. Morgan. 1983. "Symbols and Sensemaking: The Realization of a Framework." In *Organizational Symbolism*, ed. L. R. Pondy, P. J. Frost, G. Morgan, and T. C. Dandridge. Greeenwich, Conn.: JAI.

Garfinkel, H. 1963. "A Conception of, and Experiment with, 'Trust' as a Condition of Stable Connected Actions." In *Motivation and Social Interaction*, ed. O. J. Harvey. New York: Ronald.

———. 1967. *Studies in Ethnomethodology*. Englewood Cliffs, N.J.: Prentice-Hall.

Gephart, R. P., Jr. 1993. "The Textual Approach: Risk and Blame in Disaster Sensemaking." *Academy of Management Journal* 36: 1465–1514.

Gioia, D. A., and K. Chittipeddi. 1991. "Sensemaking and Sensegiving in Strategic Change Initiation." *Strategic Management Journal* 12:433–48.

Goleman, D. 1985. *Vital Lies, Simple Truths: The Psychology of Self-Deception*. New York: Simon and Schuster.

Gronn, P. C. 1983. "Talk as the Work: The Accomplishment of School Administration." *Administrative Science Quarterly* 28:1–21.

Handel, W. 1982. *Ethnomethodology: How People Make Sense*. Englewood Cliffs, N.J.: Prentice-Hall.

Heap, J. 1975. What Are Sense Making Practices? *Sociological Inquiry* 46:107–15.

Huber, G. P., and R. L. Daft. 1987. "The Information Environments of Organizations." In *Handbook of Organizational Communication*, ed. F. M. Jablin, L. L. Putnam, K. H. Roberts, & L. W. Porter. Newbury Park, Calif.: Sage.

Kahlbaugh, P. A. 1993. "James Mark Baldwin: A Bridge between Social and Cognitive Theories of Development." *Journal for the Theory of Social Behaviour* 23:79–103.

Lave, J., and E. Wenger. 1991. *Situated learning: Legitimate Peripheral Participation*. Cambridge: Cambridge University Press.

Louis, M. 1980. "Surprise and Sensemaking: What Newcomers Experience in Entering Unfamiliar Organizational Settings." *Administrative Science Quarterly* 25:226–51.

Mailloux, S. 1990. "Interpretation." In *Critical Terms for Literary Study*, ed. F. Lentricchia and T. McLaughlin. Chicago: University of Chicago Press.

March, J. G., and J. P. Olsen. 1976. *Ambiguity and Choice in Organizations*. Bergen, Norway: Universitetsforlaget.

Markus, H., and R. B. Zajonc. 1985. "The Cognitive Perspective in Social Psychology." In *The Handbook of Social Psychology*, ed., G. Lindzey and E. Aronson vol. 1. 3d ed. New York: Random House.

Maynard, D. W., and J. F. Manzo. 1993. "On the Sociology of Justice: Theoretical Notes from an Actual Jury Deliberation." *Sociological Theory* 11:171–93.

Milgram, S. 1963. "Behavioral Study of Obedience." *Journal of Abnormal and Social Psychology* 67:371–38.

Miller, D. 1993. "The Architecture of Simplicity." *Academy of Management Review* 18:116–38.

Morgan, G., P. J. Frost, and L. R. Pondy. 1983. "Organizational Symbolism." In *Organizational Symbolism*," ed. L. R. Pondy, P. J. Frost, G. Morgan, and T. C. Dandridge. Greenwich, Conn.: JAI.

O'Reilly, C. A., and D. F. Caldwell. 1981. "The Commitment and Job Tenure of New Employees: Some Evidence of Postdecisional Justification. *Administrative Science Quarterly* 26:597–616.

Rasmussen, J., B. Brehmer, and J. Leplat. 1991. *Distributed Decision Making: Cognitive Models for Cooperative Work*. New York: Wiley.

Resnick, L. B., J. M. Levine, and S. D. Teasley. eds. 1991. *Perspectives on Socially Shared Cognition*. Washington, D.C.: American Psychological Association.

Ring, P. S., and G. P. Rands. 1989. "Sensemaking, Understanding, and Committing: Emergent Interpersonal Transaction Processes in the Evolution of 3M's Microgravity Research Program." In *Research on the Management of Innovation: The Minnesota Studies*, ed. A. H. Van de Ven, H. L. Angle, and M. S. Poole. New York: Ballinger.

Sackman, S. A. 1991. *Cultural Knowledge in Organizations: Exploring the Collective Mind*. Newbury Park, Calif.: Sage.

Salancik, G. R. 1977. "Commitment and the Control of Organizational Behavior and Belief." In *New Directions in Organizational Behavior*, ed. B. M. Staw and G. R. Salancik. Chicago: St. Clair.

Scher, S. J., and J. Cooper. 1989. "Motivational Basis of Dissonance: The Singular Role of Behavioral Consequences." *Journal of Personality and Social Psychology* 56:899–906.

Schutz, A. 1964. "The Stranger: An Essay in Social Psychology." In *Collective Papers*, vol. 2. The Hague: Martinus Nijhoff.

Shotter, J. 1983. " 'Duality of structure' and 'Intentionality' in an Ecological Psychology." *Journal for the Theory of Social Behaviour* 13:19–43.

Starbuck, W. H., and F. J. Milliken. 1988. "Executives' Perceptual Filters: What They Notice and How They Make Sense." In *The Executive Effect: Concepts and Methods for Studying Top Managers*," ed. D. C. Hambrick. Greenwich, Conn.: JAI.

Staw, B. M. 1975. "Attribution of the 'Causes' of Performance: A General Alternative Interpretation of Cross-Sectional Research on Organizations." *Organizational Behavior and Human Performance* 13:414–432.

———. 1980. "Rationality and Justification in Organizational Life." In *Research in Organizational Behavior*, vol. 2, ed. B. M. Staw and L. L. Cummings. Greenwich, Conn: JAI.

———. 1981. "The Escalation of Commitment to a Course of Action." *Academy of Management Review* 6:577–87.

Staw, B. M., P. I. McKechnie, and S. M. Puffer. 1983. "The Justification of Organizational Performance." *Administrative Science Quarterly* 28:582–600.

Swann, W. B., Jr. 1984. "Quest for Accuracy in Person Perception: A Matter of Pragmatics." *Psychological Review* 91:457–77.

Thibodeau, R., and E. Aronson. 1992. "Taking a Closer Look: Reasserting the Role of the Self-Concept in Dissonance Theory." *Personality and Social Psychology Bulletin*. 18:591–602.

Thomas, J. B., S. M. Clark, and D. A. Gioia. 1993. "Strategic Sensemaking and Organizational Performance: Linkages among Scanning, Interpretation, Action, and Outcomes. *Academy of Management Journal* 36:239–70.

Turner, B. A. 1971. *Exploring the Industrial Subculture*. London: Macmillan.

Turner, J. H. 1987. "Toward a Sociological Theory of Motivation." *American Sociological Review* 52:15–27.

Wallas, G. 1926. *The Art of Thought*. New York: Harcourt Brace.

Walsh, J. P., and G. R. Ungson. 1991. "Organizational Memory." *Academy of Management Review* 16:57–91.

Waterman, R. H., Jr. 1990. *Adhocracy: The Power to Change*. Memphis: Whittle Direct Books.

Weick, K. E. 1977. "Enactment Processes in Organizations." In *New Directions in Organizational Behavior*, ed. B. M. Staw and G. Salancik. Chicago: St. Clair.

———. 1979. *The Social Psychology of Organizing*. 2d ed. Reading, Mass.: Addison-Wesley.

———. 1985. "Sources of Order in Underorganized Systems: Themes in Recent Organizational Theory. In *Organizational Theory and Inquiry*, ed. Y. S. Lincoln. Beverly Hills: Sage.

———. 1993. "Sensemaking in Organizations: Small Structures with Large Consequences." In *Social Psychology in Organizations: Advances in Theory and Research*, ed. J. K. Murnighan. Englewood Cliffs, N.J.: Prentice-Hall.

Westley, F. R. 1990. "Middle Managers and Strategy: Microdynamics of Inclusion." *Strategic Management Journal* 11:337–51.

Westrum, R. 1982. "Social Intelligence about Hidden Events." *Knowledge* 3: 381–400.

INDEX

Abegglen, James C., 172
accounting, ceremonial functions of, 97
Adams, Thomas, 81n74, 83n84
Adler, Felix, 143
Aiken, Michael, 92
Akerlof, George, 23
Alchian, Armen, 117
Aldrich, Howard E., 114, 130n6, 282
Allport, G. W., 543–44
American Farm Bureau Federation, 141
American Federation of Labor, 138
American Tobacco, 426
Anderson, Benedict, 19
antitrust law and enforcement: deconglomeration and, 189, 198–99; efficient markets versus power as explanation of, 25; history of, 424–31; large corporations, rise of and, 28–29; mergers, increasing as byproduct of, 29, 38, 196; relaxation of by Reagan administration, 7, 198–99, 430–31
Aquinas, Saint Thomas, 55, 58–59, 73n29, 74n32
arm's-length transactions, 290, 351, 360, 362
Arnold, Thurman, 428
Arrow, Kenneth, 252
asceticism: capitalism, and the spirit of, 12, 56–63; of Catholicism, 52–53, 82n76
Augsburg Confession, 69–70n26, 72n

Back, Kurt W., 334
Baker, Wayne E., 24, 366
Baltzell, Digby, 3
bank-borrower relationships: capital and, 349–51, 374–77; field research regarding, 353–60, 377–79; as networks, 24; relational embeddedness, impact of, 360–62; statistical analysis of, 364–74; structural embeddedness, impact of, 362–64; theory of embeddedness and, 351–53
Bank of England, 457–58, 463–65, 473–74
Barber, Bernard, 328, 332
Barclay, Robert, 57, 61, 76n40
Barnard, Chester I., 270n4, 530–31
Barnouw, Erik, 112, 127
battered child syndrome (BCS), 533–35
Baxter, Richard, 56–61, 63, 84n89–90
Baxter, William F., 198
BCS. *See* battered child syndrome
Beatrice Foods, 216
Becker, Gary, 249, 461, 471
Bell, Daniel, 91
Ben-Porath, Yoram, 255
Berelson, Bernard, 328
Berger, Peter, 32–35, 37
Berle, Adolf A., 443
Beveridge, Albert, 140, 147
Bhagat, Sanjai, 205, 209
Biggart, Nicole Woolsey, 475n11
Black, Bernard S., 198
Block, Fred, 296
Blumer, H., 547
Bollen, Kenneth A., 365
Boltanski, Luc, 35
bond traders, 1–2
Boorman, Scott, 341
Boswell, Terry E., 281
bounded rationality, 256, 531. *See also* rationality/rationalization
bounded solidarity, 21, 278, 280–84, 287. *See also* solidarity
Bourdieu, Pierre, 21, 35, 275–76
Bourgois, Philippe, 293–94
Bowles, Samuel, 249
Boxman, Ed A. W., 329
Breiger, Ronald, 341
Brenner, Robert, 474
Brentano, Lujo, 64n1, 66n13, 69n25, 72–73n27, 75n37–38
Britain: business recipe in, 175–76. *See also* England
Brown, J. G., 149–50
Brown, Roger, 253
Bryce, James, 82n81
bureaucracy: changing causes of, 111–12; rationalization of, 89–91; rationalized formal structures and, 87–88; rational myths and, 93
Burns, Lawton R., 193
Burns, T., 544
Burt, Ronald S., 19, 23–25, 269n, 351
business recipes, 16, 166–68, 181–82; in East Asia, 171–76; institutional environments and, 175–81; the nature of, 169–75

business systems, social construction of, 162–69, 181–82. *See also* corporations; firms
Butler, Nicholas Murray, 143

Caffey, John, 533
Calvin, John, 57
Campbell, Karen E., 328
Candolle, Augustin-Pyrame de, 228
capital: bank-borrower relationships (*see* bank-borrower relationships); character loans as source of, 286–87; of feudal craftsmen, 390–91, 396; financial, 325–26; human, 325–26; immigrant networks as source of, 285–86; industrial, transformation of all capital into, 402; movable, rise of, 398–400; relational embeddedness and acquisition/costs of, 360–62; rotating credit associations as source of, 285; separation of from landed property, 395; social (*see* social capital); social structure and rates of return, 325–28; structural embeddedness and acquisition/costs of, 362–64. *See also* capitalism; property
capitalism: asceticism and the spirit of, 56–63; child labor and, 139; labor, religious sanction and the supply of, 84–85n91; power and, 25–27; religion and, 12, 49–54; variations in, 9, 15–16 (*see also* business recipes). *See also* capital; corporations; firms
Carlyle, Thomas, 50
Carnegie, Andrew, 434
Carnegie Steel Company, 433–34
Carroll, Glenn R., 114, 130n6
Carruthers, Bruce, 26, 29–30
cartels, 10, 38–39, 416, 423–24
Catholicism: ascetism of, 52–53; casuistic ethics of, 81–82n76; economic behavior and, 49–53
Celler, Emmanuel, 428–29
Celler-Kefauver Act of 1950, 28, 188, 191, 196, 429–30
Chagnon, Napoleon, 1
Chandler, Alfred D., Jr., 27–28, 162, 452
Chicago, banking in, 354–60
Chicago School economists, 198–99
child labor: arguments supporting, 141–43; boundaries for and defining work, 145–52; controversy over regulation of, 140–41; explaining the decline of, 139; magnitude of, 135, 137; replacement by child work and weekly allowance, 152–55; restriction of, 14–15; social reformers' opposition to, 138–39, 143–45; as vital asset for working-class families, 136–38, 142–43
Child Labor Amendment, 140–41, 153, 157n24, 158n42
children: battered child syndrome, 533–35; child labor, regulation of (*see* child labor); economic roles, transformation of, 152–55; redefinition of, 135–36; scholarships for to compensate needy families, 159n59
Children's Bureau, U.S., 148, 150–51, 153
Christopher of Württemberg, Duke, 82n78–79
Cicero, 69n25
Clark, R., 172, 175
Clark, S. M., 536–37
class relations: bourgeoisie, rise of, 397; bourgeoisie, the state as a tool of the, 403–4; colonialism and, 399–400; corporate owners versus managers, implications for, 453n4; development of, 389–91; ideas of the ruling class and, 393–94; large corporations, rise of and, 439–40; the law and, 404–5; merchants, rise of separate class of, 396–97; proletariat, creation of, 403. *See also* power
Clavering, Anne, 474
Clayton Act, 425–27, 429–30
cognition, 6; conceptual machineries, 512–14; dissonance theory, 538–40; economic conventions and, 30–32; frames defined by (*see* cognitive frameworks); material premises of, 391–92; objectification of socially constructed meanings, 33–35; rationality and, 523–24 (*see also* rationality/rationalization); schemas for, 4; sensemaking (*see* sensemaking); social constructionist theory of, 32–33; social construction of meaning, religion as, 485–95; social construction of reality, 496–97 (*see also* sociology of knowledge); as social mechanism explaining economic behavior, 4, 7; subgoal formation and, 524–26, 529–30. *See also* consciousness
cognitive frameworks, 6; action, reinforcement by, 36–37; changes in firms and, 17; organizations and, 35–36; rationality and, 519–20; selective perception through, 525; sensemaking through, 536
Coleman, James S.: collective action and decision, theories of, 269n; corporate form, origins of, 194; human capital, transmission of, 328, 346n2; on social capital, 275–76,

284, 289–90; social capital and networks, 21
collective environment. *See* society
Collins, Randall, 118, 120
Commons, John R., 40, 530–31
competition: corporate structures and, 431; imperfect and social capital, 327; imperfect and social structure, 325, 327–30; imperfect and the role of trust, 331–32; predatory, 416; separation of individuals through, 405–6n6
Comte, Auguste, 241, 517n20
consciousness: acquisition of objectivity in, 506–8; collective, 490–91; common, increasing generality of, 238–41; of everyday life, 499–500; intentionality of, 498; material production of, 391–92; production of, 392–94; social institutions and, 30–32; two states of, Durkheim on, 228–31. *See also* cognition
conventions: behavior, shaping of by, 4; cognition and, 30–32; economic, differences in, 9; institutions and, 5, 17; networks and, 18–19; power and, 25–26; sociological analysis and, 39–42
corporate change: conceptions of control and, 27–28, 407–10, 415–18; deconglomeration of the 1980s (*see* deconglomeration); economic sociology, explanation of through, 7; history of and conceptions of control, 421–31; the rise of large corporations (*see* corporate revolution, the)
corporate revolution, the, 28–29, 433–35; corporations as public institutions, 448–51; efficiency versus power in explaining, 451–53; historical overview of, 443–45; institutions and, 441–43; power and, 440–43; property and, 437–40, 442–43; public and private sectors, division of power between and, 445–48; significance of, 436
corporations: boundaries of and deinstitutionalization, 215–17; changes in structure of (*see* corporate change); deconglomeration of (*see* deconglomeration); firm-as-network model, 213–14, 217; firm-as-portfolio model (*see* firm-as-portfolio model); institutional structure and control in, 413–15; mergers of (*see* mergers); national variations in (*see* business recipes); power and, 25–26; as public institutions, 448–51; public versus private basis of, 445–48; rise of large industrial (*see* corporate revolution, the); the state and, 439; structures of, 418–19, 424–25; subunit power base in, 419–20. *See also* firms
Coser, Lewis, 112
Crane, Dwight B., 352
customs, 10–14. *See also* conventions; institutions
Czarniawska-Joerges, B., 542–43, 546

Dalton, Melville, 261–63
Davis, Gerald F.: business conventions, explaining change in, 11, 16–17, 39; corporate core competencies, rise of, 7, 25, 28; poison pills as anti-takeover strategy, 351
Davis, Martin, 212
deconglomeration, 16–17, 188–92, 217–18; acquisitions, pattern of in the late 1980s and, 206–9; as challenge to organizations as institutions, 200, 214–17; diversification, changes in levels of during the 1980s, 209–11; rhetoric associated with, 211–13; takeover risk of diversified firms, 200–205. *See also* antitrust law and enforcement; firm-as-portfolio model; mergers
De Graaf, Nan D., 328–29
deinstitutionalization: deconglomeration as, 190–91; naturalizing analogies, inability to sustain, 218–19; organizational boundaries and, 214–17. *See also* institutionalization; institutions
Delacroix, Jacques, 114, 130n6
Demos, John, 137
Demsetz, Harold, 218
Devine, Edward T., 145, 154
Dickinson, Emily, 537
Didion, Joan, 292
Diekmann, Kristina, 7, 11, 16–17
DiMaggio, Paul J., 11, 13–14, 16–17, 112, 190
dissonance theory, 538–40
division of labor: contractual solidarity in, 238; development of, 388–91; expanding scope of, 227–28; knowledge and, 511–12, 514–15; manufacture, rise of and, 398–400; organic solidarity produced by, 234–35; in organizations, information and, 525; production and commerce, between, 396–98; religious calling and the, 59–60; ruling class, manifestation in, 393; Smith on, 59, 227; social attachments and, 19; social relations preceding the, 241–43;

division of labor (*cont'd*)
town and country, between, 388–89, 394–96; trade and manufacture, concentration of and, 400–403
Douglas, Mary, 193, 216, 218
Drucker, P. E., 542
Duesenberry, James, 8, 37, 248
Dunne, Reverend, 141
DuPont, 188, 426
Durkheim, Émile: on the division of labor, 3, 19, 24; generalizing from experience as a human constant, 37; network theory, contribution to, 5, 18; religion and the social construction of meaning, 32–34, 485–95; social context and economic behavior, focus on, 40–41; social facts/reality, origins of, 516n9, 516n12; social psychology, theory of, 6, 30; value introjection and, 277
Durocher, Leo, 270n2

Earle, Peter, 475n1, 476n23
East India Company, 29, 457–58, 463–70, 472–73
Eccles, Robert G., 260, 262–63, 352
ecological theory, 190
economic behavior: embeddedness of (*see* embeddedness); the Law of Indifference, 459–61, 466–67; social institutions and, 1–2; social relationships and, 460
economic modernization. *See* modernization
economic rationalism. *See* rationality/rationalization
economics: conceptions of social influences in, 247–50; game theory in, 9; legitimating function of, 96; markets, analysis of, 322; methodological individualism, premise of, 30; new institutional (*see* new institutional economics); sociology, split from, 2–3; transaction cost, 376; trust and malfeasance, arguments regarding, 250–52. *See also* economic sociology
economic sociology: contributions to and concepts of, 274–75; fourfold theory, need for, 7; origins of, 2–4, 296; scope and subject of, 39–42; social mechanisms applied, example of, 38–39; social mechanisms explaining economic behavior, 4–7 (*see also* cognition; institutions; networks; power)
Economist, 212
Edgar v. MITE, 198
efficiency: the corporate revolution and, 440–41, 443, 446, 451–53; optimized networks and, 336–37; persistence of organizations lacking in, explanations of, 126–29; structural analysis versus, 302–3, 320–21
Ellul, Jacques, 91
embeddedness: in bank-borrower relationships (*see* bank-borrower relationships); economic behavior, explanation of through, 20–21, 266–69; economic transactions, defined in terms of, 350; efficiency of hierarchical firms versus markets, argument applying, 256–66; as manifesto for economic sociology, 274; markets and, 460–61; political endogamy, 467–75; the problem of, 245–46; rationality and, 267–68; relational and capital acquisition/costs, 360–62; structural and capital acquisition/costs, 362–64; theoretical vagueness of, 275; theory of and application to lending relationships, 351–53; trust and order in economic life, explanation of, 253–56; under- and over-socialized conceptions of social relations, need to avoid, 250. *See also* social capital
Emery, Fred L., 92
enforceable trust, 21, 278–79, 284–89
England: business recipe in, 175–76; financial instruments available in, 462–63; the financial revolution, politics and markets in, 29–30, 457–60; trading and political endogamy, 469–75; trading on the London stock market, 463–69
ethnomethodology, 540

Fair Labor Standards Act, 141, 152
Federal Trade Commission (FTC), 425, 429
Feldman, M. S., 537
Fennell, Mary L., 114, 121
Festinger, Leon, 334, 342
Fichman, Mark, 365
financial theory, social embeddedness and, 349–50
firm-as-portfolio model, 188–91; change in the institutional climate of, 198–200; deinstitutionalization of, 213–15;
downfall of (*see* deconglomeration); rhetoric discrediting, 211–12, 217; rise and dominance of, 195–97; theory of, 17, 379–80n6
firms: bank-borrower relationships (*see* bank-borrower relationships); bases of control in, 413; business systems, social construction of, 162–69, 181–82; cartels, 10, 38–39, 416, 423–24; changes in structure

of (*see* corporate change); conflict between, 263–64; corporate form of, 188–92 (*see also* corporations); direct control of competitors conception of, 416, 422–26; East Asian, 171–76; efficiency of hierarchical versus markets, argument regarding, 256–58; finance conception of, 407–8, 418, 429–31; hierarchical power, efficacy of in, 261–63; ideas and practices, establishment and diffusion of, 12–14; institutional context for the transformation of, 410–15; managerial responsibility for success or failure of, 408–9; manufacturing conception of, 416–17, 426–27; midmarket, 350, 354–55; national institutions and, 16 (*see also* business recipes); network model, 213–14, 217; networks among, 258–61; networks within, 264; nexus-of-contracts theory of, 215–16, 218; persistence of small, 269; portfolio model (*see* firm-as-portfolio model); rise of large industrial (*see* corporate revolution, the); sales and marketing conception of, 417–18, 428–29; societal contexts and, 170–71 (*see also* business recipes); stabilization of through institutionalization, 98; takeover risk of diversified, 200–205. *See also* corporations
Flap, Hendrik D., 328–29
Fligstein, Neil, 7, 26–29, 39, 41, 168, 193
Ford Motor Company, 207–9
framing. *See* cognitive frameworks
France, business recipe in, 178
Francis of Assisi, Saint, 53
Franklin, Benjamin, 62, 78n56
Frederick William I, 54
Freeman, John H., 112–14
Frost, P. J., 541, 543
FTC. *See* Federal Trade Commission
Fukuyama, Francis, 20–21
Fuller, Raymond, 145–46, 149, 152

Galaskiewicz, Joseph, 113
game theory, 9
Garfinkel, Harold, 538–39
Gaudet, Hazel, 328
Geertz, Clifford, 10, 254, 290
General Electric, 207–9, 219n4
General Federation of Women's Clubs, 138
General Motors, 188, 207–9
Gintis, Herbert, 249
Gioia, D. A., 536–37
Glazer, Nathan, 281, 283
Goethe, Johann Wolfgang von, 62, 77n48
Goffman, Erving, 6, 35
Goldin, Claudia, 136
Goldner, Fred H., 115
Gould, Stephen Jay, 11
government. *See* state, the
Granovetter, Mark: community solidarity, costs of for entrepreneurs, 290; contributions of, 296; discrimination against minorities, business advantage of, 288; on embeddedness, 20, 274–76, 460–61; networks, enforcement of economic norms through, 18, 20–21, 24–25; networks, use of by job-seekers, 23, 351; organizational boundaries of the firm, national variation in, 195; undersocialized view of human behavior in economics, 40; weak-tie argument of, 328, 341–42, 345
Grief, Avner, 33
Gronn, P. C., 545
Gulf+Western, 212, 430

habitualization, 501–6, 509, 515
Hage, Jerald, 92
Haines, Michael, 136
Hall, Fred, 149
Hall, George, 152
Hannan, Michael T., 112–14
Hareven, Tamara, 142
Hart, Moses, 468
Harvard Business Review, 212
Haspeslagh, Philippe, 212
Haveman, Heather, 14
Havemeyer, Henry O., 445
Hawley, Amos H., 92, 114
Heckman, James, 368
Henry, Matthew, 77n48
Higinbotham, Harlow N., 461
Hirsch, Paul, 119
Hirschman, Albert, 33, 247, 251, 268
history: competition between nations and the development of, 400–403; of the corporate revolution, 443–45 (*see also* corporate revolution, the); of corporations, changing conceptions of control in, 421–31 (*see also* corporate change); the English financial revolution, 457–58, 463–75; manufacture, rise of, 398–400; mode of production and, 387–91; production and commerce, relations between, 396–98; property and the state, development of, 403–4; the ruling class and, 393–94; town

history (*cont'd*)
and country, relations of, 394–96; world history, transformation into, 392–93, 402
Hobbes, Thomas, 245, 247–49, 251, 255, 257, 264
holding companies, 424–25
Homans, George C., 334, 342
Homer, 513
Hong Kong: business recipe in, 16, 172–76; institutional context in, 179–81
Hoornbeek, Johannes, 83n83
Hopkins, John, 468
Huber, Joan, 139
Huberman, Michael, 365, 378
human behavior, under- and over-socialized conceptions of, 246–50
human capital, 325–26. *See also* social capital
Hurlbert, Jeanne S., 328

Imai, K., 169
immigration: bounded solidarity and, 280–84; enforceable trust and, 284–89; social capital and, 21, 276, 280
information: asymmetries, 23; networks and benefits of, 330–34; in organizations, 525, 527; private, 352, 376; structural holes and (*see* structural holes); weak ties and, 342, 344–45
Ingram, Paul, 23
institutionalization: defined, 87; of formal structures, myths and, 89–91; inertia, tendency toward, 515; organizational boundaries and, 192–95; of rational myths, 13; social nature of, 13–14; theoretical and empirical approaches to, 192–93. *See also* deinstitutionalization; institutions
institutionalized myths. *See* myths
institutionalized rules: defined, 87; success/survival of organizations and, 99–100; types of organizations and, 100–101
institutions, 5; business recipes and, 175–81 (*see also* business recipes); of capitalism (*see* capitalism); changes in and rational myths, 14–17; cognition and social, 30–32; the corporate revolution and, 441–43 (*see also* corporate revolution, the); corporate structure, 434 (*see also* corporations; firms); definitions of, 192–93; economic behavior and, 1–2; ideas and practices, establishment and diffusion of, 12–14; isomorphism of (*see* isomorphism); organizations (*see* organizations); origins of, 502–12; political parties and the London stock market, 457; as social mechanism shaping economic behavior, 4, 7–11, 63; Weber on variation and change in, 12. *See also* institutionalization
International Paper, 207
International Telephone and Telegraph (ITT), 430
iron cage, 63, 111
Irving, Washington, 76n44
isomorphism, 114; business recipes and (*see* business recipes); coercive, 115–17, 122–23; competitive efficiency and, 121; environmental of formal organizations, 91–93, 95–96; institutional, implications of theory of, 128–29; institutional school of organizational analysis, study by the, 168; managerial behavior and, 130n5; mimetic, 14, 117–18, 123, 168; normative, 118–21, 124; predictors of, 122–26; problems faced by organizations dependent upon, 101–2; in technical and institutional sectors, contrast between, 164; types of, 114–15
Italy, business recipe in, 176
Itami, H., 169

Japan: business recipe in, 16, 166, 169, 172–76, 178; institutional context in, 179–81; social construction of meaning in, 34–35
Jefferson, Thomas, 448
Jensen, Michael C., 216
Jevons, W. Stanley, 459–61
joint-stock companies, 457–58
Jones, Mary Harris "Mother," 138
Juvenal, Decimus Junius, 475n7

Kadushin, Charles, 112
Kant, Immanuel, 493
Kanter, Rosabeth Moss, 114, 120, 213
Katz, Michael B., 112
Keats, John, 54
Kefauver, Estes, 428–29
Kim, Illsoo, 292
Knoke, David, 129n3
knowledge: the division of labor and, 511–12, 514–15; of everyday life, 497–501; institutionalization and, 510–12; rational definition of the situation and, 526–28; sociology of (*see* sociology of knowledge)

Korea, Republic of: business recipe in, 16, 172–76; immigrants from, 292–93; institutional context in, 179–81
Krasner, Stephen, 11
Krugman, Paul, 3
Kuhn, Thomas, 41

Lancaster, Ryon, 24
Larson, Magali Sarfatti, 118–19
Laumann, Edward O., 113
law: corporations and, 439; property relations and, 404–5; restitutive versus repressive, 232–33; social cohesion through, Durkheim on, 228–31; types of and morality, 237–38; universality of, tendency toward increasing, 239–40
Law of Indifference, 459–61, 466–67
Lazarsfeld, Paul F., 328, 346n2
Lease, Ronald C., 477n40
LeBaron, Dean, 198
Lee, M. L., 121
legitimacy: ceremonial inspection/evaluation and, 105–6; coercive isomorphism and, 115–17; econometric analyses as bestowing, 96; formal education and, 119; institutional isomorphism of organizations and, 95–96, 99, 123; of the institutional order, 508–10, 515; institutions and, 193; of rationalized formal structures, 89; of rational myths, 93
Leibenstein, Harvey, 249, 267
Leifer, Eric M., 19, 22–23, 25, 33–34, 315
lending. *See* bank-borrower relationships; capital
Levinthal, Daniel A., 365
Lewis, Michael, 1
Light, Ivan, 285
Limlingan, Victor S., 177
Lin, Nan, 328
Lincoln, James, 263
Ling-Temco-Vought (LTV), 430
Littlefield, Douglas R., 453n7
Logan, John R., 443
London Stock Exchange: politics and public finance on the, 457–58; the politics of endogamy in, 469–75; trading on, 463–69
Louis, Meryl, 536, 545
Lozano, William B., 280
Luckmann, Thomas, 32–35, 37
Luther, Martin, 54–56, 59–60, 68–69n25, 70–73n27
Lynd, Helen, 3
Lynd, Robert, 3
Macaulay, Stewart, 259
Malaysia, business recipe in, 176
March, James C., 119
March, James G., 32, 35–37, 119, 128, 379n2, 545–46
markets: embeddedness in, 460–61; the Law of Indifference, 459–61, 466–67; "noisy trader" models of, 477–78n46; politics and, 29–30, 458–60, 465–75; production-pricing strategy, example of, 304–7; production-pricing strategy, structural analysis of, 308–15; reproducible structures, a topology of, 315–19; socially embedded ties in, 352–53 (*see also* bank-borrower relationships); structural analysis of, 22–23, 303–4, 319–22
Markowitz, Linda, 7
Mark Twain Bancshares, 352
marriage, procreation and sex for the Puritans in, 78–79n56
Marsden, Peter V., 113, 269n, 328
Marshall, Alfred, 461
Marx, Karl: class consciousness, rise of, 280; consciousness, shaping of by social structure, 31; economic behavior, study of, 2; on making history, 39–40; on power, 6, 25–27, 41; property rights, power of, 446; reification, 516n14; on social capital, 278
Maynes, E. Scott, 477n42
McConnell, John J., 477n40
McLaren, Richard, 430
Mead, George Herbert, 516n7
Mead, Margaret, 545
Means, Gardiner C., 443
Meckling, William H., 216
mergers: amicable, 38–39; conglomerate, 420–21, 429–31; encouragement of by antitrust law, 29, 38, 196; firm-as-portfolio model of corporations and (*see* firm-as-portfolio model); history of, 195, 423–31. *See also* deconglomeration
Merton, Robert, 251
methodological individualism, 30
Meyer, John W.: diffusion of conventions across corporations, study of, 11–17; institutionalization approach of, 128; on isomorphism, 114, 118, 123, 164; organizations and the state, 116, 125; social phenomenology, work based on, 33
Meyer, Marshall, 114
Miami: Cubans in, 286–87; Haitians in, 288–89
Mikkelson, Wayne H., 477n40

Miles, Matthew B., 365, 378
Mill, John Stuart, 227
Miller, James C., III, 198
Milliken, F. J., 536
Mills, C. Wright, 3
Milofsky, Carl, 116
Milton, John, 81n75
mimetic isomorphism, 14, 117–18, 123, 168
Minnesota Mining and Manufacturing (3M), 430, 544
Mirowski, Philip, 470
Mitchell, John, 430
Modell, John, 137–38
modernization: rationalization of institutions and myths of formal organization, 91; religion and, 49–50, 84n89; as societal projects, 2. *See also* capitalism
Molotch, Harvey L., 443
monopolies, 416, 427, 429
Montesquieu, Charles-Louis de Secondat, 54
Montgomery, James D., 379n2
Morgan, G., 541, 543
Morgan, J. P., 38, 433, 445
Mueller, Dennis C., 208
Murphy, Antoin E., 475n3
myths: affirmations of confidence and good faith, mechanisms for, 104–5; change in firms and, 16–17; childhood as, 15; diffusion of through networks, 13–14; formal structure and, 86–87, 106–8; formal structure, legitimacy and, 95–96; institutionalization through formal structures, 89–91; organizations and, 12–13, 86; sources of rational, 93–94; as universe maintenance, 512–13

National Association of Manufacturers, 141
National Child Labor Committee, 136, 138, 143–45, 147–49
National Consumer's League, 138
National Industrial Recovery Act, 141, 152, 427
Nee, Brett de Bary, 281–82, 292
Nee, Victor, 281–82, 292
Nelson, Richard R., 127
network complementarity, 362–63, 366–67, 372, 374–75
networks, 5; bank-borrower relationships (*see* bank-borrower relationships); in business relations, 258–61, 264; capital, impact on acquisition and cost of, 349–50, 362–64, 372, 374–77 (*see also* bank-borrower relationships); changes in firms and, 17; corporate form and, 213; design principles of optimized, 336–41; the division of labor (*see* division of labor); economic conventions and, 18–19; embeddedness argument regarding, 20–21, 253 (*see also* embeddedness); formal structures and, 89; growth patterns of, 339–41; ideas and practices, diffusion of through, 13–14; of immigrants (*see* immigration); information benefits of, 330–34; occupational, 19 (*see also* division of labor); producers in markets and, 22–23 (*see also* markets); professionalization and, 119; rational myths and, 93; small firms and, 269; social capital and, 21–22, 328–29 (*see also* social capital); as social mechanism explaining economic behavior, 4, 7; structural holes (*see* structural holes); trust in, 331–32; weak-tie argument, 341–45. *See also* social capital; social relations/structure; society; solidarity; structural analysis
new institutional economics: efficiency of hierarchical firms versus markets, argument regarding, 256–58; institutions, analysis of reduced to efficiency by, 267; the problem of embeddedness and, 246; undersocialized conception of man in, 251–52; universal logic of organizational structure, assumption of, 162
New York City, Dominicans in, 285–86
Nicklaes, Hendrick, 83n82
Nishida, Judith, 177
North, Douglass, 10
Norton, Mary Beth, 154

objectivation, 507–8, 511
Ogburn, William, 154
Olsen, J. P., 545–46
O'Mahoney, Joseph, 428
opportunism, 256–57
organizational fields: as an area of institutional life, 441–42; conceptions of control and, 415–16, 422, 428, 430; defined, 113; firm-as-portfolio model of corporations (*see* firm-as-portfolio model); large firms and, 410–11; predictors of isomorphic change in, 122–26; professionalization in, 119–21; shifts in, 421; status competition in, 121–22; structuration of, 112–13, 120–21, 125–26
organizational sensemaking, 534–35, 540, 544. *See also* sensemaking

organizations: body analogy applied to, 193–94; boundaries of, varying ideas regarding, 194–95; bureaucratization of (*see* bureaucracy); ceremonial inspection and evaluation in, 105–6; change, difficulty of, 189–90; cognitive frameworks and, 35–36 (*see also* cognitive frameworks); decoupling of formal structure from activities, 103–4; environments, efforts to shape, 94; environments, relation to their, 91–93; formal and informal, gap between, 88; formal structure, theories of, 87–88; formal structures as myths of institutional environments, 86–87, 106–8; homogeneity of, 112–14, 124 (*see also* isomorphism); institutional context for the transformation of, 410–15; institutionalization of rational formal structures, 89–91; institutionalized myths, affirmations of confidence and good faith through, 104–5; institutional structure and control in, 413–15; isomorphism across (*see* isomorphism); language of and legitimacy, 95–96; networks in and among (*see* networks); operational and nonoperational goals in, 528–29; paradox of social efficiency and dumb, 126–28; political (*see* state, the); rationality and, 111–12, 520, 530–31 (*see also* rationality/rationalization); rational myths in, 93–94; resolving structural inconsistencies in, 102–5; sensemaking in (*see* organizational sensemaking); structural inconsistencies in, 101–2; structure of, defining, 530–31; subgoal formation in, 524–26; success/survival of, 98–100; types of, 100–101; uncertainty, modeling behavior in response to, 117–18. *See also* corporations; firms; institutions
Osterman, Paul, 139

Palmer, Donald, 204
Pareto, Vilfredo, 516n15, 517n19
Park Chung-hee, 293
Parsons, Talcott, 92, 247
Pascal, Blaise, 56, 73n29, 74n34
path dependence, 10
Paxton, Pamela, 365
Pennsylvania Railroad, 434
Pepinsky, Harold, 538
performance programs, 522–23
Perrow, Charles, 25, 127
Petty, Sir William, 53, 66n11–12
Pfeffer, Jeffrey, 116, 122
Phelps Brown, Ernest Henry, 248
Piaget, Jean, 516n10
piety, commercial success and, 53–54
Piore, Michael, 4, 249
Podolny, Joel, 475n11
Polanyi, Karl, 2, 245, 274
political endogamy, 467–75
politics and political systems: business recipes and, 179–81; coercive isomorphism and, 115–17; market behavior and, 29–30, 458–60, 465–75. *See also* law; legitimacy; state, the
Pondy, L. R., 541, 543
Porter, Michael, 212
Portes, Alejandro, 18, 21–22, 24
portfolio theory. *See* firm-as-portfolio model
Powell, Walter W., 11, 13–14, 16–17, 112
power, 6, 25–26; capitalism and, 26–27 (*see also* capitalism); changes in firms and, 17, 27–29 (*see also* corporate change); the corporate revolution and, 440–43, 451–53 (*see also* corporate revolution, the); definitions of, 440; division of between public and private sectors, 446–48; property, the development of and, 388–91; as social mechanism explaining economic behavior, 4, 7; unorganized laborer's lack of, 395–96. *See also* class relations; state, the
predatory competition, 416
priming mechanisms, 353
Prisoner's Dilemma, 253–54
production: of consciousness, 392–94; division of labor and, 388 (*see also* division of labor); as a mode of life, 387
professionalization, 104, 118–21, 125
property: antagonism between town and country and, 394–95; the corporate revolution and, 437–40, 442–43; defining of in corporations, 449–50; historical development and, 388–91; law and, 404–5; manufacture, rise of and changes in, 398–99; the state and, 403–4; trade and manufacture, concentration of and, 401–3. *See also* capital
Protestantism: asceticism and the spirit of capitalism, 56–63; the calling, Luther's conception of, 54–56, 68–69n25, 70–73n27; economic behavior and, 49–54, 62–63; materialism of, 52–53; small and homogenous nature of sects, consequences of, 66n13

punctuated equilibrium, 11
punishment, Durkheim on, 230–31
Putnam, Robert, 21
Pye, Lucian W., 180

quality management, 14

Rabb, Theodore K., 474
Rachfahl, F., 63n
railroads, explaining differences in American and French, 9–10
Rands, G. P., 537, 544
rationality/rationalization: bounded, 256, 531; of business systems (*see* business systems, social construction of); changing causes of, 111–12; cognition and, 524 (*see also* cognition); cognitive frameworks as limits to (*see* cognitive frameworks); the corporate revolution and, 441; in defining the situation, 523–30; of discrimination, 459–60; embeddedness and, 267–68; embeddedness of rational choice theory, 267; of formal organizational structures, 87–88; institutionalized structures and myths, 89–91; the Law of Indifference, 459–61, 466–67; organizations and, 520, 530–31; performance programs in making choices, 521–22; rational man, classical model of, 518–19; rational man, difficulties in models of, 519–20; religion and development of, 51; satisficing versus optimizing in making choices, 521–22; selective, 267; stimulus and response in making choices, 520–21; universality of and progress in civilization, 240; variability of, 2
rational myths. *See* myths
Ravenscraft, David J., 207
Rawls, John, 245
Reagan, Ronald, 431
reality: of everyday life, 497–501; objectivity of the institutional world, 506–7; social construction of, 496–97
reciprocity transactions, 21, 277–78
Redding, S. Gordon, 179
religion: asceticism and the spirit of capitalism, 56–63; the calling, Luther's conception of, 54–56, 68–69n25, 70–73n27; economic modernization and, 49–50, 84n89; increasing abstraction of, 239; the rise of capitalism and, 12, 49–54, 62–63; science and, 492–94; the social construction of meaning and, 32–34, 485–95; as social institutions, 8; theology as universe maintenance, 513–14. *See also* asceticism
Rhodes, Cecil, 53
Richardson, George, 169
Riis, Jacob, 144, 150
Ring, P. S., 537, 544
Ritti, R. R., 115
Roberts, Peter W., 23
Rockefeller, John D., 445
Rockwell International, 430
Roosevelt, Franklin Delano, 427–28
rotating credit associations, 285
Rothman, Mitchell, 112
Rowan, Brian, 11–17, 33, 116, 123
Rowntree, J. S., 85n92
Roy, William, 6, 26, 28–29, 33, 39, 41
Rumbaut, Rubén, 291
Rumelt, Richard, 211

Sabel, Charles, 213
Sackman, S. A., 536–37
Salancik, Gerald, 116, 122
Samuelson, Paul, 268
Sarah, Duchess of Marlborough, 473
Schachter, Stanley, 334
Schelling, Thomas, 113
Scherer, F. M., 207
Schotter, Andrew, 251
Schumpeter, Joseph, 296
Schutz, A., 545
science: religion and, 492–94; universe maintenance by, 514
Scott, Richard, 164
Seabright, Mark A., 365
Seavoy, Ronald E., 451
Sedlak, Michael, 116
self-interest: cognitive frameworks and, 6; force or fraud in the pursuit of, assumptions regarding, 250–51; limited utility of the concept of, 1–2; methodological individualism, 30; in pre-modern societies, 33
Selznick, Philip, 3, 113, 200
sensemaking: battered child syndrome as an example of, 533–35; concept of, 535–37; interpretation, distinguished from, 540–42; properties of, 547–48; social property of, 543–47; uniqueness of, 538–43
Sensenbrenner, Julia, 18, 21–22, 24
Sewell, William H., Jr., 193–94
Sherman Antitrust Act of 1890, 424, 425–26
Shleifer, Andrei, 205
Shotter, J., 546

Silverman, Frederick, 533
Simmel, Georg, 40, 277, 291, 346n2, 516n8
Simon, Herbert A., 32, 35–37, 128, 270n4
Slater, Samuel, 137
Smelser, Neil, 33
Smith, Adam: on the division of labor, 56, 59, 74n31; on economic laws, 9, 13; on exchange as a propensity in human nature, 246; social atomization and competition, assumption regarding, 248; trade associations, deploring of, 258
social attachment, defined, 379n1
social capital: bounded solidarity and immigration, 280–84; competitive success and, 326–27, 329–30; conceptions of, 328–29; created by embeddedness, 21–22, 374 (*see also* embeddedness); definitions of, 275–76; enforceable trust and immigration, 284–89; immigration and, 21–22, 276, 280; negative effects of, 289–96; personal, use of to benefit a firm, 361; types and sources of, 276–80
social embeddedness approach. *See* embeddedness
social institutions. *See* institutions
Socialist Party, 138
socialization, 506–8, 512, 545
social psychology. *See* cognition; cognitive frameworks
social relations/structure: capital, impact on acquisition and cost of, 349–50, 360–62, 371–77 (*see also* bank-borrower relationships); class-based (*see* class relations); competition and, 325, 327–30; embeddedness of in economic behavior and institutions, 245, 253–56 (*see also* embeddedness); property as, 438; structural holes (*see* structural holes); under- and over-socialized conceptions of, 246–50
society: as collective ideal, construction and reality of, 487–92; collective life, precedence of in relation to individual life, 241–43; common conscience in, increasing generality of, 238–41; individuality in the development of, 235–37; institutions of (*see* institutions); mechanical solidarity in, 234; organic solidarity in, 234–35; repressive relations in, 228–31. *See also* networks
sociology: on acquisition and cost of capital, 349–50; core insight of, 4; economic behavior, limited approach to, 266–67; economics, split from, 2–3; over-socialized conception of man in, 246–47, 250. *See also* economic sociology
sociology of knowledge: habitualization in the origins of institutions, 501–6; knowledge of everyday life, foundations of, 497–501; knowledge, role of in the origins of institutions, 510–12; legitimation and control in the origins of institutions, 508–10; objectivization in the origins of institutions, 506–8; subject of, 496–97; universe maintenance, 512–15
sociology of organizations: business recipes (*see* business recipes); business systems, social construction of, 162–69, 181–82; deconglomeration, 190–91 (*see also* deconglomeration); organizational fields (*see* organizational fields)
solidarity: bounded, 21, 278, 280–84, 287; costs of community, 290–91; mechanical, 234; organic, 234–35; organic and contractual, 237–38; progress of organic, 235–37
Sombart, Werner, 63–64n1, 67n19, 75n38, 77n44, 77n48
South Korea. *See* Korea, Republic of
Speidell, Lawrence S., 198
Spence, Michael, 22–23
Spencer, Herbert, 235–36, 241–42
Spener, Philipp Jacob, 57, 77–78n50–51, 78n56, 80n63–64, 80n67, 81n72–73
Stalk, George, 172
Stalker, G. M., 544
Standard Oil, 426
Starbuck, W. H., 536
Starr, Paul, 112, 443
state, the: antitrust law and enforcement (*see* antitrust law and enforcement); bureaucratic control and the formation of, 88; child labor, regulation of (*see* child labor); commerce, regulation of, 423–29; conceptions of control, emergence of new and, 422; corporations and, 408–9, 412–13, 439; corporations, chartering of, 446, 448–51; Hobbes' conception of, 248–49; market behavior, role as arbiter of, 421; organic solidarity and, 238; property and, 438–39; public/private division as historical construct, 447; rational myths and, 93–94; trade and manufacture, expansion of and, 400–403. *See also* law; politics and political systems
Stearns, Linda, 266
Stigler, George, 36

Stiglitz, Joseph, 23
Stiles, Charles W., 159n71
Stinchcombe, A., 168
Stratford, William, 474
structural analysis, 302–3; of markets, 303–4, 319–22; of production-pricing strategy in markets, 308–15; reproducible structures, a topology of, 315–19
structural holes: defined, 334; empirical indicators of, 334–36; in networks, 23–24; optimized networks and, 336–41; the weak-tie argument and, 341–45
Swedberg, Richard, 33, 345n
Swidler, Ann, 35, 116–17
symbolic interactionism, 545

Taiwan: business recipe in, 16, 171–76; institutional context in, 179–81
Tan, Amy, 283
Tarde, Gabriel, 232
Tazelaar, F., 328
Telser, Lester G., 461
Temporary National Economic Commission (TNEC), 428–29
Tenbruck, Friedrich, 516n15
Textron, 212, 430
theology, 513–14
Thevenot, Laurent, 35
Thomas, J. B., 536–37
Thomas, William I., 284
Thompson, James D., 92, 122–23
Thompson-Ramo-Woolridge (TRW), 430
3M. *See* Minnesota Mining and Manufacturing
Tinsley, Catherine, 7, 11, 16–17
TNEC. *See* Temporary National Economic Commission
Tolbert, Pamela S., 114, 192–93
Tönnies, Ferdinand, 289
totemism, 485–88
Trist, Eric L., 92
Troeltsch, Ernst, 64n1
trusts, 424, 445
Turner, B. A., 546–47
Tyack, David, 112

Udy, Stanley H., Jr., 92
uncertainty, organizational responses to, 117–18
Ungson, G. R., 543
U.S. Congressional Commission for the Study of Immigration, 285
U.S. Steel Corporation, 426, 433
Uzzi, Brian, 19, 23–24

value introjection, 277
Veblen, Thorstein, 40, 296
vertical integration, 417
Vishny, Robert W., 205
Voet, Gisbert, 75n37–38, 76n41

Wacquant, Loïc J. D., 294
Wallas, Graham, 539
Walsh, J. P., 543
Washington, George, 448
Watson, Amey E., 154
weak-tie argument, 341–45, 375
Weber, Max: on arm's-length transactions, 290, 351; on the autonomy of the state, 412; on bureaucracy, 87–88, 111; capitalism and religion, study of, 11–12, 111; consciousness and meaning, shaping of by social structure, 31; contract law, implications of, 115; conventions and social behavior, 18; economic behavior, study of, 3; economic sociology as heritage of, 269, 274; enforceable trust and, 278–79; on institutions, 10–11, 15; power, definition of, 440; property rights, power of, 446; religion and social behavior, study of, 15; self-interest in early modern Europe, 33; social context and economic behavior, focus on, 40–41; social psychology, theory of, 6; value introjection and, 277
Weick, Karl E., 32, 37, 546
Weinstein, James, 127
Westley, F. R., 536
Westrum, R., 534–35
Whistler, Thomas, 119
White, G., 82n80
White, Harrison C.: gaps in social structures, study of, 341; network theory of markets, 19, 22–25, 33–34; reproducible structures, 315, 317; synthetic theory of, 41
White House Conference on Child Health and Protection, 148, 154
Whitley, Richard, 11, 15–17, 27
Wholey, Douglas R., 193
Whyte, William H., 3
Williams Act of 1968, 199, 201
Williamson, Oliver E.: on conglomerate acquisitions, 197; economic man, on the nature of, 250; exchanges, implications of investments associated with, 122; on markets and hierarchies, 20, 246, 256–58,

260–62, 264–65, 267; on relationship-specific investments, 195
Wilson, William J., 294
Winch, Peter, 163
Winter, Sidney, 127
W. R. Grace, 430
Wrong, Dennis, 246–48

Yanomamo, the, 1–2

Zeitlin, Maurice, 453n3
Zelizer, Viviana A., 11, 14–15, 17, 475n11
Zhou, Min, 281
Zimmer, Catharine, 282
Zinzendorf, Nikolaus Ludwig von, 79n58
Znaniecki, Florian, 284
Zucker, Lynne G., 114, 192–93